PSYCHOANALYTIC TERMS AND CONCEPTS

PSYCHOANALYTIC TERMS & CONCEPTS

Edited by

Elizabeth L. Auchincloss, MD
and
Eslee Samberg, MD

American Psychoanalytic Association

Yale UNIVERSITY PRESS
New Haven and London

Published with assistance from the foundation established in memory of Philip Hamilton McMillan of the Class of 1894, Yale College.

This book is a revised edition of *Psychoanalytic Terms and Concepts,* edited by Burness E. Moore and Bernard D. Fine, 1990 (third edition). The first edition was originally published in 1967 (revised 1968) as *Glossary of Psychoanalytic Terms and Concepts,* edited by Burness E. Moore and Bernard D. Fine.

A version of the Introduction in this volume was published as Samberg, E, and Auchincloss, EL. Psychoanalytic Lexicography: Notes from Two "Harmless Drudges," *Journal of the American Psychoanalytic Association* 58:1059–1088, 2010.

Yale University Press books may be purchased in quantity for educational, business, or promotional use. For information, please e-mail sales.press@yale.edu (U.S. office) or sales@yaleup.co.uk (U.K. office).

Designed by Mary Valencia.
Set in Adobe Garamond and Syntax type.
Printed in the United States of America.

ISBN: 978-0-300-10986-3 (cloth)

Library of Congress Control Number: 2012938404

A catalogue record for this book is available from the British Library.

This paper meets the requirements of ANSI/NISO Z39.48–1992 (Permanence of Paper).

10 9 8 7 6 5 4 3 2 1

CONTENTS

ACKNOWLEDGMENTS

This project has been carried out under the joint sponsorship of the American Psychoanalytic Association and Yale University Press. We are grateful to both for giving us this opportunity and for providing us with the support we have needed to accomplish the task. This book is the direct descendent of previous editions of *Psychoanalytic Terms and Concepts* edited by Drs. Burness Moore and Bernard Fine. Their earlier vision is the basis for this volume. Their 1990 edition provided an essential reference for us in formulating our own vision of the task.

This book represents the concerted efforts of a small army of people who devoted endless hours to its construction. At times, it seemed as though logomachy over the best terms to describe inenarrable states of mind would never end. We certainly learned many new words! More important, we made new friends. Although we are unable to thank each person individually, we have listed the names of each of our contributors and wish to thank them collectively. They devoted countless hours to the research and writing of definitions, which provided us with the essential raw material of the book. We are enormously grateful to our editorial board, whose broad range of knowledge and special expertise provided invaluable judgment, perspective, and editorial skill in the crafting of each entry. Their generosity with time and patience in the multiple reediting of many entries has been extraordinary. In the final weeks of the project we relied upon the dedicated efforts of an outstanding group of editorial assistants who constructed our master reference list and checked it for accuracy. We are grateful to them for their steadfast and painstaking help. Dean Stein from the American Psychoanalytic Association, Vadim Staklo, Kate Davis, and Margaret Otzel for Yale University Press, and Nadine Levinson from the Psychoanalytic Electronic Publishing (PEP) project also supported us with patience and wisdom. Indeed, without the PEP, this book would have been impossible; this fourth edition of *Psychoanalytic Terms and Concepts* is truly a product of the digital age. In addition, we owe thanks to Dr. Jack D. Barchas, Chair of Psychiatry at Weill Cornell Medical College, who provided time and boundless encouragement.

We owe special thanks to our families, especially to our husbands, Dr. Richard Weiss and Dr. Eric Marcus, who have both contributed mightily to this project. Their specific efforts as members of our editorial board are but a small part. Richard and Eric have provided endless emotional support and encouragement, patience, and forbearance, and a large dose of genuine excitement about the value of the project for the field.

Finally, we want to thank each other. This is not a project to go at alone. We have learned from each other and have together felt the pleasure of the work. Fortunately, we have taken turns in periods of flagging spirit, relying upon the other to keep afloat. This project has been a wonderful adventure, propelled forward by the best kind of comradeship.

Elizabeth L. Auchincloss
Eslee Samberg

COMMITTEES

Theory of Mind

    Core Concepts   J. Roiphe

    Freud   C. Hanly

    Ego Psychology   E. Marcus, A. Tutter

    Object Relations   D. Bell

    Self Psychology   J. Halpern, S. Ornstein

    Relational/Interpersonal   A. Bass, S. Cooper, J. Greenberg, C. Spezzano

    International   J. Muller, D. Scarfone

Treatment   R. Weiss

Development/Child Analysis   R. Fischer, K. Gilmore, J. Yanof

Sexuality/Gender   P. Bernstein, G. Grossman, N. Kulish

Psychopathology/Character   J. Hansell

Research/Cognitive Science/
General Psych   L. Mayes, M. Target, D. Westen

Biography/History   N. Kravis

Humanities/ Social Science   J. Lear, E. Marcus

Lexicography   B. Litowitz

CONTRIBUTORS

Samuel Abrams, MD

Mary Adams, LMSW

Karin Ahbel-Rappe, PhD, CSW

Elizabeth Allison, DPhil

Christine Anzieu-Premmereur, MD, PhD

Richard Baker, MD

Leon Balter, MD

Grace C. Barron, MD

Francis D. Baudry, MD

Silvia M. V. Bell, PhD

Antonio U. Beltramini, MD

Donna Bentolila, MSW

Kathy Berkman, MD

Susan A. Bers, PhD

Sarah A. Birss, MD

Charles Brenner, MD

John K. Burton, MD

Fred Busch, PhD

Fredric N. Busch, MD

Martin A. Ceaser, MD

Rebecca L. Chaplan, MD

Sabrina Cherry, MD

Nancy J. Chodorow, PhD

Sally D. Clement, MSW, PhD

Susan W. Coates, PhD

Robert P. Cohen, PhD

Tiziano Colibazzi, MD

Daria Colombo, MD

Cal Colarusso, MD

Allan Compton, MD, PhD

Arnold M. Cooper, MD

Susan E. Cutler, PhD

Hilli Dagony-Clark, PsyD

John J. Benjamin Davidman, MD

Diana Diamond, PhD

Norman Doidge, MD

Peter B. Dunn, MD

Dianne Elise, PhD

Steven J. Ellman, PhD

Aaron H. Esman, MD

Harvey H. Falit, MD

Theodore J. Fallon Jr., MD, MPH

Eran Feit, MD

Eric A. Fertuck, PhD

James M. Fisch, MD

Newell Fischer, MD

Michael L. Fleisher, MD

Les Fleischer, PhD, RSW

Gerald I. Fogel, MD

Peter Fonagy, PhD, FBA

James L. Fosshage, PhD

Rhoda S. Frenkel, MD

Paula B. Fuqua, MD

Ruth S. Garfield, MD

Michael S. Garfinkle, PhD

Richard A. Geist, EdD

Amarsingh Ghorpade, MD

Margaret M. Gilmore, MD

Jason Gold, PhD

Samuel T. Goldberg, MD

Cynthia L. Gordon, PhD

John M. Hall, MD

Margaret Ann Fitzpatrick Hanly, PhD

Alexandra M. Harrison, MD

James M. Herzog, MD

Dorothy E. Holmes, PhD

Deanna Holtzman, PhD

Erika F. Homann, PhD

Alexander D. Kalogerakis, MD

Navah C. Kaplan, PhD

Wendy W. Katz, PhD

Jennifer Kennedy, MD

Roger Kennedy, MD

Otto F. Kernberg, MD

Stephen D. Kerzner, MD

Keith E. Kesler, DO

Margaret Klenck, MDiv, LP

Sarah M. Knox, MD

Bernadette S. Kovach, PhD

Robert A. Kravis, PsyD

Anton O. Kris, MD

Lynn S. Kuttnauer, PhD

Claudia M. Lament, PhD

Barry J. Landau, MD

Frances Lang, LICSW

Melvin R. Lansky, MD

Ruth F. Lax, PhD

Cynthia Lee, PhD

Alessandra C. Lemma, DClinPsych

Howard D. Lerner, PhD

Lawrence N. Levenson, MD

Cyril Levitt, PhD

Zvi Lothane, MD

Andrew C. Lotterman, MD

Frances G. Martin, PhD

Corinne Masur, PsyD

Edith R. McNutt, MD

Pamela Meersand, PhD

Karen A. Melikian, PhD

Jill M. Miller, PhD

Maia R. Miller, PhD

Barbara L. Milrod, MD

David Milrod, MD

Daniel B. Morehead, MD

Edward Nersessian, MD

William R. Nixon, PhD

Jack Novick, PhD

Kerry Kelly Novick

William M. Olcott, MD

David D. Olds, MD

Shelley Orgel, MD

Anna Ornstein, MD

Paul H. Ornstein, MD

Allen J. Palmer, MD

Henri Parens, MD

Rachel Parens, MA

Sarah Paul, MD

Jean-Paul Pegeron, MD

Jane Peringer, MD

Mervyn M. Peskin, MD

David Pollens, PhD

Inge-Martine Pretorius, PhD, DPsych

Daniel W. Prezant, PhD

Satish Reddy, MD

William Robinson, MD

Marie G. Rudden, MD

Richard Rusbridger, MA

Bret R. Rutherford, MD

Andrea Sabbadini, CPsychol

Halite Sagiv, MA

David W. Schab, MD

Cordelia Schmidt-Hellerau, PhD

Anita G. Schmukler, DO

Eleanor S. Schuker, MD

Anna R. Schwartz, MD

Rachel G. Seidel, MD

Barbara Shapiro, MD

Theodore Shapiro, MD

Merton A. Shill, PhD

Michael E. Shulman, PhD

Allen M. Siegel, MD

Arietta Slade, PhD

Stephanie D. Smith, MA, LICSW

Ann G. Smolen, PhD

Stephen M. Sonnenberg, MD

Don A. Spivak, MD

Barry L. Stern, PhD

Donnel B. Stern, PhD

Naemi Stilman, MD

Charles P. Stowell, MD

Alan Sugarman, PhD

Stuart W. Taylor, MD

Judith G. Teicholz, EdD

J. Mark Thompson, MD

Johanna Tiemann, PhD

Elizabeth Tillinghast, JD, MD

Dushyant Trivedi, MD

Wendy L. Turchin, MD

Michael Uebel, PhD, LCSW

Susan C. Vaughan, MD

Jolyn Welsh Wagner, MD

Elizabeth F. Weinberg, MD

Andrea Weiss, PhD

Renee Welner, MD

Paul Williams, PhD

Samuel Wilson MD

Harriet L. Wolfe, MD

Thomas S. Wolman, MD

Léon Wurmser, MD, PhD

Frank E. Yoemans MD, PhD

Elisabeth Young-Bruehl, PhD

INTRODUCTION

This cannot be effected without framing fresh hypotheses and creating fresh concepts;
but these are not to be despised as evidence of embarrassment on our part, but deserve
on the contrary to be appreciated as an enrichment of science.

—Freud, 1938a

It is a great pleasure and honor to be introducing *Psychoanalytic Terms and Concepts*. This book represents our best effort to bring together and explicate psychoanalytic terms and concepts used in the discourse of contemporary, North American, English-speaking clinical psychoanalysis. *Psychoanalytic Terms and Concepts* has been published under the sponsorship of the American Psychoanalytic Association. It is the direct descendent, or fourth edition, of the book by the same name edited by Burness Moore and Bernard Fine (1990), published in 1990. Their book was the third edition of the original *A Glossary of Psychoanalytic Terms and Concepts*, first published in 1967 and revised in 1968 (Moore and Fine, 1968).

From its inception more than forty years ago, the mission of *Psychoanalytic Terms and Concepts* has remained the same: to help those interested in psychoanalysis achieve a better understanding of the terms and concepts used by psychoanalysts to describe the human mind, including its interaction with other human minds, in everyday life, development, psychopathology, and the clinical situation. Our aim has been to appeal to as broad a readership as possible. We hope that all intelligent readers, however naive about the subject matter, will find the book orienting and comprehensible. We also hope that experienced psychoanalytic teachers and practitioners, in need of a reading list, clarification and precision regarding terminology, or basic information in an area with which they are unfamiliar, will find the book helpful and interesting. However, our chief "imagined" audience consists of students of psychoanalysis, struggling to read our literature and to make sense of our theories and practice. We hope that by using this book as a guide, these students will better understand what psychoanalysts are trying to say.

Psychoanalytic Terms and Concepts is presented in the format of a lexicon, with terms and concepts arranged alphabetically. It is a hybrid of dictionary, encyclopedia, annotated bibliography, textbook, and intellectual history. It is closest to the first, in that it starts from an alphabetized list of words, each entry beginning with an attempt at definition. From there, it branches out to include these other forms. Indeed, the original Moore and Fine work, still commonly called "the Glossary," was expanded dramatically between the second edition (1968) and third (1990) edition, from ninety-four to more than four hundred terms, moving from a narrow glossary format to a "compendium" or "mini-encyclopedia," with references at the end of each entry. Feeling that even this combination format did not allow for the full explication of concepts, Moore and Fine (1995) followed the Glossary with the publication of an edited textbook, *Psychoanalysis: The Major Concepts*. We too have struggled with the problem of cramming complex concepts into a dictionary format. As Wittgenstein (1953/2001) described, ". . . knowledge goes beyond mere definition, but is embedded in forms of life." This hybrid book represents our best effort to manage the problem of how to bring complicated concepts to life in the basic design of a dictionary.

However, the more complex challenge we have confronted has been the problem of how to recognize, properly apply, limit, and acknowledge our own point of view. A letter from the president of the American Psychoanalytic Association described our mandate: "to maintain the same general format as the past volumes with the elimination of out-of-date terms, the revision of other entries, and the addition of a number of new items, the inclusion of which would bring the volume into better harmony with the expanded conceptual domain of current, more inclusive, pluralistic American psychoanalytic discourse." How commendable this mandate sounded when we first accepted the assignment! Almost immediately, however, we recognized how complicated fulfilling it would be. Every component of this mandate has demanded that choices be made, and choice raises the issue of authorship, even the dreaded specter of "authority," or, at the very least, the problem of "point of view." The complexity of how best to manage the inevitable fact of our having our own and, to be honest, strong opinions about everything—from broad questions about what the mind is like and how clinical psychoanalysis should be conducted, to more narrow and task-specific questions about how terms and concepts are best used—has emerged as our most interesting challenge in editing this book. While it was written by more than 170 authors and worked on by an editorial board of some 30 psychoanalysts chosen to represent a "diversity of voices, interests, and theoretical expertise" (as stipulated in our mandate), there is no escaping that the book expresses a point of view—our own, and ours alone.

How have we tried to manage the clashing directives embedded in our assignment? How have we gone about representing the whole of American psychoanalysis with sufficient integration for students to come away with something coherent, yet without having been brainwashed by our way of seeing things? Professional lexicographers describe the inevitable tension between balancing the "prescriptive" and "descriptive" functions of dictionary-writing. In other words, should a dictionary tell us how the word ought to be used? Or should it describe how it *is* used? We could have tried to handle the "point of view" issue by denying that we have one. Or we could simply have identified with the "English man of science of wide education born in the middle of the nineteenth century," as James Strachey (1966) wryly described his editing-self in his preface to the *Standard Edition*. But these options bespeak a more naive realism than we are comfortable with, not to mention being gender-discordant!

To state the matter succinctly, we define our point of view as: ego psychology or modern structural theory, with an admixture of object relations theory, self psychology, and developmental psychoanalysis, inspired by the ideal of empirical validation for psychoanalytic terms and concepts, enlivened by relational points of view, sobered by the postmodern critique of the certainty of knowledge, and tempered by realism about the impossibility of finding clear and objective referents for terms and concepts pertaining to the mind. How we might actually produce a coherent definition while representing this dizzying collection of perspectives is what we hope to explain in this introduction. Clearly, the intricacies of our approach to "point-of-view management," cannot be adequately captured in this "succinct" description.

To explain how we arrived at our approach to this balancing act, we will lead you through the journey we have made. Like all psychoanalysts, we understand that our contemporary dilemmas are always more clearly illuminated when we study the past. We outline here some of what we have learned from our study of the general history of lexicography, as well as from our study of the specific history of psychoanalytic lexicography. We will revisit the rocky terrain we encountered in considering the problems of psychoanalytic language, problems that, when contemplated from contemporary points of view, call into question the very task of dictionary-writing. Finally, we will locate the equally precarious footholds we have found in considering the problems of psychoanalytic pluralism. We end with a description of our specific methods and solutions, especially with regard to finding a balance between owning our personal point of view, and representing everyone else's.

THE HISTORY OF LEXICOGRAPHY

Research into the history of lexicography has yielded some startling results, naive as we were regarding the formidable challenges embedded in the seemingly admirable task of dictionary-making. Issues we thought were linked to the idiosyncrasies of our own field, especially in this era of theoretical pluralism and postmodern skepticism, emerged as universal leitmotifs of lexicography from its inception. While this might have deterred us, it served instead to assuage our fears of entering uncharted territory. We had learned there is no issue we would face that had not been confronted endless times before. The purported "purely intellectual" task of dictionary-making has been burdened from the beginning by politics, economics, authoritarianism, ideology, and eccentric personalities.

More than 4,500 years ago in pre-Babylonian Mesopotamia, Sumerian-Akkadian scribes, seeking to bridge the linguistic and cultural gap separating two peoples inhabiting the same land, produced the first dictionary. That the world's first attempt at lexicography served the conquering tribe (the Akkads) in their goal of assimilating the culture of their vanquished rivals (the Sumerians) chastened our vision of diverse peoples using our new dictionary to promote a shared understanding. Nevertheless, this first written effort to compile and define a given linguistic word store was undertaken with the aim of promoting coherent conversation. The role of the dictionary in promoting intelligible conversation among diverse peoples sharing terrain became important again in classical Greece, where, in the absence of a single language, *glossai* (words, or, literally, "tongues") in need of explication were compiled to deal with dialectal differences. In the early centuries of dictionary-making, editors had the primary task of translating from one language to another. Much of the emphasis that evolved was in preserving classical writers of an earlier culture who were thought to be superior to present writers. With the invention (or more properly codification) of alphabetical order in the early Renaissance, dictionaries moved away from the church-dominated, thematically organized systems of the Middle Ages toward an increasingly secular readership. Nonetheless, dictionaries also served the aspirations of the educated and the elite. Not until the sixteenth century, with the invention of the printing press, access to cheap paper, and a shift from Latin to "vulgar" tongues, did a more modern dictionary emerge, in line with the decentering trends of the Reformation and the rise of science.

Against this new potential for disseminating knowledge to the masses, a counterforce emerged with the explicit intention of maintaining the cultural, political, and linguistic status quo. In 1635, Cardinal Richelieu gathered the most distinguished minds of the time to found the Académie Française, with the expressed objective of setting down fixed rules for the French language, which seemed to be edging ever more rapidly toward "corruption." The equivalent British body for "fixing" the English language was never able to take shape, efforts in this direction repeatedly undermined by political squabbling. In this climate, the lexicographer was viewed as the high priest of authoritative laws about language, and the guardian of culture.

The thirty-seven-year-old Samuel Johnson readily accepted this exalted role when recruited by a group of British booksellers in 1746 to write the definitive English dictionary. Johnson's two-volume 2,300-page opus, highly idiosyncratic, took him nine years to produce; it was promptly vilified and extolled by equally revered critics. Johnson's *A Dictionary of the English Language* (published in 1755) remained the gold standard for dictionaries for the next century and a half. His original plan, prescriptive in nature, had been to bring order to the chaos of the English language, "composed of dissimilar parts, thrown together by negligence, by affectation, by learning, or by ignorance," but to do so in the manner of a poet. In the end, Johnson bemoaned the loss of his dream as he resigned himself to his role as "harmless drudge" or simple lexicographer, describing and cataloging the language with all its flaws. Johnson's (1755/2002) comments on the difficulty of definition seem surprisingly like our own: "When the nature of things is unknown, or the notion unsettled and indefinite, and various in various minds, the words by which such notions are conveyed, or such things denoted, will be ambiguous and perplexed."

Noah Webster, Johnson's self-declared rival, was determined to create a dictionary of the "American language," but his task became entangled in the political agenda of the day. Webster offended his Federalist comrades by declaring that his dictionary would describe the American language as it really was, a dictionary for the common man. Yet Webster was in fact motivated by two covert agendas: his own personal dogmatism about language, and his desire that his dictionary do double service as both a guide to American usage and a Christian catechism. Predictably, Webster succeeded in winning the animosity of all.[1] Fortunately for him, by the time the dictionary was published, eighteen years after he began the project, Webster had outlived most of his critics and the culture had changed. Andrew Jackson, a friend of the common man, well-known to be a dyslexic, was president. Webster's *An American Dictionary of the English Language*, published in 1828, was judged by history as a crowning achievement; despite its flaws, Webster's name has in America become virtually synonymous with the common noun *dictionary*.

According to Jonathon Green (1996), the British lexicographer and historian, the role of the dictionary in the modern world is a humble one. The lexicographer has been demystified; no longer a priestly authority performing a prescriptive role, he has been transformed into a committee identified by a publisher's name. The modern dictionary is directed at the mass market and designed to present language as it is; the subjectivity of Johnson and Webster is regarded as an amusing vestige of bygone days. However, the clamorous reception of *Webster's Third New International Dictionary, Unabridged* in 1961 belies any such complacency. While lexicography shifted ever more securely toward its descriptive task, the readership was in turmoil. The "dictionary wars" waged over *Webster's Third International* demonstrated clearly enough that a dictionary remains a formidable transference object. Reviled by some, and lauded by others, a dictionary for better or worse inevitably reflects the culture in which it lives. No dictionary, however well-intentioned, can claim to fulfill a purely "descriptive" function. A contemporary dictionary, written by committee, purportedly committed to a descriptive function, just like the bygone prescriptive dictionary written by a single individual, can never escape its role as a narrative that tells a story with all the components of time, place, and person. Above all, dictionary-making by its nature "brings with it decisions, and with decisions, however disinterested, comes choice" (Green, 1996). Through the exercise of this choice, the lexicographer reveals, deliberately or not, the story he wishes to tell.

THE HISTORY OF PSYCHOANALYTIC LEXICOGRAPHY

In our effort to better understand the "narrator position" inherent in our role as dictionary editors, we turned to the history of psychoanalytic lexicography. Again, we found that the specific problems of psychoanalytic dictionary-writing have all been cataloged and confronted on many previous occasions. We have learned much from our dictionary-writing forebears. We have been inspired by their plans and strategies, warned by their missteps, and fortified by recognizing ourselves in their universal cries of anguish and exhaustion. No less important than psychological comradeship has been the massive amount of practical help we have received from these lexicographical predecessors. For the most part, dictionaries and encyclopedias are not written, but collected, or compiled. The word *compiled* comes from the Latin verb *compilare,* meaning "to plunder"—and plunder we have! We have borrowed, used, and stolen (however you like) everything from word lists, research, and references for the entries in this book. Finally, of greatest interest to us, is the issue of how our predecessors have managed the inevitable "narrating," "decision-making," dare we say "authority" of editorship. Some of our predecessors have embraced, even vied for prescriptive authority; others have been far more leery of it.

Psychoanalytic dictionary-writing began with the problem of translation. As our interest is in the explication of psychoanalytic terms and concepts in English, we focus here on the history of German-English translation. It is well known that the English language has no words for many of Freud's terms, so that new words had to be invented by his English translators. As General Editor of *The Standard Edition of the Complete Psychological Works of Sigmund Freud,* James Strachey has been credited (or blamed) for much of the traditional translation (Ornston, 1982, 1985, 1988; Bettelheim, 1983; Wilson, 1987; Timms and Segal, 1988; Pines, 1988; Likierman, 1990; Solms and Saling, 1990). However, the story of how English-language psychoanalysis was invented is complex. While Strachey played a major role in its creation, he is not solely responsible for English psychoanalytic terminology. Freud coined some of it himself. A. A. Brill and Ernest Jones coined more of it at the beginning of the century. Brill included a glossary of some twenty terms in the second edition of his *Psychoanalysis. Its Theories and Practical Application (1914).* To

our knowledge, Brill's glossary is the first published English-language psychoanalytic dictionary. Jones (1913a) used much of this coinage plus some of his own in his *Papers on Psycho-analysis.*

The early collaboration between the American Brill and British Jones quickly turned into a battle for control over English-language psychoanalysis, with Jones and the British as the clear victors. With Freud's approval, Jones (Jones and Maeder, 1913) contributed to a "Kodex" in the first issue of the *Internationale Zeitschrift für Ärztliche Psychoanalyse,* which included "Suggestions for the translation of some of the most common psychoanalytical terms." His vocabulary was printed as a glossary of eighty terms at the end of the second edition of *Papers,* published in 1918.

Decisions about translation were made somewhat more systematically by an "Informal Glossary Committee," set up shortly after the founding of the British Psychoanalytical Society in 1919, which consisted of Jones, Joan Riviere, and Alix and James Strachey, among others. The committee, which met regularly in Jones's Harley Street office, is famous for having agreed upon the terms *parapraxis, cathexis, anaclisis,* and, of course, the *ego* and the *id.* The German-English *Glossary for the Use of Translators of Psychoanalytical Works* (Jones, 1924) was published as the first supplement to the new English-language *International Journal of Psychoanalysis,* founded in 1920 under the editorship of Jones. It included roughly four hundred words. The glossary was later revised in 1935 and again in 1943. The 1943 edition, edited by Alix Strachey, is referred to by James Strachey in his General Preface to the *Standard Edition* as the authority to which he deferred in choosing most English terms for the translation. In his preface to the first edition of this glossary, Jones (1924) described his goal of increasing "intelligibility" by providing "uniformity." He defended the choice to coin many new terms in Greek rather than English as motivated by the wish "to secure terms from the numerous accessory connotations and associations inevitable in a spoken language." Even in these early years, in the context of a clear bid for linguistic control of psychoanalysis in the English-speaking world, Jones warned that the virtues of uniformity must be balanced against the pitfalls of "prematurely fixing the mould into which fluid ideas are being cast." Perhaps with sympathy for the problems facing future dictionary-writers, Jones acknowledged that this danger would be worse had he been providing definitions rather than simply carrying out the "mere task" of suggesting the best words for translation (Steiner, 1987, 1991, 1994; Maddox, 2006).

Despite its award-winning stature,[2] a storm of controversy has raged around the *Standard Edition,* as well as the person of Strachey himself, involving almost every aspect of this "mere task" of translation. While it is impossible to review that controversy here, it cannot be ignored completely. For one thing, ignoring it would deprive us of a chance to express our boundless appreciation to Strachey and his team for their extraordinary accomplishment in creating the *Standard Edition,* which, among other things, serves as the starting place for every English-language dictionary of psychoanalysis. Indeed, we refer to "Strachey" repeatedly in our dictionary, not only to the translation and the index, but to his wonderful commentaries replete with first usages and cross-references. We also drew inspiration from his preface, in which Strachey explores with candor and humor the many challenges he faced in translating Freud.

At least two of these challenges can in our view never be solved. These problems confront anyone who attempts to translate, as well as anyone who attempts to define the words that Freud and his followers have used. All of the standard problems associated with accurately rendering ideas conceived in one language into the words of another are multiplied, first, by the particular nature of Freud's style, and, second, by the nature of the ideas that he aimed to represent. Freud's writing style has been alternately extolled and vilified; it has surely led to much confusion and misunderstanding of what he was attempting to convey. In large part, this is because Freud developed his theory over the course of many decades and did not see the need to systematize and synthesize the progression of his thinking. Freud's extensive use of metaphor has also posed a challenge, as metaphor by its nature captures depth, nuance, affect, and meaning in a highly condensed structure. Freud's use of metaphor, his frequent use of the subjunctive mood, and his choice of common words for describing technical psychoanalytic concepts have been the fodder for intense debate about psychoanalytic language. Are terms and concepts best thought of as metaphors? Or are they best conceptualized as part of a scientific theory that can ultimately be made coherent and empirically tested?

Strachey's detractors hold him responsible for the "scientification" of psychoanalysis, a criticism expressed ever more vehemently by those espousing a postmodern epistemology. We will leave a place mark here for further discussion, as this is a controversy that has only become more heated in the last two decades. For now, it is enough to say that our review of the controversy surrounding the "Strachey translation" has

taught us that attempts to make psychoanalytic language "intelligible" can never be separated from historical and sociocultural contexts, philosophy, politics, personality, and above all, point of view. In the end, we applaud the decision made by an international team of Freudian scholars who, about ten years ago, resolved that a retranslation of the *Standard Edition* was inadvisable. While they may have disagreed about the reasons, they did agree that for all the labor and expense, a new translation would succeed only in exchanging one set of problems for another (Solms, 1999).

Meanwhile, as the British were hatching their plan for the creation of the *Standard Edition,* back in Austria, the task of dictionary-writing proper had already started. Richard Sterba (1936/1937) began work on what was to become his *Handwörterbuch der Psychoanalyse,* which included English and French translations after every German term. Despite four years of work, Sterba is famous for having failed to progress beyond the letter *G.* He is also famous (among psychoanalytic dictionary-writers, at least) for having been warned by Freud (1936b) that "the path from the letter A to the end of the alphabet is a very long one. . . . So do not do it unless you feel an internal obligation . . . a compulsion. . . ." We gleaned at least two things from this cautionary tale: It is acceptable (indeed, perhaps necessary) to be half insane when undertaking the writing of a dictionary. It is also foolhardy to go it alone!

Charles Rycroft and Salman Akhtar did not find, or follow, the same lessons, having offered the only full-length, single-author English-language dictionaries of psychoanalysis we have been able to find. Rycroft (1968) wrote his *A Critical Dictionary of Psychoanalysis* in an era when reviewers would praise him for explaining the "proper meaning" of terms (Book Notices, 1970a) and for "clearing up confusions" arising from dissensions (Book Notices, 1970b). Nevertheless, the challenges described by Rycroft in his introduction are familiar: translation, jargon, reification of terms, and confusion between explanation and description, to name a few. Amusingly, Rycroft commented on the challenge of differentiating between sound ideas and those generated by the "lunatic" or "quack fringe." Most inspiring to us, Rycroft emphasized the importance of making clear his own point of view, to protect the reader from "propaganda." In Rycroft's case, this point of view was notably at odds with many around him: He was openly skeptical about causal theory, saw energy theory as outmoded, viewed neurosis as arising in an interpersonal matrix, and argued that all data are skewed by the perspective of the observer. Of note, Rycroft is among those who have called for the invention of a new psychoanalytic language, in his case, reformulated in terms of communication theory. As we will argue, we do not support this "new language" approach to solving the problems of psychoanalytic language.

Salman Akhtar's (2009) *Comprehensive Dictionary of Psychoanalysis* was published in 2009, well after our own project was under way. In contrast to Rycroft, then, Akhtar and we share the same psychoanalytic world. There is much we disagree with in Akhtar's approach. We do not aim to "synthesize" the viewpoints of differing schools "into a harmonious gestalt"; we do not seek the "prescriptive" role of providing "clinically useful hints" to readers. Finally, we feel that Akhtar offered more information about his inner state of mind (delightfully, we might add) than about his point of view—an important omission for an unapologetic "synthesizer." Nevertheless, Akhtar has assembled a wonderful array of terms, many of them quite exotic, supported by an extraordinary bibliography. We are very grateful to him for the massive amount of work he has done, and—let's just admit it—we have borrowed from his book dozens upon dozens of times.

Of greatest importance to our undertaking, of course, has been *Psychoanalytic Terms and Concepts,* edited by the remarkable team of Burness Moore and Bernard Fine.[3] The first edition of their *A Glossary of Psychoanalytic Terms and Concepts,* published in 1967, was commissioned by the Committee on Public Information of the American Psychoanalytic Association with the aim of clarifying for the public in simple and understandable language what is meant by the terms and concepts of psychoanalysis. As we have noted earlier, Moore and Fine (1990) greatly expanded the second edition of this book into what they called a "mini-encyclopedia." In their third edition, they described the point of view of the book as "primarily Freudian." While they did not further clarify their perspective, we can learn more about it from their description of the editorial board of their companion book, *Psychoanalysis: The Major Concepts* (1995), as representing "traditional mainstream psychoanalysis" made up of "ego psychology or modern structural theory with some admixture of object relations theory and Mahler's developmental theory." To contemporary eyes, Moore and Fine did not give sufficient attention to the problem of "point-of-view management." As with Akhtar, we find them too comfortable with an approach to definition that includes a lot of synthesis, or what they called "condensation." In our effort to find the proper balance between our own strong opinions and those of others, we have not been comfortable

with what we feel is the excessively "prescriptive" approach inherent in this condensation. At the same time, we have been inspired by Moore's (1990) essay "The Problem of Definition in Psychoanalysis," which prefaces the third edition. In this elegant essay, Moore tackled two problems that face any psychoanalytic dictionary-writer in choosing any approach to managing his own point of view: the problem of psychoanalytic language itself, and the associated problem of theoretical pluralism.

THE PROBLEM OF PSYCHOANALYTIC LANGUAGE

The most fundamental challenge we have faced in constructing our psychoanalytic dictionary is that the object of our study, the mind and the meeting of minds, can be known only by putting words to observations and inferences. It is inevitable that observation and inference bear the imprint of theory, and that our relationship to theory is itself subject to the vicissitudes of unconscious processes. The concatenation of subjectivities involved in these processes presents a formidable challenge to any analyst trying to think cogently and critically about inferences and theories and how best to apply them to our work. The recent explosion of theoretical pluralism is a manifestation of that challenge but does not address the nature of the challenge itself.

The struggle to think about and manage the relationship between the data we gather and the object of our study, the human mind and the clinical encounter, is at the crux of all conceptual problems regarding the language of psychoanalysis. Various writers, starting with Freud, have expressed concern about putting words to unconscious processes that are in themselves "unknowable" (Freud, 1915d). It is because the mind can be known only through inference that the language we use to describe it becomes so critically important. One hazard, repeatedly observed, is that the language of psychoanalysis becomes more than simply the way we communicate among ourselves; it becomes psychoanalysis itself (Stoller, 1975c; Rycroft, 1968; Solms, 1999). Freud (1915d) similarly warned us that we are in danger, like the schizophrenic, of mistaking "thing presentation" for "word presentation," in other words, the concrete representation for the idea.

Efforts to address the "problem" of psychoanalytic language have taken various forms over the history of the field. We will describe four approaches to the problem that are most relevant to the lexicographer's task. The first "solution" has been to systematize the language we use to describe mental experience; the second has been to address the problem at its source, that is, to find ways to empirically verify the inferences made about the mind and about the clinical situation; the third has been to devise new languages that more accurately describe the phenomena; the fourth, the postmodern solution, has been to challenge all such efforts. These four solutions to the problem of psychoanalytic language can readily be sorted into two sides of a debate that has raged since psychoanalysis began. At times this debate has been over the question of whether psychoanalysis is a natural science or a humanist/hermeneutic discipline. More recently it has evolved into an argument about whether knowledge about the human mind can be studied and "known," or whether all understanding of the mind and its processes is contextual and co-constructed. This recent debate has profound implications for whether our future as a discipline requires that we hone our vocabulary for accuracy and precision or whether we should jettison our language altogether, fearing its potential to distort and mislead. The challenge for us, as psychoanalytic lexicographers, has been to chart a path through this rocky terrain. We will keep that challenge in mind as we consider the four solutions in greater detail.

The first solution to the problem of psychoanalytic language, the proposal that we "clean up" and systematize the language of psychoanalysis is part of the earliest history of psychoanalytic controversy. Strachey's translation of the *Standard Edition* won him the animosity of more "humanistic" analysts who blamed him for Freud's "scientification," and gratitude from many others who lauded him for a monumental achievement. Jones was explicit in his aim to provide "uniformity," even while acknowledging the pitfalls of such efforts. Whether or not one is sympathetic to the efforts of Strachey and Jones, there is universal agreement that Freud's language legacy was guaranteed to create turmoil. Hartmann, in his efforts to turn psychoanalysis into a general psychology, further systematized Freud's theory and language by introducing specificity into drive theory and ego psychology. Aside from admirers of Hartmann among modern ego psychologists, his efforts at precision have been derided for moving psychoanalytic language even further into clunky, mechanistic, and pseudoscientific discourse. Others, following Hartmann, who have attempted specificity and systemization in the use of psychoanalytic language include Schafer (1976), Jacobson (1964), Kernberg (1970a, 1975), and Marcus (1992). Each of these psychoanalytic writers made explicit efforts at conceptual clarity without sacrificing complexity through a firm commitment to the precise use of categories within psychoanalytic language.

The second solution to the problem of psychoanalytic language has been to approach the problem at its source through a commitment to empirical study. Needless to say, realizing this approach is extremely difficult when the object of study is known only through inference. Rapaport, one of the first psychoanalysts who aimed for a comprehensive psychoanalytic theory based on fundamental principles of how the mind works, argued that clinical inference would never suffice and that empirical methods outside the clinical setting are necessary. Shevrin and Brakel (Shevrin et al., 1996), among others, pursued "basic science" investigation in their efforts to more precisely delineate the characteristics of unconscious mental processes. Westen (1999b), too, was also committed to precision in psychoanalytic language, achieved through empirical investigation. He drew upon advances in cognitive neuroscience to reformulate basic psychoanalytic concepts in a manner that is consistent with contemporary brain science. He argued for the use of psychometrically sound instruments with high reliability and validity to quantify clinical observations in systematic ways.

Bucci (1997), also using contemporary cognitive science and neuropsychological data, aimed at the development of an entirely revised metapsychology, named "multiple code theory." She argued that all areas of modern science operate by establishing a general theoretical framework, or "nomological network," within which hypothetical constructs are housed. Such constructs range from those that are closely inferred from observable events to those that are derived as higher-order abstractions, all connected to one another by definable links. According to Bucci, psychoanalysis lacks scientific rigor not because its data are derived from inference, but because it has failed to systematize and integrate the rules of inference by which mental events are defined. Bucci claimed that our psychological constructs, precisely defined, have the capacity to achieve at least "the same theoretical status as particles and quarks, dark matter, the big bang and life in the Bronze Age." Both Westen and Bucci were committed to the delineation of consistent and precise definitions of basic psychoanalytic concepts so that reliable and valid empirical research can be conducted.

The third solution to the problem of psychoanalytic language is the suggestion that we work to develop an entirely new language. This approach is best illustrated by Schafer's (1976) argument for what he called "action language." Schafer was motivated to rid psychoanalytic language of its mechanistic and reified terminology, and to provide a "systematic" language for clinical discourse. In so doing, his intention was to recast the analysand in the role of active "self-as-agent," a role he felt was proscribed by outdated psychoanalytic terminology. Schafer's action language was a clarion call for a psychoanalytic language based on verbs. His method has had other advocates who seek to revitalize psychoanalytic language through the prescriptive use or rejection of a particular part of speech. Kubie (1975) argued for the use of adjectives, which he felt would avoid reification; Westen (2002) argued against the use of articles for the same reason; Rycroft (1968) argued for the use of gerunds, which he felt expressed a more relational mode; and Orange (2003) argued against the use of "contaminated words" that are lurking in the form of nouns. Schafer's action language did not catch on, nor is it likely that any of these other "parts-of-speech injunctions" might provide a solution to the complex problems of psychoanalytic language.

The fourth solution to the problem of psychoanalytic language is embedded in the postmodern perspective, which at its most radical critiques virtually all assumptions about the value and use of psychoanalytic vocabulary. Orange (2003), who exemplifies a moderate, relational postmodern perspective, described psychoanalytic discourse as a "language-game." She claimed that all psychoanalytic language is embedded in and contaminated by outmoded theory, context, and history. We cannot simply move a word from one context into another without dragging along all its past history and assumptions. Invoking Wittgenstein and Gadamer, Orange cautioned that language deceives us by tempting us to think that we understand more than we actually do. She argued that words are in fact "verbal gestures" whose meanings are entirely contextual; we err when we make the mistake of treating them as if they are something real. Orange explicitly advocated for the use of "phenomenological description" within an intersubjective or "systems context," acknowledging that no perspective is without its assumptions. She was most concerned about the influence that psychoanalytic language exerts on clinical work, and believed that theoretical terminology forces a "mind-lock" on the analyst's ability to think openly and creatively about patients. This results in "authoritarian" formulations that "blame and shame" patients. Although Orange maintained that she was not advocating that we should jettison all psychoanalytic terminology, but was only cautioning us to challenge our assumptions, her positions lead irrevocably down that path.

Let us return to the question of where psychoanalytic lexicography may place itself relative to debates about the function and value of psychoanalytic language. In reviewing the introduction to Moore and Fine's 1990 dictionary, we noted that they too addressed the problems of psychoanalytic language and the role of lexicons and glossaries in the transmittal of knowledge. They focused on the linked problems of translation and metaphor in the proper reading of Freud. However, Moore and Fine also considered the big questions of how language and definition are related to science and facts, and what place to accord metaphor in the presentation of scientific theory. They acknowledged that verbalization necessarily introduces distortion into our perception, but that the solution is not reductionism. They argued for "semantic awareness," especially in the explication of science, so that "we can distinguish between symbol and referent, between inference and observation, between a valid conclusion and a statement of fact." Above all, they were unwilling to give up the richness and depth of metaphor, feeling that metaphor is particularly well suited to convey primary process phenomena. Without it, they argued, "analytic language would be dull indeed."

While we share Moore and Fine's interest in the relationship between psychoanalytic terms and concepts and metaphor, we have moved onto even more treacherous terrain. The very existence of psychoanalytic vocabulary and the act of dictionary-making is called into question by postmodern challenges to psychoanalytic discourse, and, indeed, to the nature of knowledge itself. Govrin (2006) examined the fundamental paradox that new psychoanalytic theories can emerge only when there is conviction that reality or truth about human phenomena can be explained; yet the postmodern perspective rejects that very possibility. New theories bring with them new vocabulary and new concepts, and in Govrin's view there has been no new psychoanalytic theory since Kohut. Govrin quipped that "a 'Dictionary of Postmodern Thought in Psychoanalysis' would be a thin volume indeed."

We are far from the time when consensus or prescriptive authority about language might hold sway. We are also far from the utopian vision of a psychoanalytic language that provides empirically derived precision, reliability, and consistency. However, we are heartened by the vision of scientists like Bucci and Westen, who endorsed the function of a complex and multilayered language to describe the subtleties of unconscious and conscious mental experience. They reassured us that we do not need to apologize for the use of hypothetical constructs and metaphor, as these are required in all scientific enterprises. However, while we applaud the empiricists for their efforts to subject our concepts to scientific scrutiny, we by no means align ourselves with them entirely.

We recognize that the ideal of an empirically based psychoanalytic language is difficult, if not impossible, to realize. The ineffable nature of inner life and human interaction demand poetry in addition to operationalized concepts. While empiricists want to rid language of imprecision, we fear they might rid our language of its poetry and some of its passion as well. Winnicott is a prime example of a creative innovator whose observations on the real and the imagined would never make the empiricist's cut, lacking as they are in any effort at theoretical systemization. Having signed on to the task of editing a psychoanalytic dictionary, we remain unwilling to throw away the richness of more than a century of complex psychoanalytic language and discourse. In fact, we are quite committed to ensuring that it survives. Nor do we think that inventing a new language is either possible or necessary.[4] As Moore and Fine (1990) concluded twenty years ago, "we have to use what is available." And so, having faced down the challenges presented by psychoanalytic language—a predictable outcome considering our self-imposed job description—we were no longer able to avoid confronting the problem of theoretical pluralism.

THE PROBLEM OF
THEORETICAL PLURALISM

Paradoxically, in an age of skepticism about the possibility of knowledge, psychoanalytic theories abound. Perhaps the challenge of talking about what we cannot easily articulate or measure or even apprehend leads inevitably to many points of view, each replete with its own terms and concepts. We have been intrigued by the challenge of writing a psychoanalytic dictionary in this era of increasing theoretical diversity. Hoping to facilitate dialogue among analysts with a wide range of theoretical allegiances, our first step was to assemble an editorial board made up of distinguished colleagues of different theoretical orientations. Next, we worked with these colleagues to compose a "master word list" that includes terms and concepts from many schools of thought. Our plan from the beginning has been that a diverse team of experts would "weigh in" on many of the most important terms in the book. For example, a term such as *oedipus complex* has required explication by developmental psychoanalysts, ego psychologists, self psychologists, and object relations theorists, with perhaps a disclaimer of sorts from relational psychoanalysts. We felt we were on our way to providing a platform for the exposition of theoretical pluralism.

Yet we had learned through our study of the fundamentals of lexicography and the history of dictionary-making that a psychoanalytic dictionary, like any other dictionary, cannot help but be a narrative that tells a story—a story that reflects the prejudices and biases of its authors. In fact, we had already betrayed our own allegiances in designating a collection of "fundamental" terms and concepts that we called the "core." A sampling of this core includes terms such as *unconscious, conflict, fantasy, wish, character, defense, compromise formation, primary process, structure, metapsychology, self, object, narcissism, transference,* and *countertransference.* Certainly these terms are fundamental to our way of thinking about psychoanalysis. However, we had to accept that this "core" would surely not be so designated by many others.

Twenty years ago, Moore and Fine (1990) addressed the challenge of psychoanalytic pluralism by including "terms derived from schools that are not strictly Freudian" and by having these terms "reviewed by persons thoroughly familiar with the literature of the school." We felt that this approach was no longer adequate. But we had not yet figured out how to resolve the tension between our wish to produce a coherent and useful dictionary and our wish to represent, indeed to celebrate, diversity. We were eager to accept the privileged role of constructing the narrative and telling the story. However, like Johnson and Webster before us, we were contending with a set of clashing intentions and expectations and grappling with the inevitable tension in dictionary-writing over how to balance "prescriptive" and "descriptive" functions. As amateur dictionary-writers, we have rejected the hieratic, legislative roles of the ancient lexicographers, seeking neither to instruct students in the correct reading of sacred texts nor to provide a guide to the proper use of *shibboleths.* However, we must confess that from time to time we have glanced back a bit wistfully at the days when Jones (1924) could without apology launch his quest for "uniformity," or when Freud (1936b) could commend Sterba on the "precision and correctness" of his lexicographical efforts. Yet while we have never really wished to "prescribe" our point of view, we have had to recognize that we have one. At the very least, we knew that it was essential to make it clear, lest our dictionary end up as a dizzying hodgepodge of disparate and disjointed ideas. How then to celebrate diversity, while avoiding the dangers of intellectual dishonesty and/or chaos?

As part of his extraordinary, life-long effort to contend with the challenges of theoretical pluralism, Pine (2006) offered the metaphor of the dictionary, in an attempt to imagine how contemporary analysts might make use of both the diversity in our points of view and the commonality that he, like Wallerstein

(1992), feels we share. Pine imagined this "psychoanalytic dictionary" as a compilation of theory-neutral observations, formulations, ideas, concepts, or "pieces of theory" from which analysts can draw in their work with patients. Side by side with this collection of theory-neutral "words," Pine maintained that a judicious selection of core concepts can be extracted from diverse theories to provide a conceptual base, or "grammar," from which all clinicians may work.

However, Pine's "dictionary," itself, is only a metaphor. In grappling with the assignment of writing a real dictionary, we have found it impossible to realize his vision. Every psychoanalytic theory is a complex, interlocking set of propositions and concepts that includes essential perspectives on the organization and structure of the mind, its development in relationship with other minds, and its malfunctioning in psychopathology. Every psychoanalytic theory also includes ideas about how best to understand and manage treatment. All psychoanalytic terms and concepts are components of a theory, or a model of the mind, with linked assumptions and implications. Terms and concepts cannot be separated from theory, or even from each other, without losing their coherence. Indeed, as Govrin (2006) argued, the glorious "thick descriptions" of human inner life, offered by various psychoanalytic schools of thought, depend on the fact that every element of these descriptions is embedded in a grand and complex theoretical mosaic (Ryle, 1971). At the same time, as noted earlier, despite Pine's imagined "universal core," we have found it impossible to identify a conceptual core agreeable to all. In our view, Pine's approach to pluralism through the radical deconstruction of psychoanalytic language into "words," followed by a search for the universal "grammar," cannot work.

Govrin offered us a different way to think about the challenge of theoretical pluralism that resonates with our own. In Govrin's imagined psychoanalytic world, there is a place for many kinds of positivist theory-makers who help us think about what the mind is "really" like, as well as for postmodern metatheorists who demand that we question our claims to knowledge. However, the realization of this world requires that we make fundamental changes in our institutions and organizations. In his brief history of psychoanalytic institutions, Govrin (borrowing from Freudental, 1996) argued that we have traversed an early period of confident, positivist theory-making that at its best has been essential to the field, and that at its worst has led to overconfidence and "institutional dogmatism." We are currently in a period of postmodern skepticism, which at its best challenges us to reflect on important questions of epistemology, and at its worst demands that no one believe in any particular position but rather yield to the coercions of "internalized pluralism." In Govrin's view, there is a third alternative. In a new era of "institutional pluralism," pluralism will be demanded not of individuals, but of institutions themselves, charged with the task of protecting incompatible conceptual schemes and points of view so that each may develop according to its own criteria. The ideal leader of such an institution should represent pluralistic relativism at one level, while ensuring that nonrelativist, nonpluralist theoreticians may thrive, each approaching the mind from a different point of view, and each arrayed on a spectrum from confident positivism to extreme epistemological skepticism.

As Co-Editors in Chief of the new *Psychoanalytic Terms and Concept,* we have attempted to emulate this vision of an ideal leader of a modern pluralistic institution. While Moore and Fine offered up the major share of their terms and concepts from the viewpoint of the unapologetic Freudian insider, we have attempted a more complicated balancing act. We regard our dictionary as the product of our effort to tolerate a difficult tension in which we have tried to offer the dictionary as a safe, pluralistic institution where analysts from many schools of thought and many points of view can find voice, within which we, even while functioning as Co-Editors in Chief, recognize ourselves as two nonpluralistic, individual analysts. Have we succeeded in this goal? Only our future readership can truly answer the question. However, we will describe the methodology we devised in our attempt to actualize, on a small scale, this vision.

METHODOLOGY

Devising our methodology has truly been a work in progress. Having completed the project, we finally have it all figured out, with lots of advice to spare! We will describe the process to highlight the many decisions that must be made in writing a dictionary, and the implications those decisions have for the final product. Our first step was to establish who we wanted our readership to be, since it would determine the level of complexity and clarity the writing would require. As we have said, we decided to aim for as broad a readership as possible, ranging from the intelligent but psychoanalytically naive college student to the experienced analytic teacher or practitioner. In short, our modest goal has been that our dictionary be on the shelf of every student of the mind, regardless of discipline!

We proceeded to assemble our editorial board. Aiming for diversity of theoretical orientation, academic discipline, and geographical location, we consulted with senior analysts across the country for suggestions. We started with a group of about fifteen analysts with expertise in some aspect of "North American" psychoanalysis, and also included analysts with areas of special knowledge, such as linguistics, philosophy, anthropology, and research. Another half dozen were added along the way, as we became aware of the need for additional areas of expertise or just plain manpower. Our editorial board has provided extraordinary intellectual capability and unimaginable commitment throughout this project.

Each member of the board took responsibility for a specific "section" of the dictionary based on interest and expertise, which included refining the word list, recruiting writers, and then completing the first phase of editorial review. In addition to our "core," we designated the following sections: ego psychology, object relations, self psychology, treatment, development, sex and gender, relational psychoanalysis, and psychopathology. As we have noted, the terms we assigned to the "core" represented an early acknowledgment of our theoretical commitments, although we had not fully recognized this at the time. We somewhat fancifully imagined that our experts in research, philosophy, linguistics, and so on would function as a "transverse" committee who would spring into action after all definitions were written to add an interdisciplinary focus. Time did not permit this.

As we constituted our board, we also completed two crucial tasks: the word list and the definition template. We looked for words in all the obvious places, starting with Moore and Fine and then reviewing other psychoanalytic dictionaries, journals, and textbooks. Constructing a word list is a gatekeeper function, and we needed to define our perimeter. Would we include words within the psychiatric or general psychology lexicon, or would we restrict ourselves to those words that were clearly within the psychoanalytic domain? Our decision was the latter. *Depression, psychosis,* and *borderline* are all terms attached to an extensive psychoanalytic literature, so they all made it in. Eating disorders and Piagetian terms did not make the cut. What about archaic terms? Or terms that "belong" only to a particular theory? Should they be defined separately or included within a larger exposition of their theoretical housing? Often it depended on whether the term belonged to our theory or somebody else's. So *complementary series* qualified as an independent entry, while *parataxic distortion* did not. As we had learned in our lexicographical studies, the strains of our theory narrative continued inevitably to emerge with every decision we made.

Constructing the definition template was a crucial task, as it was to serve as the model for every one of our nearly three hundred entries. We conceptualized each definition as a mini-essay, starting with a concise, contemporary definition that situates the term within its theoretical context. This "bullet definition" is followed by extremely brief definitions of closely related terms to make distinctions clear. For example, a definition of *character* distinguishes it from *ego, self, identity,* and *temperament.* Arriving at a concise contemporary definition presented a formidable challenge and might easily have left us stumped. Whose contemporary definition would qualify? Would this first paragraph end up as a linked sequence of "he says, she says," or would we actually have to bite the bullet and offer our own definition? We decided upon the latter, feeling strongly that dictionary readers need and deserve a clear definition. Our theory narrative was certainly expanding as we committed ourselves to a concise, contemporary definition that we had to recognize as our own. As we had originally conceived the entry template, the introductory paragraph was to be followed by the term's first usage; a detailed exposition of how the word has changed over time, both in terms of further elaboration within its own "school" and within other schools of thought; a discussion of the controversies that surround the term; a description of important misunderstandings and misusages of the term; a note concerning whether the term has been operationalized for research purposes, and if so, how; and important relationships with other disciplines.

As the definitions began pouring in (to our delight, from authors ranging from the most junior to the most august members of our field), the first phase of editing work was initiated. We knew how difficult it would be to conform to the definition template, as we had struggled through writing sample definitions ourselves. Our twice-yearly board meetings became essential opportunities to review definitions and consider issues such as voice, tone, and perspective.[5]

Our most profound template revision, which ultimately was our best solution to the problem of finding the right "tone," grew out of these discussions among our editors. We realized that each definition requires a critical second paragraph whose purpose is to convey to readers the term's overall importance in psychoanalysis and, in some cases, to locate it in relationship to other fields. For example, with the definition of *defense,* it is important to convey that psychoanalysis was born with Freud's revolutionary discovery of the dynamic function of defense in the etiology of hysteria, in contrast to the prevailing view of its connection to organic brain disease. Another example: In a definition of *sexual orientation,* the second paragraph must convey that psychoanalysis introduced a revolutionary view of human sexuality, but that at a later point, some of its views on sexuality were legitimately attacked as rigid and dogmatic. The contextualizing of terms is one way in which our glossary bridges the function of dictionary and encyclopedia. We realized that our board meetings also served to model a method of dialogue among analysts with different points of view, which we hope we have succeeded in representing in the entries in our dictionary.

Lost in the workload inherent in the task, we have only gradually come to recognize precisely how we have situated ourselves as dictionary-writers in a postmodern, pluralistic psychoanalytic world. We have come to understand that our definition template reflects our effort to establish a nondogmatic perch from which to view the contemporary terrain. More important, it reflects our best efforts to apply what is helpful about postmodern skepticism, while at the same time avoid linguistic nihilism. Embedded in our definition format is a stance of constant interrogation of each term, forcing us to ask: What is this term for? Why was this term invented? How has it been used? Why has its usage been accepted by some and not by others? The answers to these questions are embedded in intricacies of psychoanalytic theory. We have needed to delve deeply into theory to fully explicate terms and to fully appreciate how they are related to one another. The answers to these questions are also sometimes embedded in the politics and history of psychoanalysis. Thus, this revised edition of *Psychoanalytic Terms and Concepts* is a thick volume indeed. It is thick in the sense of the number of terms and concepts it includes. More important, it is thick in its description of psychoanalysis itself.

Our function as editors has been to provide the "glue" of this enterprise. Scores of dedicated writers brought us carefully researched definitions that served as the basis for all later work. Our excellent section editors did the first round of editing, and then it was up to us to create a consistent editorial voice so that the dictionary would cohere as a unified volume. This sometimes required extensive rewriting, streamlining, and reorganizing; unwanted repetition required that we combine several definitions into one or that we move pieces from one definition to another. Each definition became the synthesized product of the work of several contributors. We went through many rounds on the conceptually difficult definitions, passing them back and forth between us countless times. We often found that we needed to "reconcile" definitions so that references to the same set of ideas were consistent. There

was a steep learning curve, so that we would go back to definitions we felt we had completed months or years earlier, and would realize they needed rewriting. Finally, we had to know when to stop. Six years and two months after its initiation, the project was complete.

We feel confident that we have satisfied the mandate with which we were charged: to "bring the volume into better harmony with the expanded conceptual domain of current, more inclusive, pluralistic American psychoanalytic discourse." The terrain we have traversed to arrive at that goal has been far more challenging than we could possibly have imagined. We have no illusion about having contributed to the process of integrative theory building. That has not been our goal. However, we are hopeful that our effort to provide coherent and carefully considered definitions of psychoanalytic terms and concepts, to clarify the context in which psychoanalytic language originated and evolved, to consider how the same language is used differently by different theories (or not used at all), and to examine what is at stake with any particular term or concept will facilitate meaningful discourse within the field and with neighboring disciplines.

Notes

1. Indeed, we could not help but be moved by his aggrieved lament: "What is a lexicographer to do when the people of Connecticut use 'fourfold' as a verb? Is this my fault?" (*Lepore, 2006*)

2. For his work on the *Standard Edition*, Strachey was awarded the Schlegel-Tieck Prize in 1967 by the Embassy of the Federal Republic of Germany for the best translation in the United Kingdom of a "work of literary merit and general interest."

3. There are dozens of other English-language dictionaries from which we have drawn inspiration and from which we have borrowed extensively. The most important of these are the extraordinarily scholarly *The Language of Psychoanalysis*, by J. Laplanche and J.-P. Pontalis (1967/1973), which, while purporting to be a general dictionary, is focused mainly on the work of Freud; and A *Dictionary of Kleinian Thought* (Hinshelwood, 1989), whose focus is self-explanatory. At the end of this book, we append a list of the many other dictionaries, encyclopedias, and textbooks that have been important to this project (see Appendix).

4. Although Akhtar (2009) has pointed to the irony that dictionary-writing favors theorists who coin new terms and concepts.

5. A quote from the minutes of the January 18, 2007, editorial board meeting well illustrates these points. We were comparing a revised definition of *primal fantasy* with the Moore and Fine version (1990): "The

group agreed that the new (revised Glossary) approach is overall preferable to the Moore and Fine approach in that it avoids the overly confident, ex cathedra tone of the earlier volume. M and F talk to the reader as though they, 'the authors,' know exactly what the word means and how it should be used. They also talk to readers as though they know what the impact of primal fantasy or experience actually is, in other words, they present themselves as experts on the mind rather than experts on words. Finally, they go far beyond the bounds of psychoanalytic knowledge by making statements about how people in other cultures live (for example, in huts).

By contrast, the [revised] definition is more scholarly, seeking to inform the reader of a range of thought using a historical approach. It does not exceed the aims of a glossary in that it does not lecture on how the fantasy 'actually' works, but sticks to how it is 'said to work' by various writers. It also does not exceed the bounds of psychoanalytic knowledge by lecturing the reader about facts that might reasonably be said to be from another discipline . . . , for example, with the grass huts . . . anthropology."

NOTES TO OUR READERS

We hope that the following information will aid our readers in making the best use of this book.

This book follows the traditional alphabetical order format of dictionaries and lexicons. Whenever possible, we have integrated related terms within the same entry, in order to minimize repetition and provide comprehensive understanding. Therefore, there are a number of terms that have not been independently defined. These terms appear in the book in alphabetical order and are followed by a list of those terms that include their discussion. This method does not include the cognates of defined terms, which are entered in boldface in every entry but are not listed independently. We hope this provides ease of access for the reader.

Each entry follows a consistent format. The opening paragraph is a concise definition that represents our best judgment about the meaning of the term. The second paragraph is an explanation of the overall significance of the term in relationship to the field of psychoanalysis as a whole. The third paragraph identifies the term's first usage. The remaining body of the entry describes the term's historical evolution and its relevance to each psychoanalytic school of thought. The final paragraph describes any research that is relevant to the term.

All psychoanalytic theoretical schools that are identified with a particular author are listed under that author's name. These theoretical schools include the work of Bion, Fairbairn, Jung, Klein, Lacan, and Winnicott. Other psychoanalytic schools are discussed under headings that seemed to make the most sense. For example, we have included ego psychology in the entry on ego, and conflict theory in the entry on conflict. There are separate listings for interpersonal psychoanalysis, object relations theory, relational psychoanalysis, and self psychology. There are many additional, separate entries throughout the book for terms related to each of the psychoanalytic schools of thought, particularly for those terms that have entered the general psychoanalytic lexicon.

There are many places throughout the book where the adjective *unconscious* is assumed. However, in circumstances where there might be doubt, we have included it.

In general, we have defined our boundaries to include terms that are exclusively psychoanalytic and to include terms that originated within general psychiatry but have an extensive psychoanalytic literature associated with them. We do not include the phrase "as defined in psychoanalysis," in every definition, but this is assumed. We have also included some Freudian terms that are rarely used but are historically significant.

In order to avoid needless repetition, we have bundled all references at the end of the book. All in-text citations include the author's name and the year of publication. If the citation immediately follows the author's name, then only the year of publication is noted. When an author has multiple publications within the same year, we have added lowercase letters to the year of publication.

All psychoanalytic authors are referred to by last name only, except in the event of two or more authors having the same last name. In those cases, the author is identified by first initial and last name. Exceptions have been made for Sigmund Freud and Melanie Klein, who are usually identified by last name alone.

Throughout the book, third-person-singular pronouns are "he." We have adopted this format for consistency and to avoid the unnecessary and irritating repetitive reference to "he/she." The only exceptions to this format are instances where the person referred to is clearly female, or where the person referred to is the primary caregiver who, by tradition, is referred to as "she." The decision to use the male pronoun in no way represents an endorsement of attitudes of male supremacy; indeed, we are cognizant of the vexed history of psychoanalysis in this regard.

Each entry is the combined effort of multiple contributors, therefore no attribution appears on any entry. We, as Co-Editors in Chief, assume full responsibility for the final form.

A

Abreaction and **Catharsis** are terms originated by Breuer and utilized by Freud and Breuer to describe their preanalytic treatment of hysterical patients through a process by which the affect associated with a traumatic memory is discharged through speech. While the importance of these terms is largely historical, the recovery of affect-laden memories and the emotionally authentic reconsideration of the past remain valuable aspects of the psychoanalytic process.

The first use of these terms was in "Studies on Hysteria" (Breuer and Freud, 1893/1895). In this early phase in the development of psychoanalysis, Freud (following Breuer) hypothesized that hysteria, or conversion hysteria, was caused by the repression of traumatic, affect-laden memories, which prevented the discharge of the affect, resulting in its conversion into physical symptoms. Breuer and Freud observed that hysterical symptoms could be removed by the uncovering of these memories through hypnosis or by the therapist's urging. The associated affects could then be discharged through speech (abreaction). The result of the successful abreaction of a traumatic memory was a catharsis (from the Greek for "purification" or "purging"); therefore, Breuer and Freud called this preanalytic therapy the "**cathartic method**."

Freud later acknowledged the limitations of this treatment method, and when his theory of pathogenesis shifted from trauma to conflictual wishes, and the treatment shifted from hypnosis to free association and the analysis of transference and resistance, abreaction and catharsis were no longer considered to have a central role in the therapeutic action of psychoanalysis. When the term *abreaction* does appear in the literature of the 1930s to 1960s, it is often in the context of a critique of the active therapy of Ferenczi (Fenichel, 1939b) or the dynamic psychotherapy of Alexander and French (E. Bibring, 1954).

Abstinence, **Neutrality**, and **Anonymity** are three technical guidelines originally recommended by Freud for the conduct of analysis. Abstinence refers to the analyst's recognizing, but not gratifying, patients' transference wishes so as to: understand their multidetermined and multilevel character, allow for the emergence of more deeply repressed wishes, and further understand the here-and-now emotional and temporal context in which they have appeared. Neutrality, or **technical neutrality** (Kernberg, 1976b) refers to the analyst taking a position "equidistant" (A. Freud, 1936) from the patient's ego, id, and superego in the analysis of the patient's conflicts. Neutrality also refers to the analyst's persistent openness to new understandings of the patient's mental life (Schafer, 1983). Finally, neutrality refers to the analyst's self restraint and his respect for the patient's autonomy, which he protects by avoiding the imposition of his values, his personality, or his subjective view of reality (Hoffer, 1985). Anonymity refers to the analyst's relative lack of self disclosure, which has as its purpose the maintenance of sufficient ambiguity for the patient to experience a wide range of transference fantasies.

Abstinence, neutrality, and anonymity have been important throughout the history of psychoanalysis because, while Freud wrote about them only once, they have constituted the cornerstone of the analyst's technical stance. These guidelines create the framework for a psychoanalytic treatment in which the therapeutic action is based on interpretations offered by an analyst from a position of relative objectivity, and for a model of the mind that privileges psychoanalytic principles such as transference, resistance, a dynamic unconscious, and the role of free association. These guidelines also trench on core psychoanalytic concepts such as the therapeutic action of psychoanalysis, the epistemological position of the analyst, the analyst/patient interaction, and the influence of this interaction on the data of a psychoanalysis. Abstinence, neutrality, and anonymity have, therefore, been the subject of intense, often polarizing debate, as competing visions of the psychoanalytic situation and of the therapeutic action of psychoanalysis have emerged. Abstinence, neutrality, and anonymity still play a central, though controversial, role in the theory of psychoanalytic technique.

Freud (1915a) mentioned neutrality only once without actually defining it, but he related it to the analyst's need to suppress his own feelings in response to a patient's transference love. Neutrality is, however, encompassed in Freud's admonition that the psychoanalyst model himself on a surgeon, putting ". . . aside all his feelings, even his human sympathy . . ." (1912b). Freud was not directing analysts to be uncaring, but to restrain their "therapeutic ambition" lest their own emotional stake in the patient's progress interfere with their handling of resistance. Freud never used the term *anonymity*; Gitelson (1952) first used the word *anonymity* in 1952. However, Freud did recommend that "the doctor should be opaque to his patients and, like a mirror, should show them nothing but what is shown to him" (1912b). Freud's metaphor of the mirror did not aim to preserve the analyst as a blank screen for transference projection (J. Glover [1926] first used the phrase "blank screen," in 1926), but rather enjoined the analyst from sharing intimate details of his own life as a technique to overcome patients' resistances to self disclosure. Freud's stance was motivated by his desire to separate psychoanalysis from other contemporary therapies that employed suggestion or that relied on the therapeutic impact of the therapists' authority and/or personality (Makari, 1997). Freud's recommendations with regard to abstinence were embedded in his libido theory. He posited that the psychic energy required for the analytic work would be unavailable if the patient found "substitute gratifications" for the repressed wishes that his symptoms partially gratified. Freud therefore actively prohibited behaviors that he believed directly or symbolically gratified those wishes, both in the analytic setting and in the patient's everyday life. He also believed that privations within and outside of the analytic situation preserved the suffering for which the patient had originally sought relief, and thus preserved the motivation for treatment (1919a).

It is notable that while Freud proscribed some of the analyst's behaviors, he did not actually address what the analyst should do. Moreover, his own technique was apparently at odds with his own proscriptions (Lipton, 1977). Freud differentiated his response to specific transferences from his ordinary humanness and spontaneity with patients. Finally, Freud's conceptualization of abstinence, neutrality, and anonymity differs sharply from the contemporary meanings of these terms.

In light of the importance of the technical guidelines of abstinence, neutrality, and anonymity, it is striking that in the decades following their explication there was relatively little discussion or debate about them. One significant exception was the work of Ferenczi. Ferenczi's (1919, 1920) first technical innovation, "active technique," was based on Freud's libido theory. However, in contrast to the less-directive analyst described in Freud's recommended technique, Ferenczi actively issued both prohibitions and directives to his patients. His prohibitions sought to heighten the availability of libido for the treatment by blocking the gratification of unconsciously enacted disguised wishes; his directives sought to facilitate the reconstruction of early wishes by encouraging the enactment of consciously gratifying behaviors. Ferenczi's (1930, 1931) controversial second set of innovations established an analytic setting that was essentially the opposite of that recommended by Freud. Ferenczi placed "indulgence" rather than frustration or deprivation at the heart of his technique. He argued that patients are able to express a wider range of feelings when the analyst is openly warm and "relaxed" about the framework of the analytic setting, allowing patients, for example, to remain in a session until they feel comfortable about stopping for the day. He also argued that if the usual stance of the analyst too closely resembles the original prohibiting parents, the patient is more likely to repeat rather than remember his past. In place of the analytic mirror, Ferenczi was self revealing, acknowledged errors in technique, and, at one point, experimented with patient and analyst analyzing each other. Despite the dramatic challenge to Freud embodied in Ferenczi's method, his technique was not actively addressed in the literature for the next fifty years. Instead, some analysts, especially in the 1930s through the 1960s, misapplied Freud's guidelines as rigid rules, thereby creating an authoritarian and cold psychoanalytic treatment.

A second challenge to abstinence, neutrality, and anonymity was raised by F. Alexander's (1950a) therapeutic use of the "corrective emotional experience," in which the analyst does not interpret the patient's transference, but instead purposefully adopts attitudes aimed to counter the presumed pathogenic attitudes of the patient's original objects. In response, K. Eissler (1953) argued that interpretation is the model technique of psychoanalysis and that modifications of that technique that might include more gratifying interactions are "parameters" which should have only limited, temporary use and whose impact should be analyzed. In response to Eissler, Stone (1961) emphasized that, alongside transference wishes, the patient has a reasonable human expectation that the analyst's attitude should be kindly and helpful.

In the mid-twentieth century there was growing interest in the affective atmosphere of the analytic situation, the role of empathy in psychoanalytic treatment, and a growing awareness of the implicit gratifications inherent in the nontransferential emotional relationship between a patient seeking help and an analyst wishing to offer it (Fox, 1984). This relationship was cast in mother/child terms in Greenacre's "matrix transference" (1954), Gitelson's "diatrophic attitude" (1962), Modell's "holding environment"

(1976), and Loewald's (1960) descriptions of the analyst as a "new object." Greenson (1965a) wrote that the nontransferential patient-analyst relationship is characterized by the mutual respect shared by two adults: the "real relationship." Interest in the noninterpretive aspects of psychoanalytic treatment was also spurred by the treatment of borderline and narcissistic patients. While there was general agreement that abstinence, neutrality, and anonymity had been misapplied by earlier generations of analysts, and that a psychoanalytic treatment based on interpretive technique could be conducted by an emotionally engaged psychoanalyst, there were few attempts to revisit these guidelines until the 1980s.

In contemporary psychoanalysis, the principle of abstinence has been revised to reflect the understanding that a patient requires an analyst who is available enough to sustain the patient's experience of the authentically experienced illusion of transference. For example, L. Friedman (1982) wrote that the analytic situation is marked by "a peculiar blend of enticement and elusiveness," and Fox (1984) posited that the analytic situation requires an "optimal tension" between gratification and frustration for a patient's transference to be both expressed and then analyzed.

The principle of anonymity has been modified in response to the growing appreciation for the many ways that the analyst's subjectivity is unconsciously manifested in an analysis, including via role responsiveness (J. Sandler, 1976a) and enactment (Chused, 1991). While most analysts are circumspect about deliberate self disclosure because of their focus on the analysis of transference, some analysts have been critical of this restraint. Renik (1995) wrote that the analyst's clinical choices are inevitably revealing and are the object of patients' observation; he argued that if the analyst conveys an ideal of anonymity the patient may feel constrained from sharing his observations. Renik also noted that the goal of anonymity encourages the perception of the analyst as an objective observer, leading to iatrogenic idealization. In its place, Renik urged analysts to invite patients to collaborate, including sharing their views of the analyst's methods. From a social-constructivist point of view, I. Hoffman (1983) denied the possibility of the analyst's anonymity. Hoffman underscored that whatever the analyst's point of view on self disclosure, the patient assumes that he is having an impact on the analyst and senses that the analyst's behavior is an ever-present but ambiguous indicator of that impact. The patient's transference experience, therefore, is not a wholly intrapsychic experience projected onto the analyst but results from the patient's selective attention to and interpretation of the analyst's actual responses to him.

The principle of neutrality has been burdened by ambiguity. In the past, it had been conflated with both abstinence and anonymity, so that neutrality came to be equated with a stereotype of the nonreactive, unemotional, and disengaged analyst who had no interest in the outcome of the analysis. A contemporary consensus has emerged among several analysts theorizing from the ego-psychology tradition, who have offered clarifications. Schafer (1983), Poland (1984), Hoffer (1985), S. Levy and Interbitzen (1992), and Boesky (Makari, 1997) have all written that neutrality describes an attitude, not a demeanor. The neutral position is expressed in the analyst's interest in all aspects of a patient's mental life and in avoiding any foreclosure of the patient's and the analyst's understanding; this neutrality includes avoiding an unquestioning acceptance of the patient's views of himself and others. Neutrality is also expressed in the analyst's attempts to limit the intrusions of his own values, judgments, or the distorting impact of his own emotional life. Poland and Hoffer both noted that the analyst is not an objective observer; his subjective experience is inevitably drawn into the analysis so that maintaining neutrality requires ongoing self analysis. Poland also acknowledged that the analyst's allegiance to theory compromises his neutrality. Boesky described the analyst's inevitable unconscious contributions to the patient's resistance. Neutrality represents a "fictional" point to which the analyst attempts to return via self reflection; even if neutrality is impossible to maintain, the concept alerts the analyst to the constant pull away from it. Finally, Poland and Levy and Interbitzin clarified that the analyst is not neutral with regard to the outcome of the analysis; the analyst wishes to help the patient and works with a therapeutic intent.

The relational critique of this contemporary ego-psychological view of neutrality is that it underemphasizes both the analyst's ongoing participation in the interactive matrix of transference/countertransference and the patient's potential awareness of this participation. I. Hoffman (1996) wrote that the asymmetry and ritual of the analytic relationship grants the analyst a "moral authority" that, even when examined, cannot be extinguished, so that the analyst's conscious and unconscious values inevitably participate in the patient's choices. Aron (1991) noted that while the analyst may reflect on his participation in the transference/countertransference, if he doesn't inquire about the patient's observations of the analyst, he can't be fully aware of his subjective, nonneutral participation. Finally, some psychoanalytic paradigms based on postmodern philosophy challenge the entire premise of objective knowledge, truth, and correspondence to reality.

Acting Out is the tendency for unconscious transference fantasies or the defenses against them to be dramatized or symbolically realized in external reality, especially in the interpersonal setting of the analytic dyad. Acting out, like transference itself, usually functions as a resistance, because the unconscious wishes and fears actualized in the acting out oppose or impede self reflection, free association, or communication, or they intrude on the basic analytic frame. The "action" of the acting out may or may not refer to literal motor action; however, the term is most commonly used to describe discrete, observable behaviors that impinge on the analytic frame (missing, forgetting, or coming late to sessions), or to actions in the patient's everyday life that represent displaced transference feelings or defenses against them (initiating, ending, or changing the character of a particular relationship). Acting out is also used to describe the analyst's unconscious expression of countertransference. Acting out is differentiated from enactment, defined as an interaction mutually created by analyst and patient, or a joint acting out.

The term *acting out* has been used with great variability by psychoanalysts and has been incorporated, inaccurately, into the vernacular to refer to impulsive or bad behavior. This variability results from the conceptual difficulties distinguishing the resistance function of acting out from its potential communicative function, or from the intrinsic tendency of transference to seek actualization (Boesky, 1982). For these reasons, the term *acting out* is less frequently used nowadays. Furthermore, contemporary psychoanalysts of all schools recognize that the patient's communications within the psychoanalytic situation are complex and function simultaneously on many levels, including both behaviorally and intrapsychically.

Some of the ambiguities of acting out have their origin in Freud's (1914c) first description of the term in "Remembering, Repeating and Working-Through." Freud argued that patients in analysis are motivated to repeat, that is symbolically dramatize or act out the past, in order not to remember it. He conceptualized both transference and acting out in terms of the discharge of wish in action, thereby diverting thoughts and feelings from remembering, which would require the delay of discharge. Freud's list of "actions" covered a wide range, from the patient's attitudes, feelings, or manner of speaking during a session, to impulsive and potentially maladaptive

decisions undertaken in everyday life. Following Freud, several aspects of the concept have invited ambiguous interpretations (Boesky, 1982). For example, some analysts used the term *acting out* to mean actualizations that occur outside of the analytic setting, and used the term **acting in** for acting out that occurs in sessions. This also changed the original meaning of acting in, which was used to describe unconscious conflicts expressed in a patient's posture on the couch (Zeligs, 1957). The differentiation between acting out and a patient's general proclivity for action has also been blurred, so that some analysts conceptualized acting out as the expression of the incapacity to bear tension and arrest action (Greenacre, 1950b; Kanzer, 1957); acting out was consequently associated with delinquency and perversion (Reports of discussions of acting out, 1968). Finally, some analysts do not regard repetitions in analysis as resistances, but as implicit or embodied memories of early or traumatic events for which there are no potentially conscious memories (Kogan, 1992).

Active/Passive describes a polarity, or pair of opposite tendencies, with regard to degrees of physical or mental activity. While in psychoanalytic discourse, this polarity was originally used to describe characteristics of instinctual drive activity, its contemporary significance encompasses a broader view of ego defenses and character organization. For example, the extent to which an individual assumes active or passive attitudes or solutions toward his own conflicts may reflect fundamental qualities and aspects of his character and experience. The polarity has particular clinical significance in situations of trauma, where the capacity for active mastery in contrast to passive repetition often determines psychological outcome. Active mastery involves such defensive operations as "turning passive into active."

Freud's view of mind was based on several basic dualities, and the notion of opposing tendencies, or forces, appears repeatedly in both his descriptions of clinical phenomena and his metapsychology. The dualism evident in Freud's theorizing reflected the thinking of his day in the realms of philosophy and political theory. However, it has also been a basis for the criticism that Freud's theorizing often reduces more complex options into paired opposites.

Freud (1915b) considered the active-passive polarity to be one of three basic polarities that govern mental life (along with subject-object and pleasure-unpleasure). His first reference to the polarity between activity and passivity appeared in "Three Essays on the Theory of Sexuality" (1905b), where he described the component instincts that occur in pairs with active and passive aims, as seen in scopophilia/exhibitionism and sadism/masochism. While an instinct is always active, its aim may be active, achieving satisfaction through action on another, or passive, with satisfaction obtained through having the action performed on oneself. However, Freud noted that the satisfaction of passive aims may require considerable active effort. Freud saw these currents of active and passive running through all of sexual life. At times, he described a developmental progression from active/passive, through phallic/castrated, to masculine/feminine. At other times he viewed these two polarities as equivalent to masculine/feminine. However, Freud also noted that actual men and women invariably show a mixture of active and passive, or masculine and feminine traits. From the standpoint of theory, the association of activity with masculinity, and passivity with femininity is currently regarded as imprecise and misleading; however, such associations are not uncommonly represented in unconscious fantasy.

Later, in "Instincts and Their Vicissitudes," Freud (1915b) described the shift from active to passive as one of the major transformations that drive aims can undergo. He described "turning around upon the self" (with the replacement of a drive's original external object by the subject's own self) as a separate transformation, noting that these two vicissitudes can often coincide.

The active/passive polarity has major developmental significance in terms of the child's gradual acquisition of the capacity for greater activity. In the course of normal development, the child increasingly performs functions actively that earlier were performed for him by adults, and a gradual change from passivity to activity is evident in locomotion, feeding, the development of language, and the control of impulses. This process is repeated throughout life as the ego achieves active control over what had been previously experienced passively through active repetition in dreams, memory, fantasy, thought, affect, and action.

Nonetheless, both passivity and activity are on a continuum from normal to abnormal. Turning passive into active can occur in the service of adaptation and mastery, particularly in situations of trauma, or it can be part of a more-pathological picture involving identification with the aggressor and forms of projective identification. Similarly, passive behavior can range from being a component of healthy reciprocity to pathological desires to be acted on sadistically by others. Conspicuous passivity, often mistaken as a sign of impulse control, may stem from defensive denial of sadistic or masochistic impulses. The active/passive polarity is often quite ambiguous, especially when used to describe behavior; the understanding of any piece of action, or apparent inaction, requires an analysis of the underlying fantasies, wishes, and defenses involved.

Active Technique is the therapeutic strategy developed by Sandor Ferenczi (1919, 1920) for use in situations when an analysis is stalemated. Ferenczi argued that the analyst could facilitate free association and the recovery of repressed memories and wishes by forcefully prohibiting the patient from engaging in any motor activity that is the equivalent of unconscious masturbatory activity. His technique reflected the principles of early libido theory, specifically the idea that libidinal cathexes are mobile. By denying the partial discharge of libido that occurs during behavior equivalent to masturbation, Ferenczi argued that more libido would be available to cathect unconscious ideas, making these ideas more accessible to consciousness. Alternatively, Ferenczi asserted that by commanding the patient to perform actions that are not masturbatory equivalents but are the disguised enactments of unconscious conflictual wishes, the patient can gain greater access both to unconscious wishes and to warded-off shame or guilt. When a patient is conscious of the sources of his sexual pleasure, Ferenczi argued for forbidding these actions with the same goal of redirecting mobile cathexis. Ferenczi, in conjunction with Rank, also experimented with setting time limits to an analysis so as to accelerate the treatment (Ferenczi and Rank, 1925).

In moving away from the "passive" role, in which the analyst's activity is limited to making interpretations, Ferenczi stirred intense controversy. Seeking to align his technique with Freud, he differentiated active technique from suggestion, clarifying that except when the analyst is issuing commands and prohibitions, it is the patient, not the analyst, who is "active." Ferenczi defended active technique as a technical auxiliary, supplementing and not replacing the central analytic work of interpretation. Active measures are only to be used in exceptional cases for a limited time. Eventually, Ferenczi saw the limitations of the active technique, finally abandoning the method entirely. He noted that the painful frustration inherent in the method may stimulate the patient's resistance and disturb the transference. Additionally, Ferenczi observed that by formulating injunctions and prohibitions, the analyst can too easily take the place of a parental or authoritative superego.

Ferenczi is important in the history of psychoanalysis because of his influence on schools of analysis that privilege the analytic relationship as the primary factor in therapeutic action. His legacy is directly acknowledged by relational and interpersonal psychoanalysts who credit him with first describing important elements of their own clinical theory and technique. These elements include the analyst's inevitable participation in a co-created experience with his patient; the centrality of countertransference as a mutually shaping complement to transference; the impact of the analyst's actual personality and idiosyncratic ways of being and relating; attention to the potentially retraumatizing effects of the analytic encounter (Harris and Aron, 1997).

Actual Neurosis: see ANXIETY, NEUROSIS

Adaptation refers to the changes and/or compromises made by an individual in order to become better suited to his/her environment. Adaptation serves to ensure the survival of both the individual and the human species. Adaptation is a core concept linking psychoanalysis to biology; it emphasizes the important idea that human development is driven not only by conflict but also through interactions with the environment. Adaptation encompasses both the state of "fitting together," or **adaptedness**, which exists between an individual and external reality, and the psychological processes that permit and enhance that state by changing, controlling, and/or accommodating reality. Processes of adaptation are referred to as alloplastic when the individual alters the environment to meet inner needs and wishes; they are referred to as autoplastic when the individual alters himself in response to the demands of the outside world (Freud, 1924c). Hartmann added a third form of adaptation, in which an individual seeks a more appropriate environment (Hartmann, 1939a). The development of adaptive capacities is central to the process of character formation, which requires both the internalization of a stable protective environment, and identification with significant objects. Successful adaptation is recognized as one criterion of healthy ego functioning (Hartmann, 1939b). Adaptation has both active and passive components, and as such is distinguished from adjustment, an essentially passive, autoplastic phenomenon.

Strongly influenced by Darwin's theory of natural selection, Freud was always aware of the survival needs of both the individual and the species. He was also aware of the impact of external reality and the importance of adaptation. For example, Freud's early concept of defense hysteria posits a conflict between unacceptable wishes and the need to fit into society (Breuer and Freud, 1893/1895); his elaborations of the concepts of both ego and superego consider the need for adaptation to reality in the development and the functioning of these basic psychic structures (1923a); finally, his second theory of anxiety gives a central role to adaptation to imagined danger situations (1926a). In addition, Freud was aware that many aspects of the psyche are preadapted to the environment (for example, drive to object) and that inborn capacities for adaptation appear during normal maturation (for example, the gradual emergence of the secondary process and the reality principle) (Freud, 1911b). The idea that adaptation is a major function of the ego was advanced by A. Freud, who described the ego as mediating between id, superego, and external reality (A. Freud, 1936).

However, it was Hartmann (1939a) who promoted adaptation as a central theme of psychoanalysis, arguing that there is an inherited, adaptive aim of the organism that seeks "fit" with the environment. He described this adaptive aim as among what he called the "autonomous ego functions." Hartmann expanded ego psychology from a narrow conception of the ego as the agent of defense, to a broader conception of the ego, equipped with inborn preparedness, as the agent of adaptation to the "average expectable environment" (1939a). Hartmann also elucidated the concept of "change of function," which posits that the functions provided by any behavior may change during their development as they are recruited for purposes of improved adaptation (1952). Following the work of Hartmann, Rapaport and Gill (1959) added the **adaptive point of view** (along with the genetic and structural points of view) to Freud's topographic, dynamic, and economic points of view in their influential paper on metapsychology. Rado (1956a, 1956b) constructed his unique theory of the mind, which he called **adaptational psychodynamics,** around the concept of adaptation.

The concept of adaptation is important in all of developmental psychoanalysis in that this concept recognizes the importance of individual/environment interactions throughout the life cycle. Erikson, in particular (who was highly influential on Rapaport and Gill), stressed that every developmental step both solves and gives rise to problems in relation to the environment (Erikson, 1950). Bowlby's (1958, 1969/1982, 1973) attachment theory posited a positive role for caretaking with its roots in an adaptive tendency that assures the survival of the human infant. Winnicott (1965) echoed this idea in his concept of the "good enough mother." Vaillant's (1977) well-known longitudinal study of development stressed **adaptation to life** over the course of the life cycle. Emde (1988) described an infant preadapted to the infant-caregiver matrix with a basic, intrinsic motive called social-fittedness (among others). The more recent developmental concept of transactional relatedness requires successive steps of adaptational fitting between mother and infant (Sameroff and Fiese, 2000). In clinical psychoanalysis, the concept of adaptation is central to observations that analyst-analysand fit is a determinant of therapeutic effectiveness (Kantrowitz, 1986).

Adolescence is the period of life, following latency, in which psychic reorganization accommodates to the maturational changes of puberty and to the developmental challenges involved in the transition to young adulthood. Adolescence is the period of the life cycle that holds the most extensive, dramatic, and intense developmental changes relative to any other. The growth of the reproductive organs and the massive upsurge of hormonal production during adolescence focus the adolescent on issues of sexuality and gender, spur fantasy formation, and provide the impetus for the reworking of primary object ties. The most crucial challenges of adolescence are the consolidation of identity (Erikson, 1946, 1956), including sexual identity and orientation, and the transformation of attachments to primary objects so that intimacy with new objects can be established (Ritvo, 2003). Adolescence is divided into three generally agreed-upon subphases: **early adolescence** (ages eleven to fourteen), **middle adolescence** (ages fourteen to sixteen), and **late adolescence** (ages sixteen to nineteen) (Levy-Warren, 2000). Due to the tumultuous nature of this developmental period, transient adolescent disturbances may appear. Less commonly, more malignant psychopathological processes may develop and continue into adulthood.

Early adolescence revolves primarily around the adolescent's response to the onset and initial stages of puberty, which involves an explosion of physical and sexual development. As a result of this flux, the body is never far from the mind of the early adolescent. Early sexual development poses challenges and conflicts, particularly about masturbation, which serves the adolescent as a form of "practice," and about masturbatory fantasies, which may betray incestuous wishes and thereby elicit anxiety (Laufer, 1976). Struggles with authority, especially parents, may be used to defend against incestuous wishes and regressive dependency needs, as well as to express the wish for greater autonomy and independence. Wishes around the exhibition of the newly developed body may be countered by the urge to hide

from the view of others, associated with feelings of guilt, embarrassment, and shame. Sexual identity begins to consolidate, with masturbatory fantasy more explicitly depicting sexual orientation and preferred practices.

Middle adolescence revolves around the adolescent's more forceful and more permanent move into the larger world of others. Classically considered a subphase of "object removal," where a loosening of ties to the originally loved and desired objects predominates (Blos, 1962), current thinking also considers a reorganization or transformation, rather than separation or removal, of these primal ties to be a more accurate conception (K. Novick and J. Novick, 2005). Whereas physical changes give earlier trends their shape, changes in the mind of the adolescent will henceforth drive the dynamic trends of this phase. The midadolescent has new mental structures and capacities available to him that are truly revolutionary, including the shift to formal operations of cognition (the move from concrete, literalistic understanding to the emergence of abstract thinking) and the capacity for symbolic representation. The midadolescent is vulnerable to and excited by passionate, idealistic, and philosophical/existential musings. Ideas are prized, in particular those that may serve the greater good, or solve some of the ills of the world. In some individuals, creativity may peak during these years. The midadolescent gives up the anchors of prior dependencies and values, begins to see parents more realistically, looks to his peer group as a new, substitute family, and looks to other adults as alternative ego-ideal models. Superego imperatives frequently loosen, as the adolescent is more aware of and open to new forms of gratification, and as new values and beliefs are formed. The midadolescent may make the first moves toward sexual relationships, with passions that typically run quickly hot, then abruptly cold. All of this change may leave the midadolescent at times more isolated, lonely, and vulnerable to unsafe, peer-approved actions, such as sexual promiscuity and drug abuse. At times, a sense of mourning may predominate in either the adolescent and/or his parents. Trends to regression may also derail the adolescent during this phase. Defenses classically linked to adolescence, including intellectualization, denial, reversal of affect, asceticism, and narcissism (with consequent grandiosity and hypochondriasis), may peak during these middle years (A. Freud, 1958).

If these early and middle phases have proceeded well enough, the late adolescent is less vulnerable to the inevitable regressive pulls and can grapple with the tasks of the closing phase. The late adolescent must integrate past trauma, establish ego continuity, and consolidate personality organization (Blos, 1979a). The superego undergoes its final reorganization, ideally equipping the young person with his own moral standards and ideals (Blum, 1985). These processes forge a unique sense of personal identity, preparing the individual for an adaptive first step into competent, effective adult life. Altogether these accomplishments constitute the "second individuation." Though young adults will continue to face conflicts around many adolescent issues, the adolescent of these years has a more clearly defined and individualized sense of self with a core that has stability and wholeness. Sexual identity is more firmly established, as well as are work interests and goals. Affect is better regulated, and the late adolescent has a relatively mature experience of relationships, both with family and friends. The healthy late adolescent is able to love, work, and play meaningfully and pleasurably, as the real world acknowledges the newly autonomous individual. Late adolescents who have failed to consolidate earlier movements, or who surrender to regressive modes of living, are vulnerable to retreat, sometimes even prolonging adolescence for some indefinite period of time (Blos, 1979b). Interpersonal views of late adolescence similarly emphasize the importance of integrating lust and intimacy and of establishing independent values. A sturdy sense of self respect, an important component of mental health, is a special accomplishment of an optimal late adolescent phase (Pantone, 1995).

Erikson (1946, 1956) described the identity crisis as a normative experience in adolescence, providing an opportunity for developmental progression and for the reorganization of identity on a more mature level. The link between adolescence and identity crisis was supported by A. Freud's work with teenagers and the belief that turmoil is a necessary part of adolescent development. However, later authors have questioned whether identity crisis should be considered a part of normal adolescent development (D. Offer, J. Offer, and Ostrov, 1975; Emde, 1985).

Affect, a term borrowed by psychoanalysis from general psychology, is a complex psychophysiologic state comprised of: 1) a subjective experience that includes feelings; 2) associated ideas and fantasies; 3) an observable, biologically determined physiologic response pattern. Affect also includes: 4) a behavioral response or emotional expression; 5) a communication of a state of mind. The term *feeling* is commonly used to refer to the first and sometimes second aspect(s) of affect, the subjectively experienced state. Emotion is sometimes used synonymously with af-

fect, or sometimes to refer only to the third and fourth aspects, the physiological concomitants or the objectively observable behavior. Mood connotes a particular type of affective experience in which one predominant affect, such as anxiety, depression, or euphoria, spreads to include the entire self state and endures for a period of time.

Affect plays a central role in all psychoanalytic psychology. From the psychoanalytic point of view, affects are complex mental events, connecting the body with intrapsychic and interpersonal experience and conveying both meaning and motivational force. Affects originate as inborn dispositions that, over time, become both more complex and more specific to the individual as, in response to experience (especially with significant others), they become attached to thoughts and fantasies. Analysts generally agree that affects play a role in the experience of the self and others; in the evaluation of the state of the self in relation to the internal and external environments; in alerting, orienting, preparing, and motivating the individual for appropriate responses, including defenses and behaviors; and in communication between people. However, the question of how these aspects of affect are organized has long been the subject of considerable controversy. There is also a long history of discussion about the role of specific affects in psychic life, including explorations of anxiety, depression, guilt, love, hate, envy, gratitude, elation, rage, disgust, pride, joy, sense of safety, and shame, to mention a few that have received much attention. Despite controversy at the level of theory, all analysts agree that affect is at the center of psychoanalytic treatment, with the affective dimension always the most relevant in moment-to-moment interaction between patient and analyst, both as a marker for what is most meaningful and, in some theories, as an aspect of therapeutic action. Learning to identify and tolerate increasingly complex affect states is part of every analysis. Affects also play a role in generating psychopathology and may themselves represent psychopathology, as in anxiety or **affective disorders**.

Freud first used the word *affect* at least as early as 1896 in his work on the pathogenesis and treatment of hysteria and other neuroses (1896a). While his evolving theory of affect includes many different and sometimes inconsistent viewpoints elaborated at varying levels of abstraction, it is possible to divide his views on the subject roughly into three phases. During the earliest period (1892–1900), when under the influence of Breuer and the French psychopathologists, Freud viewed affect as the result of excessive cerebral excitation caused by traumatic events. In this early trauma model of psychopathology and treatment, affects are seen as basically negative and pathogenic, having the power to split the mind, become "strangulated" or sequestered like a "foreign body," and be "converted" into symptoms. Successful treatment requires discharge of pathogenic affect through abreaction or catharsis.

After the development of the topographic model of the mind and of drive theory (1900–1926), Freud conceptualized affect as the conscious perception, in the form of pleasure or unpleasure, of an underlying quantitative change in drive energy, or libido, rather than as the result of an external traumatic event. In line with his adherence to the energic "principle of constancy," Freud argued that unpleasure (or anxiety) is caused by the accumulation of unsatisfied, or "dammed up" libido (sometimes referred to as the "first theory of anxiety"); pleasure is caused by the discharge of libido. While there is some inconsistency in this model as to whether affect (mainly pleasure/unpleasure) serves to motivate behavior or is merely the surface manifestation of the drive, during this period affect definitely took a backseat to the drives in theoretical importance. Furthermore, although there is evidence that Freud was aware of the importance of the subjective aspect of affects in his clinical work (including love, hate, anger, guilt, disgust, envy, and melancholia, along with anxiety itself), in his theory-making, he was most interested in the quantitative or energic aspect of affect, sometimes writing as though energy and affect are indistinguishable.

Finally, in 1926, after undoing the equation between levels of drive energy and pleasure/unpleasure (1920a), and introducing the structural model of the mind (1923a), Freud (1926a) elaborated a new role for affect when he suggested that the ego produces an unconscious, attenuated signal of anxiety as a response to danger. This signal anxiety (or **signal affect**) has the power to mobilize defenses or adaptive action to avoid this danger. In this revolutionary new theory (sometimes referred to as the second theory of anxiety), affect is no longer conceptualized simply as a discharge product of the drive, but as an evaluative response generated by the ego in reaction to a particular situation. Thereafter, while the concept of affect as a discharge phenomenon persisted in psychoanalytic theory, over time theoretical interest gradually shifted to the subjective experience of affect, explained not as the byproduct of quantities of excitation, but as a marker, or signal, of the emotional significance, or meaning, of a situation for the person who experiences it.

In ego psychology, close attention has been paid to the relationship between affect and the ego, with affect being seen as both a stimulus to be regulated by the ego, and an ego function. Early ego psychology focused on how the ego structuralizes or "tames" affect for its own use, defends against affects, and/or develops the capacity for **affect tolerance** (Zetzel, 1949) or **affect intolerance** (Krystal, 1975). Gradually, in line with the trend started by Freud in 1926, attention shifted to the subjective experience of affect seen as a purveyor of information, often about the state of conflict or harmony between or among the structures of the tripartite model of the mind, and/or the outside world. Eventually, affects other than anxiety, beginning with depression and ultimately including all affects, were seen as capable of functioning as signals, mobilizing defense and action. Affects, themselves, were also understood as capable of serving defensive functions (A. Freud, 1936; Hartmann, 1939a; Fenichel, 1945; Rapaport, 1953; C. Brenner, 1974).

With the development of object relations theory, affects took on an increasingly important role in psychoanalytic theory. As affects always occur within and inseparable from the matrix of important relationships in childhood, attention turned inevitably to the close relationship between affective experience and the development of internalized self and object representations. Among ego psychologists, both Jacobson (1964) and Mahler (Mahler, Pine, and Bergman, 1975) were interested in the relationship between affect and the development of self and object representations, as well as of basic mood states. In the Kleinian view, affects are integral to the formation of internalized object relations, with development centering around the growing capacity to tolerate conflicting feelings of hate and love (and later, envy and gratitude) toward the object, as reflected in movement from the paranoid position to the depressive position (Klein, 1948b). J. Sandler (1987a) also saw affect as playing a central role in the development of the representational world, arguing that all experience is organized through and around feelings. For Sandler, affects play a double role; on the one hand, they provide information about the significance, or "value," of all events, and, on the other hand, they give rise to motivational states, with strivings for feelings of safety and well-being as the most basic motives. In a reversal of Freud's early view of affects as manifestations of the drives, Sandler argued that affects precede the development of the drives. He also emphasized the role of what Rado (1956a) called the "welfare emotions," especially the sense of safety, in psychological life. In his own synthesis of ego psychology and object relations theory, Kernberg (1982) viewed affects as part of the basic unit of psychological experience, linked always with self and object representations. In his view, affects are primary psychophysiological dispositions that are activated by early bodily experiences in the context of developing object relations; in early development, an individual's internal representational world is made up of multiple sets of primitive dyads, each characterized by a different one-dimensional representation of the self and other linked by a distinct affect. These dyads, or internal representations, are activated by life events and, in turn, influence how events are experienced. In the course of development, disparate one-dimensional representations of self and other become integrated into more complex, multifaceted, and modulated representations that correspond more accurately to the complexity of self, of others, and of the world. In agreement with Sandler, Kernberg argued that affects are the primary motivational force in human psychological life, serving as the "building blocks of the drives," which are conceptualized as higher-order structures, or organized, peremptory, and ongoing strivings for good experiences (libido) or bad experiences (aggression) with objects.

Over time, attention has shifted to focus not just on the affective experience of the developing child, but also on the nature of affective interactions between children and caregivers. In Sullivan's (1953a) view, anxiety is the result of "emotional contagion," an interpersonal event in which the child experiences the mother's anxiety or disapproval. In this view, anxiety ranges from the dread, loathing, and horror of the "uncanny emotions," to the absence of anxiety, or euphoria. Bion (1962b) argued that the processing of raw emotional experience is foundational for the development of the capacity for all thought and knowledge, always in the context of interactions with "containing" objects during childhood. Kohut (1971, 1972, 1977) and other self psychologists have focused on how affects reflect the state of the self, which is always understood in the context of the self-selfobject matrix. Kohut explored feelings such as narcissistic rage and shame that result from injury to the self, or pride and joy that emanate from a healthy self. Relational psychoanalysts focus on affect in the context of interaction, both in the psychoanalytic situation and in the course of development.

Much of psychoanalytic developmental theory and research has focused on the central importance of affective interactions between infant and caregivers on the development of the infant's capacities for self regulation, adaptation, object relations, moral development, theory of mind, and a host of other important psychological functions. Spitz (1959, 1965) described early somatic and affective "dialogue" between infant and mother, noting the key affects such as the social smile, stranger anxiety, and the "no" gesture to signal important developmental nodal points in the infant's mental constructions of the caregiver and of their relationship. Winnicott (1956a, 1975/1992) and Spitz both stressed the average mother's remarkable empathic attunement to her baby, and, in turn, the infant's ability to tune in to the mother's moods. Mahler, Pine, and Bergman (1975) noted that infants are capable of emotional communication with their primary caregivers, as evidenced by the "practicing" baby in his "checking back" behavior. D. N. Stern (1985, 2003) studied the effect of what he calls **affective attunements** on the development of the "core sense of the self" and the capacity for intersubjectivity. Social referencing is the term used in contemporary infant research to describe the infant's developing capacity to perceive emotional signals given by the caregiver in situations of uncertainty, as demonstrated experimentally, using the "visual cliff" (Klinnert et al., 1982; Emde, 1992). Emde (1983, 1991) studied the influence of affective interactions on the development of the **affective core of the self**, and also emphasized the role of positive emotions, such as interest, curiosity, pleasure, and pride, in psychological development and functioning. Both Emde and Stern were interested in the development of what they call the "moral emotions" (Emde, 1991; D. N. Stern, 2003). Fonagy et al. (2002) have studied the impact of **affective-mirroring** on the development of reflective function. Much of this work draws upon the explosion of research on affect in the neighboring fields of developmental psychology, attachment theory, and neurobiology. Olds (2003) has attempted to integrate psychoanalytic affect theory with semiotics.

Agency is a component of the mind as elaborated in Freud's topographic and structural models, used synonymously with system in the first model of the mind, and synonymously with structure in the second model of the mind. As such, agency represents a group of related functions. In a broader and more contemporary usage, agency also refers to an individual's capacity to effect causal action on the basis of needs, desires, or other motivations, along with the recognition and experience of this capacity, sometimes referred to as **a sense of agency**. All psychoanalytic treatment seeks to increase the patient's sense of agency in terms of an increased capacity for choice.

This broadening of the usage of agency reflects a shift in contemporary psychoanalysis away from an emphasis on structural theory and ego psychology toward an increased focus on conceptualizations of the self, often defined as the seat of personal agency. However, while Freud used the term *agency* in its more narrow sense, the issues associated with agency in its second meaning have been at the heart of the psychoanalytic enterprise from the beginning. Freud was well aware that his theory, which asserts that much of mental life is controlled by unconscious forces, was a threat to our cherished sense of free will or agency.

Freud (1900) first used the term *agency* as a synonym for system, in his topographical model of the mind, first described in "The Interpretation of Dreams." Agencies or systems were described metaphorically as "places" in the mind through which excitation or energy passed in a particular temporal sequence. The spatial underpinnings of Freud's topographical model made him prefer the term *system* to describe the conscious, preconscious, and unconscious aspects of the mind, although he tended to use agency to describe the more active notion of the censorship. With the introduction of his structural model, Freud (1923a) used agency as a synonym for structure, an enduring and organized configuration or group of functions in the mind (known in structural theory as the id, ego, and superego). In this model, the term *agency* emphasizes the dynamic aspect of structures in the mind as active participants in mental life and causative elements in mental processes, producing effects that can be discerned or inferred.

The second usage of the term *agency* within psychoanalysis has increased in recent decades, although this usage has a long tradition within philosophy and lies at the heart of Freud's view of the mind. Even as the nature of the therapeutic task shifted with Freud's evolving theory of mind, the underlying principle has always been to allow the individual increasing agency. In other words, the goal of treatment is that the individual should live rather than be lived by his aims. This idea was further developed in ego psychology's view of the executive and adaptive ego (Hartmann, 1939a). It is crucial to Winnicott's (1960a) focus on the true self and false self and to Kohut's (1977, 1984) concept of the bipolar self. Such concepts became increasingly central in Schafer's (1976) advocacy of "action language" and "action self" and G. Klein's (1976) focus on the person in motivation. The issue of how and at what level psychoanalysis conceptualizes who or what has agency, as the source of both physical and psychical action, continues to be actively explored within the literature (Warme, 1982; W. Meissner, 1993; Cahn, 1995). In other words, does agency reside within the subject, the person, a psychic structure, the ego, or the self?

Aggression is the wish to subjugate, prevail over, harm, or destroy others, and the expression of any of these wishes in action, words, or fantasy. Aggression may appear undisguised in verbal and physical combat, or disguised in a joke or in an action (or an inaction) that has the seemingly unintended consequence of causing harm. Aggression may also be turned against the self, in an expression of guilt and self hatred, resulting in self-destructive acts that can extend to self annihilation. Aggression exists on an affective continuum from mild irritation and resentment to intense envy to murderous rage. While the term is used primarily to refer to hostile thoughts, feelings, and actions, some psychoanalysts broaden the definition to include assertive, constructive behaviors directed toward mastery that seems to originate from initiative, ambition, or the demand for justice. While the meanings already described overlap with those used within common parlance, a specifically psychoanalytic meaning of the term involves the concept of the **aggressive drive**. As the fundamental constituents of Freudian drive theory, aggression and libido are regarded as the two primary instinctual drives and are considered the primary motivators of human behavior.

The clinical significance of aggression figures prominently in any psychoanalytic consideration of severe psychopathology, such as borderline conditions, sadomasochism, perversions, self destructiveness, and violence. Such pathology is regarded as the net result of multiple factors, including constitutional, experiential, and dynamic variables. Developmental factors that contribute to increased intensity of manifest aggression include early experiences of excessive pain, deprivation, loss, abuse, enforced passivity, overstimulation, and seduction (Furst, 1998). While there is considerable agreement among psychoanalysts about the clinical manifestations of aggression, considerable controversy surrounds the more theoretical aspects of the concept. In fact, a distinguishing feature of some psychoanalytic theories is the question of whether aggression should be viewed as a primary force or as a secondary force, arising only in reaction to frustration and failures in the environment. In addition, while the concept of drive has been retained by some theoretical orientations, it plays no role in relational or self psychological theories. As a topic at the interface of the biological, the intrapsychic, and the social, a complete understanding of aggression requires a broad interdisciplinary dialogue among psychoanalysis, neuroscience, evolutionary biology, and the social and political sciences.

While Freud did not accord aggression the status of a drive until 1920, he was long aware of its clinical importance, making mention of it in his early writings on resistance, sexuality, humor, obsessional neuroses, paranoia, and the conflicts of the oedipus complex. Initially, Freud (1905b) explained aggressive behavior as a component of the sexual drive, aimed at overcoming resistance in the object that, in exaggerated form, becomes sadism; later, aggression was explained as an aspect of the self-preservative ego instincts that oppose sexuality (Freud, 1915b). A. Adler (1908) postulated the existence of an aggressive instinct as early as 1908, but Freud (1909c, 1909d) objected at that time to the idea of separating aggression from the sexual drive.

However, in 1920, Freud (1920a) proposed a revision of his drive theory that gave aggression equal status with sexuality as a motivational force in mental life. In this last and most speculative drive classification, the overarching concept of a life drive, or Eros, whose aim is to build organic complexity, to synthesize, and to preserve life, is placed in opposition to a death drive, whose aim is to destroy life by breaking down organic complexity and returning it to an inorganic state. Of note, it was Freud's observations of the role of self-directed aggression and self-punitive trends in such clinical phenomena as melancholia, masochism, and negative therapeutic reactions, as well as the compulsion to repeat, which led him to his formulation of the death drive. In this model, the aggressive drive is only that portion of the death drive that is turned outward toward the external world in the individual's attempts to preserve himself. The dangers of the death drive are dealt with through fusion with the life drive, so that sexual and aggressive energies become combined. With Freud's (1923a) elaboration of his structural theory, aggression became a central aspect of relations among psychic structures, emanating not only from the id, but also from the superego's proscriptive and punitive relations with the ego.

Klein and many of her followers embraced Freud's theory of a death drive, viewing it as active in mental life from birth onward, and as playing a central role in early anxieties, defenses, and object relations. Most other theorists ignored or rejected Freud's hypothesis of a death drive, arguing that it is too speculative, goes beyond the clinical data, and is not easily reconcilable with basic evolutionary principles. Theorists who accept sex and aggression as two basic drives tend to focus more on clinically near conceptualizations of these drives, rather than on life and death drives. Within ego psychology, the concept of aggression was further elaborated as a distinct drive with characteristic developmental forms under the influence of oral, anal, and phallic phases. Through fusion with sexual drives, aggressive energy can be neutralized and become available for aims of mastery and control of reality, defense, and psychic structure building, rather than just destruction (Hartmann, 1939a; Hartmann, Kris, and Loewenstein, 1949). C. Brenner (1971) proposed that the aggressive drive operates according to the pleasure principle, rather than beyond it, and that its role in psychic conflict is comparable to that of libido. Both contemporary ego psychologists and modern Kleinians (even those who accept the death drive) view aggressive behavior as serving multiple functions of gratification, punishment, defense, and adaptation. More specifically, aggression may serve to ward off sexual excitement, to defend against passive wishes, to defend against narcissistic threats to self esteem, or to promote feelings of power and safety in the face of anxiety. Aggression may also represent a plea for external control from the environment (especially in children and adolescents), an identification with an aggressive parent, or an expression of guilt and the need for punishment.

Other theorists, particularly the British independent school and self psychologists, rejected the idea of aggression as the product of an innate drive, viewing it as a reactive response to frustrations and deprivations from the environment, particularly from early caretakers (Fairbairn, 1954; Guntrip, 1969; Kohut, 1977). In "Thoughts on Narcissism and Narcissistic Rage," Kohut (1972) presented his view of aggression, conceptualized not as an expression of a drive, but as the consequence of a perceived threat to the self. Narcissistic rage, characterized by the need for revenge and justice, is the prototype for destructive aggression. It ranges along a spectrum from trivial irritation to fanatical fury; it is triggered and accompanied by shame, humiliation, and disappointment. Insistence on the omnipotence of the grandiose self and on the perfection of the idealized selfobject underlies destructive aggression. Kohut argued that narcissistic rage is not on a continuum with other forms of aggression, such as competition and self assertion. Competition and self assertion are primary, belonging to the self's normal ambitious strivings and the need for recognition.

Others have argued that aggression does not demonstrate the rhythmicity and renewed need for discharge characteristic of a true drive. A related controversy concerns the extent to which aggression should be viewed as hostile and destructive in its primary form, with nonhostile assertion being the result of developmental modification, or whether aggression should be viewed as an initially nonhostile force, almost synonymous with activity and initiative, serving the aims of mastery and adaptation, taking on hostile and destructive qualities only in response to environmental failure. Winnicott (1950) emphasized the role of aggression in fostering very early self-object differentiation and reality testing, as well as subsequent individuation processes.

On the basis of psychoanalytically informed observation of infants and children, Parens (1973, 1979) delineated three major trends of aggressive drive behavior: 1) nondestructive aggression (seen in motoric efforts aimed at exploration, mastery, and control of the self and the environment); 2) nonaffective destructiveness (seen in feeding behaviors such as biting and chewing, in the service of self preservation, presumably evolutionarily related to prey aggression in animals); and, 3) hostile destructiveness (seen in neonatal rage reactions to unpleasurable situations; later, in biting, hitting, and other destructive behavior aimed directly at frustrating objects, or displaced onto other objects; and, beginning in the second year, a sadistic form, with pleasure in teasing and tormenting behavior).

Kernberg (1982) viewed only hostile destructiveness as a manifestation of the aggressive drive, categorizing nondestructive aggression and nonaffective destructiveness as aspects of autonomous ego functioning. In a synthesis of British object relations views and ego psychology, he viewed the aggressive drive as evolving from the gradual integration of early inborn unpleasurable affect states that become linked with internalized object relations schemas to eventually function as a supraordinate motivational system. Lichtenberg (1989) elaborated a motivational systems model in which assertion and aggression are viewed respectively as an aspect of exploratory-assertive and aversive-motivational systems.

Alexithymia: see DENIAL, ISOLATION, PSYCHOSOMATIC DISORDERS

Alloplastic/Autoplastic: see ADAPTATION

Alpha Function/Alpha Elements/Beta Elements: see BION

Altruism includes any behavior where pleasure is experienced through addressing the wishes or needs of other people. Altruism is a complex human behavior that has intrapsychic, interpersonal, and sociobiological significance. It can be seen in many situations and in many kinds of people. At one end

of a spectrum, altruism is one of the healthiest and most mature adaptive strategies; at the other end, it can be associated with severe masochism and even psychosis. Religious and cultural upbringing may promote the placement of other people's needs above one's own as particularly virtuous, a value that may be internalized into one's ego ideal.

In several of his works, Freud described altruism as the opposite of egoism, arguing that it can be distinguished from libidinal object-cathexis by an absence of longings for sexual satisfaction. However, when an individual is completely in love, altruism combines with libidinal object-cathexis. In this situation, Freud (1916/1917) described an "altruistic transposition" of egoism onto the sexual object so that the object appears extremely powerful. A. Freud (1936) elaborated on Freud's view of altruism, coining the term **altruistic surrender** to describe an individual who can only achieve gratification of instinctual wishes vicariously through a proxy. She considered altruistic surrender to be the basis of all altruism, a view that has been widely accepted by many psychoanalysts who often link altruism to reaction formation and masochism. While Vaillant (1977) described altruism as among the most mature defenses, he still considered altruism to be based on reaction formation, and to indicate some difficulty experiencing pleasure from the fulfillment of one's own desires. In contrast, Erikson's (1950) term *generativity* describes the satisfaction gained by contributing to the welfare of future generations. Unlike A. Freud or Vaillant, Erikson's concept carries no connotation of personal inhibition; he considered generativity to be essential to healthy adulthood. Amae (Doi, 1973), cherishment (Young-Bruehl and Bethelard, 2000), and primary maternal preoccupation (Winnicott, 1956a) are also concepts that include an aspect of altruism that is not conceptualized as defensive or pathological. Seelig and Rosof (2001) have described five types of altruism: 1) **Protoaltruism** has biological roots and can be observed in animals; in humans, protoaltruism includes maternal and paternal nurturing and protectiveness. 2) **Generative altruism** is the nonconflictual pleasure in fostering the success and/or welfare of another. 3) **Conflicted altruism** is generative altruism drawn into conflict, but in which the pleasure and satisfaction of another (a proxy) is actually enjoyed. 4) **Pseudoaltruism** originates in conflict and serves as a defensive cloak for underlying sadomasochism. 5) **Psychotic altruism** is the bizarre form of caretaking behavior and associated self denial, sometimes seen in psychotic individuals and often based on delusion. Seelig and Rosof's proposed classification allows for nonpathological altruism that recognizes and respects the autonomous wishes of the other and enjoys promoting the other's pleasure or success. This includes mature parental altruism, which requires that the parent distinguish among his own wishes, the child's wishes, and what the child actually needs. They suggest that this normal form of mature altruism is the heir of the earlier infantile protoaltruism.

Ambivalence is the simultaneous existence of opposite feelings, attitudes, or tendencies toward another person, thing, or situation. Within psychoanalysis, ambivalence has been used more commonly to describe the existence of both loving and hating feelings toward the same object. However, it can also be used to refer to states of mind characterized by simultaneous and contradictory wishes for dependence and independence, or domination and submission; contradictory attitudes of envy and gratitude, or idealization and devaluation; or, to the coexistence of active and passive instinctual aims or wishes.

Ambivalence, particularly the coexistence of love and hate, is a universal tendency within human relations. It can lead to pathology when the intensity or the nature of an ambivalence conflict cannot be tolerated. In such cases, it may: lead to repression of one side of the pole, sometimes accompanied by reaction formation; lead to displacement of one side of the conflict onto another object; or lead to denial and splitting, in which the two sides of an ambivalence conflict must be maintained separately within consciousness, resulting in a split in the ego and in object representations.

Freud (1912a) first used the term *ambivalence* in 1912 to account for the coexistence of negative and positive transference attitudes toward the analyst. However, he had clearly alluded to the phenomenon previously in describing the behavior of Little Hans (1909c) and the Rat Man (1909d). Freud borrowed the term from Bleuler (1910), who coined it in a 1910 lecture describing a general human tendency, but one particularly characteristic of schizophrenics, who manifest urges to act in opposite ways simultaneously, believe in contradictory propositions, and maintain loving and hating feelings toward the same person (ambivalence of will, intellect, and emotions, respectively). Freud (1913e) most often used the term to delineate this last **emotional ambivalence**, a state he saw as central to the symptoms of obsessional neurosis and of melancholia (1917c), as well as to the conflicting attitudes of the oedipus complex (1913e). However, Freud (1905b, 1915b; 1918a) also employed the term *ambivalence* in speaking of the inherent bipolarity of instincts, which is manifest in simultaneous active and passive instinctual aims, such as sadism and masochism, exhibitionism and voyeurism, and wishes for domination and submission.

Abraham (1924b) outlined a developmental schema of ambivalence that integrated ideas about libidinal drive development with object relations. He described the early oral sucking stage as **pre-ambivalent**, both the later oral biting stage and the subsequent anal-sadistic stage as ambivalent, and the genital stage, in which the infant has learned to spare the object psychically to save it from destruction, as **post-ambivalent**. These concepts had a major influence on Kleinian theory, in which the incapacity to tolerate ambivalence underlies the splitting of "good" and "bad" objects, while the capacity to become aware of and tolerate love and hate toward the same object allows for a shift from the paranoid-schizoid to the depressive position. Kernberg (1975) used this varying capacity to tolerate ambivalence to distinguish higher-level or neurotic personality organizations (characterized by tolerance of ambivalence, and the repression of it when it is very intense) from lower-level or borderline personality organizations (characterized by intolerance of ambivalence with resort to denial and splitting).

At times, ambivalence has been used very broadly and even indiscriminately, as if synonymous with conflict, to describe the incompatible or competing motives of wish and defense. In response, Brody (1956) proposed limiting ambivalence to describe loving and hating attitudes toward the same object. Holder (1975) also emphasized the importance of precise usage, noting that ambivalence may be the cause of severe conflict and pathology, but that not all conflict is due to ambivalence. However, he also argued that important ambivalent ego attitudes toward objects may exist in addition to love and hate, such as envy and gratitude, or idealization and devaluation. A. Kris (1984) noted the usefulness within clinical work of distinguishing between divergent conflicts of ambivalence (which involve intrasystemic conflicts within id, ego, or superego between directly opposing wishes, attitudes, or values), and convergent conflicts (between wish and defense). Ambivalence conflicts are central to the processes of separation and individuation in toddler development, as well as in the later conflicts of adolescence.

Anaclitic Depression is a syndrome experienced by infants more than six months old who have been separated from their primary caretaker for at least three months. Renee Spitz and Katherine Wolf

(1946a), who first delineated the syndrome, described it as an "emotional deficiency disease." Spitz and Wolf borrowed the word *anaclitic* from Freud (via Strachey's translation), who used it to describe what he called the "anaclitic object choice," modeled on the earliest relationship with the mother, who feeds and nurtures the infant; in Freud's use of *anaclitic*, which means "leaning upon," he was asserting that in this situation, libido is "leaning upon" the instinct for self preservation (1914e). Spitz and Wolf used *anaclitic* to refer to the infant's dependency on the mother, arguing that the syndrome occurs only if a good mother-child relationship has been established before the separation. Anaclitic depression is characterized by symptoms of weeping, apathy, inactivity, withdrawal, sleep problems, weight loss, and developmental regressions, as well as feelings of loneliness, helplessness, and fear of abandonment. If adequate nurturing is reestablished within a reasonable time period, the infant is expected to recover. If separation continues longer, symptoms may become more severe and may progress to insomnia, weight loss, retarded development, apathy, stupor, and even death. Spitz also observed the inhibition of normal manifestations of aggression in the second half of the first year of life. He postulated that the aggressive drive was turned back onto the self, resulting in the development of self-injurious behaviors such as head banging and hair tearing. The developmental significance of this syndrome is linked to the developmental attainment of the mother having become a consistent and recognized object for the infant (Wagonfeld and Emde, 1982). Anaclitic depression may be distinguished from hospitalism, a castastrophic condition in infancy, brought about by severe emotional deprivation from birth (Spitz, 1945).

Spitz's identification of this syndrome represents one of the earliest psychoanalytic contributions to the study of attachment behavior. In fact, Spitz inspired the work of many psychoanalytic theorists and infant researchers, including Bowlby, the originator of attachment theory, who emphasized the primacy of the early relationship between infant and caregiver and asserted that attachment is equal in motivational status to feeding and sex. Bowlby (1960a) also described the effects of maternal loss on the developing infant and observed the sequence of protest, despair, and detachment behaviors from prolonged separation. Erikson (1950) described the loss of maternal love as a cause of anaclitic depression, a "chronic state of mourning." He further speculated that infants and young children who suffer from the loss of the libidinal object during the second half of the first year

might experience a depressive undercurrent for life. Mahler (1968) understood anaclitic depression in terms of separation-individuation. She stated that after six months, once a symbiotic relationship with the mother has been established, the mother is no longer transposable and her loss produces an anaclitic depression in the infant. Fraiberg (1982) described pathological defenses of infancy, protective behaviors and states observed in infants and toddlers who have experienced recurrent severe abuse, violence, neglect, and/or deprivation. In recent years, attachment research has hypothesized that secure attachment is negatively related to depression, while insecure and/or disorganized attachment is a nonspecific but definite risk factor for both childhood and adult psychopathology.

Anality is a comprehensive term for all psychic interests, activities, fantasies, conflicts, and mental mechanisms that derive from the **anal phase** of psychosexual development. The anal phase occurs between eighteen months and three years of age. In Freud's schema of psychosexual development, the anal phase follows the oral phase and precedes the phallic phase. The psychic concerns of the anal phase arise from the child's growing pressure towards autonomy, upsurge of aggression (**anal sadism**), and struggles for mastery and control. The child in the anal phase typically evokes a response of counteraggression and, for the first time, may experience the imposition of limits and restrictions. Toilet training, now possible because of the maturation of sphincter control, may be one arena in which such conflicts are played out. The child's pleasure in defecation (**anal erotism**) ensures that the experience is highly valued along with its product, feces. The symbolic representations of such experiences coalesce around ambivalence conflicts involving activity/passivity, retention/expulsion, and control/submission, so that fantasies deriving from the anal phase typically involve preoccupations with the control or mastery of self and other. The vicissitudes of such conflicts have far-reaching effects on intrapsychic maturation, developing object relations, and character formation. The designation of **anal character** is used for individuals who are markedly orderly, stubborn, and withholding. Various aspects of the obsessive-compulsive character similarly suggest the influence of conflicts derived from the anal phase. While the concept of anality is, at times, dismissed as a vestige of early drive theory, its importance in psychoanalysis remains as an organizing motif of unconscious fantasy. In addition, Freud's discovery of anal erotism formed the basis for his recognition of the pregenital organization of the libido, that is, the groundbreaking discovery of infantile sexuality. While all mental experience is now understood as a compromise formation, the contribution of anality to psychological experience is an important reminder of the role of the body in early development.

Freud's (1897c) first reference to anality occurs in his correspondence with Fliess in which he refers to the link between gold and feces in medieval mythology about the devil. However, Freud later (1908b) observed the link between a triad of character traits, including orderliness, parsimony, and obstinacy, with childhood histories that reveal intensified anal erotism. Freud understood these traits as the product of sublimations, reaction formations, and the persistence of inborn anal erotogenicity. Freud (1905b) elaborated his view of the pregenital organization of the libido, in which the anal-sadistic phase represents the second stage of development. He emphasized that development occurs under the combined influence of constitutional and accidental factors, which together determine possible outcomes in character, neurosis, and other kinds of psychopathology. For example, Freud (1905b, 1913d) emphasized the persistence of anal erotism in the development of male homosexuality, paranoia, and obsessional neurosis.

Abraham (1921, 1924b), building upon Freud's views, divided the anal phase into two subphases and linked the sequence with developing object relations. The child's fantasy representation of the anal sphincter organizes the progression from the earlier subphase in which the part object is evacuated and destroyed, to the later subphase in which the object is contained and controlled. Abraham (1921) also described the anal character in whom the overvaluation of feces persists symbolically in the relationship to all possessions, especially money.

The attribution of phase specificity to the origin of character traits and symptoms has been supplanted by a view that favors a compromise product derived from all levels of development. In his schema of the development of life stages, Erikson (1959) linked anality to the stage of autonomy versus self doubt. However, Shengold (1985), in an effort to reestablish the role of the body ego as an organizing force in psychic development, emphasized the critical importance of mastery of anal phase conflict in healthy functioning, particularly in the management of aggression. In a less healthy resolution, defenses against anality take the form of a sphincterlike restriction of emotional depth and complexity. Chasseguet-Smirgel (1978) emphasized the contribution of anal sadism to perverse structure, in which all differentiation between genders and age is eliminated and a reductive degradation turns everything to feces.

Analytic Process or **Psychoanalytic Process** is the progressive unfolding over time of a psychoanalytic treatment during which both conscious and unconscious aspects of the patient's mind are revealed, elaborated, and explicated, so that a deepening of the exploration occurs. The engagement of both patient and analyst within a dynamic dyad is crucial to the process and is responsible for the therapeutic progression of a psychoanalytic treatment. A second, informal use of analytic process defines it as present when a patient is "in analysis," that is, meaningfully engaged in the treatment; this use connotes an evaluation of the capacities of the analyst, the patient, or both.

The nature of analytic process is fundamental to psychoanalysis because it describes the unfolding of the treatment itself. However, various schools of analytic theory differ greatly with regard to the constituents of this process. Additionally, because the concept of analytic process overlaps with views of analytic technique, therapeutic action, and indicators of therapeutic change, its usage has been ambiguous. There is disagreement, for example, about whether analytic process denotes the analyst's interventions (Arlow and Brenner, 1990), the interaction between analyst and patient (Dewald, 1978; Weinshel, 1984), or a process within the patient that the analyst facilitates (Abrams, 1987).

Freud (1913a) wrote that the analyst sets a "process" in motion by interpreting resistances, but the term *analytic process* was first used by Karpman (1950). While the term was referred to in many subsequent papers, Weinshel (1984) made the first attempt to specify its meaning, contrasting it with neighboring terms.

Psychoanalysts within an ego-psychology or conflict-theory orientation generally equate the analytic process with an unfolding of the treatment comprised of the patient's free association, the analyst's interpretation of transference and resistance, and the patient's subsequent response (Loewald, 1970; Boesky, 1990; Samberg and Marcus, 2005). Within the overall perspective of ego psychology and conflict theory, the analytic process is thought to include three phases: an opening phase, which establishes the analytic situation; a midphase, in which the core themes are identified, interpreted, and worked through; and a termination phase. The analytic situation provides a stable frame of reference within which the interaction between patient and analyst mobilizes in each participant intrapsychic processes that help the patient work toward insight and change, as the tensions generated within him are monitored and interpreted by the analyst. This interaction between patient and analyst, the analyst's modes of understanding (including empathy and countertransference), and the patient's growing awareness of his unconscious mental processes (analytic insight) are vital factors in the process.

A relational conception of process also equates it with the unfolding of the treatment, but this is posited quite differently. In the relational viewpoint, the patient's unconscious mental life strives for expression within the safety of the analyst/patient intersubjective consciousness; the analyst interprets content rather than resistance, thereby offering the patient the containing function of thought to tolerate warded-off affects (Spezzano, 1995). Reporting on a panel in which analysts of widely different theoretical orientations discussed their views of analytic process, Smith (2002a) commented on divergences in five areas: 1) the nature of analytic listening; 2) the nature of the interaction between patient and analyst; 3) concerns about the analyst imposing his experience on the patient; 4) differences in the inferential process and the methods of testing it; and 5) the influence of the analyst's doubts about the analytic method.

Psychoanalytic process research is the application of empirical measures to the therapeutic situation in an effort to determine how change occurs. Such research is complicated by controversy about what psychoanalytic process is, the subjective nature of variables connected to psychoanalytic process, the spectrum of methods that are currently classified as psychoanalytic, and the use of process by heterogeneous groups of analysts with varying levels of experience and expertise. The rate-limiting step in process research has been the development of objective measures of specific aspects of the treatment process that can be demonstrated to have validity and reliability. There has been some success in the development of measures identifying: 1) basic relationship patterns; 2) therapeutic interactions; and, 3) the effects of interventions. These measures have been used to "analyze" process from audio-recorded analytic sessions, which are then rated by trained researchers. The refinement of measurement tools is underway, utilizing larger-scale collaborative studies that attempt to determine consistency of data derived across studies. (For a review of outcome and process research, see Bucci, 2005; Wallerstein, 2005).

Analytic Third: see INTERSUBJECTIVITY, RELATIONAL PSYCHOANALYSIS (for Third: see LACAN)

Analytical Psychology: see JUNGIAN PSYCHOLOGY

Analyzability is an assessment of the patient's capacity to participate in and benefit from psychoanalysis. This includes the patient's capacity for candor; capacity to establish, tolerate, and reflect on an intense transference experience; and capacity to make beneficial use of the analyst's interpretive role. Such generally shared criteria for analyzability are based on: estimation of the patient's ego functions, including reality testing, affect tolerance, and self reflection; the nature of the patient's object relations; the patient's life circumstances; and the patient's motivation for change. These factors have been difficult to define with specificity, and analysts vary in their use of these and other criteria.

Analyzability is an important concept in psychoanalysis because it traces the evolution of analytic thinking about both the breadth and the limitations of psychoanalysis as an effective treatment for any particular patient. At the same time the concept of analyzability highlights some historical errors in psychoanalytic thinking, including the prior certainty with which analysts predicted analyzability, and the assumption among some analysts that schizophrenia had a psychological etiology and was therefore an analyzable illness. Finally, the concept of analyzability is notable because it is has been subject to empirical study.

Freud (1904, 1912b, 1917a, 1937a) made several passing references to the issue of analyzability but did not write about it at length. In his view, an analyzable patient is: educated; of good character; suffering from a "transference neurosis" (phobia, conversion hysteria, or obsessional neurosis); and not suffering from a "narcissistic neurosis" (psychosis) or organic degenerative disease. Freud's own later interest in character and especially W. Reich's (1933/1945) description of character resistances widened the indications for analysis to include various characterological problems. While the term *analyzability* was first used at a meeting of the American Psychoanalytic Association in 1948, there were many earlier discussions of analyzability, many of which extended the indications for analysis to patients with psychosis (Simmel, 1929; Cohn, 1940) and later borderline personality (A. Stern, 1938). The concept of the widening scope

(Stone, 1961) in the 1960s and 1970s facilitated the development of modified analytic treatments of patients with "preoedipal pathology," broadening inclusion criteria beyond patients with strictly oedipal-level pathology. Most contemporary analysts do not analyze psychotic patients.

From the midcentury onward, discussions of the prediction of analyzability have shifted from diagnosis as a predictor to the assessment of mental capacities; however, a robust correlation between patient characteristics and analyzability has proven difficult to establish. E. Glover (1958) noted that the psychoanalytic classificatory system, a hybrid of clinical diagnosis and metapsychological evaluations of mental function, is imprecise, lacking standardization, and is of little use in making predictions. Bachrach and Leaff (1978) reviewed twenty-four studies of analyzability, noting that both predictors and outcome measures are either not specified or are specified in abstract terms, thus diminishing their utility. Bachrach and Leaff's summary observation was that the higher a patient's functioning before analysis, the more likely this patient is to obtain a positive result. In 1983, Bachrach (1983) added that because of the considerable variability in technique among psychoanalysts, psychoanalytic treatments are difficult to compare and, therefore, their outcomes do not provide reliable data against which to measure predictors of analyzability.

Contemporary interest in the impact of the analytic dyad (the analyst/patient pair) on the course of an analysis has modified conceptualizations of analyzability to include considerations of both patient and analyst. Kantrowitz (1986) has described the previously ignored variable of the analyst-patient match, that is, how, with certain patients, the analyst's characteristic modes of relating and reacting can facilitate or impede the psychoanalytic process. Analyst-patient match (or mismatch) includes overlaps between the patient's and analyst's "conflicts or disturbances," the analyst's countertransferences, and/or other blind spots. When these qualities of the analyst and the patient/analyst interaction are understood, the analysis can proceed. If they remain unconscious, they result in a stalemate or a limitation of the analysis. In a controversial contribution, Rothstein (2006) has observed that the "evaluative" approach to analyzability has been ineffective. He has recommended a trial analysis for all but the most-ill patients; if the trial fails, a collaboration might be successful at another time or with another colleague.

Analyzing Instrument: see COUNTERTRANSFERENCE

Annihilation: see KLEIN, PROJECTIVE IDENTIFICATION

Anonymity: see ABSTINENCE, NEUTRALITY, AND ANONYMITY

Anxiety is a universal human emotion characterized by an unpleasurable experience of apprehension and anticipation of danger. Anxiety is often accompanied by physiological manifestations such as increased heart and respiratory rate, sweating, tremor, dizziness, muscle tension, and gastrointestinal distress. Intense anxiety states, characterized by a sense of utter helplessness, terror, and doom, and by multiple and severe physiologic manifestations of anxiety, are called panic attacks. In psychoanalysis, as in the general psychiatric literature, a distinction is made between anxiety, experienced in relation to internal, unconscious dangers, and fear, experienced in relation to consciously recognized, realistic external threats.

Anxiety plays a central role in psychoanalytic psychology, most notably in conflict theory, as the unconscious, unpleasurable affect (also called **signal anxiety**) that triggers defenses in both normal and pathological functioning. In addition, anxiety plays a special role in the history of affect theory in psychoanalysis, because beginning with Freud and for many years, theoretical discussion of affect almost always focused on anxiety. Anxiety plays a central role in psychoanalytic treatment, as many patients present with some conscious experience of anxiety. Furthermore, the specific story of how each patient has managed the universal anxieties of childhood is an important part of every analysis. In the here and now of psychoanalytic treatment, analysts pay close attention to anxiety as a marker for underlying conflict.

As early as 1894, Freud (1894d) argued for the delineation of a syndrome of **anxiety neurosis**, which he classified as one of the "actual neuroses," caused by faulty sexual practices. In 1909, Freud (1909c) (after Stekel) postulated that repressed libido can be transformed into anxiety in the psychoneuroses. He also described, in the case of Little Hans, how further symptoms, such as phobias, might serve to bind the anxiety resulting from undischarged libido (**anxiety hysteria**). This theory of symptom formation has often been referred to as Freud's **first theory of anxiety**, based on the topographic model of the mind and libido theory, in which anxiety (unpleasure) is caused by the accumulation of unsatisfied, or "dammed up," libido.

The development of his structural model of the mind brought with it many changes in theory, including Freud's **second theory of anxiety**, wherein anxiety was no longer seen as a byproduct of undischarged libido, but as a response generated by an active ego in anticipation of danger. In this theory, Freud (1926a) outlined two types of anxiety. In **automatic anxiety**, an overwhelming influx of "drive excitation" breaches the "stimulus barrier" creating a situation of trauma; birth is the prototype for this situation of **traumatic anxiety** (Rank, 1924). Over time, the ego develops the capacity to anticipate the danger posed by sexual and aggressive wishes (drives), and to generate a signal of anxiety, or an attenuated, unconscious version of the traumatic anxiety remembered from the past. This signal anxiety triggers defenses aimed at warding off the danger, which in turn reduce or, when successful, eliminate anxiety. The resulting compromise formation between wish and defense may or may not be a symptom. In this theory, manifest anxiety, either in waking life or in the phenomenon of **anxiety dreams**, is an indication that defenses (and/or symptoms) have failed to fully protect against anxiety.

Freud's second theory of anxiety marked a radical change in psychoanalytic affect theory, in that anxiety was no longer conceptualized simply as a byproduct of unsatisfied drives, but as an evaluative response generated by the ego in response to the emotional meaning of a particular situation. In addition, anxiety was no longer seen simply as psychopathology, but was acknowledged as a universal human experience, reflecting inevitable conflict between wishes and fears of danger. The second theory of anxiety paved the way for a view of anxiety (and of conflict in general) as playing a central role not only in symptom formation but in all psychological life. Indeed, psychoanalysis recognizes that the particular anxieties to which an individual is susceptible, along with his strategies for managing these anxieties, are among the most important determinants of his symptoms as well as his character.

As an additional contribution to understanding anxiety and conflict, Freud (1926a) outlined a developmental sequence of typical, or universal, "danger situations" in early childhood that trigger anxiety and initiate defenses. These include loss of the love object, loss of love and approval from this object, fear of bodily injury or damage in the form of **castration anxiety**, and finally, as parental disapproval is internalized and structuralized, fear of the superego and/or guilt (**moral anxiety**). Later psychoanalysts described other typical anxieties in addition to those described by Freud, including **separation anxiety** (Bowlby, 1960b), **stranger anxiety** or **eight-**

month anxiety (Spitz, 1950), **annihilation anxiety**, **persecutory anxiety** and **depressive anxiety** (Klein, 1935), **disintegration anxiety** or **fragmentation anxiety** (Kohut, 1966), and a host of others (that may not carry specific names) related to concerns about attachment, the safety of the object, separation-individuation, and the maintenance of the self. While these dangers are all developmentally phase specific, they can exist concurrently in the mind of the adult. Indeed, throughout the life cycle, any event that evokes an early childhood danger may trigger anxiety and lead to defenses and/or symptom formation. At the same time, the latent meaning of any manifestation of anxiety (or any symptom) can be obscured by the fact that almost any type of anxiety can find symbolic expression in almost any mental representation. Anxiety that appears to be without content is sometimes referred to as **free-floating anxiety**.

In addition to adding to Freud's list of typical fears, post-Freudian analysts have focused on how children develop the capacity for **anxiety tolerance** (Zetzel, 1949) or suffer from **anxiety intolerance** (Krystal, 1975). Conceptualized as an ego strength, anxiety tolerance, along with the defensive strategies used in dealing with anxiety, have many determinants, including the child's temperament, the degree of maturation of the ego, and the internalization of soothing interactions with important caregivers. How each individual manages anxiety, and whether or not anxiety becomes debilitating, reflects a complex interaction between endowment, interpersonal experiences, wishes, fears, and defenses. In Sullivan's (1953a) view, anxiety is always the result of "emotional contagion," an interpersonal event where the child experiences the mother's anxiety or disapproval. In his view, anxiety ranges from the dread, loathing, and horror of the "uncanny emotions," to the absence of anxiety, or euphoria. The threat of anxiety mobilizes what Sullivan called "security operations," analogous to defenses.

Anxiety plays a central role in the psychoanalytic approach to psychopathology because every neurotic symptom represents an attempt to avoid anxiety. When defenses fail, anxiety becomes conscious and may, if prolonged or intense, become pathological, as in **anxiety disorders**. While recognizing the biological basis of anxiety disorders, psychoanalysis emphasizes the psychodynamic underpinnings of anxiety states, as well as psychological factors that contribute to anxiety management. The psychoanalytic literature includes discussion of the psychodynamics underlying various specific syndromes related to anxiety, including generalized anxiety; phobias (A. Freud,

1977), including agoraphobia (Freud, 1926a; H. Deutsch, 1929; B. Lewin, 1952; B. Milrod, 2007); counterphobia (Fenichel, 1939a); and panic disorder (B. Milrod et al., 1997). The *Psychoanalytic Diagnostic Manual* (PDM Task Force, 2006) includes entries on anxious personality disorder, counterphobic personality (characterized by risk-taking, danger-conquering behaviors), and phobic/avoidant personality disorder (characterized by fearfulness and withdrawing). Recently, B. Milrod et al. (1997) delineated a specific psychodynamic approach for treatment of panic disorder; she also demonstrated the efficacy of psychoanalytic psychotherapy for panic disorder and agoraphobia.

At the level of general theory of mind, some theorists have pointed out similarities between the psychoanalytic concept of "signal anxiety" and the concept of "learned expectations" in learning theory. Recently, cognitive neuroscientists have become increasingly interested in the role of affects, including anxiety, in cognitive functioning. For example, Damasio's (1994) "somatic marker hypothesis," in which attenuated affective experiences generated by the body play a central role in the regulation of mental life, is strikingly similar to Freud's second theory of anxiety. Efforts continue on many fronts to integrate neurobiological and psychoanalytic models of anxiety (Alexander, Feigelson, and Gorman, 2005; Shear, 2005).

Après Coup: see DEFERRED ACTION, SEDUCTION HYPOTHESIS, TRAUMA

Archetype/Archetypal Potentialities: see JUNGIAN PSYCHOLOGY

"As If" Personality: see BORDERLINE, NARCISSISM

Attachment Theory is a theory of early development that emphasizes the primacy of the early relationship between infant and caregiver. Its central premise is that the infant's motivation to develop sustaining attachments with his caregiver is intrinsic to human existence, dictated by evolutionary pressures, and key to the survival of the species. Attachment theory asserts that there is an inborn **attachment-behavioral system** that is equal in motivational status to that of feeding and sex (Bowlby, 1969/1982). Organized patterns of attachment, evident by one year of age, are instrumental in the differentiation of one's sense of self, cognitive capacities, object relations, and the capacity for affective modulation. Insecure and especially disorganized attachment appears to be a nonspecific but definite risk factor for both childhood and adult psychopathology (Deklyen and

Greenberg, 2008; Lyons-Ruth and Jacobvitz, 2008). Moreover, the caregiver's capacity to reflect on her own attachment history is predictive of her infant's attachment pattern. These patterns are associated with **internal working models of attachment** (Bowlby, 1969/1982, 1973) and thus mental representations. A key mental capacity derived from secure attachment or resolution of attachment disturbance is self-reflective function or mentalization (Mayes and Cohen, 1992, 1996; Fonagy and Target, 1996b, 1998). Attachment history and the capacity to mentalize seem to play a significant role in mental health and certain types of psychopathology.

Attachment theory has had a long and checkered history in psychoanalysis. When introduced, it caused the expulsion of its originator, John Bowlby, from the British Psychoanalytical Society, because of Bowlby's insistence that the need for oral and other forms of libidinal gratification were secondary to an independent drive to become attached. Bowlby's focus on infant behavior and the importance of real relationships was likewise incompatible with the dominant emphasis within psychoanalysis on internal mental life and the vicissitudes of libidinal and aggressive drives. While psychoanalysts such as Hartmann (1939a), Erikson (1950), Spitz (1965), and Winnicott (1965) recognized the impact of the environment on the child's development and the simultaneous structuring of self and other that occurs during development, Bowlby's work was, nonetheless, largely repudiated (Holmes, 1993). Attachment theory as such did not begin to enter the psychoanalytic mainstream until the research paradigms introduced by Ainsworth and M. Main bridged the divide between attachment behavior and its mental representation. This work facilitated the reintroduction of attachment theory into the psychoanalytic establishment, where it has become an increasingly important theoretical modification of classical psychoanalysis, especially in the field of child analysis. Fonagy and his co-workers (Fonagy et al., 1996; Fonagy, Steele, et al., 1993; Fonagy and Target, 1996a, 1996b) have played an important role in extending the ideas derived from attachment theory and research directly into the psychoanalytic literature. For some theorists, especially for those interested in trauma, borderline personality, and dissociative disorders, attachment history has eclipsed the importance of sexual and aggressive drives in personality development.

Bowlby was heavily influenced by colleagues in a variety of disciplines, including biology, evolution, and ethology. His theorizing about attachment follows the Darwinian tradition; the infant's attachment behavior remains in the human repertoire because proximity to the mother makes survival more likely. Bowlby was inspired by Lorenz's work with imprinting in geese, by Harlow's research on maternal deprivation in primates, and by the work of Spitz (1946). Spitz's observational studies of infants demonstrated two severe, potentially fatal attachment disorders, anaclitic depression and hospitalism, which result from maternal deprivation during the first year of life. In his early work, Bowlby observed the critical importance of the child's tie to its mother in his study of juvenile offenders (Bowlby, 1944; Cassidy, 2008). Bowlby (1969/1982) went on to theorize that the infant is predisposed at birth to form an attachment to caregivers, and biologically programmed to adapt to the particular demands of his caregiving relationship.

Bowlby identified five instinctive responses that regulate proximity to the caregiver and are the key components of the attachment-behavioral system: sucking, smiling, clinging, crying, and following. When the infant becomes frightened (either by an internal stimulus, such as hunger, or by an external factor, such as a change in the environment), the attachment system becomes activated and the infant seeks reassurance from physical contact with the caregiver. When the infant feels calm and secure, the system is deactivated and the infant's attachment behaviors cease. A secure child feels free to engage in exploratory behavior at a distance from the attachment figure, using her as a secure base. For Bowlby, the quality of care and the nature of the child's earliest affectional bonds establish the child's essential orientation to and sense of security in relationships and in himself. These orientations are represented in internal working models of attachment (Bowlby, 1969/1982, 1973), which develop out of ongoing reciprocal exchanges between child and caregiver. In general, an internal working model consists of mental representations of the attachment figure, the self, and the relationship between the two that directs subsequent appraisals of interactions with attachment figures and allows the infant to predict how best to engage his caregiver in caring for him. If the attachment figure consistently acknowledges the child's need for protection and comfort, while at the same time respecting his need to autonomously explore the environment, the child is likely to develop an internal working model of the self as self reliant and valued. In contrast, if the child's need for both comfort and autonomy are rejected or not acknowledged, he is likely to construct an internal working model of the self as unworthy or incompetent (Bretherton, 1992).

Although Bowlby was expelled from mainstream psychoanalysis, he was readily embraced by developmental psychologists. His collaboration with the clinician and researcher Ainsworth established the credibility of attachment theory within academic psychology; however, this collaboration also diverted it further from the psychoanalytic community. Ainsworth developed a research procedure (The Strange Situation) to assess individual differences in attachment organization (Ainsworth et al., 1978). She described distinct patterns of attachment, each of which was found to relate in lawful ways to differences in the early mother-child relationship. These include three organized patterns of attachment: secure, avoidant, and resistant/ambivalent, and a fourth disorganized/disoriented pattern. M. Main later documented similar patterns in adult recollections of early childhood experience (M. Main, Kaplan, and Cassidy, 1985) through the **Adult Attachment Interview**. These include three organized patterns: secure-autonomous, dismissing, and preoccupied, and a fourth, unresolved/disorganized. Importantly, differences in maternal attachment organization are linked to their infants' attachment category, indicating the **intergenerational transmission of attachment**. Because of its emphasis on mental representations of attachment in adults rather than the more behavioral focus of Ainsworth's research, Main's work was instrumental in stimulating interest in attachment and related processes within psychoanalysis (Slade, 2000, 2008). For example, her work inspired Fonagy and his colleagues (Fonagy et al., 2002) to characterize self-reflective function and to develop mentalization theory, bringing together essential elements of attachment and contemporary psychoanalytic theory. However, the study of infant attachment issues was never entirely absent from psychoanalytic circles. As noted previously, the research of Spitz influenced Bowlby, and also that of psychoanalyst-researcher Fraiberg. Fraiberg (1982), in her observation of infants who experienced recurrent severe abuse, violence, neglect, and/or deprivation, described pathological attachment states that she termed pathological defenses of infancy. Researchers in other disciplines also espoused similar ideas about the critical role of the mother-infant bond in normal development, such as, for example, the pediatricians Klaus and Kennell (1976/1982), who proposed bonding theory.

Nevertheless, attachment theory has served as a critical stimulus to psychoanalytically informed infant observational research that focuses on the mother-infant dyad. Such research documents early mutual influence structures, specifying how each person is affected by his own responses, self regulation, as well as by his partner's behavior, interactive regulation (Tronick, 1989; Beebe, Jaffe, and Lachmann, 1992; Beebe and Lachmann, 2003). Observations of mutual regulations have been made in every modality examined, for example, vocalization, gaze (Beebe and Stern, 1977), and general affective involvement (Tronick, 1989). Mutual influences in the matching of affect and timing between infant and caretaker provide each partner with a behavioral basis for knowing and entering into each other's perceptions, temporal world, and feeling states. What the infant comes to represent intrapsychically is a delicately responsive interactive process: actions-of-self-in-relation-to-actions-of-other. The implication of this interactive-process model of representation is that the experiences of self and other in the social domain are structured simultaneously and are inextricably linked. The implications of derailment in the dyad can be severe for the organization of the infant experience. Usually the dyad repairs miscommunications, and the mutual-influence aspect of the interaction remains intact. But the pair may be "misattuned," or in an aversive interaction. The transmission of maternal psychopathology and the effects of maternal depression have been shown to result in insecure attachment in the infant (Beebe et al., 2008). Parent-infant observation defines precise individual and dyadic social patterns of behavior organizing early relatedness, with direct implications for early intervention.

Research focused on the mother-infant dyad and other areas of attachment research have also facilitated a more nuanced understanding of the clinical situation, in particular the contribution of intersubjectivity and the analytic dyad to treatment efficacy. Furthermore, in countering criticisms of attachment theory, Slade (2000) argued that the clinical analyst's understanding of attachment patterns does not restrict him to categorical or reductionistic thinking. It allows for a nuanced understanding of the ways in which attachment difficulties become manifest in the analytic relationship, and it provides a context in which changes in basic representational processes may take place.

Attacks on Linking: see BION, REALITY

Attention: see CONSCIOUSNESS, PRECONSCIOUS, TOPOGRAPHIC THEORY

Attunement: see AFFECT, EMPATHY

Autism: see SEPARATION-INDIVIDUATION

Autoerotic: see OBJECT, PSYCHOSEXUAL DEVELOPMENT

Average Expectable Environment is a term coined by Heinz Hartmann (1939a) to describe the external reality situation within which an individual's inborn capacities are expected to develop in a predictable and progressive manner. The concept is central to Hartmann's view of the importance of adaptation in understanding human psychology. The average expectable environment should include nurturing, love, emotional safety, and protection from physical danger. The newborn infant is equipped, or preadapted, with autonomous ego functions that allow him to make use of the average expectable environment. As the environment most relevant for infant development is the one provided by caretakers, the average expectable environment is often compared to what Winnicott (1951) called the "good enough mother."

Hartmann intended "average" and "expectable" to be understood as relative terms. Average expectable implies a good "fit" between the infant and his environment. An environment that is sufficient for some infants may be insufficient and even harmful for others (Escalona, 1963). Modern theorists have explored the factors that permit developmental progression even in the context of imperfect or atypical environments. For example, Mayes (1994) has observed the development of traumatized children and adults, with the aim of better defining an average expectable environment and of offering better understanding of the variable impact of interactions between typical and atypical environments, endowments, and experiences.

B

Basic Assumptions: see BION

Basic Fault: see NARCISSISM

The **Beating Fantasy** is a conscious or unconscious fantasy, usually originating during early latency and accompanying masturbation, which features a scenario of mistreatment. The fantasizer usually appears as the victim, however he may identify with the role of the beater. Like all fantasies, the beating fantasy undergoes a developmental evolution, serves multiple defensive functions, may be entirely repressed, and may be evident in highly disguised derivative form. In adults, beating fantasies or their manifest enactment may be a condition of excitement during masturbatory sexual activity and/or with a partner. The beating fantasy is often associated with masochistic psychopathology. The enactment of the beating fantasy, in derivative form, within the transference may serve as a powerful resistance (K. Novick and J. Novick, 1998).

The beating fantasy is important in the history of psychoanalytic thought as it contributed to Freud's formulations about both masochism and perversion. It also demonstrates the process of reconstruction, not of an actual childhood event, but of childhood fantasy that undergoes transformation during development. As such, it represents a process that is fundamental to psychoanalytic intepretation, that is, the gathering and integration of bits of data from which unconscious content is inferred and then elaborated into secondary-process narrative form.

Freud's (1913d) first reference to beating fantasies described their occurrence in the childhood of obsessional neurotics, a group of patients for whom the anal-sadistic pregenital phase of development is particularly important. In his classic study of beating fantasies, "A Child Is Being Beaten," Freud (1919b) identified the fantasy as central to masochistic functioning and, for both boys and girls, as deriving from guilty incestuous wishes toward the father. Based upon adult analytic material, Freud reconstructed three phases of the beating fantasy in girls: 1) the hated sibling rival is being beaten by the father; 2) the girl is being beaten by her father; and, 3) a group of children, usually boys, are being beaten by a father substitute. According to Freud, the second phase

is most important as it betrays the masochistic character of the beating fantasy; its meaning is now clear, as the beating is a punishment for the girl's incestuous desire for her father and, at the same time, a regressive substitute for it. However, it is the third phase that is retained as a conscious fantasy in its desexualized sadistic form.

Freud did not find a parallel sequence in the beating fantasies of boys, for whom the oedipal love for the father carries different implications. The final conscious fantasy for the boy is that his mother is beating him; his homosexual impulses have been repressed but not his "passive feminine identification." Freud viewed the beating fantasy in both boys and girls as an infantile perversion; he asserted that the adult outcome for the boy with a beating fantasy is almost always a masochistic perversion. Freud (1924a) later placed the beating fantasy within a developmental sequence of masochistic fantasy: in the oral phase, the fear of being eaten; in the anal-sadistic phase, the wish to be beaten by father; in the phallic phase, the fear of being castrated; and, in the final genital organization, primary masochism is transformed into the wish to be copulated with and to give birth. Finally, Freud (1925b) described the beating fantasy in girls as also a confession of masturbation in which the beaten child represents the clitoris.

Authors after Freud emphasized preoedipal determinants of the fantasy (Bergler, 1938, 1948b; Schmideberg, 1948). E. Joseph (1965) stressed the ubiquity of the beating fantasy, its multiple determinants and functions, the varied manifest forms and latent meaning of the fantasy, and the range of diagnostic groups in which it can occur. Other authors focused on the central role of the beating fantasy in pathological sadomasochism. Stoller (1991) highlighted the function of the beating fantasy and other perversions as protection against anxiety of merging with the mother. Chasseguet-Smirgel (1991) emphasized the attachment function of the beating fantasy. J. Weiss (1998) detailed its protective and reassuring defensive function against aggression contained in sexuality and separation. J. Novick and K. Novick (1972) and Wurmser (2007) described the archaic superego function of the beating fantasy connected with guilt and anxiety over separation issues.

The Novicks studied the role of beating fantasies in normal and pathological development, using the records of child cases from the Anna Freud Centre (then Hampstead Clinic) and observing normal children in the nursery school. They described a similar sequence to Freud's reconstructed phases and demonstrated the ubiquity of beating wishes and beating games in young children. They also identified the sexualization of the fantasy during the oedipal phase and, in accord with Freud's 1919 description, found a sharp divergence between boys and girls. Finally, they identified a transitory beating fantasy in girls, which quickly evolves into rescue and family romance fantasies, as well as a fixed fantasy, found in both boys and girls, which persists as an important organizer of severe sadomasochistic pathology. The fixed beating fantasy always includes the subject as persecuted victim, becomes the permanent focus of the child's psychosexual life, and is often impervious to years of interpretive work in treatment.

Beta Elements: see BION

Beyond the Pleasure Principle: see DEATH DRIVE, ENERGY, MASOCHISM, NEGATIVE THERAPEUTIC REACTION, REPETITION COMPULSION, WORKING THROUGH

Wilfred R. Bion, a follower of Klein, was a pioneer in the analysis of psychotic patients and in the understanding of highly primitive states of mind. Along with Segal and Rosenfeld, Bion is considered one of the leaders of the second generation of Kleinian psychoanalysts. Of these three, the work of Bion, in particular, has had an enormous impact on analysts throughout the world, both within and outside the Kleinian tradition.

Bion's work begins in the clinical situation, developing in the context of ongoing efforts to understand the forces that undermine the analyst's neutrality and his capacity to think, and the patient's ability to learn and change. Bion made extensive use of the concept of countertransference, and his papers are rich with clinical vignettes describing related phenomena. Bion's work marks a departure in the use of many of Klein's concepts. Of particular note, he radically extended the concept of projective identification both clinically and conceptually. Bion's contributions include the concepts of preconception/conception; the concepts of the container/contained; and a new model for the development of the capacity for thought. Bion's writings can be divided into three phases: the early period, during which he explored the functioning of groups; a mid-

dle period (between the mid-1950s and the mid-1970s), during which he developed the ideas for which he is best known; and a final period, during which he expressed himself in a literary form. However, there is continuity running through Bion's work in his preoccupation with thinking and the development of knowledge, and with the factors that promote or disrupt these processes.

Bion became interested in group phenomena in the context of his work in the War Office Selection Boards. He argued that the best selection process for leaders includes observing the behavior of men in a group situation. Bion (1961) described two interacting aspects of the functioning of all groups: the "work group" and the "basic assumptions group." The work group defines its task, acknowledges its purpose, and promotes its members' cooperation; it is oriented outward toward external reality. In contrast, the basic assumptions groups, characterized by one of three basic attitudes of dependency, fight/flight, and pairing, is oriented inward toward fantasy. These basic assumptions often interfere with the work task, but their energy can also be harnessed in the service of the task. Basic assumptions represent disowned parts of the individuals in a group. Because they are anonymous, they can function quite ruthlessly. Bion's theories about group processes were influential in what are called Tavistock groups and A. K. Rice seminars (Rice, 1963). During this same period, Bion worked with T. Main (1946, 1989) and others to develop concepts related to what they called the "therapeutic community."

In 1959, Bion (1959) published "Attacks on Linking," which marked the beginning of a series of papers based on work with patients who suffer from serious psychopathology involving the capacity to think. His work developed from the ideas proposed by Klein (1946) in her 1946 paper, "Notes on Some Schizoid Mechanisms." Bion's paper described how patients who have suffered "catastrophe" in the earliest relationship show profound impairments in their capacity to link thoughts together, making it difficult for them to feel linked to any object or to invest anything with emotional significance. Bion described how these patients use massive projective identification, by which they violently split off and expel from their mind aspects of their own ego. Bion argued that the capacity to link thoughts together is one of the fundamental processes that characterize thinking. He also argued that some individuals fear that bringing thoughts together and linking them will bring renewed catastrophe.

In *Learning from Experience* and "The Psycho-Analytic Study of Thinking," both published in

1962, Bion (1962a, 1962b) proposed a theory of the development of thought. This theory is articulated in a number of overlapping registers: the theory of preconceptions and its relation to absence; the concepts of the container/contained; and the theory of alpha function. Like Freud and Klein, Bion held to the view that there is a basic drive toward knowledge (the epistemophilic drive). Bion argued that the infant is born with innate structures that allow his mind to recognize objects. The expectation created by these innate structures is called a preconception. When a preconception (for example, the expectation of a breast, of being held, of being loved) is met with its realization in the external world (for example, an actual breast), the match between internal expectation and external object creates what Bion called a "conception." This matching process links the self with the object, and internal with external, forming the building blocks of thought. In other words, thought is viewed as the capacity to link together objects in increasingly complex ways. Bion called the situation where a preconception is not met by the mother's presence a "negative realization" (as, for example, when the expectation of a mother/breast is met with absence). Bion's ideas follow those of Freud (1900), who argued that thought (secondary process) develops in the face of the absence of an object that can satisfy desire. In Bion's view, if there is sufficient capacity to tolerate frustration (because of either constitutional or external factors), the nonexistence of the object can be psychically registered, allowing for the creation of the idea of an object. If there is insufficient capacity to tolerate frustration, then what might have been the idea of an absent object associated with pain and distress is, instead, experienced as a concrete presence, or a "bad object," suitable only for evacuation. In these situations, the capacity for thinking is severely compromised, replaced by violent projective identification. Ego functions are fragmented through violent, disruptive splitting.

Bion's conceptualization of the "container/contained" contributes another layer of understanding to the problem of the development of thinking. The concept of the container/contained represents an extension of the concept of projective identification into the interpersonal domain. It reflects Bion's differentiation between normal and primitive mechanisms of projective identification, the former seen as necessary for development of the capacity for empathy. In Bion's view, the capacity to think centers on the infant's need to internalize an object felt to be capable of understanding him and of giving his experience meaning. In this theory, the infant projects aspects of his own mental contents into the mother.

If the mother is able to contain these projections and to think about them, so giving them meaning, the infant has an experience of being understood. Bion called this process "reverie." Reverie does not happen consciously, but occurs unconsciously. Through repeated interactions of successful reverie, the infant develops the confidence and faith that he will be understood. He also internalizes the reverie function, thereby developing the capacity to reflect upon and understand himself. However, in situations where reverie fails (as a result of either internal or external factors), the effect can be catastrophic, leading to serious psychopathology characterized by incapacity to think. Bion also described situations where the mother, overwhelmed by her own anxieties, reprojects unwanted experience into the infant. This creates the prototype of a relationship where an individual approaches external objects in dread, with the expectation not of understanding, but with the fear that something terrifying will be forced into him.

Lastly, Bion approached the problem of thinking through the model of what he called "alpha function." Bion viewed the primitive mind as a "proto-mental" system, where body and mind are not distinct. Out of this system develops a proper mental apparatus that can think thoughts. Bion described a dialectical process; the apparatus, as well as being capable of transforming the proto-thoughts into thoughts, is itself brought into being by this process. As Bion developed a notation to describe this process, he was determined to use terms that would be devoid of associations so that we are not misled into thinking we understand what they are. He coined the term *alpha function* to describe the process by which proto-thoughts are transformed into thoughts. The proto-thoughts are called beta elements. Beta elements are acted upon by a developing function, now called alpha function, through which they are transformed into primitive thoughts, now called alpha elements. A principle characteristic of alpha elements is that they can be linked to one another. While beta elements cannot be known directly, they reveal themselves in acting out, psychosomatic symptoms, and violent projective identification. Bion developed these ideas in *Learning from Experience* (1962a) in his later books, *Elements of Psycho-Analysis* (1963), *Transformations* (1965), and, *Attention and Interpretation* (1970). In his descriptions of clinical work, he is also famous for having warned analysts of the adverse consequences of listening to patients with too many preconceived ideas or theories, advising analysts to listen "without memory or desire" (Bion, 1967).

In the final period of his life, Bion turned to a more literary form to express himself. *A Memoir of the Future,* published in 1991, is comprised of three "novels," *The Dream, The Past Presented,* and *The Dawn of Oblivion.* In these works, many of Bion's earlier ideas are reworked in a more imaginative form. Here, Bion wrote in a loose, allusive style that is difficult to penetrate. Bion described the process of "coming to know" as "K;" the failure to achieve this he called "minus-K." Bion's concept of "O" is difficult to define; some have argued that it is a mystical idea, whereas others see it as related to his earlier work.

Bisexuality, a term lacking conceptual clarity, has been used to describe behavior, conscious experience, unconscious fantasy, psychic structure, and an aspect of self experience. More specifically, bisexuality is: 1) a sexual orientation in which the **bisexual** individual experiences conscious erotic attraction to members of both sexes and pursues sexual activity with both sexes; 2) a universal human mental disposition known as **psychic bisexuality**, comprising unconscious male and female identifications and the potential capacity to experience sexual desire toward both sexes. By adulthood, one component tends to be largely unconscious so that a relatively exclusive hetero- or homosexual orientation usually evolves; 3) **bisexual object choice**, meaning the choice of an object who represents both male and female love object; and 4) a **bisexual gender identity**, in which male and female characteristics are consciously experienced by the subject and are apparent to the observer. The relationship of any of these various usages of the term *bisexuality* to psychopathology is a matter of considerable controversy as it trenches upon revised concepts of gender proposed by contemporary gender theorists.

The concept of bisexuality is important in psychoanalytic thinking because, as originally presented by Freud, it represented a radical view of the complexity of human psychosexuality. Contemporary gender theorists have justly challenged traditional psychoanalytic ideas about sexual orientation as categorical and dogmatic, especially many ideas about homosexuality. However, the complexly layered, conscious and unconscious meanings of the term *bisexuality* point to the complexity of Freud's own thinking on the subject.

The term *bisexuality* came into use in European languages at the turn of the nineteenth century with the emergence of the scientific discipline of sexology. *Bisexual* replaced *hermaphrodite,* which meant either a human who has both male and female genitals (and sometimes secondary sexual characteristics) or an invertebrate or lower vertebrate that is reproductively able to be both male and female. The sexolo-

gists also used the term for what had been called psychical hermaphroditism, meaning the interest in or attraction to both sexes; however, they usually used it to refer to individuals with homosexual object preference. Sociologists and anthropologists have described bisexuality occurring throughout history and across cultures, including "Greek love" (involving men who marry and also take younger male lovers), "Melanesia bisexuality" (involving males who, in puberty rites, are sexually approached by older males), and Native American "berdache" (shamanistic males or females who take same-sex spouses but also opposite sex lovers).

From his earliest theorizing, Freud (1905b, 1920b) explored concepts of bisexuality, his interest attributed to the influence of Fliess. In their early correspondence, Freud (1896b) famously described every sexual act as an event between four individuals. Freud's concept of bisexuality included a universal constitutional disposition that included vestigial biological bisexuality in both sexes, and also psychic bisexuality, or the capacity for sexual desire for both sexes and the presence of both masculine and feminine "mental sexual characteristics." Thus, Freud delineated three domains or types of bisexuality: physical, sexual (erotic), and mental. Freud illustrated the manifestations of psychic bisexuality in children with the universal presence of both a positive and negative oedipus complex. He posited a complex view of sexuality and gender, invoking multicausal factors both innate and acquired, in the gender preference of any individual.

Several decades later, the sexologist Kinsey (1941) demonstrated empirically that human males and females are variable in terms of their physical sexual characteristics, diverse in their gender types, and seldom either exclusively heterosexual or exclusively homosexual in their sexual preference. In other words, the majority of people are in the middle of a continuum between heterosexuality and homosexuality, manifesting bisexual desires, fantasies, and experiences.

Kinsey's data was restricted to the realm of conscious thought and behavior. However, starting in the 1960s, psychoanalytic studies of gender emerged, focusing on the complexities of gender development and sexual object choice. Psychoanalytic interest in bisexuality has reemerged more recently (G. Grossman, 2001; Smith, 2002b), demonstrating the breadth of perspectives on the topic. Chodorow (1994b), underscoring Freud's views of sexuality as an outcome of complex processes, stressed the multiplicities of genders and desires, and viewed bisexuality as a compromise formation. Other contemporary analysts have stressed the importance of bisexual identifications rather than rigid polarizations in the inner, subjective experience of gender (Bassin, 1996; J. Benjamin, 1997; Harris, 2005a). Young-Bruehl (2003) demonstrated the complex, multilayered, and multisexual nature of an individual's object choices and identifications as these emerge in the clinical situation. In this vein, Elise (1997) illuminated the wish to be and to have both sexes, that is, bisexuality in terms of object choice and object representation.

Borderline is a term first coined to describe patients who regress in unstructured situations, including psychoanalytic treatment, but who are not generally psychotic. Originally used to designate psychopathology that lies on a continuum between neurotic and psychotic, the term *borderline* has become both more precise and more varied in its meaning as it has evolved in both the psychoanalytic and the psychiatric literature. As with many terms, there is a gap between the psychiatric term, which is used descriptively in the *DSM* (*Diagnostic and Statistical Manual of Mental Disorders*) system, and the more theory-driven psychoanalytic concept. Currently, the term is used in the following ways: 1) **Borderline state**, a phrase rarely used today, has been used to designate a state of mind on the way to psychotic decompensation (Knight, 1953). Borderline states and/or transient, micropsychotic episodes can be seen in all borderline syndromes. 2) **Borderline personality disorder (BPD)** is a psychiatric diagnosis applied to patients with unstable interpersonal relationships, identity disturbance, fears of abandonment, chronic anger, frequent feelings of emptiness and boredom, diffuse impulsivity, and a tendency toward self-damaging acts. 3) **Borderline personality organization (BPO)** is a psychoanalytic diagnosis defined by Kernberg (1967, 1975), marked by: identity diffusion; nonspecific ego weaknesses, such as impulsivity, affect intolerance, and reversion to primary process thinking under stress; failure to integrate positive and negative aspects of object relations; the predominance of defenses based on splitting; the presence of generally intact but fragile reality testing. Patients with BPO function at the **borderline level of character pathology** in a four-tiered classification system (normal/flexible, neurotic, borderline, and psychotic levels of personality organization) based on assessing the psychological structure underlying the clinical presentation (Kernberg 1970a, 1984). While there is considerable overlap between BPD and BPO, the latter is a broader and more truly psychoanalytic concept, describing the shared, underlying structural and psychodynamic features of many syndromes

and/or personality types. In addition to underlying all cases of borderline personality disorder, borderline personality organization is the underlying structure of schizoid, paranoid, antisocial, and many narcissistic personality disorders, as well as certain cases of substance abuse and sexual perversion. 4) In addition to the more clearly defined BPD and BPO, the term *borderline* appears frequently in the psychoanalytic literature applied to patients with severe character pathology, by authors whose conceptualizations of the syndrome vary widely, although most include some of the descriptive elements of BPD and/or structural elements of BPO. 5) Finally, **borderline traits** or **borderline features** refer to any aspects of the above, such as a poorly formed identity, or the occasional use of splitting or projective identification, when these are observed in higher functioning individuals.

The term *borderline* in all its uses was coined by psychoanalysts struggling to describe patients who are more impaired than ordinary neurotics and who do not do well in traditional analysis. At the same time, the study of patients with borderline personality disorder and/or borderline traits has led to major developments in psychoanalytic theory, including 1) greater precision and richness in the understanding of character structure, especially with regard to ego functioning and object relations; 2) new appreciation of defense mechanisms based on splitting, such as projective identification and omnipotent control; 3) new understanding of how to apply Kleinian object relations theory to character pathology; and 4) appreciation of the interactions between defense, object relations, and interactions with other people. In psychoanalytic practice, work with borderline patients has led to significant contributions to the "widening scope" of psychoanalysis by offering a system for classifying character disorders that includes different levels of psychopathology, a better understanding of who will benefit from analysis, and modifications of psychoanalytic technique necessary for the treatment of more-disturbed patients. Work with borderline patients has also led to greater understanding of countertransference, and particularly the ways in which the analyst's countertransference functions to provide information about the patient's inner life. Finally, borderline psychopathology is an area of major overlap between the fields of psychiatry and psychoanalysis; borderline psychopathology and the treatment of borderline patients have been the subjects of much research in both fields.

The term *borderline* was introduced by A. Stern (1938) in 1938 to describe a group of patients who seemed to be on the border between neurosis and psychosis, regressing in analysis to "borderline schizophrenia." Other authors who worked with such patients include, among others: H. Deutsch (1942), who described the "as if" personality; Hoch and Polatin (1949), who described "pseudoneurotic schizophrenia"; Knight (1953), who described "borderline states"; and Frosch (1959a, 1964), who described the "psychotic character." In the 1960s, Grinker, Werble, and Drye (1968) brought diagnostic rigor to the syndrome by identifying common features through naturalistic observation of patients in the borderline spectrum; they also presented evidence that borderline patients do not deteriorate into schizophrenia, but represent a distinct syndrome; finally, they identified subtypes of borderline pathology. In the early 1970s, Gunderson and co-workers (Gunderson and Singer, 1975; Gunderson and Kolb, 1978) began research designed to more clearly delineate the features of borderline personality disorder, which was accepted as a diagnosis in *DSM III* in 1973 (and again with some modifications in *DSM IV,* with further modifications planned for *DSM V*).

Kernberg brought coherence and depth to the exploration of borderline syndromes with the introduction of his concept of borderline personality organization, described above. His concept of personality organization combines aspects of Kleinian object relations theory and of ego psychology. In his view, borderline personality disorder is characterized by an incapacity to synthesize good and bad self and object representations, and by the consequent predominance of primitive defense mechanisms based on splitting, such as projective identification and omnipotent control. These features of BPO correspond to the Kleinian concept of the paranoid-schizoid position, which is characterized by the splitting off and projection of "all bad" object relations, in contrast to the depressive position, where aggression and libido, love and hate are modulated and integrated. The borderline individual's failure of integration, based on his defensive need to separate positive from negative experiences, underlies his inability to experience a coherent picture of himself or of others. The borderline individual's fragmented and contradictory sense of self, which Kernberg called "identity diffusion," leaves him at risk for extreme and often overwhelming affects in the experience of the moment, misrepresentation of self and others, abrupt switches in the experience of self and other, and the consequent behavioral and interpersonal problems that constitute the *DSM IV* criteria for BPD.

Much controversy in the psychoanalytic literature on borderline syndromes has focused on a version of the long-standing debate over defense/

conflict versus deficit/developmental failure as the cause of psychopathology. For example, Kernberg's view of BPO emphasizes the role of overwhelming aggression in distorting internalized object relations, as "all good" and "all bad" self and object representations are actively kept apart by defenses based on splitting. In contrast to Kernberg's emphasis on active defense as the cause of borderline psychic structure, other theorists have argued that failures in infant/caregiver interactions during development are the major cause of deficits in borderline psychic structure. For example, many have argued that experiences of real abandonment by parents lead to the borderline person's inability to tolerate aloneness (G. Adler and Buie 1979; Masterson 1981), his failure to achieve object constancy (Akhtar, 1988), or his "affective identity disorder of the self" (Lewin and Schulz, 1992). More recently, Fonagy and Target (1996b) argued that borderline psychopathology results from deficits in the capacity for mentalization, which in turn results from poor infant/caregiver interactions.

Controversy over the relative role of conflict/defense versus developmental deficit in the psychogenesis of borderline syndrome is reflected in controversies over the correct approach to treatment. Debates have focused on how supportive versus exploratory the therapy should be, how actively to foster a positive therapeutic alliance versus allowing the emergence of the negative transference early in therapy, and the value of interpretation (G. Adler 1979; Masterson 1981; Gabbard and Westen 2003; Bateman and Fonagy, 2004; Gabbard, 2006b; Caligor et al., 2009). However, a consensus has emerged that psychotherapeutic work requires an emphasis on structure (a frame and holding environment), limit setting, and emphasis on the here and now (Waldinger, 1987). Analytic treatments for borderline conditions are more highly structured than traditional psychoanalytic approaches and involve greater activity on the part of the therapist.

During the 1990s, there was intense debate over the differential diagnosis between borderline personality disorder and posttraumatic stress disorder (PTSD), with the argument proposed that the concept of BPD is a misunderstanding of PTSD (Herman, 1992). Along with differences in clinical presentations, a review of the literature finds that only one-third of the BPD population has a history of severe and extended abuse, and that only 20 percent of individuals with a history of serious abuse go on to have serious psychopathology as adults (Paris, 2008), suggesting that other factors contribute to the development of borderline personality.

Currently two psychoanalytically oriented therapies have been manualized and studied empirically: transference-focused psychotherapy (TFP) (Clarkin, Yeomans, and Kernberg, 2006), and mentalization-based therapy (MBT) (Bateman and Fonagy, 2004, 2006). Links between TFP and MBT are evident, and both present a complex understanding of the borderline condition. However, whereas MBT emphasizes repairing a deficit in a mental process (mentalization), TFP, while acknowledging the presence of deficits, emphasizes working to resolve the conflicts underlying a defensively dissociated psychological structure, which is considered the root of the deficits and the specific symptoms of the disorder.

Current understanding of borderline psychopathology is increasingly informed by research at multiple levels, including neural, social cognitive, neurocognitive, and interpersonal (Posner et al., 2002; Adolphs, 2003; Depue and Lenzenweger, 2001/2005; Fertuck et al., 2009). Perhaps not surprisingly, this research supports a view of borderline psychopathology as a dynamic interaction of temperament and environmental factors, such as abuse or neglect, resulting in difficulty establishing a coherent sense of self and others in the context of an insecure working model of attachment, deficits in mentalization, and low effortful control. The lack of coherence of the self involves the lack of integration of libidinal and aggressive drives and affects, with primitive defenses based on splitting engaged as an attempt to deal with these internal conflicts (Clarkin, Yeomans, and Kernberg, 2006; Silbersweig et al., 2007). Attachment research has linked borderline pathology to a range of insecure (primarily anxious/preoccupied, disorganized/unresolved, and/or unclassifiable) attachment patterns that presuppose maladaptive and/or fragmented, inconsistent working models of self and attachment figures (Fonagy et al., 1996; M. Main 1999; D. Diamond et al., 2003; K. Levy, Meehan et al., 2006). Studies of mentalization have shown deficits in that capacity, which render the individual unable to accurately assess the contents of his own mind or the minds of others (Fonagy et al., 1996; Bateman and Fonagy, 2004). Recent research has shown changes in reflective function (RF—defined as the operationalized measure of mentalization in attachment relationships) after a year of TFP (K. Levy, Meehan, et al., 2006). The significant increase in RF can be interpreted as both an improvement in the capacity to mentalize and also as an indirect measure of improvement in the integration of sense of self and perception of others. The significant improvements in both mentalization and coherence of internal working models of attachment, as well as in symptomatology, in several studies (K. Levy, Meehan, et al., 2006; Clarkin et al., 2007), support the centrality of the quality of internal representations of self and others in borderline pathology, and they provide empirical validation for the effectiveness of transference-based psychotherapy (TFP). Empirical research on social and neurocognitive factors germane to BPD is in its early stages yet offers some evidence for psychoanalytic theories (Graham and Clark, 2006). In particular, social cognitive and neuropsychological research on patients with BPD has found a pattern of impaired information processing influenced by memory-consolidation deficits and moderate impairments in cognitive (executive) control (Fertuck et al., 2006), enhanced expression and experience of negative affect (Lenzenweger et al., 2004), and biased emotional sensitivity to ambiguous social stimuli (Donegan et al., 2003; Fertuck et al., 2009). While individuals with BPD have intact or enhanced capacity to appraise emotions in others (Fertuck et al., 2009), their abilities to trust (Veen and Arntz, 2000; Arntz and Veen, 2001), cooperate (King-Casas et al., 2008), and form secure attachments (Minzenberg, Poole, and Vingradov, 2006) appear impaired, a finding that is largely compatible with the idea that BPD involves the misperception of others through distorted internal representations, along with the misattribution of negative affect and hostile intentions to others.

Breast: see BION, KLEIN, OBJECT, PREOEDIPAL

C

Castration Complex is a constellation of wishes and anxieties associated with bodily feelings, ideas, and emotions that come together in the oedipal stage of psychosexual development. At that time, oedipal fantasies become associated with **castration anxiety,** or the fear that forbidden oedipal desires will lead to punishment in the form of loss of or injury to one's genital. In general usage, castration refers to loss of testicles or ovaries; however, in psychoanalysis, it refers to loss of or damage to the penis or clitoris, as they represent bodily parts in which the most sexual pleasure is experienced. In the clinical situation, castration anxiety may appear symbolically and is often invoked not only by fantasies of loss or injury of body parts, but by other experiences of loss.

The conceptual history of the term *castration complex* has been long and controversial. The original usage reflected Freud's phallocentric view of early development, in which the primacy of the male genital was postulated for both sexes. In addition, the unconscious fantasies in women of castration and inferiority due to the absent phallus were regarded by Freud as universal, as was the linked experience of penis envy. Consequently, the use of the term *castration* sparked considerable controversy among feminist critics and others, many of whom rejected psychoanalysis in its entirety. Within the field of psychoanalysis, views of female development have been gradually modified as the result of child observation and the analyses of adult women, which have provided evidence for the presence of a specific line of early female development recognized as "primary femininity," and a specific set of "female genital anxieties." However, also controversial is whether these female genital anxieties replace the phallic castration complex or whether they are present in some women along with fantasies of castration and penis envy. Other contemporary theorists have elaborated a symbolic or metaphorical meaning for phallus and castration, thereby maintaining their relevance for both genders.

Freud's (1900, 1908c) references to castration as a factor in mental life appeared early in his work in his description of the sexual theories of children and as a feared punishment for forbidden wishes; however, Freud (1909c) first described the castration complex in the case of Little Hans. In Freud's view, the castration complex holds a fundamental position in the development of infantile sexuality in both sexes and is closely linked to the oedipus complex, which he regarded as the organizing foundation for personality development. However, according to Freud (1924b, 1925b), the relationship of the oedipus complex to the castration complex is gender specific. For the boy, the fear of castration for forbidden oedipal wishes is the motivating force for the renunciation of those wishes. The prohibitive injunctions of the father become internalized in the boy's mind in the formation of a new structure, the superego; and the boy takes his father as the primary object for identification. In other words, the boy's castration complex brings the oedipus complex to resolution. In contrast, for the girl, the castration complex initiates the oedipus complex. The recognition of genital difference is a narcissistic blow for the little girl who feels herself to be deficient or "castrated." As she blames her mother, whom she now sees as deficient like herself, she renounces her primary attachment to her mother and turns to the father. With this change in object, the girl gives up her wish for a penis, replacing it with a wish for a child (the penis-baby equation) and taking her father as her love object. In the process, a shift with regard to sexuality occurs, in which the girl rejects her phallic attachment to the clitoris and assumes a passive receptive position in which the vagina is fully valued. According to Freud, these differences in the development of the male and female oedipus complex have important implications for male and female superego development; they also leave the female more vulnerable to narcissistic and masochistic conflicts.

With the formulation of Freud's structural theory, castration anxiety took its place in a hierarchy of anxieties arising in situations of danger in relation to phases of childhood development. Subsequent psychoanalytic theorists (Sachs, 1962; Eigen, 1974) emphasized the importance of early oral and anal precursor anxieties, which prime the oedipal child for the experience of castration anxiety. Such theorists posited that early experiences of loss and separation, such as weaning and defecation, represent the reality nidus around which castration anxiety emerges. This idea is also represented in the symbolic equation of penis=feces=baby, described by Freud and others.

Freud's findings on the central preoccupation of children with their genitals during the second and third years of life have been richly documented in longitudinal observational studies (Parens et al., 1976; Roiphe and Galenson, 1981b). Manifestations of this preoccupation include a readily observable increase in genital masturbation, self and reciprocal exploration, and concerns about injury. While the importance of anatomical difference is readily inferred and observed in the early life of boys and girls, clinical and observational findings with regard to its role in female development have been challenged and reformulated (Chehrazi, 1986; P. Bernstein, 2004). Indeed, from the beginning, many analysts have questioned the validity of the phallocentrism of Freud's psychosexual theory, especially his views on the castration complex in women. There is considerable research that documents both the little girl's preoedipal awareness of her own genital and her sense of herself as female (Galenson and Roiphe, 1976; Stoller, 1975a, 1976; Parens et al., 1976). While the awareness of genital difference in the little girl may evoke a response of penis envy, many analysts now understand penis envy to be a developmental phenomenon that evolves through subsequent vicissitudes until ultimate resolution, as well as the manifest content of a complex compromise involving narcissistic sensitivity derived from many sources and developmental levels. Many other analysts challenge Freud's ideas about the role of castration anxiety in the entry into and resolution of the oedipus complex, and the differences in male and female superego development (Kulish and Holtzman, 2008). Other analysts have also delineated a set of specifically female genital castration anxieties related to penetration, tearing, and sealing over (Mayer, 1985, 1991; D. Bernstein, 1990). Similarly, some analysts have proposed renaming the phallic phase in girls; a variety of terms are now used, including *genital phase, infantile genital phase,* and *early genital phase,* resulting in some confusion.

Another critique of the original concept of castration anxiety stems from contemporary writers who have pointed out that the anatomical penis is insufficiently distinguished from the symbolic phallus in Freud's thinking (Fogel, 1998; Harris, 2005a; M. Diamond, 2006). These writers have argued that both women and men possess a symbolic phallus, a universal metaphoric psychic construction imbued with meanings such as power and potency, or bodily or psychic dignity or majesty. They have also pointed out that since gender is constructed symbolically, psychic or symbolic castration should be separated from anatomical, biological, or material reality and should therefore be considered a threat to or loss of any valued human characteristic or function.

Catharsis: see ABREACTION

Cathexis is a quantum of psychic energy invested in the mental representation of a thought, feeling, wish, memory, fantasy, or person. Cathexis has also been used to mean the relative intensity of interest, attention, or emotional investment in a given mental content or activity. The word *cathexis* was introduced by Strachey in his translation of Freud's use of the German, *Besätzung,* meaning "that which sits on something." While Freud never rigorously defined *Besätzung,* he used it to describe the characteristics of a mental energy capable of increase, decrease, displacement, and discharge. In his view, the amount of psychic energy in cathexes can be intensified (**hypercathexis**), diminished (**hypocathexis**), withdrawn (**decathexis**), invested with libidinal and/or aggressive energies in object representations (**object cathexis**), or invested with self representations (**narcissistic cathexis**). Preconscious mental processes can be invested with intensified energies and attain consciousness through **attention cathexis** or can mobilize opposition resulting in repression and/or compromise formations (**countercathexis** or **anticathexis**). Psychic energies are easily and widely displaceable under pressure to attain discharge (**free cathexis**). Conversely, they may be more closely attached to another person, an idea, affect, memory, fantasy, or psychic structure, thereby limiting or inhibiting the pressure for immediate discharge (**bound cathexis**).

While Freud (Breuer and Freud, 1893/1895) first used the term *cathexis* in "Studies on Hysteria," the idea had been expressed as early as 1888 in a reference to "displacements of excitability in the nervous system" (Freud, 1888b). In his early work, Freud conceived of cathexis as purely physiological, as in his neuronally based "Project for a Scientific Psychology" (1895b), where he posited the idea of a "cathected neuron, filled with a certain quantity." By 1900, he spoke increasingly of what he called "psychical energy" as the force propelling mental activity, with cathexis as the investment or storage of this energy in particular mental products or structures (1900). In 1905, Freud (1905b) repudiated the use of the term *cathexis* in any but a psychological sense. With the development of drive theory, the energy involved in cathexis was conceptualized as originating in libidinal and, later, aggressive drives.

The term *cathexis* is based on Freud's theoretical assumption that mental activity can be understood economically to work with displacements of psychic energy. In more recent literature, the value of the economic viewpoint has been challenged and, for most analysts, has lost its relevance. Consequently, words such as *cathexis* and its variations are found much less frequently in current psychoanalytic literature (Holt, 1962). The term continues to be used casually to refer to the extent of emotional investment in an idea, feeling, or person, without implying that energy is involved. Indeed, despite the extensive critique of the specifics of Freud's energy theory, the psychoanalytic view of the mind includes awareness that all our experiences are accompanied by feelings of relative intensity, which is, to some extent, transferable.

Censor/Censorship: see DEFENSE, EGO, PRECONSCIOUS, REPRESSION, TOPOGRAPHIC THEORY, UNCONSCIOUS

Character is a global concept used to designate an individual's stable and enduring behaviors, attitudes, cognitive styles, and moods, as well as his typical modes of self regulation, adaptation, and relating to others. Character and **character trait** reflect the person's habitual mode of managing intrapsychic conflict. **Character organization**, a more abstract concept than character trait, refers to the synthetic understanding of an individual's overall character. Character is roughly analogous to what psychiatrists and psychologists call personality, the major difference being that character, as a psychoanalytic concept, links external manifestations of an individual's functioning to a view of underlying dynamic structure. Character must be distinguished from other global concepts such as ego (the intrapsychic structure responsible for homeostasis and adaptation); self (an individual's subjective experience of agency, and coherence); identity (an individual's stable sense of knowing who he is as a unique individual); and temperament (an individual's constitutionally determined affectomotor and cognitive tendencies). Character is most closely related to the concept of defensive style. In contrast to the popular usage of the term, character, as used in psychoanalysis, places no special emphasis on moral values, though traits involving morality are an aspect of every individual's character. While character itself implies neither health nor pathology, to the extent that someone's character is inflexible and maladaptive, he may be diagnosed with a **character disorder**. Character disorders are roughly analogous to what, in psychiatry

(and sometimes in psychoanalysis), are called personality disorders. Traditionally, pathological character traits are distinguished from symptoms by the fact that they are experienced as part of the self (ego-syntonic), as opposed to symptoms that are experienced as alien to the self (ego-dystonic).

The concept of character is important in psychoanalysis because it provides a way to think about the person as a whole. It also provides a bridge between the individual's overall personality and the psychoanalytic theory of mind. The concept of character disorder is important in that character problems present the most common indication for psychoanalytic treatment. For the most part, nowadays, psychoanalysis and **character analysis** are synonymous.

While Freud made observations about character in his earliest work, he first wrote explicitly about it in 1908, when he argued that the cluster of character traits including orderliness, parsimony, and obstinacy are the result of "exceptionally strong erotogenicity of the anal zone" defended against by reaction formation (1908b). He went on to speculate more generally that character results either from the direct expression of underlying instinctual impulses, reaction formations against them, or sublimations of them. Abraham (1921, 1924a, 1925a) expanded the project of building a theory of character based on libido theory with his descriptions of **oral character types**, **anal character types**, **phallic character types**, and **genital character types**, each derived from fixation on (or regression to) a specific erotogenic zone.

As the psychoanalytic theory of mind became more complex, so did the theory of character. In 1916, Freud (1916) argued that patterns of resistance in psychoanalysis reflect characteristic ways in which patients behave in other situations. W. Reich (1931) expanded this observation with his concept of **character resistance**, or **character armor**, understood to be a chronic "hardening" of the ego as a defense against internal or external danger. In 1933, in response to Reich, Freud (1933a) concurred that character reflects a permanent alteration in the ego to deal with an impulse. In his last works, Freud (1937a) was aware that what he called "character analyses," rather than the analysis of symptom neuroses, are often the focus of psychoanalysis. It was Reich, however, who popularized the term *character analysis* (1933/1945). Writing also within the framework of the new structural theory, Waelder (1936) and Fenichel (1954) agreed that character represents the ego's "stable and preferred solutions" to conflict between id, superego, and external reality. Character, then, like all manifestations of psychic life, serves multiple functions.

As interest in ego psychology deepened, analysts continued to explore the concept of character as the preferred solution to conflict, with most early discussion centering on the development of defensive style. They also continued to focus on the problems of character analysis (A. Freud, 1936; Fenichel, 1954). In addition, the list of conflicts underlying character expanded beyond oral, anal, oedipal, and castration issues to include conflicts surrounding attachment, separation-individuation, gender identity, and narcissistic concerns. Object relations theorists offered theories of character based on Klein's (1935, 1946) (and Fairbairn's [1952, 1954]) concepts of the paranoid-schizoid and depressive positions. In the 1960s and 1970s, Kernberg (1966, 1975) proposed a synthesis of object relations and ego-psychological perspectives, arguing that character and character pathology are the result of the structuring effect of internalized object relations. Around the same time, Kohut (1971, 1977) proposed a theory of character and character pathology based on self psychology, in which varieties of narcissistic pathology are classified according to corresponding "self-object transferences." In contrast to theories emphasizing the organizing influence of preferred solutions to intrapsychic conflict, Kohut's theory emphasized structural deficits resulting from empathic failures in the nurturing environment. Interpersonal psychoanalysts emphasized that character is shaped through adaptation to a particular culture (Sullivan, 1953a). Fromm (1941) coined the term **social character** to describe the essential character style of most people in a given culture. Horney (1945) and Erikson (1950) were also interested in the interaction between individual and cultural determinants of character. D. Shapiro (1965) offered a highly influential classification of character based on the concept of cognitive style.

Whatever their points of view, all theorists agree that character can only be understood in the context of its development. While, by definition, character is relatively stable and enduring, it forms slowly over time, beginning in childhood. As early as 1923, Freud (1923a) drew attention to the role of identification with early objects in the development of character, asserting famously, "the character of the ego is a precipitate of abandoned object cathexes," meaning that character accrues as the child's passionate libidinal strivings directed toward the parents are progressively relinquished, replaced by identifications. Post-Freudian developmental psychoanalysts have added continuously to our understanding of **character formation**, drawing attention to the influence of multiple factors, including interactions with caregivers, parental character traits and ideals, family style, culture or society, biological endowment, temperament, cognitive style, mood, fantasy, the repetition compulsion, and early loss or trauma. Most agree that character achieves its adult configuration at the close of adolescence and that consolidation of character is a central task of the adolescent process (Blos, 1968; Ritvo, 1971; Laufer, 1976; Blum, 1985). Blos, in particular, delineated four developmental challenges that must be met for character formation to occur by the end of adolescence, including 1) the loosening of infantile object ties; 2) the integration of the effects of trauma; 3) the establishment of historic ego continuity; and 4) the establishment of sexual identity.

The classification of character traits and disorders into **character types** has long posed a challenge to psychoanalysts. Attempts at classification inevitably reflect the theories on which they are based, the most famous examples being those built on libidinal stages, defensive styles, object relations, or configurations of the self. Ultimately, the names of different character types described in the psychoanalytic literature reflect a hodgepodge of theoretical concepts, including impulse-defense constellations (the passive-aggressive personality), pathological syndromes with which they are associated (the hysterical, obsessive, depressive, or psychotic characters), sexual perversions that they resemble (the masochistic and narcissistic characters), narrative themes (the "exceptions" or "those wrecked by success"), the state of the self (the "as-if" or narcissistic personalities), or the functioning of a particular psychic structure (the sociopathic character or "criminals from a sense of guilt"). Jung (1921/1957) developed a model of personality typology based on basic attitudes toward the world and on basic properties or functions of mental life. Some individuals are more excited or energized by the internal world and others by the external world; these are introverts and extroverts, respectively. Jung also identified four functions of mental life: a rational pair that includes thinking and feeling, and a perceptual pair that includes sensation and intuition. Jung's conceptual schema provides for a sixteen-category typology of personalities, which serves as the basis for several psychological tests that are used clinically as well as in educational and industrial settings.

Kernberg (1970a) proposed a widely recognized system of classifying character pathology based on levels of organization (including borderline and neurotic) defined by predominant defenses and by how successfully "good" and "bad" object relations are integrated. Psychoanalytically oriented researchers, including Shedler and Westen (1998, 2004),

Lenzenweger et al. (2001), and B. Stern et al. (2010) (among others) have developed instruments for measuring complex patterns of personality. The *Psychodynamic Diagnostic Manual* (PDM Task Force, 2006) (modeled on psychiatry's the *Diagnostic and Statistical Manual of Mental Disorders* [American Psychiatric Association, 1994]) draws on some of these efforts in its attempt to bring conceptual order to the classification of character disorders (here called personality disorders) by describing each disorder on three axes: 1) personality patterns (including placement on a continuum from health to severely disordered); 2) mental functioning (including features such as self regulation, affect expression, and coping strategies), and 3) manifest symptoms and concerns.

Child Analysis is a psychoanalytic treatment for children aimed at the internal development or revision of psychic structure and function, usually undertaken when a child's symptoms or behavior interferes with his developmental progression or causes him emotional pain. The end point of such treatment is often determined by the child's ability to resume his developmental progression. The techniques of child analysis are tailored to the developmental level of the child and the nature of the child's psychopathology, that is, whether it is thought to be due to conflict, to developmental delay or disturbance, or to some admixture. Current controversies within psychoanalysis about theory and technique are also reflected in the psychoanalytic treatment of children. Controversies related to child analysis cluster around the following issues, among others: the role of interpretive versus noninterpretive techniques; the function of the analyst as transference object; the function of the analyst as developmental object, new object, and real object; and the function of play. Also controversial is the proper role of the child's parents, whose continuing support is necessary to sustain the child's treatment. Whether to conduct regular meetings with parents may depend upon the age of the child patient, but also the analyst's concept of what is necessary for therapeutic action to occur. While the child's intrapsychic experience is the privileged arena in which to work, contact with and support of the parental role may be necessary for the analysis to be maintained. In as much as the techniques of child analysis are determined by the child's developmental level, it is clear that as the child advances, these techniques change. The child analyst moves progressively from a predominant use of play to verbalization and finally to free association proper. Interpretations become increasingly more complex as the child becomes capable of more complex symbolic representation. The techniques used in the treatment of mid- to late-phase adolescents may be identical to those used with adults.

Interpretation in child analysis is a technique whose goal, as in adult analysis, is to establish a link between overt behavior, affect and/or thought, and the unconscious mind. In the young child the meaning of the child's play is the focus of the interpretive activity. Such interpretive work is utilized most effectively in the treatment of conflict-based disturbances. Perhaps the first instance of the use of interpretation in child analysis was in Freud's treatment of Little Hans (1909c), during which Freud guided Little Hans's father in making interpretations to his young son. Following Freud's model, Hug-Hellmuth and other Viennese women educators became the first child analysts. Practicing in the children's homes, they used interpretation to instill moral values in their young patients. Melanie Klein is usually credited with initiating a play technique with children. Klein set forth a technique of play therapy in which the analyst responds to the child's activities with his toys, as an adult analyst would to free association. She advocated interpreting the child's deep unconscious fantasies from the beginning of the analysis. A. Freud disagreed, emphasizing the interpretation of defense in preparation for the analysis of unconscious conflict. This initiated the legendary debate between the Freudian and Kleinian schools of child analysis (A. Freud, 1965). Despite the theoretical and technical differences represented by the Kleinian and Freudian schools, they did agree that the therapeutic goal was to make the unconscious conscious through interpretation. The next generation of child analysts included Winnicott (1965, 1971a, 1971b), who placed particular value on the process of play in child analysis, although he followed Klein in the thematic content of his interpretations. Winnicott noted that the play of his patients became more organized in response to his interpretive intervention. Although Winnicott never formulated a theory about the role of play in child analysis, his participation in the play of his patients was clearly ahead of its time.

Defense analysis in child analysis is a technique whose groundwork was established by A. Freud (1936) through her explication of the concept of defense. She had already defined the distinct features of analytic work with children: a focus on the development of the child's capacity for insight, the use of play, the limitations of transference, and the need to work closely with parents (1927). Bornstein (1945, 1949), building upon A. Freud's pioneering work, evolved the technique of defense analysis, particularly in the treatment of latency-age children. Aware that the latency child differs from the younger child, who presents impulses and drives in relatively uninhibited form, Bornstein evolved a treatment approach that respected the latency child's need to avoid regression, defend against the experience of painful affect, and avoid any experience of hurt or shame in the analytic relationship. Rather than directly interpreting the child's warded-off feelings, wishes, or conflicts, her approach enabled the child to tolerate the analyst's interpretive work, promoted an alliance between the child and the analyst, and led to a growing technical understanding of the clinical utility of interpreting what is on the conscious surface of the patient's mind. This technique has also had a significant influence on adult clinical theory and technique, especially that of Gray (1982, 1996), who expanded on A. Freud's emphasis on defense in laying out his theory of "close process attention." While defense analysis is embraced by many North American child analysts, many contemporary child analysts in the United States and abroad have moved away from this technique in its pure form (L. Hoffman, 2007).

Bornstein was quite insistent that a transference neurosis does not develop in child analysis, and that defense analysis, which relies on a working alliance with the child, provides the best access to the child's neurotic conflict. Present-day child analysts do not universally de-emphasize the transference neurosis and transference work, but many do conceptualize transference more broadly than in adult analysis. A. Freud first parsed the analytic relationship with the child in the ways we do today (Kay, 1971). The child may utilize the analyst as a real object and a model for identification, where traits such as caring, affect tolerance, and the valuing of self reflection are underscored. The child may utilize the analyst to harbor externalized features of his own self organization that are warded off or defended against, such as unwanted aggressive feelings or vulnerabilities. Lastly, the child may utilize the analyst as a new or developmental object who can actualize or promote the child's emergence into an upcoming developmental organization. A. Freud and others (J. Sandler, Kennedy, and Tyson, 1980) also distinguished four different categories of transference: transference of habitual ways of relating, transference of current relationships, transference of past relationships, and transference neurosis. Interpretation of the analytic relationship as a manifestation of past relationships is not consistently cited as a primary vehicle for therapeutic action in the child work, and the role of the transference neurosis in child analysis remains controversial (Fraiberg, 1966; Harley, 1967; Chused, 1988).

The use of interpretation in child analysis has changed over time as a result of changes in the theory and technique of adult analysis and as a result of the emergence of new information from the field of developmental psychology, particularly infant research. Disagreements have arisen about the role and the technique of interpretation in child analysis. These focus on whether to put the interpretation into words or to leave it in displacement in the play (Neubauer, 1994; Yanof, 1996), and if put into words, whether to "decode" the meaning of the interpretation, that is, whether to bring it out of the play and into the real world of the child. Child analysts who utilize the later technique continue to argue that an interpretation must offer direct insight into the child's life in order to be effective. For example, the analyst might say, "The monster in the play is like your monster feelings when your little brother takes your toys." Analysts in the first group might instead give voice or action to the monster's victim, elaborating the underlying meaning of the play without taking it out of displacement.

Other child analysts challenge the value of interpretive techniques, asserting that the symbolic content of play will be elaborated in helpful ways without putting it into words. These analysts have concluded that pretend play has a momentum of its own that seems to move the child in the direction of healthy adaptations (Solnit, Cohen, and Neubauer, 1993; Slade, 1994; Scarlett, 1994). In fact, some consider it an ego capacity that is vital for developmental progression and resolution of conflict (Fonagy and Target, 1996b; Gilmore, 2005). Such positions are consistent with the approach utilized by relational analysts who emphasize the constructive potential of enactments, and other nonverbal relational features of the analytic relationship. These positions are also supported by work within developmental psychology and cognitive science that have demonstrated the child's limited capacity for insight and self reflection and his limited capacity to make use of typical verbal interpretations. Yet, it has been demonstrated that children are capable of creating metaphoric meaning about their inner lives in play before they are able to use comparable symbolic language (Mayes and Cohen, 1996; Yanof, 2005).

Infant research has contributed additional revelations about the young child's capacity to make meaning, not only outside of language, but outside of symbolic thought. Through nonverbal communicative exchange, infants are able to make meaning with their caregivers about affect and intention (Tronick, 1989). Such meaning making is enhanced when it takes place in a co-creative process with another person, such as an analyst (Harrison and Tronick, 2007). Incorporating such insights about the child's capacities, a child analyst might, early in a treatment, focus on making a connection with the child and regulating affect and intention. Later in the treatment, the analyst might also focus on making interpretations, either in displacement in the play or in verbal explanatory form. As in adult analysis, the child analyst is always attentive to the child's response to the interpretation.

Developmental help in child analysis is a group of noninterpretive psychoanalytic techniques used for treating non-conflict-based developmental disturbances: arrests, defects, and deficits. These techniques include verbalization of feelings and affects, clarification of cause and effect, and the demonstration of how to think about and make sense of one's own and other people's behavior, or to manage one's own behavior. Such measures lessen anxiety, facilitate play, and help strengthen the ego, with the aim of returning the child to the path of normal development. These techniques may be used alongside the classical psychoanalytic techniques of interpretation, employed primarily with neurotic children who are more capable of symbolic and reflective thinking. The technique of developmental help also involves assumptions about the analyst's noninterpretive role as a developmental object or new object, and the view that therapeutic action takes place within the actual relationship, as opposed to in the transference, and that change involves transformations through growth and consolidation of new organizations rather than integrations obtained through insight. Developmental help is a technique that has specific application to the treatment of children with developmental disturbances. However, most child analysts now recognize that all child analytic work requires a combination of interpretive methods and developmental help (Edgcumbe, 2000).

The concept of developmental help is important in psychoanalysis because it has widened the scope of child and adult psychoanalytic treatments to include a broader range of pathology and disturbance in addition to the conflict-based disturbances. For example, it has contributed to the treatment of borderline and narcissistic disturbances in adults and developmental disturbances in children. The basic assumptions of developmental help highlight the importance of early object relations in shaping mental structures and emphasize the mutative role of the analytic relationship in analytic treatment. While the latter remains controversial in adult analysis, it is generally accepted within child analysis that the analyst func-

tions as a new person, a new love object, and a new object of identification.

A. Freud and colleagues (1971, 1974, 1978, 1979) and Edgcumbe (1995) suggested a two-fold causation of childhood psychopathology: conflict, and developmental disturbance. This was later referred to as disturbances in mental representation and in processes (Fonagy and Moran, 1991; Fonagy, Moran, et al., 1993). A. Freud (1965) described the use of noninterpretive elements to treat such developmental disturbances in children. She originally viewed these noninterpretive elements as educational rather than truly psychoanalytic, because they do not focus on interpreting the unconscious, but seek to address constitutional defects or deficiencies caused by innate and environmental inadequacies. Later, these elements were elevated to the level of technique, and they became known as developmental help or developmental therapy (A. Freud, 1974). Although developmental help was originally thought to pave the way for classical interpretation, by widening the scope of child analysis beyond the neuroses, A. Freud implied that developmental help actually supplements interpretation. Edgcumbe (2000) described the essence of developmental help in terms of the distinction between making conscious by lifting repression and making conscious by creating a previously nonexistent representation.

A. Freud (1965) was the first to describe the child analyst as a new object for the child patient, different from the parents, who offers a "corrective emotional experience." She distinguished this from F. Alexander's (1950a) use of the term in which the analyst deliberately behaves in a different way than the patient expects. Tähkä (1993) first used the term *developmental object* to differentiate the analyst's function as new object from analyst as contemporary object or as past (transference) object. Child analysts were also influenced in their technique by Spitz's (1965) developmental research on the mother-infant relationship, in which he described the mother's function as an auxiliary ego. The concept of the analyst as developmental or new object is similar to the analyst's function as an auxiliary ego, but as a developmental object, the analyst works to promote the conditions for development to occur. Since their introduction, the terms *new object* or *developmental object* have been used by theorists of all persuasions, including ego psychologists, Kleinians, and relational psychoanalysts. The latter emphasize that the new object role is not solely for developmental purposes but to provide a different experience for the child that deviates from old patterns of relating. Since they include the notion of intentional stances considered therapeutic by the analyst (Altman et al., 2002), they come closer to the Alexander model. Theorists vary to the degree to which they define *new object*, based on the patient's experience and use of the analyst, or emphasize the analyst's intention.

These ideas have been supported by infancy and neuropsychology research that shows how mental structures and processes emerge, not merely in the context of, but through the impact of, primary relationships. In a similar way, other authors have stressed the importance of noninterpretive elements that support the psychoanalytic process, such as aspects of early object relations that are reenacted in the analytic relationship (Winnicott, 1965; Balint, 1968; Kohut, 1971). Attempts have been made to operationalize specific elements of developmental disturbance and developmental help (Fonagy, Moran, et al., 1993). Fonagy and Target (1996a) formulated developmental disturbances in terms of inferred deficits in mental processes assumed to generate representations, resulting in the absence or distortion of whole categories of representation and mental experience.

Chum/Chumship: see INTERPERSONAL PSYCHO-ANALYSIS, LATENCY

Clarification is a noninterpretive therapeutic intervention whereby something of which the patient is consciously aware is made more comprehensible. Clarification, often preparatory to interpretation, is one of the most frequently utilized noninterpretive techniques, and takes the form of the analyst's questions or observations about the patient's behavior or conscious, subjective experience. Clarification differs from confrontation, which directs the patient's attention to aspects of external reality or of conscious self experience that are readily observable but are avoided, or disavowed. Clarification differs from interpretation, which links the patient's conscious experience to his warded-off, unconscious defenses, motives, or affects. For example, a clarification may demonstrate a unifying psychological theme that is expressed in seemingly disparate aspects of the patient's conscious experience. Clarifications also serve to increase the patient's participation in the analytic process by heightening his self awareness and self observation (Stone, 1981).

The term *clarification* was introduced into the psychoanalytic literature by E. Bibring (1954), who credits the psychotherapist Rogers with its first use. Bibring included clarification in his list of the core interventions of a psychoanalytic treatment: clarification, interpretation, and working through.

The **Cloacal Fantasy** is a fantasized theory of birth, originating in early childhood, in which the vagina and anus are perceived as one. This childhood fantasy may persist unconsciously in the minds of adults and may be associated with unconscious anxieties about the vagina as dirty.

Freud (1908c) first used the term *cloacal theory* in 1908, describing it as a universal conviction of children that babies, like feces, are born through a process like defecation. For Freud, its origin was based on "ignorance of the vagina" (1933a, 1938a). He linked the cloacal theory to anality, with "anal" representing everything that must be repudiated from mental life. Since anal and genital processes are confused in the child's mind, sexual impulses also become repudiated. Andreas-Salome (1916) was the first to stress the importance of the cloacal theory for females, as genital and anal sensations become easily confused given their close anatomical connection. While contemporary theorists no longer hold that the vagina is unknown to children, the idea of the close connection and confusion between, anal and vaginal impulses has been retained in conceptualizations of female genital anxieties (Richards, 1992).

Close Process Attention is a technique of defense analysis in which the analyst directs his attention to the patient's moment-to-moment verbal production, in order to identify the intrusion of ego defenses that serve to divert or inhibit his verbal flow. Close process attention is most closely associated with Paul Gray (1994, 1996), who introduced the technique and the term. In close process attention, the defenses thus analyzed are preconscious and can be made fully conscious by immediately directing the patient's attention to those defenses and to the anxieties that triggered them. By working at the clinical surface, the analyst enlists the observing ego of the patient, who has had contemporaneous access to the same sequence. Close process attention is a specific extension of the recommendations of ego psychology: that analysis proceeds from the surface (conscious) to the depth (unconscious), and that resistance (conscious and unconscious) should be analyzed before warded-off unconscious wishes. However, it differs from the classical ego-psychological approach by its use of the analyst's focused, rather than free-floating, attention; by its emphasis on the microanalysis of verbal process; and by its relative lack of attention to unconscious fantasy.

Close process attention has been described as microscopic analysis, since attention is paid to small-scale moments of conflict and defense occurring as the patient is attempting the task of speaking freely to the analyst. With respect to the transference, special attention is paid to transferences of defense in which the patient's superego functions are reexternalized onto the analyst, an unconscious defensive projection that discourages further disclosure of threatening drive material.

The technique of close process attention has been criticized on several grounds. Some analysts feel that it narrows the analyst's listening because of its emphasis on preconscious resistances in the here-and-now analytic process and on conflicts over aggressive drive derivatives. Critics have also voiced concerns that the technique promotes an overly intellectualized, superficial, and mechanical analytic process. As interest in the impact of countertransference phenomena has grown, other critics have objected that close process methodology reflects an authoritarian "one person" psychology that fails to take into account the analyst's subjective experiences and contributions to the process, thus overlooking an essential aspect of the analytic exchange (Phillips, 2006). Proponents of close process attention have highlighted the advantages of an approach that hews to the patient's immediate conscious experience (F. Busch, 1993). The analyst's interventions are comprehensible to the patient, since they center on what the patient has just said in the analysis. The role of suggestive influence as an element in the therapeutic action is reduced, since the analyst is able to point out to the patient the evidence of conflict and defense that the analyst has just observed in the patient's recent sequence of associations. Proponents of this approach argue that, far from being authoritarian, close process attention engages the patient's mature observing ego capacities as a vital ally in the task of observing the patient's mental conflict in the real time of the analytic hour (Goldberger, 1996).

Compensatory Structure is a concept in self psychology that is embedded in the view that the child and the adult have multiple pathways for the development of a healthy self. A compensatory structure makes up for a defect in the self by revitalizing another sector (such as: mirrored ambition, idealized goals, or twinship feelings) so as to restore the self (Kohut, 1977). In contrast, a defensive structure camouflages a defect, becoming part of a person's psychopathology and interfering with further development. A goal of analytic treatment is the replacement of defensive structures with compensatory ones (M. Tolpin, 1997). While defensive structures underlie symptomatic behavior and protect the self, they also present obstacles to psychological change (A. Ornstein 1991). On the other hand, compensa-

tory structures permit both development and change through psychoanalytic treatment. The distinction between compensatory and defensive structures is useful in conceptualizing the working-through phase of analysis (A. Ornstein, 1991). The analyst's understanding of the self-protective function of the individual's defenses contributes to successful interpretation of resistance. By contrast, compensatory structures do not contribute to resistance.

Complemental Series is a fundamental principle that explains human behavior, normal and abnormal, as the result of the interplay of constitution and experience. Both of these factors combine to contribute to a particular behavioral outcome such that the stronger presence of one factor reduces the necessary contribution of the other. This principle represents a counterpoint to nature/nurture debates expressed over time within various scientific circles.

Freud's view that human behavior is determined by the combined influence of endowment (which he referred to variously as heredity, the endogenous, the innate, or constitution) and the environment (also referred to as the exogenous, accidental experience, reality, or trauma) operating together appears throughout his writings. He first used the term *complemental series* in an introductory lecture wherein he discussed the etiology of neurosis (Freud, 1916/1917). Here he noted that where there is more libidinal fixation present (the constitutional factor), less libidinal frustration (the experiential factor) is required to cause neurosis, and vice versa. However, he had discussed this same concept much earlier (1895c) under the name of an "aetiological equation," a term he used in various early writings about the causes of neurosis. In another introductory lecture on symptom formation, Freud (1916/1917) further elaborated these ideas, noting that both constitution and early childhood experiences together contribute to libidinal fixations, in a complemental series of their own; libidinal fixation then interacts with the accidental experiences of later life in causing adult neurosis. That trauma could occur in infancy or in later life was expressed in a complemental series of developmental inhibition versus regression. Thus, there is a layering, or nesting, set of complemental series.

The concepts expressed in the complemental series have remained central to the further development of theory within child analysis and developmental psychoanalysis. A. Freud's (1965) work on developmental lines illustrates these concepts in child analysis. Psychoanalytically oriented developmental psychologists have elaborated further complexities that occur in the interactions between biology and the environment in shaping behavior, pointing to the impact that a given infant's temperament may have on shaping and eliciting the responses of its caretakers and thus of shaping the very environment that in turn shapes the infant (Escalona, 1963; Thomas and Chess, 1977; D. N. Stern, 1985).

W. Grossman (1998) described how the model of a layered hierarchy of successive complemental series appears repeatedly in many aspects of Freud's psychoanalytic thinking, including the clinical, theoretical, and sociological domains. He described Freud's view of transference as a clinical example of a complemental series in which past and present, innate and accidental, conscious and unconscious, intrapsychic and interpersonal all contribute in a complex admixture determined ultimately by specific individual factors.

Complementary Identification: see COUNTERTRANSFERENCE, EMPATHY, IDENTIFICATION

Complex is an unconscious, organized group of thoughts, images, and associations, often originating in early childhood, which are highly emotionally charged and which exert a structuring influence on conscious attitudes and behavior. While *complex* is a term that has had little precise or ongoing use within psychoanalysis (except within the expressions **oedipus complex** and **castration complex**), it has survived within popular culture as a part of psychoanalytically informed slang to suggest the idea that psychopathology results from particular kinds of "complexes." With its denotation of organized groups of unconscious ideas and affects that exert an enduring, structuring effect on mental life, complex is related to the much more commonly used concept of fantasy. Indeed, a complex is a set of associated fantasies.

The word *complex* first appeared in a psychoanalytic context in Breuer and Freud's "Studies on Hysteria" (1893/1895), to describe groups of ideas in hysterical patients that are "currently present and operative but yet unconscious" and that account for many of their symptoms and behaviors. Later, however, Freud (1906) attributed the term to the Zurich school of psychiatry and, in particular, to Bleuler and Jung's word-association experiments conducted in the early 1900s, in which a "stimulus-word" is used to evoke associations. Jung (1906) postulated that reliable, reproducible chains of associations are evidence of unconsciously organized groups of ideas and affects, which he called "complexes." Jung considered the complex to be a central concept within his school of analytical psychology, describing complexes as

"the living units of the unconscious psyche . . . the via regia to the unconscious . . . the architect of dreams and of symptoms." Indeed, **complex theory** is central to Jung's analytical psychology, which posits that complexes are dynamic organizations of psychic content, both conscious and unconscious, represented in images, ideas, and patterns that are clustered around a common emotional theme. Complexes become "constellated," or organized and activated, when prompted by circumstance, memory, or emotion, and thereby contribute to behavior and affect (Jung, 1921/1957).

Freud's views on the term *complex* followed the larger trajectory of his relationship with Jung. In 1910, Freud (1910c) referred to the term as "a word which Jung has made indispensable." However, by 1914, having split with Jung, Freud (1914d) disparaged the term, complaining that "[n]one of the other terms coined by psychoanalysis for its own needs has achieved such widespread popularity or been so misapplied to the detriment of the construction of clearer concepts."

Component Instincts: see ACTIVE/PASSIVE, ANALITY, DRIVE, INFANTILE GENITAL PHASE, LIBIDO, OEDIPUS COMPLEX, ORALITY, PSYCHOSEXUAL DEVELOPMENT

Compromise Formation, or *compromise,* is the term for the mental product, normal or pathological, of the combined simultaneous strivings of id, ego, and superego, modified by the demands of reality. Compromise formations are initiated by conflict, and because none of the opposing mental forces can achieve complete expression, the products are called compromises. In any compromise formation, the relative contribution of each competing interest may vary and may be satisfied to varying degrees. Some contemporary conflict theorists (who call themselves modern conflict theorists) have rejected the structural theory, regarding compromise as the mental product of wish and defense. This perspective is often associated with the view that all mental products (thoughts, fantasies, dreams, character traits, behaviors, ambitions, and so on) are compromise formations (C. Brenner, 2002, 2003, 2008).

The concept of compromise formation is a cornerstone of conflict theory. Indeed, psychoanalysis began as a theory of mental conflict and compromise. Freud viewed conflict as a defining, constant, and universal aspect of the human condition. However, controversy about the role and centrality of intrapsychic conflict (and therefore the associated concept of compromise) in normal function, in determining psychopathology, and as the focus of analytic treatments is at the heart of many contemporary disagreements among different schools of psychoanalytic thought. The role of intrapsychic conflict has retained its centrality in contemporary conflict theories. It also retains a significant but modified position in modern ego psychology, Kleinian theory, and other object relational theories. It occupies a more limited place in self psychology and relational models.

Freud first used the words *compromise* and *compromise formation* in his correspondence with Fliess, in which he explained how a particular example of a phobia represents a compromise formation between unconscious underlying thoughts and the need to defend against them with repression (Freud, 1894a, 1896a). Although Freud initially focused on the compromise formations underlying pathological structures such as psychogenic symptoms and character traits, he later recognized that the same mechanism prevails in dreams and other aspects of normal mental function (1923a). Fundamental to his understanding of compromise formation is the idea repeated throughout his work, that all mental experience is the result of conflict and must be looked at from multiple perspectives.

Waelder (1936) elaborated a view of compromise formation connected to the principle of multiple function in which he described every psychic act as the ego's attempt at a compromise solution to eight groups of problems. There are four problems presented to the ego by id, superego, reality, and the compulsion to repeat, and four in which the ego actively engages with these same forces by virtue of its disposition to master the other agencies by actively assimilating experiences into its own organization. Each psychic act can then be understood as a compromise formation representing both multiple functions and multiple meanings. As no solution can be equally successful for all problems, any solution is inherently unstable and subject to change. Waelder applied his principle of multiple function to such issues as character development, dream life, and neurosis.

Some contemporary conflict theorists, known as "modern conflict theorists," advocated that all mental products are compromise formations, including symptomatic behaviors, dreams, fantasies, character traits, sublimated and adaptive behaviors, transference, and even the psychic structure of the superego. C. Brenner (1982), whose view of compromise formation differed from Waelder's in several important aspects, was the primary spokesman for "modern conflict theory." Starting from the level of clinical observation rather than from metapsychology, Brenner did not invoke the principle of multiple function to explain the significance of compromise formation. He did not privilege the role of the ego as problem solver, nor did he invoke the influence of the repetition compulsion. Similar to Freud's prestructural formulation, Brenner viewed compromise formation as the result in mental functioning of two conflicting tendencies—wish and defense. The fundamental components of compromise are therefore childhood sexual and aggressive wishes, conflict and the pleasure/unpleasure principle. Brenner's parsimonious view of mental function eventuated in his rejection of the structural theory, while maintaining the centrality of conflict and compromise. In this view, all compromise formations are regarded as essentially the same, whether they be creative products or symptoms. This is because the focus of interest is the dynamic meaning rather than specific characteristics of those elements that contribute to the compromise formation. Other contemporary conflict theorists utilize the concept of compromise formation while maintaining the value of structural considerations. In their view, the particular constituents of compromise that would distinguish one from another are considered to be of significance.

Modern ego psychologists (Bellak, Hurvich, and Gediman, 1973; Marcus, 2003) also reject Brenner's nonstructural view of compromise formation. Hartmann (1939a, 1950), a major early contributor to ego psychology, theorized that there are conflict-free spheres of the ego. He proposed that certain ego functions are relatively autonomous from their inception, and that others achieve a secondary autonomy by a mental mechanism that he called "de-instinctualization," or "neutralization" of drive energy. Controversy between these points of view is evident in the much greater emphasis placed on diagnostic and structural considerations among modern ego psychologists than by contemporary conflict theorists. For modern ego psychologists, impairments in autonomous ego function seen in some illnesses cannot be adequately conceptualized by the concept of compromise formation. In their view, the delineation of specific impairments of ego function is required to adequately define the nature of the psychopathology. There are other analysts in addition to modern ego psychologists who do not view conflict and compromise as sufficient descriptors of mental function. They view certain aspects of ego functioning, behavior, and psychopathology as either "pure" manifestations of biological givens, as the product of ego deficits resulting from severe environmental insufficiency or trauma, or as some complex combination of all of these factors (Kohut, 1984).

Compulsion: see OBSESSION

Conception/Preconception: see BION

Concordant Identification: see COUNTERTRANS-FERENCE, EMPATHY, IDENTIFICATION

Condensation is a process by which multiple ideas, images, or words and their associated affects are represented by a single idea, image, or word. While the concept of condensation was most explicitly elaborated in Freud's discussion of the dream-work, he noted its influence in jokes, parapraxes, and symptom formation. Condensation is often discussed along with displacement and symbolization, elements of what Freud called the "primary process." Later theorists have emphasized the broader role of condensation, along with other elements of what Freud called "primary process thinking" in creativity.

Freud first introduced a rudimentary concept of condensation in his discussion of symptom formation in the case of Emmy Von N., commenting on a "compulsion to link together any ideas that might be present in the same state of consciousness" (Breuer and Freud, 1893/1895). He formally introduced the term in "The Interpretation of Dreams," noting that manifest dreams are "brief, meager and laconic" in contrast to the copious associated "dream-thoughts" that they generate (Freud, 1900). A single element is selected to appear in the manifest dream because it represents the intersection of numerous associative chains of thought. Condensation operates both on the entirety of the dream's structure, compressing many latent thoughts into the manifest dream, and on the level of individual dream-elements, combining many thoughts or images into collective or composite images. The process of condensation accounts for some of the difficulty in making sense of the manifest dream. Freud explained condensation (along with displacement) as an aspect of the economic functioning characteristic of the primary process of the unconscious, which operates with free or unbound energy. Energy attached to one idea is easily displaced onto another; where numerous associative chains intersect at a "nodal point," there will be an accumulation of energy, causing a particular idea or element to gain representation in a dream. The same processes operate in symptom formation. Freud argued that the "hypercathexis" associated with condensation accounts for the particular intensity attaching to certain images in a dream. In both symptom formation and in dream-work, condensation and displacement serve to evade censorship.

As part of their effort to integrate Freud's concept of primary process thinking with the structural model, Arlow and Brenner (1964) argued that both ego and superego, as well as id, can at times function with the "rapidly mobile cathexes" characteristic of the primary process, allowing for creative thinking that makes use of condensation in art and science. Later analysts, also working from an ego-psychological perspective, employed the mechanism of condensation (along with displacement) to explain the formation of dream-elements, parapraxes, forgetting, and symptom formation (Abend, 1979; H. Blum, 2000). Lacan invoked the mechanisms of condensation and displacement to explain the separation of the "signifier" and "the signified" (Allegro, 1990). Recent studies supporting the distinction between primary and secondary process thinking provide evidence that, at times, individuals make similarity judgments according to the operating principles of condensation (Brakel et al., 2000).

Conflict or **Intrapsychic Conflict**, often unconscious, is the struggle within the mind between thoughts, feelings, or structures with opposing aims. **External conflict**, often conscious, refers to conflicts that occur between the individual and the external world, whether in the form of interpersonal relationships or the demands imposed by society. Intrapsychic and external conflict often occur together, as when unconscious intrapsychic conflict is defensively externalized. **Conflict theory** posits a sequence of events triggered by unconscious conflict: instinctual wishes come into conflict with internal prohibitions, the ego is threatened and produces the signal of anxiety, defense is mobilized, and compromise formations are created in the form of symptoms, inhibitions, and a wide variety of character traits, both pathological as well as successfully adaptive. While some contemporary conflict theorists (who call themselves **modern conflict theorists**) have rejected Freud's structural theory, they maintain the centrality of conflict and compromise (C. Brenner, 2002, 2003). In the psychoanalytic situation, the patient's use of free association allows the analyst to infer the influence of unconscious conflict on the patient's experience and behavior.

Psychoanalysis began as a theory of mental conflict. Indeed, Freud viewed conflict as a defining, constant, and universal aspect of the human condition. However, controversy about the role and centrality of intrapsychic conflict in determining psychopathology, and as the focus of analytic treatments, is at the heart of many contemporary disagreements among different schools of psychoanalytic thought. The role of intrapsychic conflict has retained its centrality in ego psychology and contemporary conflict theory; it occupies a modified position in Kleinian thinking and other object relations theories; it occupies a more limited place in self psychology and relational models.

Freud's first reference to conflict in his writings occurred in 1894, in a letter to Fliess. He classified four etiological categories of neurosis, one of which was conflict (1894a). Freud (1895a, 1896a) went on to describe the role of conflict in the genesis of obsessive and hysterical symptoms. Initially used in more circumscribed ways, the concept of conflict soon encompassed an increasingly central position in Freud's model of the mind (1899a). Ultimately, Freud viewed the nuclear or core conflict of neurosis as the oedipus complex, in which the gratification of incestuous wishes with the opposite-sex parent, and of murderous wishes toward the same-sex parent, is opposed by fears of reprisal and loss of love from the same-sex parent.

The development of Freud's metapsychological theories can be seen as refinements of his views about the sources, varieties, and consequences of conflict. In his topographical model, he described conflict as occurring between unconscious wishes and the conscious dictates of morality. In "Three Essays on the Theory of Sexuality," Freud (1905b) described the conflict between childhood sexual wishes and internalized prohibitions leading to the necessity for repression. As his drive theory evolved, Freud changed his view of what constituted the basic drives, but his theory always maintained a dualistic aspect with a pair of drives in opposition or in conflict with each other: the sexual drive versus the ego-instincts or self-preservative instincts, ego libido versus object libido, and, finally, the life drive versus the death drive. Similarly, Freud's principles of mental function express fundamental oppositions, such as the pleasure principle opposing the reality principle.

Freud's early recognition that conflict can be entirely unconscious led to his explication of the structural model of the mind, in which conflict is viewed as occurring between and within three structures of the mind: ego, superego, and id. Dangerous sexual and aggressive id wishes are in conflict with either external reality prohibitions or internalized superego prohibitions, which lead the ego to produce a signal of anxiety, thus mobilizing defense and resulting in compromise formations (1923a, 1926a). Within the structural model, conflicts between structures, such as conflicts between id wishes and superego prohibi-

tions, are referred to as **intersystemic conflicts**. Conflicts occurring within a structure, such as between sexual and aggressive drives, or conflicts between opposing superego values are known as **intrasystemic conflicts** (Hartmann, 1950). Some psychoanalysts have proposed further classification of conflict into **convergence conflicts** or **divergence conflicts**. The former are conflicts of defense, which involve an opposition between wish and defense. The latter, also referred to as **dilemma conflicts** or **conflicts of ambivalence**, involve a choice between competing alternatives, as, for example, between dependence and independence (Rangell, 1963; A. Kris, 1984).

While Freud and the early ego psychologists saw conflict as inevitable, they also viewed the goal of analysis as the "resolution," or at least the diminution of conflict. Hartmann (1939a) proposed the notion of a **conflict-free ego sphere**, in which certain ego functions have relatively primary autonomy from instinctual conflict (for example, perception, motility, intelligence, language), and others attain a secondary autonomy as they gradually become free of defensive conflict. Hartmann's emphasis on adaptation allowed for the distinction between normal and pathological outcomes of conflict and compromise. C. Brenner (Arlow and Brenner, 1964; C. Brenner, 1982) proposed a more expanded view of conflict, emphasizing that it is inevitable and ubiquitous in normal as well as pathological functioning. In Brenner's model, even adaptive ego functioning is not viewed as "conflict free," nor is the goal of analysis to eliminate conflict, but rather to shift compromise formations toward more adaptive outcomes.

All contemporary conflict theorists view conflict and compromise as essential to understanding psychological experience. "Modern conflict theorists," such as Brenner (2002, 2003), who posited the centrality of conflict and compromise in all mental activity, rejected Freud's notion of the structural theory. Contemporary conflict theorists who do not accept Brenner's position argue that structural concepts are essential to a description of the following: development, the presence of stable mental organizations that characterize any individual, psychic change that cannot be described by shifts in compromise formation, psychopathology that involves mood disorders, and other kinds of ego deficits. In addition, they argue that terms are useful for describing stable collections of conflicts, compromises, and processes that serve similar metapsychological functions, for example, relationships with reality, conscience functions, and the drives.

Contemporary psychoanalytic perspectives have increasingly appreciated the significance of developmental issues in relationship to conflict. Conflicts arise during development in response to a sequence of predictable threats known as danger situations. In normal early development, **preoedipal conflicts** arise between the child and the environment, between opposing wishes and feelings, and between superego precursors and drives. The threat to the child in preoedipal conflicts is the fantasied danger of loss of love and loss of the love object. **Oedipal conflicts**, of greater complexity, demonstrate the child's capacity for triadic object relations as well as other aspects of ego maturation and development. At the oedipal stage, the threat to the child involves the fantasied danger of injury and mutilation (the castration complex). Subsequently, through processes of internalization and identification, prohibiting forces originally associated with parental controls become forces within the child's own mind. Such a process is evident in superego formation, a developmental milestone achieved through resolution of the oedipus complex. At this stage, the threat to the child is the condemnation of the superego. While some conflicts are more or less resolved as development continues, others persist throughout life, leading to various degrees of psychopathology. The manifestations of conflict vary according to the developmental level, the nature of the psychopathology, and the influence of cultural factors. Child psychoanalysts also describe **developmental conflicts**, which are normal, characteristic, predictable, and usually transitory (Nagera, 1966; P. Tyson and R. Tyson, 1990). These are conflicts that are due to maturational forces within the child that bring him or her into conflict with the environment. When the internalization of the external demand has been more or less fully accomplished, this specific developmental conflict disappears and a further step toward structuralization and character formation has been taken.

Different schools of psychoanalytic thought have different conceptualizations of what elements are centrally involved in conflict, or of how central conflict is in the determination of pathology and/or its resolution. For example, in Kleinian thinking, much of the conflict of early development is viewed as occurring between aggressive and loving feelings toward the object. The need to keep "all good" and "all bad" objects apart, so as to protect the good, leads to an array of defensive maneuvers based on splitting and primitive forms of projection, such as projective identification. Learning to tolerate conflict between love and hate toward the object is central to the attainment of the depressive position characterized by whole object relations and concern for the object. Tolerance of ambivalence is viewed as the most crucial determinant of mental health.

Many psychoanalytic theorists of all psychoanalytic schools, including many contemporary conflict theorists, have recognized the contribution of "deficits," caused by biological givens or environmental traumas or deprivations, to some aspects of pathological ego functioning. Rather than taking an either/or perspective, these theorists recognize that psychopathology must be understood from multiple perspectives, including conflict and deficit, and that combined treatment approaches are required. Other theories privilege a deficit model; for example, self psychology emphasizes deficits in the self due to inadequately empathic parenting and views the analyst's empathic understanding as well as interpretation of conflict as central components of therapeutic action (Kohut, 1984). Still other theorists have shifted the focus from both deficit and conflict. For example, relationalists and interpersonalists emphasize that the intrapsychic realm is forged in relationship with others, a model that de-emphasizes the role of intrapsychic conflict.

Confrontation is a therapeutic intervention that directs the patient's attention to aspects of external reality or of conscious self experience that are readily observable but are avoided or disavowed. Confrontation may also be used to identify the conscious existence of contradictory ideas and actions. Confrontation and clarification are interventions that are considered preparatory to interpretation. A psychoanalytic confrontation is presented tactfully and without aggression, so it lacks the connotations of a "confrontation" in ordinary usage.

Fenichel (1938b) first used the term *confrontation* in the psychoanalytic literature; however, his usage did not clearly distinguish it from interpretation. Devereux (1951), who first used the word in its approximate current meaning, defined confrontation as an intervention in which the analyst, by modifying the patient's "actual wording," called the patient's attention to an avoidance of the obvious. Greenson (1967) established the contemporary meaning of *confrontation* and also added it to E. Bibring's (1954) core psychoanalytic interventions: clarification, interpretation, and working through.

Confusion of Tongues: see SEDUCTION HYPOTHESIS, TRAUMA

Consciousness is a mental state characterized by awareness. When conscious, an individual is aware of perception, memory, thought, action, self, or even the very act of being conscious. While neuro-scientists, philosophers, and psychologists disagree on an exact definition of consciousness, most use the term to denote this quality of mental aware-ness (Hirst, 1995). To be conscious of particular mental contents is to have the subjective experi-ence of thinking them, to have direct knowledge of their presence in one's mind. Consciousness represents a higher level of mental organization than perception. It involves awareness and inte-gration of internal and external perceptions, and readiness to respond to the environment. Many neuroscientists distinguish between **primary** or **raw sensory consciousness** and **self-reflective con-sciousness**, the latter a unique characteristic of human beings (Damasio, 1999; Edelman and Tononi, 2000).

From one point of view, the definition of con-sciousness as awareness appears circular, one term being equivalent to the other. However, it is possible to distinguish between consciousness and aware-ness. Consciousness, as used by neurologists, em-phasizes levels of arousal of brain centers, sometimes referred to as the five "A's": awake, alert, aroused, attentive, and aware. An example of consciousness used in this way is the term **altered states of con-sciousness**, which may result from psychological or physiological factors such as severe anxiety, conflict, sleep, fatigue, illness, hypnosis, anesthesia, and in-gested substances. Altered states of consciousness may involve either heightened or diminished aware-ness of external stimuli. Examples of altered states of consciousness include trances, mystical religious ex-periences, hallucinogen-induced states, depersonali-zation, derealization, and other dissociative states. Conscious awareness, as used by psychoanalysts and philosophers in describing higher mental function-ing, emphasizes the subjective aspect of conscious-ness in which the brain represents its workings to itself. Neuroscientists, when they consider conscious and unconscious, usually think of the mental life outside of awareness in terms similar to Freud's "de-scriptive unconscious," or as "non-conscious," mean-ing simply, the huge amount of brain work that goes on outside of awareness. Psychoanalysis is more in-terested in the dynamic unconscious, or those as-pects of mental life actively kept from awareness by defensive processes.

Although the fundamental contribution of psy-choanalysis to psychology involves a certain de-thronement of consciousness through its radical denial of "the equation of the psychical with the conscious" (Freud, 1915d), consciousness maintains an essential role. The clinical techniques of psycho-analysis, including free association and the use of the couch, were developed with the aim of bringing mental contents that are outside of awareness (or unconscious) into conscious awareness. While mod-ern conceptions of therapeutic action no longer view making the unconscious conscious as a suffi-cient goal of treatment, most hold it as a necessary one. The claim, still central to psychoanalytic treat-ment, that heightened conscious awareness of inner life can lead to psychological change thrusts psy-choanalysis headlong into the debate concerning what Freud called the "long looked for . . . biologi-cal function of consciousness" (1909c).

Freud's first topographic model of the mind con-ceived of the mind as divided into three parts (or systems) defined by their relationship to conscious-ness: the **system conscious** (Cs.), the system pre-conscious (Pcs.), and the system unconscious (Ucs.) (1900, 1915d). Of these, the Cs. was imagined to be the most peripheral, receiving input from both the outer and inner worlds. The Cs. perceives stimuli from the outside in the form of sensory experience. It also perceives internal stimuli, such as affects (pleasurable or unpleasurable), wishes, memories, fantasies, and thought processes. Indeed, Freud (1900) compared consciousness to "a sense organ for the apprehension of psychical qualities." In the topo-graphical model, Cs. is also closely connected with its neighboring system, Pcs.; the two are often referred to together as the **system conscious-preconscious** (Cs.-Pcs.). The Cs.-Pcs. operates according to the sec-ondary process, or logical, language-based thought that operates in accord with the reality principle. In the energy language of the time, the Cs.-Pcs. is also characterized as capable of binding mental energy and transferring it in an orderly fashion. The Cs.-Pcs. can bring mental contents from the Pcs. into con-sciousness through the investment of energy (atten-tion cathexis). However, the Cs.-Pcs. is separated from the system unconscious by a barrier of repres-sion.

Freud saw consciousness as central to any claim for the "superiority of humans over animals." With regard to its function, he ultimately rejected the idea that consciousness is a mere epiphenomenon, or, as he put it, "a superfluous reflected picture of the com-pleted psychical process" (1900). He suggested that the Cs.-Pcs. does not only perceive pleasure/unplea-sure, but contributes to the regulation of psychic en-ergy, thereby making higher-order mental processes possible (1900). Elsewhere, Freud (1909c, 1911b) sug-gested that as part of the Cs.-Pcs., consciousness contributes to the capacity for reality testing, judg-ment, and "temperate and purposeful control." In his view, the reason for making the unconscious conscious in psychoanalytic treatment is so that "repression [can be] replaced by condemning judgment carried out along the best lines" (1910a).

In 1923, Freud (1923a) moved away from the topographic model of the mind to a new structural model consisting of three agencies (ego, id, and superego) whose contents can exist in varying degrees of awareness. Part of the reason for this revision was his observation that certain mental functions previously attributed to the Cs.-Pcs. occurred unconsciously (for example, the defenses, dream-work, and the formation of secondary process fantasy). However, Freud considered the Cs.-Pcs. to be the "nucleus" of the ego, asserting that consciousness is attached to the ego. In line with his new structural model, Freud changed the goal of psychoanalytic treatment from making the unconscious conscious to the goal of strengthening the ego. However, interpreting resistance to conscious awareness remains a central aspect of all psychoanalytic treatment.

Today, questions raised by Freud and his followers about the relationship between consciousness, attention, language, integration, and higher-order mental functions, such as reflection, self monitoring, judgment, self control, and volition, are the subject of ongoing investigation and debate in psychology and philosophy (G. Klein, 1959, 1970). Among psychoanalysts participating in this debate, Solms (1997b) stayed close to Freud's earliest view that "consciousness is perception of mental activity," mental activity that itself is always unconscious. In contrast, Shevrin (Shevrin et al., 1996; Shevrin, 1997), for the most part supported by Brakel (1997), argued that the function of consciousness is to tag (or categorize) experience according to whether it is perception, sensation, dream, thought, or memory, thereby distinguishing these types of experiences from one another and shaping the organization of mind/brain. Olds (1992) saw consciousness as a "form of feedback" in which sense data are re-represented symbolically and thereby made independent of their sources. In self-reflective consciousness, then, the self and its interactions can themselves be represented, making introspection possible. F. Levin (1997) and Rosenblatt and Thickstun (1977) also emphasized that by "re-entrant" mechanisms, consciousness makes possible a whole array of "hypercomplex" functions, such as empathy, insight, object relatedness, and psychological mindedness, which allow for flexibility in the ways human beings conceptualize themselves and make decisions.

The function of consciousness has caused endless debate in the fields of philosophy and psychology, since most of the behaviors we think about can be done without awareness; indeed most brain function is not within awareness. Consciousness comes into play when a decision needs to be made or when errors in prediction must be corrected. The timing of decision making has been studied by Libet et al. (1983). They demonstrated that when an experimental subject is asked to decide which button to push, the brain begins the decision-making process shortly before the subject is conscious of it, even when the subject's experience is of having consciously decided to push the button (Pally and Olds, 1998). One way to understand the evolutionary advantage of this sequence may be that although awareness comes after the brain "makes the decision," an individual is aware of what he is about to do slightly before he does it; he does not have to wait until after the action has been executed to find out what he is doing. According to this way of understanding Libet's findings, consciousness is a representation of a brain event that has just taken place unconsciously.

Finally, Cavell (1997) asserted that any consciousness interesting to psychoanalysts is "consciousness as the necessary accompaniment of self knowledge," or "the capacity to know that we are thinking or seeing or feeling. . . ." For Cavell, consciousness, like self knowledge, can only flower in an interpersonal world. Many infant researchers and intersubjectivists agree with Cavell that consciousness and self consciousness emerge together out of the interaction of an infant and caretaker. Indeed, some would say that self awareness results from an internalization of the parent-infant dialogue, an inner representation of self as subject, and self as object (D. N. Stern, 1985).

Consensual Validation: see INTERPERSONAL PSYCHOANALYSIS

Constancy Principle: see DRIVE, ENERGY, LIBIDO, METAPSYCHOLOGY, TOPOGRAPHIC THEORY

Constellate: see JUNGIAN PSYCHOLOGY

Constitutional Factors are innate, biologically based variables that affect all aspects of personality and development. Such factors include temperamental tendencies, special vulnerabilities, and unique capacities, many of which are genetically transmitted. It is now widely recognized that a myriad of tendencies and capacities are present at birth, for example, orientation toward attachments, basic self-regulatory mechanisms, and complex sensory integration. However, the term *constitutional factors* is usually reserved for unique, individual proclivities and conditions. Constitutional factors are in constant, complex interplay with psychodynamic, developmental, and environmental variables. Virtually all psychoanalytic writers, working from various theoretical perspectives, acknowledge the importance of innate tendencies in normal development and psychopathology. The recognition that the variable interplay of inborn capacities and environmental influences cooperate to produce any particular developmental outcome has generally replaced the more static nature/nurture debates that previously dominated scientific discourse.

Consistent with medical thinking of his day, Freud (1888a, 1901, 1905a, 1905b) made reference to "constitutional factors," "constitutional disposition," and "constitutional weakness" in order to help explain individual tendencies toward certain neuroses. In fact, throughout his writings, Freud (1916/1917) acknowledged the combined influence of endowment (which he referred to variously as heredity, the endogenous, the innate, or constitution) and the environment (also referred to as the exogenous, accidental experience, reality, or trauma) as determinants of human behavior and experience. Freud referred to this proposition as the complemental series. A. Freud (1952, 1965) assumed that constitution played a significant role in children's developmental irregularities, and she elaborated her view in her work on developmental lines. In Weil's (1970) view, the child's constitutional potential places limits upon his developmental possibilities in such arenas as intelligence and object relatedness. She described how, in the first few weeks of life, the interaction between innate equipment and early experience leads to a "basic core" of developmental trends. In their seminal studies on infant temperament, Chess and Thomas (1986) described inborn tendencies that affect babies' activity level, threshold for stimulation, rhythmicity, intensity, and adaptability. Drawing on this body of work, D. N. Stern (1985) asserted that anxiety disorders have a significant constitutional component involving the early capacities for self regulation and tolerance for stimulation. In his discussion of very difficult patients, Kernberg (1998) proposed that excessive aggression results from constitutional and genetic as well as environmental factors.

In many respects, Weil's approach presaged current thinking about constitutional influences. Developmental research has greatly enhanced our knowledge about many tendencies and vulnerabilities that were previously believed to be solely dynamically based. For example, fundamental problems with relatedness or the numerous learning disabilities are now understood to have biological origins (Pine, 1974; Lichtenberg, 1981). Nonetheless, many modern psychoanalysts favor a complex approach to constitutional factors and view them in the context of conflict, defense, and interpersonal relationships (Marcus, 1999; Gilmore, 2008).

Construction: see RECONSTRUCTION

Container/Contained: see BION

Contextual Psychology: see INTERSUBJECTIVITY

Conversion: see AFFECT, DEFENSE, DISPLACEMENT, HYSTERIA, PSYCHOSOMATIC DISORDERS

Corrective Emotional Experience is a treatment technique described by Franz Alexander in which therapeutic benefit is attributed to the analyst's attitudinal and behavioral responses to the patient, rather than insight gained through interpretation. The patient's experience with the analyst is "corrective" in that it is thought to repair the unhealthy adaptations forged during childhood exposure to unfavorable parenting. Because the analyst's usual therapeutic stance is different than the parents' original attitudes, the patient's transference expectations are disconfirmed. In addition, the analyst may adopt a specific attitude toward the patient to facilitate this effect. For example, if the patient's father had been intimidating and critical, the analyst might adopt a tolerant and encouraging attitude (Alexander, 1950a). Alexander (Alexander and French, 1946; Alexander, 1950a) first used the term in his proposition that a corrective emotional experience could repair the traumatic influence of previous experiences. This proposition followed from his belief that all psychotherapies work by reexposing the patient, under more favorable circumstances, to the childhood emotional situations to which he had made an unhealthy adaptation.

The concept of the corrective emotional experience provoked considerable controversy when it was promulgated in the 1940s and 1950s. Mainstream ego psychologists argued that it could not lead to genuine intrapsychic change (Gill, 1954) because it prevents full exploration of the transference (Rangell, 1954); others argued that attempts at corrective emotional experience might simply express the analyst's countertransference (E. Glover, 1964). The debate over the appropriateness of the corrective emotional experience devolved into arguments about the differences between psychoanalysis and psychotherapy, with corrective emotional experience relegated to the latter. As the practice gained few adherents, the debate waned. However, the debate did trench on the important issue of the role of the affective relationship between patient and analyst in the psychoanalytic theory of treatment.

Contemporary analysts working within most theoretical models agree that while effective psychoanalytic treatment does not involve a specifically directed corrective emotional experience, it does inevitably include a variety of beneficial emotional experiences. Analysts differ in their conceptualizations of these experiences and their contribution to therapeutic outcome, but most agree that some kind of corrective emotional experience is both a natural and important aspect of psychoanalytic treatment.

Countertransference is a term with multiple meanings whose common thread or focus is the analyst's feelings and attitudes toward the patient in the analytic situation. While all psychoanalytic schools of thought use this term, definitions of *countertransference* have striking variation. Contemporary use of the term includes: 1) the analyst's conscious and unconscious reactions to the patient's transference; 2) the influence of the analyst's unconscious conflicts on his understanding of the patient and on his functioning in the role of analyst; 3) all of the analyst's emotional responses to the patient, including the generally expectable reactions to the patient's presentation or his reality situation, which may have little contribution from the analyst's unconscious mental life; 4) the analyst's emotional responses to the patient, which reflect, in part, an unconscious identification with the patient's unconscious mental life and which make up the chief mode of analytic understanding; 5) the result of the patient's unconscious wish for the analyst to respond to him in a way that is in keeping with the patient's transference fantasies, also known as role responsiveness; 6) the result of the patient's projective identification, in which the patient unconsciously projects into the analyst warded-off aspects of the patient's self or object representations and then interacts with the analyst in ways that promote the analyst's subjective experience of those representations; 7) the analyst's continuous and inevitable unconscious subjective responses to the patient, often understood only after the fact; and 8) a continuously changing transference/countertransference matrix that is co-constructed by patient and analyst. Thus, there is disagreement about whether countertransference refers to a psychopathological or normal phenomenon and whether countertransference feelings are the expression of the analyst's mind, the patient's mind, or some combination of the two. In fact, the term *countertransference* has become imprecise because contemporary psychoanalysts agree that the analyst's subjective experience has multiple sources and participates in an analytic treatment in multiple ways.

The concept of countertransference is important in all schools of psychoanalysis because it allows analysts to consider the place of their own subjective experience in a psychoanalytic treatment. It has been the source of long-standing controversy because differing conceptualizations of the analyst's emotional participation in the psychoanalytic dyad raise questions regarding the basic nature of the psychoanalytic situation and the therapeutic action of psychoanalysis: Are the analyst and patient in similar or dissimilar epistemological and emotional positions? Can and should an analyst maintain neutrality and anonymity? What are the processes by which the analyst understands the patient? How do the patient and analyst affect each other unconsciously? How do patients benefit from psychoanalysis?

Freud (1910c), who first used the term, defined countertransference as the analyst's "own complexes and internal resistances," which arise in response to the patient's transference (1915a). He viewed countertransference as a problem that interferes with the analyst's full understanding of the patient and that needs to be overcome by both self analysis and emotional self restraint (neutrality). Freud (1912b) differentiated countertransference from the capacity of the analyst to use his unconscious as a receptive "instrument" to understand the patient's unconscious. Isakower (B. Lewin and Ross, 1960) elaborated on the "analyzing instrument," describing it as the creation of a concomitant regression of patient and analyst in their modes of communicating, listening, and thinking.

During Freud's life and in the two decades afterward, psychoanalysts held predominantly negative views of countertransference (Jacobs, 1999). The result was that many analysts functioned with excessive, self-imposed emotional restraint (unlike Freud's own technique [Lipton, 1977]). However, some authors did comment on the importance of the analyst's subjective experience. For example, Fliess (1942) separated countertransference from empathy ("trial identification"), which does enlist the analyst's temporary emotional participation. Winnicott (1949) added that the analyst might hate the patient for objective reasons, and the analyst should be aware of such strong feelings so as to not act on them. Gitelson (1952) critiqued both the concept of neutrality and psychopathological interpretations of countertransference by underscoring the humanness of the analyst, who could be expected to have emotionally laden personal, transferential, and defensive responses to the patient. However, A. Reich's influential article, "On Counter-Transference" (1951) summarized the mainstream psychoanalytic view that while analysts understand their patients by a temporary unconscious identification, and indeed have feelings about their patients, intense feelings represent the analyst's unresolved unconscious conflicts, expressed as transferences to the patient, intolerance of the patient's transferences, or unsublimated unconscious motivations underlying the analyst's role.

Beginning in the 1950s, analysts influenced by Klein described a broader and more affirmative conception of countertransference: The analyst's emotional experience is significantly determined by the patient's unconscious mental life. Heimann (1950) wrote that patients project onto the analyst aspects of themselves or of their objects so that countertransference reflects the analyst's appreciation of the patient's unconscious mental life, before either analyst or patient is consciously aware of it. For Racker (1957), countertransference expressed the analyst's identifications with either the patient or his early objects. He distinguished between "complementary identification" (H. Deutsch, 1926), the analyst's identification with a patient's internal object, and "concordant identification," the analyst's identification with an aspect of the patient's self. Racker regarded the latter as a component of the analyst's empathy. He also described the analyst's inevitable fluctuation between concordant and complementary identifications with the patient. When unacceptable aspects of the patient's psychological life are congruent with unacceptable aspects of the analyst's own psychological life, the analyst will be intolerant of this concordant identification and will be more likely to shift to a complementary identification. If a complementary identification remains unconscious, the analyst may respond to the patient in the "rejecting" mode of the patient's original objects, and the patient may then lose the opportunity to introject a more tolerant object. Both Heimann and Racker noted that the analyst's own unconscious conflicts might interfere with his ability to sustain and/or understand the feelings stirred up by the patient's mental life, but they emphasized the central role of the analyst's emotional responsiveness.

Since then, discussions of countertransference have continued to elaborate on two basic views. The first view focuses on countertransference as an important source of information about the patient. The second view focuses on the analyst's own intrapsychic life. Expressing the first view, contemporary Kleinians Pick (1985) and B. Joseph (1985) described how by the use of projective identification, patients project "into" the analyst the part-self and part-object affects and attitudes associated with the paranoid-schizoid position, which the analyst is unconsciously invited to enact or endure. The analyst's challenge is to tolerate awareness of these intense affects and attitudes (which have their own sources in the analyst as well), to contain them, and to offer interpretations of them from a position of concern. J. Sandler's (1976a) concept of the analyst's "role responsiveness" expressed an ego-psychological/object relations view of the transference/countertransference interaction. Sandler noted that the patient wishes to actualize his transference relationship by unconsciously "maneuvering" the analyst to take on a wished-for or defensive complementary role. The analyst may become aware, instead of act on, or only after acting on the engendered response. The analyst's role response represents a compromise between his own tendencies and the patient's "prodding." Sandler differed with the Kleinians in viewing role responsiveness as the result of an unconscious interpersonal pressure, present in all human relationships, to participate in an actualized intrapsychic self-object relationship, rather than the result of the projective identification into the analyst of the patient's more primitive, part-self, part-object inner world. Role responsiveness has subsequently been incorporated into the concept of enactment (Chused, 1991), which views the patient's attempt to actualize a transference fantasy and the analyst's evoked countertransference response as a constant, shifting, intrinsic part of the analytic process.

The second basic view of countertransference is that it expresses the analyst's intrapsychic life and is a persistent, fluctuating, potentially troublesome accompaniment to the analyst's work. The patient and analyst, therefore, are in comparable, though not symmetrical, positions. Jacobs (1986) described how his countertransference responses, with sources in his own past, subtly affected his analytic technique in ways that might have been easily rationalized without his further self reflection. He contrasted these responses with the typically described stark departures from analytic technique that are more usually attributed to countertransference. McLaughlin (1981) stated that the term *countertransference* is inadequate to describe the multiple intrusions on the analyst's work ego, which include his own transferences, his current life challenges, and the unresolved conflicts stirred up by particular patients. McLaughlin and others therefore assumed that there is expectable fluctuation in the level at which the analyst functions. Renik (1993) extended this view, stating that the countertransference concept is misleading and that the analyst's unconsciously determined subjectivity is an omnipresent and necessary aspect of technique, and that the analyst's attempts to differentiate his personal motivations from technical precepts are illusory.

From another point of view, Ogden (1994) and others have viewed the analytic dyad from an intersubjective perspective in which the separate subjectivities of the patient's transference and analyst's countertransference exist in dialectic tension with a new, mutually created, intersubjective experience that Ogden called the "analytic third." The analyst's reflection on this joint creation is central to his understanding of the patient's subjective experience. Relationalists, who also utilize Ogden's concept of the analytic third, do not regard countertransference as independent of the co-created matrix of transference/countertransference that both patient and analyst together construct. In their view, the matrix is an ongoing source of essential data about the patient's object relations, defenses, self states, and affects. They view countertransference quite broadly, including not only the analyst's response to the patient's conflicts but also all elements of the analyst's person that the patient gets to know, consciously and unconsciously,

and to which he alludes through his words and interactions. In other words, the patient is a source of data to the analyst about himself, which he then utilizes in his understanding of their intersubjective experience.

Finally, some authors separate countertransference in the "narrow sense" from the analyst's human engagement with the patient that engenders attachment, loss, self doubt in the face of resistance, and the requirement to face fearful aspects of the human condition (Poland, 2006); while this experience is colored by the analyst's own psychology, it also flows from the basic interpersonal realities of the analytic situation.

Despite the apparent opposition of the two basic views of countertransference, most analysts work with some appreciation of both views, considering their subjective experience as constituted both by their own psychology and by various of the modes of patients' engagement with them noted above.

Criminals from a Sense of Guilt: see GUILT, MASOCHISM, PSYCHOPATHY

D

Danger Situations: see ANXIETY, CASTRATION COMPLEX, CONFLICT, GUILT, OEDIPUS COMPLEX

Daydream: see DREAM, FANTASY

Death Drive, sometimes referred to as the **Death Instinct**, is the name given by Freud to an innate biological urge in all living creatures to return "what is living into an inorganic state." Freud (1920a) first described the death drive in 1920, in "Beyond the Pleasure Principle," as part of his last classification of the drives, in which a life drive (Eros), whose aim is to preserve life, build organic complexity, synthesize, and unite, is placed in opposition to a death drive, whose aim is to "undo connections and so destroy things" (1930). In this theory, the sexual drives, ego-libido, and the self-preservative instincts are all subsumed under the new, overarching concept of the life drive. The death drive is sometimes referred to as Thanatos, from the Greek word for death. While Freud never actually used the term *Thanatos* in his writing, he is said to have used it in conversation (Jones, 1981). E. Weiss (1935) attempted to coin the term *destrudo* in an effort to offer an analogy with libido, but the term did not catch on.

The concept of a death drive emerged as a result of Freud's clinical observation that traumatic dreams, children's play, the patient's repetitions in the transference, and many other vicissitudes of what he called the "compulsion to repeat," often express painful events from the past. Freud attempted to solve the problem of painful repetitive behaviors that could not be accounted for in terms of wish-fulfillment by positing a drive to return to a previous state of being. He argued that this death drive operates in accord with the Nirvana (or inertia) principle, or a tendency to lower the quantity of excitation within the psychic apparatus toward zero. The concept of the Nirvana principle was borrowed by Freud from the work of Low (1920), along with her misunderstanding of this Buddhist term. Freud asserted that the death drive was "beyond the pleasure principle" in the sense of prior to it. He first posited the death drive to account for a tendency of the mind to disburden itself of energy. Only later did he explore manifestations of the death drive in the vicissitudes of aggression (1930). In this later formulation, there are two forms of the death drive: one working silently within, directed toward the self, and the other directed outward toward the world, evinced in the destructiveness of hatred and sadism. Initially, Freud had conceptualized masochism as the turning of sadism toward oneself; he now reversed this position by postulating a primal masochism as the expression of the self-destructive force of the death drive, and sadism as a secondary consequence of the death drive turned outward toward objects (1924a). However, Freud (1930) also emphasized that the life and death instincts are almost always mixed or fused in varying degrees, hardly ever appearing in a "pure form."

The death drive is one of the most controversial concepts of Freud's psychoanalytic theory. While many regard it as going beyond the clinical data, and see no requirement for the concept of a death drive, others make use of this concept at both a theoretical and clinical level. For example, from the Kleinian school, Bell (2008) and Segal (1987, 1993, 1997) used the concept of the death drive to help explain both the seductive pull toward mindlessness, and the peculiar feelings of triumph and excitement in destruction of self and object, not only on an individual level but also on the broader sociocultural level. Although early on in her writing, Klein did not fully distinguish between the death drive (destruction) and aggression, contemporary Kleinians describe aggression in the service of the life drive, as different from aggression that is more purely destructive. Laplanche (1976) also described how the concept of the death drive can be used in clinical work and to account for a variety of phenomena.

Defect: see DEFICIT

Defense is any unconscious psychological maneuver used to guard against the experience of a painful inner state. While it is generally agreed that any thought, feeling, or behavior may serve a **defensive function**, it is possible to describe some specific and commonly used **defense mechanisms**. Defensive operations begin early in childhood and continue to operate throughout the life cycle. Some defenses are associated with particular phases of development. Defense is important in both normal mental functioning and in psychopathology. An individual's stable **defensive style** is an important feature of his/her character. Rigid defensive style contributes to character pathology, with specific defensive maneuvers associated with specific character types. Defenses also contribute to symptom formation, again with specific defenses associated with specific syndromes. Defense plays a role in the phenomenon of resistance to analytic treatment. The systematic interpretation of this resistance is termed **defense analysis**. An aim of contemporary psychoanalysis is to help the patient employ less rigid and more adaptive defensive strategies.

The concept of defense is one of the cornerstones of psychoanalytic theory and treatment. While the concept first appeared in the context of Freud's new theory of hysteria, it quickly became central to his overall theory of mind. Defense lies at the center of Freud's concept of a dynamic unconscious containing instinctual drive derivatives continually pressing for discharge, countered by opposing forces, or defenses, which serve to prevent their emergence into consciousness. Although intimately associated with ego psychology and conflict theory, the concept of defense is important to most psychoanalytic approaches to the mind and to psychoanalytic treatment.

Freud's (1894c) first published use of the word *defense* appeared in 1894 as part of his revolutionary theory of **defense hysteria** (and all the **neuropsychoses of defense**), as caused not by degenerative mental weakness, but by the ego's rejection of an "incompatible idea." In "Studies on Hysteria," Freud (Breuer and Freud, 1893/1895) elaborated on the role of defense in the formation of hysteria, using the word interchangeably with two new words, *censorship* and *repression*. After 1897, Freud began to use the word *repression* almost exclusively when speaking of the ego's method of rejecting intolerable or forbidden mental contents from consciousness. While the term *defense* appeared from time to time in his work to denote a more inclusive concept than repression, it was not until 1926, in "Inhibitions, Symptoms and Anxiety," that Freud (1926a) explicitly distinguished between the two, designating repression as only one of many kinds of defense. In this same paper, Freud delineated the core of contemporary conflict theory, whereby the ego, in response to an anxiety signal, initiates a defensive process that serves to avoid a danger situation associated with an instinctual demand. When defense is mobilized, the resulting compromise is in the form of a symptom, an inhibition, or a wide variety of character traits, both pathological and normal. Failure of defense leads to the direct expression of anxiety. Even while describing the role of defense in hysteria and in the mind in general, Freud sought to specify different modes of defense characteristic of different types of neurotic illnesses. As early as the mid-1890s, in addition to repression, he described hysterical "conversion," obsessional "substitution" and "displacement," and paranoid "projection" (1894c). Later he described "reaction formation" and "sublimation" (1905b), "isolating" and "undoing" (1909c), "reversal into its opposite" and "turning round upon the subject's own self" (1915b), "disavowal" (1923b), "splitting," (1924c), and "negation" (1925a).

Various aspects of defense have been central to the development of post-Freudian psychoanalytic theory. Most notably, A. Freud (1936) made defense the focus of psychoanalytic technique and theory by delineating the ego's methods of defense, popularizing the term *defense mechanism* (used occasionally by Freud). She proposed a well-known list of ten specific defense mechanisms: repression, regression, reaction-formation, isolation, undoing, projection, introjection, turning against the self, reversal into the opposite, and sublimation. She also described "denial in fantasy, word and act," "flight," "idealization," "asceticism," "intellectualization," "altruistic surrender," "turning active into passive," "turning against the self," and "identification with the aggressor" as methods of defense. A. Freud argued that defense mechanisms are always comingled, functioning as part of a broader array of **defensive measures**; she also observed that any mental activity (fantasy, thought, behavior, and others) can be used for defensive purposes. In addition, A. Freud showed how defense can be directed not only against instinctual aims, but also against any mental activity that might give rise to unpleasurable affect, including thoughts, memories, actions, and affects themselves. Finally, she studied the chronological development of defense and attempted to correlate specific defenses with types of psychopathology.

Following the death of Freud, W. Reich explored how an individual's defensive operations are expressed in his "character armor" (W. Reich, 1933/1945). In the development of her object relations theory, Klein (1946) described **primitive defenses**, which, in her view, arise as early as the first year of life (directed against anxiety derived from the death instinct) and play a role in the formation of the inner world. The most prominent of these defenses are "splitting," "primitive idealization," and "projective identification." These defenses are prominent during the paranoid (paranoid-schizoid) position. Defenses against guilt and depression during the depressive position include turning away from the object, reversion to the depressive position, **manic defenses**, and, ultimately, reparation (Klein 1935, 1940). In the development of self psychology, Kohut (1971, 1977) distinguished between **defensive structures**, which serve to cover over a primary defect in the self, and compensatory structures, which seek to compensate for that defect. He also proposed the concept of the defensive vertical split, which serves to protect against the experience of shame and humiliation of unmet narcissistic needs, while simultaneously enacting these needs. Both Klein and Kohut expanded the list of kinds of anxiety, or affect, that have the power to trigger defense.

In the development of interpersonal psychoanalysis, Sullivan (1953a) coined the term "safety operations" (the basis for which is "selective inattention"), which are roughly analogous to defenses. However, Sullivan argued that what is defended against are not intrapsychic events, but aspects of relationships with others that, for a variety of reasons, cannot be attended to and are therefore unformulated, or dissociated. Elaborating on these ideas, D. B. Stern argued that dissociation, defined as the defensive and motivated preservation of experience in an unformulated state, is the most important form of motivated not-knowing confronting the psychoanalytic clinician (D. B. Stern, 1997). Modell (1984) extended the definition of defense mechanism to the "two-person" (rather than solely intrapsychic) context. Interpersonal and relational psychoanalysts have continued to develop this concept of **interpersonal defense** (Westerman and Steen, 2009). For example, mystification is an interpersonal defense aimed at interfering with another's capacity to think about or understand some aspect of reality by substituting a false construction of that reality (Laing, 1965; Levenson, 1972).

Other points of view include those of D. N. Stern, who argued that methods of negotiating repair in the inevitable missteps within the intersubjective field during development form the foundation for defense (D. N. Stern, 2005). Looking at defense from the point of view of meaning rather than mechanism, Schafer (1968a) stressed the narrative content embedded in all defensive operations. C. Brenner (1982) questioned the utility of the concept of defense altogether, as a distinct class of ego functions, arguing that all defenses can be recruited for nondefensive purposes, and that all kinds of mental activity and behavior can be recruited for defense. In contrast to Brenner, Gray (1994) has proposed a theory of technique called "close process attention," based almost entirely on the analysis of defenses, which he believes can be identified.

Many psychoanalytic theorists have attempted to classify and organize the defenses systematically.

Fenichel (1945) attempted to distinguish between **successful defenses** and **unsuccessful defenses**. G. Bibring et al. (1961) classified the defenses along a gradient of complexity, ranging from "first-order" or irreducible mechanisms to "second-order" defensive behavioral patterns that involve combinations of defense mechanisms. Using empirical data gathered from a longitudinal study of men, Vaillant (1992a) organized defense mechanisms into groups related to their adaptive function and developmental level: psychotic (denial, projection), immature (fantasy, projection, acting out), neurotic (intellectualization, displacement, repression), and mature defenses (humor, altruism, sublimation). From a point of view integrating ego-psychological and object relations perspectives, Kernberg (1970a) developed a hierarchical theory of personality organization (psychotic, borderline, and neurotic) based on the differential utilization of defenses, organized along an axis of less mature, or primitive, to more mature. However, Willick (1983) and others warned of the pitfalls of any system of classification, especially those that refer to primitive defenses, arguing that everyone uses all defenses in various contexts. Undaunted, Blackman (2004) expanded the catalog of defense mechanisms to a record high of 101.

Defensive operations have been the object of much empirical investigation, both within psychoanalysis and in cognitive and social psychology, where the concept of "coping mechanism" overlaps with defense. For example, much effort has been made to develop instruments to objectively measure the use of specific defenses for research purposes (Perry and Lanni, 2008). Many other investigators have studied how defenses operate in a variety of contexts (Westen, 1999b). For example, empirical studies show that defense may retain broad cross-cultural applicability (Tori and Bilmes, 2002), may differ between men and women (Bullitt and Farber, 2002), and may change with successful treatment (Roy et al., 2009). Cramer (2006) has reviewed empirical knowledge about how defenses develop, function, and change, as well as research methods for their assessment. Finally, cognitive neuroscientists have turned their attention to understanding the biological underpinnings of defense (Northoff and Boeker, 2006).

Deferred Action is the reactivation or reinterpretation of an earlier experience or memory that cannot be assimilated at the time of occurrence, usually because of maturational and developmental factors. The process of deferred action is particularly evident in the realm of psychosexuality, because the meaning of sexually charged experiences in childhood cannot be integrated until the maturational effects of puberty have occurred. It is only at this later time that the event acquires psychic force. "Deferred action" is Strachey's translation of Freud's use of the German word *nachträglichkeit,* which in various forms appears throughout the *Standard Edition* but never in a paper devoted to the concept. In fact, Lacan is credited with "popularizing" the concept in 1953, so that the term *deferred action* has received greatest attention among French psychoanalysts (Laplanche, 1991). Laplanche and Pontalis (1967/1973) identify one of the earliest references to the concept in Freud's correspondence with Fliess (Freud, 1896b). Freud described the typical "re-arrangement" or "re-transcription" of memory-traces that occurs over time, such that memories are registered in different versions. However, it is in the "Project" (1895b) that Freud explained the etiology of hysteria as the result of deferred action. An infantile sexual seduction becomes traumatic if a second event of a similar nature occurs at adolescence, at which time the memory undergoes pathological repression. Although Freud subsequently rejected the seduction hypothesis, he did not reject the concept of deferred action. Freud's (1918a) most cited illustration is in the case of the Wolf Man, whose dream at four and one-half years of age is interpreted as a deferred understanding of his primal scene exposure at one and one-half years, now evoked by the developmentally expectable emergence of castration anxiety, and coincident with the onset of a phobia. Freud cites another example of deferred action when the twenty-five-year-old Wolf Man consciously apprehends and verbalizes an experience dating from four years of age.

Laplanche (1991) added another dimension to Freud's concept of deferred action, offering a new translation: "après coup." Laplanche pointed out that Freud uses *nachträglichkeit* in two temporal directions without attempting to integrate them: from past to future in the early occurrence, which is reactivated at a later time, and from future to past in the retroactive understanding of something that occurred earlier. Laplanche tied these two directions together in his discussion of an anecdote that Freud used in "The Interpretation of Dreams" (1900) to illustrate deferred action. A young man, who is admiring an attractive wet-nurse suckling a baby, quips that he wishes he had made better use of his own opportunity. The adult's retrospective fantasy has its roots in the infant's oral erotic experience, so Freud has accounted for both the forward and backward temporality. Laplanche added to Freud's account his new concept of "the implantation of the enigmatic message," or the erotic experience of the nurse

that is communicated to the infant, which is then translated in both directions.

Deficit is an early deprivation of sufficient proportion to interfere with optimal development. The most common sources involve parental behavior, such as overstimulation or negligence; object loss, such as through divorce or death; or sensory deficiency that compromises the infant's capacity to take in environmental nutriment, such as blindness or deafness. A deficit may be distinguished from a defect, which is a constitutional impairment in the child that impacts personality development, such as an observable physical defect, neurological trauma, inborn deficiency, or developmental failure. In certain cases, there is difficulty distinguishing defect from deficit, as a defect in the individual's own neurobiological equipment, for example, the auditory apparatus, produces a deficit of "environmental provision," that is, access to auditory modes of object relations and language acquisition. Early deprivations (deficits) and constitutional impairments (defects) can compromise essential ego capacities, such as reality testing, object constancy, impulse control, or affect regulation. The use of the term *deficit* emphasizes the experiential, while the use of the term *defect* emphasizes a congenital or acquired neurobiological impairment. The concepts of deficit and defect are often contrasted with the concept of conflict, which emphasizes the intrapsychic contribution to mental experience.

The two concepts, deficit and defect, have been part of psychoanalytic thinking since its inception, waxing and waning in importance depending on theoretical controversy. The notion of deficit based on early deprivation or overstimulation is as old as psychoanalysis itself, as it is implied in Freud's earliest formulation of pathogenesis: the seduction theory. Even with the shift to unconscious conflict in the etiology of neurosis, Freud always maintained a view of the combined influence of internal and external factors on psychic development, or what he referred to as the complemental series. The concept of deficit became especially central with the rise of self psychology and relational schools of psychoanalysis, which embrace deficit models of psychopathology in contrast to the traditional conflict model. The notion of defect is implicit in arguments against the overextension of the traditional conflict model into arenas where, in contemporary thinking, there is likely a neurobiological or constitutional underpinning. Indeed, most contemporary analysts recognize the complex interplay among defect, deficit, and conflict in mental development.

Child analyst/observers, such as Spitz (1945), have documented the profound, at times irreversible, impact of environmental deprivation on child development. The famous 1943–44 controversial discussions between A. Freud and Klein and their followers formalized, for some time, the divide between those who privilege intrapsychic experience over interaction with the environment and vice versa (E. Kris 1950a; Hayman, 1994). While references to defects appear in many of Freud's early letters and papers, it was A. Freud (1952) who systematically studied the role of defects on ego development. She described both inborn (constitutional) and acquired (environmentally induced) defects as contributors to poor ego development in childhood. Weil (1978) and Pine (1994) suggested that defects in the inborn ego apparatus may need to be recognized as true, basic malfunctions that exist separate from conflicts and fantasies, but cautioned against an overly simplistic and reductionistic view. Since maturational features immediately interact with the environment (Weil, 1970), the analyst must consider the role of environmental provision, conflict, fantasy, and context. Moreover, there are patients in whom certain ego functions fluctuate over the course of analysis. Most close observers of infants recognize that the so-called congenitally determined capacities exist within a range of "potentials" that require environmental nutriment for expression and functionality (Provence and Lipton, 1962; Weil, 1970, 1978). This also applies to acquired defects due to later neurological insult or trauma, which can have a demonstrable impact on the brain and mental life.

In an attempt to bridge various psychoanalytic trends, Pine (1994) argued for an integrated approach to the concept of deficit. Deficits may lead to lifelong, psychic vulnerabilities that may become central themes in psychoanalysis, requiring the analyst's acknowledgment of the patient's early deprivations. However, Pine observed that the notion of deficit fails to illuminate all the conflictual meanings attached to childhood experience, coloring the patient's own interpretation of his early life. For example, a child embroiled in developmental conflict may reject a parent's overtures. Later, his historical narrative may minimize his own hostility and depict the parent as rejecting and depriving. This same caution applies to defects, since some inborn limitations directly impair the child's capacity to experience parental care.

Similarly, other psychoanalysts warned against concretizing a patient's sense of being defective, since, even when based on physical deformity, it inevitably evolves as a fantasy that serves defensive purposes and must be analyzed (Coen, 1986). Such analysts emphasized the evolution of a sense of defectiveness as a compromise formation. Others insisted that it is important nonetheless to recognize the specific impact of an equipmental defect on developing mental life (A. Rothstein, 1998; Gilmore, 2000; Willick, 2001). The field of neuropsychoanalysis includes the study of the interaction between specific lesions and their reverberations in the mind, as well as the technical modifications required for the treatment of individuals who have a known brain defect (Ostow and Turnbull, 2004).

Denial, sometimes called **Disavowal**, is a defense mechanism by which an individual repudiates some or all aspects of a given reality, thereby diminishing or avoiding the painful affects associated with that reality. Denial may be used to repudiate aspects of external reality (for example, someone whose spouse has had a heart attack may refuse to cancel an upcoming vacation to the Alps). It may also be directed against aspects of the self, including behaviors, character traits, and even subjective experiences that have been, or could readily become, conscious (for example, someone who is fighting back tears may be unable to recognize that he feels sad). Over time, denial has been used less to describe a discrete defense mechanism and more to describe the reality-repudiating aspect of any defensive operation, or a general defensive posture in which an individual refuses to confront any potentially uncomfortable reality. The psychoanalytic use of the term *denial* should also be distinguished from its use in everyday language, where it usually connotes the assertion that something is untrue, often with the intent to deceive.

Some element of denial plays a role in all defensive maneuvers, and denial overlaps with many other defense mechanisms. Denial differs from repression in that it serves to avoid external reality or aspects of the self that are evident and/or close to consciousness, whereas repression serves to prevent aspects of external or internal reality from becoming conscious at all. In line with this difference, in the treatment setting, denial is managed with confrontation, whereas repression is managed with interpretation. Denial differs from suppression, which is defined as a conscious effort not to think about something. The use of denial is on a continuum from massive to relatively minor impairments in reality testing, ranging from the **psychotic denial** seen in psychosis and mania (Freud, 1927b; B. Lewin, 1932, 1950) to normal. Denial is ubiquitous in the play of normal children, and some degree of transient denial is an expectable and normal reaction to stress, trauma, and the loss of loved ones at any age. Denial may play a role in normal states of optimism (Angel, 1934). Fantasy is often used to help efface a perception of reality, as when a child who feels helpless creates a fantasy in which he is powerful or omnipotent. Denial is also frequently supported by means of action (A. Freud, 1936).

Freud's first use of the words *denial/disavowal* was in "Studies on Hysteria," in connection with a patient's attempt to repudiate some aspects of his own free association (Breuer and Freud, 1893/1895). However, Freud's first specific use of *disavowal* as a defense was in reference to a child's refusal to recognize the absence of a penis in the female body (1923b, 1925a). Freud saw this refusal to recognize reality, harmless in a child, as similar to the psychopathology of psychosis in an adult (1924c). Freud also postulated that disavowal is central to the phenomenon of fetishism, in which the fetishist simultaneously disavows and acknowledges the "reality" of female castration, an inconsistency that represents what Freud called a "splitting of the ego" (1927b, 1938a).

A. Freud (1936) described the extensive use of denial in children, and added the terms **denial in fantasy**, **denial in word**, and **denial in act**. Kernberg (1975) used the term **primitive denial** in patients with borderline personality disorder to describe their elimination of the emotional significance of events when that significance is at odds with what they are experiencing at the moment; primitive denial is based on the defense of splitting. Kohut (1971, 1977) used the term *disavowal* to explain the vertical split, or, the presence in some individuals of two conscious and contradictory experiences of the self. Disavowal was cited by A. Ornstein (1985) as an important defense used by prisoners in concentration camps, which allowed daily functioning while simultaneously maintaining values and a vision of the future. Lacan (1959) extended Freud's use of *repudiation, suppression,* and/or *disavowal* into his own term, "foreclosure," whereby a fundamental signifier, such as "the phallus as signifier of the castration complex" is expelled from "the subject's symbolic universe." Litowitz (1998) placed denial at the end of a development line of negation that includes rejection and refusal.

Depression is a pathological mood state characterized by: feelings of sadness, irritability, despair, self recrimination, failure, and anhedonia; behavioral changes, including social withdrawal and diminished activity level; and psychophysiological symptoms, including anxiety, sleep disturbance, diminished appe-

tite, and blunted libido. Severe depression may also include cognitive difficulties, hypochondriacal anxieties, fears of impoverishment, and self-critical thoughts that extend to suicidal ideation and behavior. A psychoanalytic view of depression recognizes its biological substrate but attempts to understand the characterological and experiential factors that contribute to susceptibility, as well as the underlying psychodynamics and structure of depressive mood states. These factors include fragile self esteem, narcissistic conflicts, harshness of the superego, and other problems with aggression, as well as histories that include childhood trauma and object loss. Failure and loss in the present, both actual or in fantasy, may serve as triggers for depression in vulnerable individuals. Guilt and/or shame may be prominent features of depressions that involve the experience of failure. Depression is distinguished from normal grief or sadness, which is also a response to the loss of an important object relationship or any other emotionally significant loss. In contrast to depression, mourning is a time-limited process whose focus is the adaptation to a changed reality and the restoration of psychic equilibrium. Pathological grief may be indistinguishable from depression.

Depression is important in psychoanalytic clinical work because most patients in psychoanalytic treatment suffer from some level of depressed mood. In addition, failure and loss are universal experiences that may evoke depressive reactions and that may contribute to the formation of character. The capacity to tolerate and contain depressive reactions without their progressing to pathological mood states is a goal of all psychoanalytic treatment. In the history of psychoanalytic theory making, the study of depression has led to important developments in thinking about the superego, aggression, internalization, object relations, and the central role of loss in development.

Freud's early interest in the etiology of depression is evident in his letters to Fliess (1894b) where he contrasted melancholia, which occurs when "psychical tension accumulates," with anxiety neurosis, which occurs when "physical sexual tension accumulates." However, it is in his landmark paper, "Mourning and Melancholia" (1917c), in which Freud presented his most systematic discussion of depressive psychopathology. Freud viewed melancholia as a disease of the conscience, characterized by a feeling of painful dejection, loss of interest in the world, loss of the capacity to love, inhibition of activity, and, unlike mourning, a painful lowering of self regard to the point of the delusional expectation of punishment. The melancholic's self reproach represents unconscious hostility toward the lost object, which has been shifted onto the patient's ego through a process of identification. Through this shift, the melancholic succeeds in punishing both himself and his lost object. The vulnerability to melancholia is based on the harshness of the superego and the nature of the object tie, which is both highly ambivalent and required to maintain self esteem. When the object is lost, ambivalence intensifies and tremendous quantities of aggression are unleashed, directed against the self. Freud's model of melancholia became the touchstone for much of the subsequent psychoanalytic literature on depression, which has often mistakenly linked all depression to object loss and aggression turned against the self. However, through the study of depression, Freud came to understand fundamental aspects of how the mind works, including the role of identification in the internalization of object relations, the significance of aggression and ambivalence in object relations, and the function of the superego.

Both Abraham (1924b) and Rado (1928) further elaborated upon Freud's model of melancholia. Abraham emphasized preoedipal factors and characterological vulnerabilities. In contrast to Freud's emphasis on the metapsychology of depression, Abraham focused at the clinical level of unconscious fantasy, in which the lost object is treated as property that is ingested, metabolized, and anally destroyed. Rado emphasized the contribution of narcissistic pathology. While Abraham and Freud focused on the melancholic's destruction of the object, Rado focused on the melancholic's attempt to win back the ambivalently loved object through a double identification in which the good object is preserved along with the bad object.

With the growth of ego psychology, theories about the etiology and structure of depression became ever more complex. Jacobson (1953, 1971), in her synthesis of ego-psychological and object relational perspectives, emphasized the predisposition to depressive mood states based on developmental difficulties manifest in ego and superego deficiencies, unstable self esteem, narcissistic dependence on objects, constitutional tendencies toward moodiness, and problems with aggression due to endowment or trauma. Jacobson recognized that not all depression is triggered by object loss but may also be triggered by failure to live up to moral standards or worldly ambitions, either in reality or in fantasy. In the former, guilt is a prominent feature, while in the latter, shame predominates. While all moods depend upon some degree of denial and distortion, Jacobson distinguished the severity of depression on the basis of the nature of the denial used to sustain

the mood, in other words, whether denial yields to reality testing, and whether other regressive processes are set in motion. Other psychoanalytic theorists have viewed depression as a basic irreducible ego state equivalent to anxiety, essentially shifting the concept to a more pervasive if not universal experience. For example, C. Brenner (1975) defined depression as a universal signal affect, arguing that depressive affect serves as a signal for defense when danger has already occurred, in contrast to anxiety, which serves as a signal for defense when danger is anticipated. It is only when defenses prove unsuccessful that the clinical entity of depression emerges.

From the perspective of her object relations theory, Klein (1935, 1940) described **depressive anxiety** as a normal developmental attainment signifying the capacity for whole object relations. Depression is experienced as deep remorse and concern for the good object that may be lost or damaged by one's own aggressive impulses. Klein preserved all of the key features of Freud's model of melancholia including threatened loss of an ambivalent object, aggression, and superego attacks, while transforming these features into a universal developmental stage: the **depressive position**. If depressive anxieties are too great to be dealt with defensively, the depressive position cannot be consolidated and overcome, resulting in clinical states of depression, or, alternatively, the employment of what Klein called the "manic defense," consisting of fantasies of controlling the object with a sense of triumph over and contempt for the object.

Kohut's (1977) self psychology de-emphasizes the role of aggression and guilt in all unpleasurable self states, including depression. When the capacity for fulfillment and joy is impaired, states of guiltless or empty depression may ensue, characterized by subjective experiences of emptiness, lack of initiative, lack of fulfillment in one's work and relationships, lack of vitality, and shame. In Kohut's view, depressive states are manifestations of an enfeebled self, inadequately suffused with healthy narcissism, which results from a developmental failure of the archaic grandiose self to become fully integrated into the more mature personality.

In addition to exploring what has often been called **depressive neurosis**, psychoanalysts have also described the psychodynamics of chronic depressive states (also called **characterological depression** or **depressive personality disorder**), which feature chronic dysphoric affect and a tendency toward guilt and shame. Laughlin (1956) described what he called the **depressed personality**, and Kernberg (1975), noting the propensity of masochistic characters to develop depressive reactions, described the **depressive-masochistic personality disorder**. Other psychoanalysts focused on the psychodynamics of the **manic depressive personality** (Jacobson, 1953), the hypomanic character (H. Deutsch, 1933b), and the manic or elated state itself (B. Lewin, 1950), emphasizing how mania/hypomania functions as a defense against depression, supported by the use of denial, fantasies of merger with the object, and fusion of ego and superego. Based on the work of Blatt (1974), the *Psychodynamic Diagnostic Manual* (*PDM*) (PDM Task Force, 2006) distinguishes between introjective and anaclitic varieties of depressive personality disorder, the former prominently featuring self criticism, guilt, and perfectionism, and the latter featuring disrupted interpersonal relatedness, object loss, and dependency seeking. It also describes a hypomanic personality disorder.

Child observational research supports the view that in normal development, depressive responses are evoked early in life by developmentally predictable experiences of narcissistic threat or loss. Mahler, Pine, and Bergman (1975), studying the development of basic moods, described feelings of grandeur and omnipotence during the practicing subphase that are punctured by the toddler's repeated experience of helplessness and recognition of separateness, resulting in soberness or even temporary depression of the rapprochement subphase of development. Spitz and Wolf (1946a) described a severe syndrome that bears a striking resemblance to adult depression, which they called **anaclitic depression**, in infants more than six months old who have been separated from their mothers for at least three months. Spitz (1945, 1946) also documented "hospitalism," a similar syndrome seen in infants who have been emotionally deprived from birth. Pathological depressive reactions occurring later in childhood are also described (Sandler and Joffee, 1965), involving many of the characteristics of adult depression. Bowlby (1963), studying early attachment behavior, links parental separation and loss in childhood with pathological mourning in adulthood.

There have been a few attempts to study the efficacy of psychodynamic treatments for depression that have demonstrated comparable efficacy to cognitive behavioral methods (PDM Task Force, 2006). F. N. Busch, Rudden, and Shapiro (2004) specified a focused dynamic approach to the treatment of depression, complementary to adjunctive medication.

Depressive Position: see DEPRESSION, KLEIN, OBJECT CONSTANCY, PROJECTIVE IDENTIFICATION, SPLITTING

Detailed Inquiry: see INTERPERSONAL PSYCHOANALYSIS

Devaluation: see IDEALIZATION, KLEIN, NARCISSISM

Development is an organism's processes of growth, a term used widely and nonspecifically within the biological sciences. Development is the movement of an earlier or less-organized function or structure into a new more-organized, integrated, or complex function or structure. Development includes the role of the environment, in contrast to maturation, which usually refers only to the unfolding genetic blueprint. However, maturational processes prepare the way for developmental reorganization and new integrations across functional domains. In its application to mental life, development is the process by which mental structure and organization are built up in the mind in interaction with the environment over the course of a lifetime. Psychoanalysts, starting with Freud, describe development as a self-driven, interactive, biopsychosocial process, through which the individual's innate capacities unfold and are shaped in interaction with caregivers, all within a family's milieu of conscious and unconscious social values and expectations. A developmental approach differs from the genetic viewpoint of classical metapsychology (although understood to be incorporated within it) because it addresses the process of forward movement and mental transformation, in contradistinction to the backward linear search for childhood antecedents of adult behavior and emotion. The term *developmental* is also used descriptively in clinical work, especially with children, in a number of diverse ways, including **developmental conflict, developmental lines, developmental disturbance, developmental object,** and **developmental help.**

The importance of childhood development in mental life and the enlightened endorsement of the old saying "the child is father to the man" (Freud, 1913c) stand among Freud's earliest and most influential insights. His first formal developmental theory, that of psychosexual stages (1905b), set the precedent for subsequent psychoanalytic schools, which all arguably contain an implicit or explicit theory of development. Most theoretical schools subscribe to some sequential appearance of hierarchically ordered, qualitatively new configurations of the mind (phases, stages, or positions). They also acknowledge that movement, both backward and forward, and arrest along these sequences is more complex than the simple linear process suggested by the original ideas of fixation and regression. Psychoanalytic theories differ according to what components are emphasized, and frequently privilege one of these major components over another (environment over maturation, nature over nurture, or vice versa) or, more commonly, one or another feature of each of the major components, for example, a particular aspect of the environment (such as early maternal attunement) or a special attribute of maturation (emerging drives or cognitive development). Such selective preference is a potent source of difference among contemporary psychoanalytic schools. Moreover, developmental theories within psychoanalysis vary to the degree that they incorporate data from developmental research and observation. Examples of psychoanalytic developmental theories include Freud's psychosexual stages, attachment theory, A. Freud's developmental lines, Mahler's theory of separation-individuation, Erikson's stages, Spitz's psychic organizers, Klein's positions, Kohut's self-selfobject matrices, and the influence of the interpersonal/intersubjective matrix, among others.

Freud's (1888a) recognition of the importance of childhood experience is observable in his earliest clinical papers on hysteria, long before his more systematic theorizing. Placing the events of childhood at the center of adult psychopathology withstood his shift of focus from traumatogenesis to internal conflict, since the importance of childhood influences remained. With the evolution of metapsychology, the genetic viewpoint emerged as one of the pillars of psychoanalytic theorizing. In pure form, this only concerned the search backward guided by the principle of psychic determinism (Rapaport and Gill, 1959). Development was not accorded its own domain but was included in the genetic point of view. However, Freud himself expressed conviction that greater knowledge and appreciation of actual child development would enrich psychoanalytic thinking (1905b). He therefore encouraged integration with the data of observation. The developmental orientation, interfacing with empirical observations and research, examines the process of mental growth as it proceeds, observing the confluence of many influential factors that steer it in one direction or another, defying prediction and any form of determinism.

Controversy about development encompasses questions fundamental to the enterprise of psychoanalytic inquiry. Does psychoanalysis need to concern itself with forward movement, which is currently conceptualized as nonlinear and subject to broad influences of multiple systems operating on and within the individual (Abrams, 1977, 1983; Galatzer-Levy, 1995, 1997a, 1997b, 2004; Mayes 1999, 2001; P. Tyson, 2002)? For many analysts, the empirical data of developmental observations and research, however psychoanalytically oriented, have no place in psycho-

analytic theory, because they do not refer to intrapsychic life (Green as cited in J. Sandler, Sandler, and Davies, 2000; Wolff, 1996). Others think that a judicious integration of empirical and observational findings informs our current conceptualizations of psychopathology, even if its origins are unknowable through psychoanalytic methods (Gilmore, 2002, 2008; P. Tyson, 2002; Auchincloss and Vaughan, 2001).

Used descriptively in the context of clinical work, developmental is: 1) an aspect of the assessment of indications for treatment and its efficacy in children—developmental lines; 2) a type of psychopathology—developmental disturbance; and 3) a form of treatment for the management of the latter—developmental help. The assessment of indications and efficacy is derived from A. Freud's (1970) formulation of therapeutic cure in childhood as the freeing of the developmental process to resume its natural course. The implication here is that neurotic processes in childhood interfere with forward development, and a return to normal development is the indicator of therapeutic success. In this context, she proposed the concept of developmental lines, a developmental schema in which development is described as a series of predictable, interrelated, and interlocking psychic units reflecting id, ego, and superego components, as well as adaptive, dynamic, and genetic influences (A. Freud, 1963). Assessing the child's movement along these lines, for example from "dependency to emotional self-reliance and adult object relations," is an important component of her "Diagnostic Profile," which guides treatment and documents the child's progress.

Developmental disturbance is a failure in the developmental process due to severe environmental conditions or to disturbance in core ego capacities (Gilmore, 2002). It implies a theory of pathogenesis of certain disorders that are thought to originate in constitutional, neuropsychiatric, genetic, or traumatic environmental conditions. Recruitment by conflict (Weil, 1978) is secondary despite its prominence in the symptom picture. For some theorists, psychopathology in childhood inevitably involves developmental deviation or impairment, and its treatment requires the facilitation of nascent functions either by direct developmental help (Hurry, 1998) or by the reappearance in the transference of distorted or infantile modalities, which can then be examined and reworked (Gedo, 2005; Sugarman, 2006). Thus, in this context, developmental implies a specific modification of analytic technique.

Cognitive development is the emergence of information-processing skills. It is the psychic acquisition, transformation, coding, and storage of knowledge encompassing the ability to think abstractly, to learn from experience, and to organize perceptual experiences. It allows for the development of memory capacities, language abilities, and perceptual skills supporting increasingly elaborate and complex ways of understanding both the social and nonsocial world.

The characteristics of cognitive development, especially in children, have important implications for psychoanalytic developmental models and for clinical work. For example, understanding the nature of unconscious fantasy requires some accurate recognition of how children construct fantasies; these are the earliest versions in which fantasy is represented intrapsychically and bear the imprint of childhood cognitive and perceptual capacities. Psychoanalytic theorizing has increasingly acknowledged the necessity for integrative study with other disciplines.

Within the field of cognitive psychology, considerable research has focused on how a child understands the world. Beginning with Piaget (1932, 1937, 1951, 1953), theorists focused on how, across development, children use different strategies for conceptualizing their experiences. Cognitive development across the lifespan with a special focus on childhood is not just the acquisition of knowledge and experience but rather serially reorganized strategies for processing and understanding one's environment and perceptual experiences. The same event will be perceived and understood very differently by a preschool child compared to an early adolescent. While a number of Piaget's specific stages of cognitive development have not been so clearly delineated in empirical studies, the notion that children process and understand the world differently because of different cognitive strategies remains a guiding principle in contemporary models of cognitive development and within cognitive psychology.

More contemporary theories of cognitive development (Gelman, 2003; Oates and Grayson, 2004; Siegler, 1996) are informed by neurobiological theories of learning and concepts of epigenesis, which describe the impact of environment or contextual factors on gene expression. In these theories, differences in processing different kinds of information emerge with accumulated experience and increasingly integrated neural networks. It is not that there are defined developmental stages of understanding perceptions and experiences, but rather that accumulated experience stimulates learning and understanding and, in turn, these enhanced neural/learning networks make possible more sophisticated learning

and a different way of understanding any given experience.

Within this more contemporary view of cognitive development, some theorists speculate whether or not there are differences in domain-specific learning. This refers to whether or not there are specialized neural learning systems for specific information domains, such as numeracy, language, spatial orientation, visual perception, and social information. It may be, for example, that individuals develop specialized learning circuits for each of these domains that define much of human experience, or that neural learning mechanisms are highly adaptable to whatever domain of information is most common in an individual's experience. In either case, the contemporary notion of cognitive development is of an increasing elaboration of neural networks based on specific, accumulated experiences.

Developmental Conflict is conflict that is due to maturational forces within the child that bring him or her into conflict with the environment. Although such conditions can lead to symptoms or behavioral conditions similar to those seen in childhood neurosis, the symptoms are more transient, do not have the same symbolic function in terms of unconscious content, and do not represent an unconscious compromise formation in the way that neurotic symptoms do. Developmental conflict is normal, characteristic, predictable, and usually transitory. Ordinarily, conflict between external demands and inner wishes becomes an **internal developmental conflict** between two opposing tendencies, and the balance gradually shifts from the need to gratify instinctual desires toward pleasing the internal representation of the mother. When the internalization of the external demand has been more or less fully accomplished, this specific developmental conflict disappears and a further step toward structuralization and character formation has been taken (Nagera, 1966). The concept of developmental conflict derives from the assumption that: each developmental stage is based upon the previous one, whether the developmental path is normal or pathological; successive stages contain important and lasting new psychic formations that did not exist in preceding stages; and developmental processes require time for temporary regressions and discontinuities (Erikson, 1950; Hartmann, 1950; Spitz, 1959; Mahler, Pine, and Bergman, 1975; P. Tyson and R. Tyson, 1990). The intrapsychic correlates of progressive and regressive behaviors are fluctuations of internalization and externalization processes, which contribute to the gradual establishment and integration of psychic structure and increasing autonomy (Settlage et al., 1988).

Developmental conflict is a concept that has its origins in Freud's earliest theorizing about the relative import of heredity and environment and their contributions to normal and abnormal development. His concept, the complemental series, provided a schema that could account for the multiplicity of outcomes that derive from the intricate exchanges between biology and experience. The constitutional factor must await experiences before it can make itself felt; the accidental factor must have a constitutional basis in order to come into operation.

Nagera (1966), who was influenced by Freud, Hartmann, A. Freud, and colleagues, first defined developmental conflicts and delimited them to their role in normal development. Hartmann (1939a) studied phenomena that could later be understood to include developmental conflicts in an effort to understand their contribution to normal development. He assumed the influence of a developmental principle that regulated the interaction between maturational sequences and environmental conditions.

An example of developmental conflict is the experience of toilet training, which typically occurs during the second half of the second year. The child's wish for self determination and pleasure in soiling comes into contact with the wish for his mother's love and approval. Ideally, the mother's demand engages the development of capacities that are ready to be developed, rather than being introduced too soon or too late. Also, her capacity for empathy and her emotional and libidinal availability enable her to participate effectively, thus keeping her child's tensions, urges, and affects within bounds.

Developmental Lines is a term coined by Anna Freud (1963) to describe a developmental schema that captures the complexity of the developmental process by delineating multiple sequences of psychic function and behavior in specific areas of the personality. In this conceptualization, development is described as a series of predictable, interrelated, and interlocking psychic units reflecting id, ego, and superego components, as well as adaptive, dynamic, and genetic influences. The lines were designed to emphasize observable behavior and, in chorus, to represent a portrait of the total personality, which includes the individual's achievements and failures. The level that has been reached by a given child along a particular developmental line represents the results of interaction between drive and ego-superego

development and his reaction to environmental influences; that is, among maturation, adaptation, and structuralization. A. Freud (1963, 1965) identified the line from dependency to emotional self reliance and adult object relations as prototypical. She identified multiple other developmental lines, including the line leading from irresponsibility to responsibility in body management, the line leading from the body to toy, and from play to work, among others.

The concept of developmental lines is important in the evolution of psychoanalytic views of development because it is one of the first efforts to conceptualize a complete biopsychosocial assessment of a child's developmental progression. As such, it represents the application of the six broad frames of reference delineated within ego psychology's metapsychology to the clinical situation. Earlier development schemas privileged one aspect of development over others, and later developmental schemas have attempted to transcend the linearity implicit within A. Freud's model.

A. Freud (1963) first introduced the concept of developmental lines in order to facilitate a more comprehensive assessment of children than possible with specific libidinal and cognitive developmental scales. Developmental lines can also be used to: 1) capture the degree to which development is even or uneven across various lines; 2) observe the ways that myriad small areas of interaction combine over time and gradually become more fixed, and sometimes rigidified, into recognizable aspects of normal and pathological personality development; 3) help determine a child's developmental readiness to meet various life experience; and 4) pinpoint deficits in adults (Edgcumbe, 2000). A. Freud's developmental lines can be used alone or in conjunction with her Diagnostic Profile, which guides treatment and documents the child's progress.

A. Freud's (1974, 1978, 1981) views on child development became increasingly organized within the context of developmental lines. Through this organizing framework, she described how the nature of conflict and its resolution is intertwined with the level of personality development that the child has reached. She proposed that integration may or may not serve healthy development, because aberrant as well as normal functions are integrated by the synthetic function of the ego. She further proposed that the study of the vicissitudes of forward development and of the synthetic function of the ego belonged exclusively within the domain of child analysis. Her argument rested on the grounds that it is only through a study of forward development that the characteristics of the average adult personality can be understood.

Despite A. Freud's view, other analysts have regarded the concept of developmental lines as having broad utility in the understanding of basic psychoanalytic concepts. H. Blum (1979a) underlined the points of contact with ego psychology, including Hartmann's (1939a) conflict-free sphere, secondary autonomy, and developmental mastery. Blum used the concept of developmental lines as a model for psychoanalytic theory-making to link defense and resistance concepts with the parallel study of nondefensive ego functions and the problem of adaptation. Neubauer (1984) viewed the concept of developmental lines as conceptually superordinate to metapsychology because they encompass the complexity of human development through the isolation of specific developmental sequences.

The concept of developmental lines has also been criticized because they depend on a series of fixed, developmental phase- and stage-related sequences, and because assessments of normality and pathology are based on a correspondence among the various lines. Such criticisms challenge the notion of a universal fixed order and are based on findings from recent developmental research that support concepts related to systems theory and nonlinear dynamics (Coates, 1997; Galatzer-Levy, 2002). For example, Coates argued that understanding of sequence can facilitate one's understanding of the individual child's behavior in any particular domain, but cannot account for or predict the outcome of interactions among different domains that occur within the context of transactions between self and others (Coates, 1997). However, others point out that Anna Freud's concept of developmental lines can be understood as an early version of dynamics systems theory (Mayes, 2001).

Disavowal: see DENIAL, DISSOCIATION, PERVERSION, SPLITTING, REALITY, VERTICAL SPLIT

Disintegration Product/Breakdown Product: see SELF PSYCHOLOGY

Displacement is a process whereby the interest or intensity attached to one idea is redirected onto another associated idea. Displacement serves as a defense when the substituted idea is chosen because it is less dangerous, prohibited, or unacceptable. The term *displacement* was first used by Freud (1897a) in a letter to Fliess outlining his early theory of neurosis, in which symptoms are formed when the affect attached to an idea is increased, diminished, detached, discharged, or displaced. His most extensive discussion of the concept appears in "The Interpre-

tation of Dreams" (1900), where he described displacement (along with condensation) as a major feature of dream-work, wherein it contributes to the distorting disguise of latent dream-thoughts. Freud explained both displacement and condensation as aspects of the economic functioning characteristic of the primary process of the system unconscious (Ucs.) which operates with free or unbound energy. Energy attached to one idea is easily displaced onto another; where numerous associative chains intersect at a "nodal point," there will be a condensation of energy. In both symptom formation and dream-work, displacement serves to evade censorship (1900, 1915d). Elsewhere, Freud described conversion as a displacement of energy from an idea onto a somatic symptom. He also described phobia as involving displacement of anxiety, as in the case of Little Hans, where the boy's fear of his father was displaced onto a fear of horses (Freud, 1909c, 1926a). While contemporary analysts have largely dispensed with the energy (or economic) theory that underlies Freud's conceptualization of displacement, all recognize displacement as a regular feature of human psychology and behavior, both in ordinary life and in the treatment setting. For example, transference phenomena can be understood as a displacement, in that feelings and fantasies directed toward early objects are displaced on to the person of the analyst.

Dissociation is a disruption in the continuity of mental experience for the purpose of defense. Dissociation includes disruptions of consciousness, attention, memory, perception, and the sense of identity. It ranges in severity from minor lapses of attention or memory to serious and prolonged disruptions of the sense of identity, as in **dissociative identity disorder** (American Psychiatric Association, 1994). In both the psychiatric and the psychoanalytic literature, dissociation is strongly associated with trauma, especially acute (or shock) trauma. Dissociation overlaps with the defenses of denial and/or splitting, with the latter defined by Kernberg (1975) as "mutually dissociated ego states."

The term *dissociation* was made famous by the French psychopathologist Janet in his descriptions of the "dual consciousness" characteristic of hysteria. Breuer and Freud (1893/1895) used the term in this way to describe the "splitting of consciousness" in hysteria. However, thereafter, Freud used the word sparingly, taking pains to explain that in contrast to Janet and other French theorists, psychoanalysis conceptualized dissociation as the result of repression and/or conflict, and not as the result of a constitutional or degenerate incapacity for synthesis

(Freud, 1910e, 1913b). In later years, Freud (1938b) described a process similar to contemporary concepts of dissociation, which he called "splitting of the ego," in which an individual maintains contradictory views of reality.

Following Freud, the psychoanalytic literature on dissociation has developed in several overlapping directions. In the literature on psychopathology, the term appears in writing about disorders (in Freud's time, classified with hysteria, and now classified in psychiatry as **dissociative disorders**) such as multiple personality, fugue, and somnambulism, as well as disorders such as psychosis, intoxication, derealization, depersonalization, and others where altered states of consciousness are prominent. Most recently, I. Brenner has described a **dissociative character** type featuring the prominent use of dissociation as a defense, accompanied by a history of severe trauma (I. Brenner, 1994). Explorations of syndromes associated with childhood sexual abuse, written from the relational point of view, also focus on the phenomenon of dissociation (Davies and Frawley, 1992). The *Psychoanalytic Diagnostic Manual* (PDM Task Force, 2006) includes a discussion of dissociative disorders as well as dissociative personality disorders (also called dissociative identity disorder or multiple personality disorder).

While dissociation was notably absent from A. Freud's list of defense mechanisms, some ego psychologists attempted to account for the phenomenon in terms of a failure of the "synthetic function" of the ego (Nunberg, 1931) or a disconnection between "ego nuclei" (E. Glover, 1943). Sterba (1934) described what he called **therapeutic dissociation**, an essentially normal process of splitting the ego into experiencing and observing functions, allowing for self reflection in psychoanalytic treatment. However, most others defined dissociation as an abnormal phenomenon accompanied by loss of reality testing, so that it was most often discussed in relation to defenses such as denial or disavowal. Indeed, Vaillant (1977) defined dissociation as equivalent to "neurotic denial," while, at the same time (in contrast to most others) classifying it as a higher-level defense.

Dissociation was used frequently in the work of Klein and her followers with roughly the same meaning as her concept of splitting (Brierly, 1953). Kernberg (1966, 1975), in his effort to synthesize ego psychology with Kleinian theory, argued that what he calls **primitive dissociation** is equivalent to splitting, leading to a failure of the synthetic function of the ego. In later work, Kernberg distinguished between dissociation and splitting, arguing that dissociation can be a discrete phenomenon, whereas splitting is accompanied by severe distortions in object relations and other pathological defenses.

The concept of dissociation has been very important in the development of interpersonal and relational psychoanalysis. Sullivan (1947) suggested that dissociation occurs when an individual's experience is not responded to, either positively or negatively, by caregivers, so that it does not become part of the self system. Sullivan argued that dissociated experiences cannot be elaborated and cannot be known. These ideas are developed in D. B. Stern's (1997) concept of "unformulated experience," in which one or another story cannot be told because it has been actively forbidden. In Stern's view, dissociation prevents unformulated experience from ever becoming conscious; this experience is not encoded in language, but rather in action, necessitating different interpretive techniques. Stern argued that dissociation, and not repression, is the most important form of motivated not-knowing confronting the psychoanalytic clinician. In a set of related ideas, P. Bromberg (1991) argued that the task of the analyst is to move the patient from a position of dissociation to one of conflict. In Bromberg's view, dissociation is a defensive process that leads to a sequestration of an aspect of self experience, unlike repression, which involves a disavowal of content. Dissociation occurs in response to an overwhelming traumatic affect that cannot be represented symbolically; therefore, the dissociated self experience can only be accessed through behavioral enactment. Meaning is created in the treatment situation through the understanding of this enacted experience. For some relational analysts, including Bromberg, dissociation is the model for all pathological experience.

Dissociation, as conceptualized from an interpersonal and relational perspective, is roughly analogous to the vertical split in self psychology (Kohut, 1970/1978, 1971, 1977). The vertical split refers to a developmental split in the structure of the self, manifested as coexisting contradictory self states, such as grandiosity and diffidence, or as unintegrated behaviors such as perversions and infidelity.

Finally, in her efforts to integrate psychoanalysis with cognitive neuroscience and to operationalize concepts for the purpose of research, Bucci (2007) argued that psychopathology is the result of dissociation between the symbolic and subsymbolic modes of representation. She proposed that increased referential activity achieved in psychoanalysis explains how treatment works.

Dream is a mental event that occurs during sleep; in everyday parlance, a dream is the collection of images, ideas, and emotions that a person remembers following awakening. **Dreaming**, caused by the activation of specific regions of the brain that produces a hallucination generally of a visual type, occurs primarily during rapid eye movement (REM) periods of Stage I sleep, although it can also occur during other stages of sleep. A **daydream** is a conscious fantasy.

Freud (1900) considered his discovery of the meaning of dreams to be his greatest insight and famously viewed dreams as "the royal road to a knowledge of the unconscious activities of the mind." In fact, Freud elucidated crucial aspects of his first model of the mind, the topographic model, and of neurosis, through his study of dreams, aspects of which remain important to many analysts. It was through his study of dreams that Freud elaborated such concepts as primary and secondary process, regression, and the motivating power of wish-fulfillment, among others. While there are some neuroscientists today who argue that dreams are random, meaningless productions of the sleeping brain, most contemporary psychoanalysts continue to view dreams as a very valuable window into the psyche of the dreamer, whether or not they accept any of Freud's core concepts.

Dreams have fascinated mankind forever, and attempts to uncover their meaning can be found in the Bible and other ancient texts. Freud conducted detailed observations of both his patients' and his own dreams and related associations, presenting his findings and conclusions in a major work, "The Interpretation of Dreams" (1900). In this book, Freud outlined his theory of dreams, addressing two distinct though interrelated issues: the function of dreams and the meaning of dreams. The latter required an understanding of the mechanism of dream formation, which Freud then extrapolated into a much broader theory of the working of the mind.

Freud viewed the function of dreams to be the protection of sleep in the face of disturbing sensations and impulses that arise from a number of sources. Threatened disruptions can come from external or internal physical stimuli, such as noise or thirst, or from mental preoccupations, which include both current concerns and, most centrally in Freud's theory, unconscious childhood wishes that are aroused by the day's events and press for gratification. In Freud's view, it is these childhood wishes that are most central and necessary for the instigation of a dream. A dream integrates and responds to these wishes and stimuli in such a way as to help maintain sleep. A thirsty person may dream of drinking water from a fountain or a stream to avoid having to wake to satisfy his thirst in reality. Likewise, though in a generally much more disguised form, dreams represent unconscious childhood wishes as being fulfilled in order to maintain sleep. Sometimes, if the unconscious wishes are not sufficiently disguised, they will arouse enough anxiety that the dream fails to safeguard sleep, and the dreamer awakens. Freud viewed **traumatic dreams** as repetitive dreams aimed at reworking traumatic events. The difficulties Freud had in accounting for recurring traumatic dreams within his theory eventually led him to the concept of the repetition compulsion as elaborated in "Beyond the Pleasure Principle" (Freud, 1920a).

Freud's efforts to understand the meaning of dreams were part of a larger therapeutic effort to understand the meaning of his patients' symptoms. Freud's method of approaching and interpreting dreams was based on his view of their formation. What is called a dream in everyday language (that is, the dream as recalled and narrated by the dreamer upon awakening) is, for Freud, the **manifest dream**. The manifest dream must be distinguished from the **latent dream-thoughts**, the underlying thoughts and wishes expressed by the dream, which can only be understood after a process of interpretation. The **dream-work** is the process that transforms the latent dream-thoughts into the manifest dream.

Freud's elucidation of the origin of the latent dream-thoughts and the nature of the dream-work is linked to his topographical model of the mind, which he developed in tandem with his theory of dreams. In this model, the mind is divided into systems, the conscious/preconscious (Cs.-Pcs.), which operates according to secondary process, logical type of thinking, and the unconscious (Ucs.), which operates according to an archaic, primary process type of thinking. The unconscious is fueled by energy from the drives that produce wishes and wishful fantasies that constantly strive for satisfaction. When the individual is awake, various inhibitory and defensive mechanisms, which Freud labeled the "censorship," prevent these wishes from gaining access to consciousness. When the individual is asleep, however, the censorship is relaxed (in part due to the safety provided by the inhibition of motor activity), at which point the individual's unconscious wishes press for satisfaction through the hallucinatory wish-fulfilling activity of dreaming. Events from the day, known as the day residues (which may be unimportant in and of themselves) gain representation in a dream by virtue of their primary process links to events that are psychically significant. The latent content of a dream, which broadly speaking includes the day residues, the dreamer's current bodily stimuli, and his mental preoccupations, as well as the underlying childhood wishes pressing for gratification, are transformed into the manifest dream by the operation of the dream-work.

Freud also described the process of regression that occurs both in the formation of dreams and in neurotic symptoms. He distinguished among three kinds of regression: topographic regression, which refers to the movement backward along a continuum "towards the sensory end and finally reaching the perceptual system"; formal regression, which refers to a return to primitive methods of expression or representation, such as visual images; and temporal regression, which refers to the return to older psychic structures, such as early memories. Regression facilitates the operation of the dream-work, which is governed by primary process modes of thought. The primary process consists of: condensation (a process in which several ideas or images are represented by a single image or word); displacement (a process in which one idea, attribute, or image is substituted for another that is associatively connected with it); and symbolic representation (a process in which an object or idea is represented by an image that is an unconscious symbol for it, for example, ocean for mother, or money for feces). All these mechanisms act to disguise and distort the original unconscious dream-thoughts and wishes. The dream-thoughts must also be transformed into sensory, especially visual, images, by what Freud called "considerations of representability." This process allows for an abstract idea to be represented by a concrete, pictorial image, such as the idea of superiority being represented by an elevated physical location. Dream-thoughts that allow for visual representation will be "preferred" over others. A final influence on the presentation of the manifest dream is the work of secondary revision (or elaboration). Freud equivocated as to whether secondary revision is part of the dream-work itself or not. Secondary revision, which involves the influence of conscious thought and its secondary process logic, both during the formation of the dream as well as upon awakening, rearranges the dream into a more comprehensible and logical narrative, filling in gaps and inconsistencies. The influence of secondary revision may be present to a greater or lesser degree in the narration of any particular dream.

B. Lewin (1946) introduced the concept of the **dream screen**, which he described as the blank, flat surface onto which the content of the manifest visual dream is projected, analogous to the movie screen upon which a film is projected. He postulated that the dream screen is a representation of the mother's breast as perceived by the nursing infant and expresses the dreamer's underlying wish to sleep. In Lewin's view, the wish to sleep is one component of the "oral triad," a trio of wishes and fantasies that also include the wish to eat and to be eaten. He also asserted that mania is a dreamlike state in which reality is denied and conflict over two aspects of the oral triad predominate, the wish to sleep and the wish to be eaten.

Kohut (1977) proposed that certain **self-state dreams** do not reveal unconscious infantile wishes, but represent attempts to respond to current threats of self disintegration, depressive drops in self esteem, and manic overstimulation. In Jungian psychoanalysis, dreams are thought to comment on the patient's unconscious processes as well as the analytic process itself. Jungian analysts do not utilize an associative process, but attempt to dig deeper into the nature of the specific images themselves, through a process called "amplification" (Jung, 1963).

In the clinical situation, the use of free association allows for the translation of the dream. The analysand's comments prior to reporting the dream, and his subsequent associations to it, along with the analyst's knowledge of the day residue and the larger analytic context in which the dream is remembered and reported all lead to an understanding of the underlying dream-thoughts. Most analysts since Freud continue to view dreams as a very valuable source of data regarding unconscious mental content, though interpretive focus has broadened to address not only unconscious infantile wishes but also the way dreams may reveal or illustrate major defensive and adaptive modes of functioning, as well as useful information about the state of the transference. Some analysts place greater value on the manifest content of the dream, especially in the case of traumatic dreams. Furthermore, the meaning of traumatic dreams is understood not only in terms of the original trauma that it represents, but also in terms of the dreamer's experience of retraumatization by the dream itself.

There is controversy about Freud's distinction between primary and secondary process modes of thought. Some psychoanalysts and cognitive scientists have challenged the notion that these are valid categories and that there is any credibility to the developmental sequence that Freud proposed (Bucci, 2001; Westen, 1999b). Perhaps most interesting from the standpoint of dreaming is Litowitz's (2007) argument that primary process mentation does not describe childhood mentation at all, but that it does specifically describe the nature of dream-work.

Considering its importance as both a physiological event and an elucidator of unconscious conflict, until recently, the dream was the subject of rather scant psychoanalytically oriented research efforts. For a long time, Fisher (1965) was one of the few analysts who attempted to combine a neurophysiologic and psychoanalytic approach to dreaming. Freud's theory of dreams as both wish-fulfillments and guardians of sleep has been the object of great skepticism. In the field of neuroscience, Hobson (1988) vehemently challenged Freud's views, claiming that dreaming has no psychological function, and that it is an epiphenomenon of physiologic mechanisms of REM sleep. However, more recent neuroscience research has suggested that dreaming is generated by forebrain structures that appear to be involved with instinctual-motivational circuitry, offering some support to Freud's views of dreaming as connected to drive discharge and wish-fulfillment (Solms, 1997a, 2000a; Braun, 1999).

Drive, also sometimes referred to within the psychoanalytic literature as **instinct** or **instinctual drive**, is the mental representation of an endogenous motivational force, a constant pressure, in the individual's biologic needs, that stimulates mental activity and therefore all human psychological experience. In some models of the mind (including in Freud's original model of the mind), human behavior is conceptualized as reflecting the operation of libidinal and aggressive impulses or drives (whether in conflict or collaboration) under the modulating influences of already internalized regulatory agencies (ego and superego), self experience, and the experience with other important objects. In other words, drives are never seen in pure culture and are always modeled by a combination of intrapsychic and relational experience.

Drive theory has had a central, if complex and fomenting, role within psychoanalytic theory. It is a cornerstone of Freud's theory, as it refers to the basic forces that motivate human behavior. Drive theory has maintained a central role within ego psychology and modern conflict theory, however many theorists within those schools do not view drives as the only sources of motivation. These sources may also include human relations, ego function, and the self. Drives have also maintained a central role within Kleinian theory. However, endogenous drives play relatively little or no part in most relational models or the self psychological model of the mind. Many psychoanalysts utilize a concept of libidinal and aggressive drives in their clinical and theoretical work as primary motivators of human experience, without subscribing to other aspects of Freudian drive theory. Other theorists retain a concept of drives, but conceptualize them in ways quite different from Freud's original view.

The translation by Strachey of Freud's use of the word *Trieb*, as instinct rather than as impulse or drive, is misleading because the term *instinct*, within the field of evolutionary biology, has a different meaning than the psychoanalytic concept described by drive/*Trieb*. In evolutionary biology, instincts describe species-specific, inherited patterns of behavior. These may be complex, yet may not require any learning, and are often designed to elicit specific environmental responses (as, for examples, mating behaviors or an infant's smile). Freud did on occasion use the word *Instinkt* when invoking this meaning. Freud's concept of *Trieb* describes a linkage between physiologic stimuli within the body and their psychic representations within the mind, together with a motivational impulse to seek satisfaction from an object. His concept does not imply any specific or necessary behavioral response; thus, the term *drive* is generally preferable to *instinct*. However, the term *instinctual drive* is sometimes used, in which case the adjective emphasizes the innate, endogenous character of these motivating forces.

Although in his earlier work Freud often referred to concepts very similar to drives, such as endogenous excitations, endogenous stimuli, and wishful impulses, he first formally introduced the term *drive* (or *instinct*) with a description of the sexual instincts in "Three Essays on the Theory of Sexuality" (1905b). Freud characterized the drives in terms of their somatic source within the body, their aim, which is to achieve satisfaction through the reduction or elimination of tension, and their object, the thing (most commonly a person or body part, actual or imagined) through which a drive achieves satisfaction. Freud also more explicitly defined his concept of libido as the sexual energy of the sexual drives, and also described the numerous **component instincts** or subparts of the sexual drive, with their sources in different bodily organs or erotogenic zones, which predominate in a developmental sequence, only becoming synthesized with one another at a relatively late stage in development in the service of reproduction.

Freud's most cogent formulation of his drive concept was in "Instincts and Their Vicissitudes" (1915b), in which he defined a drive as "a concept on the frontier between the mental and the somatic, as the psychical representative of the stimuli originating from within the organism and reaching the mind, as a measure of the demand made upon the mind for work in consequence of its connection with the body." Freud's drive theory was intimately linked with his early formulations of energy economics. In accordance with the neurophysiological thinking of his time, he conceived of the nervous system as functioning to reduce or eliminate the stimuli that reach it (principle of inertia), or at least to keep them constant (principle of constancy). Stimuli are of two kinds: exogenous stimuli, which can be dealt with by avoidance or flight, and endogenous stimuli, or drives, which exert constant pressure and, due to their internal origin, cannot be avoided. The mental apparatus functions to attain pleasure through the reduction in drive stimulus in accordance with the regulatory process called the pleasure principle. Drives are represented in the mind by both an idea (essentially, a wish), and a "quota of affect," a registration of pleasure or unpleasure reflecting the underlying oscillations in energic tension.

Freud also described the vicissitudes, or transformations, that drives can undergo, including: 1) reversal of aim, with a change from active to passive (as seen in the shift from sadism to masochism, or of scopophilia to exhibitionism) or reversal of content (from love to hate); 2) turning around upon the self, with the replacement of a drive's original external object by the subject's own self (also seen in the shift from sadism to masochism, or in superego functioning); 3) repression (though later psychoanalytic formulations would include all the other defensive transformations that can be undergone by the drives as well); and 4) sublimation, in which a drive's original sexual aim is shifted toward more socially accepted or valued goals (as in creative or intellectual activities).

The most mutable aspect of Freud's drive theory was his evolving classification of the drives. Throughout the changes, however, his theory remained essentially dualistic in nature, with the interactions of two opposing forces or trends playing the leading role in the genesis of conflict and psychic structure. The first differentiation (approximately 1905–1914) lay between **sexual instincts**, operating with sexual energy or libido, and **ego instincts** or **self-preservative instincts**, operating with an unspecified energy Freud referred to as "interest" (1910e). At this stage, Freud conceived of drives in terms compatible with evolutionary thinking, with sexual drives functioning to insure the continuation of the species, and self-preservative instincts safeguarding the survival of the individual (and defending against the sexual drives when necessary). The second differentiation was offered in Freud's paper "On Narcissism" (1914e), when he proposed an opposition between ego-libido, or narcissistic libido (libido directed toward the ego or self), and object-libido (libido directed toward objects). In this formulation, ego instincts were now conceived of as libidinal. In his final differentiation,

offered in "Beyond the Pleasure Principle" (1920a), Freud proposed a classification of drives in which a **life instinct**, or Eros, whose aim is to build organic complexity, to synthesize and unite, and to preserve life, is placed in opposition to a **death drive**, whose aim is to destroy life by breaking down organic complexity and returning life to an inorganic state, in accordance with the Nirvana (or inertia) principle. The sexual instincts, ego-libido, and the ego (or self-preservative) instincts are now all subsumed under the overarching concept of the life instinct. With the introduction of the structural model, Freud (1923a) maintained that the two major drives, each with its own form of energy (libidinal and aggressive), could be fused or neutralized. Drives were represented by the id, with the ego functioning to modulate drive energy.

Critics argue that Freud's final drive model goes beyond the clinical data and is hard to reconcile with basic evolutionary principles. While most psychoanalytic theories ignore or reject Freud's speculations on the death drive, Klein, many contemporary Kleinians, and some French psychoanalysts make use of this concept at both a theoretical and a clinical level. Many theories that embrace drive concepts generally focus on sexual and aggressive drives, rather than on the death drive, per se. For example, within ego psychology, the concept of aggression was further elaborated as a distinct drive, operating according to the pleasure principle, rather than beyond it. Its aims can include mastery as well as destruction, and its role in the building of psychic structure has been emphasized (Hartmann, Kris, and Lowenstein, 1949). The energy formulations inherent in Freud's drive theory also became the epicenter of widespread criticisms of the theory as too experience distant, too mechanistic, and too vague. These criticisms resulted in an ongoing series of theoretical revisions and rejections (Holt, 1976; G. Klein, 1976; Schafer, 1976; C. Brenner, 1982). Brenner advocated restricting the drive concept to the clinical data of psychoanalysis, in which **drive derivatives**, that is, sexual and aggressive wishes, are defined as psychological phenomena, representations within the mind, without the need to invoke physiologic processes as their source. He argued that since all aspects of mind, not just drives, are a product of brain functioning, it is unnecessary and misleading to focus on this aspect of the drives. Furthermore, Brenner argued that the concept of drive should be understood as an abstract generalization about human motivation based on the observation of many individuals' unique and specific wishes directed at particular people (objects) over the course of their development. He also stressed the parallel role of aggressive and libidinal drive derivatives in psychic conflict and compromise formation.

Many object relations theories, with the exception of the Kleinian model, have moved away from the concept of endogenous pleasure-seeking drives as the primary engine of motivation, or have sought to integrate object relations and affect concepts with drives in explaining motivation. Fairbairn (1952, 1954) proposed that the ego, functioning with libido, is fundamentally object-seeking, rather than pleasure-seeking. He viewed aggression not as a basic motivation, but as a reaction to frustration, thus originating in the context of an object relationship. Loewald (1971) viewed drives as originating within the tensions and interactions of the mother-child psychic matrix. Kernberg (1982), while maintaining a dual drive concept, saw affects as constituting the primary motivational system. Affect states are linked to self and object representations from the beginning of development; these states are gradually integrated into libidinal and aggressive drives, and thus are viewed as the "building blocks" of the drives. Other schools of thought focus on other aspects of mental functioning as the primary motivators and organizers of human experience. Interpersonal approaches posit essential needs for satisfaction and for security, but hold that all psychological phenomena are interpersonal in origin (Sullivan, 1953a). In self psychology, the role of drives is supplanted by selfobject needs. For the intersubjectivists, the emphasis is on a basic object-related need for sharing subjective experience.

Some theorists have worked to integrate psychoanalytic drive theory with evolutionary biology (Peskin, 1997). Others have attempted to integrate drive theory with neurobiology (Panksepp, 1999).

Dynamic Viewpoint: see METAPSYCHOLOGY

E

Early Genital Phase is the phase in sexual development, occurring between fifteen and nineteen months of age, that is dominated by the discovery of and intense interest in the genitals. During this phase, children of both sexes engage in repetitive, intense, genital self stimulation, accompanied by facial expressions of excitement and pleasure, as well as by increased respiration, perspiration, and flushing. Infant researchers (Kleeman, 1976; Roiphe and Galenson, 1981b) have correlated such behavior with maturational factors and the quality of maternal care and interaction. If circumstances interfere with the infant's developing sense of body intactness or with the mother-child bond, the early genital phase may be delayed.

In Freud's (1905b, 1925b) schema of psychosexual development, the child's preoccupation with his or her genitals occurs between three to five years of age in conjunction with the "phallic-oedipal" phase and the oedipus complex. According to Freud, during that time, both genders become aware of genital difference, and only later, during the oedipal phase, does the little girl discover her vagina. Analysts and infant researchers have now placed the discovery of the genitals much earlier for both genders, and have also documented that the little girl has early sensations specific to the female genital. This revised timetable for genital awareness in children of both genders has profound implications for a reworking of Freud's psychosexual theory, contributing to a rejection of the phallocentrism evident in his view of early female development. The notion of primary femininity, while arguably requiring further refinement, has also contributed to a revised view of female development, which acknowledges the little girl's complex relationship with her own genital and her own desire.

Roiphe (1968) is credited with identifying and naming a regularly occurring "early genital phase" in both boys and girls, which he described as critical for the mental representation of the genitals to be fully integrated into the body schema. Roiphe placed the early genital phase within the developmental context of the coalescence of self and object differentiation and representations, and the typical conflicts of the anal phase. It is of interest that Roiphe cited an array of previous observations within the psychoanalytic literature that described preoedipal-phase

genital sensations and preoccupations. For example, Greenacre (1950a, 1958a) noted that starting at eighteen months and continuing through the third year of life, there is, for both genders, a gradual increase in genital feelings that has both an inner and an outer aspect. Furthermore, Greenacre asserted that through experiences of vision and touch during the first eighteen months of life, the mental representation of the body self is "built up," and serves as the core of the organization of identity.

Other infant researchers advanced observations similar to those of Roiphe about the early genital phase. Kestenberg (1968), basing her work on child observational studies, described an "inner genital phase" in both genders, occurring between two and one-half and four years of age, characterized by rhythmic patterns of sexual discharge. Kleeman (1976) also described genital awareness and manipulation as early as the first year, but noted a distinct intensification of interest and activity between fifteen and twenty-four months, which he attributed to a combination of ego maturation and the quality of the mother/child relationship. Kleeman described the earliest experience of genital sensations as becoming gradually more differentiated into anal, genital, and urethral.

Contemporary psychoanalytic views of female development have posited a set of female genital anxieties that trace the little girl's awareness of her female genitalia to the preoedipal phase (D. Bernstein, 1990; Lax, 1994; Mayer, 1995). Richards (1992) linked the awareness of vaginal clenching to the experience of toilet training, during which the little girl is able to experience sexual excitement during the mastery of the perineal musculature. However, much of the data on which this view is based involves reconstructions from the analyses of adult women. Olesker (1998b), who conducted observational studies of preoedipal-phase girls, observed diffuse genital exploration as early as the latter part of the first year of life, with a sharpened awareness of genital configuration by the end of the second year.

Some analysts use the "early genital phase" as a replacement for the "phallic-oedipal phase," arguing that phallocentric terminology does not reflect current psychoanalytic understandings of female development (Long, 2005). However, to avoid further confusion, "infantile genital phase" or "first genital phase" (rather than "early genital phase") is a preferred substitute for "phallic-oedipal phase." (See entry on infantile genital phase).

Economic Viewpoint: see CATHEXIS, DRIVE, ENERGY, LIBIDO, METAPSYCHOLOGY, PRIMARY PROCESS AND SECONDARY PROCESS, PSYCHIC DETERMINISM, WISH

Ego is the executive agency of the mind. It serves the function of homeostasis or self regulation, mediating between conflicting motivations and forging compromises among them. It also serves the function of adaptation, mediating between the demands of the inner world and external reality. Finally, the ego serves the function of synthesizing all mental processes and experiences into a smoothly operating whole. The ego is often defined in terms of its many specific capacities (called **ego functions**), which include cognition, perception, memory, motility, affect, language, symbolization, reality testing, evaluation, judgment, impulse control, affect tolerance, representation, object relations, and defense. It is also often defined in terms of its motives or interests, which include reconciling the quest for pleasure with the need for self preservation. Successful ego functioning can be pleasurable in itself, as in the experience of mastery. Mental health is often defined with reference to **ego strength** and/or **ego weakness** or **ego deficit**. The study of how the ego emerges and changes throughout the life cycle is called **ego development**. The branch of psychoanalysis that focuses on the concept of the ego and its role in psychological functioning, development, psychopathology, and treatment is called **ego psychology.**

The word *ego*, as it is used in psychoanalysis, was coined by Strachey in his translation of Freud's *Das Ich*, or, the "I." Freud used ego in a variety of overlapping ways to refer to: the person as a whole; conscious self experience; the self, conscious and unconscious; and a particular part (or agency) of the mind as described above. Freud (1923a) explicitly conceptualized the ego in this last way in his structural theory, which divides the mind into ego, superego, and id. However, his use of the term remained ambiguous so that ego did not become explicitly differentiated from person, self, and self representation until 1950 when Hartmann (1950) defined the self as the individual's whole person existing in the world, the self representation as a collection of representations of the experience of self, and the ego as an abstract agency within the psychic apparatus. While most analysts have accepted Hartmann's attempt at

greater precision, some have objected (Laplanche and Pontalis, 1967/1973; Spruiell, 1995).

Freud (Breuer and Freud, 1893/1895) first used the term *ego* in an early paper on hypnosis to refer to the "normal," conscious, experiencing self, in contrast to the "suppressed" ideas that cause hysteria. For the next thirty years (until the publication of "The Ego and the Id"), Freud continued to use *ego* in this way to mean the conscious self, encompassing the "dominant mass of ideas" (1894c, 1896c, 1900). However, even in these early years, Freud began to use ego in connection with specific functions and capacities, including defense (1894c); the capacity to repudiate, reject, or fend off incompatible ideas (Breuer and Freud, 1893/1895); the inhibition of impulses, reality testing, thinking, language, attention, and judgment (1895b); and repression, substitution, compromise, action, recollection, and working over (1899a).

In "The Interpretation of Dreams," Freud (1900) used *ego* to indicate the whole person, or the experiencing self, commenting frequently on the **egocentric** quality of dreams. For the most part, in his topographic model of the mind, the executive functions of the mind are carried out by the conscious-preconscious system (Cs.-Pcs.), which operates according to the secondary process, has the capacity for binding and regulating psychic energy, makes use of language and logic, and has the capacity for reality testing and judgment (1900, 1911b). The censor guards the boundary between the unconscious (Ucs.) and the conscious-preconscious (Cs.-Pcs.). However, at several points in "The Interpretation of Dreams," Freud used the word *ego* in connection with the concepts of censorship and secondary revision; in a foreshadowing of his later structural theory, he speculated that the most important conflict in the mind might not be between the Cs.-Pcs. and the Ucs., as proposed in the topographic model, but between the ego and what is repressed.

For the next ten years, Freud took several steps in the direction of structural theory. During this period of transition, his use of the word *ego* (among other terms) is particularly confusing, as he explores relationships among many complex themes, including different kinds of motivation, reality versus pleasure, inside versus outside, and self versus other. In 1910, he introduced the concept of **ego instincts** (also known as self-preservative instincts), in conflict with the sexual instincts. In this revised theory of conflict, he argued that the ego feels threatened by the claims of the sexual instincts, fending them off with repression (1910e). In 1911, Freud (1911b) described how the ego develops from a **pleasure ego**, operating in accord with the pleasure principle and unable to do anything but wish, into a **reality ego**, operating in accord with the reality principle and able to "strive for what is useful and guard itself against damage," using capacities for attention, judgment, thinking, restraint, and action. In 1914, Freud (1914e) differentiated between object libido and **ego libido** (or narcissistic libido), the vicissitudes of which are responsible for various kinds of psychopathology, including psychosis, hypochondriasis, and melancholia. He also introduced the concept of the **ego ideal**, foreshadowing the later concept of the superego. In 1915, Freud (1915b) added the concept of the **purified pleasure ego**, which develops after the reality ego through the internalization of pleasurable aspects of objects, now experienced as separate from the ego.

Finally, in 1923, Freud (1923a) offered a major revision of theory in his famous essay, "The Ego and the Id." His observation that censorship or repression as well as many moral imperatives operate outside of awareness presented an ongoing challenge to his topographic model, which was based on conflict between a moral, reasonable conscious system (Cs.-Pcs.) and a wishful unconscious system (Ucs.). In Freud's new structural theory, the mind is divided into three agencies or structures—id, ego, and superego—differentiated not by access to consciousness, but by stable sets of functions and motives. The id, made up of derivatives of the sexual and aggressive instinctual drives, is the heir to the Ucs. The ego, now explicitly defined as a "coherent organization of mental processes" including control of discharge, censorship, repression, thinking, and reality testing, is heir to the Cs.-Pcs. The superego (or ego ideal) is a modification of the ego made up of moral imperatives and prohibitions. Most ego and much superego functioning goes on unconsciously. Freud described how, during development, the ego differentiates from the id under the impact of perceptual stimuli from the outside world. He argued that the ego is first and foremost a **body ego**, derived from bodily sensations. He also described how the ego is formed from identifications, or "precipitates" of abandoned object ties, the most important of these identifications leading to the superego. Thereafter, the ego's role is to mediate between the passions of the id and the demands of the superego and external reality.

In 1926, in "Inhibitions, Symptoms and Anxiety," Freud (1926a) made further, major alterations in his theory of the mind. In addressing the question of where the ego gets the power to influence the id, he proposed that it generates a signal of anxiety in response to the anticipation of danger posed by sexual and aggressive drives; this signal anxiety triggers defenses aimed at warding off the impending danger. In this "second theory of anxiety," the ego finally assumed its full role as the executive agency of the mind, responsible for and capable of managing conflict and forging compromise. Soon after, in 1927 and later, Freud (1927b) introduced a new idea, the **splitting of the ego**, in which an individual adopts contradictory attitudes toward aspects of reality through the use of splitting and disavowal (1938a, 1938b). Freud's aim here was to describe patients with more severe types of psychopathology, such as perversion and psychosis, characterized by disturbances in the relationship to reality rather than conflict between ego and id.

Freud's final conceptualization of the ego as a powerful executive agency in the mind led to the development of what quickly became called ego psychology, or the study of the role of the ego in psychic functioning, development, psychopathology, and treatment. In its early years, ego psychology was often contrasted with what was called id psychology, or drive psychology. In the early years, ego psychology contributed to developments in many aspects of psychoanalytic theory and practice, as analysts began to explore ego functioning in greater detail. Federn (1926) conceptualized the **ego boundary** between the ego and the representation of the object. Nunberg (1931, 1942) described the **synthetic function of the ego**. He also explored the concepts of ego strength and ego weakness. E. Glover (1943) described the gradual integration of **ego nuclei**, built from memory traces of experience, into a coherent whole. W. Reich (1933/1945) explored the contribution of chronic **alterations in the ego** to the development of character. A. Freud (1936) explored the defensive activities of the ego in *The Ego and the Mechanisms of Defence*. She also spent much of her career exploring normal and pathological ego development (1965). Waelder (1936) elaborated on the role of the ego in conflict, proposing his well-known principle of multiple function, which asserts that every psychic act is a compromise forged by the ego in response to the multiple demands of id, superego, reality, and the compulsion to repeat.

Among the most important contributor to the new ego psychology was Hartmann (1939a), most notably in his book *Ego Psychology and the Problem of Adaptation*. In contrast to Freud, who asserted that the ego grows out of the id, Hartmann argued that it grows out of an **undifferentiated ego-id matrix**, developing from its own inborn potentials in interaction with what he called an "average expectable environment." In contrast to the earlier focus on the drives, Hartmann emphasized what he called **autonomous ego functions**, or inborn capacities that develop independently from drive and conflict, including thought, memory, perception, motility, and affect. These autonomous functions are powered by neutralized energy from the drives. Hartmann's interest in autonomous ego functions led to later views of the ego as "hard-wired" for competence and for pleasure in mastery, equipped with inborn tendencies for exploration, stimulus seeking, play, object relations, and learning (Hendrick, 1943a, 1943b; White, 1963). Hartmann was aware that during the course of development, autonomous ego functions can be drawn into conflict, as in symptom or character formation. However, an ego function may also gain "secondary autonomy," or, become "conflict free," through a "change of function." Psychopathology and health can be conceptualized in terms of success or failure in adaptation (Hartmann, 1939b). Hartmann's interest in adaptation and conflict-free ego functioning was central to his plan to expand psychoanalysis into what he called a "general psychology," as these concepts offered links between psychoanalysis and neighboring disciplines, such as biology, sociology, and developmental psychology.

In the area of **developmental ego psychology**, in addition to A. Freud and Hartmann, Erikson (1950) offered a narrative of development that, in contrast to Freud's psychosexual stages, emphasized the impact of reality, interpersonal relationships, and culture on the development of the ego. One of Erikson's most important contributions was the concept of **ego identity**, or, the consolidation during adolescence of a stable sense of oneself as a unique individual in society. Ego psychology also went hand in hand with the growth of psychoanalytic developmental theory based on child observation, including the work Spitz (1965), Mahler, Pine, and Bergman (1975), and others. More recently, Vaillant (1993) applied the concept of ego strength in a prospective study investigating normal growth and development of ego processes beginning in late adolescence and continuing into adulthood. His groundbreaking work established the lifelong developmental significance of ego defenses, **ego resilience**, and **ego integrative processes**.

The development of ego psychology also led to important changes in psychoanalytic technique and theories of therapeutic action. Freud (1896c) had originally articulated the goal of psychoanalysis as "making conscious what has so far been unconscious." After 1926, he argued that the aim of psychoanalysis is to strengthen the ego, to make it more independent of the superego, and to enlarge its organization. As he famously stated, "Where id was, there ego shall be" (1933a). A. Freud (1936) focused attention on the clinical situation, making popular the terms **ego analysis** and *defense analysis,* which, in contrast to id analysis, focuses on how defenses express themselves in the form of resistance. She also described how the analyst must listen from a point of view equidistant from id, ego, and superego (later used as a common definition of therapeutic neutrality). Finally, she explored how the ego assists analytic work. Fenichel (1938a) elaborated on this last idea, coining the phrase **observing ego** to describe how the ego is the seat of self reflection necessary for psychoanalytic work. As psychoanalysts began to consider how to modify technique for the treatment of other-than-typical neuroses, Stone (1961), Jacobson (1964), and others described their clinical approach to patients with preoedipal pathology and affective disorders. Arlow (1969b) described the formation and function of unconscious fantasy, understood from the point of view of multiple function; C. Brenner (1982, 2003) described the ubiquity of conflict and compromise in all mental life, leading to the development of what he called "modern conflict theory." Most recently, Gray (1994) offered an interpretive approach (close process attention) focusing almost entirely on the analysis of the ego's defenses.

For forty years between the late 1920s and the late 1960s, ego psychology was the dominant school of psychoanalysis in the United States. In the American psychoanalytic literature, ego psychology has often been referred to as "classical" psychoanalysis, or sometimes, simply, as "Freudian psychoanalysis. " Gradually, however, ego psychology drew criticism from many quarters; ultimately, its hegemony in American psychoanalysis collapsed with the rise of many competing approaches or theories. Challenges to ego psychology came from several overlapping points of view, including from: 1) ego psychologists themselves, especially with regard to aspects of economic theory inherited from Freud; 2) the expansion of various objects relations theories; 3) the rise of self psychology; 4) the "hermeneutic turn" in psychoanalysis, grounded in the epistemological skepticism of the postmodern era; and 5) the development of various "two-person" psychologies, including relational, interpersonal, interactional, perspectivist, social-constructivist, and dialectical-constructivist points of view, to name a few (Wallerstein, 2002).

Contemporary psychoanalysis is characterized by multiple perspectives with no consensus about whether these perspectives can be integrated or whether they are irreconcilable. For example, while there is a long tradition of attempts to integrate ego psychology with aspects of object relations theory (Jacobson, 1964; Schafer, 1968b; Loewald, 1973a; Mahler, Pine, and Bergman, 1975; Kernberg, 1975; Sandler, 1987a), others have argued that these approaches are fundamentally incompatible (Greenberg and Mitchell, 1983). Most recently, Marcus (1999) argued for what he calls a **modern ego psychology**, needed for the description of structures, functions, and processes that are crucial organizing aspects of the mind. Marcus paid special attention to the capacity of the ego to synthesize or integrate experiences from varying levels of consciousness and different levels of organization. In his view, modern ego psychology is the best hope for a psychoanalysis that can integrate divergent points of view at various levels of abstraction and can interact with neighboring disciplines of cognitive neuroscience and developmental psychology.

Ego Ideal is a component of the superego that serves as the repository of standards, values, and images of perfection of various sorts. Failure to live up to moral ideals often elicits the experience of guilt; failure to live up to those ideals involving narcissistic perfection often elicits the experience of shame. Conversely, any approximation of ideals of perfection often results in an enhancement of self esteem. Based upon identifications with the idealized objects of early development as well as on idealized self representations, the ego ideal represents a layering of preoedipal values along with the ideals and the depersonified values of postoedipal development. Moral values often refer to the ideal treatment of others, including behaviors that are both prescribed as well as proscribed. The layering of values from successive developmental phases are frequently mutually contradictory. Striving for any particular value may lead to conflict regarding other values. Conflict associated with the ego ideal invariably involves difficulties in the regulation of self esteem, and may lead to various forms of pathological narcissism.

The ego ideal serves a critical function of distinctly human significance as it is related to moral values and the treatment of others. The concept of the ego ideal has also been of critical importance in psychoanalytic theorizing, as it is tied to: the elucidation of the structural theory, particularly the structure of the superego; self-esteem regulation; the role of identification in structure building; and affect regulation. Pathology of the ego ideal has been of central importance in the elucidation of various manifestations of pathological narcissism.

Freud (1914e) introduced the term *ego ideal* in his paper "On Narcissism." The term went through many important changes in meaning throughout Freud's writings, but it was always closely related to his views on narcissism, especially to self esteem and its regulation. Defined at certain times as a function and at other times as an agency, the evolving concept of the ego ideal was also closely linked to an evolving concept of the superego, and thereby, the emergence of the structural theory. In "On Narcissism," Freud described the ego ideal as the replacement for the lost narcissism of childhood. He distinguished between the ego ideal itself and the agency that functions to guarantee that the standards of the ego ideal are met, and that also measures the ego accordingly. This distinction was repeated in "Introductory Lectures" (1916/1917), while in "Group Psychology and the Analysis of the Ego" (1921), Freud used the term *ego ideal* to designate a more active, authoritative, critical, observing, and punishing psychic agency defined by a set of interrelated functions that include conscience, self observation, and reality testing. Two years later, in "The Ego and the Id" (1923a), this psychic agency was termed the *superego*. However, the superego no longer included the function of reality testing, which was relegated to the ego.

Using the two terms interchangeably, Freud detailed the formation of the superego or ego ideal in terms of a developmental process of identifications that replace object cathexes, including the earliest ones of childhood as well as those of the oedipal phase. The superego as the heir to the ambivalent object cathexes of the oedipus complex contains both prescriptions for ideal behavior and proscriptions against assuming the sexual prerogatives of the parents. Freud briefly resurrected the distinction between ego ideal and superego in "New Introductory Lectures on Psycho-Analysis" (1933a), wherein he designated the functions of the superego as self observation, conscience, and maintaining the ideal.

Ego psychologists and conflict theorists regard the ego ideal as a distinct set of functions within the structure of the superego. While originating in early representations of idealized self and object images, the optimal developmental outcome is a set of depersonified values, which remain easily subject to regression. Jacobson (1964), and subsequently D. Milrod (1990), delineated a developmental sequence in the formation of the ego ideal. Initially, the child takes himself as his own ideal, but with increasing awareness of the reality of his limited size and strength, the child takes his primary love object as his ideal whose perfection he is still able to share through merger experiences. When a growing sense of reality no longer permits such regression, images of perfection shift to a newly formed ego structure, the "wishful" or "wished for" self image. Only with the formation of the superego does the ego ideal, as a substructure, also form and become the repository of depersonified values of moral perfection.

Much of the literature regarding the ego ideal focuses on the relationship of the ego ideal to pathological narcissism. A. Reich (1953, 1954, 1960) described the role of sadistic superego forerunners and archaic forms of the ego ideal in pathological states involving crude sexual ideals, unstable ego boundaries, and confusion between wish and reality. She also described a type of narcissistic object choice in women based on the externalization of a grandiose infantile ego ideal, in which women deify and submit to an idealized phallic man. Finally, Reich described other kinds of pathological forms of self-esteem regulation involving the ego ideal. Kohut (1971, 1977) described the origins of the ego ideal in the internalization of an early selfobject who provides necessary mirroring and empathy; when selfobject needs are not met, there is a failure of internal regulation of self esteem and a pathological reliance on an external idealized object. Kernberg (1975) emphasized the role of aggression and internalized object relations in the formation of the superego and ego ideal, and distinguished between narcissistic personalities and other forms of character pathology on the basis of the structure of the ego ideal. Kernberg described how narcissistic characters are based on a primitive fusion of the self representation and an infantile ego ideal, accompanied by a devaluation of object representations and external objects. This fusion results in a new structure, the pathological grandiose self that renders the individual vulnerable to severe narcissistic injury and to experiences of intense and archaic affects, such as rage, shame, depression, and anxiety, as well as to the derivative narcissistic affects, such as envy, jealousy, spite, and scorn. J. Sandler, Holder, and Meers (1963) attempted to distinguish between ego ideal, superego, ideal self, and ideal object in their efforts to rework basic concepts to be more consistent with the language of representation.

Elation: see DENIAL, DEPRESSION

Electra Complex is an alternative formulation for the female oedipus complex based on the Greek myth of Electra. However, most analysts since Freud have used the oedipus complex as paradigmatic for both sexes to describe the universal existence of unconscious sexual and murderous wishes toward parents or parent-surrogates. The electra complex is a term introduced by Jung (1921/1957) when he proposed

to Freud in 1913 that the girl's family complex, including unconscious fantasies, thoughts, ideas, and associations, is parallel to, as well as gender-specifically different from, the boy's oedipus complex. Based on Greek mythology, Jung described Electra taking vengeance on her mother, Clytemnestra, for murdering her husband, Agamemnon, and thus robbing her, Electra, of her beloved father. Freud did not accept the usefulness of this term, preferring the use of oedipus complex to describe the triadic constellation in children of both genders.

Other psychoanalysts, however, have utilized the myth of Electra in describing aspects of female development and unconscious fantasy. Powell (1993), a Jungian psychoanalyst, maintained that the myth expresses the girl's anguish in relinquishing incestuous bonds, delineates the psychological problems of growing up and separating from her parents, and emphasizes early problems in the mother/daughter relationship. Halberstadt-Freud (1998) emphasized the preoedipal tie to the mother delineated in the Electra myth, viewing it as most applicable to girls who have troubled and hostile relationships to their mothers and so, in consequence, idealize their fathers. Holtzman and Kulish (2000; Kulish and Holtzman, 1998) proposed the persephone complex, arguing that the myth of Persephone offers a more-accurate depiction of the compromise solutions of the female triangular situation.

Emotional Contagion: see AFFECT, ANXIETY, EMPATHY, INTERPERSONAL PSYCHOANALYSIS

Empathy is a complex affective and cognitive process of feeling, imagining, thinking, and somatically sensing one's way into the experience of another person. The capacity for empathy lies at the heart of our ability to understand other people. As such, it is central for all human relationships, especially relationships that include intimacy and concern for the other. Empathy can also be misused to coerce and control others. The capacity for empathy develops in childhood in the interaction between inborn capacities and the attunement of caregivers. Empathic responsiveness on the part of caregivers is vital to the development of many aspects of the child's psychological life, including the basic sense of self. Empathy also plays a central role in psychoanalytic treatment, contributing both to the process of understanding and, in some views, to therapeutic action. Empathy overlaps with other psychoanalytic concepts, such as mentalization, intersubjectivity, attunement, and reverie. Empathy is often incorrectly conflated with sympathy ("feeling with"), as well as with compassion, concern, engagement, rapport, oneness, and altruism.

Empathy is not a discrete function, but includes many components, conscious and unconscious. It may begin unprompted, as affective resonance and/or imitation, progressing to include hypotheses and reflection about another. However, empathy may begin with thought. Different theoretical models conceive of empathy as constituted by various processes, including inner imitation, autonomic and motor mimicry, emotional contagion, merger, symbiosis, mirroring, identification, projection, projective identification, temporary and partial regression, signal affect, affective resonance, attunement, concordant countertransference, and, most recently, embodied simulation mediated by mirror neurons.

The definition and conceptualization of empathy, as well as its clinical role, has provoked much controversy: Is empathy *sui generis,* that is, a relatively discrete, spontaneous and direct affective perception? Alternatively, is empathy the cognitive outcome of inference using analogies drawn from knowledge and experience? How do we demonstrate the accuracy of empathy? What role does theory play in empathy? Can empathy be a mode of observation, free of values, or is it always in the service of some value and motivation, whether therapeutic, sadistic, or deceptive? What are the origins of empathy, and how does it happen? Does empathy afford access only to another person's momentary subjective state, or does it also afford access to enduring intentions, beliefs, and desires? Is empathy confined to another's conscious or preconscious experience, or can we gain empathic entrance to another's disavowed, split-off, denied, repressed, unformulated experience? What role does empathy play in the therapeutic process?

The word *empathy* was coined by the psychologist Titchener in 1909 as the English translation of the German word *Einfühlung* ("feeling into"), a term originating in the works of Herder and Novalis in the eighteenth century and reintroduced in a more methodical fashion by the art historian Vischer in 1873. As Freud was launching his career, the word *empathy* had already gained considerable conceptual prominence in aesthetics, ethics, philosophy, and psychology. Lipps, whom Freud acknowledged as one of the pioneers in the discovery of the unconscious, brought the concept of empathy to the understanding of other minds. Lipps and, in divergent ways, Husserl and others in the phenomenological philosophic tradition argued that empathy is an epistemically sound, noninferential, and nontheoretical method that offers a direct and reliable way of knowing other minds. Dilthey and others in the hermeneutical tradition of philosophy linked empathy to "understanding" (the goal of psychology and the humanities) as opposed to "explaining" (the goal of the natural sciences). This dichotomy between understanding and explaining may have contributed to Freud's (and later, Hartmann's [1964] distrust of empathy and his accentuation of the "objectivity" of both the analyst's observations and the interpretive stance (Pigman, 1995).

Freud (1905d) first used empathy in "Jokes and their Relation to the Unconscious," wherein he discussed mimetics and empathy. In his paper "On Beginning the Treatment" (1913a), he urged the analyst to adopt a position of empathy (*Einfühlung* in the original, but translated as "sympathetic understanding") as opposed to a "moralizing one." Later, in 1921, Freud (1921) observed that a path from imitation and identification leads to empathy, the only means by which we are enabled to understand another's mental life. Despite the importance he attached to empathy, Freud and his immediate followers veered away from in-depth discussions of the word. Indeed, Strachey obfuscated Freud's use of empathy by often not translating *Einfühlung* as empathy in the *Standard Edition*. Ferenczi (1928) predicated technical decisions in analysis on psychological tact, equating tact with empathy; while Freud concurred, in a letter to Ferenczi, he worried that inexperienced analysts might misuse tact or empathy to justify lapses in their objectivity (Grubrich-Simitis, 1986). After Ferenczi, the first concerted effort to describe the analyst's empathy was in 1942 when Fliess (1942) defined empathy as "trial identification" (see also H. Deutsch, 1926).

In the 1950s there was a surge of interest in empathy, stimulated in large part by an undermining of notions of objectivity. Contributing to this renewed attention to empathy was the "widening scope" of psychoanalysis to include patients with narcissistic and borderline character organizations, and an expanded understanding of object relations and the analytic relationship. These trends were accompanied by a reexamination of the privileged role of insight in therapeutic action as well as by concerns that analysts were too authoritarian and too often hearing their own theories when listening to patients. Racker (1957), while he did not use the word *empathy*, described concordant and complementary processes of identification as contributing to countertransference, now conceptualized not as a problem to be overcome, but as a way of understanding the patient. Schafer (1959) (influenced by early work of Loewald [1960]) described what he called **generative empathy**, defined as a "sublimated creative act" in personal relationships (including in the psychoanalytic relationship), which combines the pleasure of intimate merger with the recognition of separateness. Greenson (1960) distinguished empathy from identification, arguing that empathy is transient in nature and preserves the analyst's separateness, allowing him to understand the patient's feelings. In the realm of developmental psychoanalysis, Olden's (1958) pioneering work described the development of the capacity for empathy between mothers and children.

A watershed in psychoanalytic discourse on empathy was the work of Kohut. In his 1959 paper "Introspection, Empathy, and Psychoanalysis," Kohut (1959) proposed that empathy (defined as "vicarious introspection") is a mode of listening, of observation, and of data collection and, as such, defines the field of psychoanalysis. For example, Kohut argued that Freud's drive is a biological concept; the psychoanalytic concept is the individual's experience of drivenness. Kohut described empathy as both an affective and cognitive mode of experience-near understanding. Empathy plays a central role in all aspects of Kohut's self psychology. The empathic responsiveness of caregivers during each phase of infancy and childhood is vital for the development of the healthy self. Serious failures in empathy during childhood, along with selfobject failures, lead to disorders of the self. In psychoanalytic treatment, unmet selfobject needs reemerge in the form of selfobject transferences.

The empathic immersion of the analyst in the patient's experience plays a central role in psychoanalytic treatment as conceptualized by self psychology. Psychoanalytic empathy requires that the analyst feel and think his way into the patient's perspective, using his own fantasies and thoughts as well as his theories, experience, and cultural knowledge. Through this complex sustained empathic immersion (rather than through isolated moments of empathy or trial identification), the analyst arrives at understanding the patient and at interpretations. Self psychology thereby shifts the focus from the analysis of the "mind in conflict" to the analysis of "complex mental states," that is, of the self in relationship to selfobjects, and the structural deficits that result from traumatic selfobject failures. Empathic immersion in the patient's inner life enables the analyst to recognize more specifically what the patient needs from the analyst to resume development.

Kohut distinguished between the analyst's empathic listening and the applications of empathic understanding, such as the communication of empathic understanding and interpretation. Empathy alone is not a therapeutic technique. Empathy is utilized to diminish the patient's need for defense and to expand his capacity for introspection, promoting the emergence of warded-off affects, memories, and selfobject needs. The examination of the analyst's inevitable empathic failures and selfobject failures promotes, through transmuting internalizations, the further development and structuralization of the self (Kohut 1959, 1984).

The work of Kohut led to an explosion in the study of empathy, both in psychoanalytic developmental psychology and in the study of psychoanalytic treatment. Working within the tradition of ego psychology, Beres and Arlow (1974) explored empathy as including signal affect, trial identification, and unconscious fantasy. T. Shapiro (1974) explored the origins of empathy, warning of its potential for inaccuracy, as did C. Brenner (1968) and Shevrin (1978). Schwaber (1981, 2010) continued to investigate the role of empathy defined as "that mode of attunement which attempts to maximize a singular focus on the patient's subjective reality, seeking all possible cues to ascertain it." Basch (1983a) offered an important review of empathy and the reasons for the ongoing confusion about its nature as well as the mistrust of the concept within the field. Basch argued that empathy is a complex amalgam of affect, cognition, perception, and communication. It begins with automatic and unconscious imitation or simulation of the sender's bodily gestures, facial expressions, and tone of voice, which generates similar or identical (although muted) affects and bodily states in the receiver. This affective communication creates reciprocal influences in which affective resonance, thoughtful evaluation, and interpretation all play an essential role. Verbal narrative adds another layer to understanding. Further interactions, reflections, and observations validate or disconfirm one's empathic discernment, contributing to increasingly accurate empathic understanding.

Kleinian analysts explained empathy as the result of mature, normal, and benign projective identification. For example, Hinshelwood (1989) defined empathy as a process in which the analyst inserts a part of his capacity for self reflection into the patient to gain, in fantasy, the patient's experience. Bion (1962a, 1970) elaborated a complex concept of reverie, operating both in development and in treatment, in which the mother (or analyst) receives, contains, and reflectively transforms the child/patient's projective identifications, before returning them to the child/patient through the interpretive process. Rosenfeld (1987), following Bion, described a "communicative" form of projective identification, which serves as the basis for all empathy.

Developmental psychoanalysts have explored both the emergence of empathy in childhood and the importance of empathic responsiveness in caregivers for the development of the child. Winnicott (1965) described the importance of the mother as a "mirror" for the true self of the developing child. Mahler, Pine, and Bergman (1975) described the importance of the mother's accurately reflecting the child's experience during the process of separation-individuation. Lichtenberg, Bornstein, and Silver (1984) offered a compilation of research related to development and empathy. Recently, attention has been paid to the more-affective, bodily, nonverbal, and procedural constituents of empathy, such as affective attunement. D. N. Stern (1985) described affective attunement as including both emotional resonance to another person and an intrinsic and spontaneous cross-modal responsiveness that conveys a shared feeling state; affective attunement is important for the development of the self and for the child's capacity for intersubjectivity. It is also essential to the capacity for empathy, as affective attunement proceeds to reflection. In a similar vein, Fonagy et al. (2002) described how the mother's ability to accurately reflect and "mark" the child's inner state is necessary for the development of the child's own capacity for mentalization.

Finally, discoveries in cognitive neuroscience, especially research in mirror neurons (Gallese, 2006), emotional recognition (Ekman, 1983; Zajonc, 1984), and the development of theory of mind in children (Premack and Woodruff, 1978) have reinvigorated philosophical controversies about the nature of empathy and its epistemological status. In philosophy and cognitive neuroscience, debates about empathy and theory of mind have frequently occurred between two (now interdisciplinary) positions known as "simulation theory" and "theory theory"; these debates have contributed to the psychoanalytic discussions of empathy (Eagle, Migone, and Gallese, 2007). In addition, overlapping debates flourish under the rubric of "mind reading," originating in cognitive neuroscience and communications science.

Enactment is a co-constructed verbal and/or behavioral experience during a psychoanalytic treatment in which a patient's expression of a transference fantasy evokes a countertransference "action" in the analyst. Enactments are "symbolic interactions" (Chused, 1991) in that they carry unconscious meanings for both patient and analyst, unconsciously initiated by the patient and evoking unconscious compliance in the analyst. Because enactments attempt to actualize unconscious fantasies, circumventing reflection by either the patient or analyst, they are resistances. However, enactments may also be communications

of something that the patient and analyst cannot yet tolerate knowing. Enactment has also been defined and conceptualized from a relational or interpersonal perspective as the expression within a psychoanalytic treatment of a patient's dissociated self state, which, from this perspective, is the only way that such experience can be accessed.

Enactment may occur as obvious, discrete behavior, or as a subtle, persistent aspect of speech, attitude, or bodily expression; enactment is defined so widely as to include silence or passivity. Enactment is distinct from acting out, which is the actualization of unconscious fantasy in one member of the analytic dyad. Enactment is similar to projective identification when the latter is defined as a bridging concept between the intrapsychic and interpersonal domains. In this view of projective identification, split-off parts of the self are forced into the object, who then temporarily experiences the affects as his or her own. In its emphasis on actualizing, and on the patient's unconscious recruitment of the analyst to serve intrapsychic aims, enactment expands on J. Sandler's (1976a) concept of role responsiveness and also on his view that there is a universal tendency and pressure toward the "actualization" of fantasies (1976b).

Enactment is an important concept because it clarifies that while transference and countertransference wishes and fears have intrapsychic origins, they seek realization, symbolically, in the interpersonal matrix of the analytic dyad. Enactments, therefore, provide information about the unconscious of each member of the analytic dyad, their histories, and a way in which the analysis might become stalemated. When understood, the emotional immediacy of enactments may lead to especially useful insights.

Although the concept of enactment has been present in the psychoanalytic literature almost from the beginning, it has been given more frequent attention in the last twenty years. This attention reflects the greater influence of object relations theories in contemporary psychoanalysis, which emphasize various aspects of the analytic dyad. The term *enactment* appeared in the psychoanalytic literature beginning in the 1950s to refer to the general human tendency to symbolically enact unconscious fantasies, the equivalent of acting out in the clinical setting. Beginning with McLaughlin (1981) and Jacobs (1986), enactment began to refer to the influence of the analyst's transferences on his work. Jacobs noted that enactments needn't be dramatic but instead might be embedded in what the analyst experienced as ordinary technique. In these articles, however, enactment was not clearly differentiated from acting out (the actualization of unconscious fantasy in one member of the analytic dyad). McLaughlin (1991) expanded the concept to include the general "evocative-coercive" functions attached to the transferences of both patient and analyst, such that each party feels he is acting in response to the other. In an influential paper, Chused (1991) defined enactments as "symbolic interactions" in analysis that have unconscious meanings for both patient and analyst, but which are initiated by the patient's attempts to actualize some aspect of the transference with which the analyst, acting on his own countertransference, unconsciously complies.

From some relational and interpersonal perspectives, enactment is the central focus of clinical technique, as enactment is directly linked to a view of the mind and of psychopathology. I. Hoffman (1994) suggested that analysis be redefined as a series of enactments that the patient and analyst come to examine and experience together. P. Bromberg (1998a, 2006) proposed that the mind, or self, is a shifting landscape of multiple "self-states"; the enactment of sequestered self-states in the treatment situation is the way in which both analyst and patient gain access to their content. According to Bromberg and other relationalists (S. Mitchell, 1997; Bass, 2003), the analyst must consult his own shifting self-states for hints about what is transpiring with his patients.

Although Kernberg (1975, 1976b) did not use the term *enactment,* his description of the treatment of borderline patients contains a similar concept. Because borderline patients often express intense transferences in the form of action, intense countertransference reactions are evoked in both acute and chronic form. These transference/countertransference enactments invariably reveal much about the patient's object relational pathology and become the focus of analytic work. In its contemporary usage, enactment has been applied more broadly to patients with all levels of pathology and includes a greater appreciation of the analyst's independent contribution to what is now conceptualized as a co-constructed phenomenon.

Endopsychic Structure: see FAIRBAIRN

Energy, also known as **Psychic Energy** or **Psychical Energy**, is a hypothetical, quantifiable force, analogous to physical energy, used to account for the relative intensities of motivational states, affects, and other mental experiences. In Freud's theory of mind and among early ego psychologists, psychic energy was also postulated to be the force behind all mental activity itself. In Freud's metapsychology, the concept of energy was elaborated in the economic point of view that considers the nature of the various energies in the mind, their quantities, the antagonisms between them, and the principles that determine their accumulation, distribution, and discharge. It is also closely associated with the term *cathexis* (used by Strachey in his translation of Freud), which refers to the investment of psychic energy in an idea or a mental process.

The concept of psychic energy is founded on both theoretical and clinical considerations. The notion of energy, borrowed explicitly by Freud from physics, is evidence of his commitment to the mandate, passed on to him from the Helmholtz School of Medicine, to explain the human organism in terms only of "forces equal in dignity to the chemical-physical forces inherent in matter" (Bernfeld, 1944). At the level of clinical theory, Freud used the concept of energy to account for the relative intensity and peremptory force of wishes, feelings, and ideas, as well as for the power of defensive operations. He also used it to account for the fundamental observation that this intensity can be separated from the idea with which it is associated, displaced from one idea to another, or transformed (converted) into symptoms. Finally, he used the concept to account for his (and Breuer's) observation that, in the treatment setting, strong expressions of emotion can be associated with improvement in symptoms (catharsis or abreaction).

Indeed, in one way or another, almost all of Freud's fundamental concepts depended on his ideas about psychic energy, including his concepts of drive, motivation, conflict, attention, primary and secondary processes, and the regulatory principles of the mind, as well as his fundamental ideas about psychopathology, including symptom formation and trauma, and psychoanalytic treatment, including resistance and transference. However, few concepts in psychoanalysis have generated more controversy than the concept of psychic energy, with many theorists recommending abandonment of both the notion of psychic energy and the economic point of view, suggesting that they add little but imprecision and confusion to the psychoanalytic model of the mind. Nevertheless, despite the critique of the specifics of Freud's energy theory, the psychoanalytic view of the mind includes awareness that all experience is accompanied by feelings of relative intensity, which, to some extent, is modifiable and transferable.

While Breuer (Breuer and Freud, 1893/1895) used the term *energy* in his contribution to "Studies on Hysteria," Freud's (1896a) own first use of the term *psychic energy* was slightly later in 1896 in an early draft of "The Neuroses of Defence." In this early phase of his work, Freud also referred to the idea of energy in concepts such as a "psychical intensity," a "sum of excitation," or "quota of affect," which "possesses all the characteristic of a quantity . . . capable of increase, diminution, displacement and discharge." In his unpublished, neuronally based "Project for a Scientific Psychology," Freud (1895b) imagined a quantity of energy analogous to an electrical impulse, which he referred to simply as "Q." By 1900, he spoke increasingly just of "energy" (or "psychical energy") as the force propelling mental activity, with cathexis as the investment or storage of this energy in particular mental products or structures (1900).

In his earliest models of the mind, including the "Project" and the topographic models, Freud proposed that the overall function of the mind (or the "mental apparatus") is the regulation and discharge of psychic energy. In these models, the mind is capable of two distinct modes of managing psychic energy, referred to as the primary and the secondary processes. In the earliest, or primary process, **mobile energy** or **unbound energy** (or mobile cathexes) seeks discharge by the fastest possible route, according to the pleasure principle; it cannot either be delayed in response to reality concerns or be stored for future use. Over time, the mind-brain develops secondary process operations with the capacity to delay discharge in response to the demands of reality, creating **bound energy** (hyper- or anticathexes) that can be used for thinking, structure building, defense, and other, more-advanced mental operations. With the development of his drive theory, Freud proposed that the sources of psychic energy are the sexual (libidinal) and, later, the aggressive drives. With the development of structural theory (1923a), he described **desexualized energy** (later called "neutralization" by Hartmann [1939a]), by which he meant energy freed from the aggressive and sexual aims of the id for use by the ego for all its functions (Freud, 1900, 1911b, 1915d, 1923a).

Finally, throughout his work, Freud proposed various regulatory principles to explain how the mind manages psychical energy. The principle of "neuronic inertia," articulated in the "Project," stated that the primary function of the psychic apparatus is to return to an inert state, divesting itself of stimulation or energy (1895b). The closely related "principle of constancy" (borrowed from Fechner) asserted that the mind aims to maintain excitation at as low and as constant a level as possible, while trying to accommodate its need for a supply of energy for mental activity (Breuer and Freud, 1893/1895). These two principles were later reworked as the Nirvana principle, invoked as the operating principle behind the death instinct, whereby the mind seeks to bring its energy level toward the zero point (Freud, 1920a). From the beginning, Freud equated the principles of inertia and constancy with the unpleasure/pleasure principle (later, renamed the pleasure principle [1911b]), arguing that unpleasure is the tension caused by the accumulation of energy, while pleasure is caused by the discharge of energy (1900). Freud, himself, recognized problems with various aspects of his energy theory (for example, that sexual behavior includes a pleasurable accumulation of energy), and his efforts to resolve these problems were never fully satisfactory. However, he never officially abandoned his view of the mind as an apparatus for managing energy, even as he became more interested in exploring its other functions. Indeed, the economic point of view and the language of energy pervaded the psychoanalytic literature until the second half of the twentieth century, when many analysts began to challenge the concept of psychic energy, criticizing it as: based on multiple tautologies; misusing metaphor as fact; pervaded by contradiction, confusion, and imprecision; lacking explanatory value; reinforcing mind-body dualism; and presenting a false link between psychoanalysis and neurophysiology. Critics have argued that variations in the intensity of felt experience, the relative strength of defensive operations, and changes in the focus of attention are all distinct phenomena that cannot be explained by shifts in amounts of a unitary concept of energy. Information, learning, and systems models from cognitive science (emphasizing the mind's capacities for information processing, representation, and symbol formation), as well as models from evolutionary psychology (emphasizing adaptation and neuronally inspired models such as connectionism) have been proposed as more suitable places from which to draw inspiration for the psychoanalytic model of the mind (Kubie, 1947; Kardiner, Karush, and Ovesey, 1959; Holt, 1962, 1976; Rosenblatt and Thickstun, 1970, 1977; Gill, 1977; Olds, 1994). Nevertheless, whatever the problems presented by the concept of psychic energy, psychoanalysts find it hard to describe mental life without some language for the experience of intensity or quantity, without which it is impossible to convey aspects of any number of clinical phenomena.

Entitlement refers to that which an individual has a right or just claim to and, more often, to an attitude bespeaking a claim to special status or treatment.

Everyone has unconscious fantasies of entitlement dating from the earliest stages of childhood. However, in some individuals, especially in individuals with narcissistic personality disorder, fantasies of entitlement are expressed in conscious and unconflicted feelings that they deserve more than other people.

Although Freud did not use the word *entitlement,* he explored the concept in relation to "The Exceptions," or, individuals who are unwilling to forego any gratifications during analytic work, as they feel entitled to reparations for suffering or deprivation endured in early childhood (1916). Many later theorists writing about narcissism and entitlement, including Jacobson (1959), A. Kris (1976), Billow (1999), and Blum (2001), referred to Freud's essay while offering a variety of theories for the origins of entitlement. For example, some have seen entitlement as the simple manifestation of unrenounced childhood omnipotence; others have stressed its defensive use to ward off feelings of helplessness and dependence or to repudiate a feeling of parental indifference. Coen (1988) explored the superego aspects of entitlement, used to justify destructive urges. A tension exists between those who view narcissistic entitlement as the expression of a normal psychological need (Winnicott, 1955; Kohut, 1971) and those who view it as a pathological narcissistic trait (Kernberg, 1975). Entitlement is not found only in narcissistic personalities. Apprey (1988) offered a developmental line of feelings of entitlement, beginning in infancy and progressing toward normal adulthood, in which there is a balance between one's own needs and the rights of others. Blechner (1987) distinguished between "attitudes" and "claims" of entitlement, pointing out that the former can be unconscious or suppressed, leading to an attitude of passivity or an experience of the self as ineffectual.

Envy: see BORDERLINE, INFANTILE GENITAL PHASE, JEALOUSY, KLEIN, NARCISSISM, PENIS ENVY, PRIMAL SCENE, PROJECTIVE IDENTIFICATION, WOMB ENVY

Erikson's Stages are a paradigm of human development organized in an eight-stage life-cycle sequence that was proposed by Erik Homburger Erikson (1950, 1959). Integrating his study of psychoanalysis, education, cultural history, and anthropology, Erikson was among the first to expand Freud's framework of the psychosexual stages of development from infancy to adolescence. He conceived of development as a lifelong epigenetic process resulting in a predictable, cumulative sequence that he called the "eight stages of man." Each of Erikson's stages is identified by a "crisis," or urgent and psychologically important central developmental task that shapes it. Healthy development results when crises are resolved in each successive stage; psychopathology results when they are not. Each stage builds upon the last. The optimal resolution of a developmental "crisis" involves a creative tension between opposing extremes.

Although Erikson's stage theory is based on Freud's (1905b) view of early development as the successive stages of the libidinal drive (oral, anal, phallic), he situated this classical developmental perspective within the context of the family and the surrounding culture. If Freud's progression consists of the sequential reorganization of drive, Erikson's schema of developmental progression consists of the sequential reorganization of ego and character structure. Through his writings on children's play, on anthropology, and on the development of the ego and identity, Erikson influenced not only the field of clinical psychology but also the general tenor of social and cultural thinking in the United States (C. Geissmann and P. Geissmann, 1998). While stage theories of development have fallen into some disfavor, Erikson's work continues to be valued for calling attention to psychosocial and cultural elements largely ignored by psychoanalysts before his time. In that vein, Erikson is credited with introducing the concept of the historical moment. Such a moment occurs when the psychology of the leader and the mass psychology of a society resonate in such a way that a transformative process occurs, as in the rise of Hitler.

In Erikson's eight-stage life cycle, each stage is described by a phase-specific psychosocial crisis and by a central life task around which there exists a conflict. Erikson proposed the following stages: Stage One, Oral-Sensory: birth to one year, trust versus basic mistrust, feeding; Stage Two, Muscular-Anal: one to three years, autonomy versus shame and doubt, toilet training; Stage Three, Locomotor-Genital: three to six years, initiative versus guilt, independence; Stage Four, Latency: six to twelve years, industry versus inferiority, schooling; Stage Five, Puberty and Adolescence: twelve to eighteen years, identity versus role diffusion, peer relationships; Stage Six, Young Adulthood: eighteen to forty years, intimacy versus isolation, love relationships; Stage Seven, Adulthood: forty to sixty-five years, generativity versus stagnation, parenting; Stage Eight, Maturity: sixty-five years until death, ego integrity versus despair, acceptance of one's life. Erikson described the favorable outcomes of each stage, which he called "virtues." The Erikson life-stage virtues, in the order of the stages in which they may be acquired, are: hope, will, purpose, competence, fidelity, love, care, and wisdom.

Erikson's paradigm of the eight stages of human development was widely accepted in the United States during the 1950s and 1960s. However, starting in the 1970s, in response to the feminist and postmodern movements, as well as in response to a growing interest in attachment theory and evidence derived from direct infant observation, Erikson's stage theory was examined more critically. For example, feminist theorists found an androcentric bias and a reflection of mid-twentieth-century sex-role stereotypes embedded in the theory's core concepts. These theorists disagreed with Erikson's emphasis on the biological distinctiveness of women and men, and with his implicit acceptance of heterosexual union as the route to healthy genitality. Erikson was also faulted for valorizing separation, autonomy, and individuation over strivings for attachment and connectedness throughout the life cycle (Gilligan, 1982; Josselson, 1996) and for failing to capture the experiences of racial and ethnic minorities.

Infant-observation research and the ascendancy of attachment theory as an explanatory model for the development of psychological health led some developmental theorists to question the validity of stage models of development. For example, D. N. Stern (1985) offered a developmental account in which new senses of the self serve as organizing principles that emerge during specific periods of the first years of life and continue over the life span, an approach he described as "normative and prospective." Stern critiqued the stage theories of Freud and Erikson for seeking in developmental phases the specific roots of later fixation (Freud) and ego and character pathology (Erikson).

Eros: see DEATH DRIVE, DRIVE, ENERGY

Erotization, Sexualization, Instinctualization, and **Libidinalization** are all synonyms for a defensive process in which a nonsexual function or mental phenomenon takes on, or is invested with, sexual meaning or sexual charge. Erotization is most commonly used in the context of discussing clinical material, as in erotization of defenses, perversion, masochistic erotization of pain, or erotization of the transference. The study of erotization or sexualization is important because it demonstrates, as with all perversion, that sexual behavior and fantasy may be recruited for the management of nonsexual conflicts.

The first use of the term *sexualization* by Freud (1911a), was in his description of the case of Schreber, who suffered from a paranoid disorder. Freud showed how Schreber's fantasies of heavenly bliss (an admixture of ideas of a "voluptuous union" with God) were an example of sexualization; Freud used this example as a further argument for his early theory of the sexual nature of mental disorders. Freud defined sexualization, or libidinalization, as a process in which a portion of the sexual drive (libido) that cannot find an appropriate outlet due to fixation or regression finds an outlet along some alternate channel. He described the infusion of other instincts with sexual drive, such as social or aggressive instincts, when libido is damned up from appropriate outlet. This process can occur at any level of development. The sexual drive is always pressing for expression, and once a nonsexual activity is co-opted as an outlet for libido, it continues to be burdened by sexual-drive expression. An early example supplied by Freud is the sexualization of thinking in obsessional neuroses. Freud (1926a) also used the term *erotization* in describing the defensive erotization of certain functions as a result of neurotic conflict. He postulated that playing a musical instrument, writing, or walking can become inhibited as the result of excessive erotization of the bodily organ involved in the particular function. For example, the hand could become linked in the individual's mind with guilt-ridden masturbation.

Hartmann (1950) used the term *instinctualization of ego functions* to designate a form of regression in which an ego function becomes invested with a sexual meaning without an obvious link to the underlying sexual component. In a similar, more contemporary usage, some theorists began to use *sexualization* to refer to sexual behavior used for the purpose of defense, without "true" sexual meaning. Coen (1981) proposed confining the term *sexualization* to describe clinical phenomenon in which a patient extensively uses sexual behavior and fantasy as a defense against anxiety. The defense has greater urgency and significance than any urge for sexual-drive gratification.

H. Blum (1973) described the erotized transference as a particularly intense erotic transference, which may occur in some patients with moderately severe character pathology. In such cases, nonsexual needs, such as needs for dependency, or aggressive urges, become erotized and directed toward the analyst. Often patients prone to such erotization have history of sexual trauma in childhood.

In self psychology, sexualization has a precise meaning related to deficiencies in selfobject functioning. Goldberg (1983) elaborated on Kohut's (1971) view of sexualization as the outcome of a structural deficiency. When a selfobject is endangered, sexualization may be used to bolster the person's sense of self and thus forestall further regression. Examples are the sexualization of loneliness or the sexualization of the triumph over others. Analytic efforts by self psychologists with patients who sexualize are aimed at understanding the underlying need for the defense; the focus of analysis is on building stable selfobjects rather than on fortifying the sublimation, neutralization, or de-instinctualization of a sexual drive.

Escape from Freedom: see INTERPERSONAL PSYCHO-ANALYSIS

The Exceptions: see CHARACTER, ENTITLEMENT, GUILT, NARCISSISM

Exhibitionism, in the broadest use of the term, is any act or fantasy in which the **exhibitionist** seeks to draw recognition or admiration to himself. Pronounced exhibitionism is a trait associated with several character disorders. However, exhibitionism is a normal part of development and of adult psychological life, so that exhibitionistic behavior and fantasy, with their attendant conflicts, are part of every analysis. In a narrower use of the term, exhibitionism refers to a perversion in which exposing the genitals to an onlooker is the preferred means of achieving sexual satisfaction.

Freud conceptualized exhibitionism as among the component instincts of infantile sexuality, pairing it with its opposite, scopophilia. In Freud's theory, perverse exhibitionism is the direct expression of this component instinct; in healthy development, exhibitionism survives as a normal aspect of foreplay (1905b). When Freud proposed the concept of the phallic phase of psychosexual development (now called the "infantile genital phase"), psychoanalysts began to describe a cluster of attitudes called phallic narcissism, which includes aggressive self aggrandizement accompanied by pronounced exhibitionism, sometimes referred to as **phallic exhibitionism** (W. Reich, 1933/1945). These attitudes were also understood as defending against and overcompensating for the castration complex in both boys and girls (Freud, 1923b). When phallic narcissism persists into adulthood, it is often referred to as the phallic narcissistic character, especially in men. Pronounced self dramatization and exhibitionism have also been described as part of hysterical character, usually in women (Easser and Lesser, 1965). As is usual in psy-

choanalytic history, understanding of the psychodynamic underpinnings of exhibitionism, both perverse and characterological, has expanded far beyond its original association with the castration complex. For example, Bergler (1956) described what he called **negative exhibitionism**, or the habit of making a "spectacle of oneself," as related to preoedipal trauma and conflict.

Kohut (1966, 1971) argued that exhibitionism, together with omnipotence, are the salient features of the normal infantile grandiose self, sometimes referred to as the **grandiose-exhibitionistic self**. With optimal responsiveness from others, exhibitionism is integrated into the totality of the personality and results in a relatively cohesive self with the capacity to regulate and take pleasure in recognition and admiration. In psychoanalysis, mobilization and interpretation of infantile exhibitionistic strivings in the transference are central to the more mature development of ambitious strivings. Exhibitionism as the expression of the grandiose self is the impetus for healthy development; when derailed, it is at the core of psychopathology.

Externalization is a group of mental process whereby an aspect of inner experience is attributed to the external world. Externalizing maneuvers may be used defensively to make painful, conflicted, or otherwise unacceptable psychic contents more tolerable by disowning them and attributing them to others. When used as a defense, externalization is often used synonymously with projection, which, in psychoanalysis, is most often defined as a defensive process. Externalization may also be used nondefensively, as in many instances where something inside the mind is attributed to the outside world. When used nondefensively, externalization is related to the prepsychoanalytic meaning of the word *projection*, which means literally "to throw in front of," as when an image is thrown onto a screen. In the field of psychology, projection is used in this way (with no implication of defense) to describe a universal tendency to find reflections of inner life in the external world. Externalization is the opposite of internalization, a process whereby aspects of the external world are "taken in" and experienced as part of the self. Both terms reflect awareness that psychological life develops and functions in interaction with an external world, with externalization and internalization describing fundamental aspects of that interaction.

Externalization encompasses a wide range of normal and pathological phenomena. Freud used the concept if not the word *externalization* (indeed, often using the word *projection*) in his explorations of: paranoid psychopathology (1894c; 1911a); creative writing (1908a); superstitions (1909d); some kinds of transference experience (1910f); fantasies about the "end of the world" (1911a); beliefs about the rewards of the afterlife (1911b); the unanalyzed analyst who mistakes aspects of his own inner life for that of his patient (1912b); magical thinking in children and "primitive peoples," including their demons and taboos (1913e); dreams (1917b); coherence in groups (1921); jealousy (1922); and phobias (1926a). Freud's accounts of these phenomena include both defensive and nondefensive aspects of externalization.

From a developmental perspective, externalization (both defensive and nondefensive) is an adaptive and normal mechanism. In 1915 (without using the word *externalization*), Freud (1915b) described how processes of projection and introjection are used to build up the ego and the concept of the external world. Klein (1927c) used the term *externalization* (interchangeably with projection) to explain play as the externalization of "phantasy" activity. Klein (1946) went on to describe how alternating defensive processes of projection (later, projective identification) and introjection work together from the earliest moments of infancy to create both the inner and the external world. J. Novick and Kelly (1970) argued that it is important to distinguish a normal and nondefensive process of "generalization," whereby children assume that others feel the same way they do. In their view, generalization is important as a stepping-stone on the way to identification. In discussing superego development, others have described how, during latency and adolescence, superego demands are often externalized onto parents and other authority figures as a phase-appropriate defense,

prior to internalization (P. Tyson and R. Tyson, 1990). In states of regression, individuals may also **reexternalize** aspects of the internal world. For example, ego and/or superego functions (such as reality testing or moral authority) may be attributed to others (Loewald, 1962b). When persistent and pervasive, externalization may become pathological, as in paranoia or psychosis. In less-severe cases, it can become a problem when it is used by an individual to avoid recognizing his own shortcomings. Parents may externalize unwanted aspects of themselves onto their children, creating the so-called "identified patient," so as to avoid responsibility for their own problems (J. Novick and Kelly, 1970).

A. Freud (1965) cautioned that externalization can be confused with transference. Expanding on this view, Berg (1977) distinguished between **externalizing transference** and classical transference. In externalizing transference, part of the patient's inner world, such as a wish, a superego prohibition, a self representation, or even an ego function, is attributed to the analyst; classical transference displaces wishes from earlier objects onto the analyst. Similarly, Klein (1946) used the term *externalization* to refer to the projection onto the analyst of good and bad self representations. Kernberg (1970b) also used externalization to describe the transferences of patients with borderline personality disorder in which all-good and all-bad aspects of the patient are split off and projected onto the analyst. Externalization of aspects of the self also contributes to the idealizing and mirror transferences described by Kohut (1971, 1977).

Extrovert/Introvert: see JUNGIAN PSYCHOLOGY

F

W. Ronald D. Fairbairn offered a theory of the mind, including its development and its functioning, based on the establishment of "endopsychic structures," which result from the internalization of fantasied interactions between self and object beginning in childhood. Fairbairn's theory has had an enormous impact on the development of psychoanalytic theory. He was both influenced by and, in turn, influenced Klein. His work was highly influential on that of Kernberg. It also influenced the development of self psychology and contemporary relational psychoanalysis. Fairbairn's work is often considered pivotal in the shift from a drive model of development to a relational/structural model. Most significantly, Fairbairn is credited with having coined the term *object relations theory* (1941, 1952, 1954). The most important explicators of Fairbairn's theory include Guntrip (1961) and Sutherland (1963).

The distinguishing features of Fairbairn's theory include the following: 1) The ego is present from birth. 2) The libido and the ego are primarily object seeking rather than pleasure seeking. 3) Libido is a function of the ego; it is reality oriented, serving to promote attachment of the infant to the earliest object, first the mother's breast and then the mother as a whole object. 4) There is no death instinct; aggression is conceptualized as a response to frustration and/or deprivation. 5) Frustration and separation lead to internalization of the object. 6) This internalized object is both loved and hated. 7) Representations of the object are split into parts, based on fantasies of love and hate. 8) Each representation of the object is paired with a corresponding representation of the self, also split into parts. 9) Configurations of these structured "object relations" form the core of the personality underlying various kinds of psychopathology.

In Fairbairn's view, the human individual is primarily motivated to seek objects and to preserve his relationship with them. In this view, development is characterized by three phases differentiated by the nature of the relationship with the object: infantile dependence; the transitional phase; and mature dependence. Psychopathology results not from conflicts over pleasure-seeking wishes, but from psychological maneuvers undertaken to preserve object ties. During the transitional phase, in response to separation

and other inevitable frustrating experiences with caretaking objects, the infant establishes internal objects within his mind that contribute to solutions to these frustrating relationships.

Fairbairn generalized from his work with schizoid patients to describe the "schizoid" core of all people, which he argued is based on the universal mechanism of splitting. Influenced by the work of Klein, who had already made extensive use of Freud's concept of splitting applied to what she called the "internal object," Fairbairn applied the concept of splitting to the ego (self) as well as to the object. In Fairbairn's view, the object is internalized in response to frustration in the early relationship with the mother. Next, both the exciting and the frustrating aspects of the internal object are split from the central core of the object and repressed by the ego. This splitting creates two repressed internal objects: the exciting (or "libidinal") object and the frustrating (or "anti-libidinal") object. Each of these internal objects carries with it into repression a corresponding, split-off part of the ego: a "libidinal ego" and an "anti-libidinal ego" (sometimes called the "internal saboteur"). This splitting of the ego leaves a "central ego" or conscious "I," which is both the center of self awareness and the agent of repression. Thus the psyche is split into three parts, or "endopsychic structures," made up of "object relations": a central ego attached to an ideal object; a repressed libidinal ego attached to an exciting (libidinal) object; and a repressed anti-libidinal ego (internal saboteur) attached to a rejecting (anti-libidinal) object.

Fairbairn's tripartite structure of the mind differs from Freud's tripartite structural theory in that all three structures are ego structures. There is no id or superego. Libido is at the disposal of the libidinal ego; aggression is at the disposal of the anti-libidinal ego, which attacks the libidinal ego. In contrast to Freud's view that an infant's core anxiety is fear of being overwhelmed by the drives, or to Klein's belief that the personality is organized by anxieties related to the death drive, Fairbairn believed that an infant's core anxiety is that his love for his mother will empty her out and destroy her, leaving the infant himself feeling despairing and depleted. Fairbairn argued that only later does the infant imagine that frustration is the consequence of his own aggression;

this aggression is then projected onto the mother to create the bad, frustrating object, which, as noted above, is then internalized.

In Fairbairn's view, psychopathology reflects various aspects of this tripartite core of the personality. For example, schizoid personality reflects the impoverishment of the central ego as a result of excessive use of splitting and/or pervasiveness of the core anxiety of depletion. Masochistic tendencies reflect excessive use of what Fairbairn called the "masochistic defense," or the all-out effort to preserve the frustrating yet needed relationship to the object through the creation of an "all-bad self" who assumes all the blame for frustration and deprivation. In psychoanalytic treatment, various of these split-off parts of the personality are mobilized in the transference. Most often, initially, the patient relates to the analyst and ideal object, experienced from the point of view of the patient's own central, conscious core. Gradually, repressed libidinal and anti-libidinal object relations emerge in the transference as well.

Family Romance is a commonly held fantasy in which a child denies his parentage and believes that he is the offspring of other parents who are typically of a more noble lineage. The precursors of the family-romance fantasy can be seen in the preoedipal conflicts of early childhood, with the splitting of objects and the idealization of the mother and father. The disappointments and disillusionment of the oedipal phase set the stage for the development of the family-romance fantasy which usually appears in latency. The family-romance fantasy can be conscious, but there are often unconscious components, including a disavowal of the real parents' sexual relationship. Analysis of derivatives of the family romance can serve as a window into narcissistic and oedipal issues.

The family romance, understood to be a primal or universal fantasy, has been described in the literature since psychoanalysis began, in both applied and clinical studies. It has been featured as a typical compensatory fantasy to manage the narcissistic injuries of childhood, as a component of mythology and tales of the hero, and, especially, as an intrinsic, more or less prominent part of everyone's oedipal solutions. Derivatives and variations of the family-romance fantasy are, in fact, a part of the actual story of Oedipus, are present (in the reverse) in the story of Moses, are pervasive in the work of authors such as Dickens, and often figure in the biographies of contemporary superheroes. They are ubiquitous, again in reverse, in adopted individuals. Many psychoan-

alytically informed studies of the arts rely on the family romance as an organizing concept.

The term *family romance* is mentioned as early as 1897 in Freud's (1897a) communications with Fliess. Freud (1909a) formalized and elaborated on the term in his 1909 paper "Family Romances." In 1920, he added a footnote to his "Three Essays on the Theory of Sexuality" (1905b) that included the family-romance fantasy as one of several primal fantasies. This marked the beginning of an interest in the phenomenon of the family romance and its recognition in myth, folklore, and fiction. Freud viewed the fantasy as both wish-fulfilling and defensive. In his view, the fantasied parents have the identical characteristics of the child's early idealized parents. The child resorts to the fantasy as a result of the discrepancy between his earlier idealizations and the subsequent more realistic and disappointing images of his parents. Freud also asserted that the fantasy can be used defensively in warding off guilt about incestuous feelings; in other words, if the child is not related to his parents or siblings, it is not forbidden to have sexual interest in them.

Rank (1909) widened the scope of the fantasy by linking it to the latency-age focus on heroes, arguing that hero worship is a way to defensively protect the child from disappointment and anger relating to his father (Frosch, 1959b). H. Deutsch (1933a) viewed the fantasy as a defensive reaction to the child's knowledge of his parents' sexuality and the ambivalent feelings that result from the discovery.

Wieder (1977) examined this theme in the fantasies of adopted children, who must grapple with the fact that the parents known to them are not the "real" (biological) parents. In his small clinical sample, Wieder discovered a typical variant amounting to a reversal of the family romance: the adopted children fantasized that they were literally cast out into the world as helpless infants and had to survive on their own until they were rescued by a savior mother (as in the Moses story). In contrast to the tendency of biological children to disavow and disparage the actual birth parents in favor of the idealized, fantasized "birth parents," adopted children imagine (often with the aid of fragments of information) that their biological parents are corrupt, immoral, sadistic, lower class, and uneducated, while the savior, adoptive parents are seen as ethical, moral, protective, powerful, and asexual. The adoptees' wish, at least in childhood, is to deny their adoption and establish a blood tie to their adoptive parents.

Widzer (1977) looked at the family-romance fantasy through the lens of comic-book superheroes. His view is that comic books are contemporary mythology and that the manner in which superheroes acquire their powers can be related to the phases of the family romance. For example, Superman, who is raised by ordinary parents on Earth, later discovers his true identity and power, which stem from his birth to a powerful mother and father on the planet Krypton.

Fantasy (or **Phantasy**) is an imagined scenario or storylike narrative that features the imagining subject in a major role, most often in an emotionally charged situation. Fantasies represent self and object interactions shaped by motivational states and by defensive operations. They may be wholly or partly unconscious. Conscious fantasies are common in the form of daydreams in which the daydreamer imagines a variety of gratifying, frightening, or punishing scenarios. Conscious fantasies are, in turn, derivatives of underlying unconscious fantasies that are stable, enduring structures that are relatively sequestered from the impact of reality. Fantasy is distinguished from wish (an unconscious mental state of desire) and complex (an unconscious, organized group of thoughts, images, and associations), neither of which need take narrative form. The different spellings of "fantasy"/"phantasy" found in the psychoanalytic literature are the result of the preference among some (mainly British) analysts for the latter, based on the German word *Phantasie* (meaning "imagination," or "visionary notion"), over the English word *fantasy* (meaning "caprice" or "whim"). Isaacs (1948) sharpened this distinction by proposing that *phantasy* be used to refer to unconscious events, and *fantasy* to more conscious ones; this convention has been followed by British Kleinians.

The concept of fantasy is central to psychoanalytic theories of mind, psychopathology, and technique. Freud's theory that hysteria does not result from childhood seduction, but is based on the pathogenic effects of childhood sexual fantasy was a revolutionary step in the development of the psychoanalysis. Over time, from its role in the etiology of neurosis, fantasy came to be seen as the dominant way in which all wishes, fears, defenses, and corresponding object relations are represented in the unconscious, comprising the core of what Freud called "psychic reality." As such, an individual's **fantasy life** exerts an organizing effect on all aspects of mental life and behavior, both normal and pathological, beginning in childhood; it also serves as a template, or mind set, that contributes to the organization of new experience (Arlow, 1969b).

In a letter to Fliess in 1897, Freud (1897e) first alluded to his dawning awareness that fantasy, rather than actual traumatic sexual experiences, plays the pivotal role in the etiology of neurosis. While he withheld publication of this view for almost a decade, his discovery opened the door to the recognition of the decisive role played by infantile sexuality and the oedipus complex in mental life. As he later summarized, "phantasies possess psychical as contrasted with material reality, and we gradually learn to understand that in the world of the neuroses it is psychical reality which is the decisive kind" (Freud, 1916/1917). Freud saw fantasy as a wish-fulfilling, illusory kind of thought that arises from the frustration of instinctual wishes. In its earliest form, fantasy is identical with the imagined satisfaction that accompanies childhood masturbation (1908e). In 1911, Freud (1911b) described how fantasy arises: "With the introduction of the reality principle, . . . (this) species of thought-activity was split off; it was kept free from reality-testing and remained subordinated to the pleasure principle alone." In Freud's view, it was the relatively sequestered nature of fantasy life, in close association with infantile sexual instincts, that accounts for the enduring impact of childhood wishes, ideas, and modes of cognition on adult mental life. Freud explored the role of fantasy in the formation of neurotic symptoms, delusions, perversion, and character traits, as well as dreams, daydreams, play, the sexual theories of children, slips of the tongue, creative acts, and mythology. Freud's most explicit formulations of fantasy predate the development of structural theory and were never fully integrated with it, contributing to long-standing ambiguities in the use of the term. For example, Freud saw fantasy as subject to repression and, therefore, as part of the unconscious; on other occasions, noting the secondary process logic of many fantasies, he saw fantasy as part of the system preconscious-conscious.

Modern ego psychologists regard fantasy as reflecting the creative and synthetic functions of the ego, which integrate instinctual wishes, superego demands, and defense in a compromise formation represented as a fantasy, with all fantasies also bearing the impact of veridical reality (Erreich, 2003). Object relations theorists and self psychologists have focused on the structuring influence of self and object representations. Furthermore, while Freud saw fantasy (like all forms of thought) as the result of frustration, most contemporary analysts see fantasy formation as an ongoing process beginning in childhood. Developmental challenges, childhood mysteries, emotionally important events, and trauma serve as special stimuli for fantasy formation. Fantasies are revised throughout life so that any given fantasy exists simultaneously in many different editions corresponding to different moments in an individual's history and reflecting the conflicts and cognitive capacities active at the time. In the adult, fantasies vary with respect to accessibility to consciousness, cognitive organization, and responsiveness to reality testing.

Ever since Freud's first formulations about the role of childhood sexual fantasy in the etiology of hysteria, psychoanalysts have privileged sexual fantasy as a particularly enduring influence on the individual's sexual behavior, personality, character, and orientation to life. **Core sexual organizing fantasies** or **masturbation fantasies** may take on different appearances and contents over time, but they retain their core structure throughout a patient's lifetime (Laufer, 1976). Often in psychoanalytic writing, **sexual fantasy** is used to describe conscious sexual fantasies, reported during psychoanalytic treatment. The reporting of sexual fantasies may have a variety of meanings in analytic work and may relate to core unconscious fantasies in a disguised or derivative manner (Person, 1995). Laplanche and Pontalis (1967/1973) refer to fantasy as the mise-en-scène of desire.

While an individual's fantasy life reflects his unique history and personal idiosyncrasies, there is a universal and shared quality to many fantasies. In contrast to Freud's concept of universal **primal fantasies** that are phylogenetically inherited, contemporary analysts see the shared aspect of fantasy as the result of universal biological imperatives and developmental experiences. In addition to core sexual organizing fantasies, common types of fantasy include fantasies of romantic gratification; fantasies of resounding success, great wealth, accomplishment, recognition, power, fame, or adulation; fantasies of expiation or reparation; fantasies of defeat, humiliation, or punishment; and fantasies of revenge or violence. Typical fantasies of childhood include fantasies that surround the mysteries of pregnancy, birth, and parental sexual life (primal scene); fantasies that surround universal wishes and fears (for example, incest, family romance, castration, penis and womb envy, and beating fantasies); and fantasies that represent the combination of wish and prohibition, often in "if-then" form (for example, "if I defeat Dad in this game, then he will attack and punish me"). The fact that human beings have fantasies in common contributes to our ability to understand and empathize with each other. E. Kris (1956a) described a kind of autobiographical fantasy to which a patient clings tendentiously, which he called the personal myth. Artistic creation is also made possible by the communality of fantasy, with the artist acting as the "daydreamer for the community" (Freud, 1908a; Arlow, 1986). Group formation and cohesion are facilitated by shared unconscious fantasies, which are often given expression in a culture's central myths (Arlow, 1995).

Ongoing controversy in the literature on fantasy includes the age at which fantasy formation is possible; the extent and type of organization of unconscious fantasy; the question of whether fantasy depends on language; and the extent to which narrative coherence might be added by the psychoanalytic conversation itself. One of the most important debates in the history of psychoanalysis (known as the Controversial Discussions of the British Psychoanalytic Society [King and Steiner, 1991]), between the followers of Klein and the Viennese analysts under the leadership of A. Freud, focused on the nature of fantasy. In these discussions, the Kleinians proposed a broad view of fantasy (for which they prefer the spelling *phantasy*), defining it as the direct mental expression of instinct, "the primary content of unconscious mental processes," occupying the position that Freud assigned to the unconscious wish (Isaacs, 1948). In this view, fantasy formation begins at birth, long before the development of language. The earliest fantasies are omnipotent and concrete, consisting of physical sensations, always interpreted as relationships with objects that cause those sensations. (For example, hunger is experienced as a bad object persecuting the infant from within; satisfaction is experienced as a blissful union with a good object.) Later fantasies, especially those related to projection, incorporation, and omnipotent control, serve as defenses against the anxieties that accompany the more primitive fantasies. In the Kleinian view, with maturation, fantasies become less connected with concrete bodily sensations and more symbolic as the child becomes increasingly able to differentiate between real and fantasied objects.

Whatever their theoretical differences, almost all psychoanalysts, including ego psychologists and Kleinians, place the exploration of unconscious fantasy at the center of psychoanalytic work. The perceptual ambiguity of the psychoanalytic situation maximizes the emergence of unconscious fantasy and allows for its interpretation. In the transference, the patient incorporates the analyst into his fantasies and attempts to enact them. Some schools of thought de-emphasize the role of unconscious fantasy, including interpersonal analysts who focus on the relationship between patient and analyst, and attachment theorists who emphasize "internal working models" of actual relationships (Bowlby, 1969/1982; D. N. Stern, 1985).

As early as the 1920s and 1930s, psychoanalytically oriented researchers used instruments such as the Rorschach Test or the Thematic Apperception Test to elicit fantasy for empirical study. In the field of psychology, the terms *schema/schemata* were introduced in 1932 to refer to a mental representation of experience (Bartlett, 1932). In the cognitive psychology of the 1970s, the idea of schemata was extended to explain how knowledge of more complex "event sequences" is represented in memory. Such knowledge structures were referred to as scripts (Tulving, 1972; Schank and Abelson, 1977; Tomkins, 1979). Cognitive psychology research on schemata and scripts has influenced a recent generation of psychoanalytic researchers, who have developed instruments designed to capture key elements of fantasy for empirical study, including Horowitz (1991) (Role-Relationship Model Configurations/RRMs); Luborsky (1984) (Core Conflictual Relationship Themes/CCRT); Trevarthen (1993) (relational scripts); Teller and Dahl (1981) (FRAMES); D. N. Stern (1985) (Representations of Interactions that have been Generalized/RIGs); Gill and Hoffman (1982) (Patient's Experience of the Relationship with the Therapist/PERT); and Sander (1997) (themes of organization).

Fate Neurosis/Fate Compulsion: see REPETITION COMPULSION

Father Hunger is an affective state of aggressive dysregulation and disorganization that occurs in young children whose fathers are absent, which can be reversed by the father's reappearance. The syndrome appears in very young boys as a night-terror-like phenomenon that seems to involve phobic mechanisms; it is manifested in older boys as an exaggerated identification with the father. Father hunger represents the boy's state of longing and need for his father, whose presence is necessary for the development of self structure, the completion of the separation-individuation process, the consolidation of core gender identity, and the management of intense affect, especially aggression. Herzog (1980; 1984; 2001), who coined the term, also described the implications of father hunger for the boy's sexuality and his ideas about the relationship between the sexes. Girls may also experience father hunger, but usually as a depressive state. For both boys and girls, at different stages, the father helps the child to negotiate the separation from mother. Other researchers corroborated observations about father hunger both empirically and clinically (Sugarman, 1997; Lamb, 2004). Father hunger underscores the father's role for both genders in the triangulation process and, for the boy, emphasizes his nonrivalrous relationship with his father.

Female Genital Anxieties are conscious and unconscious fears about damage to or loss of female body parts, as opposed to envy of and fantasies about loss of male attributes. These anxieties are often organized as unconscious fantasies whose conscious derivatives become evident in the clinical material of female patients. Some psychoanalytic theorists view the concept of female genital anxieties as replacing the phallic castration complex in women. Others view female genital anxieties and their associated fantasies as present along with fantasies of castration and penis envy (Olesker, 1998b). All such genital fantasies are rooted in the child's subjective experience of her own body, taking form within the context of the progressive differentiation of object relations and cognitive capacities, and in the awareness of anatomical differences. Early psychoanalytic views about female genital anxiety tended to focus on the little girl's (or the adult woman patient's) acceptance of her defectiveness or her position of inferiority. More contemporary views may retain the little girl's fantasies of being damaged and defective, but they place these fantasies in the context of her primary sense of femaleness and sense of possessing female genitalia. Contemporary views also emphasize societal influences that contribute to the girl's negative feelings about her own genitals.

The concept of female genital anxiety is a component of a revised psychoanalytic view of female psychology that arose as a critical reaction to Freud's early formulations about female development. Freud's early views erred in their phallocentrism, emphasizing the primacy of the phallus in the early development of both boys and girls, and centering the little girl's psychosexual development on penis envy and castration anxiety. Freud's views on female psychology became the nidus for global critiques of his theories by psychoanalysts of other theoretical orientations, as well as by critics outside the field. Early on, counterarguments were raised that girls have awareness of their own genitals, that their ideas of themselves are not confined to their distress over genital difference, and that they have anxieties and fears of damage to their female genitals (Jones, 1927, 1933; Horney, 1933). Contemporary psychoanalytic theoretical and clinical interest has moved from exclusive focus on what girls and women feel they lack, to include explorations of their fears about losing or damaging what they already possess. Central to this contemporary view is the concept of primary femininity, which establishes a distinctively female developmental pathway. The concept of primary femininity has itself been criticized for its lack of conceptual clarity; its conflation of biological, cultural, and psychological contributions; and its replacement of a phallocentric reductionism with a vaginocentric one.

D. Bernstein (1993) first coined the term *female genital anxiety* and articulated three specific anxieties, including fear of access, fear of diffusivity, and fear of penetration. Fear of access refers to the girl's sense that she does not have ready access to her vagina, which she cannot easily see or manipulate in a nonsexualized way, or which she cannot examine to determine whether her masturbation has caused damage. Fear of diffusivity refers to the nature of female sexual sensations, which spread rather than focus, challenging the little girl's effort to articulate her body image and evoking a sense of feeling uncontrolled, overwhelmed, and disintegrated (Bornstein, 1953; Fraiberg, 1972). Fear of penetration is especially prominent during the oedipal period, when girls fear damage to their small bodies in fantasies of the exciting, penetrating, large paternal penis. They feel themselves to have a vulnerable opening over which they have no control; during adolescence, they have a feeling of wetness, which they also cannot control.

Richards (1992) asserted that girls acquire a sense of control over their vaginal sphincter during toilet training, inherent in the ability to flex the perineal musculature, which also plays its role in the development of female genital awareness and sensation. The contraction of sphincter muscles during toilet training results in spreading sexual excitement, which is experienced as pleasurable. Richards also asserted that girls fear loss of their capacity for sexual excitement as a punishment for forbidden oedipal wishes. In adult women, Richards (1996) described anxieties about painful penetration, loss of pleasure, and loss of function, that is, being unable to have intercourse or bear a child.

Mayer (1995) added anxiety about the loss or closing of the genital opening, and allied anxieties about the loss of openness as a valued personality trait. She posited two separate lines of development, one rooted in primary femininity, and the other rooted in the phallic castration complex. For Mayer, conflicts about primary femininity involve fantasies of danger to the female genital, which is possessed; by contrast, the phallic castration complex involves a depressive fantasy about the loss of the male genital, which has already occurred.

Lax (1994) distinguished between primary and secondary genital anxieties, but not in terms of two separate lines of development. Like Horney (1924, 1926), she viewed primary genital anxiety, or the fear of losing the genitals the little girl possesses, as an early phenomenon; secondary genital anxieties, which can be equated with the so-called phallic castration feelings, come later in reaction to the girl's discovery that she lacks a penis.

Based on the evaluation of developmental and clinical data, Olesker (1998b) identified both female genital anxiety and the more traditional phallic castration anxiety in little girls. She argued that both fantasies occur along a developmental continuum, rather than representing separate lines of development. She described castration anxiety emerging at the end of the second year, along with the perception of anatomical differences. Female genital anxiety emerges somewhat later, during the latter part of the third year, along with the emergence of the oedipal phase. Olesker also demonstrated the presence in adult women of female genital anxieties and the castration complex, along with oedipal and bisexual conflicts.

Fetish/Fetishism: see IDEALIZATION, PERVERSION, INFANTILE GENITAL PHASE, TRANSVESTISM

Fixation: see DEVELOPMENT, HYSTERIA, LIBIDO, NEUROSIS, PSYCHOSEXUAL DEVELOPMENT, REGRESSION

Flight refers to a group of defensive processes whereby internal conflict or other problematic intrapsychic content is avoided through escape into other experiences. The concept of flight was discussed by A. Freud (1936) as typical of older children and adolescents who have access to action as well as to fantasy for the purpose of defense. The psychoanalytic literature includes explorations of several maneuvers that involve flight: S. Freud described **flight from reality** as typical of psychosis (1894c); he described **flight into illness** in hysteria symptoms that mimic illness as a defense against unconscious conflict (1909b). In contrast, in **flight into health**, symptomatic improvement may serve to avoid psychoanalytic exploration of unconscious conflict or lead to premature termination (Fenichel, 1945; Rangell 1992; Bergmann, 1997). **Flight into fantasy** was described by Freud (1917c) in his discussion of normal mourning as involving transitory immersion in fantasies in which the loss of the object is denied. Indeed all kinds of psychic refuge can be sought in flight into fantasy (Isaacs, 1933). Flight into fantasy may also represent a resistance to the analysis, disguised as compliance; for example, an excessive focus on transference fantasies may serve to keep painful realities and affects out of the treatment

(Blum, 1983). In contrast, the **flight into reason**, typical of obsessional personalities, may serve as a defense against emotional experience (Fenichel, 1932).

Fragmentation: see ANXIETY, BION, KLEIN, SELF PSYCHOLOGY, SPLITTING

Free Association is a form of mental activity achieved when a patient attempts to suspend conscious control over his subjective mental experience, thereby rendering it "free," and communicates that experience without censorship to the analyst. In psychoanalytic treatment, the directive to the patient to free associate is closely associated with what Freud called the "fundamental rule," or the directive to the patient to communicate all his thoughts to the analyst with as little censorship as possible (Freud, 1910a, 1912b). The use of free association derives from the theoretical principle of psychic determinism, that is, the principle that all mental events are caused by antecedent mental events and that there is an unconscious connection or "association" between two or more mental elements. When a patient associates freely and can attend to aspects of his experience that he would ordinarily dismiss or avoid, he is more directly self revealing, and both patient and analyst may note unexpected associative links apparent in the sequence of thoughts. Furthermore, the analyst can make inferences about the unconscious associative links that underlie and partially determine the patient's ongoing conscious, subjective experience. Analyst and patient also attend to evidence of unconscious resistances, that is, interferences in the patient's free associations that arise when warded-off conflictual mental content threatens to enter the patient's associative flow. The patient will inevitably struggle with conscious resistances, such as feelings of embarrassment, fear, shame, and guilt that prompt him to interrupt or alter his communication. Free association is facilitated by the use of the couch, the frequency of sessions, the analyst's nondirective stance, and relative silence. The analyst's interventions, especially the interpretation of transference or other resistances, facilitate free association by increasing the patient's acceptance of previously threatening aspects of his mental life.

When Freud introduced free association as a therapeutic technique, he initiated psychoanalysis as a unique treatment. His introduction of free association was a major technical advance because it provides the means by which the mind's dynamic processes can be observed at work. For both patient and analyst, free association provides the data of the method, offering a view into the interplay of mo-

tives and meanings that constitute the patient's ongoing mental concerns. In contemporary psychoanalytic schools that view psychic determinism as a key feature of mental life, free association remains a crucial part of the clinical method. While Freud viewed resistance as an obstacle to free association, the goals of free association are now seen in terms of the understanding of patients' transferences and character defenses as manifested in their struggles with the task of free association, all within the context of the analytic situation. The technique of free association is also associated with some controversy. Relational and interpersonal analysts, who focus on the exploration of meaning in the interpersonal analytic dyad, have generally de-emphasized free association because of its connection to a "one-person" psychology; however, several theorists have noted the value of free association even within a relational view of psychoanalytic treatment (Aron, 1990).

Freud gradually discovered the method of free association between 1892 and 1895, with the help of his patients; his first case example demonstrating free association was in 1907 (Freud, 1914d; Mahony, 1979). Freud first replaced hypnosis with "directed free association," a technique in which his patients were required "to associate" to their symptoms. Freud hypothesized that as his patients associated, he would hear associative chains that ultimately connected the symptom with a warded-off memory. When Freud's patients objected to the intrusions of his "directed free association," he began to utilize free, or undirected, association to bring the repressed material to consciousness.

Freud recommended free association in the context of the topographic view of the mind in which the goal of treatment was to make the unconscious, conscious. Freud (1914c) did note that resistances were not only obstacles to free association but were themselves meaningful repetitions of transference attitudes. However, he continued to advocate for overcoming resistances (1926a) rather than understanding them in greater depth. This remained true even after he shifted to the structural theory, which gave greater importance to the ego and superego in the formation of symptoms, character, and resistances. It was not until W. Reich's *Character Analysis* (1933/1945) and A. Freud's *The Ego and the Mechanisms of Defence* (1936) that the analysis of resistance was given a more central role in analytic technique. This was accompanied by a greater focus on uncovering present unconscious functioning rather than reconstructing the past. Sullivan (1953b), who founded the interpersonal school of psychoanalysis, entirely rejected the technique of free association, replacing it with a "detailed inquiry" into the patient's actual interpersonal experience, past and present. Detailed inquiry is a form of "participant observation" on the part of the analyst, whose personal involvement was regarded by Sullivan as inevitable.

For most analysts, psychoanalytic technique has shifted away from the role division of a passive/associating patient and an active/interpreting analyst, to an analytic dyad in which both patient and analyst contribute to interpretation and in which the patient's active self reflection is valued (A. Kris, 1990). However, psychoanalysts differ in their approaches to free association. Some analysts, who utilize the technique of close process attention, focus on the moment-to-moment shifts in associations, inviting patients to reflect on that experience, thereby giving the patient's self reflection a central role (Gray, 1973). Other analysts listen for the unconscious themes underlying a sequence of associations.

Fundamental Rule: see FREE ASSOCIATION

Fusion: see AGGRESSION, DEATH DRIVE, DRIVE, EGO, ENERGY, LIBIDO, SUBLIMATION

G

Gender Identity is a consistent inner experience of one's **gender** as male or female, multiply determined by biological, psychodynamic, and social components. As such, gender identity is a complex experience that demonstrates how mental representations of self, other, and self in relation to the other are co-constructed in the context of an individual's relationships over the course of life and, most importantly, that the self is always consciously and unconsciously gendered. Gender identity builds upon **core gender identity**, the most primitive sense of belonging to one biological sex and not the other, solidified by the end of the second year of life, and usually unchanging once it has been established. A gender identity perceived as deviating from the prevailing norms, on the one hand, or the wished-for self image, on the other, can be a source of extreme discomfort for an individual. In this regard, the word *abnormal* serves as the carrier of social bias, values, and fear. **Gender role** is the external expression of gender identity, which inevitably reflects the cultural role expectations associated with concepts of masculinity and femininity. Core gender identity, gender identity, and sexual orientation all contribute to the consolidation of sexual identity, which begins to form unconsciously during the oedipal phase of development and consciously coalesces during adolescence, when erotic desires become conscious, experienced, and knowable (Frankel and Sherick, 1979; Roiphe and Galenson, 1981b).

The concept of gender is an issue that challenges the limits of psychoanalytic theorizing. While gender issues figured centrally in the earliest psychoanalytic theories of psychosexual development, they have elicited controversy from the beginning. Long-standing nature/nurture debates along with a contemporary move toward the deconstruction of gender, both within popular culture as well as among some psychoanalytic theorists, have left many unanswered questions about the fundamental premises of gender theory. More recent contributions have argued for a psychoanalytic theory of gender that recognizes the actual degree and frequency of variance in human gender experience and expression (Corbett, 1996, 2009b; Ehrensaft, 2007). Gender concepts also trench upon efforts to explicate notions of the self and its development throughout the life cycle.

The term *gender* has its origins in a grammatical categorization of nouns, pronouns, and verbs that dates back to Roman times. The classification of words as male, female, or neuter was based upon nature (man as masculine) or on arbitrary prescriptive usage. Although strictly applied to word usage, gender's etymological link to other Latin words involving race and procreation has been noted by scientists and linguists. Although Freud lacked the vocabulary to distinguish clearly between the concepts of sex and gender, he attempted to delineate concepts of masculinity and femininity and to make a distinction between gendered mental characteristics and object choice. Freud's theory of psychosexual development has been criticized on the basis of gender related issues, that is, because of its phallocentric view of female development. He asserted that central to the little girl's psychosexual development is her awareness of genital inadequacy and her attempts to reconcile it. Contemporaries of Freud challenged his theory on the grounds that it lacked concepts of primary femininity, which might provide ways to conceptualize the girl's feelings about her body, her sexual desires, and her object relationships in more positive and accurate terms (Horney, 1924, 1933; Jones, 1927, 1933).

It was not until the sexual research of Money and Hampson (1955) that the term *gender* was used in the context of human distinctions. Money was attempting to define and understand the complexities of human **gender identity differentiation** through his work with intersexed and hermaphroditic individuals, and he sought to explain how it would develop in individuals born with ambiguous genitalia. Feeling constrained by the limitations of terms such as *sexual orientation* or *sexual development,* Money created the term **gender role** to acknowledge the nongenital and nonerotic aspects of gender. This term encompasses aspects of social behavior, mental content including fantasy and dreams, projective tests, and self identification, as well as erotic behavior. Money (1965) later defined the concept of **gender identity** as the private inner experience of gender role, to distinguish it from more outward or public manifestations.

Money was influenced by Stoller's extensive work with intersexed individuals. Stoller (1964) had created controversy when he published his evidence that core gender identity, which he defined as a fundamental sense of knowing one's sex as male or female, was primarily determined by the actual **gender assignment** given at birth and the subsequent parental belief and influence based upon that assignment, regardless of genetic sex. Although Stoller did not dismiss the contributions of genital anatomy, physical sensations, or biological influences, he repeatedly demonstrated that these influences were secondary to the profound effects created by the parental belief about their child's gender. Both Money and Stoller recognized that the process of gender identity differentiation—that most basic sense of boyness or girlness—was set in motion prenatally with the influence of parental expectations (conscious and unconscious).

The precursors of gender identity are the body ego, the early body image, and the sense of me/not me within the mother/infant dyad. Gender identity is developed from the extension, elaboration, and integration of these precursors into a male and female self representation. The child's own gender differentiation development is a uniquely personal and multidimensional process begun by eighteen months and generally completed by age four and one-half. Subsequent studies with young children (Coates, 1997; DeMarneffe, 1997) have confirmed that the **gendered identity** of a boy or girl precedes the oedipal phase and evolves prior to the recognition of genital difference postulated as so essential by Freud (1905b). Gender identity should be distinguished from sexual identity, a later refinement that is consolidated during adolescence and is marked by the elaboration of concepts of masculininty and femininity (as distinct from basic maleness and femaleness) and by a personal erotism expressed in sexual fantasies and object choice.

Psychoanalysts (Stoller, 1967; Ovesey and Person, 1973; Schafer, 1974; Benedict, 1976; Fast, 1978; P. Tyson, 1982a) throughout the 1960s, 1970s, and 1980s continued to reformulate and revise classical theory, fueling debate about the essence of gender: Was gender natured or nurtured? Was it essentially determined or constructively made? Did gender define sexual orientation or coexist with it? Gender soon established its usefulness in similar debates within anthropology, sociology, political science, philosophy, and neuroscience. Feminist theorists (Chodorow, 1994c; Kulish, 1998; Elise, 2000; Marshall, 2000; Gilligan, 2002; Goldner, 2005; Harris, 2005b; Layton, 2002; Toronto, 2005) found the cultural, societal, and political implications of gender theoretically useful. Gender could be explored and

appreciated as what one "does" within a family or society, one's **gender behavior**, and not just as a label that designated what one "ought" to be. Postmodernism (Gabbard, 1996; Layton, 2000; Goldner, 1991) and "Queer Theory" (G. Grossman, 2002) questioned the validity and purpose of traditional gender categories. Chaos theory (Harris, 2005b) has provided a compelling model to explore how a phenomenon such as gender can be both intricately patterned and yet dynamic, or rigidly fixed and then reorganized by subtle shifts. Current developmental literature (Mayes, 1999; Kirkpatrick, 2003) continues to contribute to the psychoanalytic understanding of the complex bidirectional interactions between biology and experience, rendering the "nature or nurture question" outdated.

Still, there is controversy about what a psychoanalytic gender theory should contain or mean. There are analysts who fear the "loss of sex and the psychoanalytic body" (Robbins, 1996) and see gender as a politically correct concession to those who deny biology. There is uncertainty about how stable a gendered identity should be. Is gender fluidity "better" for individuals? Is **transgenderedness** "normal"? The complexity of being a gendered person within a given society, family, or relationship can seem arbitrary, and yet such a categorization is required at birth. "Is it a boy or a girl?" is a question that demands an immediate answer (Toronto, 2005). Do we understand the intense interpersonal and intrapsychic distress that seems to surround any uncertainty about gender? The use of gender terminology, replete with its multiple meanings of categorizing and sexuality, continues to offer psychoanalysis a multilayered access to questions about the nature and meanings of uncertainty in human gendered categories and experience.

The pervasive reference to gender in recent psychoanalytic writing (thirty-one issues of professional journals in 1998 with *gender* in the titles [Kirkpatrick, 2003]) reflects the growing acceptance and utility of the terminology. Although definitions of *gender* vary, they do contain Money's original acknowledgment of the interweaving of private experience and public expression in the formation of a gendered identity. Gender terminology (core gender identity, gender identity, gender role) permits psychoanalysts to explore a broader spectrum of human behaviors and expressions of identity as they are experienced within an individual's "core" and evolve within the cultural environment.

Gender Identity Disorder (GID), a controversial term, has been used to refer to a childhood syndrome involving the child's persistent wish to be the opposite gender and associated deep suffering because of his or her gender assignment. GID manifests early in the second year of life and consolidates between the ages of two and three. The intensity of the child's gender dysphoria results in profound and often disabling suffering. Boys with the syndrome are referred for treatment much more frequently than girls, and psychoanalytically informed studies of the phenomenon have focused mostly on boys (Greenson, 1966; Pruett and Dahl, 1982; Coates, 1990; Coates, Friedman, and Wolfe, 1991; Silverman and Bernstein, 1993; Coates and Wolfe, 1995; Gilmore, 1995).

GID has become a contested term within psychoanalysis and psychiatry, both with regard to etiology and with regard to the clinical presentation to which it is applied. There are those theorists who would apply the diagnosis narrowly to a very rare and severe syndrome, and those who would apply it to the entire spectrum of clinical presentations, from those whose experience of gender is mildly atypical to the most severe cases. There are also those theorists who entirely reject its validity as a pathological syndrome. The controversy surrounding this diagnostic entity illustrates the contemporary debate about the validity of a variety of gender constructs and gender related diagnoses. The challenge to more traditional views about gender, which have arisen from within and from outside the psychoanalytic community, assert that gender is more variable and complex than previously acknowledged. Furthermore, traditional views have failed to adequately parse the influences of culture, biology, and psychological factors that determine outcome in any individual (Minter, 1999; N. Bartlett, Vassey, and Bukowski, 2000; Langer and Martin, 2004; Corbett, 2009a; Meyer-Bahlburg, 2010; Zucker, 2010).

First classified in the *Diagnostic and Statistical Manual* (3rd edition), gender identity disorder was introduced into the psychoanalytic literature by Friend et al. (1954). Coates, in whose clinic hundreds of boys with GID have been treated and who is one of a few psychoanalytically informed researchers who has studied this subject, has concluded that the consuming wish to be a girl and the gender crossing serve as a rigid defense against separation anxiety and rage, involving a self-fusion fantasy with the mother, which becomes compulsively enacted. In this view, GID is a complex form of attachment disorder involving identification with the problematic parent, which alters the gendered self. Coates and her colleagues have also suggested that the possibility of gender identity disturbance increases if the infant experiences trauma, or if the mother experiences trauma and is unavailable to the infant or small child. These researchers have also cited an increased risk in the case of a male child if he is of a timid constitution and hypersensitive, making him in need of especially sensitive attunement and more vulnerable to separation or loss (Coates, 1990; Coates, Friedman, and Wolfe, 1991; Coates and Wolfe, 1995).

Corbett (2008, 2009a, 2009b), incorporating into his work some views drawn from contemporary studies of gender, questioned the broad applicability of this explanation (see also Drescher, 2009). Corbett viewed the struggles of boys who lay claim to cross-gender experiences as the manifestation of natural variance in human gender expression before it is suppressed. In his view, the boys' interests are at odds with what is considered normal masculinity, as traditionally defined within a strong and oppressive binary system of gender behavior regulation. While it is broadly agreed that boys with GID are treated for an underlying attachment disorder that causes deep suffering and not for their gender role preferences, Corbett asserted that how the boy challenges the social order may too easily be mistaken for pain. He emphasized that psychoanalytic theories of sexual and object relations development, embodied in myths like the Oedipus one, are predicated on a binary categorization of gender expectations that is not only contrary to subjective experience but also highly restrictive of true self expression and creativity. Contemporary gender theorists such as Corbett view gender as self constructed but stress its fluid, even chaotic, quality through the life cycle (Harris, 1991, 2005a; Chodorow 1994b, 2002).

Widespread observation confirms that most "feminine" boys do not meet the criteria for a gender identity disorder, nor is cross-dressing in young children necessarily indicative of pathology. R. Friedman (1988) concluded from his study of healthy gay men that many recall being "feminine" or "nonmasculine" as children. Isay (1989), who stressed the biological base for homosexuality, interpreted that "feminine"-appearing traits may be observed in little boys with a predisposition for being gay, in an effort to woo their fathers. Many heterosexual boys express "feminine" interests, as well. The quotation marks around "feminine" reflect the perspective of many contemporary gender theorists who assert that the commonly accepted binary model of gender does not accurately describe the variability and complexity of experiences in people.

Generativity: see EMPATHY, ERIKSON'S STAGES

Genetic Viewpoint: see DEVELOPMENT, METAPSYCHOLOGY, RECONSTRUCTION, REGRESSION

Genitality or **Genital Primacy** is the final phase in Freud's schema of psychosexual development during which oral, anal, and phallic urges are subordinated under the primacy of the genital zone (1938a). While the beginning of development of genital primacy occurs during the phallic stage around the fourth year of life, it is not until adolescence that full genitality emerges in the service of reproduction. The concept of genitality or genital primacy has fallen out of use in contemporary psychoanalytic writings because of a shift in emphasis from a focus on sexual function to a focus on the maturity of object relations. In addition, while early formulations took for granted that psychosexual development leads to heterosexuality, a contemporary concept of genitality can also be applied to mature homosexual love.

Freud (1912d) defined a "completely normal attitude in love" as one that combines the factors of the sensual and the affectionate and rests on genital primacy. Abraham (1924b) suggested that genital primacy is correlated with the final "post-ambivalent" step in the evolution of object-love. Fenichel (1945) elaborated the relational and developmental aspects of genitality, adding considerations about object relationships. He described the evolution from early pregenital strivings to genital primacy from the perspective of both the change of the leading erogenous zones and from the change of the type of object relationships. M. Balint (1948) described genital love as genital satisfaction combined with idealization and pregenital tenderness. Erikson's "utopia of genitality" (1950) included a loving partnership within which one is able and willing to regulate the cycles of work, procreation, and recreation so as to secure satisfactory development to the offspring. N. Ross (1970) argued that in many individuals there is no correspondence between the capacity for mature relationships and for achieving orgasm, and that the relationship between levels of functioning in the genital sphere and in the area of ego activities is highly complex.

Good Enough Mother: see AVERAGE EXPECTABLE ENVIRONMENT, WINNICOTT

Grandiosity: see EXHIBITIONISM, IDEALIZATION, MAGICAL THINKING, NARCISSISM, OMNIPOTENCE, PSYCHOSIS, SELF IN SELF PSYCHOLOGY, SELF PSYCHOLOGY, SELFOBJECT

Gratitude: see KLEIN

Grief: see DEPRESSION, MOURNING

Guilt is a complex affect whose core of anxiety is linked to specific ideational contents involving moral transgressions. Failure to live up to the standards of the superego, typically due to sexual or aggressive transgressions, results in guilty feelings and associated fantasies of punishment and atonement through mental or physical suffering. Guilt is the affective experience associated with intersystemic conflict between the strivings of ego and superego. The experience of guilt may be entirely unconscious and may become apparent only through the analysis of its psychological and behavioral effects. Guilt should be distinguished from shame, an affect evoked by experiences of narcissistic failure or inadequacy, often in the context of exposure to others that is not connected to issues of morality. The experience of guilt is a developmental milestone because it requires that superego formation has occurred. In Kleinian theory, the capacity for guilt indicates attainment of the depressive position.

Guilt is both a highly adaptive social achievement and, particularly in its unconscious form, a major source of clinical pathology. Achievement of the capacity for guilt allows for the true assumption of responsibility for regulating one's impulses. However, unconscious guilt may trigger a variety of defensive operations, such as: reaction formation, either in the form of emphasized nonaggressiveness or, conversely, a lack of caring about others; turning of passive into active via provocation of guilt in others; projection, in which others are accused of intents or acts about which one feels guilty oneself; and displacement, such that the individual's experience of guilt about one issue may obscure a more intense guilt about another. Guilt also has clinical significance in relationship to: depression (a generalized mood state that is often triggered by the experience of moral failure, guilt, and associated self-directed aggression); the negative therapeutic reaction, in which unconscious guilt and the need to suffer may proscribe therapeutic gain; delinquent behavior; and other forms of self-inflicted suffering.

In Freud's "Three Essays on the Theory of Sexuality" (1905b), guilt (though not specified by that term) is one of the inherent, biologically, and phylogenetically determined "dams" erected as reaction formations against infantile libidinal trends. In this paper, Freud noted that social and cultural norms (for example, education) also contribute to the erection of these dams. Thus, guilt is seen as both biologically and socially determined, with the accent on the former. Starting with "Totem and Taboo," Freud (1913e) considered guilt to be synonymous with "social anxiety" and "fear of the community." In "Group

Psychology and the Analysis of the Ego," Freud (1921) linked social anxiety with what is called conscience. In "The Ego and the Id," Freud (1923a) developed a theory of the endogenous origin of morality. Superego formation occurs with the resolution of the oedipus complex, pertaining most centrally to impulsions toward incest and parenticide; superego formation is accompanied by the capacity for guilt. Thus Freud viewed morality as having both internal and external origins, together operating synergistically. Internally, guilt is seen as reflecting a tension between ego, as executor of the drives, and the superego, as the vehicle of internal morality. In his evolving theory, "social anxiety" became the moralistic fear of other people's disapproval, initially that of the parents, or the dread of losing love, thus indicating that it precedes the existence of a true internal conscience or superego (Freud, 1930). In a more clinical vein, Freud (1916) described "**criminals from a sense of guilt**," or individuals whose transgressions follow the experience of guilt (arising from unconscious oedipal conflicts), which then serve both as a rationalization for the crime as well as a means to secure the relief from guilt through punishment. He also described character types who experience insufficient guilt and consider themselves to be "exceptions." In this last description, Freud began the exploration of individuals and personality types characterized by impairments in the capacity for guilt, such as narcissistic personality disorders and psychopathy.

Freud also postulated a developmental line of danger situations: loss of the object; loss of the love of the object; castration anxiety, associated with the oedipus complex; and guilt, which begins to operate after the establishment of the superego. Castration anxiety and guilt often appear to be identical, as the child's castration anxiety is experienced as the punishment he expects for his rivalrous oedipal aggression. The critical distinction, however, is that the experience of guilt requires the internalization of morality, which functions as a depersonified set of moral standards. Clinically, the distinction is more difficult to delineate, as superego precursors precede the formation of the superego proper, and superego regressions occur throughout the life cycle.

The notion of guilt is closely associated with the "need for punishment" (Nunberg, 1926, 1934), although this may confuse the cause with its effect. Guilt may be experienced regressively, in a personified manner, as a consequence of the superego's developmental origin through the internalization of parental authority. This can result in fantasies of punishment, or efforts at obviating punishment in the context of an interpersonal relationship with a parental figure.

Klein (1935) described the depressive position, a specific configuration of object relations, anxieties, and defenses that persists throughout life, characterized by guilty fears of destruction of the object due to one's own aggression, and by linked efforts at reparation. Guilt then represents a developmental capacity in object relations not possible in the paranoid schizoid position. In Klein's view, the capacity for guilt is thought to occur significantly earlier than in most other contemporary perspectives on development. Winnicott (1958a) considered a healthy person to be capable of the "capacity for concern" for the object, a concept that he preferred to guilt. Kohut (1977) used the terms "**guilty man**" and "tragic man" as shorthand to distinguish paradigms of conflict theory within classical psychoanalysis from defect conceptualizations in self psychology. These terms point to the centrality of the guilt concept within the classical paradigm and its markedly diminished significance within self psychology.

H

Hatching: see SEPARATION-INDIVIDUATION

Hate: see AGGRESSION, AMBIVALENCE, DEATH DRIVE, LOVE

Hermeneutics is the theory, practice, and/or art of interpretation. Traditional hermeneutics was the practice of explicating the meaning of ancient texts, especially those with symbolic significance or multiple levels of meaning, the most obvious example being ancient biblical texts. Contemporary, or modern, hermeneutics encompasses not only issues involving interpretation of written texts but the interpretation of all human modes of communication. Contemporary hermeneutic philosophy pays special attention to how language conveys meaning and how language shapes understanding. Prominent hermeneutic philosophers include Dilthey, Heidegger, Gadamer, Habermas, and, to some extent, Ricoeur.

In the last thirty years, hermeneutic philosophy has been applied to psychoanalysis in several ways. In the 1980s, largely in response to critique of the scientific status of psychoanalysis, several prominent psychoanalysts turned to hermeneutic philosophy in an effort to find a new way to conceptualize psychoanalytic practice and theory-making. For example, Spence (1982) argued that psychoanalytic interpretation does not strive for validity or truth-seeking in the usual sense of scientific inquiry but rather aims to produce "narratives," or "stories," that offer a plausible new perspective to the patient. He referred to these accounts as "narrative truth" as contrasted with "historical truth." Schafer (1983) delineated the hermeneutic aspects of psychoanalytic interpretation, exploring criteria such as narrative consistency and coherence, critiquing the traditional view of interpretation as stemming from objective observation.

Since then, ideas borrowed from hermeneutic philosophy have become part of many controversies within psychoanalysis, including controversies over the very nature of the field. The most intense, polarized arguments have been over whether psychoanalysis is best understood as a scientific discipline or as a hermeneutic discipline. The difference between these two options has been framed in terms of controversy over whether psychoanalysis is fundamentally scientific or humanistic; aims to explain causes or to understand meanings; emphasizes the general and abstract (nomothetic) or the unique and particular (idiopathic) aspects of psychological life; and/ or searches for objective truth or accepts the idea that there is no reality beyond the subjective. In an effort to reconcile these polarized positions, Gill (1976) suggested that the clinical process is hermeneutic (in that it is based on interpretation), but that this process can be studied scientifically; therefore, psychoanalysis should be called a **hermeneutic science**.

Strong critics of a hermeneutic view of psychoanalysis have argued that while the criteria of narrative coherence may guide the process of validating interpretation in daily clinical work, these criteria are insufficient for the purpose of validating the general psychoanalytical theory of the mind (Rubovits-Seitz, 1992). Others have expressed concern that the **hermeneutic turn** (Edelson, 1985) in psychoanalysis threatens to isolate the field from the rest of mind science (Eagle, 1984; Eagle, Wolitzky, and Wakefield, 2001; Shevrin, 2003; Grünbaum, 2006; Wallerstein, 2009). L. Friedman (2000) expressed agreement with Ricoeur (1970), who argued that psychoanalysis is a unique mix of hermeneutics and science, a hybrid theory that includes both "meaning" and "force." Friedman suggested that while psychoanalytic theory and practice require abstract and general theories about the mind, hermeneutic philosophy does offer "some healthy advice for psychoanalysts," which includes the ideas that: 1) narrative may be used as a premise for understanding human meaning and action; 2) dialogue can produce discovery and change; 3) psychoanalysis must be humble in its claims to understanding; 4) analysts must accept the impossibility of capturing the patient's unique meaning; 5) understanding does not come from fitting the patient's production into a stock formula; 6) aesthetic sensibilities can be useful in clinical work; 7) theory-makers must be skeptical about fixed categories. There are always alternative abstractions available.

Heterosexuality is a sexual orientation in which the individual is erotically attracted to members of the opposite sex. In their everyday language, psychoanalysts, like others, contrast heterosexuality (attraction to other gender) and homosexuality (attraction to same gender) as two forms of sexual object choice. In clinical practice, this easy distinction falls apart. *Heterosexuality* and *homosexuality* are terms that lack clarity from a psychoanalytic perspective because either may refer to mental experience as expressed in fantasy, conscious or unconscious, and/or to behavior. Furthermore, the relationship between fantasy and behavior is not well understood. Although contemporary psychoanalysts vary in the extent to which they believe that sexual orientation is biological, they generally concur that the specifics of any one person's sexual object choice can only be understood on the individual level.

The concept of heterosexuality is important in psychoanalysis because all issues related to sexual orientation have undergone significant revision over the last several decades. With the increased interest in homosexuality in the medical profession and society, many assumptions about sexual object choice have been reformulated. Many of Freud's ideas about sexuality were radical in their day, and his views on psychosexuality changed forever the notions of its role in mental life. However, some psychoanalytic views about sexual orientation have been the source of considerable controversy. Recent contributions have aimed to be less dogmatic and to incorporate broader, less categorical, and less pejorative views of sexual orientation.

Freud (1905b) introduced the complexity and individuality of sexual orientation early in his writings. He proposed continuity rather than discontinuity between homo- and heterosexual object choice, in that everyone has both homosexual and heterosexual libidinal attachments in his unconscious. Heterosexual object choice is just as restricted in choice (whom one wants as a sexual partner) and aim (what one wants to do with that partner) as is homosexual object choice, since both, according to Freud, involve a "tyranny" of one object and aim. Thus, Freud invited his readers to be as curious about exclusive heterosexuality as about exclusive homosexuality. Freud (1920b) also distinguished between masculine and feminine identity (gender identity), on the one hand, and sexual orientation (choice of sexual love object), on the other. He disrupted the notion that being masculine always goes along with choosing a female partner, and vice versa for women, noting that a conventionally masculine, "active" man may find himself desiring male partners, while a more feminine, "passive" man may be exclusively heterosexual.

In his later work on the oedipus complex, Freud (1924b) described the "complete" oedipus complex, in which the boy both takes the mother as a love object and sees the father as a rival (the positive oedipal) and takes the father as love object and sees the mother as a rival (the negative oedipal). In his writings on femininity (1931a, 1933a), following the work of female colleagues (for example, Lampl-De Groot [1927]), Freud noticed that for women, in particular, early and deep attachment to the mother persists through all the stages of development, sometimes in conflict with and sometimes in coexistence with attachment to the father and men. He saw this attachment as problematic, a failure to resolve the oedipus complex (Freud, 1933a; P. Bernstein, 2004). H. Deutsch (1944) called this situation the women's "bisexual triangle." Chodorow (1978) challenged this view, identifying the continuing attachment to the mother and to women in heterosexual women as an important ingredient in both object choice and maternality. Her revised view of female development (1994a), like that of Kulish and Holtzman (1998; 2008), echoes the mythic pattern of Persephone.

Chodorow (1999; Chodorow and Hacker, 2003) also argued that clinically, and hence theoretically, it is necessary to talk about sexualities in the plural: heterosexualities and homosexualities. Every heterosexual person has an even more specific sexual orientation, in which only some people of the other gender, some fantasies, and some activities characterize that person's heterosexuality. A heterosexual woman is not attracted to all men, nor vice versa. Any person's heterosexuality is composed of a number of ingredients that make his or her sexuality unique. These factors include what that person finds erotic, based on bodily feelings and body image, arousal thresholds, and innate propensities toward one or another object choice; preferred sexual practices and the extent to which these are arousing, driven, obligatory, or freely chosen; an internal world that reflects both sexual and nonsexual early childhood and adolescent representations and emotions about self and other; particular affective tonalities concerning how sexuality may be laden with excitement, depression, shame, fear, anger, and resentment, and how driven or not driven it is; sexual-gender identity and sense of self; fantasies about sexual objects; and an internalized and personalized filtration of cultural stories, myths, and images of sexual-love connections.

Person (1999) proposed that sexual excitement or passion is generated by a driving personal fantasy that is developed relatively early and is relatively unchangeable. This fantasy brings together all the factors that make up the person's more specific sexual orientation. Personal fantasies may include aggression as well as lust, fantasies of power and domination or submission, the desire to harm or retaliate for humiliation, the management of anxiety about sexual performance through power, and so forth. Thus, for the psychoanalyst in the consulting room, "heterosexuality," and "homosexuality" are compromise formations in which wishes, fantasies, and fears are put together in a unique way. Psychoanalysts can sometimes help a person reconstruct, but they cannot easily predict how, among all these factors, an individual ends up primarily homosexual or primarily heterosexual.

Holding/Holding Environment: see ABSTINENCE, THERAPEUTIC ACTION, WINNICOTT

Homosexuality and **Lesbianism** (see below) are sexual orientations in which the individual is erotically attracted to members of the same sex. In their everyday language, psychoanalysts, like others, contrast heterosexuality and homosexuality as two forms of sexual object choice: heterosexual (other gender) or homosexual (same gender). In clinical practice, this easy distinction falls apart. Homosexuality and heterosexuality are terms that lack clarity from a psychoanalytic perspective, because either may refer to mental experience, conscious or unconscious, and/or to behavior. Furthermore, the relationship of sexual fantasy, conscious or unconscious, to sexual orientation is not well understood. Although contemporary psychoanalysts vary in the extent to which they believe that sexual orientation is biological, they generally concur that the specifics of any one person's sexual object choice can only be understood on the individual level. The impact on personality development of cultural attitudes toward homosexuality often contributes to the homosexual's psychic organization, conflicts, and personality attributes. Psychoanalytic theorizing about homosexuality has mostly focused on the male, but more contemporary work has broadened to include female homosexuality. *Gay,* originally a term used to describe homosexual men and women, has for the past twenty years been more narrowly defined as referring to homosexual men, and *lesbian* has been used to refer to homosexual women.

Homosexuality has been among the most controversial topics in the history of psychoanalysis. For much of the twentieth century, psychoanalysts considered same-sex object orientation to be a pathological condition, a view based primarily on an a priori assumption of the normalcy of heterosexuality (Lewes, 1988; R. Friedman, 2001; Goldberg, 2001). In addition, theories about the etiology of homosexuality reflected the erroneous conflation of psychodynamics with causality (Auchincloss and Vaughan,

2001), resulting in universal explanations of homosexuality as conflict driven and often linked to psychopathology. Contemporary views do not equate homosexual orientation with impaired object relations or other aspects of character pathology. It is now understood that the factors contributing to adult sexual orientation are varied and complex, likely involving biological, psychological, and environmental components, uniquely determined in each individual (Friedman and Downey, 2002a). The clinical counterpart of such a view is a psychoanalytic attitude of open inquiry about any patient's sexual orientation, and the avoidance of assumptions about the origins of homosexuality or the privileging of heterosexuality.

Kertbeny, an Austrian-born Hungarian writer, coined the term *homosexuality* in 1869 (to replace *pederasty*), as part of his effort to challenge Germany's sodomy laws. In the same year, Westphal, a German psychiatrist, created a new diagnostic category, "contrary sexual feelings," for individuals with same-sex attractions. Through translations from German to Italian and English, "contrary sexual feelings" became sexual "inversion." Initially a technical psychiatric term, *inversion* entered the common lexicon because of the popularity of Ellis's coauthored book, *Sexual Inversion* (Ellis and Symonds, 1897). While both Kertbeny and Westphal opposed the criminalization of same-sex behaviors, the medicalization of homosexuality as a mental illness caused by damaged heredity quickly became another justification for its prosecution. Von Krafft-Ebing added further support to the degeneracy model of homosexuality in his 1886 book, *Psychopathia Sexualis* (1886/1999).

Freud's commentary about homosexual object choice, which he generally referred to as "inversion," is complex and contradictory with references to it scattered throughout his writings (1905b; 1909b; 1910b; 1920b; 1922). While Freud rejected the classification of homosexuality as degeneracy, he did characterize homosexuality as a sexual aberration, although not necessarily as an illness (1905b). Freud's views on homosexuality occurred within the context of his revolutionary assertion of the universality of constitutional bisexuality. Freud meant by this that all humans have the capacity for sexual attraction to both genders, and that the usual outcome of heterosexuality requires the successful passage through the developmental stages of autoerotism and narcissism, culminating in heterosexual object love. In this process, homosexual libido becomes sublimated into social instincts, available for friendship, comradeship, and "love of mankind in general." However, when fixation or regression to the narcissistic phase occurs, as a result of innate or acquired factors, the outcome may be homosexuality. Alternatively, paranoia, a clearly pathological outcome, may serve as a defense against unconscious homosexuality (1911a) and may also result from some fixation at the narcissistic phase.

Freud carefully distinguished between gender attributes and sexual orientation, explaining that, for example, masculine attributes in a woman might exist independently of homosexual object choice (1920b). In so doing, Freud was aware of relying upon classifications of masculine and feminine, which devolve into the inadequate distinction between masculine as active and feminine as passive. Freud repeatedly asserted the limits of psychoanalysis in explaining or altering homosexuality, concluding that ultimately the explanation will reside within biology. While Freud delineated the psychodynamic underpinnings of homosexual orientation, he acknowledged their lack of unique association. For example, Freud described the frequency among male homosexuals of an early fixation to the mother, followed by a female identification, and then a narcissistic object choice. The male homosexual desires to love someone like himself in the manner that his mother has loved him. However, Freud noted that similar dynamics might also be present when the outcome is heterosexual object choice, strongly suggesting that "economic factors" may be the determining factor. He concluded that homosexuality is not a singular phenomenon (1920b); its origins are likely a complex mix of innate and environmental determinants, evidenced by the variety of sexual outcomes in the population. Freud (1905b) also emphasized the importance of the surrounding culture on attitudes about homosexuality, and despite contradictions within his own writings, his personal attitude toward homosexuals was one of acceptance, as demonstrated by his support of the decriminalization of homosexuality.

The original definition of the term by sexologists and most of Freud's own writings about homosexuality focused on men. An exception is Freud's 1920 case report (1920b) of an adolescent girl whose homosexuality was attributed to a confluence of dynamic factors, probably reinforced by innate predisposition. In fact, it is in this paper that Freud presented one of his most coherent discussions of homosexuality. Freud's dynamic formulation emphasized that the patient's female love object is a compromise of motives involving revenge against both parents for a painful oedipal defeat experienced during adolescence but directed especially against her beloved father. Her female love object represents the satisfaction of both her feminine and masculine ideals, thereby providing the satisfac-

tion for her bisexual strivings. Freud intended the case to demonstrate the complexity and individuality of psychosexual development, showing why it is fruitless to try to distinguish between "congenital or acquired" homosexual desire. However, others viewed the case as the basis for a panoply of pathologic formulations of female homosexuality ranging from body-ego and separation-individuation disturbances to identification with the father to prevent psychotic symbiosis with mother (Magee and Miller, 1997).

After Freud, until the 1980s, psychoanalytic perspectives on homosexuality emphasized its classification as a perversion associated with specific highly pathological genetic and structural determinants (C. Socarides, 1960). Homosexuality was thought to represent a disturbance in the whole personality, including such features as a narcissistic predisposition, primitive defense mechanisms, excessive aggression, and orality, along with ego weaknesses, such as boundary problems and low frustration tolerance. The genetic reconstructions of homosexual patients emphasized preoedipal disturbances in the mother-infant relationship creating separation fears and dread of reunion, resulting in female identifications and homosexual orientation. Often noted in the history of homosexuals is an absent or cruel father or the wish on the part of both parents for the child to be a girl. Such views were widely accepted within the psychoanalytic community with little challenge and were operationalized by the systematic exclusion of homosexuals from psychoanalytic training programs. In addition, the pessimism about changing gender sexual orientation through analysis extended to a more pervasive feeling about the unanalyzability of homosexual patients.

While some writers within the psychoanalytic community (Marmor, 1972; S. Mitchell, 1978) challenged the negative attitudes toward homosexuality, the culture continued to pathologize it, and scientific inquiry was infiltrated by moral judgments and dogma. In 1973, in response to increasing pressure from gay activists and careful review of empirical research, the American Psychiatric Association removed homosexuality from the *Diagnostic and Statistical Manual* (*DSM*). At that time, psychoanalysts were among the most vocal in their opposition to its removal (Bayer, 1981). Isay's 1983 panel on homosexuality at the meeting of the American Psychoanalytic Association (Isay and Friedman, 1986) initiated the examination of the biases and misconceptions embedded in psychoanalytic theories of homosexuality. Isay's subsequent contributions (1986, 1987, 1989) and his public acknowledgment of his own homosexuality in 1987 (becoming the first openly gay member of the American Psychoanalytic Association) were important catalysts for the changing attitudes toward an understanding of homosexuality within psychoanalysis. In 1991, the American Psychoanalytic Association voted for a policy of non-discrimination against homosexual applicants for training, candidates, and all grades of faculty.

Isay described homosexuality as a normal variant of human sexuality. While Isay noted the impact on the homosexual's psychological development of biological and social factors, he asserted the necessary but perhaps not sufficient role of genetic predisposition in sexual orientation. He challenged the view that engulfing hostile mothers and weak or distant fathers create homosexuals, and argued that critical, distant fathers and overly involved mothers are common parental responses to their sons' perceived homosexuality. In addition, Isay proposed that some of the characterization of parents by their homosexual offspring may represent the impact of defensive processes.

R. Friedman (1988, 2001) proposed a biopsychosocial interactionist model for male homosexuality that attempts to integrate psychoanalytic theory with empirical research. His theory of male homosexual development emphasizes a confluence of biological, psychodynamic, and social factors. However, invoking Freud's (1916/1917) complemental series, Friedman acknowledged the varying influence of each factor in any individual homosexual, thereby formulating a spectrum of influence for any one factor. Friedman, like Freud, did not view homosexuality as a unitary phenomenon. His research suggests that in male development, the fantasied erotic object is established between the ages of nine and thirteen. Once established, male object preference is considered to be a structure of the self, not amenable to change for either the homosexual or the heterosexual.

The issues involved in sexual identity formation in homosexuals have been recognized as more complex than in heterosexuals, whose erotic interests are congruent with familial and societal expectations. The formation of a homosexual identity, more currently referred to as a "gay identity," is a developmental achievement that implies a more complex and multifaceted phenomenon than the presence of homoerotic desires or homosexual behavior in an individual. In fact, the use of the word *gay* entered the psychoanalytic lexicon when the distinction was made between homosexual erotic attraction, behavior, or relationships and the acceptance and incorporation of homosexuality into a positive self image.

This multistage process, known as "coming out," begins with the individual becoming aware of his same-sex erotic attraction and privately identifying himself as gay and is followed by the individual revealing to significant others that he is gay. The lag time between self awareness and disclosure to others varies significantly and is strongly influenced by the degree of acceptance of sexual diversity in an individual's family and community, and by the conscious and unconscious working through of internalized antigay attitudes, often referred to in the psychological literature as internalized homophobia. In addition, because an individual's gay identity can only be known if openly disclosed, "coming out" is a lifelong process.

Auchincloss and Vaughan (2001) questioned the need for any psychoanalytic theory of homosexuality, arguing that such a theory cannot be created through psychoanalytic methodology alone. In addition, any new theory, like the old theories, will inevitably succumb to false categorizations of normal and abnormal, unsubstantiatable claims about bedrock, and the conflation of psychodynamics with causality. Contemporary psychoanalysts have focused instead on understanding the developmental experiences of homosexual men and women, as well as understanding the impact of growing up in a culture that privileges heterosexuality and denigrates homosexuality (Corbett, 1993; Cohler and Galatzer-Levy, 2000; S. Phillips, 2001; Lynch, 2002). In addition, there has been a growing interest in the psychoanalytic understanding of **homophobia**. Many studies have investigated such issues as the inaccuracy of the term, referring as it does to a variety of antigay responses besides phobic; the origins of homophobia in the fear and contempt of what is feminine (Isay, 1989); the history of homophobia within the field of psychoanalysis; **internalized homophobia**; the contributions of historical and social determinants; and others (Moss, 2003).

Lesbianism is a sexual orientation in which a woman is sexually and romantically interested in other women. *Lesbian*, or *lesbianism*, has replaced *female homosexuallity* in common and psychoanalytic usage. While it is generally recognized that there are many similarities in the characteristics of male homosexuality and lesbianism, there are also differences. For example, many authors have proposed that a distinguishing characteristic of female sexuality may be its greater plasticity, evidenced by the capacity for the later postadolescent emergence of lesbian fantasy and activity.

The term *lesbian* is derived from the name of the Greek island Lesbos, which was home to the sixth-century female poet Sappho, who wrote about female eroticism and is assumed to have had romantic relationships with women (Lester, 2002). Its usage as a term for female homosexuals began within the medical lexicon and dates back to the late-nineteenth-century psychiatric case studies (Goldstein and Horowitz, 2003). Although Freud (1920b) devoted a case history to the exploration of female homosexuality, he wrote very little specifically on the topic, especially in contrast to his interest in male homosexuality. Freud never used the term *lesbian* when referring to his patient, and the term appears only once in his work, when discussing the use of Sappho's writings in a patient's dream (1900). The earliest usage of the term *lesbian* in the psychoanalytic literature can be found in the work of Wittels (1934a, 1934b), and subsequently, *lesbian* has been used interchangeably with *female homosexuality* by other writers.

The majority of psychoanalytic writings on lesbianism and lesbian patients prior to 1993 began with a presumption that heterosexuality is the normal outcome of adult sexual development, and addressed female homosexuality as the pathological outcome of specific psychodynamic constellations (see historical summaries: O'Connor and Ryan, 1993; Schuker, 1996; Magee and Miller; 1997; Downey and Friedman, 1998). Furthermore, these writings reflected the phallocentric view of female development that characterized psychoanalytic theories of female development prevalent before the 1980s when revisions centered on concepts of primary femininity became more prevalent. The earliest writings on lesbianism focused on conflicts of the phallic-oedipal phase, which result in regression to the preoedipal mother-daughter relationship. In this context, the lesbian partner becomes a substitute good mother and the relationship is the enactment of a symbiotic union that attempts to deny the oedipal conflict. Such formulations also emphasized the lesbian's masculine identification, forged by the combined influence of penis envy, fear of passive wishes and of penetration, along with a compromised female identification resulting from the mother's characteristics as aloof, controlling, and rejecting. Subsequent writings emphasized disturbances in the mother-child relationship during the preoedipal separation-individuation phase and described lesbianism in the context of severe and pervasive character pathology. Other writings also included the impact of a father who shows contempt and criticism toward men who take an interest in his daughter, frightening or painful heterosexual encounters, disappointments in heterosexual love experiences, or the unavailability

of heterosexual objects. Analysts such as Stoller (1985) and McDougall (1986) shifted the emphasis from a single model of homosexuality to exploration of homosexualities, however they continued to conceptualize lesbianism as a compromised and less-mature outcome.

Downey and R. Friedman (1998) emphasized the common error of equating psychodynamics with psychopathology and etiology, a point they have also made in the exploration of male homosexuality. They proposed a complex interaction of biological, developmental, intrapsychic, and cultural influences with varying contributions in any individual case. However, in their view, lesbianism (like male homosexuality) may be the product of either "maladaptive unconscious conflict" or "nonpathological pathways." Other writers regarded lesbianism as one of multiple variations in adult sexuality (Burch, 1993a, 1993b; O'Connor and Ryan, 1993). This recognition has led to the exploration of unique experiences of lesbians, including internalized homophobia, coming out, motherhood, relationships, sexuality, and gender identity, in addition to the dynamics of transference and countertransference with lesbian patients (Schuker, 1996; K. Reed, 2002).

Attention has also been given to recognition of fluidity in female sexuality and sexual identity across the lifespan. Some lesbians become aware of same-sex attractions in childhood and adolescence and remain lesbian in orientation throughout their lives. Others have satisfying heterosexual relationships in adolescence and early adulthood, developing same-sex interests and lesbian identity in mid- and later adulthood. Additionally, some women who became aware of their lesbianism and entered relationships with women in adolescence and young adulthood develop opposite-sex interests later in life and form heterosexual relationships. Such a group might include college-age women who assumed lesbianism as an identity, not simply a sexual orientation, in their allegiance to ideological passions (Defries, 1978, 1979). Variations in identity are also evident, with some women who experience sexual fluidity identifying as bisexual, some as heterosexual or lesbian depending on the sex of their partner, and some who identify as lesbian later in adulthood expressing the belief that they had always been lesbian but had not realized it earlier in life (Golden, 1987, 2003; Schuker, 1996; Kirkpatrick, 2002; Notman, 2002; L. Diamond, 2008). Kirkpatrick (Applegarth and Wolfson, 1987) distinguished female sexuality from male sexuality with the emphasis in the former on intimacy, and the latter on genital release. She described the motivation for lesbianism as the pursuit of a relationship that provides greater intimacy and personal development, rather than the evidence for conflict and inhibition. She also emphasized that sexual orientation and desire to be a mother are independent, acknowledging the active desires and capacities of many lesbians to achieve motherhood.

Horizontal Split: see REPRESSION, SPLITTING, VERTICAL SPLIT

Hospitalism is a catastrophic condition that develops during the first year of life in infants who may be receiving adequate physical care but fail to receive life-sustaining psychological mothering. The clinical picture is a profound failure to thrive marked by physical deterioration, extreme susceptibility to illness, profound mental deficiencies, and even mortality. Survivors of hospitalism have a high incidence of psychiatric disturbance, mental retardation, and antisocial tendencies. Unlike anaclitic depression, which occurs when a previously normal mother-child attachment is disrupted and the child is then deprived of emotional sustenance, hospitalism is brought about by emotional deprivation from birth. Viewed from a more contemporary perspective, hospitalism is a profound disorder of early attachment, which demonstrates that adequate mothering is absolutely essential for healthy physical and psychological development.

Hospitalism was recognized as early as 1915 (Chapin, 1915) in institutionalized infants and has been observed in children whose mothers are incapable of emotionally responding to their babies (Kreisler, 1984). Spitz (1945, 1946) was the first to systematically study infants with the intent of discovering the pathogenic factors responsible for the syndrome. He studied infants who received adequate nursing, hygienic, and nutritional care, but who did not receive the normal affective supplies provided by a primary caretaker. From the third month on, physical and psychological deterioration with extreme susceptibility to infection and illness was noted, and the mortality rate from usually nonfatal disease was very high. Infants with hospitalism suffered from depression and exhibited motor retardation, complete passivity, vacuous facies, and defective eye coordination. From the second year on, the children were profoundly physically and psychologically retarded, unable to sit, stand, walk, or talk. The effects of hospitalism are long-term and generally irreversible.

Hypochondriasis: see DEPRESSION, NARCISSISM, OBSERVING EGO, PSYCHOSOMATIC DISORDERS, VERTICAL SPLIT

Hysteria designates several kinds of psychopathology or aspects of character, including 1) a syndrome characterized by somatic symptoms, diverse and often protean, that are not related to demonstrable anatomical or physiological pathology but that represent the symbolic expression of unconscious conflict, as when a conflict about "seeing" something is expressed as blindness (**conversion hysteria**); 2) an altered state of consciousness caused by dissociation, including fugue states, some amnesias, and multiple personality disorder (dissociative state); 3) a character type with a defensive style marked by the use of repression, emotionality, and somatization, in someone who is self dramatizing, emotionally labile, and/or seductive, while fearful of actual sexual interactions (**hysterical character**); and 4) a defensive style in which repression, emotionality (or affectualization), and somatization predominate, even in the absence of full-blown hysterical character (**hysterical style**). While originally, hysterical character (or style) was thought to predispose to hysterical symptoms, this relationship is far from clear. For the most part, conversion hysteria and hysterical character have been explored separately in the psychoanalytic literature.

Hysteria plays an important role in the history of psychoanalysis, as Freud invented both his new treatment of "psychical analysis" and his first psychoanalytic theories in the course of his work with patients suffering from hysteria (which, at the time, included conversion hysteria and dissociative states). Introduced by his mentors (Charcot, Bernheim, and Breuer) to the theory that hysteria is caused by ideas that have become separated from ordinary consciousness, Freud broke with tradition by proposing an etiology for hysteria, based not on degenerative illness but on psychological conflict. His view of hysterical symptoms (and ultimately of all the psychoneuroses) as the symbolic expression of repressed unconscious wishes became the foundation for all his later theories of neurosis, as well as for his general theory of mind. Ultimately, Freud's understanding of hysteria served as the foundation for his revolutionary view of the mind, forever divided (conscious and unconscious), given to overstimulating itself (wish and drive), and capable of regulating itself (defense). Hysterical psychopathology also demonstrates the many ways in which mental life finds symbolic expression through the body.

The term *hysteria* (from the Greek *hystera*, meaning "womb") was originally coined by Hippocrates in the fourth century BCE, and has been used for more than two thousand years to describe a wide array of fluctuating somatic symptoms, most often occurring in women. Freud (1886) presented his first paper to the Viennese Medical Society "Observation of a Severe Case of Hemi-Anaesthesia in a Hysterical Male," which, under the influence of Charcot, he explained as the result of trauma in combination with hereditary neuropathic disease. Over the course of the subsequent two decades, his theory became increasingly psychoanalytic, with developments in the theory of hysteria running parallel with the development of his general theory of mind. Most notably, in 1895, in his book *Studies on Hysteria* (coauthored with Breuer), Freud (Breuer and Freud, 1893/1895) introduced the new concept of **defense hysteria**, caused by ideas (most often "reminiscences" of trauma) sequestered from ordinary consciousness, not because of degenerative mental weakness but "from the motive of defense." Throughout this early period, Freud also began to search ever earlier in childhood for the causes of hysteria (at first, still the experience of trauma); by the mid-1890s, he had arrived at his famous seduction hypothesis, in which he theorized that hysterical symptoms are the sequelae of traumatic seductions during childhood (1896c). Then, from about 1897 on, in a dramatic move away from trauma theory, Freud (1897e) abandoned the seduction hypothesis in favor of the theory of internally generated overstimulation, in which hysteria represents the symbolic expression of repressed childhood sexual wishes. Freud also described **hysterical identification**, based on an unconscious imitation of the behavior of others, as contributing to the formation of hysterical symptoms (1900). Finally, by 1905, in the Dora case, these wishes include oedipal longings, as well as wishes arising in erotogenic zones, or the components of what was soon conceptualized as libido (1905a).

Freud's official theory of hysteria was based on economic principles. Indeed, the name *conversion hysteria* (coined by Breuer and Freud) was based on the theory that "the incompatible idea is rendered innocuous by its sum of excitation being transformed into something somatic" (1894c). However, in Freud's work on the subject, we find a hodgepodge of ideas ranging from the effects of heredity, to dozens of more psychological ideas, including the role of identification, unconscious fantasy (especially masturbation fantasy), symbolic communication, body language, somatic compliance (in which previous real injury to an organ lays the groundwork for its later use in the formation of hysterical symptoms), and secondary gain.

Freud used his study of hysteria to formulate a general theory of psychopathology (or neurosis) based on its underlying structure, which he saw as

any situation in which affect (later, drive energy) has become separated from its associated idea. For example, in 1909, (following Stekel) Freud (1908d, 1909b) described **anxiety hysteria**, in which repressed libido is transformed into anxiety (or, with further displacements, into phobia), analogous to conversion hysteria, in which libido is transformed into somatic symptoms. At the same time, his theory of hysteria formed the basis for his general theory of mind, characterized by a permanent division into conscious and unconscious sectors and motivated by drives.

While Freud did not write formally about hysterical character, in the course of his writing about hysterical symptoms, he did allude to a predisposing **hysterical temperament** consisting of increased excitability and affective instability (1888a). He also referred often to his patients' susceptibility to daydreaming, intense feeling, vehemence and passion, demands for love, manipulativeness, and use of "suppression." The concept of hysterical character itself was introduced into psychoanalysis by Wittels (1930) as a personality type predisposing to hysterical symptoms and fixated at the oral phase of libidinal development. Thereafter, exploration of hysterical character (rather than of hysterical symptoms) dominated the psychoanalytic literature on hysteria.

The most traditional view of hysterical character was formulated by W. Reich (1933/1945), who conceptualized it as a flight from sexuality (associated with unconscious, incestuous oedipal fantasy) to a defensive seductiveness, which reflects a regression/fixation at the early genital/phallic phase of development. In addition to the hysteric's defensive sexualization of all interactions, Reich emphasized the defense mechanisms of repression, somatization, dissociation, and identification. Others emphasized the hysteric's "flight into fantasy" (Fenichel, 1945) and the defensive use of emotionality, self dramatization, and exaggerated gender role (Easser and Lesser, 1991). More recently, authors writing from an object relations perspective described how hysterical character style is used to manage the persecutory anxiety associated with primitive object relations (Brenman, 1985; de Folch, 1984). Psychoanalysts interested in development emphasized overstimulation in childhood, particularly in the oedipal phase, often in combination with inadequate same-sex parenting (Blacker and Tupin, 1977). Contemporary views of development usually include the contributions of temperament and other innate factors, such as **hysterical cognitive style** (D. Shapiro, 1965).

Traditionally, in an era dominated by theories of pathology based on libidinal stages, hysterical character was conceptualized as the highest level of character pathology, reflecting fixation at the genital/phallic phase. However, in response to the observation that hysterics often did not do well in treatment, and to developments in theory, psychoanalytic psychopathologists began to delineate different kinds of hysterics with different levels of pathology, reflecting either earlier (oral) fixations or more primitive defenses (Marmor, 1953; Zetzel, 1968; Easser and Lesser, 1991). For example, Zetzel described the "**so-called good hysteric**" as someone who presents as a traditional hysterical character but whose functioning is more impaired and who uses more primitive defenses; Easser and Lesser differentiated between **hysteroid characters** and hysterical characters, based on overall level of ego functioning. These attempts to delineate levels of pathology in the hysteric contributed to Kernberg's (1967) work on levels of character pathology; Kernberg himself distinguished between hysterical character and borderline personality organization (including those with what he called "infantile personality"), based on level of defenses and object relations.

Over time the word *hysteria* has become so thoroughly associated with psychoanalytic theory that the term was dropped from the official psychiatric nomenclature in 1952, ultimately replaced in the *DSM* system with somatization, conversion, and dissociative disorders on Axis I, and with histrionic and borderline personality disorders on Axis II. However, in its own classification system, the *Psychodynamic Diagnostic Manual* (*PDM*) (PDM Task Force, 2006) includes on the Personality Axis: **hysterical personality disorder** (or **histrionic personality disorder**), including inhibited (sexually repressed and fearful) and demonstrative or flamboyant (dramatic, sexually provocative) subtypes; and dissociative personality disorder (referred to commonly as multiple personality), in which whole sectors of the personality are dissociated from one another, usually in the context of severe childhood trauma or abuse; and, on the Symptom Axis: dissociative disorders and somatoform (somatization) disorders (which include conversion disorder). In research that draws from psychoanalytic theory, cognitive psychology, and information theory, Horowitz (1977) tried to demonstrate changes in object and self "schemata" in what he calls **hysterical personality**, after successful treatment.

I

Id is the agency or system of the mind, described in Freud's structural model, that contains the mental representations of the instinctual drives. Within this model, the id's contents, entirely unconscious, include both inherited constitutional parts and acquired repressed parts. The functioning of the id is governed by the pleasure principle, and it operates with freely mobile drive energy and primary process modes of thought. The id is the structure of the mind most closely associated with the endogenous biologic needs of the human organism, represented mentally as sexual and aggressive drive wishes. It was Freud's (1933a) dictum that the goal of analytic treatment is to make conscious what is repressed, so that "where id was, there ego shall be."

Although Freud (1938a) described the id as the part of the mind of greatest importance throughout life, the term has fallen into relative disuse. As the id concept includes central assumptions about drives, psychic energy, and the economic viewpoint, it has been subject to all the controversies surrounding these theoretical ideas. However, even contemporary analysts who embrace drives as central to motivation and conflict tend to speak more commonly of the aggressive and sexual drives, or constellations of wish and defense, rarely invoking the term *id*.

Freud first used the term *das Es* (literally, "the It," although translated by Strachey as "the Id") in "The Ego and the Id," in outlining his new structural model of the mind (1923a). Here he acknowledged his adaptation of the term from the German psychiatrist Groddeck, who employed it to describe the way that man is "'lived' by unknown and uncontrollable forces." Freud also linked this use with Nietzsche, who used *das Es* to refer to the component of human nature that is under the control of natural law.

Freud's conception of the id had its precursor in the system unconscious (Ucs.), described in his earlier topographic model of the mind (1900, 1915d). The id maintained many features in common with the system unconscious, in particular its primary process modes of functioning and its repressed contents. However, in the new structural model, unconscious functioning is a feature not only of the repressed id but also of large parts of the repressing ego and of the superego. The id is no longer synony-

mous with the unconscious but rather with the instinctual aspects of mental functioning. Its contents include wishes resulting from the perception and memories of gratification of basic physiological needs, though the distinction between underlying biological forces and the mental content of the id is less clearly drawn than it was in Freud's description of the unconscious. Similarly, the boundaries between the id and the other two agencies, the ego and the superego, are much less distinct than those postulated between the system unconscious (Ucs.) and the system conscious-preconscious (Cs.-Pcs.). Both the ego and the superego are described as merging with the id and acquiring their own energy from the "great reservoir" of instinctual energy contained in the id. The ego originates as the portion of the id that has been modified by the direct influence of the external world (Freud, 1923a). As the id does not recognize the world outside the mind, it functions through the activities of the ego; the uneasy complexities of this relationship are noted in Freud's famous metaphor of a rider whose energies are all borrowed from the horse, and who is only sometimes successful in guiding the horse where he, the rider, wants to go. Aggressive energies of the id are used by the superego, paradoxically causing the aggression to be redirected against id wishes themselves, in the form of guilt and self punishment.

Later analytic theorists have taken note of the many ambiguities and contradictions that are present in Freud's concept of the id. Does the id have any contents, or is it totally composed of biological forces? Does it lack organization or does it have a unique organization? Do the contents of the id include secondarily repressed unconscious memories and fantasies, or do they include only what has never achieved consciousness or representability? How and to what extent can the contents of the id be apprehended? How can the complex and paradoxical relationships between the id and the ego and the superego best be understood (Marcovitz, 1963; Schur, 1966; Shulman, 1987)? Some analytic theorists have tried in various ways to integrate drives and structural theory with object relations concepts, redefining the id within the context of an object relational matrix (Loewald, 1971; Kernberg, 1982). In general, relational theories minimize or dismiss the role of drives, and thus do not use the id concept at all. Within "modern conflict theory," C. Brenner has recently advocated retiring the structural model, arguing that conflict and compromise formation are not best explained by the idea that the mind is divided into separate and functionally definable structures (Brenner, 2002). However, recent work in neuroscience provides interesting support for the idea of a deep level of mental organization that corresponds in certain respects to Freud's concept of an id (LeDoux, 1996; Panksepp, 1999).

Idealization is the attribution of exalted qualities to someone or something. These qualities may include great brilliance, beauty, strength, or goodness, even to the point of perfection. Idealization is accompanied by feelings of admiration, awe, adoration, and love; it can also be accompanied by envy and hatred. Idealization usually applies to another person, however it may apply to a group of people, such as a nation or a tribe, a place, an idea, a memory, or anything that can be aggrandized. Idealization can apply to a part of the object, such as a body part, or to an inanimate object (such as a fetish) that might symbolize a part of an object. Idealization can also apply to the self or to part of the self. The capacity for idealization is a normal and universal part of human experience. It ranges from normal experiences of being in love, parenting a child, pursuing realistic goals and ideals, and healthy moral functioning, to the painful and often dangerous experiences of those who are lovesick, are enthralled by a cult, or kill others in the service of an ideal. Idealization contributes to many forms of psychopathology, especially those involving self-esteem regulation and other problems in narcissism. The opposite of idealization is devaluation, where bad, shameful, or otherwise negative qualities are attributed to someone else, who is then held in contempt.

In 1905, Freud (1905b) described perversion as an idealization of the instinct. However, he explored idealization in greater depth in his paper "On Narcissism," where he described how an individual sets up an ideal within himself by which he measure his actual self (1914e). This **ego ideal** is the heir to relinquished narcissism of childhood. Freud went on to describe idealization, whereby the object is "aggrandized and exalted." In anaclitic object choice, based on the experience of having been fed and cared for, the object may be idealized for his/her potential to fulfill this role again. In narcissistic object choice, based on someone who resembles oneself or one's ideal self, the object may be idealized in hopes of recovering the narcissism of infancy. Freud saw ide-

alization as contributing to the "overvaluation" of the object in the normal state of being in love. He also saw idealization, especially in narcissistic object choice, as contributing to the psychopathology of those who demand a "cure through love." In later works, Freud went on to explore the contributions of idealization to fetishism (1915c); to coherence in groups, which often depends on the idealization of a leader who substitutes for the individual's ego ideal (1921); to religion (1913e, 1927a); and to war and the atrocities committed during war, in which exaltation of an ideal may combine with aggression (1933b). In a paper that foreshadowed Klein's observation of a human tendency to split images of the object (and self) into good and bad parts, Freud (1912d) expounded on a "universal tendency to debasement in the sphere of love," in which a man protects himself from the anxiety associated with incestuous fantasies by devaluing a woman with whom he has sex, while continuing to idealize the unconscious incestuous love object.

Among post-Freudian ego psychologists, A. Reich (1953, 1954, 1960) explored the development of the ego ideal, beginning with the earliest grandiose images of the self, mixed with idealized images of the parents. Reich argued that over time, this infantile ego ideal evolves into a realistic set of ideals. Trauma, narcissistic injury, or disturbances in object relationships can lead to the persistence of a grandiose ego ideal, which includes images of parental magnificence, often mixed with desires for an idealized organ, such as the breast or the paternal phallus. Externalization of this primitive ego ideal leads to a form of pathological narcissistic object choice in women, as, for example, when a woman deifies and submits to an idealized, phallic man. The masochism and subservience in this idealization may defend against aggression and envious feelings. Even small disappointments in the idealized love object may lead to his being devalued and abandoned.

Writing around the same time, Jacobson (1964) proposed a developmental sequence in the formation of the ego ideal and the superego, which includes the idealization of the object as an important component. Jacobson recognized that both superego and ego ideal always include an admixture of the grandiose wishes of the child as well as his aggrandized view of the parents. While initially, the child takes himself as his own ideal, with increasing awareness of the reality of his limited size and strength, he begins to glorify his parents, enhancing his own self esteem through fantasies of merger with them. Over time, this tendency to aggrandize himself and his parents becomes modified into a set of more reasonable moral and ethical codes, which, together with "enforcing" powers, characterize the mature super-ego. There is much that can go wrong in this developmental process, resulting in psychopathology related to the regulation of self esteem and/or feelings of shame and inferiority, such as depression, delinquency, and narcissistic personality.

Klein conceptualized idealization as the result of the universal mechanism of splitting, in which all infants (and some adults) create an "ideal object" and a "bad object" so as to protect good experiences from being destroyed by aggression. Idealization of the object may serve as a defense against annihilation at the hands of a bad, persecutory object during the paranoid position; retreat to this paranoid position may serve as a defense against depressive anxiety in the depressive position. Idealization may also result from projective identification of all-good images of the self, with consequent exaltation of the object. Ideas of perfection may themselves feel persecutory, leading to further defenses (Heimann, 1942). Rosenfeld (1983), in particular, emphasized this defensive use of idealization in various kinds of psychopathology.

Kernberg (1967), in a synthesis of the views of Reich, Jacboson, Klein, and Rosenfeld, also saw idealization as among the defenses based on splitting (along with devaluation, omnipotence, and projective identification), which underlie borderline and narcissistic personality disorders. In his view, narcissistic personality disorder is based on a pathological grandiose self, made up of a fusion between actual self, ideal self, and idealized object. In both borderline and narcissistic individuals, idealization is always accompanied by the threat of devaluation. For example, in some narcissistic people, paranoid fears of envy and of dependence on others are defended against through devaluation and/or omnipotent control of others. If an idealized object fails in some way, or if the pathological grandiose self collapses, the object or the self is quickly devalued. In later work, Kernberg (1974a) described three kinds of idealization: 1) **primitive idealization**, based on splitting, which is found in borderline personality organization and associated with unstable forms of love; 2) idealization linked to the establishment of the capacity for mourning and concern, which serves as a defense against guilty aggression in neurotic individuals; and 3) the normal capacity for idealization, achieved toward the end of adolescence, based upon realistic assessment of the love object and including social as well as personal ideals.

In contrast to Klein and Kernberg, Kohut (1971, 1977) saw all idealization of the object as a normal need, necessary for the development of the self. In Kohut's view there are two major constituents of the self: the first is the grandiose self, developing in interaction with a mirroring selfobject, out of which develop strivings for power and recognition; the second is the **idealized parental imago**, composed of the child's attributions of perfection to the parents, out of which develop enduring values and ideals. Premature or traumatic **de-idealization** of the parents leads to persistence of the need for idealized selfobject experiences to stabilize the self. In such individuals, psychoanalytic treatment will mobilize an **idealizing transference**, which offers an opportunity for renewed development of the self.

Many analysts have noted an intensification of idealization during adolescence, with Blos (1974) describing idealization as the "characteristic par excellence of youth" (see also A. Freud, 1936). This intense idealization during adolescence contributes to the consolidation of identity and is fueled by defenses against loss and separation and/or by revived oedipal strivings and fears. Akhtar (1996) has described "someday . . ." and "if only . . ." fantasies, which represent idealization of the future and the past, respectively. While these fantasies are a normal part of everyone's inner life, they become pronounced in individuals who have suffered separation trauma.

Identification is a psychological process whereby an aspect of the individual's self representation becomes modified to resemble an aspect of an object representation. Identification belongs to a group of mechanisms, collectively known as internalization, which also includes introjection and incorporation. An individual may become conscious of an identification, but the process by which it occurs is unconscious. An identification may be normal or pathological; it may be selective or broad in its scope. It may occur at an individual, group, or societal level. Identification has been used to describe both the process of changing the self representation or behavior of an individual, and the change itself. In psychoanalytic theories of development, identification plays a crucial role in the formation of all the major structures, including ego, ego ideal, superego, self representations, identity, and character, among others. Identification itself has a developmental sequence, starting with imitation and progressing to mature, specific identification. Psychoanalysis pays close attention to the multiple motivations that accompany or heighten identification, as, for example, a wish to become like a loved person, or a wish to lessen pain and loss when the tie to a significant object is disrupted or lost. The concept of identification has expanded from its original formulation as a regressive, pathological process to one involved in normal development, the molding and enriching of the self, and the development of object relations. Indeed, the concept of identification began as one psychical mechanism among many and evolved to occupy a central place in the theories about how the subjective sense of self is created (Laplanche and Pontalis, 1967/1973, Schafer, 1968b; Behrends and Blatt, 1985). The concept is also central to our capacity to understand others, contributing to the capacity for empathy, which has often been called **trial identification** (Fliess, 1942).

Freud (1900) first discussed identification as contributing to the formation of hysterical symptoms. **Hysterical identification**, based on an unconscious imitation of the behavior of others, allowed for the disguised expression of forbidden wishes, ideas, and feelings. In 1913, he linked identification with the concept of incorporation, describing how primitive people took on the qualities of others through cannibalism; he also described how the sons in the primal horde "accomplished their identification" with the father, acquiring his strength after eating him in the first totem meal (1913e). Freud (1905b) also described the concept of incorporation as linked with his newly described oral (sometime called cannibalistic) phase, and as the prototype for identification. In 1917, in his exploration of melancholia, Freud (1917c) described several phenomena related to identification. First, he argued that in melancholia, there is a regression from a narcissistic object tie to a **narcissistic identification** with the object; in other words, the libido withdrawn from a lost object is used to establish an identification with that object within the ego. As he famously stated, "the shadow of the object" falls upon the ego. The painful experience of self reproach, so characteristic of melancholia, is produced when another part of the ego, called the "critical agency" (later, the superego), attacks this object within the ego. Freud contrasted the narcissistic identification of melancholia, in which the object tie is completely abandoned, with the previously formulated hysterical identification, in which the object tie is maintained. The narcissistic identification of melancholia is, according to Freud, a pathological one that exists only for the duration of the pathological state of melancholia. As such, it does not result in a permanent change within the self but instead functions as what contemporary analysts might call a temporary introject. Elsewhere in this paper, Freud placed identification in a developmental sequence of object relations (a problem he was

working on at the time), by describing it as "a preliminary stage of object-choice . . . the first way in which the ego picks out an object," based on the oral phase of libidinal development.

In 1921, in his exploration of group psychology, Freud (1921) proposed that there are three kinds of identification: first, the original form of emotional tie with an object or, **primary identification**; second, a regressive substitute for a libidinal object tie; and, third, a new kind based on the perception of common quality shared with another person, which provides the basis for solidarity in groups. Here, Freud began to describe identification as a normal process. He also related identification to the capacity for empathy. Finally, in 1923, Freud (1923a) explored the role of identification in the normal development of major psychic structures: the ego and the superego. In his view, identification was central to the resolution of the oedipus complex, leading both to the formation of the superego and to the development of character. In this exploration, identification is not only a normal process but is, according to Freud, perhaps the only way in which an object tie can be given up (see also 1924b).

Following Freud, the development of the concept of identification has proceeded in several directions. For example, later analysts attempted to clarify Freud's idea of identification as an early and primitive way of relating to objects, calling this mode of relating "primary identification." In contrast, **secondary identification** was conceptualized as occurring at a higher level of development, after self and object have been differentiated and object ties established. Thus, secondary identifications are often a response to object loss, as Freud had described in melancholia, or may serve other defensive purposes (A. Freud, 1936; J. Sandler, 1960b, Loewald 1962a, Jacobson 1964). Specific forms of identification were also described, as in A. Freud's **identification with the aggressor** (1936) and **identification with the lost object** (1967b). Jacobson (1964) described the development of identifications in childhood, beginning with the earliest **affectomotor empathic identifications** to more mature **selective identifications**. Depressed and psychotic patients are prone to **psychotic identifications**, which represent regressive wishful fantasies of merger with the object. Loewald (1962b) described a tendency to "reproject" or externalize superego functions in situations of regression. Greenson (1954, 1968) emphasized the processes of **disidentification** needs for separation from early objects, especially boys from their mothers.

Klein and her followers generally preferred the terms *incorporation* and especially *introjection* over *identification* in their efforts to describe the development of object relations and the internal world. In Kleinian theory, internalizing processes (including identification) play a major role in normal psychological development. Heimann (1942) introduced the term *assimilation* to describe how internal objects become part of the ego; unassimilated objects remain alien to the self. In Kleinian theory, assimilation is often used synonymously with the words *identification* and/or **introjective identification**. This last term is contrasted with the term **projective identification**, whereby parts of the ego are imagined to be separated off and forced into the object (Klein, 1946). Kleinian theorists also developed the concept of **adhesive identification** (Meltzer, 1975; Bick 1986), a type of relating to the object characterized by sticking to or imitating the object, as opposed to projecting into it. This type of identification occurs when there is a failure to develop either an internal space or a space between objects that together allow for the normal processes of introjection and projection and for the development of object relations in depth. Sohn (1985) has described what he called the **identificate**, formed when part of the ego, through projecting itself into an object, acquires an omnipotence that forms the core of a narcissistic organization. Exploring concepts of identification arising in the treatment setting, Racker (1957) described **concordant identification** and **complementary identification**, which occur in the analyst in response to different aspects of the patient's inner life.

All analysts from all schools of thought use some variant of the concept of identification, recognizing it as central to the development of the self concept and of object relations. However, some contemporary psychoanalysts, drawing from the fields of evolutionary biology, genetics, infant observation, and neuroscience, have questioned the extent to which structures of the mind previously thought to arise from identifications may, in fact, be constitutionally based (Olds, 2006).

Identity is a sustained sense of the self as a unique, coherent, and authentic individual. Identity is both an intrapsychic phenomenon, with conscious and unconscious components, and an interpersonal phenomenon, relying on corroboration by the social group. While the word *identity* was used occasionally by Freud and others, it is most closely associated with the work of Erik Erikson, who included it in his well-known series of developmental stages as the developmental accomplishment of adolescence. Erikson also coined the terms **identity crisis**, which refers to the expectable onslaught of doubts and anxieties that accompany the reorganization of self image during adolescence, and **identity diffusion**, which describes the pathological state of failure to integrate earlier identifications into a coherent identity (1946, 1950, 1956, 1959). More recently, the concept of identity has been used in the study of **gender identity**, **core gender identity**, and **sexual identity** (Stoller 1964; Money, 1973; R. Green 1975; S. Frankel and Sherick, 1979; Roiphe and Galenson, 1981b).

Identity has particular importance in developmental theory, as well as at the interface between sociology and psychoanalysis. Indeed, identity differs from self, or self representation, as it specifically includes an individual's sense of self in relation to the surrounding culture. In addition, according to many developmental theorists, the crystallization of identity is the most important specific task and achievement of adolescence. However, Erikson emphasized that identity is continually reworked throughout the life cycle.

Erikson (1946) defined the term identity, which he initially called **ego identity**, as the individual's sense of "conviction" of "a defined ego within a social reality" that emerges out of developmental experiences within his cultural and social world. Erikson identified identity as "a subsystem of the ego," whose function is to integrate the self representations derived from prior psychosocial crises of childhood into a stable, though modifiable, sense of the reality of the self within its social world. He compared the ego identity to ego ideal, from which it is partly derived, which he defines as a set of goals for the self (1956). Indeed, Wallerstein (1998) suggested that Erikson's conceptualization of identity laid the groundwork for the subsequent emergence of interest in the self, including self psychology.

Many psychoanalysts dismissed Erikson's conceptualization of identity as excessively sociological because, in their view, it refers primarily to the adaptation of the individual to his or her particular culture. However, many others have made use of the term or similar concepts to refer to the individual's capacity to internalize, synthesize, and integrate identifications over the course of development. Greenacre (1958a) argued that the sources of identity lie in the development of body image. Mahler (Rubinfine, 1958) discussed identity in terms of the successful negotiation of the process of separation. Jacobson (1964) explored what she called **personal identity**, which consists of the integration of increasingly realistic representations of the self. Lichtenstein (1961) described the origins of identity in the earliest dyadic interactions with the mother, who shares needs and expectations with the child. D. N. Stern (2005) also argued that identity is formed in interaction with others and has its basis in intersubjectivity. Kernberg (1967) elaborated on the concept of identity diffusion present in borderline personalities, arguing that identity diffusion should not be confused with identity crisis, which is a normal process. Wilkinson-Ryan and Westen (2000) have attempted to study various kinds of identity disturbance in borderline personality disorder using empirical methods.

Usage of the term *identity crisis* in the psychoanalytic literature has been markedly inconsistent, spanning levels of abstraction and conceptual focus. For example, the term has been used to describe institutional upheavals (Gitelson, 1964), shifts in conscious self representation due to hospitalization (Will, 1965), or the confrontation with unconscious secrets that challenge the self image (Margolis, 1966). Thus, *identity crisis* is used loosely to refer to any shift in self representation and in the experience of self in the social context.

Illusion, from a psychoanalytic point of view, is any belief that is heavily influenced by wish-fulfillment. In ordinary usage, the word *illusion* means an unreal, deceptive, or misleading perception, without any implication that the distortion of reality is caused by wishfulness. Unlike a delusion, an illusion is capable of correction. Illusion is not necessarily a sign of psychopathology, although it may play a role in the persistence of irrational ideas. While Freud's initial view of illusion was somewhat pejorative, psychoanalysts have come to appreciate the importance of illusion in the development of object relations, as well as for many kinds of experience that rely on creativity and imagination.

Freud's most famous discussion of the term *illusion* appears in "The Future of an Illusion" (1927a), where he introduced the idea that religion is an illusion based on the most "urgent wishes of mankind." Freud argued that religion is an illusion created to cope with man's feelings of helplessness, and that the idea of God is modeled on the child's relation to his father. Freud asserted that science, and psychoanalysis in particular, are not illusions, concluding provocatively that it would be illusion to suppose that religion can substitute for what science cannot give us. In 1930, Freud (1930) revisited the concept of illusion, this time drawing attention to its positive value, especially in the realms of imagination and aesthetic enjoyment, as in daydreams and art.

Winnicott (1945, 1953) further expanded on the positive value of illusion in his descriptions of children's play. Winnicott argued that illusion is essential in the creation of transitional space and of the transitional object, and indeed, in the formation of the first object tie. The hungry baby and the feeding mother come together in a moment of illusion in which the baby is free to experience the satisfying breast either as a hallucination of his own creation or as something belonging to the reality of the external world. In other words, rather than insisting on a sharp distinction between reality and unreality, Winnicott staked a claim for the importance of an intermediate state of illusion as part of the baby's growing ability to recognize and accept reality. Winnicott, like Freud, connected the capacity for illusion to the concept of the soul, to religion, to art, and to many forms of group cohesion. Illusion can coexist with sound reality testing, but madness results when an adult puts too powerful a claim on the credulity of others, forcing them to acknowledge a sharing of illusion that is not their own.

Imaginary Register: see LACAN

Impingement: see WINNICOTT

Implicit Relational Knowing: see INTERSUBJECTIVITY, MEMORY, RESISTANCE, THERAPEUTIC ACTION, UNCONSCIOUS

Imposter: see BORDERLINE, NARCISSISM, PSYCHOPATHY

Incorporation: see INTERNALIZATION, ORALITY

Individuation: see JUNGIAN PSYCHOLOGY, SEPARATION-INDIVIDUATION

Inertia Principle: see DEATH DRIVE, DRIVE, ENERGY, LIBIDO, METAPSYCHOLOGY, TOPOGRAPHIC THEORY

Infancy, a word derived from the Latin *in fans*, or "without speech," is the period of childhood between birth and toddlerhood (from zero to twelve–eighteen months of age). However in the psychoanalytic literature, the term is more often used to encompass the first three years of life. Infancy is a critical time in development wherein the newborn progresses from a state of total psychological and physical dependency into an individual with a host of dawning capacities, including self regulation, symbolic communication, and the motor skills supporting independent and self-determined activity. Depending on theoretical orientation, the intrapsychic accomplishments of infancy include well-differentiated representations of self and other, integration of good and bad part objects and part selves into whole object and whole self representations, well-differentiated ego and id, experiences of conflict and anxiety and the emerging defenses to manage them, early internalization of a self-regulating function, a core sense of self, and a cognitive advance from sensorimotor to preoperational thought. Evidence of the capacity for make-believe is present in the first year of life (Gergely and Watson, 1996), and by age three, there is a full flowering of language and symbolic play. Infancy is also a time when attachment bonds are firmly established and the infant's attachment style can be assessed. These remarkable achievements are accompanied and enhanced by physical development affecting locomotion, gestural communication, and burgeoning motor skills, both gross and fine.

Conceptualizations of infancy, specifically the central role of infancy in the development of mental life, have shifted dramatically within the history of psychoanalysis. Early psychoanalytic conceptualizations, including those of Freud and Klein, were primarily based on clinical reconstructions in adult and child analyses. Freud's model depicted the infant as narcissistic and drive dominated, while Klein posited the existence of an inborn capacity for object relatedness grounded in a complex set of innate images or "phantasies," colored by powerful aggressive and libidinal drives. Freud encouraged observational research to support ideas about infancy and childhood. The pioneers of early observation include A. Freud, Spitz, Mahler, Winnicott, and Bowlby. These contributors looked at babies in naturalistic settings and developed their theoretical views based on what they saw. A growing recognition of the importance of interaction with and provision by the environment produced innovations in developmental theorizing. Mahler, Winnicott, and Bowlby privileged the crucial role of the mother-baby relationship over the importance of the drives. Despite their differences in emphases and theoretical orientations, these contributors all operated from the Winnicottian principle: "There is no such thing as an infant, meaning, of course, that whenever one finds an infant one finds maternal care, and without maternal care there would be no infant" (Winnicott, 1975/1992).

A. Freud is credited with launching the observational research in this country that has revolutionized our contemporary view of infancy. Increasingly, naturalistic observation has melded with empirical research, profoundly influencing current-day thinking about infancy. The data obtained by developmental and cognitive psychologists have confirmed and illuminated the remarkable inborn capacities of infants and their readiness to engage in interaction

with the world. Whether these findings are useful or even relevant in psychoanalytic theorizing about infancy is a subject of some debate (Fajardo, 1993, 1998; Wolff, 1996). The findings of developmental and cognitive psychology have documented the complex array of the newborn's capacities to perceive and learn from the surrounding world, as well as the real limitations of infant representations (Emde, 1991; Gergely, 1992; D. N. Stern, 1992; Fonagy et al., 2002). "Baby watchers" within psychoanalysis have sought to integrate psychoanalytic thinking with new findings and have delivered a new picture of infancy and of early development, which presumably affects their clinical work with adults. Especially relevant for the latter are those who have sought direct correlations between the dyadic relationship of infancy and the patient-analyst relationship (Emde, 1990; Beebe and Lachman, 1998).

Infantile Genital Phase, formerly known as the **Phallic Phase** or **Phallic Genital Phase**, is the third stage in Freud's schema of infantile psychosexual development, spanning the years from about three to five, during which the child's interest in his genitals acquires psychological dominance along with an upsurge of exhibitionistic impulses. It follows the oral and anal stages and merges into the succeeding oedipal phase. The infantile genital phase marks the beginning of an organization that subordinates other urges to the primacy of the genitals. This phase is distinguished from the "early genital phase" or "pre-oedipal genital phase," occurring between fifteen and nineteen months of age, during which the infant first discovers and takes an interest in his genitals. It is also distinguished from the "genital phase" that emerges when the adolescent discovers the significance of the genitals for reproduction.

The renaming of this phase from "phallic" to "infantile" genital phase represents a rejection of Freud's phallocentric theory of psychosexual development, which asserts that the penis is the principle object of sexual interest for children of both sexes, that the little girl has no awareness of her own genital until later in development, and that her fantasies of castration and penis envy are "bedrock" rather than serving defensive purposes. Contemporary perspectives on female psychosexual development focus on the notion of primary femininity and a uniquely female set of genital anxieties. However, the renaming of the phase does not invalidate the importance that genital difference holds for every child; nor does it diminish the importance of "phallic" phase conflicts for the little boy, or the universal symbolic significance of the phallus for both genders.

Freud introduced the concept of the phallic phase rather late in his career (1923b; 1924b; 1925b); however, he introduced various related issues much earlier, for example, the concept of infantile or pre-genital sexuality (Freud, 1897g), the primacy of the phallus for both genders, and the associated castration complex (Freud, 1909c). In Freud's theorizing, **phallus** conveys a symbolic meaning that encompasses more than the male genital organ, involving notions of power and generative forces in nature, as, for example, illustrated by its substitutive function in the unconscious equation of baby=feces=phallus. According to Freud's theories of infantile sexuality, the fantasy of a **phallic mother** is formed in the course of the child's psychosexual development. Freud did not use the term *phallic mother* until late in his writings, although Little Hans's fantasy that his mother possessed a penis is clearly discernible in the case (1909c). However, in his papers on fetishism, Freud (1927b) described how the little boy had to construct a fantasy of a woman with a phallus to ward off the recognition of the threatening reality of a castrated, penis-less creature, the woman, and the possibility of his own castration.

In Freud's view, the psychosexual development of boys and girls is the same until the discovery of genital difference. The little girl's phallic phase involves the recognition of her deficient castrated genital, while the little boy's phallic phase involves pride in his genital and anxiety that his genital can also be destroyed. According to Freud, the little girl's discovery of her own genital, the vagina, does not occur until the resolution of the oedipal phase. At that time, the little girl has renounced her mother as her primary love object, holding her mother responsible for her absent penis, and has turned to her father in the hopes of obtaining her substitutive penis, a baby. With that libidinal object shift, the little girl also renounces masculine clitoral masturbation and discovers the passive receptive sexual attitude involving the vagina (1924b, 1925b).

The challenge to Freud's phallocentric view of psychosexual development was immediate, based upon data derived from adult psychoanalyses; however, some of the most interesting critique has come from childhood observational studies that followed. For example, Erikson (1950), noting significant differences in boys' and girls' drawings and play patterns, was reluctant to generalize that the infantile sexual organization was phallic for both sexes. Similarly, Parens et al. (1976) found no evidence for phallic aggression in girls. Roiphe and Galenson (Roiphe, 1968; Roiphe and Galenson, 1981a) found substantial evidence of genital preoccupation in all children

from fifteen months of age on, and proposed that an early genital phase occurs between fifteen and twenty-four months of age in both boys and girls. Meanwhile, many other studies offered evidence of the little girls' vaginal awareness as early as infancy (Greenacre, 1958a; Kleeman, 1976; Chehrazi, 1986), and an early sense of herself as female (Stoller 1968c, 1976; H. Blum, 1976b; Money and Ehrhardt, 1972; Parens et al., 1976; P. Tyson and R. Tyson, 1990). With further maturation of cognitive capacities and later opportunities for the reworking of early narcissistic conflicts, the girl is able to resolve her penis envy and then value her own genital, feminine body and female capacities, especially when parental attitudes support such a positive view (Chehrazi, 1986). Other studies (Parens et al., 1976) challenged the traditional notion that the girl's wish for a baby followed upon her penis envy and castration complex, and proposed instead that there is a preprogrammed psychobiological urge to have a baby, which thrusts the girl into the oedipal phase. For all of these reasons, some analysts proposed renaming the phallic phase, resulting in some confusion, because a variety of names are now used in addition to the "infantile genital phase," including the "genital phase," and "early genital phase."

For the boy, the transition from anal to phallic concerns is marked by a tremendous emotional investment in the penis, and a cluster of personality characteristics, known as **phallic narcissism**, involving pride, self confidence, exhibitionism, and aggressive self aggrandizement. During this phase, boys evince a preoccupation with such toys as guns, knives, airplanes, and racing cars, and an interest in games and fantasies that symbolically celebrate the phallus. Such attitudes may also serve to defend against and overcompensate for castration anxiety. Little girls can show such traits as well, with exhibitionism regarding the whole body, arguably as an adaptation to the recognition of genital differences (Edgcumbe and Burgner, 1975). The persistence of these attitudes into adulthood has been called the **phallic character** or **phallic-narcissistic character** (W. Reich, 1933/1945), which in some cases may be accompanied by an unconscious fantasy of the **body as a phallus** (B. Lewin 1933).

Writers following Freud have elaborated on the role of the fantasized phallic mother in defending against the boy's castration anxiety. Bak (1968) described the **phallic woman** as the ubiquitous fantasy in perversions. Stoller's work (1975a) emphasized the importance of the fantasy in male homosexuals, transvestites, and fetishists. In dressing up as a woman, for example, the transvestite acts out the unconscious fantasy of a woman with a penis. Greenacre (1968) also pointed to the underlying castration anxiety and fantasy of the phallic mother in understanding the meaning of the fetish in the male. Both Stoller and Greenacre stressed the role of childhood trauma, such as an overly seductive mother, in the reinforcement of the fantasy.

H. Deutsch (1965) felt that the presence of this fantasy could also be discerned in homosexual women. While the concept of the phallic mother has been seen primarily as a denial of castration anxiety, it has also been understood as expressing earlier, more infantile fears. Brunswick (1940) asserted that the fantasy is a regressive compensation: The phallic mother not only possesses a penis but is also seen as all-powerful. The fantasy of a penis is projected back upon the early infantile image of the active, caretaking mother and her breast. Chasseguet-Smirgel (1964) asserted that the image of the omnipotent mother survives in everyone. Kubie (1974) explained the fantasy from a unique perspective: as a manifestation of the ubiquitous "drive to become both sexes."

Fantasies such as the phallic mother illustrate the symbolic significance of the phallus, its distinction from the anatomical penis, and its use as universal psychic construction representing power and potency—values that may be aspired to by both men and women (Fogel, 1998; M. Diamond, 2006). However, there is generally less reference in the psychoanalytic literature to phallic fantasies, as notions of the primacy of the phallus and penis envy in female development have been challenged. Feminist writers have reinterpreted the fantasy of the phallic mother in terms of cultural influences on images of women. For example, a male's original and early feelings of awe toward a powerful mother may be hidden beneath devaluing images of women (Birksted-Breen, 1996; Elise, 1998).

In an entirely different context, the term *phallus* is used in contemporary psychoanalytic discourse as a central organizing concept in Lacanian theory involving the structure of the oedipus complex.

Infantile Neurosis is the universal and persisting psychic structure and organization that coalesces during the oedipal phase of development as a result of oedipal conflict. Underlying this structure is the developmental achievement of superego formation and consolidation. This intrapsychic organization forms the basis of later adult neurosis, although it need not eventuate in pathology. As such, infantile neurosis is a metapsychological concept rather than a manifest clinical entity (Tolpin, 1970). It requires (re)construction through analysis of the adult neu-

rotic, often facilitated by its manifestation in the transference neurosis. Considerable confusion has surrounded the term throughout the history of psychoanalysis because of failure to maintain this distinction, resulting in its usage for disparate entities, including normal development, any oedipal-level conflict, and neurotic illness. In the interest of clarity, the words *infantile* and *neurosis* have been decoupled, except in the very specific metapsychological meaning described above. Neurotic psychopathology in childhood is best described as childhood neurosis or neurosis of childhood; adult symptomatology is best described in terms of neurosis.

Despite the confusion surrounding the term *infantile neurosis*, it has central significance within the history of psychoanalysis, as it connotes some of the most fundamental of psychoanalytic propositions. These include the universality of internalized conflict, the developmental significance of the oedipus complex and its resolution for psychic structure building, the pathogenesis of neurosis, and the importance of the genetic perspective in a complete metapsychological view of the mind. Finally, the concept of infantile neurosis parallels the history of psychoanalytic understanding of neurosis, which in turn is indistinguishable from the overall history of psychoanalysis.

Freud (1909c) first presented the concept of the infantile neurosis in his case study of Little Hans, in which he described repressed infantile sexuality as the motive force for neurosis. However by 1918, in his case study of the Wolf Man, Freud (1918a) used the term to describe the manifest anxiety hysteria of the four-year-old. This conflation of metapsychology with manifest illness was further complicated by Freud's use of other meanings at other times, including a characteristic group of symptoms organized around oedipal conflict with origins in childhood, for example, hysterias, phobias, and compulsions (1918a), and the consolidation of oedipal conflict resolution in superego formation (1923a).

Following Freud, confusion about the meaning of infantile neurosis persisted (New York Psychoanalytic Institute, 1956; Tolpin, 1970; Blos, 1972; Ritvo, 1974). For Klein (1932), infantile neurosis was a stage of life during which the depressive position could be expressed, worked through, and overcome. Both A. Freud (1954) and Loewald (1974) viewed neurotic conflict as inevitable in personality formation, and in this context, used infantile neurosis as a concept equivalent to neurosis and neurotic conflict. A. M. Cooper (1987a, 1987b) has suggested that a "modern" view of the infantile neurosis should regard it as "an unprivileged set of current fantasies rather than historical fact."

Inferiority Complex: see COMPLEX, NARCISSISM

Inhibition: see NEUROSIS

Inner Genital Phase: see EARLY GENITAL PHASE

Insight: see INTERPRETATION, MENTALIZATION, THERAPEUTIC ACTION

Instinct/Instinctualization: see DRIVE, EROTIZATION, PSYCHOSOMATIC DISORDERS, TRAUMA

Intellectualization is a defensive process whereby intellectual activity is used to control and ward off unacceptable or intolerable impulses, thoughts, and feelings. It is exemplified by abstract, theoretical, or philosophical speculation that avoids emotional or somatic feeling. The term has been used interchangeably with flight into reason (Fenichel, 1932), and is closely related to isolation of affect (A. Freud, 1936). One form of intellectualization is rationalization, a term coined by Jones (1908), whereby an individual avoids deeper examination of a troubling reality with the offer of a so-called reasonable explanation. Intellectualization is the opposite of what has been called "affectualization," where emotion is used as a defense against understanding (G. Bibring et al., 1961). Intellectualization is commonly associated with obsessional and/or paranoid disorders (Freud, 1909d).

A. Freud (1936, 1945) defined intellectualization as a defense, linked by its avoidance of feeling states to isolation of affect. She described the extensive use of intellectualization in adolescents who manage an increase in instinctual demands with their newly acquired ability for abstract reasoning. Hartmann (1939a) emphasized the reality-oriented, adaptive aspects of intellectualization, which serves to enrich knowledge and enhance intellectual functioning. However, extreme intellectualization may also limit access to emotions and affects and contribute to obsessive and paranoid symptoms and traits. During psychoanalytic treatment, intellectualization, or "pseudo-insight," can be used to resist emotional insight and engagement with the analyst.

Intergenerational Transfer (or **Transmission**) **of Trauma**, sometimes referred to as secondary or vicarious traumatization (Scheeringa and Zeanah, 2001), is the unconscious psychological process by which the effect of trauma in a parent is passed on to the child. Parents with unresolved trauma who are unable to reflect upon or contextualize their trauma are at risk for experiencing their child's helplessness, crying, and rage as re-creations of their own original trauma. This experience may then serve as a trigger to both avoidance of the child's distress—thereby exacerbating it—and to flashbacks. In the moment of a flashback, parents may confuse their child with a tormentor from their own childhood. This confusion can, in turn, trigger a rageful, withdrawing, and/or otherwise nonprotective response that may traumatize the child in a way that reenacts the parent's trauma. Current research suggests that when parents have resolved their own traumatic experiences, by contextualizing them in time and place and integrating them into their life narratives, they rarely pass these traumas on to their children.

The term *intergenerational transmission of trauma* was first used by H. Barocas and C. Barocas (1979) in the context of children of holocaust survivors. However, the concept had already been a powerful organizing concept in psychoanalytically informed parent-infant research and clinical work. Beginning with Fraiberg, Adelson, and Shapiro's (1975) description of "ghosts in the nursery," and leading to Fonagy, Steele, et al.'s (1993) elaboration of "reflective function" in the mother as a key determinant of the attachment category of the child, the assumption that unconscious traumatogenic experience can be communicated by parents to their young children is present throughout contemporary psychoanalytically informed infancy studies and attachment theorizing. With regard to adult psychopathology, the concept has influenced self psychology, contemporary object relations and relational theory, and research into the etiology of borderline personality, all of which, explicitly or implicitly, emphasize the importance of the parents' capacity to think about their own and their infant's separate, unique minds. Recurrent transmission of trauma to the infant by a nonreflective traumatized parent initiates or exacerbates dissociative processes that are postulated to be the core disturbance in adult symptomatology (Coates, 1998; Fonagy et al., 2003).

Intergenerational transfer of trauma is a concept that came into being in the 1960s as clinicians began to see the adult children of Holocaust survivors. These individuals presented with a range of emotional difficulties that appeared to echo the effects of their parents' traumatic experiences in various ways (Krystal, 1968; Auerhahn and Laub, 1998). The concept is a specific illustration of the process of unconscious communication described by Freud.

In the clinical situation, the concept of intergenerational transfer of trauma is useful in several different ways. In working with children whose symptoms stem from unresolved parental trauma, parental intervention serves to modify the parental behavior and attributions that sustain the child's symptoms. Traumatized parents may be helped to understand and identify current trauma-triggered inappropriate behavior and attitudes that may be outside of awareness, such as hostile negative identifications, in relation to their children. They may then be able to modulate behavior that can be traumatizing to their children by identifying repetitive reenactments and recognizing their underpinnings in repressed trauma and their elaboration in unconscious fantasy. The construct is also useful in helping adults understand anxieties and specific fantasies in themselves that do not seem to stem directly from traumatic events in their own life, but may have been passed down to them by their parents' unresolved anxieties and fantasies around trauma-related experiences. Finally, the concept of intergenerational transfer of trauma can sensitize the clinician to ways that powerful unconscious processes, below the level of flashbacks and other signs and symptoms of traumatic stress, can be activated in adult patients by their children's traumatic experiences, suggesting the reverberation of trauma across the generations. Contemporary research (Schechter et al., 2007) focuses on the mediating process involved in intergenerational transfer of violent trauma from one generation to the next.

Internal Saboteur: see FAIRBAIRN, OBJECT, SPLITTING

Internalization comprises a group of psychological processes whereby the inner world is altered by taking in real or imagined aspects of the external world. Internalization is the opposite of externalization, a group of processes whereby aspects of the internal world are attributed to external reality. Both terms reflect the fact that the inner world develops in interaction with an external world, with internalization and externalization describing basic aspects of this interaction. Internalization is closely related to the terms *incorporation, introjection,* and *identification.* Historically, these terms have at times been used interchangeably and are often confused with one another. There have been numerous attempts to clarify their distinct, if overlapping, meanings, using various criteria, such as original meanings, most common use, level of abstraction, level of development, association with kind of psychopathology, whether whole or part objects are taken in, and the extent to which

what is internalized has become integrated with the self, to name a few.

In all schools of psychoanalysis, internalization plays a major role in all psychic development and occurs throughout the life cycle. It allows the mind to record the history of interactions between the individual and the outside world, especially other people. Attitudes, behaviors, values, and functions of important objects, as well as interactions with these objects are internalized, so that over time the individual can assume the functions originally supplied by others. Internalization contributes to the development of the basic structures of the mind (the ego, the superego, self and object representations, and others). It also contributes to the development of character traits and cultural attitudes (as in the painful **internalized homophobia**, which underlies the self hatred so common in gay individuals) (Malyon, 1982). Internalization is dependent upon ego functions such as perception, memory, and the capacity to form representations and symbols, which encode aspects of self-object interaction in the mind. Internalization is an aspect of normal maturation, and it may also be a motivated event and/or function as a defense. A key motivation for internalization is the wish to preserve the gratifying and/or need-fulfilling functions normally fulfilled by the object, by making them a part of the self. During development, internalization can be a means by which the child holds on to object-related gratifications that are lost as greater autonomy is achieved. Internalization may be stimulated by periods of transition and loss or of anxiety. The processes of internalization reflect the stage of development at which they occur, and represent both real as well as fantasied interactions with others. Internalizations vary in the extent to which they are complete, stable, and/or reversible. Internalization of various aspects of the analyst-patient relationship play a major role in theories of the therapeutic action of psychoanalysis (J. Strachey, 1934; Loewald, 1960). For example, the concept of the **transmuting internalization** of the analyst's selfobject function is central to the theory of therapeutic action proposed by self psychology (Kohut, 1977).

Most analysts follow Hartmann in using internalization as a generic concept to subsume the others. In line with his interest in psychoanalysis as a general psychology conceptualized within the framework of biological and evolutionary considerations, Hartmann (1939a) emphasized the adaptive function of internalization to transform regulating interactions with the environment into self regulation or function. Schafer (1968b) agreed with Hartmann that internalization is the overarching concept that subsumes the others, but emphasized the motivational (dynamic) and later narrative aspects of internalization. Loewald (1960, 1962a), who emphasized that internalization in psychoanalysis applies mainly to relationships with others, distinguished between **primary internalizations**, which contribute to the development of concepts of internal/external or self/other, and **secondary internalizations**, which occur after these boundaries have been established.

Freud first used the term *internalization* in a 1912 letter to Jones, referring to the "internalizations of resistances," internal repression being the outcome of an external obstacle (1912f). Freud (1913e) introduced the concept of incorporation in 1913 while discussing the myth of the primal horde, linking incorporation to the cannibalism of primitive peoples and describing how the sons acquire the strength of the father by eating him in their first totem meal. He went on to describe incorporation as related to his new oral phase, conceptualizing incorporation as the aim of the oral libido, an aim with three parts: to obtain pleasure by taking the object into one's body, to destroy the object, and to appropriate the object's qualities (1905b, 1915b). He also stated that incorporation was the prototype for identification (1905b). Contemporary analysts, many of whom no longer adhere to the drive theory attached to the original concept of incorporation, still use the term as a fantasy whereby an individual imagines that an aspect of the object is being taken into the interior space of his body. Such fantasies are the way in which the mental processes of introjection and/or identification are represented. The opposite of incorporation is a fantasy of expulsion (Abraham, 1924b). Fantasies of incorporation are often accompanied by fantasies of being incorporated by others (B. Lewin, 1950). Incorporation is not limited to the oral mode, and may also include other modes, such as auditory, respiratory, and anal. Fantasies of incorporation may be aggressive, loving and protective, or both. Incorporative fantasies are central to Kleinian theory, representing the subject's experience of taking the object inside the body; *introjection* is the term used by Kleinians to describe the mental process involved (Hinshelwood, 1989).

Introjection is a term introduced by Ferenczi (1909) in 1909 to distinguish neurotic psychopathology (characterized by the use of introjection) from psychotic (characterized by the use of projection). Freud (1915b) adopted the term in 1915 as the process by which the ego takes into itself an object experienced as a source of pleasure (in contrast to projection); he used the term again in 1921 (also in contrast to projection) when he described identification as a process whereby a lost object is introjected into the ego, as in melancholia (1921). From the outset, introjection has been used in highly confusing ways, often synonymously with incorporation and/or identification. The concept has been used extensively by the Kleinians in describing how processes of introjection and projection are crucial to the development of the internal world of the infant, as anxieties linked with aggression and associated with good and bad objects are managed using these defensive operations. E. Weiss coined the term **introject**, used as a noun, to designate an object that has been taken inside the ego (or self), similar to what the Kleinians often call the **internal object** (E. Weiss, 1932). More recently, Schafer (1968b) proposed that the term *introjection* be used to designate a type of internalization whereby an object representation is changed into an introject, or an "inner presence," with which the individual feels an ongoing relationship.

Identification (see separate entry) refers to a type of internalization whereby an individual's self representation or behavior or both are modified so as to resemble the object. In contrast to introjection, identification, as defined by Schafer, refers to an internalization in which what was external is now integrated into the self representation, rather than experienced as an internal presence. Freud introduced the term *identification* first as an aspect of symptom formation in hysteria (1900) and later as central to symptom formation in melancholia (1917c). In the latter formulation, he also placed identification in a developmental sequence of object relations: the first way an individual relates to the object, prior to the formation of real object ties. Finally, Freud began to explore identification as a normal process, first in the formation of group ties (1921), and soon in the formation of basic psychic structures, including the superego, and the ego (1923a). All subsequent psychoanalysts from all schools of thought have used the concept of identification to describe the ubiquitous process by which the self is modified on the model of the object.

Interpersonal Psychoanalysis, introduced by Henry Stack Sullivan in the mid-twentieth century, is a psychoanalytic theory of the development and functioning of the mind and of psychoanalytic treatment, based upon the perspective that psychological meaning can only emerge, evolve, and become known in an interpersonal environment. From its inception, interpersonal psychoanalysis defined its commitments in opposition to those of Freudian psychoanalysis, which Sullivan regarded as too focused on drive/instinct. Instead, Sullivan espoused a focus on social and cultural factors and on the experience of the external world. The early interpersonalists also de-emphasized or rejected the role of intrapsychic structure, the dynamic unconscious, and internalized object relations. Other salient characteristics of the interpersonal school include a view of the self as the seat of personal experience and agency, conceived of dynamically rather than structurally and as the product of interactive processes with others; a view of pathology that is based upon disruptions in the equilibrium and integrity of the self; and a view of the mind that privileges cognition over affect and regards cognition as the outcome of interpersonal relations. Salient characteristics of interpersonal treatment include an interactive view of the clinical situation with a "here-and-now" focus to interpretation; a focus on what is observable in that interaction; and an attempt to understand the human experience in terms of what "really" happens.

However, it is easiest to define interpersonal psychoanalysis in terms of what it is not, perhaps because more than any other psychoanalytic school, it is characterized by diversity in both theory and in clinical practice. From its inception, interpersonal psychoanalysis has attracted individuals who are noncomformists and who have had wide-ranging commitments beyond the realm of the clinical situation. Sullivan was influenced by the social sciences and education; Fromm, an early founder of the school, had a lifelong commitment to political and cultural issues. Those early contributors whose major commitments were to clinical work had very specific areas of interest. Thompson, who is credited with conceiving of interpersonal psychoanalysis as an entity, devoted her attention to the psychology of women and to interpersonal conceptions of character; Fromm-Reichmann, another early contributor, independently developed clinical views and conceptions of the treatment of psychotic patients.

The early interpersonalists were deeply influenced by the work of Ferenczi (Ferenczi and Rank, 1925; Dupont, 1988), although Ferenczi never actually rejected his allegiance to Freudian psychoanalysis. However, Ferenczi exerted the greatest influence on schools of analysis that privilege the analytic relationship as the primary factor in therapeutic action. His legacy is directly acknowledged by interpersonal analysts because of his recognition of the impact of real-life experience on the course of development (Ferenczi, 1933), his portrayal of psychoanalysis as the interaction of two real personalities, his encouragement of the analyst's active participation, his recognition of the centrality of countertransference as a

mutually shaping complement to transference, and his attention to the potentially retraumatizing effects of the analytic encounter (Harris and Aron, 1997).

Sullivan, who was not a psychoanalyst, devised a psychological theory and technique that remained independent of the Freudian theoretical hegemony that existed in the early twentieth century. Sullivan was influenced by Ferenczi, however American values of pragmatism, empiricism, and pluralism are most apparent in his work, presumably through the influence of American philosophical perspectives espoused by James, Pierce, Mead, and Meyer, among others. In Sullivan's view, the self develops in relationships with others and can be understood as a set of reflected self appraisals; it is nothing more than habitual interpersonal patterns, and the notion of a private, essential self is a narcissistic illusion. Sullivan's position that the self is interpersonal led him to shift the treatment focus to the observation of the patient in relation to other people, including the analyst (1953b). He rejected the technique of free association in favor of a "detailed inquiry" into the patient's actual interpersonal experience, past and present. The detailed inquiry was a form of "participant observation," by which Sullivan (1940, 1953b) meant the analyst's inevitable personal involvement in the unfolding relatedness of the detailed inquiry. However, Sullivan also felt that it should be possible for the analyst to consistently guide that participation in a way that served the patient's interest. In other words, he did not accept the analyst's inevitable unconscious and personal involvement with the patient, a principle that by the 1970s had became synonymous with the interpersonal orientation.

Sullivan (1953a) contributed his own theory of psychological development, including an intensive focus on mother-infant relatedness and the events of early childhood. In Sullivan's view, the infant, through a process of "empathy," experiences the disruptive presence of the mother's anxiety, which then serves as a motivational factor in the infant's attempts to maintain psychic equilibrium. The infant utilizes a process of splitting, resulting in separate visions of the good and bad mother, which later become integrated and organized as "personifications," and then ultimately "complexes." The infant develops reciprocal self personifications of "good me" and "bad me" that are ultimately integrated into a dynamism called the self, and a self system that utilizes defensive self protective operations. The outcome of this process is based upon the nature of the infant's interactions with others and, most importantly, the level of the mother's anxiety that the infant must endure. Probably the most widely recognized of

Sullivan's (1953a) developmental innovations was his description of the "chumship" of preadolescence, the first authentic self/other intimacy in a child's life, in which the feelings and perspective of the other matter at least as much as one's own. If all goes reasonably well, the chumship is integrated within a healthy expression of lust, resulting in adult sexual intimacy. In Sullivan's view, many people progress only as far as the chumship because of cultural and societal trends that make sexuality, and especially homosexuality (Blechner, 2005), extremely difficult to negotiate.

Sullivan regarded experience that is not admitted to awareness as characteristic patterns of relatedness with significant others. Similarly, in Sullivan's view (1940, 1953a, 1956a, 1956b), what are defended against are not internal dynamic events but "selectively inattended" or "dissociated" aspects of relationships with significant others, which cannot be known in symbolic, linguistic form. Instead, these patterns are enacted in ways invisible to the actor but observable to the properly trained clinician. For Sullivan (1940, 1953a), language in its most highly developed form is used in a way that allows for the public verification, or "consensual validation," of meaning. The meanings that are conveyed in language, or could be if so desired, are classified as the "syntaxic mode" of experience. The "parataxic mode" is composed of "private" meanings that participate in the structuring of experience but that cannot be known by oneself in the explicit terms of language. Experience is maintained as parataxic by ongoing selective inattention or dissociation. In this sense, parataxis cannot be considered in the explicit public terms of language, because it is unconscious.

A significant aspect of treatment for Sullivan was the identification of parataxis and its conversion to syntaxic experience. "Parataxic distortion" was Sullivan's term for the patterns of incompleteness and distortion, based on selective inattention and dissociation that an individual characteristically employs in the creation of his images of other people. The result is interpersonal misunderstanding and difficulty. Sullivan encouraged the detailed study of interpersonal relations in the consulting room but without assigning oedipal conflict a central organizing role, a role that was taken for granted in Freudian theories of transference and transference neurosis of the era. Later interpersonalists built on Sullivan's interest in cognition and language (Schachtel, 1959/2001; Tauber and Green 1959/2008; Barnett, 1966, 1980a, 1980b; Arieti, 1967, 1976; Levenson, 1972, 1983, 1987; Greenberg, 1986, 1991; D. B. Stern, 1994, 1995, 1997).

Fromm, another early founder of interpersonal psychoanalysis, received formal psychoanalytic training at the Berlin Institute. Fromm also had a lifelong commitment to political and cultural issues, having been a member of the tenured faculty at the Institute of Social Research at Frankfurt University, with Horkheimer, Adorno, and Marcuse. Fromm developed his social critique in his concepts of: social character (1947); the "escape from freedom" (1941), which he felt explained the success of fascism; the idea that not only individuals but also societies could be either sane or insane (1955a); as well as other ideas. Although Fromm never wrote the clinical manifesto that he promised, his humanistic, existential inclinations—his emphases on authenticity, directness, spontaneity, affective immediacy, and core-to-core interpersonal contact—were highly influential on early interpersonalists and, through them, on later generations (Fromm, 1955b). In fact, Fromm's most important influence on his colleagues was his clinical perspective, which differed greatly from Sullivan's. For Fromm, the existence of an authentic, agentic self was fundamental. Fromm's (1951) interest in dreams and other aspects of the nonrational also contrasted with Sullivan (1940, 1953a), who included dreams among phenomena of the inner life that could not be directly observed and therefore did not repay close study. Fromm's attitude to dreams predominates in contemporary interpersonal psychoanalysis (Bonime, 1962; Ullman, 1996; Blechner, 2001; Lippmann, 2002; P. Bromberg, 2006).

Sullivan left a notable legacy to contemporary interpersonal psychoanalysis through his work on dissociation, which has expanded into distinctly interpersonal models of mind. P. Bromberg (1998a, 2006) proposed that the mind, or self, is multiple, a shifting landscape of "self-states." Shifts between states take place as a result of the mind's need to maintain its equilibrium and continuity, the sense of being the same person one has been. Dissociated, or "not-me," states are inconsistent with that sense of continuity and therefore must be sequestered from other self-states. When ongoing interpersonal life makes it impossible to avoid experiencing oneself as not-me, the continuity of the self is threatened; it can be preserved only by unconsciously enacting not-me, thereby avoiding the intolerable experience of feeling that one is not "oneself." The ideal is to "stand in the spaces" between self-states, able to accept all one's parts, and in that way to feel like one person while being many. Bromberg detailed the way he works with clinical process, particularly its affective aspects, continuously consulting his own shifting self-states for hints about what is transpiring with his patients.

D. B. Stern (1997, 2010) proposed a dissociation-based model in which unconscious phenomena are defined as "unformulated experience." Unformulated experience is potential experience; it has not yet been given articulate or symbolic shape, and so it cannot be reflected on. Dissociation is understood as the defensively motivated preservation of experience in its unformulated state. The shape taken by unformulated experience is not entirely predetermined, although it is constrained by reality. The explicit form that experience takes depends on the nature of the interpersonal field within which the formulation takes place. Therefore the meanings and events of the analytic relationship are the prime influence on which articulations of experience come into being between patient and analyst. In later work, D. B. Stern (2010) expanded these ideas into the realm of enactment.

The writing that most fully expresses today's interpersonal sensibility is the perspective on clinical practice created by Wolstein and Levenson. Wolstein (1959) introduced what he called the "transference-countertransference interlock," by which he meant that transference and countertransference inevitably play a role in creating and maintaining one another. Later, Wolstein addressed the irreducibly unique nature of each psyche and each therapeutic dyad and conceived of treatment as the engagement of the "psychic center of the self" (Wolstein 1981, 1983, 1987; Hirsch 2000; Bonovitz 2009).

But it was Levenson (1972, 1983, 1987; Levenson, Hirsch, and Iannuzzi, 2005) who took the decisive step, arguing that, as Mitchell later expressed, "you can't not interact." Analyst and patient are inevitably and unconsciously involved with one another in personal, affectively charged ways, which Levenson described as the heart of psychoanalysis. Levenson's insight lies at the core of both interpersonal and relational psychoanalysis. Contributors to the ongoing expansion of the conception of therapeutic relatedness that began in Levenson and Wolstein's work include Hirsch (1985, 1996, 2002, 2008), Ehrenberg (1992), Buechler (2004, 2008), Feiner (2000) and Fiscalini (2004).

Interpersonal psychoanalysis has been critiqued both from within its own ranks and also from several generations of mainstream "Freudian" psychoanalysts. From its inception, interpersonal psychoanalysis was regarded as diminishing the importance of the intrapsychic and the biological dimensions of human experience and focusing exclusively on the interpsychic domain. Interpersonal theory rejects the concept of drives as the motivator of human experience but does not offer another integrated point of view. Sullivan posited the role of anxiety; others have expanded motivation to include other affects or cognition as primary sources of motivation. Freudians have also critiqued interpersonal psychoanalysis because of its de-emphasis of the role of unconscious fantasy in mental life. Later, starting in the 1980s, some relational analysts (J. Frankel, 1998) offered their own criticisms, including insufficient concern with developmental theory and issues; underemphasis on unconscious processes, including fantasy and internal object relations; and too much emphasis on resistance as consciously willful or oppositional. Too frequently, according to these critics, interpersonal analysts created a challenging and confrontational atmosphere in the consulting room, accompanied by an emphasis on clarity, directness, and honesty that can make it difficult for patients to adopt a nondefensive, exploratory attitude toward their own experience. Interpersonal psychoanalysis has also been criticized for its failure to integrate or to address the inconsistencies and contradictions introduced by a diverse set of theoretical propositions. This has sometimes resulted in confusion and a failure to fully acknowledge the implications of any particular position (Demos, 1996).

The interpersonal group has played a critical role in the paradigmatic shift that has taken place over the last several decades in the United States from the unquestioned dominance of drive and structural theory to the interpersonal-relational model of psychoanalytic treatment and human growth and development. The interpersonal perspective, with its focus on the interpersonal field, contributed a major current to the emergence of the relational school in the 1980s. Greenberg and Mitchell (1983) are credited with creating the concept of the relational school (see RELATIONAL PSYCHOANALYSIS) which serves to link the interpersonal perspective with the British object relations school. Mitchell went on to become one of the major contributors to relational theory, if not its intellectual leader (S. Mitchell, 1988, 1993, 1997, 2000). Although today's psychoanalytic world is unquestionably pluralistic, it is also the case that interpersonal and relational influences are apparent in other psychoanalytic theories.

Interpretation is the analyst's verbal communication to the patient of his understanding of the patient's unconscious mental life as it is expressed in the patient's speech, thoughts, affects, fantasies, and behaviors. An interpretation connects aspects of the patient's conscious experience with those mental experiences that he has actively kept from awareness, thereby making unconscious mental life accessible to conscious understanding. Interpretation leads to insight. While there is a clear informational component to interpretation, effective interpretations usually encompass more than intellectual understanding and resonate with some aspect of the patient's emotional experience. Interpretation differs from clarification, which expands on what is already in the patient's consciousness, and from confrontation, which addresses aspects of the patient's conscious experience whose meanings are denied or dissociated. The analyst's interpretation is offered in the context of the transference/countertransference relationship and therefore carries both conscious and unconscious, transference-laden meanings for the patient. An interpretation also reflects both conscious and unconscious aspects of the analyst's subjective experience, which may be expressed in his choice of what to interpret, his language, or tone of voice. In the course of the analysis, both analyst and patient modify or add to any interpretation as new information emerges.

Interpretation has significance within psychoanalysis both historically and within the present. It is the intervention that is uniquely psychoanalytic, and thereby distinguishes psychoanalysis from treatments that are based upon the analyst's suggestion. The function of interpretation is tied to a view of the mind that features a dynamic unconscious actively excluded from consciousness through the processes of defense. However, the role of interpretation is at the center of core psychoanalytic controversies: Are interpretations about true things that can be discovered about a patient's mental life, or do they offer the patient a plausible and coherent narrative about themselves (the hermeneutic perspective)? Is the analyst in an epistemologically privileged or objective position from which to know things about the patient's mind? Do interpretations convey meanings that are intrinsic to and persistent in the patient's own mind, or are they co-constructed in the unique dyadic interaction between a particular patient and analyst? Are interpretations, in fact, the central feature of the therapeutic action of psychoanalysis? How do interpretations help patients? There are also controversies about the technical use of interpretations: What are the salient aspects of mental life to interpret? Should interpretations focus solely on the transference or on the patient's extra-transference mental life as well? Should interpretations refer to mental contents close to the patient's conscious awareness, or to those to which the patient has little conscious connection?

The concept of interpretation, and the word itself, first appeared in "Studies on Hysteria" (Breuer and Freud, 1893/1895) in Freud's treatments of Elisabeth von R. and Lucy R. However, it became a technical term in "The Interpretation of Dreams" where Freud (1900) asserted that dreams, like symptoms, have meaning. More specifically, the interpretation of a dream attempts to reestablish a link, or a "lost connection," between unconscious and conscious mental life. In Freud's topographical theory, he posited that while unacceptable wishes are repressed, their continuing pressure for gratification is expressed in symptoms. To interpret the meaning of a symptom, that is, to make it conscious, allows the patient to replace repression with conscious, rational, and moral judgments (1909c). When Freud (1923a) elaborated the structural theory, he reconsidered the goal of interpretation. Freud conceptualized the ego as a mental agency responding to the demands of unconscious wishes derived from the drives (the id), unconscious punitive prohibitions (the superego), and reality; in this conceptualization, interpretation becomes the way to extend the ego's mastery.

Following Freud, Fenichel (1938b) elaborated on this theme, noting that interpretations should be directed to the psychological surface, to defenses with which the patient has some resonant connection. By first interpreting the unconscious aspects of defense and resistance, interpretations gradually help the patient's observing ego to master the underlying anxiety associated with repressed wishes, awareness of less-distorted expressions of those wishes, and awareness of unconscious superego (conscience) demands.

In his book *Character Analysis* (1933/1945), W. Reich made a significant contribution to the technique of interpretation. Reich observed that until a patient's character resistances are addressed, little analytic progress can be made by the interpretation of other aspects of the patient's unconscious life. Reich's prescient appreciation for the way characterological defenses suffuse the patient's experience of an analytic treatment became the foundation for contemporary ego-psychological analytic technique. However, Reich's rigid and adversarial approach to the interpretation of character resistances presented new problems and has not been incorporated into contemporary technique.

J. Strachey (1934), using Kleinian concepts of projection and introjection, formulated the concept of the **mutative interpretation** (one promoting change). Strachey theorized that patients in analysis are freed up for normal development by introjecting the analyst's benign "auxiliary super-ego," thereby diminishing the ferocity of the patient's superego and lessening both aggression and the consequent need for pathological defenses. Strachey posited that this introjection, which occurs when the patient can see the difference between his own aggression and the analyst's more benign superego, is stimulated only during the intense affective experience of the transference. Strachey is remembered for having asserted that only transference interpretations are mutative; however, he also recognized the importance of other interventions that serve to facilitate the analytic process.

What, how, and when an analyst interprets follows from his theoretical orientation. However, regardless of their theoretical orientation, most analysts agree that the process of formulating and making an interpretation is largely a preconscious process. Some analysts place major emphasis on the role of empathy in the interpretive process, but all analysts strive for some level of empathic attunement in formulating interpretations and in assessing the patient's capacity to integrate the information at any particular moment in the treatment.

Three widely utilized types of interpretations that are intrinsic to the theory of therapeutic action have specific designations: 1) **transference interpretation** is the analyst's communication to the patient regarding unconscious, warded-off aspects of the patient's relationship to the analyst. The interpretation may focus on the patient's here-and-now relationship to the analyst or may identify the repetition in the here and now of aspects of internalized, conflictual past relationships. The representation of these relationships in the patient's mind includes both fantasy and reality elements. A minority of analysts have posited that only transference interpretations are mutative or of therapeutic benefit (J. Strachey, 1934; Gill, 1982). The timing of transference interpretation has also been debated. Freud (1912a) recommended that transference should be interpreted only when it has become a resistance. E. Glover (1955) theorized that transference should not be interpreted during the initial phase of treatment, during which a "gathering the transference" occurs. In contrast, Gill (1954, 1982) stressed the importance of analyzing transference manifestations from the beginning of the treatment. 2) **genetic interpretation** links present wishes and fears to those first experienced with important figures in the past. It may focus on childhood experience or fantasy that is consciously remembered or that has been reconstructed during the analysis. 3) In contrast, **dynamic interpretation** focuses on here-and-now conflicts.

Contemporary ego psychologists emphasize the interpretation of all psychological contributions to intrapsychic conflicts organized in multiple unconscious fantasies, especially as these are organized within transference and resistance; these analysts underscore the need for an open-ended inquiry (S. Levy and Inderbitzin, 1992). Kleinian analysts focus on the experience of split-off aspects of the patient's part-self and part-object representations. The analyst becomes aware of these part-self and part-object representations through the patient's associations and by the patient's projective identification, which invites or induces the analyst to subjectively experience the affects associated with these part-self, part-object images. Because of the centrality of projective identification in Kleinian theory, Kleinian analysts are especially attuned to transference/countertransference enactment. Kleinians influenced by Bion (1962a) may choose to interpret or to contain and tolerate the projected subjective experience until the patient is able to reintroject it (Schafer, 1997). Self psychologists interpret patients' defenses against the mobilization of selfobject transferences, and patients' experience of the analyst's inevitable empathic and selfobject failures (Kohut, 1984). From the point of view of self psychology, sustained empathic immersion, rather than isolated moments of empathy, enables the analyst to arrive at understanding of the patient and to make interpretations.

Relational analysts may subscribe to self-psychological, interpersonal, intersubjective, or object relations theories. The umbrella title of *relational* refers to the view that both intrapsychic and interpersonal contributions to any relationship, including the analytic relationship, must be taken into account. Interpretations, therefore, are offered in the context of a patient/analyst relationship in which it is understood that the subjectivities of both participants have shaped the patient's experience that the analyst interprets. The patient may also be aware of and comment on aspects of the analyst's experience of which the analyst is unaware. Interpretations are offered in the setting in which the analyst and patient negotiate the many ambiguities of the experience. The analyst must be flexible enough to present himself as a new object, thereby creating the safety from which to explore and interpret the impact of old objects in the transference (Greenberg, 1986).

Intersubjectivity, a concept borrowed from the philosophy of Husserl, is: 1) the dynamic emotional and psychological interaction of two (or more) different persons, each with their own subjective experience of themselves, each other, and the interactions between them; intersubjectivity includes the idea that this dynamic interaction is best understood by examining the contributions of each person's subjective experience; and 2) the capacity to understand, feel, participate in, and share the subjective experience of another person. The intersubjective perspective is not meant to replace an intrapsychic one but to contextualize it, both developmentally and in the here and now. The clinical situation is a specific example of the intersubjectivity of human relatedness. The capacity for intersubjectivity has been distinguished from the related concepts of empathy and mentalization in a variety of ways; most often, intersubjectivity is considered the broader concept, encompassing the ongoing human interaction that serves as the foundation for the more specific capacities of empathy and/or mentalization. Empathy is most often defined as the affective and cognitive process of feeling/thinking one's way into the experience of another person. Mentalization is most often defined as the ability to understand the behavior of others in terms of mental states, such as beliefs, desires, feelings, and memories, and as the ability to reflect upon one's own mental states.

While psychoanalysis has always included an implicit concept of intersubjectivity, in as much as analyst and patient are able to understand each other largely because each has a mind, in recent decades the concept of intersubjectivity has emerged in the forefront of many psychoanalytic theories about the mind and about treatment. It is the basis for the contemporary shift among some analysts from a "one-person" to a "two-person" psychology, also known as a "contextual psychology" (Orange, Atwood, and Stolorow, 1997). This shift is represented in several schools of thought, including intersubjectivist, interactional, interpersonal, and relational schools, as well as some approaches to contemporary self psychology. All these various approaches share the goals of undermining what Stolorow and Atwood (1979) have called the "myth of isolated mind." This shift also informs much of the contemporary discourse in all psychoanalytic theories about enactment and countertransference, both of which involve recognition of the analyst's conscious and unconscious participation in the analytic encounter. While dozens of psychoanalysts have contributed to the study of intersubjectivity, there are excellent reviews contributed by Aron (1991), Dunn (1995), S. Mitchell (2000), and D. N. Stern (2005).

Stolorow and Atwood (1979) are credited with introducing the term *intersubjectivity* into psychoanalytic discourse. The intersubjective point of view includes several assumptions: 1) An urge toward intersubjectivity, intimacy, or a feeling of **intersubjective orientation**, is a basic and irreducible force within the mind, while **intersubjective disorienta-**

tion results in anxiety. 2) Many important mental structures, capacities, and functions are best understood as having their basis in intersubjectivity, including motivation, defense, empathy, identity, identification, superego, object, self-reflective consciousness, and the self, to mention a few. 3) Intersubjectivity contributes to the capacity for falling in love, feelings of intimacy and belonging, successful parenting, and effective participation in groups. Controversies and questions about intersubjectivity include the following: Is it restricted to what is conscious, or does it include unconscious processes? Is it sometimes asymmetrical, or one-way, or is it always bidirectional? Is intersubjectivity about understanding or about feeling? Is it verbal and/or nonverbal?

Intersubjectivity has many implications for understanding and managing the psychoanalytic clinical situation, including the views that: 1) the material that emerges from the clinical situation is always co-created by the interaction between the analyst's and patient's subjectivities; 2) neither the analyst nor the patient can claim an objective (or "third-person") perspective about what is "really going on," because what happens in a session is always co-created through the interplay of their interacting subjectivities; 3) the patient's psychic reality is not "discovered" in the session but emerges from the relational matrix of the moment; 4) psychoanalytic exploration should focus on understanding the **intersubjective field**, including misunderstandings and processes of repair as well as "moments of meeting," as these unfold in the here and now of the psychoanalytic situation (Boston Change Process Study Group, 2002); and, 5) processes of development and change may be understood to occur within a nonverbal **intersubjective matrix** called "implicit relational knowing" (D. N. Stern et al., 1998; Fonagy, 1999; Lyons-Ruth, 1999). Psychoanalysts with an intersubjective perspective may draw upon some combination of these views within the clinical situation.

Stolorow and Atwood (1992b) emphasized that the development and the structuring of intrapsychic experience is embedded in an intersubjective context that contributes shape and meaning. They view the unconscious from that perspective and distinguish among: a dynamic unconscious, which is comprised of defensively repressed conflicted content; the prereflective unconscious, which is comprised of internalized structure established in the context of the early intersubjective dyad, and then serves as the organizing principles of subjective experience; and the invalidated unconscious, which is comprised of content that cannot be articulated at all because of selfobject failure of validation. The analyst's participation within the intersubjectivity of the analytic situation enables the patient to investigate, articulate, validate, and reorganize his unconscious experience.

J. Benjamin (1990), a relational intersubjectivist, described the intersubjective and the intrapsychic as two realms of human experience that exist together in a state of dynamic tension. The development of the capacity to appreciate the subjectivity of the other is always challenged by the wish to "negate" the other in the effort to maintain omnipotent control. In the clinical situation, the patient and analyst together create an asymmetrical intersubjective matrix, the space in which therapeutic process occurs. Ogden (1994) is credited with the formulation of the "analytic third," a term now used widely to describe the intersubjective matrix. Ogden also viewed the third as an asymmetrical creation in both its contribution from analyst and patient and in their experience of it; he focused on the therapeutic value for the patient of the analyst's capacity to put language to their experience together. In Ogden's view, the analytic third may at times represent a formidable resistance for both patient and analyst, but if it can be understood by the analyst and communicated effectively to the patient, it provides the most fertile and critical data for analyzing the patient's inner experience. Renik's (1993) argument that the analyst's epistemologic position is always one of "irreducible subjectivity," challenged the traditional technical principles of neutrality, abstinence, and anonymity; Renik argued that the analyst's participant-observer role is not only inevitable but entirely desirable. In fact, therapeutic action requires it. In a similar vein, Renik rejected traditional notions of countertransference and enactment because they fail to recognize that the analyst's subjectivity is the fabric of the treatment, not a departure from it.

Developmental psychoanalysts and psychologists have observed phenomena that are closely linked to the development of intersubjective capacities. They have offered a view of early infant development that emphasizes the emergence of the self in relationship to others. In addition, they have recognized greater perceptual capacities in the infant than had been previously recognized. Moreover, by the age of seven to nine months, the infant comes to the momentous realization that inner subjective experiences— the subject matter of the mind—are shareable with someone else (Trevarthen, 1980; Bretherton, McNew, and Beeghly-Smith, 1981; D. N. Stern, 1985). The baby now has a sense of subjective self and is aware that two separate minds can communicate with one another, sharing and comparing perceptions, affects, and intentions or wishes. Furthermore, such recognition stresses the importance of lifelong human relatedness while challenging the assumption that the hallmarks of healthy development are separation, autonomy, and independence.

Emde (Emde, 1988; Emde et al., 1991) also elaborated a theory of an "affective self" that is intrinsically social. He described social referencing as a phenomenon that originates during infancy but that may be utilized at any age. It is a phenomenon in which an individual, encountering a situation of uncertainty, looks to a significant other person for an emotional signal in order to resolve the uncertainty and to regulate behavior accordingly. In Emde's developmental scheme, or "we" psychology, autonomy with connectedness and the evolution of an ever-more-differentiated sense of "we-go" are fundamental to normal ego and object relations. Intersubjective theories of psychology are consistent with contemporary views of development as nonlinear, interactive, and relational.

Intersubjectivity is a term that also intersects with neighboring disciplines of cognitive neuroscience. Many developmental psychoanalysts are hopeful that mirror neurons will provide the beginning of a neurobiological understanding of the capacity for intersubjectivity.

Introject/Introjection: see INTERNALIZATION, OBJECT

Inversion: see HOMOSEXUALITY

Isolation is any defensive process in which an individual separates events, thoughts, or parts of mental experience from one another so as to lessen their emotional impact. The most commonly used term related to isolation is **isolation of affect**, in which an individual separates an idea, experience, or memory from the feelings connected with it, thereby lessening its emotional power.

Freud first described isolation of memories (along with the "dissolving thought connections") as characteristic of obsessional neurosis (1914c). In 1926, he delineated the role of isolation in normal thought processes as serving to facilitate concentration by reducing distraction from irrelevant details and bothersome feelings (1926a). A. Freud (1936) included isolation in her famous list of defense mechanisms, eventually coining the term *isolation of affect*. She linked isolation of affect to intellectualization, in which the intellectual content of material is focused on to defend against its emotional meaning.

The use of isolation of affect ranges from ordinary to extensive. It includes the discrete isolation of feelings connected to certain ideas; the discrete isolation of certain feelings themselves; and the more-global isolation of emotions in general. Isolation of affect also typically contributes to symptoms and/or character traits, especially obsessional and paranoid symptoms and traits. Isolation of affect can also lead to altered states of consciousness, such as derealization, in which a person feels detached or surreal. Extensive use of isolation of affect can lead to the experience of no emotion at all (Fenichel, 1941). Alexithymia is an extreme variation of isolation of affect in which there is an apparent absence of emotions, or an inability to describe specific emotional reactions or to distinguish one affective state from another; alexithymia is seen in schizophrenia, psychosomatic disorders, and addictions (Sifneos, 1973).

J

Jealousy is a set of painful feelings and thoughts associated with the experience of the actual or imagined advantage of a rival, especially in regard to the love of an object. Jealousy is often accompanied by suspicion that one's own love object prefers someone else. The feeling of jealousy ranges from mild to intense and preoccupying **pathological jealousy** accompanied by paranoia (Freud, 1911a, 1922). Jealousy is generally distinguished from rivalry, which is a feeling of competition with another person in a struggle for advantage, often felt among siblings. It is also distinguished from envy, which is a negative feeling that accompanies the wish to possess an attribute of another, including, for example, the penis or breast or the fame and power (Neubauer, 1982).

Jouissance: see LACAN

Jungian Psychology or **Analytical Psychology**, introduced by Carl Gustav Jung in the early twentieth century, is a psychoanalytic theory of the development and functioning of the mind and of psychoanalytic treatment that features the mind as a self-regulating dynamic psychic system that is organized in dissociable feeling-toned complexes and that manifests through images and symbols (Jung, 1921/1957). Jung established his school of psychology after leaving the Freudian fold. Although he was initially enthusiastic about Freudian theory (based on his recognition that his own experimental work with word association confirmed Freud's findings regarding repression), their thinking diverged (Jung, 1906). This was due in large part to Jung's rejection of Freud's focus on sexuality as the prime motivator of mental life.

Complex theory is at the core of Jungian psychology (Jung, 1934). It posits that complexes are dynamic organizations of psychic content, both conscious and unconscious, which are represented in images, ideas, and patterns that are clustered around a common emotional theme. The ego complex is considered the most important of these complexes, in the sense that it serves an integrative function among the others and also accounts for functions such as memory and thought. Complexes themselves become "constellated," that is, organized and activated when prompted by circumstance,

memory, or emotion, and thereby contribute to behavior and affect. Jungian theory does not posit a concept of drives or defenses that keep unacceptable impulses out of awareness. In fact, Jungian theory emphasizes that the unconscious is always present and that it is always commenting and communicating through images, dreams, language, metaphor, narrative, and physical symptoms.

Jungian theory views all psychic energy as libido that is freely mobile between the conscious and unconscious. The conscious and the unconscious mind are themselves in a dynamic relationship to each other, a state known as "in tension." Jung used the term *unconscious,* as Freud did, to refer to mental contents and also a psychic system with its own character, laws, and functions. However, Jungian theory posits two aspects of the unconscious—the personal and the collective unconscious. The personal unconscious is comprised of unique experiences, of, for example, an individual's personal mother. The unconscious image of mother has a set of specific attributes, such as nurturing or neglectful, all of which have specific meaning for that individual. Those experiences of mother live in conscious memory, in behavior, and in unconscious patterns of expectation.

The collective unconscious is comprised of archetypal potentialities. These are innate, inherited patterns and structures of psychological meaning that are linked to instinct and, when activated, become manifest in behavior and emotion. It is erroneous to delineate too rigid a divide between the personal and collective unconscious, for the archetype, as a skeletal concept, requires ordinary experience to become fully elaborated. Through that process of elaboration, archetypes become organized into complexes. For example, "king" is an archetype with the attributes of male, leadership, and social status, which has some variant form in every culture. The archetype of king becomes constellated into a complex based upon the tension between the archetypal potential and the individual's personal experience with parents and other authority figures. This process might be considered analogous to the role of the oedipus complex in Freudian theory, which has some innate organizing potential structure, and becomes elaborated within the context of individual propensities and experience within the object relational environment.

Those aspects of self experience that are disallowed by the ego because they are judged to be unacceptable, inferior, worthless, or primitive are called the "shadow." Aspects of the shadow are often dealt with by projection onto others. However, they are not repressed and are always striving for expression through all the means that the mind utilizes to communicate its message. Jung emphasized that everyone has a shadow; everything substantial casts a shadow; the ego is to shadow as light is to shade, and it is the shadow that makes us human. Jung gave Freud the credit for calling the attention of modern humanity to this aspect of ourselves. As the shadow cannot be eradicated (this should not even be attempted), the best that can be hoped for is to come to terms with it.

Jung developed a conceptual model of personality typology to demonstrate and ascertain different modes of psychological functioning among people. He used basic attitudes toward the world and certain properties or functions of mental life to delineate several psychological types. Some individuals are more excited or energized by the internal world, and others by the external world; these are introverts and extraverts respectively. Jung also identified four functions of mental life: a rational pair that includes thinking and feeling, and a perceptual pair that includes sensation and intuition. This conceptual schema provides for a sixteen-category typology of personalities that is the basis for several psychological tests used clinically and in educational and industrial applications.

The concept of development is central to Jung's ideas, but he was little concerned with early childhood development. Instead he conceived of life as divided into two periods. The first half involves establishing one's place in the world and making the essential choices of occupation, mate, values, and interests. The second half is primarily concerned with confronting and adapting to mortality. The sequential progression of life is directed toward individuation, a lifelong process in which a person becomes "a psychological 'in-dividual,'" that is, a separate indivisibility or "whole." Individuation involves a continual pressure to make available to consciousness the potential that is latent in psychic structure and to relieve inherent tensions by reconciling or balancing opposites. Individuation, in Jung's view, is a universal human process, which aims at a smoothly functioning, integrated individual, capable of achieving the full potential of his personality while being fully engaged in the world.

A major aim of analytical psychology is to develop a deep and flexible dialogue within the individual among the elements of his psyche, mediated through the ego complex but not dominated by a rigid conscious structure. In this way, unconscious content can be integrated, which is the main endeavor of analytical psychology. Another stated purpose of analytical psychology is to facilitate the patient's achieving a nonjudgmental attitude toward his instinctual side, or shadow, in order to extract what is of worth within it. Jungian theory views dreams as a very valuable source of information from the unconscious; in fact, Jung thought that dreams were purposive, direct communication from the unconscious to the conscious (Jung, 1963). Jung believed that dream images were specific and not to be associated away from. Rather, an individual should dig deeper into the nature of the specific images themselves, through a system of amplification, to reveal the patterns that need to be brought into consciousness. Analytical psychology relies on dreams to continually comment on both the analysand's unconscious processes and the analytic process itself. Information derived from dreams is regarded as "compensatory" to conscious thought processes, providing a more elaborated vision of the individual's full range of feelings and attitudes. From this perspective, when symbolic communication from the unconscious is taken seriously and the tension of opposing attitudes is tolerated, new psychic energy emerges to facilitate healing and growth. Jung called the energy that is shared by the analyst and analysand the "Transcendent Function."

Illness occurs when psychic energy is blocked and cannot flow freely among the various mental entities. This might occur as the result of an archetype potentiality taking supremacy over the ego complex and thereby disrupting a desirable state of dynamic tension and fluidity within the psychic system. A Jungian psychoanalyst looks for the tension points between and among the various psychic entities, complexes, images, narratives, and layers of consciousness to find both the source of illness and the indication for healing. Jungians use the reductive method, but, importantly, they also use what Jung called the "synthetic method." The synthetic method has a teleological orientation, assuming that the nature of the illness, as expressed by image and symptom, holds a clue to the path to wellness. Because the psyche is self regulating, it will indicate, through symptom, dream image, and within the transference dynamic, the nature of what will provide the path toward healing. In other words, the nature of the disturbance guides the analyst toward what difficulties must be addressed within the treatment.

Analytical psychology has met with some criticism. These criticisms include that 1) some Jungian analysts cross the boundary from a clinical psychology to a metaphysical domain; 2) Jung's ideas have been misappropriated by "New Age" movements; and 3) some of Jung's theories have little clinical applicability. Historically, the long-standing rift between Freudian and Jungian theory has resulted in little communication between the two schools.

K

Melanie Klein was one of the most important figures in the history of psychoanalysis. Her ideas and their development have been highly influential on the entire world of psychoanalysis, not only within the community of those who call themselves "Kleinians" but much more broadly. Through her development of play technique, and the access this provided to very early experiences, Klein radically extended psychoanalysis, making it possible to understand and work with patients with more-severe levels of disturbance. Her clinical work with adult patients also provided a window into the more-primitive and archaic aspects of mental life in general.

Although the tradition that Klein founded is broad, there are several core theoretical and technical concepts that characterize the Kleinian school of thought. Theoretical developments include: 1) enriched understanding of unconscious "phantasy"; 2) the importance of the world of internal objects; 3) the formulation of development as a constant interaction between feelings of love and hate, striving toward integration of these contradictory feelings; 4) the description of typical early anxiety situations; 5) the discovery of a primitive and archaic superego; 6) the emphasis on and broadening of the understanding of the significance of early aggression and sadism in mental life; 7) the recognition of two fundamental ways in which the mind is structured—the paranoid-schizoid and the depressive positions; 8) the significance of envy; 9) the centrality of the concepts of the life and death drives, which in Kleinian work are given a clinical as well as theoretical significance; and 10) the crucial role in development of the internalized good object, the source of security and integration. Technical developments include: 1) new approaches to understanding of the transference, and 2) the attention to the nonverbal aspects of communication and to countertransference phenomena. In addition, Klein introduced the concept of projective identification, the exploration of which has been a central focus of contemporary psychoanalysis. While the Kleinian school is one of the foremost representatives of object relations theory, it is distinct in the importance it continues to give to drive theory. Furthermore, although there have been many developments in technique within the Kleinian school, its approach remains "classical,"

in the sense that it views insight and understanding as basic to change and emphasizes the neutrality of the analyst (Spillius et al., 2011).

Segal (1964), who did much to explicate the work of Klein, divided Klein's theoretical development into three broad phases: an initial phase, during which Klein laid the foundations of child analysis, ending with the publication of *The Psycho-analysis of Children* (Klein, 1932); a second phase, which led to the formulation of the depressive position and manic defense mechanisms, ending in 1940; and a final phase, during which Klein developed her theory of very early primitive mental mechanisms, ending in the publication of "Notes on Some Schizoid Mechanisms" (Klein, 1946) and the papers collected together in the book *Envy and Gratitude* (1975). Klein's early work focused on infantile aggression, sadism, and hatred, along with their implications and consequences; however, from 1935 on, her work focused on the importance of good objects, with the central struggle being to protect, repair, and securely establish the good internal object.

Central to all of Klein's work, and to those who followed in this tradition, is the careful, detailed description of unconscious phantasy, and the attention paid to the ever-present dialectical movements between internal and external and between projection and introjection. Freud used the concept of unconscious fantasy in various ways, both as an expression of the pleasure principle, a wish-fulfillment, and a primary mental content, as in "primal fantasy." For Klein, unconscious phantasy is a core primary activity, an original expression of both impulses and defenses. In her well-known paper on the subject, delivered as part of the Controversial Discussions of the British Psychoanalytic Society between the followers of Klein and the Viennese analysts under the leadership of A. Freud (King and Steiner, 1991), Isaacs (1948) made explicit what was already implicit in Klein's views on phantasy. In this paper, Isaacs described phantasy as the direct mental expression of instinct, "the primary content of unconscious mental processes," occupying the position that Freud assigned to the unconscious wish. In this view, phantasy begins at birth, long before the development of language, as the manner in which the mind represents its own activities to itself (Wollheim,

1984). The earliest phantasies are concrete bodily experiences, consisting of physical sensations, always interpreted as relationships with objects, which are experienced as causing those sensations. (For example, hunger is experienced as a bad object persecuting the infant from within; satisfaction is experienced as a blissful union with a good object.) Projection and introjection are also experienced as bodily phantasy. (For example, projection might be experienced as vomiting; introjection is experienced as swallowing.) Klein pointed out that unconscious phantasies have real effects. (For example, a patient who says, "I feel empty," may be expressing a true observation about his feeling that, as a result of projection, he really has emptied his mind.) Spillius (2001) distinguished three registers of phantasy that permeate Kleinian thinking: unconscious phantasies of the body; phantasied objects as having existence in the internal world (for example, a phantasied primal couple who have relations with each other and with the self); and lastly, phantasies as defenses. These three registers have technical as well as theoretical implications, for in communicating to the patient (for example, that he has introjected a bad object), the analyst might talk to the patient not about a mental mechanism but about an experience (for example, the feeling that he has something very bad inside him).

A core feature of Klein's theory is the distinction drawn between two fundamentally different psychic organizations, which she called the "paranoid-schizoid" and the "depressive" positions. Klein used the term *position* to emphasize that she was not describing a stage in development that can be passed through, but rather an enduring mental structure constituted by its characteristic pattern of object relations, anxieties, and defenses. Furthermore, the concept of position emphasizes that these configurations are ways of "being in the world" that are never completely superseded.

Klein described the mental processes of splitting and projection, which constitute the paranoid-schizoid position in her early work (1929, 1930). However, it was not until the groundbreaking paper "Notes on Some Schizoid Mechanisms" (1946) that she fully elucidated the concept. In this paper, drawing on her own work and that of Fairbairn, Klein defined and elaborated the processes characteristic of what she now termed the *paranoid-schizoid position* (formerly, *paranoid position*). From the earliest periods in life, the infant is faced with fundamental anxieties derived from the life and death drives. These anxieties develop into a lifelong struggle between love and hate toward the object. In Klein's

view, the infant experiences an inner persecutory state that results in his projecting what are felt to be "bad objects." This process, though vital to survival, creates a paranoid world, as the infant now feels threatened by the external object that was the target of projection. Indeed, for Klein, the mind develops in the context of an endless interplay between projection and introjection, so that the external persecuting object is repeatedly internalized and then reprojected in response to anxiety. The source of this anxiety is both inherent and experiential: The former derives from the operation of the death instinct; the latter derives from frustration. Inevitable deprivation and associated frustration stimulate infantile sadism, resulting in ruthless attacks upon the mother/breast, felt to be the source of frustration. In turn, these attacks result in an object that is felt to be vengeful. For example, "the breast" attacked with the force of oral sadism becomes a breast that will retaliate by consuming the infant, tearing him to pieces. The paranoid-schizoid world is characterized by an absence of feelings of remorse and guilt; survival of the self is paramount. This contrasts with the depressive position, where guilt and remorse are central.

The paranoid-schizoid position is characterized by the presence of specific anxieties and the use of specific defenses. Splitting serves to protect good, pleasurable experience from bad, persecutory experience. On the one hand, the infant has the experience of a mother who is present, who is felt to provide for his material and emotional needs, and with whom he has an idealized relationship; on the other hand, the infant has the experience of a mother who is unavailable, who is felt to be frustrating, and with whom he has a persecutory relationship. The infant cannot manage this degree of complexity, instead maintaining these contradictory experiences as separate and distinct. The creation of an idealized object is vital to development, as it serves to protect the self from the persecuting, bad object. For Klein (following the work of Fairbairn), the object cannot be split without a concurrent splitting of the self. The paranoid-schizoid position is also characterized by the use of denial, in that what is split off from self or object is, in effect, denied existence or even "annihilated." In her 1946 paper, Klein used the term *projective identification* for the first time, defined as a process whereby unwanted, split-off parts of the self are forced into the object so as to control the object from inside. With this new concept, Klein emphasized something already implicit in her descriptions—the object that is the target of projection becomes identified with the part of the self that has been projected.

Klein described several clinical phenomena that are expressions of the paranoid-schizoid position. For example, projection of good parts of the self can result in a compulsive clinging to objects that have now become identified with what is vital to life. Projection of bad persecuting aspects can result in terror and flight. Later Kleinian analysts have confirmed a further feature, particularly found in borderline states, wherein the individual oscillates between flight and compulsive clinging, as the pattern of what is projected alternates.

The principal developmental task in this earliest phase of life is the establishment of a stable, internalized good, albeit idealized, object that can serve as a source of security, thus lessening the need for projection and allowing for the integration of "all good" and "all bad" experiences. Although there is some limited capacity for integration of experience even in the earliest periods of life, in the middle of the first year, small quantitative shifts reach a tipping point and a qualitative transformation takes place, allowing for a new level of integration. The development of an integrated experience is a major developmental achievement, which Klein called the "depressive" position (1930, 1935, 1940).

The depressive position describes a constellation of object relations, defenses, and new anxieties. It is accompanied by an acute and poignant mental pain made up of a number of components. First, the awareness of separateness from the object brings with it pain, a pining for a loved object not present but absent. In addition, the object is now understood as having a life of its own, beyond the subject's control, including relationships with other objects. This new awareness introduces the triangulation essential for the oedipus complex. Finally, recognition that the good object and the bad object are one and the same causes acute anxiety as to the state of the object, now seen as vulnerable to the infant's attacks. Instead of fearing for his own safety (as in the paranoid-schizoid position), the infant now fears for the safety of his object, at risk of being destroyed because of the infant's own sadism and aggression. This new fear is experienced as depressive anxiety, or guilt.

The capacity to manage these new forms of pain and anxiety has lasting consequences for psychic health. If all goes well, if there is sufficient external and internal support, the mourning processes brought on by pining and guilt can be borne. As the ego grows stronger, there is a release of reparative impulses, which aim to restore the object, internal and external (Klein, 1929). Because "reparation" requires time and patience, it is, by nature, never complete. There is always danger of regression to paranoid-schizoid

modes of functioning or, alternatively, the danger of an attempt to deal with the situation through manic mechanisms ("manic reparation"). The latter represents a magical solution in which it is imagined that the object has been completely and instantly restored. Attainment and mastery of the depressive position depends on a variety of environmental factors, including the experience of an ordinary loving mother who can provide security and support, and innate and constitutional factors, including capacity to bear frustration.

For Klein, the establishment of the depressive position brings with it a number of fundamental changes to mental life, including: 1) the ability to manage separation; 2) the capacity for guilt and concern; 3) the capacity for symbol formation; 4) the recognition of the internal world as distinct from the external world, yet having a valued reality of its own and thus providing an important basis for the free use of imagination; 5) the instantiation of the self in time and history; 6) a capacity for broader engagement with the world; and 7) a capacity for creative work.

There are several pathological consequences to the failure to establish a reasonably stable depressive position. For example, the phenomenon of depressive illness, characterized by splitting and projection, reflects a schizoid state of mind and often derives from the lack of capacity for the depressive-position mode of functioning. Manic illness may reflect the manic defense. Undue regression to the paranoid-schizoid position may also result in serious character pathology.

In addition to her description of the paranoid-schizoid and the depressive position, Klein made important contributions to the study of envy and its role in psychological life (1928, 1932, 1945, 1975). Klein described envy as what the child feels when he becomes aware that another possesses something he desires/needs. The feeling of envy is complex, including intense feelings of anger and a wish to destroy the object, spoil it, and rob it of its contents. Feelings of envy are stimulated by frustration; however, they are also stimulated simply by the fact that the object is "good." Indeed, Klein cites Chaucer as arguing that envy is the deadliest of the deadly sins because it is directed against goodness itself. For Klein, envy is directed toward the very object upon whom life depends; it is an inborn manifestation of the death drive. In her mature work, Klein (1975) saw the capacity for gratitude and generosity as the antithesis of envy and as deriving from the life instinct.

Klein described envy as a source of a deep dread, as objects who are envied become hostile and persecuting. Envy is also one of the deepest sources of guilt in relation to the damage done to the object during the depressive position. Finally, although envy is distinct from jealousy based on a triangular situation from which the subject feels excluded, it can make feelings of jealousy intolerable. Envy has a number of profound consequences, including: interference with the normal splitting necessary for development (as the good object is enviously spoiled and therefore becomes indistinguishable from the bad); interference with introjection, leading to failure to learn; paranoid dread of retaliation; and interference with oedipal development, as jealousy becomes suffused with envy.

Klein based her concept of envy on Freud's (1937a) description of a particular form of resistance to analysis linked to the death drive. This concept was developed by Abraham (1919), who described patients who do not progress in analysis because they begrudge the analyst's work. Horney (1936) and Riviere (1936) both argued that the negative therapeutic reaction may be related to envy of the analyst, that is, a wish to spoil the analyst's work. There has been considerable development of the concept of envy from both a theoretical and clinical perspective by analysts working within the Kleinian tradition. Spillius (1993) stressed the painfulness of the experience, clarifying the different forms it can take (see also Spillius et al., 2011). Rosenfeld (1971a) linked envy to narcissistic object relations, describing a rigid internal narcissistic organization which functions to continuously undermine and enviously attack all good objects and prevent progress. Devaluation of the object is both an expression of envy and a defense against it.

Major figures in the second generation of Kleinian psychoanalysis include Segal, Rosenfeld, and B. Joseph, among others. (The work of Bion is addressed in a separate entry.) Segal's work falls into three overlapping areas: her theories about symbolism, her work on aesthetics, and her contributions to the psychoanalytic understanding of sociopolitical processes (Segal, 1981, 2001; Bell, 1997, 1999). Segal is also the principal explicator of Klein's work, and her introductory text is a classic in the field (Segal, 1964).

Segal's work both with schizophrenic patients and artists struggling in their creativity led to her interest in the nature of symbolism and the function and dysfunction of symbol formation. Segal studied the tripartite relationship between the symbol, the thing symbolized, and the symbolizer. She demonstrated that psychotic patients do, in fact, form symbols, but that these symbols are equated with the thing symbolized, forming what Segal called "symbolic equations." Symbolic equations underlie the concrete thinking characteristic of psychotic disorders, as in her famous example of a violinist who experienced playing the violin concretely as an act of masturbation. In later work, Segal (1957, 1979b, 1991) explored the relationship between projective identification and symbol formation.

Segal's papers on aesthetics (1952, 1974) comprise a major contribution to aesthetic theory and to the understanding of creativity in general. Building on Klein's theory of the depressive position, Segal placed the capacity to mourn at the center of the creative process. Creative work is a reparative activity in which the capacity to bear the pain associated with damaged internal objects is central, serving as the activating or motivating force for the artist. Response to creative work derives from the audience's capacity to empathize with the artist's unconscious inner struggles.

Finally, Segal is unique among the second generation of Kleinian psychoanalysts in her application of psychoanalytic ideas to sociopolitical issues. She cofounded the psychoanalytic movement against nuclear weapons, delivering a classical paper at the opening conference (Segal, 1987). Segal's (1997) warnings about the dangers of "triumphalism" after the ending of the cold war have been highly influential. Segal's last book, entitled *Yesterday, Today and Tomorrow,* was published in 2007.

Rosenfeld's early work with schizophrenic patients led to his making important contributions to the understanding of fragmentation of the ego in disturbed patients, and of what Rosenfeld called "confusional states" (1947, 1950, 1952, 1954). Rosenfeld (1971b) also extended the concept of projective identification, distinguishing the different motives that underlie communicative or evacuative projective identification. In the former, the patient aims to make the analyst aware of the patient's own disturbed state of mind; in the latter, the patient seeks to deny all ownership of what has been projected.

Rosenfeld also made important contributions to the understanding of narcissism. He clarified how narcissistic patients identify themselves with idealized objects, taking in all the good qualities and projecting all unwanted aspects of themselves (1971a). He also described how some very destructive patients idealize the destructive elements in their internal world, denigrating the more loving, or "libidinal," aspects (1971b). Rosenfeld described how these patients make frequent references to gangs or mafialike organizations. This observation led to the understanding that his patients' destructive elements have a pathological internal organization or structure, which he likened to an "internal mafia." If the patient remains loyal to this internal mafia, the mafia, in turn, offers the patient protection. The internal mafia also functions as a kind of internal propaganda machine, advertising the superiority of hatred, destructiveness, and omnipotence, while treating ordinary dependence, vulnerability, and love with contempt. In Rosenfeld's view, envy is the source of both this pathological internal organization and some kinds of negative therapeutic reaction.

In the last phase of his work, Rosenfeld focused on the problems associated with difficult analyses, especially those in which the patient comes from a deprived background. During this phase, he focused on the subtle ways in which the analyst's unwitting errors may result in a retraumatization of the patient. This work was controversial among many Kleinians who viewed it as moving too far in the direction of focusing on external factors (in both the early environment and in the analyst) at the expense of understanding psychological factors within the patient. Rosenfeld's last book, *Impasse and Interpretation* (1987), gathers together many of his major contributions on projective identification, destructive narcissism, psychotic transferences, and impasses in treatment.

B. Joseph has been a major innovator in the area of psychoanalytic technique within the Kleinian group (Hargreaves and Varchevker, 2004). Her work in this area is closely linked to her understanding of psychic change. Joseph's paper "The Patient Who Is Difficult to Reach" (1975) includes some central themes of her work. In this paper, Joseph described patients who are not obviously seriously disturbed and who appear to be working well in psychoanalysis, but who fail to progress. She demonstrated how this failure reflects a subtle collusion between patient and analyst with the patient's defensive organization. Joseph made extensive use of countertransference exploration in the here and now of the psychoanalytic encounter. In this exploration, she expanded the concept of projective identification, examining how it is expressed in the clinical situation.

In later work, Joseph explored the concept of what she called "psychic equilibrium." Patients seek analysis at a point when psychic equilibrium is disrupted. While the patient seeks change, he also seeks to use the analysis to restore the previous equilibrium (B. Joseph, 1989). Many patients maintain their equilibrium by making it appear as if change has taken place, when it has not, as, for example, in what Joseph (2000) described as the "agreeable patient." This distinction between real and apparent change is a hallmark of Joseph's work.

L

Jacques Lacan proposed an independent theory and technique of psychoanalysis that views the human condition as one of individual alienation and estrangement, linked to an experience of desire of and for the "Other" that can never be satisfied. Lacan promoted a "return to Freud," by which he meant a privileging of the unconscious in his theory of the mind, and a focus on Freud's special interest in language. In fact, Lacan offered a reinterpretation of Freudian theory, rejecting the concept of the ego as synthesizer and integrator, and the role of the drives as motivators of psychic experience. Unlike Freudian metapsychology, which affirms the biological underpinnings of mental life, Lacan viewed the unconscious as structured like a language, a premise that is associated with various interpretations but consistently linked to Lacan's use of linguistic concepts and terminology to explain the workings of the unconscious. These concepts include the structural descriptors of metaphor and metonymy (essentially equivalent to Freud's description of the primary process mechanisms of condensation and displacement), and of signifiers (essentially equivalent to Freud's description of the primary process mechanism of symbolization). Similarly, Lacan's motivational concept of desire has its roots in philosophy, especially the existential philosophy of Hegel and Heidegger, unlike the Freudian motivational concept of drive, which has its roots in a metapsychology of empiricist positivism. According to Lacan, the organizing narrative of the human psyche is the oedipal configuration, which inevitably leaves as its residue a desire for the mother, which can never be escaped but whose satisfaction is foreclosed by the rule of the father. Hence, the alienation and decenteredness of the human condition, which stands in contrast to Freud's assertion of man's capacity to achieve sublimated or compromise satisfaction in both love and work (Felman, 1987; Lacan, 1966/2006).

Lacan's theory draws heavily from philosophy, mathematics, linguistics, and aesthetics, as well as from his psychiatric experience with psychotic patients. The exposition of Lacan's theory has been complicated by the legendary nature of his writing style, which has been noted to resemble the associative nature of unconscious thought, replete with wordplay, punning, contrived language, neologisms, ambiguity,

and contradiction. Lacan also modified his theory throughout his career and made no attempt to systematize it, leaving many ambiguous and contradictory formulations. For many readers, Lacan's written discourse borders on incomprehensible, however his theory has gained substantial currency within various academic disciplines. Lacan's enduring psychoanalytic legacy is perhaps most apparent in his native France, and perhaps least apparent within North American clinical psychoanalysis. Lacan has inspired controversy throughout the international psychoanalytic community because of both the radical nature of his theoretical ideas and his clinical technique. For all of these reasons, providing a concise and lucid summary of Lacanian theory presents formidable challenges. In fact, just as Lacan viewed the synthetic and integrative function of the ego as a distortion of unconscious meaning, he argued that to impose clarity on his ideas is to distort their intent.

Lacan took up what he called Freud's last will and testament, *Wo Es war, soll Ich werden,* usually translated as "Where id was, there ego shall be" (Freud, 1933a). Lacan's oft-quoted retranslation typifies the highly condensed ambiguity of his prose: "Where it was . . . it is my duty that I come into being" (Lacan, 1966/2006). From Lacan's perspective, the "I" is not the ego but the "subject," the "it" is the unconscious, and the path between "was" and "come into being" is established by satisfying the ethical imperative to be true to one's (unconscious) desire. It is the function of the analyst and the goal of psychoanalysis to reconnect the patient with his desire and the language of his unconscious. Just as the unconscious is formed through the structuring influence of language and the social structure, psychoanalysis is a dialogic and intersubjective process whereby the patient's unconscious can be revealed to him through a spoken process with the analyst. Lacan's focus on the relationships among the unconscious, language, and speech centers his interest on the clinical situation.

Lacan's theory of mind features the developmental acquisition of three modes of experience or systems of thought, which Lacan identified as "registers." These include the Imaginary, the Symbolic, and the Real, which come into place as distinct registers only at the resolution of the oedipus complex.

The Imaginary consists primarily of images, or pre-verbal experience, which Lacan viewed as governed by narcissistic strivings and inevitable disappointments. The Symbolic is not limited to language, but includes all semiotic systems, including the domains of ritual and art. The Real is the arena of trauma, psychosis, and death, also described at times as the external world. Lacan's theorizing about human development always involves an element of retroactivity, so that what is seen looking back is affected by the level of differentiation that has already been achieved, and does not imply that this same clarity is available in the original forward movement of time.

The ego emerges in what Lacan called the "mirror stage" when, between six and eighteen months of age, the young child is able to recognize his reflection in a mirror and responds with jubilation to his capacity to control his movements. Because his reflected image manifests coherence and unity felt as lacking by the child at this age, the child narcissistically identifies with the masterful image, installing it as a defensive illusion that serves primarily as a protective illusion of unity, guarding against the threat of fragmentation and the loss of coherence. When this threat is felt, the ego responds with aggressive retaliation in the form of imagined or intended fragmentation of the Other. For these reasons, Lacan referred to the ego as the human symptom par excellence and the mental illness of all humanity. In the mirror stage, two pre-Symbolic registers of human experience begin to emerge: the Real as the chaos of the fragmented body, and the Imaginary as "image" in the mirror. Mirroring reflects back the illusion of sameness, while difference is a function of the Symbolic register, that aspect of experience whereby signification is introduced as distinct from representation or resemblance.

It is through Lacan's description of the evolution of the oedipus complex, which follows the mirror stage, that other important concepts emerge, such as the role of the phallus, the perception and elaboration of "lack," and the function of the "Other." The phallus serves as a conceptual pivot around which Lacan elaborated his central hypothesis that lack drives the structuring that comes to be called the oedipus complex and simultaneously leads to the development of an unconscious that is structured like a language. Each of the three stages of the oedipus complex—frustration, privation, and castration—evoke in the infant an experience of lack. From the start, the child is immersed in the world of signs, initially a jumble of perceptions, that ultimately includes communicative language and is the basis of what Lacan called the Symbolic order. In the stage of frustration, Lacan described how the coming and going of the mother, especially in feedings at the breast, create an off/on phenomenon in which the child is first confronted with times when need is present but the breast is absent. Since the Imaginary is the register of similarity and identification with images, this is the beginning, not just of an experience of absence of the breast, but of a break in Imaginary completeness. This phenomenon of a shifting presence/absence is also the beginning of Symbolic order. In summary, the first stage of the oedipus complex, frustration, is the lack of a real object (the breast) whose agent is Symbolic (the Symbolic mother) and is registered in the Imaginary realm.

In the second stage of the oedipus complex, privation, the child becomes aware that the mother is not complete herself, that she is lacking something that Lacan described as the desire of the "(m)Other." Lacan called this kind of lack "desire," because it is the experience of lacking something one wants. The term (m)Other indicates that the mother and the Other have a primal relationship to each other, and, according to Lacan, remain unconsciously linked. Because the mother spends time interacting with someone else, the child recognizes that he does not totally occupy and satisfy her. This lack in the mother occurs in the register of the Real. The child imagines a rival, the Imaginary father, who is or has what could complete the mother. This total filling of the lack in the mother is what Lacan called the phallus, conceptualized, at least retrospectively, as a Symbolic object that has a quasi-symbolic relation to the desire of the mother. In summary, the second stage of the oedipus complex, privation, involves an agent, the Imaginary father, who possesses what would complete the mother. This object, the phallus, at this stage is not a real object but a Symbolic object, in so far as it stands for the desire of the mother, which is felt as a real lack in the mother.

In the third stage of the oedipus complex, castration, the child is confronted by the Real father, who shows the child that he (the father) has what the mother lacks. The child realizes he cannot compete, because he has been deprived of the phallus, here understood as an Imaginary object. At this point, the child shifts from experiencing lack in the (m)Other to accepting that he does not have the phallus and therefore cannot satisfy the mother's desire. The child's acceptance of this state also constitutes fully entering into the Symbolic order. The child's experience of lack at this stage, the agent of which is the real father as the representative of the law of the Symbolic order, is what forbids incest and establishes the Symbolic order proper. In a secondary manner, the child makes a partial identification with the father on a symbolic basis (the Symbolic being the realm of naming and making of distinctions). Thus the desire of the mother sinks into repression while the "Name of the Father" takes the position above the bar of repression. What is vital here for Lacan is that there is a kind of "fathering of naming" that is necessary for the Symbolic order to develop and for the unconscious to be created as such. According to Lacan, the mystery of the desire of the mother is something that can never really be escaped; it remains in the founding of the unconscious as that which creates us as desiring beings. In effect, the origins of the unconscious are in the (m)Other, and are structured by the father (Leavy, 1977). Tracing the stages of the oedipus complex in this way also sheds some light on Lacan's complex and ambiguous usage of the term *Other* as an overarching framework that encompasses the mother, the unconscious, governing authority, the "code," and the fault line of psychotic states.

Lacan's assertion that the unconscious is structured like a language rests upon the interlocking premises that the unconscious is contingent upon the acquisition of the Symbolic order, and that the unconscious functions as "the matrices that organize the rules of the social order, rather than as a dynamic and personal system" (Leavy, 1977). Used as such, Lacan has drawn upon the work of the structural linguists Jakobson and Saussure. Utilizing their vocabulary, Lacan described the unconscious as a "network of signifiers" revealed by inference through language, which is organized by the processes of metaphor and metonymy. The unconscious is created and revealed through its relationship to the Other (that is, an intersubjective process) and becomes recapitulated in the analytic relationship, where the patient's unconscious is again revealed by the Other (the analyst) through the function of language and speech. Lacan asserted that the individual's unconscious fantasy of its position in relation to the Other's desire determines the nature of those symptoms (hysteric, obsessional, or perverse) that develop as responses to the question "What does the Other want from me?" In hysteria, the individual attempts to be the phallus for the Other, attempting to satisfy the Other's desire and being unable to satisfy one's own. In obsessional neurosis, the emphasis is on a passive-aggressive refusal to satisfy the Other's desire while waiting for the death of the Other before enjoying one's own

desire. In perversion, the individual enjoys the Other by placing oneself in a fantasy one enjoys as if in the place of the Other. So, according to Lacan, the unconscious originates within the Other, as does the experience of desire.

Lacan's meaning of Other as the governing authority refers to the father's function as the "Third," that is, the regulator of speech and relationships. In general, Lacan viewed the Third as serving to contextualize the dyad, grounding it in the signifying network of language and culture (Muller, 2007). Dyadic relations risk becoming narcissistic bubbles, lost in the Imaginary register, subject to intense regressive pressures. In this way, Lacan referred also to the role of the analyst. The analyst's proper place is to be available for ego-to-ego love/hate transference relations and mutual projections while maintaining perspective on these projections from the position of the Third.

Since the Other is "the very foundation of intersubjectivity" (Lacan, 1956b), it also contains the faultline of psychotic states. In Lacan's view, the Other serves as a constraint or a boundary, tied as it is to the resignation to the state of lack or incompleteness. Lacan also described the father as the one whose role is to proscribe the "child becoming the desire of the mother or her phallus" (Oliner, 1998), thereby enforcing the gap or lack. In the psychotic individual, however, there is a state of undifferentiated chaos due to the breakdown of boundaries, a closure of the gap, and a denial or "foreclosure of the name of the father" (Oliner, 1998). Lacan described this as the "unbarred Other," which is no longer subject to constraint and operates by showing rather than speaking. The absence of constraints on the Other contributes to the subject's terror in these states. For this reason, according to Lacan, the analyst must be alert to the development of a psychotic transference in which the patient begins to experience the analyst as "unbarred," that is, as omniscient, omnipotent, and arbitrary, and intent on "enjoying" the patient, or, in Lacan's terms, making the patient into an object of the analyst's "jouissance," a term with critical meaning in Lacanian theory.

Jouissance is a French word, not readily translated into English, bearing on the notion of wildly "getting off" on something. *Enjoyment* is in contemporary usage too weak a term, although the older English term *joyance* has resonances. *Pleasure* is not the appropriate term, since jouissance, which is unbound, and pleasure, which is bound, are antithetical. *Orgasm* as a term is more closely related to jouissance, but it is too specific. The term *jouissance* is therefore usually left untranslated and refers to an out-of-bounds pursuit of pleasure beyond pleasure, to the detriment of pleasure, even to the point of death and the end of all possibility of pleasure. Jouissance operates along a broad arc, from the vitality of flesh as such to the mystical union in ecstatic religious experience and to the psychotic terror of becoming fused with the unbarred Other. Perhaps the most important effect of the structuring of human desire—which can be said to be the main goal of analysis—is that desire serves as a constraint on the impetus toward jouissance. Likewise the chief function of anxiety is to provide a signal that the framework of desire is disintegrating and desire is folding into jouissance, thereby creating a mortal risk.

While Lacan and his theory have evoked considerable controversy, some analysts within the mainstream have acknowledged his contribution. Their appreciation has generally focused upon Lacan's insistence on the analyst's role as interpreter of the patient's unconscious, and not as an agent of empathy or relational needs; his challenge to ego psychology; and his affirmation of the unconscious as the preeminent psychoanalytic fulcrum of therapeutic action.

Lack: see LACAN

Latency is a developmental stage of childhood that occurs between five–six and eleven–twelve years of age. Originally used to describe a biologically based phase characterized by decreased sexual-drive intensity (compared to the preceding oedipal phase and the succeeding adolescent phase), contemporary psychoanalysts and developmentalists use the term *latency* to describe developmental behaviors that are much broader than the inhibition or control of drives. During latency, a greater equilibrium is established between defenses and drives. Due to brain growth and development, a variety of other changes occur within the neuropsychiatric, cognitive, sociocultural, and intrapsychic domains. The latency child experiences a greater capacity for mastery of mental and physical operations, is able to establish himself within a social community beyond the family system, and develops the capacity for subliminatory activity, all of which contribute to a heightening of self esteem (Schecter and Combrinck-Graham, 1980). Data from a variety of disciplines show that the chronological age of seven (plus/minus one) years of age is a reference point for a discontinuous development that is marked and recognized in many different societies, both historically and in the present (T. Shapiro, 1976). Most

notably it is the beginning of formal education for children.

Freud (1905b) borrowed the term *latency* from his colleague and mentor Fliess and first used it to refer to a period in childhood between early childhood and puberty when sexual drive, or libido, is markedly diminished. He distinguished this period of sexual quiescence from the more active sexual periods before and after latency, the oedipal period, and adolescence, respectively. Freud asserted that latency was set in motion by inborn, unfolding, developmental factors (1905b; 1923a, 1924b), along with the contributions of environment, education, and culture (1911b, 1915/1916). At times, Freud attributed the diminution in sexual drive to an actual biological decrease in drive activity (1926a), and at other times to the fact that latency is a defensive solution to the oedipal conflict (1921). In order to resolve the oedipus complex, the child erects defenses (reaction formations, repression, shame, morality) against forbidden infantile sexual wishes and sublimates drive energy into nonsexual activities (1924b, 1926a).

Bornstein (1951) divided latency into an earlier phase (years five and one-half to eight) and a later phase (years eight to ten). She argued that during early latency, children experience more intrapsychic turmoil as they struggle against still-active incestuous wishes, the temptation to masturbate, and the demands of a much harsher superego. There is also a regression to preoedipal impulses, which are experienced as less dangerous than genital impulses. In late latency, sexual impulses are better defended against and superego demands are less strict.

A. Freud (1965) described latency as a period of biologically based diminished drive pressure, during which libido is transferred from parents to peers, teachers, ideals, and sublimated interests. She noted the efflorescence of unconscious fantasies, such as the family romance, aimed at denigrating the parents, as children move from their almost exclusive involvement with family to the greater social world of the community. A. Freud (1963) also noted the latency child's progression from play to work and his transition from dominance of the pleasure principle to that of the reality principle. In a similar way, Erikson (1950) described the central developmental task of latency as resolving the conflict of "industry versus inferiority." Erikson argued that a successful resolution to this crisis results in a feeling of competence and mastery, an important ego capacity.

Piaget (1932, 1954) described the development of cognition in the seven- or eight-year-old, which moves from preoperational logic to the stage of concrete operations and moral development. Kohlberg (1963), similarly, discussed the developing stepwise progression of children's moral judgment. Sarnoff (1976), viewing latency from a narrow perspective, argued that it is not biologically determined but much influenced by the environment, citing that in societies or families where sexuality is encouraged, there is no period of latency. He emphasized that the latency-age child is able to use symbolic thought and fantasy to discharge drive impulses and reduce conflict; therefore, he is less likely to act out impulses. The child deals with breakthrough of oedipal or pre-oedipal impulses with repression, displacement, and fantasy formation. Other authors (R. Friedman and Downey, 2002b) have noted gender differences in latency, including a universal kind of play observed only in latency-age girls (Goldings, 1974). Interpersonal theorists do not use the term *latency*, with its implied emphasis on psychosexuality, but instead refer to the juvenile era as a time of significant interpersonal development and a shift away from fantasy to logical thought. Sullivan (1953a) suggested that the juvenile gradually moves beyond cooperation with peers to the formation of a "chumship," that is, a same-gender friendship in which the child develops a true empathic connection and a sense of himself as an interpersonal being. Chumship forms the foundation for the capacity for mature love (integrating sex and intimacy) in adolescence.

Lesbianism: see HOMOSEXUALITY

Libidinization: see EROTIZATION

Libido, derived from the Latin for "wish" or "desire," is Freud's general term for sexual desire or sexual appetite, as well as his more specific term for the mental energy of the sexual drive as distinct from the ideational content of the drive. Freud's propositions regarding the origins, transformations, and effects of libido have been collectively referred to as the **libido theory**. Libido came to designate the idea that sexual interest or stimulation is continuous throughout life, and that it is a causal factor not only in direct sexual desire but also in affectionate and social bonds; more generally, libido is the causal factor in mental interest in any thought or activity.

Freud's libido theory, situated at the center of his conceptualizations about drive and energy and thus his theory of motivation, was an early cornerstone of psychoanalytic theory. The focus of libido theory on the effects of sexuality and of unconscious conflict is central to all of Freud's models of the mind. Freud's revolutionary expansion of the concept of

sexuality beyond genital functioning is regarded by many analysts as one of his central contributions to understanding human psychology. His concept of libido and infantile sexuality radically expanded the role of sexuality as a motive force, often in disguised or derivative form, manifest in symptoms, behavior, character, and fantasy. Many contemporary analysts regard the concept of libido as crucial to their clinical and theoretical understanding of human motivation and mental functioning, even as they have discarded certain aspects of Freud's drive theory and energic propositions. Others object to Freud's emphasis on the pleasure-seeking aspect of the libidinal drive, viewing this emphasis on infantile sexuality as diminishing the importance of object seeking and attachment. For such analysts, particularly those working within an interpersonal and self psychological mode, as well as for attachment researchers and theorists, sexuality has a much more diminished role in their conceptualizations of the mind and its development. Other theorists have retained the concept of libido but conceptualize it in ways quite different from Freud's original view.

The term *libido* probably had some currency in Freud's contemporary scientific circle when he adopted it for psychoanalysis. It first appeared in Freud's writings in an 1894 draft to Fliess in which he described libido as a mental representation of an underlying somatic process involved in sexuality (1894b). If libido became "damned up" and could not be properly discharged, it was transformed into anxiety. In his "Three Essays on the Theory of Sexuality," Freud (1905b) more explicitly defined his concept of libido as the sexual energy of the sexual instincts or drives. In a very broadened conception of sexuality, Freud described the sexual drive as consisting of wishful ideas (**libidinal aims**) associated with exciting sensations (libido) that have as their source the intimate sensual stimulation of the body's erotogenic zones (for example, mouth, skin, anus, genital). Stimulation of these erotogenic zones occurs in the course of normal caretaking by the parents and their surrogates, who tend to become the **libidinal objects** of such wishes. The sexual drive is made up of numerous component instincts that only come together in the service of reproduction at a relatively late stage in development during puberty and adulthood. This theory of psychosexual development was later elaborated by both Freud (1915 addendum to 1905b, 1923b) and Abraham (1924b) as a temporally ordered developmental sequence of **libidinal stages**, or **libidinal phases**, in which the libido's organization and mode of object relatedness reflected the predominant influence of the underlying oral, anal, and phallic erotogenic zones. Fixations or regressions of libido to particular stages could lead to various forms of psychopathology or character organization.

Freud's concept of libido was a central component of his evolving drive theory, which viewed opposing forces in the mind as playing a leading role in the genesis of conflict and psychic structure. In 1914, Freud (1914e) formally described his libido theory, in which he viewed libido as a form of mental energy that might be invested in (or cathect) various mental representations or structures of the mind. Freud postulated a reciprocal relation between the amount of libido invested in oneself (**ego libido**) and the amount of libido invested in one's objects (**object libido**). He also described a reservoir of ego libido used to fuel the development of psychic structure and sustain self esteem. Failure to discharge libido might result in a "dammed-up state," resulting in the formation of neurotic symptoms. In response to frustrations in the external world, the ego might defensively withdraw object-libido back into itself. In its most pathological form, this process could lead to psychosis (also referred to as narcissistic neurosis) with its associated megalomania and loss of interest in, and relation to, reality and the external world.

In 1915, in an expansion of this theory, Freud (1915b) described the operation of the drives in relation to the pleasure principle. He conceptualized libido as a hypothetically measurable force whose increase produces unpleasure and whose decrease and discharge produces pleasure. Sexual energy is a mutable, slippery, constantly transforming force, capable of shifting both its object and its aim. These transformations, referred to as **libidinal vicissitudes**, occur as the sexual drive: shifts its object (for example, with displacement from one external object to another, or back to the self), its content (for example, from love to hate), or its aim (for example, from active to passive); undergoes repression; or is sublimated, in which the original sexual aim is shifted toward more socially accepted or valued goals, in particular creative or intellectual activities. In 1920, Freud (1920a) outlined his final and most speculative drive model, in which libido is conceived more broadly and abstractly as the energy of the life drive, or Eros, whose aim is to build organic complexity, to synthesize and unite, and to preserve life, opposed by the coequal aggressive energies of the death drive, whose aim is to destroy life by breaking down organic complexity.

In 1923, with Freud's (1923a) introduction of the structural model, libidinal and aggressive energies are located in the id, as the prime motivating forces of mental life. Fusion, neutralization, and sublimation of libido and aggression are central concepts in Freud's final theory, as processes essential to the formation of psychic structure. Desexualized libido provides the energy involved in thinking, the synthetic functioning of the ego, and the formation of identifications. In the structural model, anxiety is no longer conceptualized as a transformed product of undischarged libido, but as the ego's response to the threat of libidinal or aggressive discharge that is opposed by the superego (1926a).

With subsequent developments in psychoanalytic thought, some analysts viewed libido theory as occupying a more limited place within a larger psychoanalytic formulation of motivation and mental functioning. Other theorists rejected the usefulness of the libido concept entirely. The energy formulations inherent in Freud's libido theory (and larger drive theory) were widely criticized as being too experience-distant, mechanistic, and vague, resulting in a series of proposed theoretical revisions and rejections (Holt, 1976; G. Klein, 1976; Schafer, 1976). Hyman (1975) countered that such criticisms misunderstand that libido, and psychic energy more generally, are concepts striving to capture the experiential aspects of intrapsychic fantasy and experience, in particular the quantitative changes or intensities in mental life. C. Brenner (1982) argued that drives should be understood as an abstract generalization about human motivation based upon the observation of many individuals' unique and specific libidinal (and aggressive) wishes directed at particular people over the course of their development. In this way, Brenner emphasized the more experience-near aspects of the libido concept that were present in Freud's initial descriptions of it.

Freud's libido theory was also revised by theorists who sought to further emphasize or integrate the role of object relations in motivation. Fairbairn (1954) reconceptualized the innate aim of libido as fundamentally object seeking, rather than pleasure seeking. Loewald (1971) stressed the role played by tensions and interactions within the mother-child psychic matrix in the origins and development of libido. Kernberg (1982) viewed pleasurable affect states linking self and object representations from the beginning of development as the building blocks of both libidinal and aggressive drives. Interpersonalists, relationally oriented infancy researchers such as D. N. Stern (1985), and attachment theorists have recast the psychoanalytic understanding of the libidinal nature of the child in terms of relational needs while downplaying the sexual intensity of early childhood. In self psychology, while Kohut initially maintained an allegiance to the terminology of libido theory in his early theorizing, in his later work, he and other self psychologists replaced the role of libido with selfobject needs.

Love is a complex, affectively charged state of mind characterized by strong positive regard for the love object, which may include any of the following: sexual attraction, special affection, attachment, devotion, tenderness, longing, adoration, idealization, and/or concern. Love is most often felt toward another person, but may be felt toward almost any object, including a thing, a place, an activity, or an idea. There are many types of love, including romantic, passionate and sexual love, brotherly love, love for a friend, parental love, or love of one's country or god. Self love is also a vital component of all psychological life. Love is contrasted with hate and/or indifference.

From the beginning, love has played a central role in the psychoanalytic theory and practice. In his earliest work with patients, Freud noted that "difficulties attached to the idea of love" play a central role in neurosis (Breuer and Freud, 1893/1895). He also observed that most people place love at the center of their lives and, despite the suffering associated with love, experience it as the "prototype of happiness" (Freud, 1930). Indeed, psychoanalysts from every school of thought work with patients' struggles in the domain of love, as these struggles play a central role in everyone's psychological life. While recognizing that love can be conceptualized at all levels, from the biological to the cultural, psychoanalysis has made important contributions to understanding: the importance of being and feeling loved in psychic development, the development of the capacity for love and self love, the barriers and problems associated with loving and feeling loved, and the relationship between love and many other issues, including sexuality, attachment, aggression, narcissism, object relations, intimacy, and morality, to mention a few. From most points of view, the goal of psychoanalytic treatment includes increased capacity for love, feeling loved, and appropriate self love.

In "Studies on Hysteria," Freud (Breuer and Freud, 1893/1895) noted that his patients suffered from the pathogenic effects of repressed ideas associated with what he called "unconscious love." For the most part, after the development of libido theory (1905b), Freud used the word *love* interchangeably with the word *libido*. Freud (1915b) defined love as an attitude of the whole ego toward the object of pleasure, becoming possible only after "all the components of

libido have been subsumed under the genitals in the service of reproduction." He conceptualized the affectionate aspect of love as an expression of "aim-inhibited libido" (1921, 1925d, 1930). In later works, Freud conceptualized love as a vicissitude of Eros, or the life instinct (that includes libido), which binds people to each other (Freud, 1920a; Lear, 1990). Throughout his writing life, Freud explored many aspects of love, offering overlapping insights, which have contributed to all subsequent discussion, such as the following: 1) The earliest object, usually the mother, provides the prototype for all later love objects, so that the finding of a love object is always a "refinding" of the object; all later love objects, including the analyst, are substitutes for the earliest object; the love object is often chosen for his/her resemblance to the original nurturing object (anaclitic object choice) (Freud, 1905b, 1914e, 1915a, 1938a). 2) Anxiety is associated with the loss of the mother's love, upon which the child is dependent (1905b, 1926a). 3) In the state of being in love, boundaries between self and other break down, as in psychosis (1930). 4) Children have the capacity for love long before puberty (1907c). 5) The need for the object (mother) and her love is crucial to the development of the superego and morality (1923a). 6) All psychopathology results from the repression of ideas associated with love; in other words, neurosis is always a "love story" (1907d). 7) Too little or too much love during childhood can result in psychopathology (1905b). 8) Some types of people are characterized by the intense need for love; other types of people are characterized by various kinds of incapacity for love. For example, neurotics suffer from too much repression, interfering with the ability to love, whereas criminals are defined by the incapacity to love at all (1928, 1931b). 9) During the latency period of development, there is a split between the sexual and the tender currents of libido, leading to later psychopathology that reflects difficulties integrating these two currents (1905b). 10) Many "pathologies" involving love (including special types of object choice, sexual impotence and inhibition, difficulties integrating sexual attraction with tenderness, homosexuality, and pathological jealousy) can be traced to conflicts originating in the oedipal period (1908e, 1910d, 1912d, 1918b). 11) In contrast to situations of psychopathology and inhibition, success in love correlates with success in other areas of life (1908e). 12) While marriage may begin with passionate love, over time it becomes characterized by aim-inhibited "affectionate sympathy" (1908e). 13) Love is experienced in relation to three sets of opposites: love versus indifference, love versus hate, love versus being loved (1915b). 14) Love and hate are closely related and can easily be transformed into each other (1905b, 1923a); most love is characterized by ambivalence; intense ambivalence predisposes to melancholia in the face of object loss (1909c, 1915b, 1917d). 15) Love is also intertwined with narcissism, defined as the libidinal investment of the self; for example, in addition to anaclitic object choice, the love object may be chosen because of his/her resemblance to the self or the ideal self (narcissistic object choice); the love object is always idealized; the need to recapture one's lost narcissism plays a role in parental love; object love is inversely proportional to the self love, leading to the sense of humility (at times, depletion) in the face of the idealized love object (1914e). 16) There is a fundamental incompatibility between civilization and love, in that civilization depends upon aim-inhibited affectionate bonds between people, while at the same time, civilization cannot tolerate unrestrained expression of libido (1930).

While Freud's clinical work reveals a nuanced approach to his patients' struggles with love, his theory suffers from his view that love can be reduced to a vicissitude of libido. For example, for the most part, Freud saw the caregiver's importance as an object in terms of providing drive satisfaction rather than love. Over time, the psychoanalytic theory of love has shifted toward understanding love as a primary emotion, not reducible to libido. It has also placed loving interactions between child and caregiver at the core of development. In post-Freudian psychoanalysis, the experience of love has largely been conceptualized in terms of object relations, rather than libido. At the same time, developments in theories of narcissism have challenged Freud's views of object love and self love as inversely proportional to each other.

While several of Freud's immediate followers, including Abraham, Hartmann, and A. Freud elaborated on the development of the capacity for love and the role of the mother in development, for the most part, their ideas continued to be conceptualized in terms of libido theory. For example, Abraham elaborated on Freud's ideas about preoedipal stages of development and on the role of internalization, identification, and other aspects of developing object relations. Abraham also added the important idea of "post-ambivalence" to his concept of the "genital character," expanding Freud's concept of "genital primacy" (Freud, 1938a). Abraham's ideas about the central problem of ambivalence contributed to later elaborations of genitality in terms of object relations, the capacity for love, and the capacity to master ambivalence (Abraham, 1924b). In a similar vein, Hartmann's important concept of object constancy (1952), while initially conceptualized by him in terms of libido theory, was also ultimately conceptualized in terms of object relations and the capacity to master ambivalence. Finally, in her extensive work with children, Anna Freud was certainly aware of the important role of the mother in all aspects of child development; however, she did not conceptualize this role in terms of the centrality of loving interaction (A. Freud, 1965).

With the advent of various forms of object relations theory, love took its place as a central component of the psychoanalytic theory of mind and of development. Ferenczi adumbrated some of these developments with his concept of "amphimixis," a diffuse amalgam of pleasurable experiences in infancy, whose aim is not drive discharge, but an exchange of "tenderness" between infant and caregiver. In Ferenczi's view, adult passion intrudes on this experience, resulting in an inappropriate erotization of childhood attachment, which he referred to as the "confusion of tongues." At the same time, Ferenczi described how children who feel unloved feel forever unwelcome in the world, often developing depression characterized by lack of desire to live (Ferenczi, 1929, 1933, 1938).

However, it was Klein (1937) who offered a radically altered view of the importance of love in psychological life. While most famous for her theories on the role of aggression, Klein saw love as central to all psychological development and function. Moving away from Freud's views on the primacy of libido, Klein conceptualized love not as a derivative of libido, but as a fundamental feature of the infant's psychic life. At the same time, while she did not emphasize the role of the actual mother, it is clear in her work that the mother's consistent love for the child and their loving interaction are vital to normal development. Klein described the infant's earliest experience as a mixture of drive, emotion, and "phantasy," all experienced in relation to the object (mother/breast). In her view, "feelings of love and gratitude arise directly and spontaneously in the baby in response to the love and care of his mother." The first "good object" is created through the projection of the infant's loving feelings, which are a fundamental aspect, rather than a result, of libidinal attachment. For Klein, the earliest experience of boundless and perfect love in relation to the object serves as the core of the ego, as well as the foundation for creativity, hope, trust, and belief in goodness. This earliest experience of love also brings with it gratitude, the drive for reparation, guilt, and concern for the object, all of which are crucial for development. Indeed, for Klein, development is characterized by the constant interaction between love and hate, striving toward the integration of these contradictory feelings. The child is motivated to control aggressive impulses because of love for his parents, leading him from the paranoid-schizoid to the depressive positions. Love for the parents also motivates the child to renounce his oedipal wishes (Klein, 1937, 1940, 1945, 1946, 1952, 1957, 1958).

Various other early object relations theorists, influenced to varying extents by both Ferenczi and Klein, elaborated on the importance of love and loving interaction in development. Fairbairn, famous for having declared the infant to be fundamentally "object-seeking," wrote of development in terms of love, describing the infant's need to feel loved by the mother and to feel in return that his love is felt and valued by her. Fairbairn (1952, 1954) also described how the child must overcome his fear that his love has damaged his mother, making her unavailable to him. From his own point of view, Winnicott (1965) described the "holding environment" created by the loving mother in interaction with her infant as crucial to development. For Winnicott, this holding environment predates and provides the matrix for instinctual satisfaction. The mother's consistent, loving presence is necessary for the child's development of creativity and play, as well as for his own capacity for love and concern. Also from an independent point of view greatly influenced by Ferenczi, A. Balint (1949) wrote about **archaic love**," and M. Balint (1952) described "**primary love**" as an innate infantile propensity, not reducible to libido. M. Balint (1948) also reworked the concept of genital primacy, separating the experience of genitality from **genital love**, arguing that love must include the experience of tenderness, idealization, and mutual identification.

Finally, from his own distinct point of view influenced both by Klein and by contemporary ethologists, as well as by his studies of war orphans and hospitalized children, Bowlby (1951) described how "**mother-love** in infancy and childhood is as important for mental health as are vitamins and proteins for physical health." Indeed, Bowlby's attachment theory is based on the concept that attachment between mother and infant is primary, rather than based on the gratification of drive needs. Others who studied hospitalized children reached conclusions similar to Bowlby's, including Ribble (1943), who coined the term *TLC,* or "**tender loving care**," needed by all infants, and Spitz (1965), who described anaclitic depression in hospitalized infants deprived of mother's nurturing and love. Indeed, as the importance of the mother's love gained concep-

tual dignity within psychoanalysis, D. Levy (1943) described the effects of too much maternal attention or love, coining the phrase "maternal overprotection." Meanwhile, Sullivan (1953a), working somewhat independently on the development of his own interpersonal psychoanalysis, asserted that the development of an integrated self dynamism depends upon the consistent presence of the loving mother. Fromm (1957) drew heavily from the work of Sullivan in his book written for the public, *The Art of Loving,* in which he explores (among other things) the balance between the quest to love, which offers the "answer to existence" with the need to maintain individuality.

Writing in the tradition of American ego psychology augmented by direct infant observation, Mahler elaborated her developmental psychology in which the fundamental conflict between wishes for symbiosis and wishes for separation-individuation are intertwined with conflicts between love and hate and mediated by the experience of loving and being loved; the mother's constant loving attitudes toward the child in the face of the aggression mobilized in the rapprochement crisis allows the child to move through the crisis toward object constancy (Mahler, Pine, and Bergman, 1975). Contemporary developmental theorists have continued to stress the importance of various aspects of loving interaction between mother and child, emphasizing love as part of the interactional system or relational matrix (D. N. Stern, 1977, 1985; Beebe and Lachmann, 1988; Lichtenberg, 1982, 1983).

Bergmann, Person, Kernberg, and S. Mitchell (among others) have all written extensively about the adult experiences and pathologies of love. Heavily influenced by Mahler, Bergmann (1971, 1982, 1987, 1988, 1995) asserted that the experience of bliss associated with falling in love involves recapturing the pleasures of the symbiotic phases of development. Bergmann explored the ego functions necessary for falling in love and maintaining the experience of love, as well as the consequences for the adult of disturbance at various phases of separation-individuation. In an overlapping argument, Bak (1973) asserted that the experience of object loss is inherent in love; the intense bliss of passionate love may serve to defend against the experience of loss.

In contrast to Bergmann, Person (1988, 1991) argued that the experience of romantic or passionate love is not universal, but arises at the intersection between the individual psyche and surrounding culture. In cultures where passionate love is encouraged, the essential features of the experience include the idealization and yearning for the beloved, based on narcissistic strivings, which seek to recapture lost perfection and/or redress disappointment. Fantasies of love draw from both the mother-infant relationship and the parental couple. Experiences of passionate love offer unique opportunities for personal growth and the expansion of meaning. Like Person, Chasseguet-Smirgel (1984) also argued that the power of passionate love derives from the search for union with the original narcissistic object.

Writing from his unique point of view integrating ego psychology with Kleinian object relations theory, Kernberg (1974a, 1974b, 1977, 1982, 1985, 1988, 2011) explored subjects such as the barriers to falling and remaining in love, and the prerequisites for **mature love**. In Kernberg's view, mature love is a complex emotional disposition, which integrates sexual excitement, tenderness and concern for the object, normal idealization, genital identification, and aggression. It depends upon the development of object relations in depth, the superego, and mastery of oedipal conflicts. Mature love must withstand many major contradictions, including: feelings of merger with the love object combined with firm boundaries between self and other; idealization of the love object combined with strong reality testing; tenderness and concern for the love object combined with playful aggression; the excitement of re-finding former objects without succumbing to the incest taboo; and the excitement of finding new objects in the face of attachments to the old. Kernberg has explored specific pathologies of love in narcissistic, borderline, and neurotic individuals, stress-

ing, for example, that an inverse relationship between love and self love is seen only in psychopathology. Kernberg has also explored the complexities of the relationship between the couple and the larger group or society.

In his book *Can Love Last?*, written from the point of view of relational psychoanalysis, S. Mitchell (2002) challenged what he described as Freud's fundamentally tragic view that love and desire cannot coexist. In Mitchell's view, individuals often create lifeless relationships because of their need for safety and their wish to avoid the risks of intimacy presented by dependency, sexuality, aggression, and idealization. In argument with Mitchell, Goldner (2004) argued that the safety of attachment, rather than providing a hiding place from passionate love, is a necessary foundation for love. For love to remain passionate, lovers must balance inevitable tensions between recognition and negation and/or destruction and reparation, as well as the dramas of love lost and found and of romantic victory and defeat. Also arguing with Mitchell, R. Stein (2006) asserted that the challenge of maintaining passion in love depends more on the "unforgetting" or retrieval of the poignant and transgressive feelings of childhood.

With regard to the place of love in the psychoanalytic clinical situation, L. Friedman (2005) has offered a review of the literature along with reflections on the question "Is there a special kind of psychoanalytic love?"

M

Magical Thinking is a kind of cognition characterized by a belief in the omnipotence of thoughts, or the belief that thoughts have the power to alter reality. Magical thinking is commonly observed in children during fantasy and play. In normal adults, it appears in dreams, fantasy, uncanny experiences, and states of regression. Magical thinking is observed psychopathology that involves a significant failure in reality testing, including psychosis, perversion, and obsessional symptoms. For example, magical thinking is seen in obsessions and/or compulsions employed to ward off a feared disaster. Magical thinking is also observed in severe character disorders, such as borderline or narcissistic personalities.

In "Totem and Taboo," Freud (1913e) described three stages—animistic, religious, and scientific—in the evolutionary and developmental progression of human thought. Freud understood animism (a belief system in which spirits inhabit animate and inanimate objects) as rooted in narcissism and a lack of self-object differentiation; spirits and demons represent man's own emotional impulses projected into the world. Freud described the magical, omnipotent thoughts characteristic of animism as reflecting the dominance of primary process and the pleasure principle. He noted that in magical thinking, control over one's inner thoughts is mistaken for an ability to control outer reality. Freud (1914e) described magical thinking as grandiose, representing the remnants of infantile narcissism. In Freud's (1919d) view, "uncanny" feelings may arise in situations where the infantile belief in the "omnipotence of thoughts" seems plausible once again. Jacobson (1964) explicated the magical nature of the internalizations formed in the preoedipal period, remnants of which persist throughout life. As a result of the child's undeveloped reality testing, aspects of the object are attributed to the self, resulting in the illusory belief they are under one's control.

Mania/Manic Defense: see DENIAL, DEPRESSION, KLEIN, MOURNING

Masculine Protest: see MASCULINITY/FEMININITY

Masculinity Complex: see MASCULINITY/FEMININITY, PENIS ENVY

Masculinity/Femininity is a constellation of character traits and aspects of self experience associated with one's gender identity, experienced on a conscious and unconscious level, and manifest in such attributes as manner of speech, posture, physical mannerisms, and style of dress. It is the developmental outcome of a complex interaction among: biological factors, including anatomy and hormones; psychological factors shaped in large part by internalizations of important early objects; and cultural factors that organize characteristics, attitudes, and values about all of the above. Masculinity and femininity are aspects of sexual identity (a more complex structure than gender identity), established during adolescence, which also involves an individual's personal erotism expressed in sexual fantasies and object choice. However, one's sense of masculinity or femininity is a dynamic developmental process that spans the life cycle, during which the associated attributes may become more nuanced, flexible, and varied. The relative contributions of and interplay among nature, nurture, and culture to the development of a sense of masculinity or femininity have not yet been delineated.

Psychoanalytic understandings of masculinity and femininity have changed markedly in the more than one hundred years of psychoanalytic discourse. Freud (1905b, 1923a, 1925b) understood that masculinity and femininity are both developmental achievements, rooted in anatomy, emerging from conflicted identifications, and further shaped by sociological factors, however his views on both female and male psychosexual development also suffer from gender bias. Although his views on female development were challenged during his time by psychoanalysts Adler, Horney, and Jones, it was not until the late twentieth century that psychoanalytic researchers and theorists, and gender theorists of other disciplines, began to comprehensively delineate theories of gender and its development, resulting in new insights and controversies. The concept of **primary femininity** emerged in response to the phallocentrism of Freud's theories of female psychosexual development. Challenges to Freud's views on male development and masculinity have emerged more recently, at first in connection to a growing interest among psychoanalysts in the development of male homosexuality, and then as an obvious counterpart to the focus on femininity. Post-modern approaches to gender critique the idea that there can be any stable, "essentialist" (meaning true and enduring across time and culture) definition of masculinity (Flax, 1990) or femininity.

Freud's (1892/1899) first reference to the concepts of masculinity and femininity are in his letters to Fliess, where he described his abandoned attempts to explain the elements of repression in terms of this polarity. In his landmark paper "Three Essays on the Theory of Sexuality," Freud (1905b) introduced many of his views on male and female psychosexual development, which he elaborated subsequently (1908c, 1923b, 1924b, 1925b). Freud recognized that the psychological attributes of masculinity and femininity are not related in a simple way to anatomy, and that both men and women demonstrate a mixture of masculine and feminine character traits rooted in a universal bisexual potential. Furthermore, the attainment of masculinity in men and femininity in women is vulnerable to conflict and psychopathology. The attributes of masculine and feminine evolve via a developmental sequence that begins with the emergence of active and passive instinctual strivings during the anal sadistic stage of psychosexual development, which is evident in both girls and boys. Active strivings are associated with the musculature and the instinct for mastery and represent proto-masculine sexuality, while passive strivings are associated with the anal mucus membrane and represent proto-feminine sexuality. In Freud's view, although male and female characterological differences are evident from early childhood, the girl's femininity is not consolidated until adolescence, when she affects a transfer of erotogenic zone from clitoris to vagina and fully represses masculine sexual strivings. The boy's development is more straightforward, as he maintains both the same erotogenic zone throughout life and the same gender of his libidinal object. However, strong passive propensities and feminine identifications in the boy may lead to neurosis or perversion. Subsequently, Freud (1914e) distinguished between feminine and masculine object choice, describing the former as narcissistic and the latter as anaclitic, yet also acknowledged the admixtures of object choice in both men and women. Subsequently, Freud (1925b) delineated the role of penis envy and the castration complex in the girl's psychosexual development, describing the girl's renunciation of masculine clitoral masturbation after the humiliating discovery of genital difference. Freud (1931) argued that the boy's masculinity is primary and the girl's femininity is in large part the outcome of feelings of disappointment and inadequacy. This

leaves women more vulnerable to neurosis, a repudiation of sexuality, a persistent "masculinity complex," and possibly homosexual object choice. Furthermore, the feminine preference for passive aims and behavior, combined with the culturally and constitutionally determined suppression of aggression, lead to masochism. However, Freud (1924a) also described **feminine masochism** in men who adopt passive and feminine sexual fantasies of being castrated and abused (as a defense against oedipal fears).

Using the terms *masculine* and *feminine* as metaphors for strength and weakness, Adler (1924) postulated the **masculine protest** as a cluster of traits in both sexes overcompensating for feelings of inferiority and predisposing to neurosis. Later he used the term in a more limited way to women's protest of the feminine role. Adler considered Freud's concept of penis envy too literal and biological, asserting that women feel inferior not because of a conviction of physical deficiency but because of culturally ordained male dominance. This early critique of Freud's psychology of women grew from Adler's focus on power as a dominant influence in human psychology. Arguing against the term *masculine protest*, Freud (1914e) equated it with castration anxiety, which he defined as the boy's anxiety concerning his penis and the girl's envy of the penis.

Horney (1924) and Jones (1927, 1933), who did not view the girl's phallic phase and castration complex as a genuine developmental stage, also challenged Freud's views on female psychosexual development. Instead, they argued that the girl's castration complex is a secondary defensive response to disappointment that occurs after a female love-relation to the father has already been formed. In effect, they argued that the girl's femininity is primary rather than forged from disappointment and humiliation over gender difference.

Subsequent studies with young children (Stoller, 1965; Coates, 1997; De Marneffe, 1997) have challenged Freud's views on gender development in both boys and girls. While Freud emphasized the monumental discovery of genital difference, child researchers have observed that the child's sense of himself or herself as boy or girl, and the child's sense of his or her genitals as part of a bodily self representation, are established by the end of the second year of life. However the link between one's genital and one's gender is a cognitive recognition that may be consolidated somewhat later. Also observed is the child's genital satisfaction regardless of gender. In contrast to Freud's idea of the primacy of masculine sexuality, Stoller argued that the earliest state for both boys and girls is **proto-femininity**, which results from the mother-infant symbiosis. According to Stoller, the boy's masculinity develops later as the result of biological factors and the encouragement of a male father figure, which together aid the boy's defenses against the regressive pull of the symbiotic tie with mother. The girl's feminine development follows a more direct path and is not so tied to issues of separation as with the boy.

Nonetheless, understanding the evolution from a sense of maleness and femaleness to the emergence of a complex sense of masculinity and femininity leaves much room for theoretical controversy. The concepts of masculinity and femininity are seen as comprising a number of constituents: gender identity, gender role, physical appearance, anatomy, sexual identity and behavior, and social behavior (Torsti, 1998). However, the specifics of these constituents can vary widely across cultures and history. What is considered particularly masculine or feminine in terms of style of dress or personal grooming varies with time and place, yet small children fixate on those superficial differences as the essential differences between what is identified as masculine and feminine, and such early experiences become deeply ingrained. Changing notions of what comprises femininity or masculinity surely emphasize the impact of culture on their content, however the universal imperative to maintain a distinction between the genders has been challenged by some gender theorists who espouse more fluid conceptions.

Contemporary efforts to rework the early phallocentric views of female psychosexual development produced an extensive literature under the umbrella of primary femininity, a concept with broad and differing usages, whose common thread or focus is the girl's earliest sense of herself as female. Efforts to understand masculinity emerged from studies of male homosexuality and gender identity disorders and have evolved into more subtle explorations of the highly individualized experience of masculinity that comprises every man's unique and subjective attempt, consciously and unconsciously, to integrate the familial, cultural, and psychosexual experiences associated with masculine gender. Therefore, some psychoanalysts now speak of "masculinities," rather than reductively assuming that there is such a thing as a singular masculinity (Chodorow, 1994b; Person, 2006).

M. Diamond (2006), exploring the development of masculinity over the life cycle, challenged the view that a boy must disidentify with his mother in the process of early separation. Instead he viewed healthy masculinity as a developmental process in which both masculine and feminine identifications are integrated along with a progression from phallic to genital values internalized within the ego ideal. Other authors emphasize that contemporary Western society and the familial patterns it engenders have restricted the psychological experience of masculinity, such that much of what comes to be felt as masculine for boys is actually a renunciation of the traits valued by the culture as feminine. Important psychological experiences, such as the capacity to experience a full and rich affective life (Reichbart, 2006) and the ability to integrate a sense of genital interiority or receptivity (Fogel, 1998) are experienced as prohibited to men. In practice, much psychoanalytic work with male patients consists of helping them analyze such restrictions in order to experience a richer, more-nuanced sense of masculinity.

Masochism is the pursuit of pain, humiliation, and/or suffering for the purpose of finding hidden pleasure or gratification. The term *sadomasochism* is often used, referring to Freud's pairing of the instincts of sadism and masochism. In the psychoanalytic literature, masochism refers to: 1) sexual behavior characterized by conscious sexual arousal or pleasure in the experience of pain or humiliation (**sexual masochism**); if pain or humiliation are absolute requirements for sexual arousal, sexual masochism is defined as a perversion (**masochistic perversion**); 2) nonsexual behavior characterized by the pursuit of pain or suffering with the aim of finding satisfaction or pleasure (**psychic masochism**); in the latter, either the pursuit or the pleasure (or both) is unconscious; 3) **masochistic personality disorder**, describing someone whose whole character is organized around the hidden search for suffering or disappointment.

Masochism must be distinguished from depression, a mood state often accompanied by self-directed aggression. However, depression may at times serve masochistic aims, thereby increasing the risk of its occurrence in individuals with masochistic personality disorder. Masochism must also be distinguished from the suffering that accompanies all psychopathology but which is not necessarily sought. Recognizing that some degree of suffering is involved in many of life's positive achievements, masochism should be reserved for situations in which pain or suffering is sought beyond what is required for appropriate pursuit of goals and where the capacity to enjoy legitimate achievement of one's goals is significantly impaired.

Masochism plays a central role in clinical psychoanalysis because self-defeating behavior, accompanied by various degrees of hidden gratification, is ubiquitous or even universal; indeed, some degree of masochism is a feature of everyone's psychological life. From the point of view of theory, masochism is important in that its existence demands consideration of psychological factors that operate (or appear to operate), as Freud (1920a) described it, "beyond the pleasure principle." In the history of theory-making, masochism has been intimately linked with the study of aggression and of the superego. More recent literature has sought to understand masochism in terms of problems in object relations or attachment and/or narcissism.

The term *masochism* was coined by Von Krafft-Ebing in 1895 to describe a sexual perversion in which pain is a necessary element for achieving sexual satisfaction. His new word was based on the novel *Venus in Furs,* by von Sacher-Masoch, which describes the pain and suffering of a man hopelessly in love with a woman, whom he induces to enslave him. Freud adopted the term *masochism* initially to refer to masochistic sexual perversion. He dealt with the paradox of pleasure-in-pain by positing an "intimate connection between cruelty and the sexual instinct," explained in evolutionary/biological terms as derived from the need to subjugate the object; because of this innate aspect of libido, "every pain contains in itself the possibility of a feeling of pleasure." In this early work, Freud (1905b) described masochism as the "reverse" or "passive" expression of sadism, with which it is always associated. As his instinct theory developed, Freud (1915b) conceptualized masochism as a manifestation of aggression (still an aspect of libido) turned against the self, now in response to guilt and/or fears of castration. Freud (1919b) linked masochism with the beating fantasies of children, which represent a defensive regression from oedipal strivings to anal-sadistic strivings, and which, in the face of guilt and demands for self punishment, have been turned against the self. The "essence of masochism," then, is the "convergence of the sense of guilt and sexual love."

Prior to 1920, Freud conceptualized masochism as a vicissitude of the sadistic aspect of libido (and thereby as operating in accord with the pleasure principle). In "Beyond the Pleasure Principle," Freud (1920a) posited a death drive, operating outside of the pleasure principle, which results in **primary masochism**. In this formulation, sadism is now a secondary phenomenon resulting from masochism directed outward. In a further convolution, sadism may be turned against the self to produce **secondary masochism**, the source of most clinically observable pain-seeking behavior. Finally, in "The Economic Problem of Masochism," his fullest account on the subject, Freud (1924a) proposed three kinds of masochism: 1) primary **erotogenic masochism**, the basic type underlying all others, which results from the "fusion" of the death drive with libido; 2) **feminine masochism**, described in men who adopt "passive" and "feminine" sexual fantasies of being castrated and abused (as a defense against oedipal fears); and 3) **moral masochism**, a dramatic expansion of the concept of masochism, which describes apparently nonsexual, self-defeating behavior resulting from an "unconscious sense of guilt" and a "need for punishment." In the clinical situation, moral masochism may be evinced in a "negative therapeutic reaction." While almost all analysts have rejected Freud's notion of the death drive as the explanation for masochism, his concept of moral masochism opened the door for all later explorations of nonsexual psychic masochism.

In post-Freudian psychoanalysis, discussions of masochistic perversion and psychic (or moral) masochism have diverged; masochistic perversion is generally explored in the literature on perversion, whereas psychic masochism is explored in the literature on character. As the range of psychodynamics underlying psychic masochism has expanded beyond the psychosexual, the link between the two basic forms of masochism has become less clear than it was to Freud. In discussions of psychic masochism, all theorists have stressed the universal aspect of masochism, its existence on a continuum from neurotic to normal, and its association with sadism. All, following Freud, have emphasized the role of aggression and the contribution of the superego. Many theorists have questioned whether the pain and suffering of masochism is pursued for its own sake or whether it is the condition or price paid for any type of pleasure or success (Reik, 1939; C. Brenner, 1959). Freud (1916) too described such individuals as "those wrecked by success" or "criminals from a sense of guilt."

In addition to self punishment for forbidden sexual or oedipal strivings, later theorists have emphasized the interpersonal, attachment, and (predominantly preoedipal) object relations aspects of masochism, including its provocative, exhibitionistic qualities (Reik, 1939), its attempt at magical control of the object (Eidelberg, 1959), and its attempt at "seduction of the aggressor" (Loewenstein, 1957). Some of these theorists have connected masochism with the need to preserve a tie to an object at whose hands one has suffered in childhood (Berliner, 1942). Fairbairn (1954) described what he called the "masochistic defense," or the all-out effort to preserve the frustrating yet needed relationship to the object through the creation of an "all-bad self" who assumes all the blame for frustration and deprivation.

In a formulation that stressed the self-esteem enhancing, or narcissistic, aspects of masochism, Bergler (1948a, 1949) labeled masochistic individuals as "injustice collectors," describing a three-step process of relating to others, which includes 1) the perception of a situation in which the individual feels injured, cheated, or humiliated; 2) a "pseudo-aggressive" response, meaning an aggressive response that is mistimed, misdosed, and misdirected, leading to further "mistreatment"; 3) further defeat, with anger giving way to self pity, depression, and feelings of "this only happens to me." Bergler (1961) also described **malignant masochism** in severely ill patients. Following Bergler, A. M. Cooper (1988) has argued that narcissistic and masochistic elements are so closely intertwined that conceptual clarity is gained by considering a single entity, the **narcissistic-masochistic personality disorder**. In Cooper's view, even in the case of "good enough" caregiving, the universal experience of weakness and helplessness in childhood leads always to the deployment of some masochistic defenses, with their promise of "victory through defeat" (Reik, 1939). Self psychologists have described how chronic narcissistic rage may become embedded in the structure of the self, resulting in sadomasochism, characterized by contempt, injustice collecting, self recrimination, self pity, and suicidal behavior (A. Ornstein, 1991).

Despite the universality of psychic masochism and the widespread prevalence of masochistic personality disorders, psychiatric nosologists have consistently decided not to include a proposed "self-defeating personality disorder" in the *DSM* system out of deference to those who argue, following Freud, that the diagnosis is linked to passivity and femininity and might lead to discrimination of women and others who might be blamed for their suffering. The *Psychodynamic Diagnostic Manual* (*PDM*) divides masochistic (or self-defeating) personality disorders into moral masochistic personality disorder (characterized by diminished self esteem, refusal of experiences of satisfaction and success, and unconscious guilt) versus relational masochistic personality disorder (characterized by suffering or victimization in relationships). It also includes a sadistic/sadomasochistic personality disorder, which it argues always functions at the borderline level (PDM Task Force, 2006).

Mastery is the capacity to achieve competence or superior skill at a particular task, accompanied by a feeling of pleasure, effectiveness, dominance, or power. Mastery may be experienced in relation to some aspect of the environment or of oneself, such as a developmental task, an inner conflict, or a psychic trauma. Strivings for mastery contribute to many aspects of human behavior, with particular significance in the understanding of children's play and in the management of trauma. Conflicts over mastery are common among reasons for seeking treatment.

Freud (1905b) first described the **instinct for mastery** in relationship to sadism as a nonsexual instinct to dominate others by force, which attaches itself to the sexual instinct in acts of cruelty. He posited the muscular apparatus as the source for this instinct for mastery. Freud (1913d) discussed mastery in connection with the pair of opposites activity/passivity. In 1915, Freud (1915b) described the instinct for mastery as among the ego instincts. In 1920, Freud (1920a) considered the instinct for mastery in a different way, conceptualizing it as the form taken by the death drive when attached to the sexual instinct, contributing to overpowering the object at various stages in psychosexual development. Freud also discussed mastery, not to describe control of the object or in connection with aggression, but to describe the binding of excitation, thereby explaining the role of repetition in children's play, traumatic neurosis, and traumatic dreams.

Following Freud, many analysts have continued to observe strivings for mastery in a variety of situations. These include childhood development, play, work, creativity and art, and the effort to survive trauma. During the era of ego psychology, strivings for mastery were increasingly conceptualized as an ego function. For example, Hartmann (1939a) mentions mastery in connection with the tasks of adaptation. Hendrick (1943a, 1943b) described an instinct to master connected to the ego, with the aim of controlling or altering the environment by the skilful use of perceptual, intellectual, and motor techniques. He compared his concept of the striving for mastery to A. Adler's (1927) concept of "will to power." Later, White (1963) introduced a new concept, effectance motivation, described as an inborn tendency to explore and influence the environment; White suggested that the "master reinforcer" for humans is personal competence. While Erikson (1950) did not use the word *mastery,* the concept is implied in several of his stages of ego development, that is, in ideas such as autonomy, initiative, and industry. Although A. Freud (1965) did not make special note of the term *mastery,* she distinguished between competence and psychopathology.

There was a mixed response to the work of Hendrick and White, with debate raging for years over the proper conceptualization of strivings for mastery within a traditional drive theory of motivation.

With the collapse of the hegemony of ego psychology and increasing comfort with multiple sources of motivation, strivings for mastery have assumed a variety of roles in contemporary psychoanalytic theory. Kohut (1977), who posited a separate line of development for narcissistic strivings of all kind, conceptualized pleasure in mastery as fundamental to the smooth functioning of the bipolar self. Developmental psychoanalysts take for granted the idea that the exercise of capacities has a self-propelling quality, manifest in strivings for mastery beginning at birth and continuing throughout the life cycle. For example, D. N. Stern (1985) included striving for mastery among the organizers of the self. Emde (1991, 1999) included mastery as an aspect of all of his five basic inborn motivations, also describing the pleasure associated with "getting it right" as an important aspect of infant experience. In the area of treatment, J. Weiss, Sampson, and Caston (1976) have proposed what they call the **Control-Mastery Theory**, which explains the therapeutic action of psychoanalysis as based on an innate need to achieve order and coherence by testing one's beliefs in the world.

Masturbation is a technique of producing sexual pleasure by the self stimulation of erogenous zones, which are usually but not exclusively the genitals. It occurs throughout the life cycle and may be a feature of normal or pathological functioning. Masturbation may be accompanied by a variety of feelings and both conscious and unconscious **masturbation fantasies**, which may be split off from physical masturbation through defensive processes. Masturbation fantasies, like all fantasies, evolve throughout development, reflect the predominant conflicts of each phase, and represent compromise formations serving multiple functions. However, some analysts regard the **central masturbation fantasy** or **core masturbation fantasy** as the final configuration of the repressed oedipal complex, which then forms the basis for subsequent masturbation, sexual preferences, and personality organization (M. Laufer, 1976). Masturbation fantasies for both genders often involve masculine and feminine, heterosexual and homosexual, active and passive, and sadistic and masochistic fantasies, in which the person unconsciously identifies with all the roles (Lampl-De Groot, 1950; Arlow, 1953). Masturbation is necessary for normal development, and its complete absence is considered a poor prognostic sign (I. Bernstein, 1975). In analysis, masturbation, including how it is done and the masturbation fantasies that accompany it, are considered windows into the uncon-

scious. It is usually a sign of progress if, in the course of treatment, someone who does not masturbate begins to do so (Freud, 1912c).

Masturbation has figured significantly throughout the history of psychoanalytic thinking, however, the vicissitudes of its emphasis within different theoretical orientations correlate with levels of interest in infantile sexuality and sexuality in general. It is important in the earliest history of psychoanalysis because Freud and his followers were trying to move beyond the moral prohibitions of the day to discover the meaning of sexuality in human development and its contribution to psychopathology. Freud's central discovery of infantile sexuality importantly features the role of masturbation in psychosexual development.

While the act of self stimulation to orgasm is represented throughout history in art and literature, the term was probably introduced by the medical profession and popularized in the nineteenth century. Beard, a nineteenth-century American psychiatrist, developed the concept of sexual neurasthenia, to which young males were particularly prone due to excessive masturbation. Like most physicians of his era, Freud (1912c) thought masturbation could be harmful because it was an inadequate discharge of sexual tension that could lead to a fixation on infantile sexual aims. However, over time his emphasis shifted from the behavior to its meaning and its accompanying fantasies.

Masturbation and masturbation fantasies play an important role in most psychoanalytic views of development. Infantile masturbation or genital play is one of the various types of autoerotic activity of infancy. It is a normal, developmentally progressive activity that provides an outlet for tension, fosters early differentiation of body boundaries and boundaries between self and other, facilitates self exploration and self awareness, and indicates satisfactory relations with the caretaking environment. Boys usually masturbate by manipulating the penis; girls manually stimulate the clitoris or may use objects or engage in thigh rubbing. A relatively mature ego is necessary before true masturbatory fantasy is associated with the activity. Masturbation fantasies promote gender identity, contribute to the development of genital primacy over pregenital wishes and fears, neutralize aggression by binding it with sexuality, and aid in the mastery of anxiety and trauma. They also facilitate the progression from narcissistic to object love, and the transformation from incestuous to nonincestuous object relations. Oedipal masturbation fantasies are object related and often concerned with conquest or the dread of retaliation (castration anxiety). Latency is associated with struggles against masturbation and fantasies that reflect the developing superego. Such defenses as repression, regression, and reaction formation contribute to character development in the latency phase. The struggles with masturbation continue into adolescence, and the regressive aspects of the activity must be counteracted by new achievements in ego development. Masturbation in adolescence may serve to assist development by facilitating genitality, in learning sexual pleasure and how to have an orgasm, and in fostering object relatedness through masturbation fantasy. The setting aside of sadomasochistic omnipotent fantasies and beliefs is the major developmental task of late adolescence (as well as during termination of treatment), and late-adolescent and adult masturbation practices and fantasies may serve to retain and sequester sadomasochistic pathology.

Contemporary perspectives on masturbatory activities and fantasies consider their contribution to self regulation, affect modulation, and impulse control, that is, in the assessment of ego functions and controls. While past theories of masturbation often focused on its pathological aspects (E. Kris, 1951; Bornstein, 1953; Wurmser, 2007), contemporary authors take a more balanced position on adolescent and adult masturbation, recognizing multiple motives and determinants, with an emphasis on the positive developmental functions served, for instance, in relation to trial action (M. Laufer, 1976; M. Laufer and M. E. Laufer, 1984). It is noteworthy that many contemporary psychoanalysts are relatively uninterested in masturbation, which parallels the sharp decline of psychoanalytic interest in sexuality itself (Fonagy, 2008). It is primarily in the context of perversion that current theory privileges masturbation fantasies as critical to understanding (K. Novick and J. Novick, 1987, 1991).

Memory is a function of the mind by which impressions once perceived, learned, or experienced are retained and reproduced. The term also applies to the capacity to remember and to the content of what is recalled. The processes employed in memory are very complex, involving perception, apperception, recognition, encoding, retrieval, and activation. Memories may be evoked by voluntary cognitive recall, affective and sensory experiences, and verbal association. Like all mental experiences, memories are a complex amalgam of cognitive and affective processes, such that both the storage and the recall of memory are shaped by the conscious and unconscious emotional conditions associated with that experience. Psychologically determined alterations of memory range

from the normal experience of déjà vu (a sense of erroneous familiarity evoked by a situation that both symbolizes and stimulates the revival of memories, wishes, or fantasies) to pathological dissociative states in which one's entire sense of identity may be disrupted. Within psychoanalysis, such categories as **recognition memory**, **recall memory**, **screen memory**, and **telescoping of memory** have been described.

Memory plays an important role in the history of psychoanalytic theorizing, starting with Freud's first model of pathogenesis, in which he viewed the repressions of **traumatic memory** or "reminiscences" as the cause of hysteria. Although Freud extensively revised his theories of the mind over time, he never abandoned the genetic point of view, a central premise that the past lives within the present in powerful and complex ways. The concept of transference is a manifestation of that premise, illustrating that memories may be experienced in complex ways, or "acted out," rather than consciously remembered. Many current controversies within psychoanalysis focus on aspects of memory, for example: How is experience encoded in the mind in both normal and pathological conditions? What is the role of remembering in psychoanalytic treatment? Are retrieval and reconstruction necessary for therapeutic action? Can change result from shifts in a type of interpersonal process memory called "implicit relational knowing" (D. N. Stern et al., 1998; Fonagy, 1999; Lyons-Ruth, 1999)? These ideas are at the core of psychoanalytic theorizing about how the unconscious mind is structured and organized and how treatment works.

In Freud's earliest theorizing (1895b, 1900), he ascribed perception and memory to separate systems of the mind and conceived of memory, or "mnemic traces," as structural modifications that are linked through association. Some of those traces within the system unconscious are charged with intense sexual energies and are forcibly kept out of consciousness by a "censor." Access to consciousness is possible if the censor distorts and disguises memory traces enough to be tolerated by the system conscious-preconscious. Within the system preconscious, memories can become conscious by receiving sufficient "attention cathexis" and in this preconscious form are already linked with a symbolic representation. The clinical correlations of such formulations involve a view of hysteria in which symptoms can be understood as symbolic representations of traumatic memories, the recall of which is prevented by repression. Treatment consists of attempts to recover the traumatic memories and to discharge or abreact through speech the affect associated with them.

A shift in Freud's (1914b) theory of therapeutic action is evident in his papers on technique, in which his earlier view of memory retrieval gives way to a more complex vision of the motivating power of unconscious wish and its expression through repetition or enactment within the transference. In Freud's (1900) view, wish too is a concept inextricably linked to memories of previous gratifications that press for satisfaction in the present. Freud described this repetition in relationship to the concept of transference, which is a "new edition" or "facsimile" of impulses and fantasies from the past that replaces the analyst with an early object relationship. Object choice is always the "refinding" of an object, or, in other words, every object choice is shaped by the memory/representation of an early object choice. Freud placed remembering in opposition to repetition: The analyst asks the patient to remember, but knows that the patient will repeat his memories, symptoms, inhibitions, and character traits through action without conscious awareness of doing so. Freud acknowledged that such repetition is, in fact, a form of memory that is necessary for analytic work; it is responsible for the here-and-now aliveness of the psychoanalytic situation and thereby, its therapeutic leverage. In this vein, Freud (1912a) famously argued, "it is impossible to destroy anyone in absentia or in effigie."

Freud (1914c) understood that memory is a complex process and that it exists in different forms that serve different functions. He distinguished four categories of memories that have clinical significance in psychoanalytic process: 1) memories of external experiences that the patient claims he has never forgotten but has no understanding of their psychological significance; 2) screen memories or rigidly fixed, seemingly innocuous recollections of childhood that conceal or "screen" (Freud, 1899a) a more affectively charged, sometimes traumatic recall of something more significant; as such, screen memories are condensations or displacements of latent ideation, affects, or drives in a manner comparable to dreams or neurotic symptoms; 3) internal psychical processes that have never been conscious but have become "remembered," such as fantasies or thought connections; 4) memories of experiences that were not understood at the time they were recorded, but are subsequently understood through the process of reconstruction (Freud, 1937b). With the advent of the structural theory, Freud (1923a) retained a concept of the centrality of memory both in his view that all structure building involves the internalization of mnemic traces of past object ties, and in his concept of signal affect (1926a), which involves the ego's reproduction in attenuated form of the memory of traumatic anxiety. Freud also referred to processes of remembering (or forgetting) in his discussion of traumatic dreams, childhood amnesia, the compulsion to repeat, and deferred action.

E. Kris (1956b) described the dynamic relationship between the recovery of childhood memories and therapeutic action, emphasizing that the essential issue is not the content of the memory but its contextual meaning. In his view, interpretation does not produce recall of childhood memories but establishes the dynamic conditions under which recall becomes possible. In other words, the conflictual themes represented by the memory have already become central within the transference relationship through interpretive work. The analytic work is conducted at the psychic surface, at the border between the preconscious and unconscious, so that the patient's experience is one of recognition memory, or déjà raconté, as if the meaning of the memory is understood rather than that the memory is recovered. Kris also described the telescoping of memory that occurs during childhood, such that a specific memory comes to represent a condensation of conflicts from different developmental phases and that become progressively integrated into personality structure and patterns of behavior.

Many analysts have challenged the notion that memory retrieval is responsible for therapeutic action in psychoanalytic treatments. For example, it is argued that the curative factor is the gradual modification of "mental models of object relationships" (Fonagy, 1999) or "implicit relational knowing" (Lyons-Ruth, 1999) or "way-of-being-with-the-other" (D. N. Stern, 1994; D. N. Stern et al., 1998) that become activated within the transference relationship and become understood in the here and now. Fonagy cited data from cognitive-science research that distinguishes between two distinct memory systems, **declarative** or **explicit** memory, and **procedural** or **implicit** memory. He described declarative memory as that which may become conscious, and implicit memory as content free and therefore that which cannot be remembered but can be accessed only through subjective experience. So, in the view of Fonagy and others, change occurs through the modification of procedures or implicit memory that can be connected to unconscious fantasy only when accessed through experience. Similarly, P. Bromberg (1991, 2006) designated dissociated self states as the form in which early trauma is "remembered," requiring behavioral enactment within the analytic dyad for access and the creation of meaning. Such dissociated states are not the result of repression and are also not conceptualized as aspects of the dynamic unconscious. All such views assert that there are aspects of unconscious experience that are better described as the descriptive nondynamic unconscious.

Westen and Gabbard (Westen and Gabbard, 2002; Gabbard and Westen, 2003) agreed that memory retrieval is not the key factor in therapeutic action and argued instead for the role of multiple modes of therapeutic action, including insight, those utilizing the treatment relationship, and various secondary strategies. Citing cognitive-science research that features a connectionist model, they did not focus on procedural implicit memory but rather **associative memory**, another subtype of implicit memory. They described associative memory as unconscious networks created through experience of cognitive, affective, and other psychological processes. The unconscious activation of these networks effects behavioral and psychological experience at all times, as, for example, in the patient's transference. Other networks represent unconscious wishes, fantasies, beliefs, defenses, compromise formations, and internal object relations. Change occurs through the deactivation of networks, the loosening of links, and the creation of new associative links. Gabbard and Westen view free association and interpretation as methods that engage the patient's ability to explore their unconscious associative networks, especially when the focus of interpretation is the transference. They view the analytic relationship as critical for change in multiple ways, including internalization of functions, affective attitudes, and conscious strategies for self reflection, as well as through the identification of transference-countertransference paradigms.

Drawing from the principles of hermeneutics, analysts such as Spence (1982) challenged the fundamental premise that interpretation aimed at connecting the patient's past with present experience is possible. Spence argued that the value of interpretation is in constructing a "narrative truth," because the nature of memory precludes reconstructing "historical truth."

Memory or Desire: see BION

Mentalization, or **Reflective Function**, is the ability to understand the behavior of others in terms of mental states such as beliefs, desires, feelings, and memories; the ability to reflect upon one's own mental states; and the ability to understand that one's own states of mind may influence the behavior of others. The capacity to understand or describe one's own and others' behavior in terms of underlying mental states and intentions is an innately human ability that is intrinsic to emotional regulation and productive social relationships. Beginning at around four years of age, the child develops the awareness that feelings and thoughts are mediating variables that cause him and others to behave as they do, and that these feelings and thoughts are also affected by how they behave toward each other. In essence, a crucial developmental attainment is the child's realization that there is a mind, consisting of mental functions and contents, which both affects and is affected by experiences in the world, most commonly interpersonal interactions. Mentalization is considered a specific aspect of the broader capacity for intersubjectivity, which is the capacity to understand, feel, participate in, and share the subjective experience of another person.

Mentalization has achieved considerable importance within contemporary psychoanalysis, arising simultaneously from a number of separate schools of thought, including attachment theorists, developmental psychoanalysts, and classical theorists. It is viewed as a crucial developmental accomplishment of the four-to-six-year-old child, an indication of secure attachment and/or resolution of attachment disturbance, a central aspect of mental life, and an achievement of successful treatment. Capacities that are required for mentalization have been long recognized within psychoanalytic discourse. These include the attainment of a variety of ego functions, including the differentiation of self from other; observing ego, the mental function that mediates the capacity for self reflection; empathy, a mode of perceiving by vicariously experiencing the psychological state of another person; and mature object relations, which through processes of internalization enable the capacity for recognizing and responding to the needs and motivations of others. However, the recognition that the attainment of these multiple capacities represents a specific developmental achievement reflects a growing appreciation of the self as a motivational sphere of influence.

The term *mentalization* first appeared in 1883 in a medical journal where it was defined as "mental activity" (*Oxford English Dictionary,* 2009). By the 1960s and 1970s, mentalizing acquired the additional connotation of reflecting on one's own mind as in a mindful or meditative state. Fonagy and his colleagues (Fonagy and Target, 1996b; Target and Fonagy, 1996; Fonagy et al., 2002) were among the first to apply the term in a psychoanalytic context. The work of Fonagy and Target intersected with a body of developmental research known as children's emerging theory of mind (Premack and Woodruff, 1978), which began to document the development of mentalization capacities and a range of developmental achievements that require mentalization. The latter include the capacities to take the perspective of another, to distinguish fantasy from reality, and to participate in fantasy play (Leslie, 1987; Lillard, 1993; Fonagy and Target, 1996a). Mayes and Cohen (1996) were instrumental in elucidating the mutual enrichment of psychoanalytic theories of development and theory of mind developmental research, because while theory of mind has focused on the attainment of cognitive capacities, psychoanalytic developmental theory has focused on the attainment of internalized object relations and the capacity for fantasy and play (Mayes and Cohen, 1992). The term *mentalization* has become the more common term in the analytic literature.

Mayes and Cohen (1996) described the child's gradual attainment of three cognitive abilities required for mentalization (the same also needed for imaginary or symbolic play), which become fully evident by four to six years of age. These include 1) the ability to use an object or person for representational purposes; 2) the recognition that an object or person may be connected with different representations; 3) the recognition that a person is internally motivated by his own needs, perceptions, and beliefs. The demonstration of such capacities has emerged from multiple empirical studies that utilize some version of the false-belief situation, which tests the child's ability to recognize another person's perspective and understanding of a situation that differs from the child's own. Drawing upon clinical data from child analyses, Fonagy and Target (1996a) have similarly described the attainment of a reflective mode of mental function at the oedipal stage, based upon the integration of two modes of psychic reality experienced as separate by the young child—"psychic equivalent" and "pretend" modes. In the "psychic equivalent" mode, the child equates internal and external reality; in the pretend mode, the child is able to maintain thoughts and feelings that are separate from his reality experience.

These studies also demonstrate that the child's attainment of mentalization capacities does not occur in a vacuum. Mentalization abilities have been linked to attachment theory and other models that describe the child's early relationship with his significant objects. Children learn about the link between mental states and behaviors by the facilitating impact of having others reflect on and make that link for them. For example, in comforting a crying toddler by saying how much he must miss his grandmother, a parent makes a link between an observable behavior (crying) and an internal state

(loneliness). Similarly, the developmental progression of mentalization can be disrupted by emotional deprivation, strain or shock trauma, or internal conflict. Fonagy, Steele, et al. (1993) demonstrated that external stressors, particularly early attachment disruptions from abuse or neglect, could lead to the inadequate development of this mental process, or to conflict about its use. Securely attached individuals usually have had a primary caregiver with sophisticated mentalization abilities, and thus have more developed capacities to represent the states of their own and other people's minds. The profound inhibition, or even absence, of mentalization capacity in serious psychopathology is associated with far-ranging developmental disruptions, due to its importance for internal development and adaptation. A failure to develop mature mentalization leaves the child or adult patient with a world of inadequately formed representations, thereby undermining self-object differentiation, separation-individuation, reality testing, secondary process thinking, affect regulation, empathy, and deeper understanding of social interaction.

Some psychoanalysts view the fostering of mature mentalization processes as an important aim of child and adult psychoanalytic treatment and a source of therapeutic action. In the context of child treatment, mentalization is sometimes referred to as insightfulness (Sugarman, 2003, 2006), to differentiate it from the developmental process occurring in the rest of the child's world. Other psychoanalysts view treatment aimed primarily at promoting mentalization as distinct from psychoanalysis proper, which they define as a therapy aimed at helping the patient reclaim repudiated mental contents (Bleiberg, 2003; Bateman and Fonagy, 2004, 2006). Still others (Lecours and Bouchard, 1997; Sugarman, 2003, 2006) believe this to be a false distinction and argue that all patients present with difficulties in the capacity to fully and successfully utilize crucial and stable mental functions to self regulate, and require the remobilizing and reintegrating of these functions so that they work optimally and harmoniously. These analysts believe this is best accomplished by helping patients consciously experience and expound on all their inner workings with a minimum of restriction. As applied to child analysis, this position suggests less focus on making patients aware of the complex "whys" of their difficulties, and instead more focus on making them aware that they have an inner world, that it arises out of important experiences with and fantasies about the environment, and that it contributes to their emotions, self esteem, symptoms, and behavior. With children, mentalization capacity can be promoted through play or the relationship with the analyst, as much as by verbal interpretation. From this perspective, therapeutic work with adult analysands who need help in gaining mentalization capacity importantly occurs through transference-countertransference enactments and the analyst's willingness to reflect on his own participation, as well as through the use of verbal interpretations. Hence, redefining the aim of psychoanalysis as promoting mentalization (or insightfulness), as well as realizing its central contribution to therapeutic action, may broaden the tools in the analyst's technical armamentarium to include ways of working that are usually seen as outside the purely analytic. Some psychoanalysts argue that mentalization is a concept that can serve to synthesize the multiple models populating today's pluralistic psychoanalytic landscape.

Fonagy and colleagues (George, Kaplan, and Main, 1985; Fonagy et al., 1996) developed a method for evaluating reflective function (RF) from M. Main's Adult Attachment Interview (AAI). Recently, this method of evaluation has been computerized (Fertuck et al., 2004) and used to study changes in reflective function in psychoanalytic psychotherapy, especially in borderline patients treated with Transference Focused Psychotherapy (Levy et al, 2006). Bouchard et al. (2008) examined the relationship among mentalization capacity, attachment status (using the AAI), and the severity of Axis I and Axis II pathology. They measured mentalization capacity on three axes: reflective function, mental states, and verbal elaboration of affect; their studies have shown that only reflective function correlates with attachment status.

Merger/Remerger: see DEPRESSION, EGO IDEAL, EMPATHY, IDEALIZATION, IDENTIFICATION, OBJECT, OBJECT RELATIONS THEORY, OMNIPOTENCE, SELF PSYCHOLOGY, SELFOBJECT, TRANSFERENCE

Metapsychology, a word coined by Freud, is a conceptual structure for psychoanalytic theories of how the mind works at the level of generalizable principles and concepts. The broadest possible view of metapsychology might define it as equivalent to psychoanalytic theory in its entirety. The narrowest view equates it with Freud's (1915g) theory of mind as presented in his "Papers on Metapsychology." Most often, metapsychology is defined as the highest level of abstraction in a hierarchy of psychoanalytic conceptualization, described in ascending order: clinical observation and data, clinical interpretation, clinical generalization or theory, and metapsychology (Waelder, 1962). A traditional view defines metapsychology as encompassing

six broad frames of reference or viewpoints from which to conceptualize observations about the mind: topographic, dynamic, economic, structural, adaptive, and genetic. While many psychoanalysts regard metapsychology as an essential element in psychoanalytic understanding of the human experience, metapsychology has been the subject of considerable controversy for many often-contradictory reasons. These arguments have mostly focused on whether or not psychoanalytic theory requires a level of abstraction that goes beyond clinical observation to include broad principles borrowed from the rest of the natural sciences.

Freud (1898a) first used the term *metapsychology* in a letter to Fliess. In an era when psychology addressed only conscious phenomena, psychoanalysis was revolutionary in being a psychology of the unconscious, going literally "beyond psychology," hence "metapsychology." In Freud's (1901) first published use of the term, he described mythological or religious accounts of the world as the projections of psychology into the external world, which might then be translated back into the psychology of the unconscious. In Freud's (1915g) "Papers on Metapsychology," only five of which survive, he published his view of the basic foundations of psychoanalytic theory. In these papers, Freud expanded his definition of metapsychology beyond the topographic point of view to include the dynamic and economic points of view, as he now considered all three necessary for a complete description of mental processes.

As Freud had predicted, the development of psychoanalytic theory required further expansions of what constituted a complete metapsychological description. Rapaport and Gill's (1959) influential paper, regarded as an authoritative standard by many psychoanalysts, presented the then-current status of metapsychology, reflecting half a century of development in psychoanalytic theory. They increased Freud's three required aspects to five, which they referred to as "points of view." In their schema, the topographic was replaced with the structural, and they added the genetic and the adaptive. However, many analysts continue to utilize both the topographic and structural points of view.

The topographic viewpoint describes mental contents in terms of their relationship to consciousness, an enduring aspect of all psychoanalytic theory. Freud also used the terms *conscious, preconscious,* and *unconscious* as nouns, designating three regions of the mind, neither anatomical nor spatial, but metaphorically arranged on a vertical axis from surface to depth. Freud replaced his topographic model of the mind with a structural one but never discarded the former.

The dynamic viewpoint postulates that all psychic phenomena involve the continuous interplay of multiple psychological forces (or motivations) defined by their function and meaning. These forces provide the basis for concepts of intrapsychic conflict, compromise formation, and unconscious fantasy.

The economic viewpoint postulates that mental events and structures are "fueled" by psychic energy, used to account for the relative intensities and peremptory force of wishes, feelings, and ideas, as well as for the power of defensive operations. Freud also used the concept of energy to account for the fundamental observation that this intensity can be separated from the idea with which it is associated, displaced (or transferred) from one idea to another, or transformed (converted) into symptoms. The term *cathexis* is used to describe the investment of drive energy in mental products, structures, activities, and objects. While the economic viewpoint is the most controversial of the metapsychological viewpoints, it remains essential to any description of the quality of intensity of mental experience and the understanding of psychic change. Energic concepts are also implicit in the dynamic and topographic viewpoints.

The structural viewpoint postulates that recurring and enduring psychic phenomena achieve more or less stable and organized representation in the mind as structures. Freud's tripartite model viewed the mind as divided into three structures—the id, ego, and superego, defined by their functions rather than their relation to consciousness. In this model, an executive ego must balance the demands of id drive derivatives against both reality concerns, and the moral and ethical pressures from the superego. The operation of forces and energy is also implicit in the structural viewpoint, embedded in concepts such as inter- and intrasystemic conflict.

After Freud, with the emergence of ego psychology, additional substructures were described within the ego and superego, such as the psychic representations of the self and object, the wishful self image, and the ego ideal (Hartmann, 1964; Jacobson, 1964). Kohut (1971), who postulated the self as a superordinate structure in the mind, attempted initially to work within a classical framework, but eventually, his theoretical formulations departed entirely from the assumptions of traditional metapsychology.

The genetic viewpoint examines psychological phenomena with a focus on finding the historical precursors or origins of its form, motivation, and meaning. It further posits that earlier psychic forms, though superseded by later ones, remain active and may become prominent through regression. The genetic point of view, explored from the perspective of psychic reality and closely related to the therapeutic process of genetic reconstruction, should be distinguished from a developmental point of view, which examines developmental processes as they proceed from the perspective of external observation and reality.

The adaptive viewpoint focuses on the relationship of any psychic phenomenon to their environment, including the physical and human aspects of the external world that exist at every stage of life. There is a mutual aspect to adaptive relationships. Not only does the external world have a significant impact on the developing child, in the process affecting the child's pattern of adaptation, but the child, through its various phases of development, plays a significant role in the parents' psychology and may affect their patterns of adaptation.

Interest in metapsychology was greatest during the rapid growth of ego psychology. The specific goal of early ego psychologists such as Hartmann, Kris, and Lowenstein was the systematization of metapsychology as a general psychology. They shared a view of psychoanalysis as an empirical science and metapsychology as the basic science of it. As such, they regarded metapsychology as the most general laws of mental life on the most abstract level, consistent with scientific thinking, in general, which tends toward objectivity and depersonalization. At the same time they understood that the use of these laws requires a more personal clinical method. However, with the emergence of other theoretical views, metapsychology receded in its central importance. Object relations theorists and self psychologists (Klein, Fairbairn, Winnicott, Balint, and others) developed substantially different assumptions and propositions that are not easily mapped onto the five (or six) conventional viewpoints of metapsychology, nor did they particularly concern themselves with these viewpoints within their formulations.

Controversies about both the proper definition and the value of metapsychology have gained momentum within the pluralistic landscape of contemporary psychoanalytic theory. Some anti-metapsychology voices assert that any theory that is excessively abstract and/or mechanistic is too removed from clinical experience and runs the risk of inviting analyst and patient to describe the patient's choices in terms of structures and forces rather than personal agency (Schafer, 1976). A strong version of this critique maintains that the fundamental premise of metapsychology is wrong, as it is inextricably rooted in Freud's misguided and never-abandoned attempt to link psychoanalysis to the natural sciences, specifically neurophysiology (Gill, 1976). Such critics tend to equate metapsychology with

Freud's economic theory, viewing it as a pseudoscientific enterprise since its formulations are not verifiable by data derived from the clinical situation. In contrast, clinical theory, while often abstract and theoretical, is closer to and may be extrapolated from clinical observation (G. Klein, 1976).

Some analysts who argue against psychoanalysis as a natural science describe it instead as a hermeneutic discipline, one whose method is the interpretation of meaning and whose clinical situation is its text. A hermeneutic view includes such perspectives as psychoanalytic explanation as narrative, the questioning of historical truth, and the relativity of views of reality (Spence, 1982). Some hermeneuticists argue that psychoanalysis can be scientific, and they further reason that man's biological nature is not ignored but rather understood from the standpoint of its psychological meaning (Gill, 1988). Metapsychology also has little currency within relational, interpersonal, and some intersubjective psychoanalytic theories where greatest emphasis is placed upon the analytic dyad and the co-constructed interpersonal field.

Modern ego psychologists and some contemporary conflict and object relations theorists remain committed to metapsychology as a potent tool in informing and conceptualizing clinical interventions. They argue that since theoretical formulations based on abstract assumptions inevitably underlie all clinical therapeutic endeavors, there is enormous value in clearly explicating those assumptions. Others argue that psychoanalysis should include the goal of constructing the best abstract theory of mind precisely because it allows the field to maintain contact with the rest of contemporary mind science (Shevrin, 2003). Such theorists draw upon information, learning, and systems theories; models from cognitive science emphasizing the mind's capacities for information processing, representation, and symbol formation; models from evolutionary psychology emphasizing adaptation; and neuronally inspired models (such as connectionism) which emphasize parallel processing.

Midlife Crisis is a revolutionary turning point in an individual's life, occurring in middle age, involving sudden and dramatic changes in commitments to career and/or spouse and family and accompanied by ongoing emotional turmoil for both the individual and others. The powerful unconscious conflicts that precipitate such behaviors are centered on the difficulty in facing growing awareness of the inevitability of limited time and personal death, and the refusal to engage the narcissistically injurious reality that not all of one's goals, ambitions, and dreams

will be realized in this lifetime. The result is a frenzied attempt to throw away the present and the past to magically begin life anew. Although relatively rare, true midlife crises are real phenomena that are often encountered in clinical practice; they present technical challenges in part because of the pressure toward action. As a period of great turmoil, a midlife crisis may also provide the potential and the impetus for tremendous positive growth and change, often not possible during more static periods of life. The term **midlife transition** (D. Levinson et al., 1978) has great clinical utility because aspects of the phenomenon are seen in every midlife patient. Quasi-universal in extent, the examination of one's life may be quite conscious and apparent or more subliminal and unconscious. Because the term *midlife crisis* has become part of popular culture, the psychoanalytic origin and understanding of the phenomenon have been minimized.

Elliott Jacques (1965) coined the term *midlife crisis*, however Freud (1915f), during his own midlife, laid the foundation for psychoanalytic thought on the subject in discussing the transient nature of human existence and the inevitability of death. Freud (1919d) also eloquently described both the universal reaction to the anticipation of one's death and the universal fear of the dead. Other writers have focused on the issue of time sense. Kernberg (1980) described change in the perspective of time, and Colarusso and Nemiroff (1981) defined the midlife developmental task as the acceptance of time limitation and personal death.

Mirror Stage: see LACAN

Mirroring: see SELF PSYCHOLOGY

Moments of Meeting: see INTERSUBJECTIVITY, THERAPEUTIC ACTION

Mood, a term borrowed by psychoanalysis from general psychology, is a type of affective experience in which one predominant affect, such as sadness or joy, spreads to include the entire self state and endures for a period of time. A mood is a complex state of mind consisting of the following: a predominant coloring of emotional tone (the affective component), a narrowing of mental content consistent with the emotional tone (the cognitive component), and a tendency to particular actions (the behavioral component). For example, in a depressed mood, someone may feel sad and guilty, believe that he is worthless, and withdraw socially. In an elated mood, someone may feel overjoyed, believe that he is smarter than others, and behave in an extroverted or impulsive manner. Mood must be distinguished from affect, which is a relatively short-lived psycho-physiologic state. Moods are also distinct from persistent affect states, such as love or hate, in which feelings are directed toward specific objects in stable, ongoing ways. Mood should be distinguished from the larger concept of character, although mood may become embedded in character structure (as in depressive or anxious characters). Moods that are unduly pervasive, unresponsive to reality testing, and/or disruptive to adaptive functioning may be considered pathological, as in **mood disorders** (or **affective disorders**).

Mood is important in psychoanalysis as a major, organizing component of many self experiences. Moods alter self and object representations with corresponding emotional tones, often to the extent of creating a sweeping and uniform worldview. They are characterized by a selective focus on ideas, memories, attitudes, beliefs, assessments, and expectations that are consistent with the emotional tone of the mood, and an exclusion of dissonant mental content. Moods have a self-perpetuating aspect, both through this process of selective attention and through mood-concordant behaviors, which may lead others to confirm the validity of the mood. Moods arise in response to internal or external, conscious or unconscious, psychophysiological events; they represent a response to the current meaning of the event, as well as to associated conscious and unconscious memories and fantasies. Moods arise when the evocative experience is of such high intensity that the response cannot be contained as a focal affect. Moods originate in inborn dispositions; however, developmental factors, including both temperament and experiential variables, may predispose individuals to certain moods. Like all mental states, moods serve a compromise function, simultaneously defending against and allowing for expression of various feelings and fantasies. Moods also serve an interpersonal, or communicative, function. As with affect, in the psychoanalytic situation, the analyst pays close attention to mood states as indicators of the underlying state of the self. The psychoanalytic literature includes discussion of the general concept of mood, as well as some specific moods, such as depression (Jacobson, 1971) and elation (B. Lewin, 1950), to mention two that have received most attention.

Freud (1917c) wrote little about moods, except in his landmark paper "Mourning and Melancholia," in which he distinguished between the normal mood state of mourning and the pathological mood state of melancholia. In his description of mourning, Freud described the economic function of mood as the repetitive discharge of affect that, over time, liberated psychic energy from fixated positions, allowing for new emotional investments.

Post-Freudian ego psychologists, most notably Jacobson (1957, 1961, 1971), described mood from a structural point of view, as the ego's attempt to integrate and control affective responses that threaten to overwhelm it. Jacobson stressed the usefulness of moods in economic terms, as allowing for the prolonged discharge of affect in small, modulated quantities, thereby contributing to self regulation. In her view, an experience causes a change in mood only if it leads to changes in the representations of the self and object world. Jacobson also discussed mood from a developmental point of view, arguing that, over time, individuals develop the capacity to experience and derive pleasure from more nuanced or complex moods, often characterized by higher tension states. In her view, vulnerability to pathological moods results from both constitutional predispositions and early experiences of excessive gratification, deprivation, or trauma that become structuralized in the form of ego and superego weakness. Many analysts have noted that depressive mood in adults is strongly associated with loss and/or deprivation in childhood (Mahler, 1966). Others, such as Greenacre and Mahler, focused on how specific developmental phases might be associated with characteristic moods, creating "fixation points" around which later states of mind are organized. For example, elation is associated with the young child's "love affair with the world" (as described by Greenacre [1957]), or with the practicing subphase of separation-individuation (as described by Mahler [1967]). On the other hand, depression is associated with the rapprochement subphase of separation-individuation (again, as described by Mahler). Finally, pathological mood states, such as depression, have been described as occurring as early as infancy (Spitz, 1945; Spitz and Wolf, 1946a). More recently, infant researchers have explored how the mother and infant mutually create the infant's mood (Tronick, 2001).

M(Other): see LACAN

Motivation is the impetus for mental and physical activity that is represented in the mind in the form of needs, fears, wishes, purposes, and intentions. The concept of motivation is not specific to psycho-analysis, and has currency within common discourse, as well as within the disciplines of biology, philosophy, psychology, and the social sciences. In psycho-analysis, however, motivation is understood to have a significant unconscious component, and any aspect of mental life is assumed to have multiply determined, possibly conflicting, sources of motivation. Psychoanalysts also recognize the concept of agency, an individual's capacity to effect causal action on the basis of needs, desires, or other motivations, the individual's conscious recognition and experience of this capacity, and the individual's responsibility for the results of his actions. Many key technical aspects of psychoanalytic theory, such as free association, transference, and resistance, implicitly reflect an underlying unconscious motivational model. While variously conceptualized by different theorists, these technical terms reflect a central, motivated human tendency to maintain a previously established psychic equilibrium and to repeat familiar patterns of relatedness, even though these states and relationships may also be the source of considerable pain and distress.

Psychoanalysis is at its core a theory of motivation, beginning with Freud's revolutionary theory that hysteria originates not from pathogenic brain states but from motivated processes of defense. Motivation is of critical importance both as an overarching concept—delineating what motivates human behavior—and in a more specific sense, identifying what motivates an individual under certain conditions at a certain time. To trace theories of motivation within psychoanalysis is to trace the history of psychoanalysis itself, from Freud's view of sexual and aggressive drives as the prime motivating forces, to the inclusion of motivations stemming from the ego and from affects, and then shifting to include or to be replaced by attachment needs, object relational needs, and self strivings. Contemporary psychoanalytic theories of motivation attempt to account for biological imperatives that are present at birth, their representations and transformations through contact with the relational environment, and their increasing complexity through maturation and development. Rather than restricting motivation to two sources, as in Freud's drive theory, contemporary theories tend to account for the presence of multiple sources of motivation that capture the full range of human strivings. Although controversy about the sources of motivation distinguishes psychoanalytic theories from one another, within the clinical situation, most analysts focus on what motivates patients in their moment-to-moment interactions with the analyst, as well as within their life experience, past and present.

While Freud did not use the term *motivation*, his evolving drive theory was a motivational systems model. As part of his attempt to connect his new psychological science to biological, evolutionary roots, Freud (1895b) originally posited endogenous biological forces as the prime motivational elements in mental life. Freud (1905b) formally introduced the term *drive* in 1905, as a concept at the interface of mind and body, that is, the mental representation of an endogenous force that stimulates mental activity and therefore all psychological experience. Drives are represented in the mind by both an idea (essentially, a wish), and a "quota of affect," a registration of pleasure or unpleasure reflecting the underlying oscillations in energic tension (Freud, 1915b). In Freud's view, the "goal" of the mental apparatus is to attain pleasure through reduction in drive stimulus, in accordance with the economic regulatory process that he called the "pleasure principle." In Freud's early model, affects are "perceptions" of the underlying state of drive tension, and thus play an important subsidiary role in motivating behavior. Eventually, Freud (1926a) accorded anxiety a special role as the unpleasurable affect that the ego uses as a signal to mobilize defense in situations of danger.

Freud's (1905b) description of infantile sexuality radically expanded the role of sexuality as a motive force, often in disguised or derivative form, manifest in symptoms, behavior, character, and fantasy. As Freud's drive theory evolved, he identified different classes of drives as the central motivating forces in mental life. In a model compatible with evolutionary thinking, Freud (1910e) delineated between the sexual instincts, which functioned to insure the continuation of the species, and the ego or self-preservative instincts, which functioned to safeguard the survival of the individual (and defend against the sexual instincts when necessary). With his later work on narcissism, Freud (1914e) distinguished between object-directed and ego-directed, or narcissistic, libidinal drives. In this way, Freud introduced motivations connected to the relationship with objects and motivations derived from the needs of the self. Freud (1915b) also described the transformations that drives can undergo to satisfy different aims, such as desexualized or sublimated ones that include socially accepted or valued goals, in particular creative or intellectual activities. In effect, the "fuel" of the drives, according to Freud's theory, serves the multiple needs, wishes, and aspirations of the individual throughout development. Later, under the rubric of the death drive, Freud (1920a) placed aggression on a par with the sexual drive as central motivating forces within mental life. Allied with Freud's notion of the death drive was his observation that individuals are compelled to repeat their past experience, even when it is painful. Freud viewed the motivation to repeat as a characteristic of the drives and of mental life in general. In Freud's view, repetition serves as a way of remembering; but he viewed the repetition compulsion as a more primitive form of repetition that operates beyond the pleasure principle. In 1923, with the introduction of the structural model, the dual drives libido and aggression are located within their own structure, the id (1923a). While the drives press for satisfaction, the ego channels and modulates their motivational impetus or force through the processes of neutralization and fusion. The ego's defensive, synthetic, and integrative function enables the formation of compromise formations that facilitate the simultaneous satisfaction of drive derivatives and a vast array of ego and superego aims. Aggressive drive energy serves a special function in fueling the critical and punitive function of the superego, while libido serves its other functions; both drives thereby provide the energy for morality.

One nearly universal objection to Freud's drive theory was his view that the aggressive drive is a reflection of a death drive, an innate biological urge in all living creatures to return to an inorganic state. This thesis was hard to reconcile with basic evolutionary principles, and with the exception of Klein and some of her followers, most theorists have rejected it. A more adaptive view of aggression was adopted by many analysts, in which its function was expanded beyond destructive forces to include initiative, mastery, and the response to obstacles, frustration, injury to the self, and even trauma. However, there remains considerable controversy as to what motivational status to accord to aggression, and whether its hostile, destructive forms or its assertive, adaptive forms, or both, are to be viewed as primary (Hartmann, Kris, and Loewenstein, 1949; Fairbairn, 1954; Kohut, 1977; Parens, 1979; Kernberg, 1982).

Ego psychologists built upon Freud's motivational theory by adding to or emphasizing other dimensions of dual drive theory. While an adaptive perspective was implicit in Freud's metapsychology, Hartmann (1939a) explicitly developed the model of an adaptively motivated ego operating with its own primary autonomous functions and conflict-free sphere and powered by neutralized energy from the drives. (Many analysts rejected Freudian drive theory because it required complex convolutions of energy theory to provide neutralized drive energy for the ego.) While Hartmann's theory was steeped in Freudian dual drive theory, he focused on the ego's motivated function in its relationship to reality. In his delineation of the principle of multiple function, Waelder (1936) implicitly accounted for the competing motivational contributions of the id, ego, and

superego to compromise formations forged by the ego to maximize the satisfaction of their competing motives. Waelder's inclusion of reality as another "problem" that the ego must engage also implicitly included an adaptational motive to the ego's efforts at compromise. Others have also emphasized the ego's developmental and adaptive push toward mastery and the exercise of its capacities, suggesting that the mind operates not only in a manner to reduce tension but also to seek out stimulation (Hendrick, 1943a; White, 1963). A clear advocate of this perspective was Schafer (1968b), who (ultimately dispensing with energy concepts entirely) focused on the motivating function of wishes that express the strivings of each agency and all constituents of mental activity. Conflict theorists, such as C. Brenner (1982), argued that drives are to be understood as abstract generalizations about human motivation, based on the observation of many individuals' unique and specific wishes directed at particular objects over the course of their development.

Other analysts sought to integrate drive theory with object relational motivations. For example, Loewald (1971) saw drives as coming into being within the tensions and interactions of the mother-child matrix, and thus drive and object relationship together comprise an inseparable motivational unit. The Kleinian model maintains the centrality of drives but views them as inseparable from internal objects from their inception. Fairbairn (1954) proposed that the ego, functioning with libido, is fundamentally object-seeking, rather than pleasure-seeking. He viewed aggression, not as a basic motivation, but as a reaction to frustration, and thus originating in the context of an object relationship. Kernberg (1982) combined dual drive theory with an object relational model but viewed affects as the primary motivational system. In his theory, pleasurable and unpleasurable affect states are the primary motivational elements that are linked to self and object representations, then gradually organized into libidinal and aggressive drives, which are developmentally later, superordinate motivating forces.

Attachment theorists, starting with Bowlby (1969/1982) viewed the infant as object-seeking and identified attachment as the primary motivator of human experience, diminishing or eliminating the role of drives entirely. Interpersonal and relational psychoanalysts similarly view attachment, intersubjectivity, and the establishment of social relations as primary motivators (D. N. Stern, 2005). Sullivan (1953a) referred to two kinds of motivations called dynamisms—the lust dynamism and the self dynamism. For self psychologists, this role is occupied by narcissistic aims and/or selfobject needs, which allow for the establishment of adequate self cohesion, vitality, and self esteem. Kohut (1971) posited a separate line of development for narcissistic aims.

Historically, various psychoanalytic schools of thought have privileged one motivational source over others; however, many contemporary theorists have broadened the concept of motivation to include multiple sources. For example, Pine (2005a) did not reject the notion of the drives as a "core motivational theory" but added motivational spheres of influence that include human relations, ego function, and self. He emphasized that all motivational sources, including the drives, become connected with highly specific personalized meanings. Westen (1997), in an effort to present a clinically relevant motivational theory that is consistent with experimental data and current neuropsychological hypotheses, argued that affects, not drives, serve as the instigator for a complex hierarchically organized set of conscious and unconscious motivations. Westen's theory retains many pieces of classical theory but reassembles them in a different way. In Westen's model, affects are rooted in the body and are elicited by drive states, learned associations between mental representations and feelings, and environmental features such as object relations and culture. Affects serve as adaptive behavioral regulators by providing emotional feedback that activates responses to maximize pleasure. Compromise formations result from the effort at satisfying multiple motives.

Child researchers have documented the presence of more highly sophisticated perceptual and discriminatory capacities than previously appreciated, both in newborns and preschool-aged children. Consistent with such findings is Emde's (1988) description of a hierarchy of motivational structures that are built upon basic intrinsic motives, present from birth: activity, self regulation, social fittedness, and affective monitoring. In concert, and requiring facilitation by the emotional availability of the caregiver, these four basic motives establish more complex motivational structures, including the self system and early relationship motives, which together establish a "we" psychology. D. N. Stern (1985) described the development of similar capacities as the intersubjective self and the capacity for "self with other."

Mourning or **Grief** is a painful intrapsychic process that occurs in response to the loss of an important object relationship or any other emotionally significant loss, such as a job, a possession, an ideal, or one's health or youth. The work of mourning, in the case of a lost love object, is the gradual adaptation to a changed reality. The mourner must slowly accept the reality of loss, relinquish the object tie as it has been known, and accept a transformed internalized object relationship that remains deeply connected to loving memories. Loss is an inevitable part of life, and the capacity to mourn in the face of loss reflects the healthy depth of human attachments. **Uncomplicated grief** or **uncomplicated mourning** following object loss may include somatic distress, preoccupying thoughts about the lost object, diminished capacity to make new emotional investments, loss of interest in the usual activities of life, guilt, hostility, and identifications with the lost object. The mourning process is inevitably shaped by the psychological capacities of the bereaved, including the ability to tolerate painful affect, the nature and function of the object relationship that has been lost, the capacity to derive support and comfort from other object relationships, and in some cases, the resilience of one's self esteem. Also relevant is the condition under which the loss has occurred, such as whether it is sudden or whether some emotional preparation has been possible. In childhood, the outcome of mourning depends upon age, cognitive and emotional developmental capacities, and particularly if it is a parent that has been lost, whether a suitable replacements object is available. In the clinical situation, the work of termination is often conceptualized as a mourning process. **Pathological mourning** may take many forms but is usually characterized by a prolonged depressive state that fails to resolve, which may feature intense feelings of anger and guilt.

Freud's (1917c) most comprehensive discussion of mourning occurs in his landmark paper, "Mourning and Melancholia," however he made reference to the clinical manifestations of pathological object loss in earlier works (Breuer and Freud, 1893/1895; Freud, 1909d). Freud juxtaposed mourning and melancholia as two distinct clinical states that are precipitated by identical conditions, but while mourning is not a pathological response, depression is. The phenomenological difference, in Freud's view, is that in melancholia there is a painful loss of self regard, while in mourning there is not. Freud described the work of mourning during which reality must be acknowledged; the object tie must be relinquished, and it requires time and great emotional effort. The melancholic is unable to give up the object because of the ambivalent nature of the object tie, resulting in the regressive formation of a narcissistic identification with the lost object, upon which aggression is released, thereby explaining self attack and the loss of self regard. Although the identification formed during the pathological state of melancholia does not persist after the episode has resolved, Freud's (1923a) notion that an object tie may be replaced by identification became a central thesis in his view of normal ego and superego structure building. In Freud's (1926a) later elaboration of his second theory of anxiety, object loss is identified as the first of a developmental sequence of danger situations. While anxiety is the response to threatened object loss, pain is the response to actual loss of the object.

Jacobson (1971), using distinctions similar to those of Freud, distinguished between grief (and the broader category of sadness), as the response to the experience or fantasy of loss, uncomplicated by aggression toward the self; depression, also triggered by object loss, is characterized by aggression directed toward the self and/or the lost object. The latter is a more likely outcome when underlying narcissistic conflicts are prominent.

In contrast to Freud, loss of a love object, in Klein's (1940) view, always evokes a conflict of ambivalence, and the pain of mourning is associated with that conflict. She described the reactivation of frightening, painful, and guilty unconscious "phantasies" associated with the depressive position that the good internal object will also be destroyed when the external object is lost. The mourner, like the child, utilizes manic defenses to cope with the painful "pining" for the lost love object by establishing an idealized internal object. Such processes alternate with aggressive attacks against the hated love object, which further threaten destruction of good internal objects. The successful work of mourning involves the slow and painful testing of reality, the rebuilding of the inner world, and the reconnection with the external world. Pathological states of mourning may be evident when manic states become prolonged or when regressive paranoid processes are evoked.

Bowlby (1961), the originator of attachment theory, advanced the thesis that even in very early childhood, object loss evokes a mourning process comprised of basic psychological processes that may be observed in adult pathological mourning, and that early object loss often predisposes to later psychopathology. Bowlby was influenced by the work of Spitz (1945) and Spitz and Wolf (1946a), who described catastrophic reactions to maternal loss in the first year of life, but he challenged a commonly held view that young children do not mourn. Bowlby described three phases of mourning that follow from his thesis that attachment is mediated by an inborn instinctual system that is equal in motivational status to that of feeding and sex. When separated from a love object the response is 1) disappointment, separation anxiety, grief, protest, and angry efforts to recover the lost object; 2) cessation of focus on the lost object and the effort to recover it, which is replaced by disorganization of the personality, pain, and despair; 3) completion of mourning via reorganization of the image of the lost object and the connection to a new object or objects. Bowlby, unlike Freud, viewed anger at the lost object as a universal response to loss; unlike Klein, he did not view guilt and fears of retaliation as components of normal mourning. Bowlby concurred with Lindemann (1944) who distinguished between normal and pathological mourning by describing the latter as an exaggerated version of the former, rather than as two fundamentally different structures. Pathological mourning in Bowlby's view is most often a failure to progress beyond the first stage. Bowlby also concurred with Lindeman and Klein, as well as with Engel (1961), that while mourning may be "uncomplicated," the enormous disruption, suffering, and disorganization involved constitutes a state of illness. Finally, Bowlby, like Pollock (1961), emphasized that the capacity to mourn is an adaptive response based in biological function, as it is a response to a real external event that has similar characteristics to that of birds and lower mammals who experience object loss.

Kernberg (2010) proposed that the work of normal mourning stimulates healthy reparative impulses, strengthens the internal object relationship to the lost object, facilitates the further development of the superego and ego ideal, and deepens the capacity for love. The love object may not be fully appreciated until it is gone, when the mourner may experience guilt over lost opportunities, not because of aggression toward the lost object. In Kernberg's view, the memory of the lost love object remains intensely present forever, evidenced by sadness and tearfulness when thoughts of the lost object are evoked.

Multiple Code Theory: see PRIMARY PROCESS, SYMBOLISM/SYMBOLIZATION/REPRESENTATION/ SYMBOLIC REPRESENTATION

Multiple Determination, or **Overdetermination**, often used interchangeably, are theoretical constructs that emphasize that multiple psychological explanations and motivations account for any given manifestation of mental life. Thus a dream, symptom, or piece of behavior will derive its outward shape from more than a single wish or conflict, and analysis will reveal that a particular thought or dream is determined both by the intent consciously perceived and by multiple unconscious factors, including drive derivatives, the defensive operation of the ego, and complex transference feelings. Ultimately, the analyst must choose among several avenues or levels of interpretation when approaching any particular piece of a patient's productions, depending upon the immediate clinical situation. Multiple determination builds upon the fundamental principle of psychic determinism, which asserts that all mental events are caused by antecedent mental events and follow the laws of cause and effect.

Freud first wrote of overdetermination in relation to hysterical symptoms (Breuer and Freud, 1893/1895a). These, he argued, achieve their manifest form as a result of the coming together of numerous chains of thought and memory radiating out from the repressed contents of the unconscious. These chains, having been subjected to various degrees and strategies of resistance, will ultimately converge in a "nucleus" leading to the creation of one "overdetermined" symptom. In fact, a patient's entire neurosis can be viewed as overdetermined because its etiology is inevitably related to multiple factors. Freud (1900) continued to invoke the concept of overdetermination in later work on dreams, symptoms, and slips of the tongue. In "The Interpretation of Dreams," he illustrated how the manifest content of a dream is determined by a variety of unconscious themes that are both reflected in and disguised by the processes of condensation and displacement. The condensation of the dream-work insures overdetermination, as elements that find their way into a dream must possess contacts with a great number of the dream-thoughts, constituting overdetermined "nodal points."

With the advent of the structural theory and the development of ego psychology, Waelder (1936) offered the principle of multiple function as an alternative to overdetermination, a concept he viewed as flawed. Waelder, like Freud, emphasized that all mental experience must be understood from multiple perspectives, and that every psychic act must "be understood as the expression of the collective function of the total organism." He described every psychic act in terms of the ego's attempt at a compromise solution to eight groups of problems: four presented to it by id, superego, reality, and the compulsion to repeat, and four that the ego actively assigns to itself in relationship to these same forces. Each psychic act can then be understood as representing both multiple functions and multiple meanings. Waelder argued that the concept of overdetermination does not follow the laws of natural science, which require that an occurrence be determined by necessary and adequate causes. He illustrated that in mathematics, a triangle is determined by exactly three components, and cannot be determined by four. He further argued that the principle of multiple function provides a bounded limit to the determinants of any psychic act. For these reasons, it may be preferable to use the term multidetermination rather than overdetermination.

Waelder's objections notwithstanding, the issue of how and when to interpret the various possible meanings of a patient's productions has remained central to psychoanalytic discourse and may be influenced by the analyst's theoretical orientation as well as other individual factors. On the one hand, multiplicity of interpretation should not be confused with wild interpretation (Schafer, 1985), while a too-narrow theoretical focus can limit the perception and interpretation of multiple meanings. Lacan has connected the endless referentiality of linguistic meaning to the structure of the unconscious, suggesting that unconscious elements are inevitably multiply determined (Lacan, 1956a).

N

Narcissism, a term lacking conceptual clarity, includes a vast array of ideas whose common thread or focus is the relationship with the self. Narcissism is often wielded in common parlance as a pejorative label for traits such as self preoccupation, pride, perfectionism, vanity, grandiosity, entitlement, and exploitation of others. In contemporary psychoanalysis, narcissism most frequently refers to: 1) the overall well-being of the self, including feelings of aliveness, initiative, authenticity, coherence, and self esteem; 2) self esteem, in both its normal and pathological forms; 3) **narcissistic pathology**, in the form of **narcissistic character** or **narcissistic personality disorder**, which exists on a continuum of severity from higher-level neurotic disorders to more-pervasive character pathology; narcissistic personality disorder includes defensive self inflation; lack of integration of the self concept; inordinate dependence upon acclaim by others; poor object relations; vulnerability to feelings of humiliation, shame, rage, and depression; entitlement; relentless pursuit of self perfection; and impaired capacities for concern, empathy, and love for others; 4) **narcissistic defenses**, including self aggrandizement or omnipotence, idealization, and devaluation, used to regulate self esteem; 5) **pathological narcissism**, a term describing narcissistic pathology from a specific perspective closely associated with the object relations school of the British Kleinians; 6) the clinical and theoretical emphasis of self psychology that views narcissism as a normal line of healthy development, subject to developmental arrests.

Much of the conceptual confusion surrounding the term *narcissism* results from its use as both a metapsychological concept and a description of experience, as well as from the persistent use of earlier definitions at differing levels of abstraction alongside more contemporary ones. Freud himself contributed to this confusion by using *narcissism* in a wide variety of ways also at varying levels of abstraction, including: 1) a sexual perversion (the prepsychoanalytic meaning); 2) the self as a libidinal object; 3) an early developmental stage that precedes object ties; 4) primitive, omnipotent, and magical aspects of thinking and feeling; 5) a type of object relationship; 6) a mode of relating to the environment characterized by an apparent withdrawal of libidinal

investment from objects (as in his concept of the **narcissistic neuroses**); and 7) self esteem.

The concepts associated with the term *narcissism* remain central to any psychoanalytic formulation of the self and its relationship to the object world. As such, narcissism is a universal feature of all mental life. Delineating the complex relationship between the experiences of the self, self-esteem regulation, and object relations has been a critical focus of psychoanalytic theorizing since Freud. Freud's efforts to untangle the concept of narcissism initiated major advances in his theory-making, contributing to the development of ego psychology and to object relations theories. Struggles with narcissistic disorders also provided the impetus for the theory of self psychology.

Freud (1914e) credited both Ellis and Näcke with introducing the term *narcissism*. Ellis, in 1898, compared individuals with autoerotism to Narcissus, the youth from Greek mythology who fell in love with his own reflection and languished from unfulfilled desire. Näcke used the word *narcissism* in 1899 to describe a sexual perversion. Freud (1899b) alluded to the concept of narcissism (although not by name) in an 1899 letter to Fliess, referring to the vicissitudes of libido in psychotic conditions. Freud's (1905b) first published use of the term was in a 1910 footnote appended to his "Three Essays on the Theory of Sexuality," describing object choice in homosexuals.

Freud's (1914e) theory of narcissism is elaborated most fully in his landmark essay, "On Narcissism," motivated in part by increasing pressures (and defections) from a number of theorists who challenged the centrality of his libido theory. Jung, in particular, had asserted that libido theory was unable to account for clinical phenomena associated with psychosis and schizophrenia. In this paper, Freud defined narcissism as the libidinal investment in the ego. He also described narcissism as a stage in the development of object relations, a normal, halfway phase in a progression that begins with autoerotism and proceeds to object love. The original stage of autoerotism is succeeded by the stage of **primary narcissism**, in which libido is invested in the now-differentiated ego, prior to the formation of object ties. From this stage of development, the ego establishes libidinal ties to external objects (object love).

However, thereafter, in response to frustration, the ego may withdraw libido back into itself, resulting in **secondary narcissism**. Elaborating further, Freud distinguished **narcissistic object choice** from what he called "anaclitic object choice." In anaclitic object choice, rooted in the self-preservative instincts, a child loves the woman who feeds him, the man who protects him, and, in adult life, the people who resonate with those roles. In contrast, in narcissistic object choice, a child (or adult) loves someone who resembles himself, someone who reminds him of a promising earlier self, someone he hopes to be, or someone experienced as part of himself, such as his own child. The aim of narcissistic object choice is the preservation of self regard.

Freud used his new concept of narcissism to account for schizophrenia and psychosis, arguing that the withdrawal of libido back into the ego explains both the megalomania and the withdrawal from the external world typical of these disorders. He also used the concept of narcissism to explain other diverse phenomena such as: taking oneself as a sexual object, homosexuality, omnipotent thinking, hypochondriasis, idealization, and, above all, the vicissitudes of self regard. According to Freud, self regard has two additional sources besides the satisfaction derived from object libidinal ties: first, the residue of **infantile narcissism**, and, second, the fulfillment of one's ego ideal, a concept first introduced in his paper "On Narcissism." The ego ideal is heir to the lost perfection of childhood. By projecting before him his ego ideal, the child attempts to recover the omnipotence he is forced to relinquish as a result of the reproaches of others and his own emerging critical judgment. The ego ideal, by which an individual measures his actual ego, is a rudimentary conscience (superego). Freud also argued that **narcissistic libido**, or the energy withdrawn back into the ego from an abandoned object-cathexis, is now available for many other nonsexual ego functions, including the building of psychic structure (an idea that was later elaborated in terms of sublimation, internalization, and identification). Indeed, Freud's concept of narcissism went hand in hand with the development of the concepts of the ego, the superego (ego ideal), the self, and object relations.

Freud did little further to revise his theoretical formulation of narcissism. However, the growth of ego psychology facilitated more-complex concepts of narcissism, incorporating elements of structural theory and the role of aggression. For example, Hartmann helped clarify Freud's ambiguous use of *ego* to refer both to the experiential "I," and to the more abstract psychic structure. Hartmann (1950) redefined narcissism as the libidinal cathexis of the self or self representation. Jacobson (1964) elaborated on the work of Hartmann, integrating Freud's focus on drive with concepts of ego function, affect, and object relations. She detailed the complex development of the self in tandem with the development of objects relations and the associated vicissitudes of self esteem. She explored the dynamics of how self esteem is stabilized through the structure building of superego, ego ideal, and wishful self image. Over time, conceptualizations of the self became increasingly important in psychoanalytic approaches to narcissism, as did greater understanding of the superego and ego ideal. For example, analysts such as J. Sandler and Joffee (1965) attempted to define narcissism in entirely nondrive terms, locating its meaning instead in terms of affective states. They defined narcissism as an "ideal state of well-being," and narcissistic pathology as an overt or latent state of pain.

From the beginning, the concept of narcissism was important to understanding different kinds of psychopathology. Early on, Freud (1915d) distinguished between transferences manifested by neurotic patients (with hysteria, anxiety, and obsessional neurosis) and those with **narcissistic neuroses**, a group comprising what would now be considered narcissistic and borderline personality disorders, as well as "paranoiacs, melancholics, and sufferers from dementia praecox." He (1917c) argued that narcissistic object ties predispose individuals to form the **narcissistic identification** characteristic of melancholia and others kinds of psychopathology. The contribution of narcissistic issues to character was also evident early on in Freud's (1916) description of "The Exceptions," a character type organized by the demand for reparations for early **narcissistic injury**. A. Adler (1925) had already argued that the child's sense of inferiority relative to powerful adults, and compensatory grandiosity, result in an inferiority complex that motivates all subsequent psychological development. Jones (1913b) had already described what he called "the God complex." However, the growth of ego psychology allowed for fuller elaboration of the concept of character and for gradual development of the specific diagnostic category of narcissistic personality disorder. W. Reich (1933/1945) described the **phallic narcissistic character**, identifying phallic aggressive, domineering, arrogant behavior as a stable defense against regression to passive-feminine and anal strivings. The phallic narcissist has suffered severe frustration of phallic and exhibitionistic strivings at the height of his development, usually by the opposite sex parent, laying the groundwork for the motive of sadistic revenge. Reich described a spectrum of severity ranging from a healthier form of phallic narcissism to pathological, pregenital forms involving addiction, sexual sadism, and criminal behavior. A. Reich (1953) described narcissistic disorders in women whose early feelings of gender inferiority are reflected in a persistent infantile grandiose ego ideal, externalized onto an idealized love object that is used to satisfy narcissistic needs and stabilize self esteem. She (1960) also described narcissistic disorders in men who have suffered early trauma resulting in regressive withdrawal from love objects and overvaluation of the body, especially the phallus. Such individuals rely on narcissistic fantasies of self aggrandizement that they experience as magically fulfilled. H. Deutsch (1934) described severe narcissistic disorders that present as "as if" personalities. H. Deutsch (1955) and Greenacre (1958b) both described severe narcissistic disorders with prominent sociopathy that present as "imposters." M. Balint (1968) described how parental lack of primary object relatedness, that is, a lack of understanding, recognition, and comfort creates in the child a "basic fault" often manifested as narcissism. A. M. Cooper (1988) described the **narcissistic-masochistic personality disorder**, arguing that narcissistic and masochistic elements are so closely intertwined that they should be considered a single entity.

Pathological narcissism is a term closely associated with object relations theories emerging from the British Kleinians. Klein argued that even earliest infancy is not objectless, as Freud had proposed, but rather is characterized by primitive object relations. Her view was the basis for several developments in the theory of narcissistic pathology. For example, Rosenfeld (1964) disputed Freud's claim that, in the narcissistic neuroses, a coherent transference does not unfold. He argued that in narcissistic transferences, the separateness of self and object is denied, as a defense against dependence and envy. In his view, the apparent inability of narcissistic patients to cathect an object is a defensive phenomenon concealing richly elaborated but primitively organized object representations. Rosenfeld (1971a, 1971b) later distinguished between **libidinal narcissism**, where rejection of the object is a defense against intolerable experiences of separateness and envy, and **destructive narcissism**, where rejection of the object is a manifestation of the death drive. Van der Waals (1965) was the first to use the term *pathological narcissism* to describe theories of narcissistic pathology based on distorted object relations, as opposed to theories that conceptualize narcissistic pathology as reflecting a fixation at an early, normal point of development.

Kernberg (1970a, 1970b, 1975, 1984) followed Rosenfeld in elaborating the centrality of distorted object relations in the syndromes of narcissism. Integrating this idea with many others from Klein, A. Reich, and Jacobson, Kernberg posited a view of pathological narcissism in which early and severe splitting, utilized as defense against intolerable aggressive wishes, leads to a distortion in the basic structure of the self. In place of a normal self representation that integrates good and bad aspects of the self, the narcissist develops a pathological grandiose self (a term he borrowed from A. Reich and Kohut), a structure that is the product of a defensive fusion of the actual self with ideal self and ideal object representations. The pathological grandiose self defends the individual against intolerable fears of dependence and envy. Unintegrated bad aspects of self and object are projected onto the object world, leading to the experience of external objects as malevolent, mechanical, and unreal. In addition, the appropriation of ideal images into the self prevents their normal integration into the superego. Some narcissists function very well. In others, paranoid fears of envy and of dependence on others are defended against through devaluation, omnipotent control of objects, and **narcissistic withdrawal**. Some exhibit a more-severe disturbance, **malignant narcissism**, in which the severe deformations in the superego result in prominent sociopathic features (Kernberg, 1984).

The work of Kohut (1966, 1971, 1972, 1977, 1984) was a major landmark in the theory of both normal and pathological narcissism, leading to the development of a branch of psychoanalysis known as self psychology. Kohut's contributions to understanding narcissism include: 1) his positing of narcissism as an essential and irreducible driving force in psychological life, with its own **narcissistic line of development** distinct from the development of object love; healthy narcissism is characterized by the emergence of a bipolar self, with the grandiose self and the omnipotent object as its two poles; 2) his account of selfobject functions in the development and maintenance of the self; selfobject functions refer to the process by which the presence and actions of an object (originally a caretaker) enlivens and stabilizes self experience; 3) his conceptualization of extreme forms of aggression as **narcissistic rage**, conceptualized not as a vicissitude of an aggressive drive but as secondary to an experience of injury to the self or disruptions of the self-selfobject matrix; 4) his conceptualization of narcissistic pathology (later called disorders of the self) as the result of developmental arrests that occur when selfobject needs are not adequately met; and 5) his elucidation of the **narcissistic transferences** (later called selfobject transferences) based on the patient's continuing need for the selfobject functions of mirroring and idealization to maintain his precarious sense of self cohesion and self esteem.

Much controversy surrounding the concepts of narcissism centers on differences between the views of Kohut and Kernberg. Kohut saw narcissistic pathology as reflecting a developmental delay due to an environmental deficit; Kernberg distinguished between normal infantile or adult narcissism and pathological narcissism, seeing the latter as a manifestation of a pathological psychic structure deformed by defensive operations. Some have suggested that the disagreement between Kohut and Kernberg reflects different patient populations. For example, Rosenfeld (1987) distinguished between "thick-skinned" and "thin-skinned" narcissists, the former inaccessible and defensively aggressive, and the latter fragile and vulnerable. Similarly, the *Psychodynamic Diagnostic Manual* (PDM Task Force, 2006) separates narcissistic personality disorder into two types: arrogant/entitled (characterized by haughtiness, charisma, and devaluing others), and depressed/depleted (characterized by envy and a search for people to idealize).

Westen (1990a), in response to the conceptual confusion surrounding metapsychological concepts of narcissism, identified four phenomena (egocentrism, relative emotional investment in self and others, self concept, and self esteem) as most often associated with the concept of narcissism. After reviewing the relevant developmental research data, he concluded that these phenomena vary independently from each other and that therefore, any one alone fails to accurately define the concept of narcissism. As a result, Westen argued for a broad definition consistent with his clinical and experimental data: "Narcissism refers to a cognitive-affective preoccupation with the self."

Narcissistic Rage, a self psychology term, is a complex mental state that arises when the cohesiveness of the self-selfobject matrix is threatened or injured. Narcissistic rage is characterized by the relentless and ruthless need to exact revenge and rectify a perceived injustice, accompanied or preceded by intense shame and humiliation. The individual may be unconscious of his rage, he may disavow it, or he may be exquisitely aware of it. He may feel preoccupied with his feelings and bring sharpened rational thought to bear in achieving retribution. The expression of narcissistic rage can range from mild annoyance to the full-blown rage that lends its name to the concept. Rage is both a sign of a fragmenting self and a response to the experience of selfobject failures. In treatment, the analyst focuses attention on

the primary self-selfobject pathology behind the rage with the aim of strengthening of the self and improving the hair-trigger vulnerability to narcissistic rage with its relentless intensity.

In contrast to Freud's conceptualization of aggression as a drive that must be "mastered" by the ego, or to Klein's theory based on the death drive, Kohut viewed hostile aggression as the inevitable manifestation of a primary, unmet selfobject need that creates a disturbance in the individual's narcissistic balance. Narcissistic rage must be distinguished from self assertion, which is a normal part of the striving self and which unfolds along a separate line in the development of ambition. In self assertion, the target of the individual's competitive ambition or anger is experienced as a separate person; the anger subsides once the goal is reached. In narcissistic rage, the target of the individual's rage is not experienced as a separate person; even with successful retaliation, the sense of injury and the rage persist. The denial of the "otherness" is not in itself an expression of hostile aggression or a defense against dependence. The rage itself may serve to avert further disintegration and to repair the integrity of the self.

Kohut's (1971) controversial views on aggression were based on his understanding of narcissism. He proposed that narcissism and object libido have separate lines of development and that narcissism is transformed from primitive to mature forms in the context of phase-appropriate empathic responsiveness from caregivers. He argued that unintegrated manifestations of isolated drive derivatives, including narcissistic rage, should be conceptualized as disintegration products (occasionally referred to as breakdown products), which are symptomatic of defects in the self. Kohut (1972) first commented on the relationship between narcissism and aggression when he described idealization as an aspect of normal development rather than a defense against aggression. He argued that underlying all rage, from minor grudges to paranoid vendettas, is the insistence on the perfection of the idealized selfobject and on the limitless power of the grandiose self. Rage results from traumatic frustrations of the phase-appropriate need for omnipotent control of selfobjects during childhood.

When acute rage reactions do not subside, rage may permeate the psyche with the gradual establishment of **chronic narcissistic rage**. Chronic narcissistic rage is characterized by fantasies of redressing injustice, disdain for compromise, and heedlessness of injury to oneself. Chronic rage may become embedded in the structure of the self, resulting in sadomasochism, contempt, injustice collecting, self recrimination, self pity, and suicidal behavior (A. Ornstein, 1998). Narcissistic rage may also contribute to group psychology; humiliation and deflated fantasies of omnipotence can lead to a group's propensity for highly organized, aggressive action (Kohut, 1970/1978).

In the psychoanalytic treatment situation, the analyst must understand that narcissistic rage cannot be transformed into constructive aggression. The aim of treatment is the gradual transformation of the narcissistic imbalance from which the rage arises. This transformation occurs in the context of the analyst's recognition of the legitimacy of the rage within the patient's narcissistically perceived world. The analyst interprets the underlying disappointments in the idealized other, and the underlying need for validation and admiration. During the working-through process, the analyst focuses on the meaning of the trigger as an affront to one's sense of self. The goals of this therapeutic process include the strengthening of the self, diminishment of vulnerability to narcissistic rage, and greater capacity for self assertion.

In the last twenty years, infant research (D. N. Stern, 1985; Beebe and Lachmann, 1988; Lyons-Ruth, 1991) has lent support to Kohut's view that the baby at birth is not rageful but assertive; his assertion allows him to make demands on his selfobjects to offer him average empathic responsiveness. The most explicit statement regarding the difference between aggression and self assertion was made by Stechler (1982, 1987) and Stechler and Kaplan (1980), who concluded that assertion and aggression have different origins in our biopsychosocial heritage, serve different functions in our lives, and are accompanied by different affective experiences.

Narrative: see HERMENEUTICS, FANTASY

Nature/Nurture: see COMPLEMENTAL SERIES, CONSTITUTIONAL FACTORS, DEFICIT

Negation is a process that permits something that is repressed access to consciousness, but only in the negative form (as for example: "That woman in the dream? She's not my mother!"). The concept of negation is related to the concept of denial, in that a conscious thought or feeling is rejected. While Freud (1925a) noted the phenomenon of negation on several occasions, his most thorough exploration of it is in his paper "Negation." In this paper, Freud asserted that there is no better evidence that the analyst is on the correct track with an interpretation than the patient's words "I never thought that." Freud was aware that the use of this kind of evi-

dence opened the analyst up to charges of claiming to be infallible, finding in whatever the patient says a confirmation for interpretation. Grünbaum (1979) called this Freud's "tally argument." Freud (1937b) refuted this charge by noting that the analyst must always search for further confirmation of his interpretations through the overall context of the treatment. The many issues surrounding the possibility of confirmation in the analytic setting pose an unsolved problem in psychoanalytic epistemology, a problem that is actively discussed in contemporary psychoanalysis from multiple points of view (Grünbaum, 1982).

Negative Therapeutic Reaction is the paradoxical clinical deterioration of a psychoanalytic patient that may occur following the understanding of an important insight or other indication of progress in the analysis. It was originally understood as the expression of unconscious guilt and a need for punishment, but many other psychodynamic explanations for its occurrence have been proposed. Negative therapeutic reaction has also taken on the broader connotation of any tendentious stance the patient unconsciously takes against progress in treatment. In its broadest interpretation, negative therapeutic reaction is understood as the universal fears of loss and separation that underlie the inherent resistance to change. In response, some authors note that the term has lost its usefulness (Pontalis, 1980; J. Sandler, 1980). The negative therapeutic reaction is differentiated from negative transference, which is unconscious hostility toward the analyst.

Negative therapeutic reaction is a significant clinical concept within psychoanalysis because it is linked to patients in whom masochism, sadomasochism, depressive trends, superego issues, pathological envy, and aggression are prominent issues in mental life. Such patients seem unconsciously intent on suffering while simultaneously evoking experiences of helplessness, guilt, and anger in their analysts. They present formidable clinical challenges especially in the management of transference and countertransference. The concept has also evoked controversy because of claims by some theorists starting with Freud (1920a) that it is a manifestation of the death drive, which operates "beyond the pleasure principle." The death drive is one of the most controversial concepts of Freud's psychoanalytic theory, as many analysts regard it as going beyond the clinical data and do not see its usefulness.

Freud (1918a) initially attributed "negative reactions" to the patient's need for autonomy. Freud (1923a) first used the term *negative therapeutic reac-*

tion in "The Ego and the Id," noting that it exemplified the unconscious functioning of the superego. He explained that the patient's conscious experience is one of feeling ill, not of feeling guilty, the latter manifest as a resistance to recovery. In "The Economic Problem of Masochism," Freud (1924a) replaced the concept of "the unconscious feeling of guilt" with "the need for punishment" and "moral masochism," which are responses to sexual and aggressive oedipal wishes. Finally, in "Analysis Terminable and Interminable," Freud (1937a) proposed that a constitutional factor, the death drive, accounted for the intensity of the aggression invested in the superego and expressed in the negative therapeutic reaction. He viewed it as one of the limiting factors in a psychoanalytic treatment. However, earlier, Freud (1916) described related behavioral phenomena in individuals who experience any positive life experience as threatening and have a negative response. Examples include categories of criminals who are "criminals from a sense of guilt" and those "wrecked by success."

Abraham (1919) described patients who do not progress in analysis because they begrudge the analyst's work. Similarly, Horney (1936) interpreted the negative therapeutic reaction as organized by some patients' hostile competitiveness, fear of retaliation, narcissistic vulnerability marked by envy and shame, and also wishes for affection.

Several analysts working in the ego psychology tradition subsequently reaffirmed the role of unconscious guilt in the negative therapeutic reaction but disagreed with Freud regarding the necessity to invoke the death drive to explain it (C. Brenner, 1959; Loewald, 1972).

The concept of negative therapeutic reaction has had a central role in Kleinian theory. In fact, Klein (1957) based her concept of envy on Freud's description of the negative therapeutic reaction as a particular form of resistance to analysis, linked to the death drive. Kleinians have emphasized the role of aggression in the negative therapeutic reaction. Riviere (1936) linked the negative therapeutic reaction with the patient's envious need to destroy the analyst's work. She described a complex clinical picture in which a patient's manic defensive stance, which is expressed in an omnipotent denial of dependency on the analyst and on the treatment, wards off both paranoid and depressive anxieties. The depressive anxieties are consequent to the patient's "phantasies" of having destroyed inner objects, which must be repaired before the patient can tolerate greater awareness of what he fears is a desolate internal world. Rosenfeld (1971a) described negative thera-

peutic reaction in narcissistic patients as the expression of sadistic wishes to retain a sense of power and to deny feelings of dependency, weakness, and envy. Kernberg (1971) offered a similar understanding.

Other dynamics invoked to account for the negative therapeutic reaction include fears of separation and abandonment, negativism to protect against a feared emotional surrender (Olinick, 1964), the need to evoke an angry rebuff from the analyst to ward off a wish for merger, and a masochistic bondage that stems from wishes for acceptance in the context of traumatic overstimulation and consequent shame (Wurmser, 2000, 2007).

Neurasthenia: see NEUROSIS

Neurosis or **Neurotic** is any excessively rigid, inflexible, or stereotyped pattern of thought, feeling, attitude, or behavior that results from the expression of and/or solution to unconscious conflict. The hallmark of neurosis is that it does not change in response to ordinary experience or learning, even in the face of considerable suffering and pain. For this reason, it is often defined as a maladaptive solution to unconscious conflict. Psychoanalysis attempts to elucidate the motivations and/or meanings embedded in the apparent unreasonableness of neurosis by exploring the underlying unconscious conflict. In the psychoanalytic literature, neurosis is used in various ways: 1) In a narrow sense (the original meaning), neurosis is used to designate a group of symptoms (**symptom neurosis**), traditionally including conversion hysteria, **obsessive compulsive neurosis**, anxiety or panic attacks, phobias, psychogenic sexual dysfunctions, or **depressive neurosis**. Symptom neurosis also includes inhibitions such as sexual inhibitions, or writer's block. Symptom neurosis is often described as ego-dystonic (experienced as alien to the self) as opposed to character disorders that are described as ego-syntonic (experienced as part of the self). 2) In a broad sense (the most common contemporary meaning), neurosis is used to designate any inflexible or maladaptive pattern of behavior, which may not be a symptom but which nevertheless interferes with optimal functioning, such as repetitive problems with authority, acts of self sabotage following success, or an endless search for love in the wrong places. If a neurotic pattern of this sort is pervasive enough, it may be called a character disorder. Indeed, at one time, nonsymptomatic but maladaptive patterns of this sort were referred to as **character neuroses**, to distinguish them from the symptom neuroses while emphasizing their similar structure. 3) In a specific sense, **neurotic styles** have been described based on the concept of cognitive style (D. Shapiro, 1965). 4) In addition to the above designations, neurosis is often used to distinguish one type or "level" of psychopathology from other types/levels. For example: 1) In the nineteenth century, prior to Freud, neurosis was distinguished from psychosis, usually on the basis of the presence/absence of reality testing. 2) In his early work, Freud (1905b) distinguished neurosis from the perversions, on the basis of whether unconscious infantile wishes were disguised as symptoms (neurosis), or expressed directly (perversion). 3) Among contemporary psychoanalysts, neurotic behavior is distinguished from **nonneurotic** (or normal) behavior, usually on the basis of whether or not it is excessively rigid or maladaptive (Hartmann, 1939b). 4) In contemporary usage, **neurotic character organization** is distinguished from borderline character organization, usually on the basis of the types of defense and/or the organization of object relations (Kernberg, 1970a).

Neurosis plays an important role in the history of psychoanalysis, as Freud derived both his new treatment and his most important psychoanalytic theories in the course of working with patients suffering from the symptom neuroses, beginning with hysteria. His view that neurotic symptoms represent the symbolic expression of repressed, unconscious conflict became the foundation for all his theories of psychopathology, as well as for his revolutionary theory of a mind divided into conscious and unconscious and motivated by conflicting wishes and defenses. The analogies Freud found between neuroses and dreams led him to describe the peculiar but creative primary processes that characterize the unconscious. The analogies he found between neuroses and the sexual life of adults, of children, and in perversion led him to his radical ideas about the many, often highly disguised vicissitudes of psychosexuality. While psychoanalysis initially borrowed the term *neurosis* from the surrounding culture of general medicine, over time it has become almost exclusively associated with psychoanalysis. Indeed, the history of the psychoanalytic understanding of neurosis is indistinguishable from the overall history of psychoanalysis, which in large measure is the story of changing approaches to understanding neurotic suffering. Despite confusion and controversy surrounding the term, its use has persisted because of our need to identify a category of troublesome thoughts, feelings, and behaviors that result from unconscious conflict.

The term *neurosis* was coined by the Scottish physician Cullen in 1777 to designate functional disturbances of the nervous system for which there was no demonstrable "inflammation or structural lesion" in the afflicted organ. In the nineteenth century, the neuroses included a wide variety of diverse ailments, including many that are now considered neurological (such as epilepsy and Parkinson's disease), as well as hysteria. In his own work, Freud (1888a) addressed neurosis as a purely nosological category as early as 1888. However, Freud's (1894c, 1896c) first psychoanalytic writings on the subject were his explorations of what he called the neuroses (or **neuropsychoses**) of defense, which included hysteria, obsessional neurosis, phobias, and some kinds of paranoia, all of which he explained as representing "the return of repressed" sexual ideas or memories. In this early period, Freud (1898b) distinguished between what he called the **psychoneuroses** and the **actual neuroses** (predominantly anxiety neurosis and neurasthenia), which result not from psychological conflict but from faulty sexual practices. At other points (following the work of Jung), Freud (1915b) divided the psychoneuroses into **transference neuroses** (hysteria, obsessional neurosis, phobias) and **narcissistic neuroses** (manic depression, hypochondriasis, and some psychotic disorders), so designated because patients were thought unable to form transferences. He (1919c) also compared/contrasted the **war neuroses** (or **traumatic neuroses**) and the **peacetime (psycho-) neuroses** by arguing that in both, the ego fears being damaged, either from without or from within.

In Freud's final formulation, symptom neurosis reflects a fixation and/or a regression to pregenital libidinal strivings in the face of conflict associated with the oedipus complex. These reawakened infantile libidinal strivings come into conflict with superego and ego, leading to anxiety, defense, and compromise in the form of a symptom. Every symptom provides both the primary gain of a solution to unconscious conflict, and a secondary gain associated with the benefits of being ill. Freud (1918a) also introduced the concept of **infantile neurosis**, by which he meant the inner organization of the personality, which dates from childhood and reflects defenses and compromises resulting from the oedipus complex, and which forms the basis for adult neurosis. Indeed, in Freud's classical formulation, the oedipus complex is the basis for all neurosis. Freud's work also includes speculation about each person's **choice of neurosis**, influenced by his choice of defense and by his particular developmental fixation. In the domain of technique, he (1914e) argued that psychoanalytic treatment works through the successful analysis of an **artificial neurosis** (or later **transference neurosis**), the expression of the infantile neurosis within the psychoanalytic setting.

Following Freud, child analysts expanded the concept of neurosis to include **childhood neurosis** (A. Freud, 1945) , a neurotic condition that occurs during childhood. Neurosis also came to include nonsymptomatic behavior patterns and character traits (as described above). Then, with the introduction of the concept of borderline personality organization, the term *neurotic* became used commonly to designate a level of psychopathology (again, see above). At the same time, developments in psychoanalytic theory led to increased complexity in the psychoanalytic theory of neurosis. For example, emphasis on preoedipal development raised questions about Freud's obligatory link between neurosis and the oedipus complex; interest in object relations and the development of the self led to consideration of structural elements of neurotic suffering beyond id, ego, and superego. Meanwhile, developments in the theory of treatment challenged the classical definition of psychoanalysis as the recapitulation of a definable infantile neurosis in the form of a **regressive transference neurosis**, which could then be analyzed (Gill, 1954).

Because of this expanding (and arguably increasingly confusing) understanding of and use of the concept, neurosis has fallen into relative disuse as a discrete nosological category, even within psycho-analysis. In the field of psychiatry, the term *neurosis* was decried as vague, overinclusive, and impossible to verify empirically; in 1980, it was dropped from the official psychiatric nomenclature in favor of the word *disorder* (American Psychiatric Association, 1981). However, despite its relative disuse as a formal nosological category, neurosis remains one of the most important concepts in clinical psychoanalysis, as all psychoanalytic treatment seeks to help patients gain freedom from neurotic suffering, defined as inflexible, maladaptive behaviors that represent solutions to unconscious conflicts.

Neutrality: see ABSTINENCE/NEUTRALITY/ANONYMITY

Neutralization: see DRIVE, EGO, ENERGY, SUBLIMATION

New Object: see CHILD ANALYSIS, INTERPRETATION, RELATIONAL PSYCHOANALYSIS, THERAPEUTIC ACTION, TRANSFERENCE

Nirvana Principle: see DEATH DRIVE, DRIVE, ENERGY, ID, METAPSYCHOLOGY, REPETITION COMPULSION, TOPOGRAPHIC THEORY, UNCONSCIOUS

O

Object is the word used in psychoanalysis to refer to another person. The object is contrasted with the self. The term *object* has been used variously to refer to: 1) a real, tangible, other person who exists in external reality (**interpersonal object**); 2) the mental representation, or set of representations, of another person (**object representation**, **intrapsychic object**, and occasionally, imago); 3) a theoretical construct, different from both a real object and a simple object representation, in which the organizational structure of an object representation is invested with drive and affect (as for example **internal object**, introject, and some aspects of the superego); and 4) a nonhuman thing, or representation of a thing (non- or prepsychoanalytic meaning). In Klein's theory, the object (always intrapsychic) is further differentiated into the internal object (see above), defined as an internal representation of another person, who, in "phantasy," has been taken inside the body, and the **external object**, defined as an internal representation of another person who is not experienced as having been taken inside the body. In other words, confusion has been created by the fact that the term *external object* is used variously to mean both a real person who exists in the external world (the interpersonal meaning), and the intrapsychic representation of another person who is imagined to be exterior to the body (Kleinian theory). The word *internal*, with regard to Klein's internal object, also has several meanings, including "mental," "imaginary," and "inside" (A. Strachey, 1941). While most analysts accept the use of the term *object*, with all its flaws, a few reject the term, feeling that it **objectifies**, or denies the subjectivity of the other person. The word **objective**, meaning the ability to perceive and know the world from a perspective outside one's subjective position, appears in many debates about psychoanalytic epistemology.

The concept of the object is important in all schools of thought in psychoanalysis, as it provides a way to talk about the importance of other people in every aspect of mental life. Interactions between self and other, the experience of these interactions, and the internalization of these interactions are important in the development of the mind and in its everyday functioning. Disturbances in the interaction between self and other, and/or their representa-

tion in the mind, contribute to understanding of some, if not all, psychopathology. Finally, interactions and their internalization are important in understanding the relationship between patient and analyst in the treatment situation; patient-analyst interactions, and/or the meanings associated with those interactions, are central to all concepts of therapeutic action.

While every psychoanalytic theory includes object(s), the schools of thought or perspectives that place special emphasis on self and object interactions and the mental representation of these interactions, in their conceptualizations of development, mental functioning, psychopathology, and treatment, are called variously and confusingly: **object relations theory**, interpersonal psychoanalysis, and relational psychoanalysis. Roughly speaking, in the original Kleinian/object relations point of view, *object* almost always refers to representations of objects in the mind; by contrast, in the original Sullivanian/interpersonal point of view, *object* is used to mean the real object in the external world. However, in contemporary psychoanalysis, most who call themselves object relations theorists or interpersonal theorists use *object* in both ways. Relational psychoanalysis has presented itself as a broad perspective whose adherents are united in the view that no strict separation can be made between the intrapsychic and interpersonal realms of experience. While relational psychoanalysis claims to subsume object relations theory, many object relations theorists reject this designation.

Analysts who use *object* in the sense of a real person generally agree that: real interactions with significant others are important in development, ongoing mental functioning, and every aspect of the treatment situation; experiences of interaction are internalized, contributing to all aspects of psychological functioning; and the subjective state of each person in the interaction contributes to the experience of this interaction. Theorists who place special emphasis on interacting subjectivities call themselves intersubjectivists. All such analysts also describe the psychoanalytic situation in terms of a two-person psychology.

Analysts who use *object* in the sense of the mental representation of an object generally agree that:

object representations are both conscious and unconscious; object representations are both stable and changing, based on both internal and external circumstances; object representations range on a spectrum from realistic to distorted; object representations are shaped by interpersonal interactions with real objects that have been internalized; object representations are also shaped by multiple intrapsychic factors, including cognitive development, fantasy, motivational state, and conflict, to mention a few; object representations are made up of multiple **object images** more or less integrated into a coherent whole (J. Sandler and Rosenblatt, 1962); object representations, especially in early development and serious psychopathology, often consist of unintegrated "parts" of an experience of the object, more or less concrete (as, for example: Freud and Abraham's **oral objects**, **anal objects**, and **phallic objects**; Hartmann and A. Freud's **need-satisfying object**; Klein's **internal object** and **part objects**, such as the **good object** [sometimes called the breast], **bad object**, and **persecutory object**; Winnicott's **transitional object**; Kohut's **selfobject** and idealized parental imago; "objects" described by Fairbairn, Bion, and others). The capacity to construct and maintain representations of objects that are reasonably realistic and integrated is an important developmental task (as in Hartmann's **object constancy** or Klein's **whole object** of the depressive position). The failure to construct or maintain well-integrated object representations correlates with various kinds of psychopathology.

Every theorist, beginning with Freud, has been interested in the complex processes of internalization by which objects and interactions with objects are represented in the mind. Processes of internalization include introjection, identification, and/or projective and introjective identification. Such processes may be psychically represented by fantasies of incorporation. Every school of thought offers its own view of how these processes operate in development, in psychological functioning, and in the treatment situation. However, all agree that internalization of objects and interactions with objects contributes to the organization of mental life and the development of psychic structure. Processes of internalization are important in the therapeutic action of psychoanalytic treatment.

Furthermore, every theorist since Freud has also noted that it is difficult, if not impossible (for either the theorist or the individual), to fully differentiate representations of the object from representations of the self. Self and object representations are created in interaction with each other, beginning in childhood. The boundary between self and object is always somewhat porous, ranging on a continuum from reasonable differentiation to complete confusion, depending on many factors, including cognitive immaturity, psychopathology, high affect states, and psychological stress. Serious failure to differentiate between self and object representations is characteristic of psychosis.

Throughout his writing life, Freud used the word and the concept of object in all the ways enumerated above, without clearly differentiating among them. Freud's (1905b) first use of the object as a conceptual term was in "Three Essays on the Theory of Sexuality," where, in elaborating his new drive (or libido) theory, he described source, aim, and object as aspects of the drive (instinct). In this conceptualization of object (sometimes called **sexual object**), the object is defined as "the thing in regard to which or through which the instinct is able to achieve its aim." In 1910, Freud (1910d) offered a different use of object as a **love object**, to mean, quite simply, the person whom someone chooses to love. These concepts of object are distinct but overlapping, in that for Freud loving (indeed, all human behavior) reflects the activity of the drives, and the concept of object is always linked to the concept of the drive.

Freud offered many overlapping insights in connection with the concept of object that have been used and argued over ever since: 1) The object is not intrinsic to the drive but is only "soldered" onto it (1905b). 2) In any individual instance, the object is highly particular to the individual. 3) Because the sexual drive is "anaclitic" (or "leaning on" the instincts for self preservation, such as hunger and thirst), the object of the drive is often modeled on objects who satisfy the self-preservative instinct (as for example, the mother who feeds the child). 4) In the early stages of development, the object of the drive is not a whole, integrated object but is always connected to a "component" of the drive, such as the oral, anal, or phallic components. 5) The object of the drive may be extremely concrete (as for example, a body part, such as the mouth, anus, or phallus). 6) Symbolic substitutions may occur between objects (as for example, feces=child=gift or penis=man) (1917d); in other words, investments of interest or energy (cathexis) may be displaced from one object to another (1909b). 7) The object may be shaped by the vicissitudes of narcissism, as in idealization or **narcissistic object choice** (1914e). 8) The object may be split into parts, as in idealization accompanied by debasement (1912d). 9) The object may be both loved and hated, as in the concept of ambivalence (1912a). 10) Vicissitudes of the drive (later conceptualized as defenses) can be described in terms of the object (as for example, "turning round upon the subject's own self" [1915b]). 11) Object choice, or "the finding of an object is, in fact, a refinding of it," or, in other words, every object choice represents or is shaped by the memory/representation of an earlier object choice; this fact is reflected in the phenomenon of transference (1905b). 12) Many phenomena are best understood as reflecting atypical object choice, as in homosexuality or fetishism. 13) **Object loss** is an important and painful psychological event, which sets in motion complex processes with many consequences, including mourning and melancholia (1917c). 14) Self and object representations are not always clearly differentiated.

In addition to the above ideas, scattered among his many writings, Freud offered a developmental schema for the individual's way of relating to the object. Rendered as perhaps more coherent than it is, this developmental schema begins with autoerotism, whereby the drive is satisfied through interaction with the individual's own body, in the absence of a concept of self or object. It progresses through primary narcissism (in which libido is invested in the self, before the concept of the object), primary identification (the first way an individual relates to the object, prior to self-object differentiation or the formation of real object ties), and, finally, object love (libido invested in objects) which exists side by side with secondary narcissism (libido withdrawn from the object back into the self). Object love is further differentiated into various pregenital stages (marked by relationship to only a part of the object, experienced as a source of pleasure in relation to a component of the drive) and the oedipal/genital stage (in which the whole object is loved). Finally, Freud talked of the importance of adolescence as a stage marked by the challenge of finding a new, nonincestuous object. As part of his developmental schema, Freud (1926a) also offered a timetable of object-related danger situations (including fear of loss of the object, fear of loss of the love of the object, and fear of castration at the hands of the object), the anticipation of which triggers defense (signal anxiety).

Finally, Freud explored many of the complexities of internalization and externalization by which self and object representations and intrapsychic structures develop, beginning in childhood. The most important of these internalizations is the formation of the superego, constructed through a set of complex processes of projection, introjection, and identification, which occurs with the resolution of the oedipus complex. Freud (1923a) also described structure building within the ego, which results when object cathexes are abandoned, an insight that would

become very important in later object relations theories. Of note, while Freud was certainly aware of the concept of representation (understanding that it is not possible to internalize an object without a mental representation of it), he did not use the term *object representation*. Occasionally, he used the word *imago* (borrowed from Jung) to mean the "model" of the infantile object in the mind of the adult that influences object choice. Finally, while Freud (1917d) used the word **object relationship**, he did not use it in the same way as it has been used in object relations theory, that is, internalized interactions between self and other serving as the fundamental building block of the psyche (Fairbairn, 1952).

As Freud was developing his views on the origins of the superego, Klein proposed a theory that has had a lasting effect on all subsequent psychoanalytic theory-making. Building on Freud's theory of the superego as the agency for inner moral authority, constructed through complex processes of projection, introjection, and identification, Klein proposed that the entire inner world is built out of multiple internalizations, or internal objects, in processes that begin in the first days of life. Klein defined the internal object as a phantasy of an object, located in the interior of the body. She described many features of the internal object, all of which reflect her belief that phantasy, drive, the experience of the body, and the experience of the object are all inseparable. (Of note, confusion is created by the fact that Klein used *ego, body,* and *self* interchangeably.) In Klein's view: 1) the internal object is a phantasy; 2) the internal object is a bodily object; it has a quality of concreteness that is never fully lost; this fact is reflected in Kleinian synonyms for the internal object, such as the "breast"; 3) the internal object is suffused with experiences of pleasure and pain; 4) the internal object is experienced as an alive, powerful presence; 5) the internal object is defensively split into "all-good" and "all-bad" part objects, so as to protect good experience from aggression; 6) part objects become integrated into whole objects in the course of normal development; 7) internal objects can be good or "helpful," although most of Klein's work focused on descriptions of the internal bad object; 8) all representations of object and self are constructed through ongoing processes of projection and introjection, so that these representations can never be fully differentiated from each other; 9) the internal object is distinct from the external object, defined as a representation of an object that is not experienced as having been taken inside the body.

In Klein's theory, the experience of the object develops over time from the concrete internal object to the more abstract and symbolic representations of object; in the course of this development, the internal object comes to resemble the external object, with both becoming more realistic. Most importantly, psychological development progresses from the paranoid-schizoid position, dominated by defensive processes of splitting and projective identification and characterized by split, part objects (and parts of the self), to the depressive position, characterized by the ability to tolerate ambivalence (or love and hate toward the same object) and by the integration of good and bad aspects of the object into a whole object. Psychopathology reflects various aspects of either the paranoid-schizoid position or the depressive position. In Klein's (1929, 1935, 1946) view, all processes related to the internal objects are related to management of anxieties associated with aggression; in other words, like Freud, her theory was essentially drive-based. However, unlike Freud, her final stage of development (the depressive position) is characterized by the capacity to integrate contradictory attitudes of love and hate toward the object, rather than various components of the drive.

All psychoanalytic theory since Freud and Klein has focused increasingly on interactions between self and object and the internalization of these interactions. Various theoreticians have drawn from the work of either Freud or Klein or, more often, from both. Important developments in psychoanalytic concepts related to the object include: 1) Sandler's effort to reconceptualize much of Freud's and Klein's views of the object in terms of *object representation* (a term coined by Fenichel [1932]); 2) object constancy, or the capacity to tolerate ambivalence toward representations of the object, conceptualized within the tradition of ego psychology (Hartmann, 1952; Spitz, 1965; Mahler, 1968); 3) *introject,* a term coined as a noun by Eduardo Weiss as roughly the same as Klein's internal object; Sandler and Schafer, conceptualizing within the tradition of ego psychology, agreed that an introject is an object representation with the quality of an "inner presence" with which the individual feels an ongoing relationship; developmentally, introjects precede the development of the depersonified superego (J. Sandler and Rosenblatt, 1962; Schafer, 1968b); 4) the role of the analyst as a real person in the therapeutic interaction of psychoanalysis, such as "new object" (A. Freud, 1978) or "developmental object" (Tähkä, 1993; Hurry, 1998); and 5) Kohut's selfobject and internalized parental imago, crucial to normal development as conceptualized by self psychology. Dozens of other kinds of "objects" have been offered over the years by theorists who have been interested in self and object rela-

tionships, including Bowlby, Spitz, Fairbairn, Winnicott, Bion, Jacobson, Mahler, Loewald, Kernberg, Kohut, Sandler, Sullivan, D. N. Stern, Fonagy, and Greenberg and Mitchell. These theorists have been variously identified as ego psychologists, object relations theorists, self psychologists, interpersonalists, relationalists, or some combination of these.

Blatt and others have attempted to integrate the concept of the object with concepts from social psychology and cognitive neuroscience (Blatt and Lerner, 1983). There have also been several attempts to study self and object representations in various kinds of psychopathology (Nigg et al., 1992). Finally, there have been attempts to study the change in self and object representations with treatment (Bers et al., 1993).

Object Constancy is a developmental attainment enabling an individual to preserve a stable internal representation of an object in the face of complex or contradictory affects experienced toward the object. Object constancy is most often described as the ability to maintain positive feelings toward a loved object in the face of anger and disappointment; however, it also refers to the ability to maintain appropriate negative feelings toward an object in the face of contradictory positive experience. The establishment of object constancy is a multidetermined process requiring growth in a number of areas of psychic functioning. Usually established by the age of three, object constancy can develop earlier or later, as the process is open-ended. It requires the earlier attainment of **object permanence**, usually in place by eighteen months, which is a purely cognitive capacity to maintain a representation of an object (animate or inanimate) even when it is not within perceptual awareness (Piaget, 1954). Object constancy develops in tandem with **self constancy**, or the capacity to sustain a unified self representation even in the face of conflicting experiences of the self. Object and self constancy are roughly equivalent to the object relations described in Klein's depressive position. Object constancy is a pivotal point in development, as its attainment is required for all subsequent progression in object relations. Failures in the capacity for object constancy are universal at times of stress, however, pervasive failures are characteristic of serious psychopathology.

The concept of object constancy was introduced by Hartmann (1952) to describe a quality of object relations in the developing child. He (1953) defined object constancy as the relation to the love object that endures and remains stable and permanent, "independent of the state of needs." Prior to this achievement, the object is characterized as "need satisfying." For Hartmann, object constancy implies a cognitive and a drive element and presupposes some neutralization of the aggressive and libidinal drives.

Spitz (1959, 1965) understood the infant's reaction to strangers at eight months as an indication that the mother had become a **constant libidinal object**, a consistently preferred and loved object; Spitz stressed the mother's irreplaceability and her safety-keeping function. A. Freud (1965), who included object constancy as the third stage in her developmental line of object relationships, added that the infant's investment in the object needed to be maintained regardless of whether the mother frustrated or satisfied.

Among the many elements necessary for object constancy is the capacity to recognize and tolerate loving and hostile feelings toward the same object, to keep feelings centered on a specific object, and to value an object for attributes other than its function of satisfying needs. Mahler (1968; Mahler, Pine, and Bergman, 1975) constructed her own notion of object constancy, **emotional object constancy**, understood as the successful outcome of the rapprochement phase of the separation-individuation process. Mahler stressed differentiation of self from other, and also the unification of good and bad objects into a whole representation (or the resolution of anal-phase ambivalence) in the development of object constancy (McDevitt, 1975). With the establishment of object constancy, the relationship between the mother and child becomes more stable and durable and persists despite frustrating or gratifying experiences (Burgner and Edgcumbe, 1972). While it is sufficiently permanent in the normal three-year-old child, it can remain open-ended, so that Mahler often referred to this final stage in the separation-individuation process as **on the way to object constancy**, reflecting the fact that its attainment is a lifelong process.

P. Tyson (1996b) and Settlage (1993) explored the development of object constancy in tandem with the capacity for affect regulation. Tyson suggested three stages along a continuum toward affect regulation and the development of object constancy. The infant's use of the mother's affective signals at eight months grows into **representational object constancy** at eighteen months, eventually resulting in affect regulation and **self-regulating object constancy**.

It is not possible to study the development of the object separately from the development of the self (Mahler and McDevitt 1982). **Self constancy** develops in tandem with object constancy through similar codetermined processes (P. Tyson and R. Tyson, 1990; Settlage, 1993). Self constancy is the capacity to sustain a unified self representation within all the different, affectively toned ideas about one's self. The process of developing self constancy begins through the "refueling" dialogue between mother and child and requires self-object differentiation (A. Sandler, 1977). It is the attainment of two levels of a sense of identity: the awareness of being a separate individual and a growing awareness of a gender-defined self (Mahler, 1975). The attainment of self constancy makes self reflection and introspection possible (Tähkä, 1988).

From the perspective of modern cognitive developmental theory and theory-of-mind research, Gergely (1992) described how between eighteen and twenty-four months, representations of significant attachment figures contain mental attributes. The developmental task of representing an important object as a mental agent who retains its identity leads to a new level in mentalization of integrated object representations. Gergely hypothesized that the integration of different intentions within the representation of another is not guided by Piaget's theory of object permanence but by the principle of coherence or consistency, a core assumption of theory of mind.

Although object constancy most frequently refers to the child's relationship with the mother, there are other significant people in the child's life, most notably, the father. Settlage (1993) and Akhtar (1994) suggested that object constancy is further structured in interaction with others, and if experience with these others is markedly different, problems may arise. Solnit (1982) noted that children can develop integrated, autonomous object constancy when several caregivers are involved, but there is a limit as to how many. Attachment research has shown that different types of attachments form with different objects, based on the history of interactions with that object (Steele, 2003). Solnit, in his studies of children's reactions to loss and deprivation, described the initial pathway to recovery as "regaining a capacity for object constancy through aggressive behavior." Only later does object constancy become associated with affection and closeness.

Kernberg (1975) described failures of object constancy in borderline and narcissistic psychopathology. Akhtar (1994) described challenges to object constancy at each phase in the life cycle and noted how failures in object constancy contribute to many kinds of serious and subtle forms of psychopathology. Clinical work with such patients requires special technical considerations. Various theorists (Fleming, 1975; Settlage, 1993; Akhtar, 1994; Woods 2003) emphasized the ways in which the therapeutic process and the developmental process complement one another, and also that the experience of being in a safe relationship makes it possible to address transference issues and contributes to the establishment of self and object constancy.

Object Permanence: see OBJECT, OBJECT CONSTANCY

Object Relations Theory, one of the major schools of thought within psychoanalysis, is a theory of the development and functioning of the human psyche, based on the dynamics of basic structures within the mind, called object relations. An **object relation** is an intrapsychic representation, or structure, consisting of three parts: a self representation, an object representation, and the representation of an affectively charged interaction between self and object. An object relation is sometimes termed **object relationship**; either term, especially the latter, is often misused to mean the interaction with a real, external object (best termed *interpersonal interaction*). Object relations range on a continuum from distorted to realistic; they are formed from the combined interaction of fantasy and real interaction; they range from fleeting to enduring, the latter forming stable intrapsychic structures. Certain core features of structured object relations follow a developmental timetable. There are at least three ways to define object relations theory: 1) The broadest point of view defines all psychoanalysis as object relations theory, as all theories include a view of internalized self and object interactions. 2) The narrowest point of view defines object relations theory as including only the work of Klein, Fairbairn (who is widely credited with having coined the term), and Winnicott. 3) The most balanced point of view defines object relations theory as including any school of thought that places object relations at the core of psychological life and at the center of efforts to understand psychoanalytic treatment. In this definition, the most important object relations theorists include Klein, Fairbairn, Winnicott, Bowlby, Spitz, Jacobson, Mahler, Loewald, Kernberg, J. Sandler, Bion, Sullivan, D. N. Stern, Fonagy, and Greenberg and Mitchell, each emphasizing a different aspect of the theory. These writers have been variously identified as object relations theorists, ego psychologists, interpersonalists, relationalists, or some combination of any of these.

Object relations theories have several shared features: 1) All psychological experience, from the most fleeting fantasy to the most stable structure, is organized by object relations. In other words, object relations are the basic unit of experience. 2) The human mind is object-seeking from birth; the basic motivation for object-seeking is not reducible to any other motivational force (as, for example, drive, in Freud's theory). 3) Internalized object relations are built up in the course of development through the interaction of innate factors (such as inborn affect dispositions and cognitive equipment) and relationships with others (primarily caregivers). 4) Interpersonal relationships reflect internalized object relations; psychopathology, especially serious psychopathology such as psychosis, and borderline and narcissistic personality disorders, is best conceptualized in terms of object relations. These basic features lead to theoretical attitudes about basic aspects of the psychoanalytic model of the mind, including motivation, structure, development, and psychopathology. Object relation theory provides natural links to the study of family and group dynamics. It also provides natural links to developmental psychology, as for example, the development of affects.

Object relations theories differ from each other along several parameters: 1) the relationship to drive theory; Klein, Jacobson, and Mahler stayed intimately connected to drive theory; Fairbairn and Sullivan, for the most part, abandoned drive theory; Loewald, Kernberg, Sandler, and Winnicott maintained a version of drive theory, with the concept of drive substantially reworked from that of Freud, placing major emphasis on affect and object relations as the building blocks of drives; 2) the importance of aggression in psychic life; Kleinian theory gives aggression a central role in psychic life; 3) the importance of actual versus fantasied interaction; Sullivan's interpersonal theory emphasized real interactions; Klein's theory emphasized "phantasy"; 4) the question of whether the clinical situation is shaped primarily by internalized object relations or by the real, dyadic patient-analyst interaction; Klein and Kernberg emphasized the former; Greenberg and Mitchell emphasized the latter.

Object relations theory differs from ego psychology in its emphasis on: 1) the idea that the drives are always attached to object relations; 2) the idea that all psychic structures (not just the superego) are structured object relations; 3) the contribution of preoedipal development in the structuring of the mind; 4) the view that the basic unit of experience is an object relation, not the conflict between wish and defense. Object relations theory differs from self psychology in that the latter does not include the role of an internalized "bad object."

Freud used the term *object* throughout his writing life. In fact, there is no aspect of his theory, including motivation, structure, conflict, development, and psychopathology, that does not depend on the concept of an object. Indeed, Freud offered dozens of overlapping insights in connection with the concept of object, which have been used and debated ever since and which have reappeared, unmodified or altered, in later object relations theories. Finally, while Freud (1917c) used the term **object relationship**, he did not use it in the same way as it has been used in object relations theory to mean internalized interactions between self and other, serving as the fundamental building block of the psyche. Freud's (1905b, 1938a) theory of mind focused always on the drive, with object attached to the drive; successful development culminates in the attainment of the "genital phase," where all psychosexual strivings—oral, anal, phallic, and other component instincts—are subordinated under the primacy of the genital zone.

Immediately following the death of Freud, psychoanalysis developed in several directions, in part differentiated by the place given to the role of the object and object relations in psychological life. A. Freud stayed closest to Freud in her allegiance to drive theory, developing Freud's last structural model of the mind (later called ego psychology) through her work with children and the study of defense. However, her interest in development led her to consider the development of object relations beginning in childhood. In her important contribution of the concept of "developmental lines," A. Freud (1963) considered the development from dependency on the object to emotional self reliance and "adult object relations" as prototypical. In her view, this development proceeds through predictable stages, including an early state of undifferentiated self and object representations, suffused with narcissism; an anaclitic phase, where the object is experienced as need-satisfying; attainment of object constancy, wherein stable object representations can be maintained even in the face of strong contradictory feelings; oedipal phase conflicts over rivalry and possessiveness; preadolescent return to archaic ways or relating to the object; and adolescent struggles to find new, nonincestuous objects.

At roughly the same time, Klein proposed a very different theory of the mind, generally considered the first, true object relations theory, which has had a lasting effect on all subsequent psychoanalytic theory-making. Building on Freud's theory of superego development from complex processes of projection, introjection, and identification, Klein proposed that the entire inner world is built out of multiple internalizations, or internal objects, in processes that begin in the first days of life. In Klein's view, development progresses through "positions"— the paranoid-schizoid position and the depressive position—characterized by stable configurations of self and object representation built out of drive, phantasy, and interactions with caregivers, under the influence of internalizing and externalizing processes. Successful development reflects the growing capacity to tolerate conflicting feelings of hate and love (and later, envy and gratitude) toward the object, as reflected in movement from the paranoid position to the depressive position. Klein believed that all processes related to the internal objects are related to management of anxieties associated with aggression; in other words, like Freud and A. Freud, her theory was essentially drive-based. However, unlike the theories of Freud and A. Freud, Klein argued that the ego, as well as the superego, is built from structured object relations. Klein (1932, 1946, 1975) described her final stage of development (the depressive position) as characterized by the capacity to integrate contradictory attitudes of love and hate toward the object, rather than the capacity to integrate various components of the drive (as in Freud) or to achieve relative independence from the object (as in A. Freud). The struggle between A. Freud and Klein (and their followers) for dominance and influence in psychoanalysis in the aftermath of Freud's death is legendary in the history of psychoanalysis (King and Steiner, 1991).

Even as A. Freud and Klein were locked in struggles over theory and power, Bowlby (1969/1982, 1973, 1980) was developing a different object-relations-based theory called attachment theory. Attachment theory is an empirically derived theory of early development that emphasizes the primacy of the early relationship between infant and caregiver. Its central premise is that the infant's motivation to develop sustaining attachments with his or her caregiver is intrinsic to the human mind, dictated by evolutionary pressures and the survival needs of the species. This motivation for attachment is realized through an inborn attachment-behavioral system, operating between infant and mother. Bowlby's attachment theory, with its view that libidinal gratification is secondary to the motive for attachment, and its emphasis on the importance of real relationships and inborn behavior patterns, led to Bowlby being expelled from the British Psychoanalytic Society. Subsequently, attachment theory did become a major force in developmental psychoanalysis through the work of Ainsworth and M. Main, D. N. Stern, and Fonagy.

Finally, working independently in the United States, Sullivan (1953a) was developing his interpersonal theory of psychoanalysis based on the internalized interactions between self and other, or infant and caregiver. For many years, interpersonal psychoanalysis developed separately from mainstream psychoanalysis, with a separate language and distinct following, until recently, when Greenberg and Mitchell (1983) integrated Sullivan's work with that of Fairbairn and other object relations theorists in their view of relational psychoanalysis.

For seventy years following the death of Freud, object relations theory, ego psychology, attachment theory, and interpersonal psychoanalysis developed relatively independently of one another. However, within the tradition of ego psychology, theorists described the object relations accomplishments characterizing genitality, the final stage of psychosexual development. For example, Abraham (1924b) suggested that genital primacy is correlated with the final "post-ambivalent" step in the evolution of object love. Abraham (who greatly influenced Klein) outlined a developmental schema of ambivalence that integrated ideas about libidinal drive development and object relations. He described the early oral sucking stage as "pre-ambivalent"; both the later oral biting stage and the subsequent anal-sadistic stage as ambivalent; and the genital stage, in which the infant has learned to protect the object from the infant's own aggression, as "post-ambivalent." Fenichel (1945) also elaborated the relational aspects of genitality, adding considerations about object relationships to the concept. Erikson's (1950) "utopia of genitality" included a loving partnership and the capacity to care for children. Spitz (1965) studied early interactions between infant and caregivers, exploring how deprivation and object loss leads to serious psychopathology in children. However, it was largely through the work of Jacobson and Mahler that object relations entered mainstream ego psychology. Jacobson (1964) described the development of the ego and superego in tandem with self and object representations, placing a major emphasis on the role of affect. Mahler (Mahler, Pine, and Bergman, 1975) also described the development of psychic structure conceptualized in terms of object relations, focusing on the separation-individuation process. Mahler emphasized the attainment of object constancy (based on the tolerance of ambivalence) as the final stage of development. Loewald (1973a), one of the great innovators within the tradition of ego psychology, worked from the basic assumption that mental activity and psychic development are fundamentally relational and intersubjective. In Loewald's view, the internalization of interactions is the major force in both development and in psychoanalytic treatment.

Meanwhile, influenced by and influencing Klein, Fairbairn (1952, 1954) developed his theory of the mind based on the establishment of "endopsychic structures" that result from the internalization of fantasied interactions between self and object. It was Fairbairn who coined the term *object relations theory*. Fairbairn stressed that the individual is primarily object-seeking rather than pleasure-seeking (drive oriented); in addition, his three basic endogenous structures are all "ego structures" (in distinction from the ego, id, and superego of Freud's structural theory). Working within the same Kleinian tradition, Winnicott (1945, 1950, 1951) proposed a theory of object relations, particularly the development of object relations that describes the development of the infant's sense of self, his way of relating to others, and his sense of reality, all in relation to the mother. Indeed, Winnicott's famous sentence "There is no baby without the mother" was the starting point for the development of relational psychoanalysis. In contemporary psychoanalysis, modern Kleinian theorists have emphasized the development of symbol formation, cognitive functions, and the relationship to reality (Segal, 1957; Bion, 1967). Bion's (1962a) work extending the concept of projective identification in his concepts of the container/contained has been especially influential. Kohut (1971, 1977) also was greatly influenced by Winnicott in the development of his self psychology, which is based on the development of the self in relation to selfobject functions provided by caretakers. However, self psychology is not generally classified as an object relations theory.

Several analysts made efforts to integrate object relations theory with other schools of thought. For example, in his concept of the representational world, J. Sandler (1976b, 1987a, 1987b) attempted to integrate object relations theory with the concepts of ego psychology. Kernberg wrote extensively with the aim of synthesizing object relations and ego psychological perspectives, arguing that both character and character pathology are the result of the structuring effect of internalized object relations. Both Kernberg and Sandler were interested in integrating psychoanalysis with the rest of mind science. Greenberg and Mitchell (1983) attempted to integrate objects relations theory with interpersonal, intersubjectivist, and relational points of view.

Westen and others attempted to integrate object relations theory with aspects of attachment theory, social psychology, and cognitive neuroscience (Blatt and Lerner, 1983; Westen, 1990b, 1991b; Calabrese, Farber, and Westen, 2005). In addition, there have been several attempts to operationalize concepts related to object relations for the purpose of empirical study using projective tests (Blatt et al., 1976; Westen, 1991a) and/or other kinds of rating scale, such as the Social Cognition and Object Relations

Scale (SCORS) (Westen, 1995; Porcerelli et al., 2005). There have been several attempts to study self and object representations in various kinds of psychopathology (Nigg et al., 1992). There have also been attempts to study the change in self and object representations with treatment (Bers et al., 1993; Blatt, Auerback, and Levy, 1997). Westen (1990b) has summarized empirical evidence that both supports and challenges several aspects of objects relations theories, concluding that: object relations is not a unitary phenomenon or developmental line but rather a broad rubric encompassing a large number of cognitive, affective, and motivational processes that are interdependent but distinct in their functions and developmental trajectories; unidimensional stage descriptions are inadequate in accounting for the richness of the data about object relations; object relational development is best understood in terms of multiple interacting but discrete developmental lines, such as complexity of representations, understanding of social causality, and capacity for emotional investment in relationships; object relations pathology has multiple etiologies, including biological and environmental factors.

Observing Ego is the aspect of conscious mental functioning that mediates the capacity for self reflection. Observing ego function is necessary for many aspects of everyday psychic functioning, including learning and moral functioning, both of which depend on self monitoring and self evaluation. It is also necessary for a patient's effective participation in a psychoanalytic treatment, contributing to introspection and insight. In normal states of consciousness, an individual is relatively aware of his conscious experience and his reactions to it. Self reflection is diminished but not entirely abolished during experiences such as daydreaming and fantasizing. Strong wishes or feelings and peremptory needs also interfere with the function of observing ego, as can intoxication, fatigue, and hypnosis. Impairments of observing ego contribute to disorders characterized by dissociation, such as depersonalization, posttraumatic disorders, and identity disturbances; they also contribute to failures in reality testing ranging from denial to psychosis. On the other hand, excessive self observation can acquire pathological intensity, for example in ongoing feelings of self consciousness and shame, hypochondriasis, and delusions of observation and persecution.

Although the term *observing ego* refers to a function at a high level of abstraction, which likely combines several aspects of mental functioning, there has been little discussion or controversy about its specificity. Freud (1914e, 1917c) was certainly aware that the mind is capable of observing itself, describing this feature as central to the functioning of the "critical agency," which later became the superego. The concept of the observing ego itself was first used by Fenichel (1938a), during the early phase of ego psychology, in a discussion of the analysis of patients whose conflicts were not expressed in disturbing symptoms but were embedded in their character and therefore experienced as untroubling (ego-syntonic) aspects of the self. The challenge for the analyst is to demonstrate to the patient's observing ego, or "reasonable ego," the conflicts expressed within the "experiencing ego." Fenichel used the term *observing ego* to clarify the apparent paradox of the ego's dual role in the facilitation of self knowledge and in the prevention of self knowledge by repression. Sterba (1934) had earlier described this same division in ego functioning as a "therapeutic dissociation" in the ego. In the treatment situation, it is expected that observing ego may be transiently impaired under conditions of high affect intensity, such as the experience of transference. The capacity to reinstate observing ego contributes to the patient's therapeutic alliance (Zetzel, 1956), or working alliance (Greenson and Wexler, 1969). For analysts working within the close-process-attention model, the development of a more effective observing ego is a central goal of psychoanalysis (F. Busch, 1996).

From the point of view of developmental psychoanalysis, D. N. Stern (2005) has argued that self-reflective consciousness has its origins in social interaction, which contributes to the "second point of view" necessary for self observation. Fonagy et al. (2002) have studied an aspect of the development of observing ego that they have named mentalization and/or reflective function (RF), which denotes the understanding of one's own as well as another's behavior in mental-state terms. They have developed a method for evaluating reflective function (RF) from M. Main's Adult Attachment Interview (AAI) (George, Kaplan, and Main, 1985; Fonagy and Target, 1998). Recently, this method of evaluation has been computerized (Fertuck et al., 2004) and has been used to study changes in reflective function in psychoanalytic psychotherapy, especially in borderline patients treated with Transference Focused Psychotherapy (K. Levy et al., 2006).

Obsession is an intrusive and persistent idea, thought, image, or sensation that a person cannot avoid even though it creates significant distress. Typical obsessions include fears of loss of control or contamination, worry about whether things are in proper order, doubts about whether one has behaved responsibly, or images involving violent or sexual acts. Obsessive ideas must be distinguished from delusions, which are fixed, false beliefs that are not recognized as unreasonable. They must also be distinguished from more normal preoccupations that might, in common parlance, be called "obsessions" (for example, with a love object or a favorite pastime). A **compulsion** is a repetitive, excessive, seemingly meaningless activity or mental exercise that a person feels compelled to perform, often to ward off distress or worry. Examples of compulsive behaviors are hand washing, checking whether a stove is turned off, and rearranging items in a set order. Examples of compulsive mental acts are counting or repeating specific words. Someone may be diagnosed with **obsessional neurosis** (or **obsessive-compulsive disorder**) if his obsessions or compulsions take up large amounts of time or cause significant distress. This disorder is quite common in latency-age children. **Obsessive-compulsive character** (or personality) is a long-standing pattern of insistence on control, orderliness, and perfection, accompanied by rigid efforts to control emotion and an overly intellectualized approach to life. The interpersonal life of the obsessional is beset with struggles over power and control. Obsessive-compulsive character may or may not include obsessional symptoms; it also ranges along a spectrum from a relatively healthy person whose **obsessional character traits** or **obsessional defenses** may lead him to excel in fields that demand conscientiousness and attention to detail, to a seriously impaired person whose rigid obsessionality merges with paranoia.

Obsessions and/or compulsions play an important role in the history of psychoanalysis. Early on, Freud (1894c, 1896c) recognized obsessional psychopathology as similar in structure to hysteria, in other words, as representing the symbolic expression of repressed unconscious conflict; he included both disorders among his first descriptions of the neuropsychoses of defense. His investigations of obsessional neurosis contributed to the development of core concepts such as compromise, unconscious guilt, aggression, ambivalence, and pregenital sexuality (most specifically, anality). They also led to early descriptions of new defenses beyond repression, including reaction formation, displacement, regression, undoing, and isolation. Freud's observations of obsessional personality traits, in the form of what he called "anal character," opened the door to the psychoanalytic study of character. Finally, all obsessional psychopathology illustrates how cognitive processes can be recruited for the management of psychological conflict.

Descriptions of patients with obsessions and/or compulsions have been reported since the fifteenth century in religious and psychiatric literature, and the English word *obsession,* in the sense of a fixed idea, goes back at least to the seventeenth century. The term *obsessional idea* was introduced by Von Krafft-Ebing in 1867. The concept (and the term) obsessional neurosis, however, originated with Freud (1894c) in his early work on the structure of the neuropsychoses of defense and their relation to sexuality. Freud hypothesized that in obsessional neurosis, the repressed idea (or memory) is replaced with a seemingly meaningless idea or action, while the distressing affect (usually anxiety or remorse) remains conscious (in contrast to hysteria, where the affect associated with a repressed idea is converted into somatic symptoms). In this early period, dominated by his seduction hypothesis, Freud (1894c, 1896c) argued that obsessional neurosis results from an early and traumatic active sexual experience (in contrast to hysteria, which results from a traumatic passive sexual experience).

A decade later, after abandoning the seduction theory, Freud returned to the subject of obsessional neurosis, finding its origin now in the conflict between the temptation associated with repressed instinctual urges and the "special conscientiousness," which, through a process of reaction formation, has been created to defend against these urges. Every obsession and/or compulsion, then, is a compromise between urge and defense. Freud (1907b) went on to compare the neurotic ceremonials of the obsessional to the sacred acts of religious ritual. He (1909d) also went on to link obsessional symptoms to both sadistic fantasy and ambivalence and, finally, to the influence of (newly described) pregenital, specifically anal-sadistic libidinal strivings (Freud, 1913d), also described by Jones (1918a). During this same period, Freud made his first observations of an anal character type with the traits of orderliness, parsimony, and obstinacy, associated with a history of struggles during toilet training. Ultimately, in Freud's (1908b, 1913d) classical formulation, both obsessional neurosis and obsessional (or anal) character traits reflect fixation to anal-phase libidinal strivings, and regression from frightening oedipal strivings; activated anal wishes are then defended against with reaction formation, undoing, and isolation. Predisposed individuals are those with strong biological propensity to what Freud called "anal erotogenicity." Symptoms reflect the "return of the repressed" in those whose defenses are relatively unsuccessful.

Post-Freudian analysts interested in either obsessional neurosis or obsessional character have elaborated on: the vicissitudes of anal libido expressed in struggles with dirt, money, and time (Jones, 1918b; Abraham, 1921); ego defenses, such as those noted above, along with magical thinking and intellectualization (A. Freud, 1936); conflict-free aspects of ego functioning, such as rigid cognitive style (Horowitz, 1977; D. Shapiro, 1965); harsh and punitive superego functioning, often referred to as "sphincter morality" (Ferenczi, 1925); object relations characterized by conflicts over aggression, ambivalence, and dependency; and interpersonal relationships characterized by power struggles (MacKinnon and Michels, 1971). Developmental theorists have emphasized: the role of parental attitudes toward aggression, impulse control, and emotional expression; the quality of mother-infant interactions; and the experience of toilet training (D. Levy, 1956; A. Freud, 1966). Child analysts, who see a high incidence of obsessional symptoms in children, have noted the close association between the development of obsessional character traits and the latency phase of development.

In the psychiatric literature, the term *neurosis* was replaced by the term *disorder* in 1981. Indeed, the *Diagnostic and Statistical Manual of Mental Disorders* (American Psychiatry Association, 1981) and the *Psychodynamic Diagnostic Manual* (PDM Task Force, 2006) include both obsessive-compulsive personality disorder and obsessive-compulsive symptom disorders (OCD) in adults and children. For the most part, advances in understanding the neurobiological basis for OCD and the success of biological and/or nonpsychodynamic psychotherapy treatments for the disorder dominate the literature on obsessions and compulsions in the broader field of mental health. However, psychoanalysts in clinical practice continue to confront obsessional character traits and obsessional defenses as part of many analyses.

Oedipus Complex is the universal constellation in both genders of related conflicts, identifications, fantasies, and object relations that emerge between three and six years of age, at the height of the infantile genital phase of psychosexual development. The hallmark of **oedipal conflict** is that it arises from a triadic relationship; it consists of the complex web of love and hate, desire and jealousy, disappointment and hope that arises in the context of the child's relationship to two parents (real or imagined). It transcends the simple problem of wishing for the affection and admiration of a single parent without regard for the rival. The latter is considered preoedipal, dyadic, and narcissistic (Edgcumbe and Burgner, 1975). Oedipal conflict is more complex, inevitably involves ambivalence, and contains passionate sexual desire. It arises from the wish for sex-

ual union and the love of one parent with the concomitant jealousy and the wish to be rid of the other, also-beloved parent. The child desires to be the primary if not the sole recipient of the love of the coveted parent, and fears retaliation from the rival parent who may become aware of the child's jealousy and murderous wishes. These fears, known as the castration complex, are usually experienced in terms of bodily injury, especially castration anxiety in boys and genital injury in girls. These fears are also experienced in terms of loss of love and loss of the object, which are fears that derive from earlier stages of development. Sexual wishes for the opposite-sex parent, with hatred and fear of the same-sex parent, is called the **positive oedipus complex**, while sexual longings for the parent of the same sex with concomitant hate and fear of the opposite sex parent is called the **negative oedipus complex**. As they inevitably coexist, with varying intensities, the child experiences ambivalence of desires and fears toward each parent. However, in heterosexual development, the positive oedipus complex dominates this psychosexual stage; its progressive resolution leads to identification with the person and the ideals of the same-sex parent, facilitating the consolidation of the superego, sexual orientation, and gender identity. In homosexual development, the opposite constellations prevail. The child's relationship with both parents is both preserved and deepened.

Freud's discovery of the universality of the oedipus complex with its profound impact on psychological development is considered one of his major contributions, along with infantile sexuality and unconscious conflict. In classical psychoanalytic thinking, the oedipus complex was considered the nuclear reorganizer of the psyche, since it leaves in its wake the superego and thereby contributes to the definitive shape of the adult mind (Tolpin, 1970; T. Shapiro, 1977; Simon, 1991). As a consequence, the exploration and resolution of these conflicts were seen as the sine qua non of clinical psychoanalytic work. Such views have been modified so that conflicts from all developmental phases are seen as overlapping and contributing to any individual's dynamics and character development. Nonetheless, the complex link between superego development and oedipal resolution guarantees the importance of the oedipus complex in the view of many psychoanalytic theorists. The formation of the superego is essential not only to the growth of the individual but to society as a whole; the child internalizes the morals of important adults in his immediate family, who in turn sustain the standards of the surrounding culture. In other psychoanalytic theories the oedipus complex is considered central to the child's development and adult life but is not considered the fundamental core of personality and psychopathology. Those psychoanalytic theories that do not privilege the oedipus complex as an important organizer of the human psyche generally do acknowledge the triangulation process as a critical developmental attainment. In that process, the child's object relations advance to incorporate a complex ambivalent relationship to two other important persons, which includes the awareness of their relationship to each other.

Freud first formulated the oedipus complex in 1897 through his self analysis in the year following his father's death, positing it as the universal psychological experience of childhood and naming it for the classical myth of Oedipus Rex as rendered by Sophocles. Freud (1897f) first wrote of this theory in his correspondence with Fliess, and he (1900) first published this thesis in "The Interpretation of Dreams." Freud developed his theory of the oedipus complex while struggling with inconsistencies in his seduction theory of neurosis and posited its role in the genesis of neurosis. Freud (1923a, 1924b, 1925b) identified the **dissolution of the oedipus complex** as both a developmental and intrapsychic concept that described the fate of the oedipus complex as it succumbs to repression and identification in the mind of the child, results in the formation of the superego, and ushers in the developmental stage of latency. Freud posited that oedipal conflict reaches its full intensity during the years from three to five, and then fades or dissolves for maturational, intrapsychic, and social reasons. It leaves in its place the **oedipal constellation**, which persists in the unconscious as the psychic organizer of mental life. The sequence of this dissolution was described by Freud (1924b) as follows: As a result of oedipal disappointment, frustration, and fears (fear of castration, loss of the object, or loss of love), boys and girls abandon their incestuous desires and ambitions regarding their parents. The object-cathexes of both parents are then given up and replaced by identifications. Sexual desire for the parent is transformed into affectionate impulses and is also sublimated. Idealizations of the parents are transformed into an ego ideal, while guilt and fear of parental punishment become depersonified and structuralized in the formation of the superego, considered the "heir of the oedipus complex." However, Freud (1925b) also delineated different tasks for each gender in typical heterosexual development: The boy shifts his identifications from his mother to his father, while the girl's task is to change her primary love object from her mother to her father. The boy, in the grip of castration anxiety from actual or imagined threats to his penis, relinquishes his sexual yearning for his mother and

identifies with his father, internalizing the father's morals and ideals to consolidate his superego. For the girl, recognition of genital difference leads to disappointment and deflation; she blames her mother for her "castrated state." For her, the oedipus complex is the sequelae of this initial blow; she turns to her father and (indirect) possession of his penis for consolation and then wishes for his baby as further compensation. In this way the girl changes love objects from mother to father, however, the impetus for the girl's renunciation of oedipal desires is never so complete and thorough as the boy's. Her conviction of castration and penis envy leads her into oedipal conflict, and its repression is only achieved through her struggle to come to terms with her father's preference for her mother. Thus, her internalization of her mother's morals and ideals occurs under little urgency and pressure, and her superego consolidation is compromised. For both genders, the state of latency that follows is a moratorium from the pressure of the drives until full genital organization is reached after puberty. Oedipal impulses remain primarily unconscious. However, depending on the extent of the dissolution and the nature of current life events that can trigger these impulses, the oedipal complex and its remnants (**oedipal situation**) can be recognized in behavior, attitudes, object relationships and object choice, character structure, sexual identity, fantasy formation, and later sexual patterns and preferences in the adult.

New findings have affected our thinking about the origins of oedipal conflict and the emergence of its legacy, the superego. The oedipal phase was seen as ushered in by a biologically based upsurge of genital excitation, curiosity, and erotic desire for one or the other parent. The residual repressed oedipal constellation was thought to form the basis for the "central masturbation fantasy," which determines the specific requirements for sexual arousal (Laufer, 1976). It is now understood that while it may be possible to link conditions for sexual arousal to the features of the oedipal configuration, these accrue not only from all prior development but also from a hypothesized biological substrate. Human sexuality is now conceived of in much more inclusive terms, including behavioral genetics, psychoneuroendocrinology, and research occurring outside the domain of psychoanalysis (R. Friedman and Downey, 2004).

It is now recognized that cognitive growth, an increased capacity for object relatedness, and the general expansion of affect range and tolerance, especially tolerance of ambivalence and the experience of guilt, are important contributors to the emergence of the oedipal phase and are essential for oedipal resolution and superego formation. Many psychoanalytic authors believe that the oedipus complex and the structure of the superego are subject to maturational modification until adulthood and are not entirely completed at five or six years old. Others believe resolution of the oedipus complex is not as complete as Freud originally suggested. Loewald (1979), for example, wrote of the "waning of the oedipus complex," rather than of its dissolution. He argued that the oedipus complex is not destroyed but returns and requires repeated repression, internalization, transformation, and sublimation. Other theorists view Loewald's vision of the oedipus complex as driven by the child's need for separation and the development of autonomy (Chodorow, 2003; Ogden, 2006). The child atones for the oedipal parricide by internalizing the parents, which results in the formation of the superego, the essence of which, according to Loewald, is responsibility to oneself. Holder (1982) posited revisions to Freud's concept, based on a review of indexed child analytic cases at the Hampstead Clinic. He suggested that superego development and functioning begins before the phallic-oedipal stage, that evidence of intrapsychic oedipal conflict continues to be found in quite a number of latency-aged children, and that the resolution of the oedipus complex does not seem to be a precondition for the development of fully structured, relatively autonomous superego functioning.

Gender differences in oedipal conflict have been revised in light of current thinking. Psychoanalytically informed child observation has demonstrated that the oedipal sequence for the girl can show many variations. For example, the wish for a baby can usher in the complex rather than serve as consolation (Parens et al., 1976; Parens, 1990). Recent literature on the female superego demonstrates that the female superego is different but in no way inferior to the male (D. Bernstein, 1983). Penis envy, while certainly seen in some adult women, is now understood to be the result of early deprivation and/or defenses against normal female genital drives and fantasies (Frenkel, 1996). Castration anxiety is still considered an essential motivation for the resolution of the oedipus complex in boys. However, contemporary theory suggests that for boys and girls, the love and protection of both parents remain important contributors to the initiation and resolution of both positive and negative oedipal conflicts. Finally, current thinking about normal homosexual development has led to a rethinking about oedipal conflict and the potential for the so-called negative oedipal conflict to be the primary configuration, based on a homosexual predisposition (Auchincloss and Vaughan, 2001).

The concept of **oedipal victory**, or oedipal triumph, has been described, which may occur in fantasy or reality, and is recognized as tragedy, as it was in the tragedy of Sophocles' Oedipus Rex. The tragedy is seen in the consequent disturbances in personality development, with unmitigated narcissism, distortions in reality sense, disturbances in sexual function and object choice, inhibitions in achievement of any sort, and incomplete coalescence and consolidation of the superego.

Klein (1945) offered a different formulation of the oedipus complex. In her view, it emerges in a primitive form in the first year of life and, in ideal circumstances, matures in early childhood to the version described in Freud's formulation. The primitive early oedipus complex is configured around part objects—the breast and penis—about which the infant has innate awareness. Because libido is fused with aggression, and primitive defense mechanisms of projection, introjection, and splitting predominate, the infant separates his part objects into good and bad, projects aggression, and reintrojects the aggressive bad object that forms the superego, making him vulnerable to persecutory anxiety and unable to contain and integrate ambivalence. If aggression is not overwhelming, the superego can facilitate the movement toward the depressive position, where love and guilt toward whole objects gains ascendance.

In the self psychology view of oedipal development, if the child enters the oedipal phase with a firm self, it is the caretakers' responses to the child's oedipal passions that play the decisive role in the outcome of the oedipal phase. The parents' aim-inhibited counteraggression to the child's competitiveness, and their aim-inhibited responses to the child's sexual assertions are crucially amalgamated with their pride and joy in the child's developmental achievements expressed by his vigor and self assertion. The child must be able to reliably idealize both the same-sex parent and the opposite-sex parent and to elicit optimal mirroring for his budding capacity to vigorously compete and to have his sexual, affectionate, and competitive feelings validated. The child's unconscious use of his caregivers to elicit optimal selfobject responsiveness for these developmental needs will result in a strengthening of a self that has the capacity to enthusiastically pursue love interests and passions, realistically contend with others, and experience pleasure in sexual desire. If the oedipal selfobject needs are not optimally met and optimally frustrated, the child cannot successfully traverse the oedipal phase and develops an oedipus complex. Disappointments in the same-sex parent during the oedipal phase of development may be pathogenic and result in deficits in the pole of ideals in the bipolar self and, more specifically, to a sense of shame and inferiority around one's sense of being masculine or feminine. Unmet idealizing needs during this period can lead to sexualized yearnings to merge with and to be admired by the same-sex parent. Self psychology conceptualizes the negative oedipus complex as a deficit in the idealization of the same-gendered parent that leads to homoerotic incestuous yearning (A. Ornstein, 1983).

Omnipotence refers to the fantasy of power with no limits, or "all power." As a psychoanalytic concept, omnipotence has been used to describe: 1) a fantasy about self and object; 2) a mechanism of defense; 3) an element of a pathological psychic structure (the pathological grandiose self; and 4) in self psychology, a characteristic of the normal infantile grandiose self that contributes to the development of healthy self esteem.

Freud (1909d) first discussed omnipotence in reference to the Rat Man's belief in the power of his own thoughts. Freud credits the Rat Man himself with the first use of the word *omnipotence* in this way. Thereafter, Freud associated omnipotence of thoughts with obsessional neurosis. In "Totem and Taboo," Freud (1913e) used the word *omnipotence* to describe a characteristic of thinking in infants and in primitive cultures. Omnipotent thinking lies behind the animistic mode of thought in early human societies. It also contributes to creativity and art as well as to the thinking of all neurotics. Freud linked omnipotence of thought to his new concept of narcissism, describing it as the "libidinal hypercathexis of thinking." In his paper "On Narcissism," Freud (1914e) described how the developing ego attempts to regain powerful aspects of the original narcissistic state by fulfilling the demands of the ego ideal; this effort to recapture lost narcissism is accomplished, in part, by the confirmation of one's omnipotence by experience. Freud (1919d) also described how uncanny experience results, in part, from the sensation that the infantile belief in the omnipotence of thoughts seems plausible once again.

Ferenczi (1913/1952) added to Freud's ideas about omnipotence by describing how the child develops a sense of reality through retaining some feeling of omnipotence throughout development. To the extent that the infant has his omnipotence affirmed by optimally responsive caretakers, he experiences mastery over his environment and begins to perceive reality with greater accuracy. In this model, omnipotence is not relinquished but rather modi-

fied, leading to an increasing ability to know what is real.

Klein (1935) elaborated on Freud's ideas about omnipotence in her formulations of infantile mental life, describing how "phantasies" of omnipotence play a role in what she called the "manic defense" against the anxieties of the depressive position. Phantasies of total control soon became referred to as **omnipotent control** (Riviere, 1936). Klein (1946) later described how, during the paranoid-schizoid position, in order to defend against overwhelming anxiety, the infant splits the object into all-good and all-bad aspects with the aim of protecting good experience from aggression. As part of this split, the infant idealizes the good object, which is imagined to be omnipotent; he also maintains a phantasy that he has the power for omnipotent annihilation of the bad, persecutory object. Working within the Kleinian framework, Rosenfeld (1971a, 1971b) later described the role played by omnipotent control in narcissistic object relations. The object, or part object (usually the breast), may be omnipotently incorporated and treated as the infant's possession; or the mother (or breast) may be used as a container into which unwanted parts of the self are omnipotently projected.

A normal phase of childhood in which either the self and/or important others are experienced as omnipotent has been viewed as developmentally crucial in a variety of ways by a range of other psychoanalytic theorists. For example, Winnicott (1965), following Freud's, Klein's, and Ferenczi's view that omnipotence is an important feature of the infant's experience, introduced the concept of the transitional space as a way to think about how omnipotence is given up in development. In his discovery of the first "not-me possession," the infant believes he has created the object. This omnipotence is not questioned by the "good enough mother"; the infant is permitted this illusion. In the course of development, the mother incrementally disappoints the infant, resulting in disillusionment. In this context, the infant's omnipotence is modified to better perceive reality but not relinquished, as it remains a potential source of creativity throughout life.

Fenichel (1945), following the ideas of Freud and Ferenczi, regarded self esteem as the expression of nearness to or distance from the infantile feeling of omnipotence. In a similar vein, A. Reich (1954) described how, through identification with the aggrandized object, omnipotence can be attained for oneself. The overvaluation of the object serves as a detour to obtain otherwise unreachable magnificence for the ego. Jacobson (1964) also described the preoedipal child's belief and participation in his parents' omnipotence. As ego development proceeds, a sense of pride and strength in one's own real accomplishments begins to replace early omnipotent fantasies. Mahler (1975), studying the development of basic moods, described feelings of grandeur and omnipotence in the practicing subphase, which are punctured by the toddler's repeated experience of helplessness, leading to the rapprochement crisis.

The omnipotent object plays a crucial role in Kohut's theory of normal narcissistic development. Kohut (1970/1978, 1971, 1977, 1984) posited two major psychic configurations—the grandiose self and the omnipotent object—as central in the development of healthy narcissism. The omnipotent object is the basis of what he calls the idealized parent imago, a narcissistically invested image of the parent as the source of power, joy, and perfection. The young child needs to feel a continuous connection with this omnipotent, idealized object in order to feel strong and resilient. In analysis, the idealized parent imago is reactivated in the transference, which Kohut called the idealizing transference. In the course of optimal development, the omnipotent object plays a transitional role in the development of a sense of efficacy. In narcissistic personality disorders, a strong need for merger with omnipotent selfobjects is maintained, and in psychotic disorders, the omnipotent internal object may be delusionally experienced as persecuting or controlling.

Kernberg (1975, 1984, 1995) drew from the work of Klein, Rosenfeld, A. Reich, Jacobson, Mahler, and others in his conceptualization of omnipotence and omnipotent control in various kinds of psychopathology. Kernberg viewed omnipotence and the related idealization and devaluation as derivatives of the defense of splitting, crucial in early development to protect the self from projected aggression. A fantasy of omnipotence is translated into omnipotent control of the object through projective identification, whereby intolerable elements of the self are projected into an object, which then must be controlled. Kernberg views this defensive constellation as important in the development of narcissistic personality disorder and in the psychopathology of hatred. The phantasy of omnipotence and the defense of omnipotent control help to maintain a pathological psychic structure, the pathologic grandiose self, which forms the basis for the narcissistic personality disorder.

One-Person/Two-Person Psychology: see COUN-TERTRANSFERENCE, ENACTMENT, INTERPERSONAL PSYCHOANALYSIS, INTERSUBJECTIVITY, OBJECT, RELATIONAL PSYCHOANALYSIS, THERAPEUTIC ACTION, TRANSFERENCE

Optimal Frustration/Optimal Responsiveness: see SELF PSYCHOLOGY, THERAPEUTIC ACTION

Orality is a comprehensive term for all psychic interests, activities, fantasies, conflicts, and mental mechanisms that derive from the **oral phase** of psychosexual development, which occurs during the first eighteen months of life. Oral themes are typically organized around the most primary and basic aspects of emotional experience: hunger, satisfaction, attachment, and dependency. According to Freud's theory of psychosexual development, the infant's earliest feelings of pleasure, and manifestations of aggression, originate in the upper digestive tract, also known as the **oral zone**. States of psychic excitation and tension arising in the oral zone are conceptualized as resulting from psychic forces known as the **oral drives**. Although the role of the oral zone diminishes as subsequent developmental phases emerge, orality persists in its effect on personality, and derivatives of oral themes are universal in all analyses. While the classification of character types based upon psychosexual phases is now considered reductionistic, when issues of dependency and neediness or other **oral conflicts** predominate in an individual's total makeup, the designation of **oral character** is still sometimes used.

While the concept of orality is often dismissed as a vestige of early drive theory, its importance in psychoanalysis remains as a universal organizing motif of unconscious fantasy. Historically, interest in orality has stimulated explorations in early infant development, mood disorders, character, and mental processes of internalization. However, at times, interest in orality has contributed to the erroneous attribution of adult psychic content to a particular early phase of development, an example of psychoanalytic genetic fallacy. From a contemporary perspective, the persistence of oral themes in the adult patient is understood as a compromise formation serving multiple functions, which has been reworked in the face of ongoing developmental challenges and mental structure building.

Freud's (1897b) first reference to the oral sexual zone is in his correspondence with Fleiss in which he described it as a region whose sexual significance is normally extinguished by adulthood but may persist in pathological states, such as perversion. Freud's (1905b) drive-based theory of psychosexual development is more fully elaborated in "Three Essays on the Theory of Sexuality," in which he described the oral zone as the first erotogenic zone, whose stimulation through the ingestion of food produces a pleasurable experience of satisfaction. Freud also explained that this link between oral ingestion and pleasurable satisfaction establishes the prototype for mental processes of internalization that persist into adult life in both normal and pathological forms. Linking psychosexual stage to the development of object relations, Abraham (1916, 1924a, 1924c) divided the oral stage into a "pre-ambivalent" auto-erotic phase, followed by a "cannibalistic" ambivalent stage, during which **oral aggression** plays a more prominent role. He described the underlying **oral incorporative fantasy** as the wish to devour the love object. Abraham also described the fixation to **oral erotism** (which he attributes to overindulgence or deprivation during the oral phase), evident in the unconscious fantasies of some neurotics, and its contribution to the formation of the oral character, marked by **oral traits**, such as demandingness, compulsive talking, and acquisitiveness.

The relationship of orality to mood disorders has a long and complex history. Some analysts have argued that oral conflicts predispose to both depression and mania, and many analysts have cited the preponderance of oral themes in the dreams, fantasies, and characters of depressed patients. Furthermore, according to Freud and others (Abraham, 1911; Freud, 1917c; Rado, 1928), the structure of melancholia involves introjection of a lost love object, a mental process that may be linked to an unconscious fantasy of oral ingestion. D. Milrod (1988) challenged the view that orality predisposes to depression, arguing that the prominent orality of depressed individuals represents a desperate effort to restore self esteem by obtaining needed narcissistic supplies. B. Lewin (1950) posited an **oral triad**, a trio of wishes or fantasies that originate during the oral phase and persist in the unconscious, which include the wish to eat, to sleep, and to be eaten. He asserted that mania is a dreamlike state in which reality is denied and conflict over two aspects of the oral triad predominate, the wish to sleep and the wish to be eaten.

Overdetermination: see COMPROMISE FORMATION, MULTIPLE DETERMINATION

P

Parameter is a conscious and deliberate therapeutic intervention that departs from an analyst's usual stance or technique. Originally a mathematical term, in ordinary usage, a parameter is a factor that limits or determines a range of variation. Modifications in technique over a wide range of an analyst's actions might be considered parameters: the relative activity of the analyst, the analyst's self disclosure, fee arrangements, or any change in the usual freedoms and constraints of the analytic situation. A parameter differs from an enactment, which refers to the analyst's unconscious participation in the transference/countertransference dialogue. First used by K. Eissler (1953) in a psychoanalytic context, he contrasted the "parameter of a technique" with interpretation, the "model technique" of psychoanalysis. Parameters, or noninterpretive interventions, were to be used only in specified circumstances, for a limited time, and were not to prevent a return to the "model technique." Unfortunately, Eissler's usage carried a distinctly pejorative cast, and his unjustifiable theoretical and technical certainty was characteristic of some of the ego psychology literature for decades.

The historical shift from an analytic focus on warded-off wishes to ego functions, including defensive processes, became especially relevant as psychoanalysts attempted to treat patients with more severe psychopathology, a shift described by Stone (1954) as the "widening scope." However, in contrast to Eissler, Stone's attitude was nonpejorative, and he remained committed to the analysis of transference for patients with ego weakness or distortions. Stone argued that such patients required the warmth and flexibility of an analyst who could provide the support necessary to facilitate the analysis. The term *parameter* is used rarely in contemporary psychoanalytic literature, and when used, it is no longer connected to a conceptualization of technique in which interpretation is the only acceptable psychoanalytic intervention. Parameter may refer to a departure from the analyst's usual technical stance but does not have the negative connotation implicit in Eissler's use, nor is it necessarily linked to the specific constraints listed by Eissler.

Paranoia is an unfounded or exaggerated distrust of others. Individuals with paranoia suspect the motives of those around them and believe that certain individuals, or people in general, are "out to get them." Paranoia may reach delusional proportions and appears as a feature of many different mental illnesses, including depression, mania, schizophrenia, toxic syndromes, dementia, and delirium. At the same time, **paranoid** thoughts and feelings can appear in any situation that evokes extreme feelings of helplessness, humiliation, and/or vulnerability. Psychoanalytic approaches to paranoia focus on the underlying psychodynamics in all paranoid states of mind. Unfortunately, the psychoanalytic literature has failed to clearly distinguish between paranoia and psychosis. In the clinical situation, analysts deal most often with patients who suffer from transient **paranoid ideation**, **paranoid personality traits**, or **paranoid personality disorder**, rather than patients with full-blown delusions. Individuals with paranoid personality disorder tend to be self referential and suspicious and to feel easily slighted. They relate to the world through hypervigilant scanning of the environment for clues that validate their biases. Paranoid personalities lead constricted emotional lives, characterized by difficulty achieving intimacy with others. Their romantic relationships are often made difficult by pathological jealousy. Full-blown paranoid personality disorder is among the most severe personality disorders, generally functioning at the level of borderline personality organization. Paradoxically, however, some degree of paranoid experience is probably part of every person's experience when under duress and, therefore, of every analysis.

The study of paranoia is important in the history of psychoanalysis in that, early on, Freud (1894c, 1896c) recognized some paranoid states of mind as similar in structure to hysteria, in other words, as representing the symbolic expression of repressed unconscious conflict. He included both paranoia and hysteria among his descriptions of the neuropsychoses of defense. In his study of paranoia, Freud first observed what he called "projection," the defense whereby forbidden or intolerable thoughts and feelings are attributed to others. The concept of projection opened the door for exploration of the interaction between defense, object relations, and interactions with other people. Ultimately, Klein (and others) recognized the potential for paranoid fears as a universal aspect of human psychology.

The word *paranoia* (from the Greek *para,* meaning "outside" and *nous,* meaning "mind"), has been used as far back as ancient Greece to mean "madness." The history of its use as a nosological term in modern mental health is complex, overlapping with the nosology for psychotic illnesses, of which paranoia is a frequent symptom. Irrespective of his views on paranoia as an illness category (which changed frequently and are mainly of historical interest), Freud's (1895a) initial view was that the purpose of paranoia is to "fend off an idea that is incompatible with the ego, by projecting its substance into the external world." In his early work on paranoia, Freud (1896a) also commented on the paranoid's propensity to hostility as well as to feelings of "mortification."

A decade later, Freud (1911a, 1922) returned to the subject of paranoia, finding its origin now more specifically in the vicissitudes of the homosexual component of libido. In his discussion of the Schreber case, he developed his well-known formula for paranoid ideation as a series of transformations of a homosexual wish: The thought/feeling "I love him" is transformed through repression and reaction formation into the thought/feeling "I hate him," which is then transformed through projection into the thought "He hates me." Variations in the formula result in erotomania, pathological jealousy, and/or megalomania, all of which Freud saw as expressions of paranoia. During this period, Freud also explored the origins of paranoia in fixation and/or regression to the narcissistic stage in the development of the libido, which, in his view, included homosexual object choice (or the choice of an object similar to the self). Throughout, Freud's theory of paranoia was closely related to his theory of psychosis (and/or delusions) in which there is a withdrawal of libido to the autoerotic stage of libidinal development, with paranoid delusions representing an "attempt at recovery," or effort to reestablish ties with the object world through paranoid fantasy.

For the remainder of his writing life, Freud's views of the origins of paranoia did not undergo substantial change. However, post-Freudian ego psychologists interested in paranoia had to contend with the observation that paranoid ideation does not always appear to be accompanied by unconscious homosexual strivings; at the same time, some overtly homosexual persons suffer from paranoia. Some theorists eager to preserve Freud's theory linking paranoia and repressed homosexual libido argued that paranoia results only from repressed passive, anal-sadistic homoerotic wishes (as opposed to all homosexual wishes) (Frosch, 1981). Other theorists focused on the paranoid's primary struggles with aggression, asserting that his intense need to be loved, often expressed in the fantasy of homosexual surrender, represents a wish for reassurance that aggression has not destroyed the object, or that the object does not wish to retaliate (Knight, 1940). Developmental theorists focused on experiences of shame, humiliation, and abuse (often sexual) in the childhood of people who become paranoid, leading to low self esteem, mistrust, and a need to control others (Niederland, 1951; Sullivan, 1953a, 1956b). H. Blum (1980a, 1981) argued that paranoid psychopathology cannot be explained solely on the basis of conflicts over either libidinal or aggressive drive derivatives. In his view, at the core of paranoid pathology are failures in the separation-individuation process resulting in a lack of object constancy. A response to this inability to maintain object constancy is the effort to maintain constant contact with the actual person. Later theorists have elaborated on the paranoid person's use of magical and concrete fantasies of connectedness to objects to deal with object inconstancy (Auchincloss and Weiss, 1992). Others have focused on conflict-free aspects of ego functioning, such as paranoid cognitive style (D. Shapiro, 1965). Still others have elaborated on the narcissistic function of paranoid fantasy with regard to stabilizing the self (A. M. Cooper, 1993b).

All post-Freudian theorizing about paranoid ideation reflects the influence of Klein (1935, 1946), who provided a basis for understanding paranoid fears as a universal aspect of the human condition. Impressed by the intensity of children's struggles with aggression, Klein began by describing persecutory or **paranoid anxieties** that result from the projection onto the mother of primitive sadism and aggression. The prevalence of this persecutory anxiety, aggravated by what she called the **paranoid vicious circle**, led Klein to posit a **paranoid position** (later, renamed **the paranoid-schizoid position**), the earliest organization of the psyche characterized by active splitting of good and bad aspects of internalized object relations, accompanied by violent projection (later, projective identification) of the bad. The paranoid position precedes the depressive position, which is characterized by anxiety over the fate of the whole, integrated, internalized good object in the face of one's own aggression (depressive anxiety). In Klein's view, the infantile paranoid position forms the basis for future paranoid psychopathology. However, in all persons, these two positions fluctuate with each other; retreat to the paranoid position often serves as a defense against intolerable depressive anxiety.

Psychiatry's *DSM* system clearly separates delusional paranoid disorders (listed on Axis I) from paranoid personality disorder (on Axis II). The *Psychodynamic Diagnostic Manual* (*PDM*) also separates paranoid personality disorder from psychotic disorders (PDM Task Force, 2006). In the broader field of mental health, the literature on paranoid psychoses is dominated by efforts to understand the neurobiological basis for these disorders. However, psychoanalysts in clinical practice continue to confront paranoid states of mind, paranoid character traits, and paranoid defenses as part of many analyses.

Paranoid Position/Paranoid-Schizoid Position: see FAIRBAIRN, KLEIN, OBJECT, PARANOIA, PROJECTIVE IDENTIFICATION, SPLITTING

Parapraxis, also known as a symptomatic act, is one of a number of cognitive or functional errors, such as slips of the tongue, forgetting of names or words, slips of the pen, or bungled actions.

Parapraxes have long been important in psychoanalysis as providing evidence for a dynamic unconscious mental life. Strachey coined the term *parapraxis* from a translation of Freud's *Fehlleistung*, meaning "faulty function." In "The Psychopathology of Everyday Life," Freud (1901) argued that such errors are not, as conventionally believed, accidental and meaningless (or, in the case of slips of the tongue, based on purely linguistic confusions) but rather are motivated events determined by unconscious conflicts (generally over sexual or aggressive wishes) and provoked by current "disturbing factors." As psychoanalytic theory developed, parapraxes, like all symptom formations, came to be seen as compromise formations that serve the multiple functions of wish, defense, and adaptation. Looking at parapraxes from the point of view of the unconscious, Lacan classified verbal slips and bungling acts as "successful acts" (Mahony, 1993). Although some linguists have been skeptical about Freud's contentions regarding slips of the tongue, there is some empirical research to support his views (Motley, 2002).

Parataxic Mode: see INTERPERSONAL PSYCHOANALYSIS

Participant Observation: see FREE ASSOCIATION, INTERPERSONAL PSYCHOANALYSIS, TRANSFERENCE

Pathological Defenses of Infancy are protective behaviors and states observed in infants and toddlers who have experienced recurrent severe abuse, violence, neglect, and/or deprivation. The phrase is misleading, as the pathology lies not in the defense but rather in the attachment relationship with the maltreating caregiver who has failed in the nurturing and protective functions. These defenses help protect the infant from overwhelming affects of recurring unbearable pain and distress but are fragile and limited. As the defenses collapse, the infants frequently descend into states of extreme and frenzied disorganization and disintegration characterized by screaming and flailing, and ultimately into states of total exhaustion.

Pathological defenses of infancy as a concept is linked to a larger group of observational studies of infant attachment behavior. These behaviors are similar to those described by Spitz as hospitalism and anaclitic depression, which also involve the infant's catastrophic reactions to maternal deprivation or loss. While the psychoanalytic establishment initially rejected Bowlby's attachment theory, ideas about attachment, such as pathological defenses of infancy, have been more quietly within the psychoanalytic mainstream for decades.

Selma Fraiberg (1982) introduced the phrase "pathological defenses of infancy" to describe five groups of aberrant behaviors that she observed repeatedly in infants and toddlers who had been maltreated by their parents. They are understood to be behaviors and states rooted in primary psychobiological responses to danger and not as actual defense mechanisms, which are defined within a structural model that does not apply to infants. Infants of maltreating and depriving parents may use one, many, or all of these defenses in developmental sequence. Fraiberg was influenced by the work of Spitz (1961), who, based on his observation of institutionalized infants, proposed that inborn neurophysiologic functions are processed psychologically and later evolve into mechanisms of defense.

The five groups of defenses Fraiberg described are: 1) selective avoidance; observed by three months of age, every sensory and motor modality available is selectively utilized in the total or near-total avoidance of a parent or parents, but not other people; the infant does not gaze, smile at, or reach for the parent, and, once mobile, does not approach the parent for comfort, and may even run away or hide; 2) freezing; observed as early as five months of age, the infant becomes immobile and mute; it is speculated that intense psychophysiologic energy is required to maintain the frozen state; 3) fighting; emerging in the second year of life with the development of motor coordination and mobility, wild and flailing outbursts of fighting are triggered by the anticipation of danger; this defense precedes "identification with the aggressor" and is understood not only as a response to terror but also as a temporary means to keep at bay total helplessness and dissolution of the self; 4) transformation of affect; appearing between nine and sixteen months of age, giddy laughter is triggered by the anticipation of danger; related to this behavior is the infant's excited and apparently pleasurable participation in recurrent sadistic teasing by the caregiver; 5) reversal; the turning of physical aggression against the self is observed by Fraiberg as early as thirteen months of age, but is described by Spitz in infants as young as eight months of age.

Galenson (1986) described defensive aggression in infants arising from a variety of stimuli, including traumatic but lifesaving medical interventions and hospitalizations; extreme deprivation; and violence, chaos, and poverty in the social environment. Osofsky (1993) also confirmed the presence of these defenses in infants of adolescent mothers at high psychosocial risk. She argues for a dynamic interactional model that takes the entire social context into consideration. Hesse and Main (2000) described the odd, disoriented, and anomalous behaviors of a group of infants with disorganized attachment patterns whose behaviors include freezing and avoidance. They suggested that such behavior, as well as later psychopathology, is predictable when a primary attachment figure recurrently maltreats the infant.

Pathological Grief: see DEPRESSION, MOURNING

Penis Envy, or the **Masculinity Complex**, as it is sometimes called, is a girl or woman's feeling of discontent with her own genital equipment, often accompanied by an aggressive urge to identify with and take over the genital apparatus and imagined superior achievements and potency of the male. There may also be an unconscious fantasy/belief that her lack of a penis is due to the negligence or evil intent of her parents (usually the mother) or is a punishment for misconduct, usually for masturbation. The girl or woman may fantasize a hidden penis of her own. Penis envy, or the masculinity complex, may also manifest itself in learning inhibitions, self-defeating behavior in the workplace, and sexual inhibitions. Penis envy may be present in boys, who compare themselves with their fathers, and in adult men, who compare themselves with other men whose penises appear larger, more potent, and more perfect than their own. Contemporary psychoanalytic perspectives view penis envy as the manifest content of a complex compromise involving conflicts and narcissistic vulnerability derived from many sources and developmental levels.

The concept of penis envy is central to Freud's theory of female psychosexual development and to his view of the female character. While current psychoanalytic theories of female development accord penis envy a place in the girl's experience, it is generally viewed as arising in the context of her primary femininity, her own female genital anxieties, her own ways of masturbating, and a social context where males may be favored. Penis envy is no longer considered to be fundamental to feminine development or to be the "bedrock" of female psychology, as Freud had thought.

Freud (1908c) first mentioned the girl's envy of the penis in an early paper on the sexual theories of children, in which he argued that only the male genital is taken into account and that the vagina remains undiscovered by both sexes until adolescence. In his most extensive exploration of the role of penis envy, Freud (1925b) argued that the little girl is psychologically "a little man" until she notices the penis of her brother or playmate, a discovery that is momentous and life changing. The girl instantly perceives the deficiency of her own organ (the clitoris) and suffers a narcissistic wound that leaves her with a permanent sense of inferiority and a driving wish to obtain what she has been denied. Furthermore, according to Freud, it is penis envy that propels the girl into the oedipal phase. Depreciating her mother as penis-less like herself, and resenting her for her failure to give her a penis, she turns away from her mother to her father. She gives up her wish for a penis, replacing it with a wish for a child (the penis-baby equation); with this purpose in mind, she takes her father as a love object. In this way, Freud explained the redirection of the girl's libido from her mother, until now her primary love object, to her father, and the rivalry with the mother that characterizes the girl's oedipal situation. Whereas in boys the oedipus complex is destroyed by the fear of castration, in girls the oedipus complex is the result of the castration complex, which leads the girl to reject her mother for her father. In boys, fear of castration and identification with the father contribute to the formation of the superego. In Freud's view, because castration is a fait accompli for girls, the female superego can never be so "inexorable" and "independent of its emotional origins" as in the male superego. Finally, because of her feelings of inferiority and humiliation, the girl renounces clitoral masturbation and assumes a passive, receptive position with regard to sexuality; the renunciation of clitoral sensitivity paves the way for the cathexis of the vagina and true womanhood (a change in erogenous zone). Freud (1937a) regarded penis envy in women as "bedrock," and therefore never fully resolvable by psychoanalysis.

Horney (1924, 1926) quickly challenged Freud's argument that penis envy lies at the center of the female psyche, asserting views that have formed the foundation for current psychoanalytic theories of female psychology. She agreed that during the infantile period, when scopophilic and exhibitionistic instincts predominate, little girls do envy the boy's very real advantages. For example, the little girl's primary penis envy is focused on the boy's having an organ to show off, on his ability to direct the urinary stream, and the social permission accorded to males to touch themselves during urination (which is perceived by the girl as masturbation). However, Horney asserted that beyond the infantile period, the woman's sexual advantages are unmistakable. She rejected the notion that the woman's wish for and pleasure in motherhood was derived from or compensating for the lack of a penis. Horney also argued that the masculinity complex observable in adult women is a regressive neurotic position, a "flight from womanhood" in the face of oedipal anxieties, guilt, and disappointment.

Freud remained unmoved either by Horney's arguments or by the objections of others in his circle. However, over time, Freud's theory has been revised in the light of material drawn from both the psychoanalyses of women and direct child observation (Kleeman, 1976). A male developmental model for both sexes and a phallocentric bias in which female genitals are devalued are, for the most part, no longer accepted (H. Blum, 1996). One exception is Lacanian theory, which is organized around the phallus and the impact of the mother's "lack" on the girl's development. More typically, contemporary theorists such as W. Grossman and Stewart (1976) regarded penis envy not as universal in women but as a symptom that requires analysis, and one that may occur within the context of varying levels of psychopathology. For example, at the more severe end of the spectrum, it may come to represent a coalescence of narcissistic injuries within a narcissistic character disorder. At the neurotic end of the spectrum, it may represent a regression from oedipal-phase conflicts. Views of superego development in general have also been revised to include preoedipal precursors and to accord castration anxiety a minor role in the development of morality. Penis envy is not regarded as the impetus into the triadic phase.

Other contemporary writers have emphasized the distinction between the anatomical penis and the symbolic phallus in Freud's thinking (Fogel, 1998; Harris, 2005c; M. Diamond, 2006). The symbolic phallus may serve as a universal psychic construction representing power and potency, values that may be aspired to by both men and women.

Persephone Complex is an alternative formulation for the female oedipus complex, based on the ancient Greek myth of Persephone, which some psychoanalysts argue is a better elucidation of the typical dynamics, conflicts, and compromise solutions of the female triangular situation than the Oedipus myth (Kulish and Holtzman, 1998, 2008; Holtzman and Kulish, 2000). The Persephone myth illustrates the intense closeness of mother and daughter, the sexual danger for the girl in straying from her mother's protection, the girl's readiness and desire to enter into the heterosexual incestuous erotic relationship, and her need to maintain a relationship with her mother. It also encompasses the themes of menstruation, cyclical fertility, birth and rebirth, and other uniquely female vicissitudes of drives, object relations, and resolution through compromise. Many contemporary psychoanalysts argue that the girl's entry into the triangular stage does not require the change in erotic love object from mother to father, as originally theorized by Freud. The persephone complex demonstrates how the girl's identification with her mother contributes to the construction of her sense of female identity, her maternal desires, and her acceptance of female sexuality. It is consistent with contemporary perspectives on female development in which the woman revisits, reexamines, and resynthesizes representations of self-versus-mother and self-with-mother over her lifetime (P. Bernstein, 2004). The persephone complex also illustrates a defense frequently used by women, which is abdication of agency over her sexuality. Persephone depicts her sexual initiation as forced and forever keeps her sexuality hidden in the underworld, thereby avoiding the alienation of her mother upon whom she still depends. In this vein, Gilligan (1982) related the myth of Persephone to her research on contemporary female adolescents, in which she documented a loss of assertiveness and voice; and Krausz (1994) interpreted Persephone as portraying the voicelessness and invisibility of womanhood. For the feminist psychoanalyst Irigaray (1991), Demeter and Persephone represent femininity divided by patriarchy. Jung (1921/1957) suggested that Demeter and Persephone are archetypal mother-daughter imagoes. Interestingly, Jung introduced the electra complex as an alternative formulation for the female oedipus complex, however it did not gain wide currency, as Freud regarded the oedipus complex as paradigmatic for both genders.

Personal Myth is a detailed, conscious autobiographical narrative of one's past that is highly valued and presented to oneself and others as comprehensive and complete. It serves to support a particular wished-for vision of the self and contains important defensive distortions. It can be a formidable resistance within an analysis. While E. Kris (1956a) originally coined the term to describe the self presentation of a specific and circumscribed set of individuals with a particular kind of developmental history and dynamics, its use has expanded to describe a larger set of clinical circumstances.

Kris described individuals who come to analysis with a seamless description of their childhood history, which they treat as a "treasured possession" and which they are extremely resistant to explore or modify in any way. Analysis of these "personal myths" reveals that they function as an extended screen memory, expressing disguised versions of early fantasy wishes (Freud, 1899a). At the same time, they defend against recollection of more traumatic aspects of the past. Kris proposed that patients who present this type of personal myth typically display analerotic character features and a history of precocious ego development, particularly with regard to memory function and fantasy life. They develop autobiographical "memory nuclei" at a time when fantasy and reality are still intermingled. As a relatively undisturbed preoedipal period is followed by oedipal-phase traumas, these patients fuse "memories" of the past with an early developing family romance fantasy (Freud, 1909a). As oedipal conflicts are revived in latency and adolescence, the personal myth, with its wish-fulfilling and defensive functions, crystallizes further.

Later analysts have suggested that personal myths are also seen in patients with predominantly preoedipal and narcissistic pathology (Lester, 1986; Baratis, 1988; Hartocollis and Graham, 1991). They have also proposed that this kind of mythification of one's past is a universal and not necessarily pathological process. Some analysts have taken issue with the view that analysis of the personal myth can uncover the "truth" about the past, arguing that the goal of analysis is to allow the patient to recognize the constant and inevitable myth-making ("mythopoetic") activity of the unconscious in both its defensive and creative aspects (Ellenberger, 1970; Potamianou, 1985).

Personality Typology: see JUNGIAN PSYCHOLOGY

Personification: see INTERPERSONAL PSYCHOANALYSIS

Perversion (from the Latin word meaning "to turn the wrong way") in traditional usage is sexual behavior that deviates from accepted norms. Synonyms for *perversion* include sexual deviation, sexual aberration, neosexuality (McDougall, 1995), and paraphilia (the term used in the *DSM* system in psychiatry). Typical examples of perversion include fetishism, voyeurism (scopophilia), exhibitionism, sadomasochism, bestiality, and pedophilia. In contemporary psychoanalysis, use of the term *perversion* is quite divided, with many eschewing the judgmental connotations of the word with its implication of a clear line between "normal" and "abnormal." Others feel that the term is worth preserving to describe expressions of sexuality that are qualitatively different and problematic relative to the "norm." Most analysts agree that extremely unusual and rigidly enacted sexual preferences should be called "perversion"; however, short of this, there is little agreement as to what should be called perverse, with varying emphasis on the extent of deviation from genital intercourse, on the rigidity of the behavior and/or the extent to which it is required for arousal, or on the nature of the underlying fantasy, psychodynamics, and/or object relations. All agree that perversion is on a continuum with "normal," with all sexuality including an element of the perverse. Certainly, usage of the term *perversion* has evolved to reflect changing social norms. For example, homosexuality is no longer considered among the perversions. In the last forty years, perversion has been used ever more loosely to describe aspects of character found in people who do not exhibit structured sexual perversions, as in: "**character perversion**," "**perverse defense**," "**transference/countertransference perversion**," "**perverse attitude**," or "**perverse modes of thought**." In some cases these states of mind are understood to be substitutes for sexual perversions; in other cases, they are conceptualized as reflecting defenses or attitudes similar to those found in sexual perversion, such as a disturbed relationship to reality, or the misuse of others (Arlow, 1971; L. Grossman, 1996; G. Reed, 1997; Coen, 1998; Zimmer, 2003; Purcell, 2006; Smith, 2006; W. Katz, 2009).

Perversion is important in the origins of psychoanalysis in that Freud's study of perversion was at the heart of his revolutionary challenge to traditional views of sexuality. His observations of similarities between perversion, normal infantile sexuality, neurosis, and normal adult foreplay allowed him to see beyond conventional divisions between child and adult, or normal and deviant in the realm of sexuality. His explorations led to his radical conceptualization of psychosexuality as a universal motivational force, present at birth as a **polymorphously perverse disposition**, and capable of infinite transformations. Among Freud's first contributions to psychology was his observation that sexuality plays a role in phenomena that are apparently nonsexual. Conversely, the study of perversion demonstrates how sexual behavior/fantasy can be recruited for the management of nonsexual conflicts. In addition, the study of perversion led Freud and later analysts to important observations about splitting, disavowal, and other dramatic defenses against the acknowledgment of reality.

Freud (1905b) initially followed Von Krafft-Ebing and Ellis in his designation of a group of common deviations in sexual behavior, including sadism, masochism, inversion (homosexuality), and fetishism as perversion. He conceptualized these behaviors as representing the direct expression of "component instincts," or the unintegrated and immature components of libido (including sadism/masochism, exhibitionism/voyeurism, and pregenital oral and anal sexual aims) that emerge during development, beginning in infancy. In Freud's view, perversion represented a regression from genital sexuality to a pregenital point of libidinal fixation in which there is a preference for the expression of these component instincts in place of heterosexual genital intercourse. Freud famously described neurosis as the "negative of perversion" in that in the former, symptoms are caused by the return of repressed drives and fantasies, whereas in the latter these same drives and/or fantasies are not repressed but seek direct satisfaction.

With the development of ego psychology and a more elaborated theory of defense, Freud (1927b) began to conceptualize perversion as the product of compromise rather than simply the expression of unmodified instinct. For example, he argued that fetishism in men defends against castration anxiety aroused by the sight of the woman's genitals through the creation of the fetish as a substitute for her missing penis. In addition, Freud's study of fetishism led him to explore defenses based not on repression but on disavowal and splitting. This emphasis on the connection between perversion and more primitive defenses has been retained and elaborated in the work of subsequent theorists.

Post-Freudian analysts continued to emphasize the role of castration anxiety and the importance of the fantasy of the phallic woman in the psychodynamics of perversion (especially in fetishism) (Bak, 1968). At the same time, many began to explore the role of difficulties with attachment, conflicts over separation-individuation, aggression, and/or the experience of early trauma. As attention turned to the internal object world of the person with perversion, many noted the factor of dehumanization so prevalent in perverse sexual behavior, and/or the subject's incapacity for integrating sexual expression with love and concern for another person experienced as separate from the self (Fenichel, 1945; Greenacre, 1955; Bak, 1956; Khan, 1969; McDougall, 1980, 1986; S. Mitchell, 1988; Parsons, 2000). For example, Stoller (1975a) referred to perversion as "the erotic form of hatred," asserting that cruelty and the wish to degrade one's sexual partner are defining features of perversion. In accord with others, his view of perversion included the attempt to preserve a fragile gender identity and to achieve a victory over trauma. In his later work, Kohut (1977) expanded his concept of the vertical split to account for perversion (as well as addiction). More recently, Goldberg (1995, 1999, 2000) conceptualized perverse behavior as an attempt to deal with an impaired self through the generation of enlivening excitement; he also used the concept of the vertical split to account for perverse behaviors such as cross-dressing, which are secretively split off. In her study of female perversions (including kleptomania, homovestism, extreme submissiveness, mutilations, female impersonation, anorexia, and the "incest wife"), Kaplan (1991) also emphasized both the importance of triumph over trauma and the centrality of gender roles, conceptualizing perversion as the exaggeration of female stereotypes, which also express disguised and unacceptable masculine wishes.

Post-Freudian analysts have also continued to explore impaired ego functioning in perversion, with particular emphasis on distortions in the relationship with reality. For example, Chasseguet-Smirgel (1984) argued that perversion is based on an unconscious fantasy that denies the importance of the two main human differences that constitute the core of the oedipus complex: the difference between the sexes (represented by castration) and the difference between the generations (represented by the primacy of heterosexual, procreative intercourse, which excludes the sexually immature child). In her view, perversion reflects a set of omnipotent and magical beliefs characteristic of the anal phase, accompanied by primitive sexualized fantasies of destruction. Others have emphasized the role of enactment and sexualization in perversion, emphasizing how the valorization of excitement and arousal serves to bolster the denial of reality and/or to give the stamp of reality to enacted fantasy (Bak, 1956; Coen, 1998; W. Katz, 2009). As noted above, this emphasis on the distortions in relation to reality has led many theorists to extend the term *perversion* to include many nonsexual phenomena, including attitudes, defenses, behaviors, and aspects of character that share the feature of pronounced disavowal, often in the context of sadomasochistic object relations (Coen, 1998).

Phallic/Phallic Phase/Phallus: see EGO IDEAL, IDEALIZATION, INFANTILE GENITAL PHASE, LACAN, NARCISSISM, PSYCHOSEXUAL DEVELOPMENT

Phantasy: see FANTASY, KLEIN, OBJECT, PROJECTIVE IDENTIFICATION

Phobia/Phobic Character: see ANXIETY, HYSTERIA

Pleasure Principle: see CATHEXIS, DEATH DRIVE, DRIVE, ENERGY, LIBIDO, METAPSYCHOLOGY, MOTIVATION, PRECONSCIOUS, PRIMARY PROCESS, PSYCHIC DETERMINISM, REALITY, REPETITION COMPULSION, UNCONSCIOUS

Practicing Subphase: see SEPARATION-INDIVIDUATION

Preconscious describes mental contents that are not conscious but that are not repressed and can become conscious under certain conditions. The **system preconscious** (Pcs.), as described in Freud's topographic model, designates a hypothetical region or system in the mind between consciousness and the unconscious, in which mental contents are capable of becoming conscious if attention is paid to them. The preconscious operates according to the secondary process. The concept of the preconscious is important because it is an aspect of Freud's revolutionary idea that mind cannot be equated with consciousness. In addition, the concept of the preconscious allows for the differentiation between a "descriptive unconscious" (preconscious) and a "dynamic unconscious" (the unconscious), a foundational idea for psychoanalysis.

Freud (1897b) first described the preconscious in a letter to Fliess. Freud's (1900) first published use of the term was in "The Interpretation of Dreams," where he delineated the three systems of his topographic model of the mind, consciousness (Cs.), the preconscious (Pcs.), and the unconscious (Ucs.). Describing the nature of the preconscious, Freud asserted that the "excitatory processes" occurring in the preconscious can enter consciousness without further impediment if certain conditions are fulfilled: if they reach a certain degree of intensity, or if they receive the function of attention. While the contents of the preconscious are descriptively unconscious, unlike the contents of the unconscious, the thoughts, memories, and wishes of the preconscious are not actively pushed out of awareness by

the force of repression. Thus, these contents can enter consciousness readily at any moment either from the pressure of outside stimulation, or from the person's own mental effort of attention.

Freud acknowledged the fluidity of the boundary between consciousness and the preconscious by frequently using them interchangeably, often referring to them together as one system, Cs.-Pcs. In contrast, the preconscious is separated from the unconscious by the barrier of the censor. As Freud (1915d) developed his model, he moved away from a topographic definition toward a more-dynamic definition in which he conceived of preconscious mental contents as characterized by the degree and nature ("bound versus unbound") of psychic energy (or cathexis) with which they were invested. Preconscious thoughts are less mobile than those in the unconscious, and, as such, operate according to the linear, organized principles of the secondary process.

When Freud (1923a) reformulated his model of the mind in structural terms, the qualities and functions of the preconscious system—including inhibition of discharge, reality testing, judgment, dream-work, and defense—were subsumed into the concept of the ego. However, he continued to employ the term *preconscious*.

Some authors have pointed out that in his post-1923 efforts to map the topographic and the structural models of the mind onto each other, Freud entertained various, somewhat-contradictory concepts of the preconscious. Arlow and C. Brenner (1960) noted a general tendency among analysts to conflate Freud's earlier definition, in which preconscious thoughts are equated with those that are latent but easily accessible to consciousness, with Freud's (1938a) later definition, in which the preconscious is equated with secondary process functioning but may nevertheless be largely inaccessible to consciousness (especially preconscious superego elements). They proposed abandoning the term *preconscious* altogether because of semantic imprecision and a lack of clinical utility. Other authors have found it useful to retain a concept of preconscious mental processes, noting their complex qualities and characteristics. E. Kris (1950b) described a continuum of content, ranging from purposeful reflection to fantasy, and of form, ranging from logical formulation to dreamlike imagery. He noted the contribution of preconscious mental processes to the recovery of memories in psychoanalysis as well as within the creative process. Interpretation facilitates, first, recognition of forgotten memories, and, ultimately, recall, when preconscious mental processes have been assimilated through the synthetic function of the ego. The concept of preconscious is related to technical advice about the optimal depth of interpretations (A. Green, 1974; J. Ross, 2003) and the potential "resonance" between patient and analyst when both parties "relax their customary cognitive controls and permit the emergence of preconscious responses" (Jeffrey, 1992; Kantrowitz, 1999). The concept of preconscious mental life is also present in the experimental psychology literature in relation to the study of subliminal perception and memory (Fisher, 1954; W. Meissner, 1983).

Preoedipal (sometimes referred to as **Pregenital**) is a developmental stage in childhood that precedes the oedipal period, spanning the time from birth to about three years of age. During this **preoedipal stage**, critical aspects of maturation and development occur, including the development of early ego capacities such as perception, reality testing, cognition, and defense; the growth of internalized object relations; the emergence of the self; early stages of psychosexual and gender development; and the early differentiation of affects and drives. All psychoanalytic developmental theories describe the preoedipal period somewhat differently, featuring some aspects of development over others. Classical Freudian theory emphasizes the vicissitudes of the sexual drive in its sequence of pregenital phases: oral, anal, and phallic-narcissistic. Kleinian theory (Klein, 1958) places oedipal conflicts (involving part objects—breast and penis) and superego nuclei in what is commonly considered the pregenital phase, during the first year of life. Other object relations theories differ from the classical schools by their emphasis on relationships to objects as opposed to the focus on drive. Mahler's separation-individuation theory emphasizes the establishment of internal self and object representations and the actual process of separation from the primary caretaker. Attachment theory focuses on the attachment bond to the primary caretaker and the establishment of an organized pattern of attachment that becomes represented in the mind. Disturbances during the preoedipal phase due to constitutional defect or environmental deficit contribute to and shape the organization of subsequent developmental issues and conflicts, particularly the oedipal constellation, but also throughout the life cycle. **Preoedipal issues** and **preoedipal conflicts** in the adult patient are considered to be "dyadic" and "primitive," referring back to the early relationship with the primary caregiving object (usually the mother), in contrast to the "triadic" issues of the oedipal period that involve a third person (usually the father). Such issues and conflicts typically involve dependency, attachment, and control, among others, and are sometimes identified by the pregenital psychosexual stage that features such themes, for example oral, anal, and phallic issues or conflicts. Preoedipal issues and conflicts are present in the psychological life of all adults but may be more prominent in the psychological life of individuals who have experienced early maternal deprivation or loss, or other kinds of physical and/or emotional trauma. When preoedipal conflict is prominent and it is also accompanied by impairment in ego functions, such as reality testing and affect tolerance, the diagnosis of **preoedipal pathology** is sometimes made. This is unfortunate shorthand, as it conflates dynamics with ego dysfunction and implies that such disturbances necessarily arise during the preoedipal phase of development. In fact, the relationship of conflict to ego dysfunction is complex, and the assumption that such pathology has its etiology in the preoedipal phase of development is an example of the genetic fallacy. Such psychopathology is best designated as moderate to severe character pathology or, at its most severe, borderline personality disorder.

As psychoanalytic theory and practice traditionally focused on the oedipal conflict, preoedipal issues were considered outside the realm of psychoanalytic concern. The emergence of interest in this period, stimulated in part by the escalating growth of infant and child observation research in the past fifty years, generated considerable controversy. There is now an appreciation of the omnipresence of preoedipal issues and their universal interdigitation with oedipal issues. Within the widening scope of psychoanalytic practice, analysis has become the treatment of choice for many patients whose psychological issues include preoedipal components.

Freud (1931a) first used the term *preoedipal* in the form of the "pre-Oedipus phase in women," which he described as a longer and more-important phase than for the boy. During this "negative oedipal phase," the girl's intense and passionate love for her mother is pursued in an active or masculine form. However, the girl's recognition of her deficient castrated state precipitates hatred for her mother, whom she holds responsible. The girl changes her love object and also her way of loving, ultimately assuming the passive feminine attitude. Freud's schema for female sexual development sparked immediate controversy and has been subject to extensive revision. Most of Freud's (1905b) interest in the preoedipal phase of development focused on the neurobiologically determined vicissitudes of the sexual drive in a sequence of instinctual stages, including the oral, anal, and phallic stages. In his view of the preoedipal child, Freud also emphasized the predominance of the pleasure principle, infantile narcissism, primary process mentation, fantasies of omnipotence, and the gradual emergence of the ego and object relations.

By the mid-twentieth century the controversy between A. Freud and Klein over the level of complexity of mental development in infancy concentrated attention on the preoedipal years. A. Freud (1963) focused on ego development and introduced the concept of developmental lines, while Klein's (1928) focus was on early "phantasy" formation, the predominance of aggression, and the development of internalized object relations. In fact, Klein saw evidence of ego development and oedipal fantasies during the first year of life, thereby effectively eliminating the concept of a preoedipal stage in Kleinian theorizing. Because libido is initially fused with aggression, the infant's primary struggle is with the management of aggression and destructiveness through projection and splitting. The nucleus of the superego is formed by projection and reintrojection of the infant's own aggression. The first version of oedipal conflicts, evident as early as four to five months, is directed at gratifying and frustrating part objects—breast and penis. The paranoid-schizoid position is characterized by the splitting off and projection of aggressive affects, thereby creating persecutory anxiety. Over the course of this period, the infant arrives at the depressive position, when aggression and libido, love and hate are modulated and integrated. This is comparable to the traditional oedipal struggle, with love, guilt, and the urge for reparations predominating. Other psychoanalysts, such as Jacobson (1964) and Kernberg (1975) attempted to bridge the gap between ego psychology and object relations, and formulated sophisticated schemas for preoedipal development that focused on the emergence and differentiation of self and object representations, facilitated by the maturation and growth of ever-more-complex ego capacities and functions.

Efforts to validate theoretical models of early development, which had been reconstructed from clinical work with adult patients, have stimulated infant and child observational research. Spitz (1965), one of the earliest psychoanalytic infant researchers, introduced the concept of psychic organizers, an indicator of the attainment of a stage in psychological development, which is, in turn, the precondition for further progress in the structuralization of the mind. Spitz borrowed the concept from embryology and applied it to psychological development. He proposed three psychic organizers: 1) the social smile, which appears between six weeks and three months of age and represents the beginning of social relations; 2) the stranger anxiety reaction seen in children normatively around eight months of age, in which the infant displays obvious signs of distress, such as crying, frowning, and fussing, when approached by a stranger; 3) The expression of "no," which is normatively seen at eighteen months of age and demonstrates the child's first capacity to assert autonomy and make judgments. Piaget (1969) studied mental processes of children, seeking to understand how knowledge is constructed and organized in order to promote adaptation to the environment. Mahler and her co-workers (Mahler, Pine, and Bergman, 1975) introduced separation-individuation theory, dividing the first three years of life into subphases during which the infant-mother relationship evolves and the beginning of object constancy is established, a state in which there is a solid sense of self and other. Galenson and Roiphe (1976), studying the impact of body sensations on instinctual and ego development in young children, identified the recognition of genital sensations as early as eighteen to twenty-four months, resulting in the formulation of an early genital phase of development. Bowlby (1969/1982), who introduced attachment theory, asserted that there is an inborn attachment-behavioral system that is equal in motivational status to that of feeding and sex, and described organized patterns of attachment that become evident by one year of age. D. N. Stern (1985), using detailed observations of infants and mothers, described the evolution of self experience beginning at birth and also described more-complex and organized mental capacities at a much earlier age than other researchers.

More recently, a linear developmental theory has been replaced with one in which there are overlapping and interacting systems (P. Tyson, 1996b; Gilmore, 2008). Attention has turned to the recognition of early moral development (Emde and Buchsbaum, 1990; P. Tyson and R. Tyson, 1990), the early relationship with the father (Abelin, 1975; Herzog, 2001), attachment styles (M. Main, 1993), mentalization (Fonagy, 1995), affect theory (Emde, 1999), vicissitudes of the mother-infant interchanges (Tronick, 2007), a return to the importance of the body (Balsam, 2001), gender development (Chehrazi, 1986; P. Bernstein, 2004), and neurophysiological and neuropsychological considerations (Solms, 2000b).

Primal Fantasy is a particular type of fantasy that is found universally in all individuals regardless of their unique personal experience and history. Primal fantasies include fantasies of parental intercourse (primal scene), seduction, and castration. The con-

cept of primal fantasy is important in psychoanalysis because it emphasizes the fact that powerful
structuring ideas exist in the unconscious, which
cannot be fully explained by the lived experience of
the individual; it is psychic rather than material reality that is decisive. Like all fantasies, primal fantasies often play an important role in the formation
and expression of neurotic symptoms.

Throughout his career, Freud struggled with the
question of whether actual "real" experiences or
"imagined" fantasies were the source of his patients'
neurotic symptoms. Over time, his clinical work led
him increasingly to view fantasy rather than actual
experience as the principal organizer of his patient's
symptoms; however, he never fully abandoned the
idea that real traumatic experiences are important.
In 1897, Freud (1897e) wrote that hysterical symptoms are the delayed result of actual early sexual
experiences, which he referred to as "primal scenes."
Over the next two decades, as he developed his ideas
about the role of fantasy, Freud (1915e) shifted his
focus from primal scenes to what he would eventually call "primal fantasies." In his "Introductory Lectures," Freud (1916/1917) elaborated his views on the
origin of these universal fantasies, arguing that primal fantasies are a "phylogenetic endowment" in
which "the individual reaches beyond his own experience into primaeval experience at points where his
own experience has been too rudimentary." Freud
asserted that many fantasies that emerge in analysis—
the seduction of children, the inflaming of sexual
excitement by observing parental intercourse, the
threat of castration (or rather castration itself)—
were once real occurrences in the "primaeval times
of the human family." In their fantasies, children
are simply filling in the gaps in individual truth
with "prehistoric truth."

Most analysts have dismissed Freud's idea of
phylogenetic inheritance, adopting the point of view
that the universality of primal fantasies is explained
by the basic human need to solve the central mysteries of procreation, childbirth, sexuality, and the an-
atomic difference between the sexes. The child forms
both conscious and unconscious fantasies as his version of a "theory" to account for these enigmas.
Freud (1909d) had, in fact, expressed a similar view
earlier in a note in the Rat Man case; he later changed
his formulation. Klein (1927a) and Bion (1962b),
however, articulated ideas quite similar to Freud's
notion of inherited fantasies. In Klein's view, the
infant is born with inherent knowledge of body organs, birth, and intercourse. Bion proposed the idea
of "pre-conceptions," as inherited schema, which are

waiting to combine with experience to form "conceptions."

Primal Horde is a term introduced by Freud (1913e)
in "Totem and Taboo" to describe a small, organized
group of women and young men led by the primal
father at the dawn of human history. The primal
father maintained a monopoly over sexual access to
the women and girls, expelling (or later, castrating)
younger males from the horde. These younger males
feared and hated as well as admired and loved their
father. Freud acknowledged the influence of Darwin, Atkinson, and Smith in this formulation. The
theory of the primal horde represents an example of
Freud's phylogenetic speculation, generally rejected
by contemporary psychoanalysts.

Freud argued that the dissolution of the primal
horde led to the advent of civilization and laid down
the primordial contours of the human psyche. He
argued that the sons, expelled from the horde by
their father, banded together and killed and ate
him. Remorse and guilt led the sons to exaggerate
the slain father's power and benevolence and to ele-
vate his status to that of a god. Similarly, the sons
renounced their claim to sexual access to their mothers and sisters, thus introducing the practice of ex-
ogamy and the system of religion and kinship known
as totemism. This instinctual renunciation, expressed
in the incest taboo, led to the foundation of religion
and civilization. It also provided the phylogenetic
underpinning for the oedipus complex. In his exploration of the concept of the primal horde, Freud
explored early ideas about the oral phase (sometimes
referred to as the cannibalistic phase), incorporation, and identification in his description of how, in
the totem meal, the sons acquire some of the father's
strength. In later work, Freud (1919e, 1921, 1925d,
1930, 1939) claimed that any structured group with a
defined leader can recapitulate dynamics of the primal horde, in which group solidarity is maintained
by the illusion that the leader loves each of the members equally and treats each justly.

Primal Scene is the child's actual experience of wit-
nessing sexual intercourse between the parents, or
unconscious fantasies of this experience and the derivatives and transformations of such fantasies. Primal scene fantasy occurs frequently and most often
in the absence of the actual experience; it serves to
organize ideas and feelings about the nature of sexual intercourse, and feelings attached to the experience of being excluded from intimate relationships
between others, including feelings of inadequacy,

humiliation, or anger often linked to feelings of jealousy and excitement. As an actual experience, the primal scene has traditionally been regarded as inevitably traumatic and pathogenic for the child, though this view has been challenged. Primal scene fantasy is, perhaps, the most well known and culturally iconic of the universal, primal fantasies delineated by Freud. Primal scene fantasy finds frequent representation in art, literature, and myth.

Freud (1897e) first used the term *primal scenes* in a letter to Fliess, referring to early sexual experiences that he regarded as the cause of later hysterical symptoms. Although Freud did not so specify in this paper, he was for the most part referring to experiences of childhood seduction. In numerous subsequent papers, Freud (1900, 1905b, 1908c) commented on the impact of the observation of parental coitus on the child. He argued that observing parental intercourse is a source of anxiety because of its production of excess sexual excitement. He also described how children have a tendency to interpret parental intercourse as a violent and sadistic act. Over time, as Freud's theory developed, he shifted his focus from the impact of the actual experience to the impact of universal fantasies about this scene, which he felt were acquired through phylogenetic inheritance. It is not until Freud's (1918a) account of the Wolf Man that the specific scene of intercourse between the parents acquired the label of the "primal scene." In this case report, Freud most fully elaborated his views on the clinical sequelae of the primal scene, attributing the Wolf Man's infantile neurosis, castration anxiety, and consequent wolf phobia, as well as homosexual orientation, to the impact of this scene. He also described in detail how the emotional impact of primal scene experience may be delayed, subject to what he called "deferred action."

Many subsequent analysts have provided clinical material that confirms and enlarges upon Freud's conclusions regarding the traumatic and pathogenic impact of primal scene experiences. Esman (1973) provided an important counterpoint to this chorus of views, marshaling clinical, cross-cultural, and other evidence to challenge the logic that a common experience and/or a universal fantasy are invariably sources of pathology. Others (H. Blum, 1979b) have stressed the importance of a more-nuanced view of the consequences of primal scene experience and fantasy, which takes into account: the larger context in which such a scene is experienced; the nature of the surrounding object relationships; the cognitive and developmental level of the child who has such

an experience; the differential impact of a single event as compared to a repetitive trauma; and, of course, the crucial distinctions between actual experience and fantasy. Strongly influenced by Freud's case of the Wolf Man, Klein argued that the sense of exclusion associated with primal scene fantasy contributes to the intense envy and sadism of what she called the "oedipal situation." Klein (1928) described the fantasy of the "combined parental figure," a universal fantasy of the parents locked in intercourse forever; so united, these parents contribute to the child's fears of retaliation and terrifying persecutory anxiety. Klein (1946) and later theorists explored how an inability to tolerate anxieties associated with the primal scene leads to psychosis (Bion, 1957), to failures in the development of abstract thought (Britton, 1989), and/or perversion (McDougall, 1972; Chasseguet-Smirgel, 1984).

Primary Femininity is a term with broad and differing usages, whose common thread or focus is the girl's earliest sense of herself as female. The term, which arose as a response to the phallocentrism of early psychoanalytic theories of female development, lacks conceptual clarity because it stems from different frames of reference, with varying attributions to biological, psychological, and cultural influences (Kulish, 2000). Primary femininity has been used to mean: 1) core gender identity and gender identity; 2) a nonconflictually derived bedrock of femaleness; 3) an unconscious identification with the first caretaker—mother—occurring in both girls and boys; and 4) an early positive sense of femaleness derived from early perceptions of one's female genitalia (Elise, 1997). Primary femininity has also been used to explain persistent conscious and unconscious fantasies, derived from early female development, of an array of female genital anxieties.

The idea of a primary femininity represents a challenge to Freud's (1925b; 1933a) theories of female psychosexual development, which were founded on notions of primary masculinity. Freud's views emphasized the primacy of the phallus in the early psychosexual development of both boys and girls and centered the little girl's psychosexual development on penis envy and castration anxiety. Primary femininity is an attempt to redress the distortions of such a view of female development, one that recognizes the girl's earliest experience of a female body and a female sense of self. While the concept of primary femininity is regarded among many psychoanalysts as a crucial step in a much-needed revision of female psychosexual development, it has been compellingly critiqued on a variety of grounds. These include a concern about the ambiguity of the terms *primary* and *femininity* (Elise, 1997) and a more-general concern that it replaces a phallocentric reductionism with a vaginocentric one, among others.

For Freud (1933a), the little girl's journey into heterosexuality and the triangular oedipus stage is based on her sense of lack and her penis envy. He believed that the sexual development of the little boy and the little girl is identical at first, as captured by his now-notorious words "the little girl is a little man." The girl's future sexual development depends on a reaction to or a renunciation of her original, primary masculinity. The primary object of sexual interest and desire for both boys and girls is the mother. With the discovery of the anatomical difference between the sexes, the girl realizes that she lacks a penis, and in her disappointment turns away from the mother toward the father, with the envious wish for a baby as a compensation for the missing penis. Furthermore, the little girl's knowledge of her vagina is only discovered at puberty.

Contemporaries of Freud challenged his theory on the grounds that it lacked concepts of primary femininity, which might provide ways to conceptualize the girl's feelings about her body, her sexual desires, and her object relationships in more-positive and more-accurate terms. Horney (1924, 1933) did not use the term *primary femininity* but advanced such a concept in her argument that a little girl's sense of being inferior is not primary but acquired and culturally reinforced. Horney (1926) also argued that a girl's reproductive urges do not necessarily stem from a compensatory substitution of a baby for a missing penis but via identification with her mother, an idea that reemerges in contemporary concepts of primary femininity (P. Tyson and R. Tyson, 1990). Horney and others such as Jones (1927, 1933) and later Greenacre (1950a) insisted that the girl does have early knowledge of her own vagina, although it is often repressed. It is in these early writings that the first usage of the idea of a primary quality of femininity is to be found, in the sense of early feelings about the female body, which do not carry with them meanings of inferiority. Jones also questioned the concept of a phallic phase in girls, which he argued is secondary and defensive. He posited that there is a primary femininity for girls as well as an inborn bisexuality. As described by Jones, this primary (heterosexual) femininity takes the form of early, inborn, oedipal impulses that impel girls toward their fathers and evoke genital fears of penetration.

While these first conceptualizations about primary femininity were advanced in the context of the early formulations about psychosexual drive development, the term *primary femininity* per se first emerged in an entirely different frame of reference. Stoller (1968c) first used the term *primary femininity* in his studies of the development of core gender identity, a concept based on the combined influence of biology, sexual assignment, parental rearing, and cultural attitudes. However, on a different basis, he attempted to counter Freud's notions about the primacy of masculinity, which in part rested on the nineteenth century's knowledge of embryology. In Freud's time it was believed that in the fetus, the male state is primary and that female sexual organs are then differentiated. Stoller (1976) pointed out that modern embryology tells us the opposite: the female state is primary, and with the secretion of testosterone, male sexual organs are differentiated from the female. Finally, Stoller (1975b) argued that femininity for both females and males was primary in another sense, in that the first object of identification for the infant is female—the mother. Here, using the concept of primary femininity as a particular kind or state of object relatedness, Stoller suggested that boys have the difficult task of disidentifying from their mothers to establish their gender identities and sense of masculinity.

Many psychoanalysts have questioned Stoller's ideas. Birksted-Breen (1996) pointed out that many British and French psychoanalysts do not accept the notion of a nonconflictual primary femininity, because there is no area of cognition free of ambiguity, conflict, and unconscious fantasy. Person and Ovesey (1983) criticized Stoller's views along different lines, questioning whether an early undifferentiated symbiotic state is one that confers gendered behavior or identity as the infant separates from the primary object. Coming from the perspective of sociology and object relations, Chodorow's (1978) early writings resemble Stoller's ideas of a kind of primary femininity in the development of the sense of self and gender identity. Although Chodorow did not use the term *primary femininity* as such, her ideas about gender-based differences founded in early maternal identifications or disidentifications imply concepts of primary femininity in the establishment of gender identity.

Another major context for discussions about primary femininity is the concept of female genital anxieties, anxieties related to fears about damage to or loss of female bodily parts, as opposed to envies of and fantasies about loss of male attributes. D. Bernstein (1990) articulated three specific "female genital anxieties." Expanding on Bernstein's classification, Richards (1996) anchored female psychosexual development in the little girl's early experience of the flexing of the perineal musculature. Richards also described her view of the primary fear of castration in women in terms of a loss of pleasure or function of the female genital apparatus. Richards's use of *primary femininity* suggests the meaning of *primary* as early and basic, ideas that have commonalities with Kestenberg's (1968, 1982) theories of the centrality for a girl of inner genital sensations. Mayer (1985) proposed another primary feminine genital anxiety, which she called "female castration anxiety." Mayer argued that a little girl's primary femininity, that is, her knowledge of her uniqueness, of her own body and of her genitalia, inform her feminine identity and can contribute to a valued sense of herself. Mayer's contributions have led many analysts and analytic therapists to focus clinically on their female patients' conflicted yet positive feelings about their femininity. Mayer (1995), in elaborating these ideas further, compared female castration anxiety with male castration anxiety. The girl values her feminine parts and she fears losing them, hence, she experiences signal anxiety at the anticipatory threat of such a loss. While the concept of female genital anxieties has been viewed by some psychoanalysts as a replacement for earlier concepts of penis envy and castration anxiety, Olesker (1998b), based on observational studies of young girls as well as the clinical analyses of adult women, identified both female genital anxiety and the more traditional phallic castration anxiety, along with oedipal and bisexual conflicts.

In some writings, particularly earlier ones, primary femininity is pictured as one side of an inborn bisexuality (Parens, 1980; H. Deutsch, 1982). Parens described a basic inborn bisexuality and neutral genital libido, from which primary masculinity and primary femininity differentiate.

Concepts of primary femininity have also led to ideas about renaming or revising the traditional psychosexual stages of development, particularly the phallic phase. Thus, instead of a primary masculine or phallic phase through which all children must traverse, some have suggested that we might think in terms of a "primary feminine" phase, an early "genital" phase. Glover and Mendell (1982) suggested that psychoanalysis replace the *phallic* in "phallic" stage with a "preoedipal genital" or "genital" stage. The dominant zone in this stage would be the genital, characterized in the case of the girl by penetration anxiety. Others, including Chehrazi (1986), Parens

(1990), P. Tyson (1994), and Dorsey (1996), have made similar proposals, which have grown in many instances out of ideas associated with primary femininity. There is some confusion surrounding the renaming of this phase because Roiphe and Galenson (1981a, 1981b) proposed an "early genital phase" that refers to an earlier stage of development, one that is between sixteen and twenty-four months, concomitant with the rapprochement phase, which includes manipulation of genitals, sexual curiosity, and a generally heightened genital awareness. For this reason, infantile genital stage is the preferred renaming of the phallic phase.

Kulish (2000) cogently critiqued the concept of primary femininity as conceptually problematic in the domain of theory but quite useful in the clinical realm. In a careful review of the literature, Kulish identified confusion about the term, including the lapses of many writers into biological reductionism, resulting in a view of primary femininity as a kind of bedrock, emerging independent of fantasy and conflict. Elise (1997) has proposed a revision of the term to a "primary sense of femaleness," to refer to the mental representation of the female body that develops in the first years of life.

Primary Maternal Preoccupation: see WINNICOTT

Primary Process and **Secondary Process** are two fundamentally different modes of representation and/or organization of psychological life, which, at the descriptive level, account for two types of "thought," different in both form and content. Primary process thinking, well illustrated by dreams, is nonlinear, often nonverbal, and makes use of the mechanisms of concrete symbolization, displacement, and condensation. It is characterized by a disregard for logical connections, for contradictions, and for the realities of time. The content of primary process is dominated by wishes, affects, conflict, and/or unconscious fantasy. By contrast, secondary process thinking is logical, usually verbal, and reality-based. It is oriented toward judgment, solving problems, or achieving goals. While the traditional psychoanalytic perspective has been that primary process predominates in unconscious thought, and that secondary process predominates in conscious and preconscious thought, most contemporary analysts recognize that both primary and secondary process thinking occur at all levels of awareness.

Central to a psychoanalytic perspective is the recognition that all mental life is influenced by unconscious conflict and fantasy and that, therefore, the qualities of primary process thinking are always present, side by side with, albeit largely obscured by, secondary process thinking. When mental life is dominated by intense affect and/or conflict, or when the organizing constraints of reasonableness are relaxed, primary process modes of organization become more evident in conscious thought. For example, characteristics of primary process are evident in the play of children, dreams, daydreams, jokes, slips of the tongue, neurotic symptoms, and psychosis. In the clinical setting, primary process becomes evident in free association, when the patient is invited to suspend concerns for logic and appropriateness. The analyst listens for primary process elements in the patient's communications as clues to his private, unconscious, inner world of fantasy and personal meaning. The characteristics of primary process are also evident in metaphor, poetry, art, and religious ritual. Indeed, the psychoanalytic concept of primary process is a major contribution to the study of how art, religion, and other cultural products represent and communicate complex, emotional, often unconscious human experience.

Through his study of symptom formation and the analysis of dreams, Freud first identified and distinguished the primary and secondary process modes of thought. In his unpublished "Project for a Scientific Psychology," Freud (1895b) used the term *primary process* to designate the mental functioning of the infant. Thus, *primary* refers to what comes first in development; *process* refers to the method by which "neurons" (in this neuronally based early model) handle excitation or "energy." At first, in this model, "energy" in the system moves quickly and cannot be either delayed in response to reality concerns or "bound" for future use. With growth and learning, the mind-brain develops secondary process operations with the capacity to delay discharge and store or redirect energy in response to the demands of reality.

Although Freud abandoned efforts to build a brain-based model of the mind, he retained the concepts of the primary and secondary processes along with the "energy" concepts on which they were based. Freud (1900, 1911b, 1915d) elaborated on these concepts in chapter 7 of "The Interpretation of Dreams," and other papers, as part of his effort to elucidate the unconscious mental processes underlying symptom and dream formation. In the topographic model of the mind, Freud assigned the primary process to the system unconscious (Ucs.), where, as in the previous model, energy is highly

mobile, seeking immediate discharge in accordance with the pleasure principle. He described specific mechanisms that characterize the primary process (illustrated through dream-work), including displacement (where one idea can substitute for another with which it is affectively associated) and condensation (where one idea can express several others). Freud assigned the secondary process to the system conscious-preconscious (Cs.-Pcs.), where, in accord with the demands of reality, it has the capacity to bind energy and use fixed, denotative symbols, thus leading to reality-oriented, language-based thought. As before, in this model, the primary process is the more primitive of the two, or the first to develop. The secondary process develops only when the infant learns, in the face of what Freud called "bitter disappointment," that wishing alone (including hallucinatory wish-fulfillment) does not bring satisfaction, and that more complex maneuvers (in other words, thinking and action) are necessary to achieve satisfaction. However, the primitive, timeless, amoral, wish-driven world of unconscious fantasy continues to be organized by the primary process.

In his structural theory, Freud reassigned primary process functioning to the id, and secondary process to the ego. While with this move to the structural theory, Freud (1938a) explicitly rejected the idea of a unified "unconscious" characterized by one type of mental processing, he confused matters by continuing to refer to a systemic unconscious governed by primary process. At the same time, there was growing recognition among ego psychologists that the equation of id with primary process functioning and of ego with secondary process functioning is too simple, and that there are many mental states that lie between primary and secondary process thinking, partaking of both. For example, Arlow (1958) argued that the primary process is a general aspect of mental life, characterizing id, ego, and superego under certain conditions. E. Kris (1950b), Loewald (1960, 1978), and others argued that the ego can "regress" to a state with primary process characteristics, promoting creativity in art and science and allowing for progress in analysis. Schafer (1968b) defined introjects as **primary process presences**, or representations of the object with which the subject (self) has an ongoing relationship. More recently, Dorpat (2001) has argued against a notion of primary process as an archaic infantile residue, extolling primary process cognition as an essential and vital aspect of relatedness.

Also over time, there has been a gradual abandonment of other elements of the conceptual framework proposed by Freud for the primary and secondary process. For example, while Arlow and C. Brenner (1964) argued that primary and secondary processes should be defined not as types of thinking but by the "degree of mobility of cathexes" underlying various phenomena, analysts with less allegiance to energic elements of theory began to use primary and secondary processes simply to mean different modes of thought (Rapaport, 1951; Holt, 1967). Others challenged the developmental sequence of primary and secondary processes proposed by Freud. For example, while recognizing the importance of primary process as a piece of clinical vocabulary useful for describing a particular organization of thought, Cavell (2003) drew on philosophy of language and developmental psychology to argue against the idea of a kind of mental content that precedes the orientation to reality. Litowitz (2007), in elaborating a contemporary conceptualization of unconscious fantasy, rejected entirely Freud's idea that primary process modes of thought characterize childhood thinking. Citing contemporary developmental research, she refuted the notion that four features of primary process thinking (including condensation, lack of negation, pervasiveness of reversals, and timelessness) have any relationship with childhood mentation. In effect, she relegated primary process to the domain of adult dream-work. Marcus (1999) argued for the concept of **tertiary process**, coined by Arieti (1976), defined as a third mental process that organizes the relationship between primary and secondary process thought, producing synthetic experience at many levels of consciousness. Tertiary process joins inside and outside; drive derivative, defense, and superego conflict elements; thing presentations and word presentations; and percepts, affects, and concepts. It brings reality experience and emotional experience together to form a complex psychic reality.

A number of psychoanalytically oriented researchers in cognitive and developmental psychology have attempted to empirically test the concepts of primary and secondary process. Holt (2002) developed a scale to measure the presence of primary process thinking, reporting a correlation between the adaptive use of primary process thinking and both artistic achievement and positive outcome in psychotherapy. Brakel and colleagues (2002) drew from theories of category formation in cognitive psychology to generate empirical support for the existence of primary process (represented by categorizations based on concrete, perceptual attributional similarities) and secondary process (represented by

categorizations based on abstract, rule-bound, relational similarities). Brakel's work (2004) also supports the idea that primary processes are more active outside of awareness, in children, and in anxiety states (used as a marker for unconscious conflict).

Borrowing also from the methods of cognitive psychology, Bucci (1997) proposed a "multiple code theory" of processing that moves beyond the concepts of primary and secondary process to include a symbolic verbal mode, a symbolic nonverbal mode, and a subsymbolic mode. These three modes of processing are linked together through the integrating activity of what she called referential activity. The subsymbolic mode, characterized by continuous rather than discrete representational modes, is used to represent motoric, visceral, sensory, and emotional experiences of all kinds; access to the subsymbolic mode is vital to a vast array of important life functions, from creativity to emotional communication between individuals. In Bucci's view, while both symbolic nonverbal and subsymbolic modes of processing have features in common with primary process, they are neither intrinsically primitive nor associated with either wish or conflict; all three modes of processing can be either intentional or automatic and can operate both within and outside of awareness.

Bucci agreed with Westen (1999a), who asserted that data now clearly indicate that many qualities Freud attributed to primary process thought (unconscious, imagistic, wish-fulfilling or drive-dominated, irrational, developmentally primitive, prelinguistic, and associative) constitute different kinds of thought, both conscious and unconscious, and may be present independent of one another. Nevertheless, while concepts of mental organization have developed considerably in the past century under the influence of both psychoanalytic observation and research from other branches of psychology, most analysts continue to use the terms *primary process* and *secondary process* (albeit not necessarily attached to the conceptual framework proposed by Freud) to refer to distinct modes of thought. *Primary process,* in particular, continues to be used to describe how the mind represents and communicates experience dominated by wishes and feelings associated with unconscious fantasy in highly condensed form.

Primary/Secondary Gain: see NEUROSIS

Principle, Constancy: see DRIVE, ENERGY, LIBIDO, METAPSYCHOLOGY, TOPOGRAPHIC THEORY

Principle, Inertia: see DEATH DRIVE, DRIVE, EN-
ERGY, LIBIDO, METAPSYCHOLOGY, TOPOGRAPHIC
THEORY

Principle of Multiple Function: see COMPROMISE
FORMATION, EGO, METAPSYCHOLOGY, MULTIPLE DE-
TERMINATION, STRUCTURAL THEORY

Principle, Nirvana: see DEATH DRIVE, DRIVE,
ENERGY, ID, METAPSYCHOLOGY, REPETITION COM-
PULSION, TOPOGRAPHIC THEORY, UNCONSCIOUS

Principle, Pleasure: see CATHEXIS, DEATH DRIVE,
DRIVE, ENERGY, LIBIDO, METAPSYCHOLOGY, MOTI-
VATION, PRECONSCIOUS, PRIMARY PROCESS, PSYCHIC
DETERMINISM, REALITY, REPETITION COMPULSION,
UNCONSCIOUS

Projection is a defensive operation whereby an individual attributes an unacceptable or intolerable idea,
impulse, or feeling to another person. Projection may
also include the defensive attribution of aspects of
the self representation, the superego, or an internal
object to another person. Projection is sometimes
used synonymously with the broader term *externalization,* the attribution of something within the
mind to the outside world, which does not necessarily serve defensive purpose (as, for example, a happy
person seeing the world through "rose-colored
glasses"). Externalization is related to the prepsychoanalytic meaning of the word *projection,* as it has
been used in many fields in connection with its literal meaning: "to throw in front of," as when an
image is thrown onto a screen. In the field of psychology, *projection* is used in this way to describe a
universal tendency to find reflections of inner life in
the external world; Rapaport refers to this tendency
as the **projective hypothesis** (Rapaport, 1944). An
example of this use of projection is **projective tests**
(as, for example, the Rorschach Test or the Thematic Apperception Test [TAT]), in which ambiguous stimuli are presented to a subject with the
understanding that the subject's interpretations will
reflect his inner life. Projection is also often used
this way (by Freud, among others) to describe the
animistic thinking of children and "primitive"
people, who assume that others think as they do or
that nature resembles inner life. J. Novick and Kelly
(1970) have argued that this process should be called
"generalization" rather than projection.

Projection, when used as a defense, ranges from
the normal and the universal, contributing to every
child's beliefs and fears about the world, to the highly
pathological, contributing to delusions and hallucinations in psychosis. Projection, when pathological,
is most often associated with paranoid states of
mind. Projection is distinct from but often used
interchangeably with **projective identification**, defined by Klein (1946) as a defensive process by which
parts of the self are forced into the object so as to
control the object from inside. The concept of projective identification has a long and complex history
of its own.

Like all processes of externalization and internalization, the concept of projection is important in
that it reflects the fact that psychological life develops and functions in interaction with an external
world; words such as *externalization, internalization, projection,* and *introjection* describe the processes of that interaction. More specifically, projection
reflects the fact that when children become aware
that other people have minds of their own, this
knowledge of other minds can be used for defensive
purposes. In his earliest observations of processes of
projection, Freud initiated an ongoing exploration
of the interaction between defense, object relations,
and interactions with other people.

Freud's (1894c) first published use of the term
projection was in 1894, when he explained paranoia
as the misuse of projection for the purpose of defense. In this comment, he notes awareness that the
concept of projection was already in use as a broader
concept; in his view, projection is a normal mechanism as long as the individual remains aware of his
own inner state. Thereafter, Freud's discussion of
projection focused sometimes on its role as a defense, and sometimes on its role as a universal,
nondefensive externalizing process. Freud (1911a) described projection as a defense most often in paranoid individuals who use projection to defend
against homoerotic wishes that have been transformed into hatred. However, he (1915b) also asserted
that projection can be used to rid the ego of any
mental contents that threaten displeasure, in contrast to introjection, which serves the opposite purpose. In other works, he noted the role of projection
(both defensive and nondefensive) in the formation
of superstitions (1909d), certain kinds of transference experiences (1910f), fantasies of the "end of the
world" (1911b), the overconfidence of the unanalyzed
analyst (1912b), beliefs about the rewards of the
afterlife (1913e), demons and taboos, works of art
(1913e), dreams (1917b), jealousy (1922), and phobias
(1926a).

Klein used the word *projection* interchangeably
with her new concept of projective identification;
these concepts play a major role in Kleinian theory.
In Klein's view, alternating processes of projection

and introjection work together from the earliest moments of infancy in the creation of both the inner and the external world. Ultimately, Klein (1946) began to use the term *projective identification* rather than *projection,* defining the former as the prototype of an aggressive object relationship. In her view, every individual must traverse a paranoid (later called paranoid-schizoid) position in which the projection of split-off, bad aspects of the self and/or the internal object results in persecutory anxiety. Failure to progress from the paranoid to the depressive position, characterized by anxiety over the fate of a whole, integrated, internalized good object in the face of one's own aggression, leads to paranoid psychopathology in the adult. Following the work of Klein, the psychoanalytic literature has been dominated by discussion of the complex processes of projective identification rather than projection.

An exception is the work of J. Novick and Kelly (1970) who sought to differentiate between processes of externalization, generalization, and projection. In their view, defensive externalization includes attribution of cause or responsibility to another (as, for example, when an individual admits to having a feeling or thought but blames it on another person); attribution of unwanted or devalued parts of the self to another person, usually to avoid narcissistic pain; and attribution of unacceptable wishes (or drive derivatives) onto another as a defense against anxiety. In their view, only the last should be referred to as projection.

Projective Identification is a process whereby unwanted, split-off parts of the self are forced into the object so as to control the object from inside. Projective identification is used variably to mean: a fantasy, a defense, and an object relationship; in some definitions, it is also a mode of communication. Among the various motives for projective identification is the wish to: rid the self of unwanted experience, control the object, avoid separation, and communicate about a state of mind. Projective identification is a normal and universal process, contributing to the development of the internal world and influencing how every adult experiences the world. However, pervasive use of projective identification is a manifestation of severe psychopathology. While projective identification was originally described as an aggressive action, it also refers to the attribution of positive parts of the self to others. Projective identification is strongly associated with the work of Klein, who coined the term in 1946. However, the term has taken on a life of its own, both within and outside of the Kleinian tradition. While controver-

sies as to the definition of the term abound, the concept of projective identification reflects efforts to understand the complex interactions between self and object, and internal and external worlds, in normal development, serious psychopathology, and the psychoanalytic situation. In many of its uses, projective identification has served as a bridging concept between the intrapsychic and the interpersonal domains.

Many theorists distinguish between projection and projective identification, with the latter defined as a primitive form of projection characterized by intense aggression, lack of differentiation between self and object, and continued "empathy" with the unwanted feeling, leading to an ongoing need to control the object (Kernberg, 1975). However, Klein and many of her followers do not distinguish between projection and projective identification, arguing that: every "phantasy" of projection includes part of the self; impulses and parts of the self never vanish when projected, but are felt to go into an object; the individual always maintains some contact with projected aspects of himself (Spillius, 1988; Hinshelwood, 1989; Spillius et al., 2011). Klein and others have also made the point that it is difficult, if not impossible, to distinguish between projection and identification, with each including aspects of the other. Projective identification results in the object's being perceived as having acquired the characteristics of the projected part of the self, but it also results in the self becoming identified with the object of its own projection. While theoretically, projective identification implies its opposite, **introjective identification**, this term has not had much use. Additional confusion surrounds the question of whether projective identification is best defined in terms of the subject's phantasies, or whether the definition should include aspects of a real interaction between subject and object. In other words, while Klein defined projective identification as a phantasy of the subject about his relationship to the object, some definitions include the real efforts of the subject to control the object, along with the real responses of this object. Other definitions of projective identification specifically exclude this aspect.

Freud (1910b) described the concept of projective identification in his exploration of the psychic life of Leonardo da Vinci. Freud described how Leonardo took his mother inside himself, becoming identified with her; he projected his own infantile self into the young men who became the object of his erotic interest. In other words, Leonardo attributed to the objects of his devotion characteristics that were really his own; by treating them with devotion, he was able to maintain the central relationship between a devoted mother and her son. The concept of projective identification was also adumbrated by A. Freud (1936), who described several complex defenses (such as altruistic surrender) that involve projecting parts of the self into another.

Klein (1946) first used the term *projective identification* in "Notes on Some Schizoid Mechanisms." She delineated several points related to projective identification: 1) Projective identification is closely associated with the paranoid-schizoid position, in which split-off, all-bad parts of the ego (self) are forcibly projected into the object. 2) The complex motives for projective identification include ridding the ego of unwanted aggressive parts so as to protect the internal world from aggression, and controlling the object from within. As a result of these combined motives, projective identification leads to what Klein called the "prototype of an aggressive object-relation." 3) While projective identification is most often used in relation to aggression, it can be used for good parts of the self, as for example, in the concept of **projection for safekeeping** (Heimann, 1942). In her later work, Klein (1955) described a type of projective identification characteristic of the depressive position, in which projection of good parts of the self serves to enrich the ego through securing a relation between it and a world endowed with goodness. 4) Projective identification occurs at the level of bodily phantasy, in that parts of the self are often associated with parts of the body; for example, the hated parts of the self are often associated with excrement, and the loved parts of the self are associated with the breast. Phantasies of forcefully ejecting aspects of the self follow the bodily model of vomiting or defecating. 5) Projective identification is a normal and universal part of development, contributing to creation of the internal world and to the differentiation between self and other. Indeed, projection and introjection represent two fundamental movements of the mind that take place in two locations: between the ego and its objects, and between the ego and the external world. Parts of the self and of objects that have been projected are subsequently reintrojected and then reprojected, this being a constant movement throughout life. 6) Projective identification is pathological when it is used excessively or when it continues to dominate the functioning of the personality. The pathological consequences of projective identification include paranoid fears of the object who is now felt to be menacing or, in turn, to be threatening to invade and control the subject; feelings (often psychotic) that the world has become

"strange," in that the object seems to have access to parts of the self; impoverishment of the self, sometimes to the point of extreme feelings of emptiness and unreality (as in schizoid states of mind); and/or excessive clinginess to an object who is experienced as containing valuable aspects of the self. When good parts of the self have been projected, the object may be idealized, often to the point of extreme submissiveness. The subject may even feel persecuted by the idea of perfection itself (Heimann, 1942). In the most extreme form of projective identification, the whole self is projected into an object with the aim of appropriating all the qualities of the object for oneself. This wholesale identification of the self with the object is typical of psychotic states where the subject feels that he has become someone famous (Klein, 1955).

Various of Klein's followers elaborated on the concept of projective identification. For example, Segal (1957, 1978) explored the effects of projective identification on the capacity to form symbols. In pathological situations, the patient confuses those aspects of himself that he has projected into an object with the object itself: The symbol is confused with the thing symbolized. Segal described this as forming a "symbolic equation," quite distinct from true symbolism, which can only occur when there is separation from the object.

Bion (1959) made a fundamental contribution to the understanding of projective identification, elaborating on its role in psychological development and in the clinical situation. He distinguished between pathological and normal types of projective identification. Pathological projective identification is characterized by extreme hatred and violence, the quality of omnipotent control, and the specific aim of destroying awareness of reality. Normal projective identification is characterized by an effort to communicate with another about one's state of mind, by putting this state of mind "into" the other. Bion (1962a) introduced the metaphor of the container and the contained to represent this process, both in the clinical situation and in normal development. When all goes well, the object (analyst/mother) receives the projections of the patient/baby and contains them within her own mind through a process called "reverie" and returns them to the patient/baby in a more manageable form. In his work, Bion defines projective identification in a new way that includes its actual effects on the real object and the object's responses. This extension of the concept has had a major influence on theories of development and of psychoanalytic treatment.

Expanding on the work of Bion, Ogden (1979) offered a definition of projective identification which includes an individual's fantasies of placing an unwanted part of himself in another, his real-life efforts to pressure the other into behaving in accord with these fantasies, and his reintrojection of the projection, as modified by the other. In this view, Ogden stressed how projective identification serves to bridge the intrapsychic and the interpersonal domains, shedding light on how best to understand both development and the clinical situation.

Rosenfeld (1971a, 1971b), along with Bion, further clarified the distinction between different kinds of projective identification, delineating: **communicative projective identification** (a benign form in which the patient wishes to make the analyst endure experiences that the patient cannot manage himself) and **evacuative projective identification** (similar to Klein's original concept). Rosenfeld also explored the important connections between projective identification, narcissism, and envy. In his view, the desire to get inside the object becomes very intense just at the point where the object is felt to be separate from the self and possessed of good and valuable qualities. At this moment, the subject may project himself into the object so as to possess its good qualities, avoid awareness of separation, and abolish painful feelings of envy. Rosenfeld described how this defensive strategy contributes to narcissistic object relations. He also described the various contributions of projective identification to psychosis (Bell, 2001).

Kernberg (1975) described the predominance of projective identification (and other defense mechanisms based on splitting) in borderline and narcissistic personality disorders, and the contributions of projective identification to understanding countertransference in the clinical situation.

J. Sandler (1976b, 1987b) attempted to integrate Klein's concept of projective identification with his own views of the representational world. Sandler recognized fantasies of projective identification as important in development, in psychopathology, and in the clinical situation, but he rejected Klein's emphasis on the death drive, her developmental timetable, and much of her emphasis on bodily phantasy. Sandler also rejected Bion's extension of the concept of projective identification to include interactions between the baby and mother, or patient and analyst, in terms of the container and the contained. While recognizing the importance of Bion's observations, Sandler saw them as reflecting a universal tendency to "actualize" fantasies rather than as the

result of projective identification itself. Joseph (1989) explored how the analyst can identify and manage the effects of projective identification in the clinical situation, describing the many ways in which the phantasies of projective identification can become "actualized."

Psychic Apparatus: see EGO, ENERGY, METAPSYCHOLOGY, STRUCTURAL THEORY, TOPOGRAPHIC THEORY

Psychic Determinism is a broad theoretical principle that asserts that all mental events are caused by antecedent mental events, or that all mental events follow the law of cause and effect. Freud (1915/1916) used the principle of psychic determinism to argue that mental phenomenon including thoughts, symptoms, dreams, and slips of the tongue should never be regarded as accidental; all mental phenomena are meaningful, although the meaning may be discovered to be unconscious. Psychic determinism is the principle that justifies the "fundamental rule" of the psychoanalytic method in which the patient is asked to say whatever comes to mind. As Freud argued, when conscious control of the flow of thought is relaxed in free association, it is possible to observe how conscious experience is "determined by important internal attitudes of mind which are not known to us at the moment."

The principle of psychic determinism did not emerge from psychoanalysis itself but was borrowed by Freud from the surrounding scientific culture, wherein it was assumed that the mind, as a product of a biological organism, must follow natural laws. In Freud's view, determinism was "the whole Weltanschauung of science." In "Studies on Hysteria," Breuer and Freud (1893/1895) described how the "strict" application of the principle of psychic determinism to the data generated by the new technique of free association led to the concept of defense hysteria in which psychogenic ideas are forced from awareness by the motive of defense. In "The Interpretation of Dreams," Freud (1900) found intentionality in the chaotic productions of sleep. In "The Psychopathology of Everyday Life," he (1901) argued that "nothing in the mind is arbitrary or undetermined," providing exhaustive evidence for the underlying reasons for parapraxes, superstitions, and seemingly chance actions and choices of daily life.

While belief in the principle of psychic determinism has remained a central tenet of psychoanalysis (C. Brenner, 1955), many authors have sought to clarify ambiguities in Freud's use of the term. For instance, several have noted that Freud spoke of determinism both to indicate that a piece of behavior or mental life has meaning and to indicate that it has causality (Basch, 1978; M. Phillips, 1981). The emphasis on the latter aspect has led to a variety of debates, such as the degree to which all human behavior is preordained by biological drives and early life experience, or whether Freud's statements on causality conflict with the possibility of free will, psychic change, and the development of an autonomous ego (Knight, 1946; Lipton, 1955). Basch (1978) suggested that analysis creates change by providing a new set of mental experiences based in the transference, which then serve as determinants of later thought and behavior. Rosenblatt and Thickstun (1977) argued that psychic determinism should best be understood in probabilistic rather than absolute terms. Other questions related to psychic determinism in psychoanalysis include: Does it matter to psychoanalysis if the strict determinism, which it borrowed originally from physics, has broken down? Should psychic determinism really be used as a heuristic rather than a hard fact of science (Erdelyi, 1985)?

Psychic Energy: see ENERGY

Psychic Organizers: see PREOEDIPAL

Psychic Reality is the subjective experience that results from the interplay and integration of sensory perceptions of an objective, incompletely knowable, external or material reality, with the conscious derivatives of unconscious internal motivations and structural determinants. Analysts of different theoretical persuasions may variously define these underlying unconscious structural determinants as consisting of unconscious fantasies, self experiences, or internalized object relationships. A second definition of psychic reality, more in line with Freud's original usage, equates it with unconscious experience only, usually unconscious desire and its associated fantasies. In this usage, psychic reality is the inner source of subjective experience, as the external world is its outer source. The conscious derivatives of psychic reality and the sensory perceptions of external reality together influence the individual's mental representation of the world.

With either usage, the concept of psychic reality underscores the fundamental psychoanalytic discovery that unconscious motivations and structures are as "real" and determinative for the individual as anything in the external world. Through understanding these unconscious determinants as fully as possible, psychoanalytic treatment aims to expand the individual's sense of agency within that experiential world. In other words, through psychoanalytic exploration, the individual becomes increasingly aware of how he is impelled by motives that were previously unknown to him, thereby providing him with greater capacity to make conscious choices and decisions.

Freud (1895b) first distinguished "thought reality" from "external reality" in his 1895 "Project for a Scientific Psychology." In "The Interpretation of Dreams," Freud (1900) changed *thought reality* to *psychical reality,* using it to describe the nature of the unconscious and asserting that neither the unconscious nor the external world could be fully apprehended by consciousness. The mental representations, dreams, and fantasies of conscious subjective experience are transitional and intermediate derivatives of psychical reality, modified by secondary processes.

Freud's recognition of the centrality and influence of psychic over material reality came with his dawning discovery in the late 1890s, that fantasies rather than actual traumatic sexual experiences play the pivotal role in the etiology of neurosis. Most subsequent theorists, however, have inverted Freud's formula, using the term *psychic reality* to refer to conscious subjective experience, with the unconscious entering into psychic reality only to the extent that it exerts an influence on conscious awareness. From this vantage point, psychic reality cannot be opposed to external reality, as the two are inextricably intermixed. To the extent that external reality can only be known subjectively, it is a part of psychic reality (Loewald, 1960; W. Meissner, 2000). In his famous double-movie-projector metaphor, Arlow (1969a) described psychic reality as the screen on which images from the side of external reality become inextricably intermingled with images from the side of internal unconscious fantasy. Psychic reality is then the psychic admixture of fact and fantasy. Subsequently, Arlow (1996) advocated dropping the term altogether, arguing that with increasing pluralism of psychoanalytic theory, the concept of psychic reality had lost its usefulness due to the lack of any agreement as to the nature and quality of its unconscious mental constituents.

Intersubjectivists emphasize an intersubjective psychic reality that is co-created between patient and analyst, while Meissner argued that the inherent subjectivity of psychic experience precludes any form of direct intersubjective communication (W. Meissner, 2000).

Psychoanalysis is a discipline introduced by Sigmund Freud and developed by others, whose focus is to understand the nature of human mental life.

Psychoanalysis includes a theory of the mind, a theory of some aspects of psychopathology, a medical treatment, and a method of investigating the mind (Freud, 1923c). Psychoanalysis also includes a professional enterprise made up of mental health practitioners who engage in psychoanalytic clinical practice, as well as theoreticians and investigators in a variety of disciplines who contribute to the development of psychoanalytic theory or who apply psychoanalytic theory to other disciplines.

The psychoanalytic theory of the mind emphasizes the interaction of several aspects of psychological life, including: 1) the influence of unconscious mental life, especially unconscious conflict; 2) the vicissitudes of motivation, including wishes, moral imperatives, attachment needs, and narcissistic strivings; 3) the many specific organizing structures and/or processes of the mind, including self and object representations, fantasies, conflicts, character, as well as the many ego functions that contribute to self regulation and adaptation, such as defense, compromise, and reality testing, and the dynamic relationships between and among them; and 4) the developmental point of view, from which the previous aspects of mental life are understood, which includes attention to both inborn and environmental factors and considers the complexities of how past experience lives on in the present.

The psychoanalytic theory of psychopathology addresses how these interacting psychological factors play a role in various kinds of mental suffering including neurosis and character pathology. Psychoanalytic treatment is based on a deep exploration of psychological life. It places special emphasis on the exploration of how the patient manages psychological conflict, how he avoids full awareness of psychological life (resistance), and, how he enacts or expresses psychological life in the treatment experience, itself (transference and resistance). The aim of psychoanalytic treatment is to deepen and expand the patient's psychological experience with the goal of ameliorating suffering and improving adaptive functioning.

The psychoanalytic method of investigation coincides with the psychoanalytic treatment situation. Both are based on a process of communicated introspection that takes place between analyst and patient. Traditionally, the psychoanalytic method of investigation includes the technique of free association and the exploration of the treatment experience itself, most importantly the vicissitudes of the patient's transference and resistance. While psychoanalytic theory is largely derived from clinical data, it is also influenced by findings from neighboring

disciplines, including developmental psychology, general psychology (including cognitive neuroscience and social psychology), psychiatry, the social sciences (including anthropology and sociology), and the neighboring humanities (including philosophy and literature). At the same time, psychoanalysis has had an impact on all of these neighboring disciplines, as well as on education, law, and the study of culture. Finally, while psychoanalysis is only one of many types of therapy practiced in the mental health community, it has contributed to almost all forms of psychological treatments for emotional suffering.

While in his early work, Freud referred to his treatment of patients as "psychical analysis" (Freud, 1894c) or "psychological analysis" (Freud, 1894e), he coined the term *psychoanalysis* in 1896 to describe his method of treatment (Freud, 1896d). In the same year, Freud (1896b) wrote to Fliess that he was also well on his way to inventing a "new psychology," based on the idea of mental "registrations" characterized by "unconsciousness." During the course of his writing life, Freud offered several definitions of psychoanalysis. The most famous and oft-quoted of these definitions appeared in an encyclopedia article in which Freud (1923c) argued that "psychoanalysis is the name: 1) of a procedure for the investigation of mental processes which are almost inaccessible in any other way, 2) of a method (based on that investigation) for the treatment of neurotic disorders and 3) of a collection of psychological information obtained along those lines, which is gradually being accumulated into a new scientific discipline." Elsewhere, Freud made various attempts to define these components with greater specificity, sometimes referring to these more-specific components as "shibboleths," which separate analysts from nonanalysts. These included the nuclear role of the oedipus complex (1905b), the theory of dreams (1914d, 1933a), and the division of the "psychic apparatus" into id, ego, and superego (1938a). However, most often Freud (1898a, 1901, 1923a, 1925d) defined psychoanalysis as "the science of unconscious mental processes." More specifically, he argued that the theory of repression is the "cornerstone" upon which the edifice of psychoanalytic theory rests, leading inevitably to the phenomena of transference and resistance; Freud (1914d) asserted that any investigation of the mind that starts from the phenomena of transference and resistance may call itself psychoanalysis. Finally, Freud (1898a) made an attempt to define psychoanalysis in terms of his concept of "metapsychology," going "beyond psychology" to become a psychology of the unconscious. In his elaboration of the concept of metapsychology, Freud (1915g) argued that the topographic, dynamic, and economic points of view are all necessary for a complete description of mental processes. (Rapaport and Gill [1959] later elaborated on this approach to defining the essence of psychoanalysis in terms of its metapsychology, adding the structural, genetic, and adaptive points of view.) Jones (1946) summarized Freud's definition of psychoanalysis as the study of the unconscious that utilizes the technique of free association to analyze the phenomena of transference and resistance.

Despite the specificity of Jones's summary, controversies about the theory and technique of psychoanalysis have been present since its earliest history. A number of different schools of psychoanalytic thought have emerged over time, such that the contemporary psychoanalytic landscape is characterized by theoretical diversity. These schools are differentiated from one another on the basis of a model of the mind, a view of psychopathology and development; a theory of therapeutic action, and a technique of clinical practice. Examples of these schools of thought include ego psychology, Kleinian psychoanalysis, varieties of object relations theory, self psychology, interpersonal psychoanalysis, relational psychoanalysis, Jungian psychology, and Lacanian psychoanalysis, to mention a few.

There is disagreement within the field as to whether these various schools of thought share "common ground" (A. M. Cooper, 1985; Wallerstein, 1992; Rangell, 2007), or whether they are fundamentally irreconcilable. The manifestations of such diversity within the clinical situation are vast. Although many contemporary psychoanalysts of different theoretical orientations continue to privilege the use of free association and the analysis of transference and resistance, those same analysts may also disagree about the relative contributions of conflict versus deficit to the patient's psychic organization, and may also disagree about the role of the analyst's empathy and/or countertransference in their interpretive function. Other analysts may reject the interpretation of transference and resistance in favor of the exploration of the here-and-now relationship between the analyst and patient, emphasizing intersubjectivity, the co-construction of the analytic situation, and/or the therapeutic benefit of nonverbal aspects of the analytic relationship. Contemporary analysts also disagree about adherence to what have been regarded as the universal clinical principles of abstinence, neutrality, and anonymity. Some analysts argue that the analyst's judicial self disclosures may facilitate the analytic process, and that neutrality is an obstructive fiction and ought not be held as an ideal. Other sources of controversy include the proper frequency of a psychoanalytic treatment, the use of the couch, the length of the sessions, and even whether it may be conducted by telephone, and so forth. However, in contradistinction to the rampant controversy within the field, a "relational tilt" among all analysts has been frequently noted. In other words, psychoanalysts of all theoretical persuasions have increasingly recognized the contribution of the analytic relationship to therapeutic action.

Controversies about the definition of psychoanalysis have also emerged related to fundamental challenges to psychoanalytic epistemology. Some of these overlapping controversies include questions such as: 1) Should psychoanalysis be defined as a "general psychology," as argued by Hartmann (1939a, 1939b, 1964), or should it be defined more narrowly, as for example, when Kris (1947) argued famously that psychoanalysis is the study of "human behavior viewed as conflict"? 2) Does psychoanalysis need an abstract theory (metapsychology) that goes beyond clinical observation as argued by Rapaport and Gill (1959), Hartmann (1964), and more recently Shevrin (2003), or can it be simply a clinical theory (Schafer, 1976; Gill, 1976; G. Klein, 1976)? 3) Should psychoanalysis be included among the natural sciences, as asserted often by Freud (1913c, 1925e, 1933c), or is it best understood as an interpretive discipline and therefore classified among the humanities (Spence, 1982; Schafer, 1983, Edelson, 1985)? Others have argued that psychoanalysis is a hybrid discipline with features of both science and the humanities (Ricoeur, 1970; Gill, 1976; L. Friedman, 2000). Developments in cognitive neuroscience, as for example the "rediscovery of the unconscious," place additional pressure on psychoanalysis to define its unique approach to the study of unconscious processes (Kihlstrom, 1995). Developments in postmodern philosophy pose challenges about the very nature of psychoanalytic data and knowledge.

Finally, there are intense controversies in the professional domain about how to define and regulate the title *psychoanalyst* and how best to organize and regulate psychoanalytic education.

Psychoanalytic Psychotherapy, also known as **Psychodynamic Psychotherapy**, **Insight-Oriented Psychotherapy**, and **Expressive Psychotherapy**, is psychotherapy based on the theory and technique of psychoanalysis. The practice of psychoanalytic psychotherapy has greatly expanded the universe of patients who may benefit from treatments that utilize the application of psychoanalytic principles. There has been considerable controversy about the specific techniques, indications, and therapeutic action of psychoanalytic psychotherapy, and about the degree to which it differs from both psychoanalysis and supportive psychotherapy. Like psychoanalysis, psychoanalytic psychotherapy usually makes use of a psychoanalytic model of mental functioning, and the technique of interpretation of defenses, resistances, and transference. It differs from psychoanalysis in formal ways, for example, patients usually sit up facing the therapist and there are fewer sessions per week. In addition, psychoanalytic psychotherapy may have a more-focused therapeutic aim than psychoanalysis, the analysis of transference may play a less central role, and there may be greater attention paid to the realities of the patient's daily life. A patient may be referred for psychoanalytic psychotherapy rather than psychoanalysis because: the presenting problem is not expressive of global, long-standing, maladaptive patterns necessitating the intensive time commitment of psychoanalysis; the patient is facing a specific crisis and requires a brief and more-focused treatment; the patient is unable to tolerate the intimacy or the interpersonal ambiguity of the psychoanalytic treatment setting without psychological deterioration; the patient's current life circumstances are tumultuous or unstable, requiring more active, reality-oriented intervention; practical considerations make a four-to-five-times-weekly treatment impossible; and/or the patient is unmotivated for more intensive work. Psychoanalytic psychotherapy is distinguished from **supportive psychotherapy**, in which various noninterpretive techniques aim to strengthen adaptive functions such as defenses, without deeper exploration or the fostering of insight; and the transference relationship is not interpreted but is utilized to promote growth and change.

Psychoanalytic psychotherapy involves the application of psychoanalytic ideas within therapies other than formal psychoanalysis, thereby extending psychoanalytically based treatment to a wider range of patients. It is of further interest because it has been the stimulus for attempts to characterize what it is about a treatment that makes it psychoanalytic and how treatments may differ from psychoanalysis proper.

Freud used the terms *psychoanalysis* and *analytic therapy* interchangeably throughout his writings. However, in 1919, he (1919a) differentiated psychoanalysis, which employed interpretation, from the

"psychotherapies." The latter were utilized to treat a wider patient population, and they combined interpretation with "suggestion." While various psychotherapies, including psychoanalytic therapies, were discussed in the psychoanalytic and psychiatric literature throughout the early decades of the twentieth century, they were not described as psychoanalytic psychotherapy (Kitson, 1925). The first usage in the psychiatric literature of the term *psychoanalytic psychotherapy* was in Fromm-Reichmann's (1943) description of her treatment of psychotic patients; Obendorf (1946) first used the term in the psychoanalytic literature. In the same year, F. Alexander and French (1946) described the technique of the "corrective emotional experience" in their book *Psychoanalytic Therapy: Principles and Application*, and Fromm-Reichmann (1950) described her Sullivanian interpersonal treatment of psychotic patients as psychoanalytic psychotherapy in *Principles of Intensive Psychotherapy*. These publications provided impetus for efforts to differentiate psychoanalysis from psychoanalytic psychotherapy, because each of the authors used techniques at odds with mainstream psychoanalysis, yet claimed their treatments were, in essence, psychoanalytic. In response, Rangell (1954), E. Bibring (1954), and Gill (1954) emphasized that psychoanalysis is characterized by the establishment of a transference neurosis, and by the exclusive use of interpretation to achieve structural change through insight and to resolve the transference. Each author contrasted these techniques and aims with psychotherapies that achieved therapeutic benefit by the therapist's active interventions, manipulations to promote experiential learning, and an emphasis on interpersonal rather than intrapsychic functioning. Gill, however, noted that some intensive psychotherapies were closer to psychoanalytic treatments in both their techniques and outcomes.

Alexander and French's corrective emotional experience never achieved prominence, but the practice of psychoanalytic psychotherapy based on psychoanalytic technique became widespread. The debate about the boundaries of psychoanalytic psychotherapy with both psychoanalysis on the one side and supportive psychotherapy on the other continued actively for the next thirty years, with little empirical data to support qualitative divisions among the three. Some earlier authors (Tarachow, 1962) emphasized the distinctions between psychoanalysis and all other psychotherapies, while others (Dewald, 1964) underscored the similarities, differentiating both psychoanalysis and psychoanalytic psychotherapy from supportive psychotherapy. Paradoxically, Wallerstein (1993) found that aspects of what had been called supportive treatment, especially the therapeutic benefit of the patient's unanalyzed positive attachment to the therapist, are beneficial components of both psychoanalysis and psychoanalytic psychotherapy. Others have explored the use of combined supportive and exploratory elements in the psychodynamic treatment of depression (F. N. Busch, Rudden, and Shapiro, 2004). Kernberg (1999), however, has argued that the inclusion of supportive elements interferes with transference analysis in psychoanalytic psychotherapy. Some contemporary authors (Zerbe, 2007) underscore the similarities between psychoanalysis and psychoanalytic psychotherapy, and include the previously unacknowledged role of the dyadic relationship in both treatments.

Several manualized psychoanalytic psychotherapies, for which therapist adherence can be rated, have been developed: 1) Luborsky's (1984) **Supportive-Expressive Psychotherapy** (whose name explicitly acknowledges the role of both supportive and interpretive elements) operationalizes psychoanalytic concepts and uses the CCRT (Core Conflictual Relationship Theme), a scored, reliable measurement that captures essential components of subjectively experienced interpersonal interactions. 2) Clarkin, Yeomans, and Kernberg's (1999) **Transference-Focused Psychotherapy for Borderlines** is a manualized treatment that uses an object relations approach to the interpretation of transference as it is experienced in the here-and-now treatment relationship, avoiding interpretations linking present and past experience. 3) B. Milrod et al.'s (1997) manualized **Brief Psychodynamic Treatment for Panic Disorder** has demonstrated the efficacy of psychoanalytically informed treatments of panic and agoraphobia. 4) **Mentalization-Based Psychotherapy** (Bateman and Fonagy, 2004, 2006) is based on the authors' finding that secure attachment, facilitated by an affectively attuned parent, is required for the small child's development of the capacity to mentalize (understand the mental states of one's self and others). Mentalization treatment involves the establishment of a secure therapist-patient relationship in which the therapist responds in a contingent, congruent way to the patient's affective states while accepting rather than interpreting the patient's transference experience.

Psychopathy is a set of personality traits that includes incapacity for empathy, lack of remorse for one's own misdeeds, and exploitation of others, often accompanied by violations of social, moral, and legal norms. The term **psychopathic** is often used interchangeably with *antisocial, dissocial, asocial, sociopathic,* or *amoral,* with each term carrying a slightly different connotation depending upon whether it is used in psychiatric, legal, or sociological context. In general, the term *antisocial* refers to aspects of a socially deviant lifestyle, such as lying, cheating, and stealing (as in the antisocial personality disorder in the *DSM*), while the term *psychopathic* refers to underlying personality features, especially moral weakness and lack of empathy and/or concern for others (Cleckley, 1941; Hare, 1980). Psychoanalysts have long recognized the complex biological and environmental determinants of psychopathy; they have also long been aware of the fact that psychopathy is not best treated in psychoanalysis. Nevertheless, psychoanalysis has made important contributions to the psychology of morality and, conversely, of immorality.

The origins of the concept of psychopathy go back as far as Theophrastus, a student of Aristotle, whose description of the "Unscrupulous Man" includes many characteristics of psychopathy. Modern efforts to categorize different kinds of "moral imbeciles" (Maudsley, 1874) began in the early nineteenth century and continue to this day. However, it is only by the middle of the twentieth century that the terms *psychopathy* and/or **psychopathic personality** came to be used to describe people with impaired moral functioning, most systematically in the work of Cleckley (1941). In psychoanalysis, the term *psychopathic* appears in Freud's (1907a) work with the nonspecific meaning of susceptibility to develop neurosis. He preferred the simple word *scoundrel* to refer to people whom he deemed morally unfit, contrasting them unfavorably to neurotics, whom he judged to be morally intact. Freud was famously pessimistic about treatment for "scoundrels," counseling a colleague to "ship such people ... across the ocean ... to South America." However, Freud (1916) did offer a psychoanalytic explanation for people he called "The Exceptions" (for example, Shakespeare's Richard III), whose demand for reparation for early narcissistic injury leads them to exempt themselves from the limits imposed by ordinary reality and morality. He also described what he called "criminals from a sense of guilt," or people who commit crimes with the aim of finding punishment for an unconscious sense of guilt.

Aichhorn (1925) offered the first major psychoanalytic exploration of antisocial behavior, arguing, "Delinquency is the consequence of an inhibition of development . . . along the path from primitive reality adaptation to social adaptation." He proposed a therapeutic strategy designed to promote enough positive transference to allow the delinquent to move beyond a sole reliance on the pleasure principle by incorporating some influence from the reality principle. In his introduction to the book, Freud (1925c) praised Aichhorn's *Wayward Youth* as an important contribution to "applied psychoanalysis."

Later psychoanalysts writing about psychopathic personalities continued to explore the role of pathological identifications (R. Eissler, 1949). For example, A. Johnson (1949) introduced the term *superego lacunae*, which result when a parent consciously or unconsciously encourages delinquent actions by a child for his or her own gratification. Other analysts explored the contributions of excess aggression, pregenital libido, ego weaknesses such as poor impulse control and anxiety tolerance, primitive defenses, and primitive objects relations (Michaels and Stiver, 1965). Psychoanalysts interested in development have focused on childhood histories of trauma and abuse and on childhood behaviors that predict for adult psychopathy. For example, in his work with juvenile offenders, Winnicott (1956c) described what he called the "antisocial tendency." Later, Winnicott (1960a) described antisocial tendencies in terms of what he called the "true self," and the "false self."

Other analysts have focused on countertransference responses evoked by psychopathic behavior (Gabbard, 1994b), with some arguing that criminals serve as scapegoats for the rest of us seeking acceptable outlets for our own aggression (R. Eissler, 1949). Several authors have explored the "imposter" as a variant of psychopathic personality (Abraham, 1925b; H. Deutsch, 1955; Greenacre, 1958b), with Gediman (1985) offering the important reminder that conflicts around authenticity and truthfulness lie on a continuum from the normal to the psychopathic. More recently, Kernberg (1984) has argued that psychopathy is best understood as a primitive variant of narcissistic personality disorder, most similar to what he calls "malignant narcissism," but more extreme in terms of a complete inability to invest in any relationship that is not exploitative.

The *Psychodynamic Diagnostic Manual* (*PDM*) distinguishes between aggressive and passive/parasitic forms of antisocial personality disorder, the former characterized by violence and predatory behavior resulting from identification with an abusive parent, and the latter characterized by nonviolence and manipulativeness (PDM Task Force, 2006). Most re-

cently, Fonagy, Sharp, and others have reported evidence linking childhood conduct disorder, adolescent delinquency, and some kinds of violence to impaired capacity for mentalization. His team has developed and investigated psychoanalytically based treatments emphasizing mentalization for the treatment and prevention of delinquency and violence (Mentalization-Based Psychotherapy) (Sharp et al., 2009).

Psychosexual Development is a theory of human development that is conceptualized according to the neurobiologically determined vicissitudes of the sexual drive, a sequence outlined by Freud in 1905 (1905b) and elaborated in subsequent contributions (1923b). The early phases, which appear sequentially but with considerable overlap, correspond with the area of the body—the pregenital erotogenic zone—that is most invested with libido at a given time. The sequence culminates in the oedipus complex. Each of the pregenital psychosexual phases (oral, anal, and phallic) is associated with its own specific modalities of desire and forms of aggression linked to the dominant bodily zone; each phase likewise engenders specific fantasies and conflicts related to parents and other significant objects in the environment. Such fantasies and conflicts may persist throughout life and shape aspects of character or psychopathology. Freud also described his notion of infantile sexuality in terms of component instincts of the sexual drive, with their sources in the erotogenic zones, which only become synthesized with each other in the service of reproduction at a relatively late stage in development. The child's sexual constitution, under the sway of the component instincts, is polymorphously perverse and in its early stages is satisfied through autoerotic activity. In this formulation, the earlier pregenital stages (component instincts) are left behind or incorporated into adult foreplay, unless specific difficulties lead to pathological fixation or regression. According to Freud's original schema, the overarching shape of psychosexual development shows a psychobiologically determined "diphasic" pattern, which he attributed primarily to repression of the oedipal constellation, resulting in a period of latency. Recent studies suggest that latency is more likely the result of multiple developmental and cultural influences (T. Shapiro, 1976) but that the diphasic nature of childhood sexuality is clearly demonstrable (Friedrich et al., 1998). It is during puberty or later that the final, adult genital stage of sexual organization is attained.

The concept of psychosexual development, which remains more or less present in most psychoanalytic theories (Michels, 1999), raises important theoretical questions with regard to the fundamental nature of human development and the role of the body in mental life. While Freud's discovery of infantile sexuality and its formative role in adult character and psychopathology were groundbreaking at the time, his theory of psychosexual development has been critiqued on multiple grounds. Psychosexual development implies the emergence of hierarchically organized, sequential mental organizations, thus a discontinuous developmental sequence, but the closely associated notions of fixations and regressions suggest that linear movement backward to previous states is possible. Modern psychoanalytic developmental thinkers argue for a more-complex, dynamic systems model (Abrams, 1983; Coates, 1997; Mayes, 2001; P. Tyson, 2002) that cannot be described by a linear sequence. Other critiques challenge the impact of the theory on the interpretation of concrete bodily imagery in the psychoanalysis of adult patients. These authors (W. Grossman and Stewart, 1976; Melnick, 1997) agree that early experience is encoded in bodily experience and imagery, but they argue that inevitably these images come to have multiple complex meanings, including defensive ones, as development proceeds. Contemporary developmental theories have either shifted the focus to other specific features critical to development—for example, attachment, separation-individuation, the self—or have attempted to delineate a more-complex, integrated perspective of the development of the total personality, for example developmental lines. Finally, Freud's theory predates empirically derived concepts of gender development and revised formulations regarding female psychosexual development, and it moreover presumes that heterosexuality is the normal outcome of sexual development. Consequently, contemporary gender theorists have rejected it.

In Freud's schema, during the oral phase, corresponding roughly to the first eighteen months of life, the mouth, lips, tongue, and upper digestive tract play a dominant role in the organization of the psyche. The early oral stage is primarily associated with oral satisfaction and gratification. Later, coinciding with the development of teeth, more aggressive aspects of orality develop and pleasure is derived from activities such as chewing and biting.

The anal phase emerges toward the end of the oral phase, beginning at approximately one year of age and extending to the third year of life. Corresponding to the development of sphincter control and ultimately to the environmental demand for toilet training, the child's attention and libidinal investment shift to the anal zone. Similar to the evolution of the oral phase, the anal phase is divided into anal erotism and anal sadism, the later facilitated by the child's muscular development. During this time, the active/passive polarity also emerges as the psychic organizer of drive activity and experience and serves as the forerunner to conflicts of ambivalence and other more-complex polarities such as masculinity and femininity. This polarity is demonstrated by pleasure and unpleasure associated with the expulsion and retention of fecal matter. Later in this phase, pleasure is derived from soiling and destroying, holding on to, or trapping. It is also evident in the typical patterns of compliance or defiance that emerge in the child's relationship to the parent around the accomplishment of bowel and bladder control. Freud described the emergence of aggression during the anal phase in terms of the component instinct for cruelty and also the instinct for mastery, both relatively independent of any erogenous zone.

In the phallic phase, spanning the years from three to five, the external genitalia become the primary sources of interest and pleasure. This phase is associated with a generally heightened interest in the naked body, its activities and processes, and with pleasure in the component instincts of looking (scopophilia) and showing (exhibitionism). The phallic phase is the most controversial of Freud's pregenital stages of development; it has been revised on several grounds, which is reflected in its also having been renamed the infantile genital stage. Firstly, infant researchers have found substantial evidence of genital preoccupation in all children from fifteen months of age on, and have proposed that an early genital phase occurs between fifteen and twenty-four months in both boys and girls (Roiphe, 1968; Roiphe and Galenson, 1981a, 1981b). Secondly, Freud's use of phallocentric terminology, which reflected his view that the early psychosexual development of boys and girls is in most respects identical and that in the mind of the child the only proper genital organ is the penis, has been rejected and subject to numerous contemporary revisions (Parens, 1980; Mayer, 1985; Chodorow, 1995, 1996; Dorsey, 1996; Olesker, 1998a). Stoller's (1976) argument that the little girl's femininity arises from her genetic endowment and that it is promoted and elaborated by sex assignment at birth and by parental attitudes and handling, supports the observation from research that the girl's sense of herself as a girl is well established long before the phallic phase (De Marneffe, 1997). However, both boy and girl struggle throughout the third year of life to establish the equation between gender and genital (that is, the child knows clearly his or her gender but cannot reliably equate that with the corresponding genital). This is only firmly in place by thirty-six months. Contemporary writers disagree about whether the little girl experiences her own uniquely feminine "genital anxieties" prior to the recognition of genital differences, with its associated deflation and penis envy, or whether these follow thereafter (Olesker, 1998a).

Most psychoanalytic theorists agree that boys and girls accomplish the watershed configuration of the oedipal complex in different ways. In Freud's formulation, penis envy and the "recognition" of her "castrated" state leads the girl into the oedipal complex, where she identifies with the mother and seeks to obtain the father's phallus and then a baby as consolation. For the boy, recognition of sexual differences and castration anxiety lead out of the oedipus complex to renunciation of competitive strivings and compensatory identification with the father in order to safeguard possession of the penis. Both boys and girls must contend with the added blow that they are little and not suitable partners for the desired parent and must await adulthood for their envied gratifications, a potential source of narcissistic mortification. The superego—the mental agency formed from the identifications with the parents and an important internalized source of self esteem—is formed from the child's oedipal struggles. It is now understood that superego precursors can be observed prior to the oedipal resolution and that the superego undergoes revision well into early adulthood (H. Blum, 1985; Chused, 1987; E. Blum and H. Blum, 1990).

The period of latency follows, characterized by Freud as a phase of decreased sexual-drive intensity, as compared to the preceding oedipal phase and the succeeding adolescent phase. Contemporary theorists emphasize the greater equilibrium between defense and drive during latency, resulting in the child's greater capacity to master mental and physical operations, to establish himself within a social community beyond the family system, and to sustain sublimatory activities, all of which contribute to a heightening of self esteem (Schecter and Combrinck-Graham, 1980). Latency has been divided into two phases (Bornstein, 1951), the first distinguished by a very active struggle against masturbation, when the superego is still experienced as a harsh and alien "foreign body," and the second in which the superego is better integrated and the child more securely immersed in typical school-related and peer-oriented activities.

With puberty, the child experiences a biologically determined upsurge in libido, ultimately associated during late adolescence with the attainment of adult genitality. A new focus on sexual intercourse incorporates the "component instincts" of the individual's prior psychosexual development into forepleasure (foreplay) and achieves the final adult organization, with the corresponding biological capacities for orgasm in the male (the female having attained this capacity prior to puberty), impregnation, and childbearing.

Abraham (1924a) built upon Freud's schema of psychosexual development by integrating ideas about libidinal drive development with early object relations. He also more systematically accounted for the influence of aggression, which Freud had not yet designated as a drive, equal in significance to the sexual drive. Abraham described the early oral sucking stage as pre-ambivalent; both the later oral biting stage and the subsequent anal-sadistic stage as ambivalent; and the genital stage, in which the infant has learned to spare the object psychically to save it from destruction, as post-ambivalent. These concepts had an influence on Klein (1948a, 1948b), who ultimately replaced Freud's notion of sequential libidinal stages with the concept of "positions" (paranoid-schizoid and depressive) that have characteristic patterns of object relations, anxieties, and defenses and are present throughout life. Klein emphasized the role of aggression, more so than libido, in the early development of object relations.

Erikson (1950) was among the first to expand Freud's framework of the psychosexual stages to a process that spanned the life cycle. Erikson's stage theory retained Freud's developmental perspective but situated it within the context of the family and psychosocial/cultural surround. While Freud focused on drive, Erikson's focus was on the sequential reorganization of ego and character structure.

Psychosis is a diagnostic term used in general psychiatry to designate a syndrome that includes delusions (fixed false beliefs) and/or hallucinations (compellingly real sensory perceptions that occur without external stimulation). Other features of psychosis include loss of ego boundaries, impairment in reality testing, and severe functional impairment, among others. In contemporary psychoanalysis, *psychosis* is also used variously to describe a mental state in which there is a loss of reality testing; the presence of paranoid, erotic, or other kinds of intense transference states; the presence of highly aggressive primitive conscious fantasies; problems in self-other differentiation. Before the term *borderline* became widespread in the 1960s, **psychotic** was often used to refer to a variety of ego weaknesses underlying severe character psychopathology (as in **psychotic core** or **psychotic character**). The psychoanalytic literature has also been confusing in its failure to clearly distinguish between psychosis and paranoia, or psychosis and schizophrenia. While recognizing that most psychosis appears in illness with underlying biological determinants, some psychoanalysts try to understand the psychological factors that contribute to susceptibility to psychosis, as well as the psychodynamics and/or specific psychic structures that underlie different kinds of psychotic states.

Psychosis plays an important role in the history of psychoanalysis in that, from the beginning, explorations of psychotic patients led Freud to a deeper understanding of the complex role of reality in psychic experience. Specifically, the observation that disturbed relationship to reality is an essential feature of psychosis contributed to the development of the concept of the "ego," the psychic agency responsible for adaptation to reality. The study of psychosis led to the study of pregenital (oral and anal) phases of libidinal development (Abraham, 1911). It also contributed to the development of the concept of self, needed to describe psychotic states of mind, often characterized by a disintegration of the self experience, an apparent lack of relatedness to others, and/or to confusion between self and other. Finally, work with psychotic adults and especially psychotic children played a major role in the development of both Klein's theory and that of several of her followers (Klein, 1946; Bion 1967). Work with psychotic patients was also important in the development of interpersonal psychoanalysis (Sullivan, 1953a). Painfully, the study of psychosis also led to some of the most egregious errors in psychoanalytic theory-making, as when psychotic patients' difficulties relating to others were blamed on faulty or even "schizophrenogenic mothering" (Fromm-Reichmann, 1950). Reexamination of some of these errors have highlighted the need for psychoanalytic theory-makers to avoid psychoanalytic forms of the "genetic fallacy," in which present-day failures in functioning are blamed on failures in development, most often on parent-child interactions (Willick, 1983).

The word *psychosis* entered medical discourse in the mid-nineteenth century. While initially it was used synonymously with *madness* or any severe mental illness, its use gradually became more specific, depending on the nosology of the day. While Freud's (1894c) explorations always focused more on the study of neurosis, he did apply his new concept of defense to some of the psychoses, even while taking note of the drastic mechanisms (including outright "rejection" of ideas and/or "projection") used by psychotic patients in their relationship to reality. With the development of libido theory and the concept of narcissism, Freud (1911a, 1914e) explained psychosis (including paranoia) as a fixation at the narcissistic phase of libidinal development. This was described as a withdrawal of object libido (decathexis) to ego libido, with secondary reconstitutive efforts to reinvest in the object world appearing in the form of hallucinations and delusions. For the most part, Freud (1915d) considered psychotic illnesses (now classified as narcissistic neuroses) not analyzable because of what he saw as a failure to develop transference. With the development of the structural theory and the concept of the ego, Freud (1924c) again argued that the essential characteristic of psychosis is that the ego "withdraws from a piece of reality."

Post-Freudian analysts writing on psychosis have focused on several aspects of psychosis, sometimes focusing on psychotic illnesses and sometimes on severe character pathology (not always clearly distinguished from one another, with the latter now largely conceptualized as borderline, especially in the United States). Many analysts have proposed the notion of a "psychotic core" of the personality, which, while elaborated from various theoretical points of view, is characterized by: pregenital conflicts and anxieties, a preponderance of aggression, poorly differentiated self and object representations, a tendency to regress to primary process thinking and primitive defenses, and a tenuous or destructive relationship to reality (Bychowski, 1953; Bion 1957; Frosch, 1959a, 1964). Klein (1930, 1946) proposed a notion of persecutory or **psychotic anxiety** related to the projection of intense aggression and sadism, arguing that certain primitive defense mechanisms are characteristic of psychotic patients, including splitting and projective identification. She also described impairments in symbol formation in psychosis. Bion (1957, 1967), elaborating on the work of Klein, further explored the consequences of a hatred of reality in psychotic patients who use primitive forms of nonverbal and nonsymbolic communication. Self psychologists have conceptualized psychosis as severe, protracted damage to the self. Lacan, in an elaboration of Freud's concept of repudiation of reality, also described failures in symbol formation in psychotic illness (Laplanche and Pontalis, 1967/1973). Burnham and colleagues (Burnham,

Gladstone, and Gibson, 1969) focused on what he called the "need-fear dilemma" in psychotic disorders, in this case, fear being related to threats to autonomy. Going beyond the general concept of ego impairment, Bellak and colleagues described a variety of specific, complex ego dysfunctions in psychosis (Bellak, Hurvich, and Gediman, 1973). Marcus (1992) utilized a similar approach to describe the specific ego structure of hallucinations and delusions found in psychosis and **near-psychosis**. This structure is comprised of specific ego dysfunctions, psychodynamics, and object relations, which together form a **psychotic symbolic representation**, a dynamically meaningful condensation of specific aspects of reality experience and conflicted emotional experience.

Psychosomatic Disorders are medical illnesses or syndromes in which psychological factors are thought to play a central role in the etiology, development, course, and/or outcome of the disease. Traditionally, psychosomatic disorders are distinguished from conversion disorders, in which symptoms have specific symbolic content, although sometimes conversion disorders are included among psychosomatic disorders. Psychosomatic disorders are also distinguished from factitious disorders (Munchausen syndrome), or malingering, in which an individual feigns illness. Hypochondriasis, an exaggerated fear of illness seen in many different syndromes, overlaps with psychosomatic disorders; however, while hypochondriasis may include symptoms, it is defined by excessive fear rather than by the presence of symptoms.

While it is difficult to pinpoint the exact origins of the term *psychosomatic,* it began to appear in the psychiatric and medical literature in the first decades of the twentieth century, coming into its own in 1939 with the introduction of a new journal, *Psychosomatic Medicine: Experimental and Clinical Studies,* under the editorship of Flanders Dunbar (Dunbar, 1938). The related word **somatization**, meaning the process by which psychological distress is expressed as physical symptoms, began to appear in the medical literature around the same time. The coining of the new term *psychosomatic* was an attempt on the part of clinicians from many specialties to avoid an artificial separation of mind from body in thinking about disease processes, especially in complex illnesses. In the current *DSM* diagnostic system in psychiatry, **somatization disorder** includes conversion disorder, body dysmorphic disorder, hypochondriasis, somatization disorder, and pain disorder. Factitious disorder is listed separately (American Psychiatric Association, 1994).

Beginning with its origins in the study of hysteria, psychoanalysis has long been interested in interaction between the life of the mind and the life of the body. Freud (1905a) coined the expression "somatic compliance" to describe the participation of parts of the body in the formation of symptoms. Early on, he (1894d) distinguished between the psychoneuroses, which represent the symbolic expression of psychic conflict, and what he called "actual neuroses," which represent the failure to manage psychic excitation in a healthy manner. These two strains of thought—symbolic expression and general emotional disturbance—find echoes in all subsequent psychoanalytic writing about psychosomatic illness (Knapp, 1995). In the psychoanalytic literature, use of the term *psychosomatic* has ranged widely from the highly specific to the more general. Famous examples of the former include Fenichel's (1945) concept of "organ neuroses" to designate somatic symptoms resulting from conflict; and F. Alexander's (1950b) proposal that there are seven psychosomatic disorders: peptic ulcer, bronchial asthma, ulcerative colitis, rheumatoid arthritis, hypertension, neurodermatitis, and hyperthyroidism, each characterized by a specific psychic conflict. In recent years, efforts to link specific ailments to specific underlying conflicts have largely been abandoned in favor of a more general use of the term to suggest only a pronounced contribution of psychological factors to the etiology or expression of any medical syndrome.

Schur (1955) coined the term **desomatization** to describe the developmental process whereby bodily feelings are increasingly replaced by psychological experience, and **resomatization** to describe the situations where this process is reversed, especially in situations of deprivation and trauma. More recently, attention has been paid to the common finding of alexithymia, a term coined by Sifneos (1973), in somatizing patients. Alexithymia, meaning "no words for mood," refers to a marked inability to identify, name, or experience emotions. Following the work of French psychoanalysts Marty and de M'Uzan (1963), who called this characteristic "*la pensée operatoire,*" Sifneos suggested that somatizing patients may suffer from a constitutional inability to experience emotion. McDougall (1985) has also described how patients with psychosomatic disorders suffer from an impoverishment of inner experience. However, in her discussion of the concept of alexithymia, she argued that the inner deadness of psychosomatic patients results not from defect but from the drastic and primitive defensive mechanism of "fore-closure" (Lacan's translation of Freud's [1894a] *Ver-werfung*) (Laplanche and Pontalis, 1967/1973), in which threatening experiences are violently repudiated prior to achieving symbolic representation. The result of foreclosure is the radical splitting of the emotional component of affect from the physiologi-cal component, so that only the latter remains, dis-charging itself in the form of bodily symptoms. The *Psychodynamic Diagnostic Manual* (*PDM*) (PDM Task Force, 2006) describes a somatizing personal-ity disorder (characterized by a habitual tendency to express feelings through somatization often accom-panied by alexithymia) and somatoform disorders.

R

Rapprochement Subphase/Crisis: see SEPARATION-INDIVIDUATION

Reaction Formation is a defensive process whereby psychic content is turned into its opposite so as to transform intolerable thoughts, feelings, or impulses into more acceptable or desirable ones. Reaction formation is often used as a disguise for varied aspects of aggression. For example, contempt may be turned into admiration; murderous feelings toward someone may be replaced by excessive concerns about that person's health. Reaction formation may be specific and transitory, contribute to symptom formation, or play a role in the development of character. It plays an important role in the development of the superego.

Freud (1896c, 1907b, 1908b, 1913d) first used concepts related to reaction formation, and later the term itself, in his exploration of the obsessional neuroses to account for special conscientiousness seen in these disorders. Freud (1908b) went on to explore the role of reaction formation in the traits of cleanliness, orderliness, and trustworthiness in anal character. However, in 1905, in his first use of the precise term *reaction formation,* Freud (1905b) explored its role (along with sublimation) in the development of the attitudes of disgust, shame, and morality, so important in the "civilized and normal individual." In this early period, Freud (1915b) conceptualized reaction formation simply as a vicissitude of the instinct (reversal into its opposite); later Freud (1926a) viewed it as a function of the ego, or a form of defense. In 1925, Freud (1925a) was explicit about the contribution of reaction formation to the development of the conscience (superego). Writing at the same time, Ferenczi (1925) described what he called "sphincter-morality" to describe a situation in which a child complies with a command given by the parents, especially a command to be clean. A. Freud (1936) included reaction formation in her landmark list of defense mechanisms, and it has found a place on almost every list of defenses thereafter (Vaillant, 1992a; Blackman, 2004).

Real Relationship: see CHILD ANALYSIS, THERAPEUTIC ACTION, THERAPEUTIC ALLIANCE, WIDENING SCOPE

Reality, as most often used in psychoanalysis, designates everything that exists independently of human volition outside the human mind, or what is objectively perceived or consensually agreed upon to be "actually out there." Reality is often contrasted with phenomena such as fantasy, illusion, hallucination, projection, wishful thinking, dreams, and the like. In this sense, reality is generally equated with material reality, in contrast to what Freud called **psychic reality,** or the world of unconscious fantasies and wishes. Recently, psychic reality has been equated with the totality of **subjective reality** or **inner reality,** made up of the integration of thoughts, feelings, and fantasies with perceptions of the external world. **Reality testing** is the capacity to differentiate between subjective experience and external reality; the **sense of reality** or **feeling of reality** is the feeling that what is happening is real and not imaginary. In the experience of **derealization,** this feeling is lost (Freud, 1936a). **Relationship to reality** is the extent to which appropriate responses to a given reality are maintained (Frosch, 1964).

Broad concepts such as externalization and internalization describe fundamental aspects of the interaction between internal and external realities. Defenses such as denial and disavowal are defined as efforts to ward off aspects of external reality. In addition, Bion (1959) has described defensive "attacks on linking," which attempt to destroy awareness of reality. In general, the severity of psychopathology is roughly correlated with the extent of disturbance in aspects of reality testing. At the same time, preoccupations with external reality, being reasonable, or excessive rationalization may themselves serve defensive purposes (Jones, 1908; Inderbitzin and Levy, 1994). While all processes of externalization and internalization can be used for defensive purposes, Freud and later analysts have noted nondefensive, innate tendencies in the human mind to experience what is inside as outside, and vice versa. For example, Rapaport (1944) described the "projective hypothesis," or the universal tendency to find reflections of inner life in the external world; J. Sandler (1976b) described actualization, or the universal tendency to make inner fantasies seem real.

From the beginning, psychoanalytic theory has reflected awareness that psychological life develops and functions in interaction with the external world. However, for the most part, Freud took material reality as a given, choosing not to enter explicitly into philosophical debate about epistemology, metaphysics, or ontology. Although aware of the distinction in German philosophy between reality and actuality, Freud seems to have ignored it, almost always preferring the former term in his writings. On several occasions, Freud (1927a) argued that science is the best means of understanding reality, famously contrasting science and reality favorably with religion and illusion. More recently, some psychoanalysts have entered into debate over philosophical issues related to reality, many influenced by aspects of postmodern philosophy that cast doubt on whether psychoanalytic theories or clinical work should adhere to values such as objective knowledge, truth, and correspondence to reality. In contemporary psychoanalysis, there is considerable controversy about how best to consider these philosophical questions in relation to psychoanalytic questions, or whether such consideration is useful or harmful to the field (C. Hanly, 1990; C. Hanly and M. Hanly, 2001; Govrin, 2006).

In his earliest theories of psychopathology, developed under the influence of his mentors, Charcot and Breuer, Freud (Breuer and Freud, 1893/1895) argued that hysteria resulted from the repression of memories of real trauma. By the mid-1890s, Freud (1896c) had arrived at his famous seduction hypothesis, which posited that hysterical symptoms result from real seductions during childhood. However, from about 1897 on, in a dramatic move away from trauma theory, Freud (1897e) concluded that his patients had not experienced real sexual seduction but were conflicted over fantasies or wishes of a sexual nature. He abandoned the seduction hypothesis in favor of a theory in which hysteria represents not the repression of real trauma but the symbolic expression of repressed childhood sexual wishes. This dramatic change in theory represented a major shift in Freud's thinking, from a focus on external to internal reality in the etiology of neurosis. However, ultimately Freud (1916/1917) understood neurosis to be caused by a complex interaction between endowment and/or internal factors (such as fantasy) and the environment (including accidental experience, trauma, or reality), operating together in what he called a complemental series. Freud (1924c) also recognized that several kinds of psychopathology, such as perversion and psychosis, are characterized by marked disturbance in the relationship to reality.

While Freud was revising his theory of pathogenesis, he was also at work developing his theory of mind. In his "Project for a Scientific Psychology," he

(1895b) described the capacity to distinguish between **thought reality** and **external reality**, a capacity that he linked with the functions of perception, inhibition of impulses, thinking, language, attention, and judgment, all described in connection with his earliest conceptions of the ego. The distinction between internal and external reality played an increasingly important part in Freud's (1900) theories, introduced (in a footnote in 1914) into the final pages of "The Interpretation of Dreams," where he compared **psychical reality** with **factual reality** (later called **material reality**). In line with the shift in his theory of the pathogenesis of hysteria from external to internal reality, Freud asserted that "the unconscious is the true psychical reality," both as unknown to consciousness and as powerful in its effects as the reality of the external world. Freud also described how the developing mind learns to take reality into account as it moves from the primary process (which functions according to the pleasure principle) to the secondary process (which is capable of reality-oriented, logical thought). In his view, secondary process develops only when the infant learns, in the face of bitter disappointment, that wishing alone (including hallucinatory wish-fulfillment) will not bring satisfaction and that more complex maneuvers such as thinking and action are necessary.

A decade later, in his essay "Formulations on the Two Principles of Mental Functioning," Freud (1911b) again described development from a pleasure ego, operating in accord with the pleasure principle, which can do nothing but wish, to a **reality ego**, operating in accord with the **reality principle** which is able to "strive for what is useful, and guard itself against damage." The reality principle, introduced in the essay for the first time, does not supplant the pleasure principle but only modifies it in accord with the constraints imposed by the external world. In this paper, Freud also introduced the term **reality testing**, or a kind of trial-and-error approach to mapping the contours of reality. He argued that fantasy is a type of thought activity that is not subject to reality testing and that remains tied to the pleasure principle. Finally, he asserted that the goal of treatment is to replace repression with the impartial passing of judgment, which decides whether a given idea is true or false, or whether it is in agreement with reality. Another decade later, in "The Ego and the Id," Freud (1923a) offered his structural (or tripartite) model of the mind, in which the ego is formally conceptualized as the executive agency within the mind, developing out of the id under the impact of external reality, and thereafter charged with the task of mediating between id, superego, and external reality. In this work, he also noted that processes of internalization (for example, identification), whereby the inner world develops by taking in aspects of external reality, are far more common than he had first imagined, contributing to the development of both the ego and the superego.

In his considerations of the relationship between individuals and reality, Freud laid the groundwork for all future exploration of the subject, including the role of interactions with reality in the development and functioning of the mind, and in the genesis and expression of psychopathology (Wallerstein, 1983b). However, for the most part, for Freud (1930), external reality was a source of constraint, danger, and/or frustration: Reality provides a spur to development, both for the individual and for civilization itself, through its offering of bitter disappointment, or *Ananke* (the Greek word for "necessity"). In contrast to this somewhat grim view of the uneasy relationship between the individual and reality, Hartmann (1939a) suggested that the infant comes into the world preadapted for survival in an average expectable environment, which includes nurturing, love, emotional safety, and protection from physical harm. Loewald (1951) agreed with Hartmann that the infant is not born into a hostile reality. In his view, the neonate is unable to distinguish between internal and external reality or between ego and outer world, so that the epistemological creation of one occurs simultaneously with the creation of the other. At the same time, in contrast to Freud's somewhat pejorative view of illusion, Winnicott (1945, 1953) argued that illusion is essential in the creation of transitional space and of the transitional object, and in the formation of the first object tie. Rather than insisting on a sharp distinction between reality and unreality, Winnicott argued for the importance of an intermediate state as part of the baby's growing ability to recognize and accept reality.

Views of the human infant entering the world preadapted to a reasonably friendly reality paved the way for all contemporary developmental psychoanalysis, which has explored the complexities of interaction between the growing child and the caretaking environment. Contemporary psychoanalysts debate the extent to which real experience or intrapsychic experience is the primary organizer of psychological development and functioning. For example, some developmental psychoanalysts have described the positive emotion associated with "getting it right" as a core source of motivation in infancy, suggesting that there are pleasures associated with operating in accord with reality (Emde, 1991). In recent years, the evolution of psychoanalytic theorizing has followed a general trend toward greater emphasis upon the impact of real experience, both during development and in the clinical situation. A shift away from what some have called Freud's naive realism is most evident in the literature on the clinical situation, with controversies raging on such topics as: whether it is possible to distinguish between transference and the **real relationship** (Greenson and Wexler, 1969), whether anyone has the authority to say what is really going on between patient and analyst, the extent to which treatment seeks to make patients more realistic, whether the goals of treatment include a search for narrative or historical truth, whether reality (psychic or external) is there to be discovered or whether it is always co-constructed by patient and analyst, and whether the therapeutic action of psychoanalysis includes the analyst as a real object, to mention several among many ongoing controversies. Schafer (1970), arguing that any view of reality is always partly subjective, explored four **visions of reality** characteristic of psychoanalytic thought: comic, romantic, tragic, and ironic.

Reconstruction or **Construction** is a formulation, usually initiated by the analyst, about significant experiences and/or organizing fantasies in a patient's early life, the content and/or meaning of which the patient has repressed along with their associated affects. Conceptualized as facilitating the recovery of memories, it connects significant, repressed past experiences to the patient's assumptions, fantasies, beliefs, and behaviors in the present. It also represents an attempt to recover and correlate evidence of such experiences in order to deepen understanding of the genetic factors that have contributed to character formation and psychopathology. Because the patient has repressed the experiences and their meaning, the analyst must rely upon the patient's free associations, transferences, dreams, parapraxes, screen memories, enactments, and other unconscious communications from which to make inferences and formulate the reconstruction. For the patient, the transference contributes an especially persuasive force in the process of reconstructions, as it is accompanied by affectively charged experience in the here and now. As traditionally conceptualized, reconstruction was thought to play a major role in therapeutic action.

Reconstruction is an important concept in psychoanalysis because it highlights controversy within the field about how psychoanalysis works and whether attempts to integrate past with present experience is a critical aspect of therapeutic action. The integration into psychoanalytic discourse of contemporary cognitive-science views of the organization of memory has shifted attention from narrative memory to implicit processes that, in the view of some analysts, are thought not to be recoverable in the same ways. The concept of reconstruction (or construction) also touches upon some of the greatest difficulties posed by psychoanalytic inquiry. These involve the very nature of unconscious processes, which can never be directly known and therefore always require acts of translation to become available for examination and discussion.

Freud (1937b) devoted only one paper to the specific topic of reconstruction, which he wrote rather late in his career, "Constructions in Analysis." However, Freud (1918a) demonstrated the process much earlier, in his case histories, most famously in the case of Wolf Man, and in the construction of the three stages of the beating fantasy, which Freud (1919b) believed occurred commonly in the childhood of obsessional neurotics. However, Freud's reference to the process as construction emphasizes its fundamental role in his view of the mind and the work of treatment. All information about the unconscious is derived through inference, and is therefore constructed from bits of "raw material." In his paper on constructions, Freud compared the process to archeological excavation and described the use of memory, free associations, parapraxes, the patient's behaviors, and transference in helping patients to remember certain childhood experiences. The analyst draws inferences from fragments of data, reconstructs a piece of the patient's forgotten early history, and communicates it to the patient. The reconstruction, which is a conjecture, ideally results in the patient's recovery of new memories that confirm and extend the reconstruction, and the process continues. Freud emphasized that the analyst seeks to create a picture of a patient's forgotten years that is trustworthy and complete, but he acknowledged the impossibility of that goal. Freud argued that in situations when the reconstruction does not result in the recovery of memories but the patient has conviction of its veracity, the same therapeutic effect is achieved. In Freud's view this was evidence of a compromise between the pressure toward the recovery of the memory and the forces that continue to exert their repressive influence.

Despite the fact that Freud wrote "Constructions in Analysis" (1937b) long after he introduced structural theory in 1923, the essay emphasized the topographic model and focused on lifting repressions and making the unconscious conscious (although his focus on replacing infantile impulses with more mature responses clearly implies ego functions). After 1937, as ego psychology gained ascendancy, especially in American psychoanalysis, the concept of reconstruction declined in importance. There was, however, a resurgence of interest in the topic beginning in the 1970s. Greenacre (1975) emphasized that reconstructions are the joint work of analyst and patient. The patient contributes dreams, associations, and other unconscious material; the analyst facilitates the formation of a relationship that makes tolerable the pain of uncovering the past. This serves as a catalyst for healing by means of empathic understanding, which is the analyst's contribution to the basic transference that facilitates the process of reconstruction. In the context of that safe relationship, analyst and patient can reconstruct and understand the past experiences that culminate in the patient's current psychopathology.

H. Blum (1980b) emphasized the integrative function of the reconstructive process. What is reconstructed is not the historical events of childhood but their intrapsychic meanings and their ramifications on adult life. The opportunity for reliving the past under new conditions with the analyst establishes a new set of meanings, causes, consequences, and relationships for the patient that could not have been experienced in childhood because of developmental immaturity. Blum (2003) famously argued this perspective with Fonagy (1999, 2003), who, along with others (D. N. Stern et al., 1998), concluded that the recovery of childhood memories plays no part in the therapeutic action of psychoanalysis. Drawing upon cognitive-science research that divides memory into declarative and procedural, and explicit and implicit systems, such analysts proposed that pathology may relate to problematic object relational representations that are formed too early to be stored as declarative memories. These object relational representations are instead encoded within procedural memory, which is not subject to retrieval through psychoanalytic interpretation. Analysts can learn something about those early experiences from how patients relate to them within the relational dyad. In their view, therapeutic action occurs in psychoanalysis not through the recovery of actual memories but through the process of restructuring experience, which is curative.

Within relational psychoanalysis, the term *construction* has an entirely different usage, as it relates primarily to the co-construction of experience within the transference/countertransference matrix. Therapeutic efforts are aimed at understanding the mutual influences between patient and analyst in the here and now. I. Hoffman (1994), who suggested that analysis be defined as a series of enactments that patient and analyst examine together, conceptualized the treatment situation with the descriptor "social constructivism."

Analysts with a hermeneutic orientation reject the notion that the past can be recovered in any accurate way, but they see the value of constructing coherent narratives that enable the patient to view himself from a contextualized perspective. Schafer (1982), who argued from this position, described constructions of the infantile past and the transferential present as temporally circular, their content determined primarily by theoretical commitment. In his view, reconstruction of the past is burdened by the difficulty of distinguishing imaginary infantile events from perceptions, locating memories in time, and separating single memories from multiple memories collapsed into one.

Reflective Function: see MENTALIZATION

Refueling/Emotional Refueling: see SEPARATION-INDIVIDUATION

Regression is a movement backward to an earlier state in psychic functioning, which may relate to libidinal stage, ego functioning, and/or object relationship; regression therefore has theoretical, developmental, and clinical significance. Developmental regression can occur in clinical and nonclinical settings, can be normative or pathological, can serve a defensive function, and can be observed throughout the life cycle. The concept of regression has held a central place in psychoanalytic theory and practice from its beginning. Regression links together other core concepts in psychoanalysis, such as the need for a developmental understanding of the mind, the idea of the dynamic unconscious, and the centrality of the transference in clinical psychoanalysis. There is some contemporary disagreement about the underlying premises of the term. For example, many analytic theorists contend that a literal return to a prior level of functioning is impossible. However, regression continues to appear regularly in the literature as part of clinical theory, often with the caveat that it not be understood concretely as a return to prior functioning. There are also analysts who do not endorse the use of regression in the analytic situation.

Freud (1897g) discussed regression for the first time in 1897 in Letter 79 of his correspondence with Fliess. He distinguished between the deferred effect of childhood sexual experiences that involve the genitals and those that involve the mouth or anus. In the former, libido is produced, and in the latter, internal disgust, a regression from libido. However, it is not

until a paragraph added to "The Interpretation of Dreams" in 1914, that Freud (1900) delineated three types of regression that he understood as interrelated: **Topographic regression** is the movement backward along a continuum "towards the sensory end and finally reaching the perceptual system." **Formal regression** is a return to primitive methods of expression or representation, such as visual images. **Temporal regression** refers to the return to older psychic structures, such as early memories. As Freud (1905a, 1911b) developed libido theory, he began to explore the concept of regression (and fixation) in relation to psychosexual development, and he proposed that regression to a specific libidinal stage might be associated with specific psychopathology. For example, Freud (1913d) proposed that regression to anal erotism is associated with obsessional neurosis. Freud theorized that regression occurs to a point of fixation or a point in development, unsatisfactorily traversed, which exerts a regressive pull within the mind. Freud introduced two metaphors, both frequently cited, to illustrate his notions on regression and fixation. The first metaphor (Freud, 1905a) is the image of a stream getting dammed up, leading the water to flow backward, possibly into old channels that had previously dried up. The second metaphor (Freud, 1916/1917) is of a migrating people leaving some of their number behind at settlements along their path, with those who have pushed on needing to return to these locations in times of trouble. Both metaphors include two key ideas: that present difficulty leads to backward movement, and that retreat allows for the possibility of renewed forward movement. Both of these ideas continue to inform modern debate on regression.

With the ascension of ego psychology, psychoanalysts began to apply the concept of regression to the structural model. Regression was viewed as one of the mechanisms of defense, appearing on A. Freud's (1936) list of basic defense mechanisms, but also was seen as a process that can involve any agency of the mind, as well as object relationships. Other pathological ego regressions occur as part of the clinical picture in severe psychiatric disturbances. E. Kris (1936) offered the idea of a type of ego regression described as **regression in service of the ego**, or controlled regression, important in creative pursuits of all kinds. In this usage, Kris was highlighting a nonpathological, nonclinical type of regression.

Child analysts and others interested in normal development have also noted the ubiquitous occurrence of regression in children, often manifested by a temporary relinquishment of a new developmental accomplishment. Play involves many adaptive and creative aspects of regression. Frustration, conflict, danger, physical illnesses, and new developmental challenges are common triggers for regression. For example, the birth of a sibling may produce regression in children, as may experiences of separation and loss. Addressing these commonplace observations, A. Freud (1965) formulated the idea of **regression in the service of development**, which describes its necessary and facilitating aspects for the process of development. Similarly, Neubauer (2003) suggested that unless such regressions lead to fixation points—sometimes referred to as developmental arrests—they are unlikely to be pathological but rather can allow for resolution of earlier conflicts. Thus, in the context of child and adolescent development, regression is viewed as an observable phenomenon that is commonplace and self reversing.

Many analysts view regression in the clinical situation as a facilitating phenomenon, observable in the transference and the transference neurosis, which involve some degree of a return to earlier modes of object relating. It is an important aspect of the free association process, which is used to facilitate the emergence of memories, images, preconscious thoughts, and unconscious derivatives. The use of dreams is another illustration of the value of regressive mental processes in the treatment situation. Also noted by many writers are the beneficial aspects of controlled regression in the analyst, allowing for greater attunement and access to his own subjectivity. A parallel from outside the analytic situation would be the regression that parents use to play and communicate with their children, thus facilitating growth.

Contemporary critics have focused on several aspects of the concept of regression. For example, Inderbitzin and Levy (2000) stated that the fixation-regression model posits simple links from early to later behavior but that modern developmental understanding of the mind does not support this view. Dowling (2004) similarly asserted that there is no such thing as a regressive return to the past. These writers also observed that regression has a pejorative connotation and that it has become concretized in a way that impedes analytic understanding. They suggest alternative concepts, such as "transformation" or "a continuously constructed present," to refer to many of the phenomena associated with developmental regression. Using Freud's metaphors, these critics suggest that one can never go back to a settlement or point in the stream and find it to be exactly the same.

Interpersonal and relational psychoanalytic schools do not utilize a concept of regression in the clinical situation. Sullivan (1940, 1953a, 1953b) specifically rejected the free-association technique in favor of the analyst's "detailed inquiry" into the patient's past and present experience. The focus on the here and now, in both interpersonal and relational perspectives, implicitly challenges the idea of returning to past modes of function. Relational theory also emphasizes the importance of some degree of symmetry between patient and analyst, who provide mutual regulatory functions. I. Hoffman (1983) argued that the patient is a less-naive and more-sophisticated observer of reality than generally appreciated. Others have objected to the comparison made between the patient/analyst relationship and the mother/infant relationship (J. Benjamin, 1988; S. Mitchell, 1984).

Holt (2002) and others, seeking to test aspects of Freudian theory experimentally, developed a research tool entitled the Adaptive Regression Index. This instrument is used to distinguish adaptive use of regression from maladaptive or pathological regression and to connect these measures to other measurable clinical phenomena. For example, schizophrenic patients score at the extreme low end on the ARI (more maladaptive use of regression). In nonpsychotic patients, high ARI scores predict successful psychotherapy outcomes.

Relational Psychoanalysis is a psychoanalytic perspective, broadly represented within contemporary psychoanalytic discourse, whose central theme is that no strict separation can be sustained between the intrapsychic and interpersonal realms of experience, and that the intrapsychic is forged in large measure out of relations with others. Relational perspectives have been less focused on models of the mind and of development than on the implications of their common theme within the clinical situation. Terminology within relational psychoanalysis that highlights its central theme is its description as a two-person psychology (in contrast to the one-person psychology of a classical view) in which the analyst is a participant observer; patient and analyst together function within an interpersonal field, co-constructing a transference/countertransference matrix or co-creating an intersubjective space in which analytic work transpires. Such descriptors also emphasize that much of the interpretive and working-through aspects of treatment focus on the here and now of the analytic situation as it is enacted and experienced within the analytic dyad.

Some of the overarching principles of the relational theory of technique include the following: 1) Interpretation and clinical understanding are usually embedded in the enactments between patient and analyst and are not issued from outside the unconscious participation of either patient or analyst (S. Mitchell, 1997). 2) The analyst's forms of participation include both discipline and spontaneity, such that the analyst employs ways of understanding affect, defense, unconscious conflict, and elements of dissociation in a disciplined way, but the analyst is also learning about his patient and about himself as analytic work proceeds (I. Hoffman, 1994). 3) The analyst's participation as an old and new object for the patient is inevitable; that interaction and intrapsychic phenomena are not in opposition to each other but instead are inevitably in dynamic relationship with each other (S. Cooper and Levit, 1998). 4) While the analyst's containment of the patient's affects and unconscious conflict are the primary current of analysis, patients also experience, contain, and respond to the analyst, including aspects of the analyst that may be consciously unknown to him (Aron, 1991; S. Cooper, 1998; Davies, 2004). 5) Countertransference transparency and expressiveness is desirable and may also be a crucial source of analytic data to be utilized in the interpretation of internalized object relations, interpersonally expressed elements of enactment, defense (disavowed elements of experience), and a variety of self states and affects. 6) Each dyad is unique, and while general guidelines and technical precepts are useful, they are also potential interferences with understanding the uniqueness of each patient.

The word *relational* entered the psychoanalytic lexicon in 1983, following the highly influential publication of "Object Relations in Psychoanalytic Theory," authored by Greenberg and Mitchell (1983). This work of comparative psychoanalytic theory constituted a deep structure interrogation of a range of psychoanalytic theories that the authors proposed share common, underlying perspectives on development, motivation, psychopathology, and clinical theory. Greenberg and Mitchell coined the term "relational structure model" to distinguish it from Freud's "drive structure model" to describe and link theories that placed relationships themselves—conscious and unconscious, interpersonal, interacted, and internalized (the world of internal objects and their relations)—at the center of their developmental, motivational, and clinical theories. The relational structure model proposed by Greenberg and Mitchell suggested that conflict is not constituted so much among the different agencies of mental structure (drives, ego, superego) as between different internal representations or relational configurations. Such relations can be either conflict-laden or dissociated.

Thus, diverse analytic theories associated with a range of object relations, interpersonal, self psychological, and intersubjectivist theories that shared these common features came under the Greenberg and Mitchell "relational" umbrella. While Greenberg and Mitchell cogently argued their rationale, some theorists within their synthesis, such as Kleinian and other object relations theorists, do not generally identify themselves as relationalists.

The defining elements of relational clinical theory and technique were first described by Ferenczi (1932), particularly in the clinical experiments that he traces in his clinical diary. Ferenczi's influence, through his writing as well as directly through his supervision and analysis of major contributors within the object relations tradition (for example, Balint) and the interpersonal tradition (for example, Thompson) is well documented (Harris and Aron, 1997). Ferenczi noted the centrality of countertransference as a mutually shaping complement to transference. He highlighted for the first time the role of reciprocal influence in the analytic relationship, and he underscored the crucial importance of the analyst's recognition of his own impact on the patient, a factor that he recognized would go a long way toward ameliorating the inevitable iatrogenic risks of retraumatization. Ferenczi highlighted the implications for analytic treatment of recognizing the analyst as a real person, ideas developed in the British schools by Fairbairn, Guntrip, and M. Balint, and in the interpersonal school by Thompson, Singer, and Levenson, among others. Ferenczi's influence on interpersonal psychoanalysis, a major contributing forerunner to relational psychoanalysis, is well documented. M. Balint (1950) is credited with having first described the psychoanalytic situation as a "two-body" situation, and with also using the terminology "two-person psychology" when describing object relational issues.

Contemporary relational analysts regard the analysis of transference as essential to analytic work, but transference is defined in ways that overlap and differ with some other analytic approaches. Relational analysts tend to think about transference as one dimension of a transference-countertransference field or matrix of experience. Thus transference-countertransference is seen as a unity, a complementarity that constitutes a form of mutual influence. While the patient's transference reactions are partly formed by enduring elements of conflict, internalized object relations, and fantasies, transference is intrinsically related to and expressed through elements of the contemporary interpersonal relationship. The relational analyst is always asking, "Why is a very particular story about the past being told now to the analyst?" Countertransference is not defined more restrictively as the analyst's response to the patient's conflicts; instead, countertransference is seen as including all elements of the analyst's person that the patient will get to know and consciously and unconsciously allude to through his words and interaction.

Transference-countertransference engagement becomes the vehicle through which patient and analyst enact elements of the patient's conflicts and affective states. Rather than define psychoanalysis as a series of the patient's free associations, I. Hoffman (1994) suggested that we redefine analysis as a series of enactments that the patient and analyst will come to examine and experience together. While the analytic situation is highly asymmetrical in terms of varying responsibilities as patient and analyst, mutual influence and mutual containment occupy the analyst's attention. Hoffman offered his conceptualization of the treatment situation as alternatives to traditional views of transference and countertransference. Initially using the terminology of "social paradigm," Hoffman's descriptors evolved to "social constructivism" and then ultimately "dialectical constructivism." The "dialectics" that Hoffman described in the treatment situation include the dialectic between "interpretive reflection on transference-countertransference enactments and the fact of those enactments per se"; the dialectic between "the analyst's personal visibility and the relative invisibility"; the dialectic between "noninterpretive interpersonal interactions and the interpretive interactions"; and the dialectic between "the analyst's inclination to reveal and the inclination to conceal aspects of one's personal experience in the analytic situation."

The perspectival (Aron, 1996) and constructivist (I. Hoffman, 1998) views of the analytic situation suggest that the dyad must explore the patient's past in terms of what is happening in the present of the analytic relationship, not only through the interpretive inferences by the analyst but through observed experiences by both patient and analyst, which become an important point of departure for analytic experience and interpretation. The analyst's interpretations are focused on affective states, defenses, and conflicts of the patient, but he learns about these various shifts within the patient partly through elements of his own experience. The analyst's self-reflective participation is demonstrated through his curiosity about how and when elements of conflict and dissociation are enacted between patient and analyst (S. Mitchell, 1997; Bass, 2003). Ogden (1994), while not identified as a relational

psychoanalyst, is credited with a significant contribution to the relational perspective through his formulation of the "analytic third," an unconsciously communicated intersubjectivity created by the personal subjectivities of both patient and analyst in their work together. Ogden viewed the third as an asymmetrical creation in both its contribution from analyst and patient and in their experience of it; he focused on the therapeutic value for the patient of the analyst's capacity to put language to their experience together. In Ogden's view, the analytic third may at times represent a formidable resistance for both patient and analyst, but if it can be understood by the analyst and communicated effectively to the patient, it provides the most fertile and critical data for analyzing the patient's inner experience.

J. Benjamin (1990), an intersubjective theorist who has also contributed to feminist psychoanalytic critique, distinguished between the interpersonal, that is, between people, and the intersubjective, that is, the mutual recognition of the other's subjectivity. She viewed intersubjectivity as a developmental attainment that is maintained in a dynamic tension with the intrapsychic realm of experience. In all relationships, a tension exists between the subject's wish for omnipotence and the associated negation of the other, and the wish for mutuality and contact with the other. In her developmental propositions, Benjamin challenged Mahler's separation-individuation theory as incomplete, arguing that Mahler left out the important attainment of intersubjectivity, or shared reality, between infant and mother, a process to which the mother contributes her own subjectivity. In her view, pathology is manifest in the patient's aggressive negation of the analyst's subjectivity, resulting in a power struggle between patient and analyst. The challenge for the analyst is to reestablish the intersubjective space, to restore dialogue, often requiring some creative act.

Relational theorists have reformulated the concepts of defense and defense analysis from that of the traditional ego psychological view. A number of relational theorists have suggested the ubiquity of dissociation as a defense for all patients, not necessarily unique to a particular diagnostic group, such as to hysteria, or to traumatized patients (P. Bromberg, 1998a). The analysis of dissociated states is central to the relational analyst's focus on the patient's self integration and the reclaiming of previously sequestered or vanquished self states. In D. B. Stern's (1997) view, dissociation prevents "unformulated experience" from ever becoming conscious; this experience is not encoded in language but rather in action, necessitating different interpretive techniques. Stern argued that dissociation, not repression, is the most important form of motivated not knowing confronting the psychoanalytic clinician. In a set of related ideas, Bromberg (1998a) argued that the task of the analyst is to move the patient from a position of dissociation to one of conflict. In Bromberg's view, dissociation is a defensive process that leads to a sequestration of an aspect of self experience, unlike repression, which excludes content from consciousness. Building on Balint's (1968) and Winnicott's (1969) elaboration of the way that some patients form defenses against object failure (false self), relational theorists have focused on the patient's needs to experience continuity of self as they open up new avenues of experience.

Many forms of countertransference expressiveness that have been emphasized in relational theory have been formulated in the context of analyzing defenses. Relational analysts sometimes verbalize elements of their own experience when they believe that the patient is unable to feel states that the analyst has been recruited to feel. In Davies's (1994) controversial discussion of her decision to reveal her erotic countertransference to her patient, she argued that it provides the only access to certain disavowed elements of the patient's own sexual experience. Arguing from the position of a two-person psychology, Davies linked the problematic denial by the oedipal parent of his own state of desire to the traditional analyst's nondisclosure of erotic desire for his patient and the negative impact this may have on treatment. In contrast, while many contemporary Kleinian analysts believe that the analyst is often being recruited to repeat and enact elements of unconscious object relations, the Kleinian analyst will rarely make reference to his own experience in the effort to elaborate the patient's experience (Feldman, 1997).

Relational theory emphasizes some degree of symmetry between patient and analyst as affective participants and mutual regulators of affect. The patient is regarded as a less-naive and more-sophisticated observer of reality than had previously been appreciated (I. Hoffman, 1983). A number of relational theorists have questioned the assumption that the mother-infant relationship is a rigidly held prototype of later relationships. Relationally oriented authors in agreement with some infant researchers, such as Tronick (2003), have also criticized various models of therapeutic action that liken the analysis of adults to the workings of the mother-infant relationship. Others have refined the view that the mother-infant relationship serves as a model for the analytic situation. Benjamin (1988) and S. Mitchell (1984) critiqued the "developmental tilt model" of Winnicott. In their view, Winnicott focused exclusively on the important

and necessary functions of the analyst, who, like the mother, coalesces and tries to understand, contain, and metabolize the patient's (infant's) experience. What Winnicott left out is the complexity of the analyst's (mother's) subjective participation with his patient (her infant), including the inevitable and growth-producing impact that his (her) subjectivity has on the patient (child).

Mitchell (1991) introduced a different developmental model in distinguishing among such concepts as need versus wish or demand. His approach was constructivist, integrating the analyst's countertransference experience into his observations. He argued that what may seem like a need on the part of the patient at one point in analysis may, at another point, be experienced as a wish or demand, with the differences carrying crucial implications for the forms that analytic participation and intervention might take. However, most relational theorists have viewed the addition of a constructivist perspective as complementary to thinking about and applying a range of developmental models for understanding clinical work. In other words, relational analysts do not dispense with the notion of thinking about enduring personality features but instead see this as incomplete because the analyst as observer/participant also figures into the determination of analyzing these unfolding patterns in the interactive matrix of analytic work.

Over the last three decades, relational perspectives have gradually penetrated the work and thinking of analysts from a variety of major orientations. A relational sensibility about the analyst's participation in the analytic process has become evident in most discussions about the theory of analytic technique. Concepts such as enactment, mutual influence, constructivism, transference-countertransference engagement, and intersubjectivity are prominently represented within the psychoanalytic literature. Attempts to distinguish the role of the analytic relationship from the role of interpretation on therapeutic action have given way to more-complex recognition of their interdependence.

However, relational psychoanalysis is not without its critics. Some interpersonal analysts have seen the integration of object relations ideas into its theory as a hidden acceptance of the very drive-based theory that it critiques. Analysts from other schools have criticized relational theory for its focus on a theory of technique while neglecting a coherent theory of the mind. Such critics argue that relational theory lacks a complex concept of development, motivation, affects, and unconscious conflict, and that it diminishes the role of sexuality and aggression in mental life. Others argue that the valorization of a kind of dyadic subjective reality, and the overemphasis on countertransference expressiveness, may shift the focus too far from the patient's intrapsychic experience to the analyst's intrapsychic experience. Such analysts caution that a relational perspective is best viewed as an essential addition to other theoretical perspectives but cannot be viewed as a replacement.

Repetition Compulsion, or **Compulsion to Repeat**, is the tendency to repeat or to act out aspects of past experience, especially painful experience, without awareness of the meaning of present behavior, its connection to the past, or one's own role in initiating the repetition. The repetition compulsion is evident in both normal and neurotic behavior, including symptoms, character, life choices, play behavior in children, and treatment experiences, including transference, countertransference, acting out, and enactments. It is especially evident in situations involving trauma. The compulsion to repeat is the essential feature behind what Freud (1920a) called the "fate compulsion" (later, "fate neurosis"), in which the lives of certain people have an uncanny way of repeating the same unhappy scenarios, as if fate itself were conspiring to make this person unhappy.

While the explanation for and even the definition of the repetition compulsion is much debated among psychoanalysts, the concept is important in that it describes a fundamental feature of human psychology and behavior. It touches on questions such as the role of repetition in mental life, how action is related to thought, how experience is represented in the psyche, how the past lives on in the present, and how psychic pain and trauma are handled in the human psyche, to mention a few. The repetition compulsion also underlies the therapeutic action of psychoanalytic treatment, which makes use of the fact that inner life, including memories of the past, is enacted in the treatment setting, especially in the transference.

From the beginning, Freud (Breuer and Freud, 1893/1895) was aware of the role of repetition in psychic life and of repetition as a form of remembering. For example, in his earliest work, he described symptoms as "mnemic symbols" of feelings and thoughts. Later, in the postscript to the Dora Case, Freud (1905a) described how he had overlooked much of Dora's transference experience because she "acted out" many of her transference fantasies instead of verbalizing them. Freud (1914c) first named this compulsion to repeat in his 1914 paper, "Remembering, Repeating and Working-Through," again in re-

lation to the patient's acting out in treatment. He understood this acting out as both a defense against remembering and a form of remembering through action; he also understood it as both a form of hiding something and a method of communication. He argued that the compulsion to repeat lies behind the central phenomena of resistance and transference. Its persistence requires that much time be spent "working through." However, Freud also pointed out that the compulsion to repeat is responsible for the here-and-now aliveness of the psychoanalytic situation and, thereby, its therapeutic leverage.

Freud (1920a) returned to the compulsion to repeat in 1920, this time emphasizing the tendency to repeat the most painful experiences of the past, as in traumatic dreams, children's play in situations of loss, and the patient's repetitions in the transference. At one level, he explained the tendency to repeat as an attempt at active mastery over a painful or traumatic event. At the metapsychological level, he argued that repetition serves to bind excess, or traumatic excitation prior to its being discharged. Finally, he went on to argue that the repetition compulsion is "beyond the pleasure principle," representing the expression of the death drive, a conservative tendency inherent in the organism to return to a previous state of being.

While all analysts agree that the phenomenon of repetition is an important feature of how people conduct their lives and how they behave in treatment, there is widespread disagreement about the precise definition of the repetition compulsion and about the proper explanation for the phenomenon. Areas of controversy include: What kinds of repetitive behavior should be included as part of the compulsion to repeat? Should the concept be reserved only for the repetition of traumatic or painful experiences, or can it be used for the repetition of pleasurable experiences as well? Must the concept be used in connection with Freud's last drive theory, or can the term be used for phenomena conceptualized in another way? How is the compulsion to repeat related to a search for mastery? How is it related to the encoding of what some call "unformulated experience" or to preverbal experience? Do people only repeat the past, or can they also be in search of something new? Controversy is made more confusing by the fact that Freud himself used the term in more than one way, at more than one level of abstraction.

Representation/Representational World: see OBJECT, OBJECT RELATIONS THEORY, SELF, SYMBOLISM/SYMBOLIZATION/REPRESENTATION/SYMBOLIC REPRESENTATION

Repression is the unconscious defensive process by which mental experiences are not allowed access to conscious awareness. Repression is distinct from the conscious process of judgment or condemnation. It is also distinct from suppression, or the conscious, deliberate attempt to avoid thinking about something. Traditionally, repression is distinguished from denial (disavowal), in that denial serves to avoid external reality or aspects of the self that are evident and/or close to consciousness, whereas repression prevents aspects of internal reality from becoming conscious at all. Repression is also distinguished from dissociation, which is a disruption in the continuity of conscious mental experiences. However, most analysts agree that defense mechanisms overlap with each other, and that repression, in particular, plays a role in almost every other defense.

Freud (1914d) famously asserted that the theory of repression was not only among the most original of his ideas but was "the cornerstone on which the whole structure of psycho-analysis rests." In psychoanalytic theory, repression is a universal mechanism of defense that contributes to all mental experience, pathological and normal. More importantly, it is a process that plays a role in establishing the dynamic unconscious as a realm in the psyche separate from consciousness. Throughout his work, Freud (1930) described the foundations of civilization itself as resting on the repression of instinctual life. Work with understanding and undoing repression is part of every psychoanalytic treatment.

In his early work, and in some parts of "Studies on Hysteria," Freud (Breuer and Freud, 1893/1895) agreed with the French psychopathologists that the essence of hysteria lay in the "splitting of the mind." However, gradually, Freud introduced his revolutionary concept of defense hysteria, which asserts that hysteria is caused by ideas (most often "reminiscences" of trauma) sequestered from ordinary consciousness not because of degenerate mental weakness (as Janet and others had argued) but "from the motive of defense." Freud used the word *repression* to describe the process by which incompatible ideas or memories are separated from consciousness. Freud's early discussions of repression include many of his most important ideas about the concept: repression is a dynamic or intentional process motivated by the need to avoid distressing affect; repression is carried out unconsciously; repression is an act of censorship; repressed ideas constitute an unconscious psychic nucleus capable of attracting other ideas to it (the pull of the push-pull feature of repression); repressed ideas continue to be psychically active; repression lies behind the clinical phenomenon of resistance; repressed

ideas are potentially pathogenic. Freud (1894c, 1896c, 1900) also applied the concept of repression to psychopathology other than hysteria, including obsessional neurosis. For the most part, *repression* was used interchangeably with *defense*; at other times, "the repressed" was used interchangeably with "the unconscious" itself, in what became the topographic model of the mind.

Freud (1915c) offered his most elaborate discussion of the concept of repression in his 1915 paper "Repression." Written after the formulation of drive (libido) theory, repression is directed against the psychic representations of the instinct. As structural theory was yet to be invented, repression is conceptualized as a vicissitude of the instinct. In this paper, Freud distinguished between three stages of repression: The first stage is **primal repression** (or **primary repression**), the process by which drive derivatives are denied access to consciousness, forming the original nucleus of the unconscious, which exerts a pull on all later drive derivatives; the second stage is **repression proper**, in which all ideas and/or trains of thought associated with repressed drive derivatives are denied access to consciousness through the application of an "after-pressure"; the third stage is **the return of the repressed** (first noted in 1896c), in which derivatives of the repressed instinct force their way into consciousness as "substitutive formations," in the form of dreams, jokes, parapraxes, and neurotic symptoms. Various forms of substitute formation correspond with different kinds of neurosis. In a 1915 footnote to "Three Essays on the Theory of Sexuality," Freud (1905b) noted that the distinction between primal repression and repression proper is analogous to the distinction between infantile amnesia and hysterical amnesia. In his same 1915 paper, "Repression," Freud also elaborated on many of his earlier ideas about repression, including the push-pull aspect, the extent to which repressed ideas continue to be active, the reasons why ideas (or instinctual representatives) become more virulent when repressed, how free association is used to discover what has been repressed, and the fact that repression is not a single occurrence but requires a constant expenditure of force (countercathexis).

After the development of the structural theory and the elaboration of ego psychology, Freud revived the word *defense* to describe all the techniques the ego makes use of in conflict, with repression meaning only one of the defenses, characteristic of hysteria. In Freud's (1926a) new theory, defense is conceptualized as initiated by the ego in anticipation of danger; anxiety is no longer conceptualized as the result of repression but the cause of it. During this period, Freud (1924c, 1927b, 1938b) began also to explore defenses (such as denial and/or splitting of the ego) that are not based on repression.

For the most part, post-Freudian psychoanalysts have continued to view repression as a central and universal feature of psychological life. A. Freud (1936) listed repression first on her famous list of defense mechanisms. However, Klein (1940) and Fairbairn (1952) continued to deepen Freud's earlier explorations of defenses based not on repression but on splits within the ego. More recently, Kernberg (1970a), following the work of Klein and Fairbairn, argued that only the neurotic level of personality organization is based on the use of repression, whereas the borderline level of personality organization is based on splitting. Self psychologists have also placed emphasis on what they call a vertical split in the psyche as the cause of psychopathology rather than repression (horizontal split) alone. Some interpersonal psychoanalysts have argued that dissociation and/or "unformulated experience" and not repression (analogous to Sullivan's [1953a] "selective inattention") are the most important forms of motivated not-knowing confronting the psychoanalytic clinician (D. B. Stern, 1997)

There is an array of empirical studies in psychoanalysis, cognitive psychology, and social psychology exploring the concept of repression, variously referred to as "motivated forgetting," or "warding off of conflictual cognitive contents." Among psychoanalysts, Shevrin et al. (1996) developed experimental paradigms to explore repression and dynamic unconscious processes, approaching these concepts from psychodynamic, cognitive, and neurophysiological points of view. Singer (1995) brought together investigators from both psychoanalytic and cognitive psychological perspectives to examine the historical, theoretical, psychobiological, and methodological issues surrounding the concept of repression, as well as research models and empirical data. Westen (1997) tried to integrate the psychoanalytic approach to repression with empirical data from cognitive and social psychology. Gassner et al. (1982) studied the emergence of warded-off contents in the clinical setting. Karon and Widener (2001) studied the phenomenon of repressed memories. Eagle (2000) and Weinberger, Schwartz, and Davidson (1979) reviewed the empirical evidence related to the concept of **repressive style**, examining costs and benefits, as well as physiological correlates.

Resistance is the patient's unconscious opposition to the unfolding and deepening of a psychoanalytic process. It may be expressed through mental processes, fantasies, memories, character defenses, and behaviors. Resistance reflects the patient's unconscious anxiety about relinquishing familiar compromises and facing emotionally painful self awareness. Usually unconscious at first, it may persist long after it is consciously recognized. Resistance, in contrast to the general concept of defense, is a concept specific to the treatment situation.

Sterba (1953) conveyed the centrality of resistance with his assertion that psychoanalytic therapy was born when resistances were taken into consideration. Freud wrote that the analysis of resistance and transference is the fundamental hallmark of a psychoanalytic treatment, and it is only through their interpretation that an analytic process is established. This technique distinguishes psychoanalysis from other treatments based on suggestion or persuasion to facilitate change. The term *resistance* is often tied to a model of mental organization that features conflict and compromise and is not explicitly utilized by analysts with other points of view. However, all psychoanalytic perspectives recognize, in some form, the dynamic tension that exists within the treatment situation between the analyst's focus on facilitating the patient's understanding of his own mind, and the patient's unconscious wish to oppose this process and preserve the intrapsychic status quo.

Freud's earliest references to resistance appear in "Studies on Hysteria" (Breuer and Freud, 1893/1895), in which he observed resistance to the process of hypnotic suggestion. The forces that had resulted in the original forgetting of the traumatic event now opposed the physician's attempt to undo the dissociation through hypnosis. His recognition that resistance was something to be understood rather than overcome established a psychoanalytic cornerstone and paved the way for a technical shift to the free-association method. Resistance was then defined as any action on the part of the patient that interrupted the flow of his free associations. Making a link between resistance to the treatment and his early views of motivated defense, or repression, represented a conceptual leap in the development of Freud's theory.

Freud's understanding of resistance became progressively more complex as he came to recognize its pervasive presence and its multiple determinants. In "Papers on Technique," Freud (1914b) identified resistance broadly as anything that interferes with the continuation of the treatment and therefore recovery, but his primary concern was to explicate the relationship between transference and resistance. Freud's discovery that transference is resistance but also the strongest vehicle for cure was of paramount importance. In these papers, Freud identified the unconscious nature of resistance (a critical recognition leading to his elucidation of the structural theory), the relationship of resistance to the necessity of the working-through process, and the contribution of the analyst's unconscious resistance to the course of treatment.

In "Inhibitions, Symptoms and Anxiety," Freud (1926a) identified ego, id, and superego sources of resistance. **Transference resistance** is only one of three ego resistances and involves affects, ideas, and attitudes directed toward the analyst that stand in the way of expanded knowledge. Early in an analysis there might be resistance to the awareness of transference wishes, fantasies, and thoughts, and, later, resistance to the evolving manifestations of transference attitudes. Because of the immediacy and emotional intensity of the patient's experience, the interpretation of the transference resistance provides the greatest leverage for change. A second **ego resistance** Freud described is repression, which is the active exclusion of conflictual ideas from awareness. The third ego resistance is the secondary gain from illness that contributes to its continuation. Freud identified an **id resistance** in the compulsion to repeat, which accounts for the necessity for the working-through process. Freud described this resistance as the attractive force exerted by the unconscious, or the "adhesiveness of the libido." Freud defined **superego resistance** as the need for punishment based on unconscious guilt. This resistance is expressed in the unconscious refusal to relinquish suffering or to benefit from analysis. The most intense form of superego resistance is manifest in the negative therapeutic reaction in which constructive and effective therapeutic work is followed by a paradoxical worsening of the patient's condition. This resistance is an expression of moral masochism. The concept of superego resistance has had great clinical import in the understanding of impasses in analysis. In "Analysis Terminable and Interminable," Freud (1937a) considered the impact of resistance factors that might reside outside the realm of interpretive intervention, such as the influence of early trauma and the constitutional strength of the instincts.

With the ascendance of ego psychology, W. Reich (1933/1945) and A. Freud (1936) provided competing visions of **resistance analysis**. Reich took a combative approach to the patient's "character armor," while A. Freud's more-balanced position of therapeutic neutrality removes the analyst from the adversarial position. Efforts to redress Reichian extremes dominate much of the subsequent conceptualization of resistance analysis. Reich's approach may also account for persistent negative perceptions of the concept of resistance, which connote an adversarial relationship between patient and analyst.

Most contemporary analysts maintain a broad view of resistance as a ubiquitous and integral aspect of all psychoanalytic treatments, rather than as an episodic intrusion. The nature and quality of the patient's resistance may change depending on the phase of the treatment, but it is often characteristic for that patient, as it is rooted in character structure and core neurotic conflicts and fantasies. Therefore, interpretation of resistance may be experienced as a narcissistic threat and may evoke narcissistic defenses. The timing of resistance interpretation is key, and premature or incorrect interpretation may result in the intensification of resistance. While resistances become conscious through interpretation, it is the painstaking analysis of resistance that comprises the working-through process and leads to substantive change (Samberg, 2004).

A singular focus on the analysis of resistance was advocated by Gray (1996) whose close process monitoring focuses the analyst's attention on breaks in the free-associative process as evidence of the ego's defensive activity. This view adheres to an earlier and narrower conceptualization of the term.

Some contemporary analysts have rejected the concept of resistance, perhaps because it continues to be viewed as an adversarial concept. Other analysts maintain the concept but emphasize the contribution of the analytic dyad to resistance. Such perspectives focus on the impact of specific qualities of the analyst, the analyst's inevitable empathic failures (Kohut, 1959), and countertransference. Resistance may also be regarded as a joint creation by patient and analyst from both ego psychological (Boesky, 1990) and intersubjective (Ogden, 1996b) perspectives; these enactments express unconscious collusion between analyst and patient.

Kohut (1977) distinguished between defensive structures and compensatory structures in their relationship to resistance. Compensatory structures serve to revitalize one sector or pole of the self (mirrored ambitions, twinship feelings, or guiding ideals) by compensating for defects in other sectors of the self. They are not part of the patient's resistance. However, defensive structures serve to hide defects in the self, impeding healthy development and contributing to resistance.

Modern Kleinians view resistance within the context of the total transference situation. They emphasize the intrapsychic nature of resistance but may describe its expression within the process of projective identification. Alternatively, the primary interest may be the co-constructed aspects of resistance looked at from an interpersonal rather than intrapsychic perspective (Stolorow, Brandchaft, and Atwood, 1987). Fonagy et al. (2003) viewed some aspects of resistance as the expression of a nondynamic deficit in the mentalization capacity, which is the ability to reflect on one's own and others' affective mental states. D. N. Stern (Stern et al. 1998) argued that resistance is a concept that can only be applied to the workings of the dynamic unconscious, and yet there are aspects of the mind that are organized differently. For example, according to Stern, concepts like "implicit relational knowing" and "how-to-be-with-others" describe aspects of the analytic experience that are linked to early preverbal experience.

Reverie: see BION, EMPATHY

Role Responsiveness: see COUNTERTRANSFERENCE, EMPATHY, ENACTMENT

S

Sadism: see AGGRESSION, DEATH DRIVE, MASOCHISM, NARCISSISTIC RAGE, PERVERSION, ANALITY, PSYCHOSEXUAL DEVELOPMENT

Schizoid: see BORDERLINE, FAIRBAIRN, KLEIN

Scopophilia: see ACTIVE/PASSIVE, EXHIBITIONISM, INFANTILE GENITAL PHASE, PERVERSION, SHAME

Secondary Process: see PRIMARY PROCESS

Secondary Revision: see DREAM

Seduction Hypothesis is Freud's (1896c, 1898b) early effort to understand the etiology of neuroses in general and hysteria in particular, by proposing that symptoms serve as defenses against the threatened eruption into consciousness of memories of childhood traumas caused by sexual seduction on the part of adults. The repressed memory of this childhood event becomes traumatic later, after puberty has set in, through a process of deferred action. Freud acknowledged that these purported events were not actually recalled by his analytic patients but were reconstructed by him from fragmentary associations and memory traces. Initially he attributed these seductions to a variety of persons—for example, older siblings, relatives, and nursemaids—but increasingly he focused on fathers as the putative seducers.

Gradually, Freud (1897e) came to doubt the correctness of his seduction hypothesis, both because the interpretations did not appear to resolve the patients' symptoms and because he found the ascription of widespread incestuous seduction by fathers (including his own) increasingly implausible. He concluded that supposed memories of seduction were usually not of actual events but of the patient's fantasies, ultimately derived from oedipal wishes and associated masturbatory acts. This represented a major shift in Freud's thinking from a focus on external reality to a focus on intrapsychic conflict as the determining factor in the etiology of neurosis. His abandonment of the seduction hypothesis led to the development of his concepts of psychic reality, the oedipus complex, and infantile sexuality.

Some recent commentators (for example, Masson, 1985a) have accused Freud (and by extension psycho-analysis) of minimizing or denying the actuality of childhood sexual abuse. Freud, like the psychoanalysts who have followed him, was aware of and concerned about the seriousness of sexual abuse. Much has been written in the psychoanalytic literature about the specific role of sexual abuse and overstimulation in the creation of psychopathology. Soon after Freud abandoned the seduction hypothesis, Ferenczi (1913/1952, 1933) offered a variant in his view of the traumatic effects of a parent's unempathic sexual seductiveness on early character development ("confusion of tongues"). More recently, Laplanche (1997) described the consequences of asymmetry between infant and caretaker in the domain of sexuality, arguing that the "sexual message originate[s] in the adult other." Others have written about the consequences of overstimulation and/or childhood sexual abuse (Shengold, 1989; Davies and Frawley, 1992).

Selective Inattention: see DEFENSE, INTERPERSONAL PSYCHOANALYSIS, REPRESSION

Self is used variously in psychoanalysis to refer to: 1) one's whole person in the external world, including one's body and mind; 2) the subjective sense of self, or the "I"; 3) a representation or set of representations within the ego; 4) a fantasy of the self in its various aspects; and 5) from the perspective of self psychology, a personal psychic core that governs experience and action. The self is contrasted with the other, usually called the object. The term *self* is distinguished from several other terms, including *ego* (the intrapsychic structure responsible for homeostasis and adaptation), *identity* (one's stable sense of self as a unique person situated in a surrounding culture), and *character* (one's stable behaviors, attitudes, cognitive styles, and moods, along with typical modes of self regulation, adaptation, and relating to others). Recently, some psychoanalysts have preferred the term *subject,* arguing that *self* has come to mean a mental structure that is too sequestered, reified, and misleadingly unified (Ogden, 1996b). The word *person* has not found much theoretical place in psychoanalysis, in part because it is not an intrapsychic term.

The term *self* is important in almost all schools of thought within psychoanalysis as providing a way to talk about the core of subjective experience, which is always organized around an experience of "I." *Self* also serves as a reminder that an integrated and coherent core of mental life remains after we try to break it down into its component parts. Finally, most analysts agree that some kinds of psychopathology are best described in terms of disturbances of self experience, or of self and object representations.

Most analysts who use the term *self* agree about some of its core features: it is both conscious and unconscious; it is both realistic and subject to defensive distortion; it is made up of multiple self experiences, more or less integrated into a coherent whole; it is both stable and changing based on both internal and external circumstances; and it has a complex developmental history that includes inborn characteristics, maturation, and internalized interactions with others. However, there has always been controversy about how to integrate the word used to describe our immediate, subjective experience of self, with words needed to describe more abstract aspects of agency and motivation. For example, in traditional ego psychology, the primary motivators are the drives, with the ego consisting of a set of functions used for managing the drives and mediating between the drives and the outside world. The self is conceptualized as a representation, or a set of contents within the structure of the ego. In contrast, other theorists, most notably self psychologists, argue that the self is a structure with its own driving force or motivations that are primary and irreducible. Other controversies regarding the concept of the self include: 1) how much of self experience is private and independent from the experience with the other? 2) how possible is it to have a unified self experience? 3) are there universal attributes of the self? 4) does the self include unformulated or nonrepresentational experience?

Throughout his writings, Freud used the terms *self* (*Selbst*) and *the ego* (*das Ich*) flexibly, using *das Ich* (translated into English in the *Standard Edition* as "the ego" rather than "the I") to refer both to a mental agency and to the subjective experience of a personal self. The concept of the self as distinct from the ego developed only gradually in response to clinical and theoretical pressures. For example, in 1914, largely in reaction to Jung's criticisms of libido theory, Freud (1914e) conceptualized narcissism as the libidinal investment in the ego, using this new concept of narcissism to explain phenomena such as omnipotence, grandiosity, idealization, and narcissistic object choices. In particular, Freud traced the roots of **self esteem** to the omnipotence of infantile narcissism, arguing that self esteem is reinforced by fulfilling one's ideals, loving another who possesses qualities similar to the ego ideal, or by being loved. Jung went on to elaborate a distinct concept of the self as an organizing archetype separate from the ego, which leads to experiences of greater wholeness. Freud (1923a), however, never really fully distinguished between ego and self. He continued his ambiguous use of ego, even after 1923, when he posited the ego as the executive agency within an impersonal "psychic apparatus." In a foreshadowing of future theory, he also emphasized the development of self in terms of object relations, drawing attention to the role of identification; he asserted that "the character of the ego is a precipitate of abandoned object cathexes," by which he meant that character accrues as the child's libidinal strivings directed toward the parents are relinquished, replaced by identifications.

In addition to Jung, there were several other theorists who proposed various concepts of a self to describe the subjective, creative, or experiencing aspects of the psyche (Ticho, 1982). For example, while Federn (1952) kept the term *ego,* he used it to refer to the subjective experience of one's own mind and body, or one's **sense of self**. Sullivan (1953a), in particular, rejected Freud's structural theory, speaking instead of the self, defined as the subjective "I" at the core of the personality, which serves as the locus of interaction between the individual and the external world, and which develops through internalization of "reflected appraisals" of caregivers. The self includes various **self personifications**, including the "good-me," which develops in interaction with an approving and calm mother and leads ultimately to self esteem and confidence, and the "bad-me," which develops in interaction with an anxious or distressed mother and leads to a punitive conscience. A third component of the self, the "not-me," develops in response to the mother's "forbidding gestures," and consists of "unformulated experience" that is not available to conscious awareness. The **self system**, or **self dynamism**, consists of all defensive maneuvers that serve to prevent the emergence of experience inconsistent with the self. Rado (1956b) also preferred **action self** to ego, feeling concepts of self should be less mechanistic and more descriptive.

Within mainstream psychoanalysis, it was Hartmann (1950) who differentiated the concepts of person, self, and ego. The person, like the external object, exists in the external world. The self, or **self representation**, is a collection of mental representations of the "I," which correspond to object representations. Self representations (and object representations) are descriptive concepts within the structure of the ego. The self is not on the same abstract metapsychological plane as the ego, as it is not a system or agency within the psychic apparatus. Hartmann attempted to correct Freud's terminological imprecision by defining narcissism as the libidinal cathexis of the self, or, more correctly, self representation as opposed to the ego. Jacobson (1964) further honed the distinction between self and ego. She described the development of the self (and self representation) in tandem with the development of object relations. She viewed self esteem as reflecting the distance between the self representation and the wishful concept of the self. Around the same time, Erikson (1950, 1956) proposed the concept of ego identity (later called identity, in deference to Hartmann's effort to differentiate between ego and self), the end result of stages of development leading up to identity formation in adolescence. Erikson's concept of identity includes many of the same ideas referred to later by others as self. Schafer (1968b) delineated the many various narrative aspects of self experience, describing **self as place**, **self as agent**, and **self as object**. He also described the contribution of the **reflective self representation** (or its absence) in many aspects of mental life. W. Grossman (1982) also emphasized the fantasy aspects of self experience.

Unlike Hartmann and Jacobson, Klein generally used *self* and *ego* interchangeably, preferring the latter term. In Klein's theory, the ego (or self) develops in tandem with object relations amid the dangers associated with potentially annihilating aggression. Her paranoid/schizoid and depressive positions describe fundamental ways in which love and hate, along with self and object, are managed in the development of the internal world.

The concept of self went through a profound change with the advent of the British Middle School. In the 1940s, Fairbairn (1941) challenged the supremacy of libido as the core of psychological motivation, applying the term *ego* in ways that are closer to current ideas of self. Unlike Freud's ego, it does not arise from the id as a result of unpleasurable experiences of reality; Fairbairn's ego is present from birth with its own object-seeking aims. In Fairbairn's view, an original "pristine ego" is split into three parts, in response to frustration in early relationships: 1) the "central ego," or "I"; 2) the "libidinal ego"; and 3) the "antilibidinal ego," or "internal saboteur." Each of these ego states (or selves) is paired with a corresponding internal object. Winnicott (1958b, 1960a, 1960b, 1963a) followed Fairbairn in redefining the ego as the whole person, or self, that seeks recognition and support in relationship with others. Winnicott's self is the origin of the "sponta-

neous gesture and personal idea." In contrast to Fairbairn, he placed somewhat more emphasis on the real person of the mother and on her subjectivity. For Winnicott, the infant's initial experience of himself as omnipotent within a maternal holding environment is necessary for the development of a healthy and creative self. Gradually the "good-enough mother" introduces the world to the child by mirroring the child's experiences and gestures. When the child looks, he is seen, and so he exists. Winnicott distinguished the **true self**, a subjective sense of aliveness, creativity, and authenticity, from the **false self**, the experience of futility, exploitation, and fragmentation.

The work of Kohut (1971, 1977) was a major landmark in the theory of both narcissism and the concept of the self, leading to the development of **self psychology**. Kohut viewed the self both as an experience-near concept, that is, as the locus of subjective experience, and as a more experience-distant, metapsychological concept, that is, as a superordinate structure with its own specific program of action. For Kohut, the self is the source of agency, the initiator of actions, and the seat of affect regulation. It is also the source of self esteem and the sense of continuity in time and space. Ultimately, Kohut posited a **bipolar self**, comprised of strivings for power and recognition on one pole and idealized goals on the other. Between these two poles is a tension arc consisting of basic talents and skills that allow for the realization of ambitions and ideals. Similar to Winnicott, Kohut believed that a structurally sound self depends on an empathic relationship with another person (a **selfobject**) who provides essential functions not yet part of the developing self. Indeed, for Kohut, the self is inextricably embedded in a **self-selfobject matrix**. Also like Winnicott, he contrasted cohesive self experience with **fragmentation of the self**, or **disorders of the self**, brought on by the absence of environmental support. Disorders of the self reflect a dissociated **self state**, especially an unintegrated, infantile **grandiose self**. In psychoanalytic treatment, patients with disorders of the self experience a reactivation of the original needs of the self in the form of a variety of **selfobject transferences**.

In his own synthesis of the work of Klein, Jacobson, Fairbairn, Winnicott, and Kohut, Kernberg (1975) proposed an integration of object relations theory and ego psychology, emphasizing the importance of the two basic tasks in the development of healthy object relations: the differentiation of self from object, and the integration of "all good" and "all bad" experiences of self and object into normal and "whole" self and object representations. Following the work of Mahler, Kernberg referred to the capacity to integrate contradictory aspects of self experience as **self constancy**. In Kernberg's view, failure to accomplish these developmental tasks is associated with psychotic and/or borderline psychopathology. Narcissistic pathology reflects the formation of a structure called the **pathological grandiose self** (borrowing from A. Reich and Kohut), which is the product of a defensive fusion of the **actual self** with the **ideal self** and ideal object representations.

Contemporary interpersonal and relational psychoanalysts, emphasizing the development of the self and the self system in the interpersonal matrix, view the clinical situation as allowing for the emergence of dissociated experience that exists as unformulated, unconscious self states; therapeutic interaction offers the possibility of attaining a more coherent **self definition** (P. Bromberg, 1991; D. B. Stern, 1997). From an overlapping point of view, Fonagy et al. (2002) have argued that experiences that are inadequately mirrored by the mother remain unintegrated, experienced thereafter as an **alien self**. Increased capacity for mentalization achieved through treatment offers the possibility for greater integration. In the last forty years, in response to the work of infant researchers, the concept of self has taken an increasingly developmental turn as many psychologists and psychoanalysts have continued to explore models for the development of the self, stressing the contributions of temperament, the early experiences of the body, and infant-caregiver interactions, and integrating knowledge from neighboring fields such as social psychology, cognitive psychology, attachment theory, and informational processing. For example, D. N. Stern (1985) described four and, later, five senses of self that develop in infancy in the intersubjective matrix of baby and caregiver: an **emergent self**, based on the integration of sensations and affects; a **core self**, rooted in the sense of agency, personal emotions, and personal history; a **subjective self**, established through the awareness of other minds with whom one can communicate about subjective experience; a **verbal self**, able to communicate about experience in symbols; and a **narrative self**, arising from autobiographical histories, co-constructed with parents and siblings, which further organize all earlier senses of self. Stern also described how the infant forms both a sense of **self versus other** and a sense of **self with other**, as part of his growing capacity for intersubjectivity. Emde (1988) included **self regulation** among the basic intrinsic motives, present from birth. Similar to Stern, Emde has proposed a concept of "autonomy with connectedness," suggesting that separateness and relatedness coexist.

Various aspects of the concept of self have been subject to empirical investigation. Auerbach and Blatt (1996) studied self representation in severe psychopathology. Westen (1985, 1990a) delineated four aspects of self: egocentrism, level and quality of emotional investment in self and others, **self concept**, and self esteem. He explored the relations among these four phenomena and concluded that they are interdependent but distinct developmental lines. Both Westen and Horowitz (1987) attempted to integrate the psychoanalytic concept of self with empirical evidence from cognitive, social, and developmental psychology. Bers et al. (1993) attempted to study how aspects of self representation change in the course of treatment. Gallese and Ulmità (2002) attempted to integrate concepts and empirical evidence from cognitive psychology and cognitive neuroscience related to self concept with concepts from psychoanalysis.

Self in Self Psychology is a predominantly unconscious structure at the core of the personality, which is the center of initiative, the recipient of impressions, and the source of a sense of recognizable sameness. The self is constituted by the individual's ambitions, ideals, and talents, and develops through interplay between inherited and environmental factors. It has its own driving force toward the realization of its own program of action. It is always contextualized in relation to **selfobjects**. Kohut considered the lived expression of the ambitions and values of the self as the central motivating force in human life. While he thought it was impossible to define or know the essence of the self, it is possible to access its manifestations through introspection and empathy. Indeed, the self develops through introspective and empathic experiences that become the subjective sense of "I," but it is not identical with this subjective "I." An individual with a **cohesive self** experiences an enduring sense of personal agency and initiative, continuity through time and space, stable self esteem, values and ideals, the capacity to regulate affects and tension states, and the ability to seek out others with whom to share **selfobject responsiveness**. In an individual with a **fragmented self**, these capacities are compromised or not evident, resulting in a **self disorder**.

Following Hartmann's (1950) distinction between ego and self, Kohut (1971) initially defined the self in a narrow sense, as a structure within the ego. As his thinking developed, he conceptualized the self in a broader sense, as a superordinate structure at the core of the personality. In placing this superordinate self at the theoretical and clinical forefront of psychoanalysis, Kohut's self psychology shifted the emphasis from the vicissitudes of sexual and aggressive drives to the vicissitudes of **selfobject needs** as they contribute to the development of self cohesion, ambition, and ideals. Kohut asserted that the self cannot be conceptualized outside of the **self-selfobject matrix**.

Kohut argued that the self has its origins in the parents responding to the infant as though he already has a self—a **virtual self**. In the context of the parents' empathic responsiveness, a **core self**, or **nuclear self**, develops. There are two major unconscious narcissistic developmental lines, or **constituents of the self**, acquired in interaction with the parents, who are experienced as selfobjects. One constituent, or pole, is the **grandiose self** (sometimes referred to as the **grandiose-exhibitionistic self**), from which emanate strivings for power (omnipotence) and recognition (exhibitionism). The grandiose self develops in interaction with a **mirroring selfobject**, who confirms, validates, and takes pleasure in the child's unique sense of self and achievements. The other pole is the idealized parental imago, which results from the child's attribution of omnipotence and perfection to his parents in relation to whom he feels powerful and special. The idealized parental imago develops in interaction with an **idealized selfobject**, who provides the strength and the calming response needed for the child to feel safe and to develop the capacity for tension regulation. An intermediate area consisting of the child's basic talents and skills is activated by the tension arc between these two poles. Kohut used the term **bipolar self** to describe these two poles, or developmental configurations, which he thought could be reconstructed in an analysis. Later, he added another line of development by positing a third selfobject experience, originally conceived as a subcategory of mirroring, which he called the **alter ego** or **twinship selfobject**.

In the course of development, the self grows stronger through the gradual internalization of **selfobject experiences**. These transmuting internalizations occur in the context of the parents' optimal responsiveness to the child's selfobject strivings, as well as in response to optimal frustration of these strivings. Transmuting internalization consolidates the self by propelling: 1) the maturation of the grandiose self through modification of the child's initial sense of omnipotent perfection, leading to stable self esteem, self assertion, and realistic ambitions; 2) the maturation of the idealized parental imago through modification of the child's perceptions of parental perfection, leading to enthusiasm and enduring ideals; and 3) the maturation of twinship needs through modification of the child's feelings of likeness to others, leading to the feeling of belonging within a community.

Disorders of the self (initially called narcissistic disorders) result when a caregiver does not accept, mirror, and/or participate in the child's grandiosity or does not help the child to modulate it. In such cases, the grandiose self is repressed and/or disavowed (undergoing what Kohut called a "vertical split"); this grandiose self becomes poorly integrated within the adult personality, retaining its archaic and infantile quality and resulting in struggles with self esteem. In severe cases or under stress, individuals with disorders of the self may have trouble organizing reality, as in psychosis or perversion.

In psychoanalytic treatment, patients with disorders of the self experience a reactivation of the original needs of the self in the form of a variety of selfobject transferences (originally called narcissistic transferences). With the mobilization of mirror transferences, the patient's archaic grandiose self is revived; with the mobilization of idealizing transferences, the patient's idealized parental imago is revived. The mobilization of these transferences offers an opportunity for renewed development of the self. In contrast to the interpretation of the defensive function served by the transference, the analyst's interpretive focus is on the inevitable failures of empathy or selfobject function (Kohut, 1966, 1971, 1977, 1984; Kohut and Wolf, 1978).

Self Psychology, introduced by Heinz Kohut, is a theory of the development and functioning of the individual and of treatment based on a structure at the core of the personality—the self. The self is defined as the center of initiative, the recipient of impressions, and the source of a sense of recognizable sameness. The self is established, preserved, restored and transformed in the context of selfobjects, defined as others who are experienced as part of the self and who serve essential functions for the self. A healthy self is characterized by feelings of cohesion and continuity, feelings of energy and initiative, mature self assertion and pride, and enthusiasm for a stable set of ideals and goals. It is also characterized by the ability to avail oneself of selfobject responsiveness. When an individual has a fragmented self, or a self disorder, these feelings are compromised or not evident. The distinguishing features of self psychology include: 1) its use of sustained vicarious introspection (or empathy) both to define the field of psychoanalysis and as a mode of observation; 2) its recognition of selfobject functions and selfobject transferences in structuring the self and the analytic situation; 3) its approach to the understanding and treatment of patients with narcissistic vulnerabilities; and 4) its perspectives on shame and narcissistic rage.

Many of the developments in self psychology were anticipated by other psychoanalysts. Ferenczi (1913/1952) emphasized the patient's subjective experience, the central role of empathy, the traumatic effects of the parent's unempathic responsiveness, and the patient's fear of repeating this trauma in the transference. He introduced the idea of lines of development (in addition to libidinal stages), especially in reference to the ego's original omnipotence and the sense of reality. Balint (1968) described how parental lack of "primary object relatedness," or a lack of understanding, recognition, and comfort creates in the child a "basic fault," often manifested as narcissism. Balint viewed treatment as a resumption of interrupted development, "a new beginning," in which the patient is allowed to exist in the analytic situation as if the analyst were a primary substance, "such as oxygen or water." Fairbairn (1952, 1954) viewed the central activity of the personality as a search for an object who will provide what is needed; significant frustrations result in arrested development. In discussion of narcissistic object choice in women, A. Reich (1953) also anticipated some of Kohut's ideas. Although Winnicott (1960a, 1960b, 1965, 1969) did not build a systematic theory in the way Kohut did, there are profound similarities in their work. Kohut's elaborations of the selfobject concept in the development of a sense of self overlap with Winnicott's ideas of the subjective object, the mirroring function of the mother's face, the holding environment, the ordinary devoted mother, the transitional object, subjective omnipotence, potential space, illusion, and the false self. In addition, Winnicott stressed the importance of the mother's meeting the omnipotence of the infant in the development of a true self.

Self psychology has had an important impact on the field of psychoanalysis, influencing and challenging how psychoanalysts conceptualize basic aspects of the structure, functioning, and development of the mind. Central to this contribution is the concept of selfobject functions and selfobject transferences. In addition, self psychology has contributed to thinking about self, narcissism, motivation, aggression, and about various kinds of psychopathology. Self psychology has influenced developmental psychoanalysis. It has also influenced how analysts think about the clinical situation, the analyst's listening and interpretive stance, the understanding and management of transference, and the conceptualization of therapeutic action. Finally, self psychology has contributed to debates about the nature of psychoanalytic epistemology by arguing that introspection and empathy define the field of psychoanalysis.

In his first major paper, "Introspection, Empathy, and Psychoanalysis," Kohut (1959) proposed a psychoanalytic epistemology based on subjectivity rather than on the more "objective" mode characteristic of Freud, Hartmann, and others. He argued that the empathic-introspective modes of observation define the psychoanalytic field and are the central observational tools in the clinical situation.

In his next major paper, "Forms and Transformations of Narcissism," Kohut (1966) argued that narcissism, still defined (in conformity with Freud and Hartmann) as the libidinal investment of the self, is a driving force in the personality with its own line of development. The development of narcissism does not proceed to object love but instead has the potential for transformation from archaic to mature forms, such as creativity, humor, wisdom, and empathy. Building on Freud's (1914e) paper on narcissism, Kohut proposed that narcissistic development, prompted by inevitable disruptions in the infant's blissful state, takes two directions toward establishing new systems of perfection. One direction is the development of the narcissistic self (later renamed the grandiose self), in which everything pleasurable and perfect is experienced as part of the self, and all that is imperfect or bad is experienced as outside the self (similar to Freud's [1915b] purified pleasure ego). The second direction is the development of the idealized parent imago. Following Freud and Ferenczi, Kohut agued that the infant's original perfection and omnipotence is projected onto the rudimentary "you," the adult caretaker. Within the line of development for narcissism, these two branches follow their own paths. Nontraumatic disappointments in the parent's perfection lead to internalization of small quantities of parental omniscience, resulting in structuralization of the ego ideal. Gradual frustrations lead to integration of the exhibitionism and the grandiose fantasies of the narcissistic self into a realistic and goal-directed ego.

In his first book, *The Analysis of the Self*, Kohut (1971) distinguished patients with transference neuroses, for whom traditional views of oedipal pathology and technique are satisfactory, from patients with narcissistic transferences, for whom new views of narcissism are needed. He defined narcissism not as the libidinal investment of the ego, but by the quality of the object relationship, or by the way an individual experiences an object as a part of the self, performing essential psychological functions. Kohut designated objects used in this way as selfobjects. Selfobject experiences form the core of narcissistic transferences. Optimal frustration of selfobject needs leads to internalization and structure building, a process that Kohut called transmuting internalization. He described two types of narcissistic transferences: mirror (which he subdivided into merger, alter ego or twinship, and mirroring proper) and idealizing.

In his 1971 book, Kohut also distinguished narcissistic idealizations from idealizations of the oedipal object, in which the object is experienced as a separate individual. Disturbances in the idealized parental imago create deficits in tension regulation; weaknesses in the superego because its functions are not cherished; or the sexualization of narcissistic needs. Exhibitionistic demands of the grandiose self may be repressed (horizontal split), or split off from integrated awareness (vertical split). Kohut referred to a vulnerable self's reaction to a failure in selfobject responsiveness as fragmentation, and its symptomatic manifestations as disintegration products (or, occasionally, as breakdown products).

In "Thoughts on Narcissism and Narcissistic Rage," Kohut (1972) presented his view of aggression, conceptualized not as an expression of a drive but as the consequence of a perceived threat to the self. Narcissistic rage, characterized by the need for revenge and justice, is the prototype for destructive aggression. Narcissistic rage ranges along a spectrum from trivial irritation to fanatical fury. It is triggered and accompanied by shame, humiliation, and disappointment. Insistence on the omnipotence of the grandiose self and on the perfection of the idealized selfobject underlies destructive aggression. Kohut argued that narcissistic rage is not on a continuum with other forms of aggression such as competition and self assertion; these latter kinds of aggression are primary strivings of the self.

With publication of *The Restoration of the Self,* Kohut (1977) explained why he thought a distinct psychoanalytic psychology of the self was necessary to supplement classical psychoanalytic theory. In elaborating the self as a new structural model, self psychology broadened its theoretical and clinical scope beyond the understanding and treatment of narcissistic personalities to include all individuals who suffer from "disorders of the self." Kohut rooted his developmental theory in the strivings of the self in a selfobject matrix, rather than in the drives. In a final break from Hartmann, he viewed the self as superordinate to the mental apparatus rather than as a representation within the ego. He replaced the term *narcissistic transference* with the term *selfobject transference.* He also introduced the concept of compensatory structures in contradistinction to defensive structures. Compensatory structures serve to revitalize one sector or pole of the self (mirrored ambitions, twinship feelings, or guiding ideals) by compensating

for defects in other sectors of the self. They are not part of the patient's resistance. On the other hand, defensive structures serve to hide defects in the self, impeding healthy development; they do contribute to resistance. While Kohut argued that his new bipolar self could not be fully integrated with Freud's tripartite model of the mind, he suggested that the two theories could be used side by side. For the most part, however, self psychology has developed independently.

At the same time, Kohut's new self psychology assigned the oedipus complex a less prominent role in the development of psychopathology. He proposed a metaphor that contrasted Freud's "guilty man" with a new "tragic man," to illustrate his differences from Freud. In Kohut's view, guilty man, propelled by the pleasure principle, seeks incestuous satisfaction only to be vanquished by the emergence of inner conflicts whose hallmarks are castration anxiety and guilt. Tragic man strives to realize the self's program of action but is disillusioned by the tension between his unrealized ambitions and goals and his inescapably disappointing talents and skills. Tragic man struggles with fears of fragmentation, depletion, defectiveness, shame, and rage.

In his last book *How Does Analysis Cure?* Kohut (1984) further considered the extent to which empathy has, in itself, a mutative and curative role in treatment. He concluded that empathy is neither a therapeutic technique nor the active agent of cure, but a method of gathering data. The communication and interpretation of this data to the patient, however, means that empathy inevitably changes the relationship between the analyst and patient and is therefore necessary for psychological change. Kohut further elaborated on his concept of the interpretive process, which consists of empathic understanding followed by explaining what has been understood. The therapeutic consequence of the analyst's empathy is a lessening of the patient's need for defense, accompanied by an expanded capacity for introspection, which promotes the emergence of warded-off affects and memories. The working through of defenses against the mobilization of selfobject transferences characterizes the early part of an analysis. Central to the therapeutic action is the examination of moments of disruption in the selfobject transference, accompanied by shared understanding of what is required for its repair. Finally, in his last book, Kohut distinguished the twinship selfobject function/transference from mirroring. With this change, he modified the structural model of a bipolar self into a tripolar self.

Since Kohut's death, self psychology has developed in three directions, sometimes referred to as traditional, intersubjective, and relational. P. Ornstein (1990, 1993) and P. Ornstein and A. Ornstein (1980, 1985) explicated the role of empathy, selfobject transferences, and narcissistic rage in the interpretive process and in therapeutic action. A. Ornstein (1991) explored the patient's dread to repeat traumatic selfobject disappointments and hope for a new beginning in treatment. Goldberg (1995, 1999) applied the concept of the vertical split to the study of perversion and narcissistic behavioral disorders, as well as to behaviors that are covertly split off from avowed experience, such as binge-eating, cross-dressing, and infidelity.

Stolorow, Atwood, Orange (Atwood and Stolorow, 1984; Stolorow and Atwood, 1996; Stolorow, Atwood, and Orange, 1999; Orange, Atwood, and Stolorow, 1997), and others incorporated self psychology into a more general view of intersubjectivity. They regarded the selfobject as a crucial dimension in the experience of an object but emphasized how the subjectivity of that object creates an intersubjective field that contextualizes interactions, all viewed as inherently reciprocal. They introduced further selfobject functions related to affect differentiation, integration, regulation, and articulation. Critical of self psychology's "one-person" notion of empathic immersion, they prefer the term *empathic inquiry* to reflect the analyst's participation in and impact on the psychoanalytic process.

In developmental psychoanalysis, Lichtenberg (1989) has described five motivational systems in the development of the self, including the need for: 1) psychic regulation of bodily requirements; 2) attachment and affiliation; 3) exploration and assertion; 4) aversive reactivity; and 5) sensual and sexual needs.

There has also been cross-fertilization between self psychology and many analysts who endorse a relational perspective. For example, the role of the other as selfobject is highlighted in "specificity theory," which proposes that each analyst offers something unique to a particular patient, including but also transcending technique and theory (Bacal and Herzog, 2003). Bacal (1998) and others identify themselves as "relational self psychologists" because their focus is on the context of the subjective relationship rather than the relationship per se. Bacal (1985) and Stolorow (1986) have both questioned the role of "optimal frustration" in development and treatment, arguing that "optimal responsiveness" is a better description of what is needed for the self.

Self psychology has met with much controversy and criticism, which include: 1) the view that resistance is an expression of legitimate, developmentally arrested needs; 2) the view that pathology is the result of arrested development rather than conflict; 3) the homogenous broadening of Kohut's conceptualization of narcissistic disorders to neurotic disorders in general; 4) the undertheorizing of object relations, in contrast to selfobject relations; 5) the view that idealization is a developmental need, rather than a defense against envy and hostility; 6) the concern that aggression is de-emphasized by being conceptualized as a secondary phenomenon; 7) the focus on the development of the self at the expense of exploration of the unconscious and unconscious fantasy; and 8) the relative emphasis on the effects of pathogenic parenting, rather than the effects of the infant's constitutional endowment. In addition, self psychology has been criticized for its reification of "self" and for its narrow view of a bipolar or tripolar self as opposed to a multidimensional self.

Selfobject is a concept in self psychology that describes a quality of a relationship in which another person serves functions necessary for the development and maintenance of the self. A **selfobject function** is an action or communication by the other person that contributes to the development of the self. The selfobject concept is based on the idea that the infant's psychological capacities develop in the context of a caregiver's empathic responsiveness to the infant's **selfobject needs**. In the course of development, selfobject functions are offered by the parents without the child's awareness that the provision comes from another, so that the selfobject is experienced as part of the self. Selfobject responsiveness enables the child to internalize a specific set of functions that contribute to a sense of self, characterized by: 1) feelings of cohesion in spite of the complexity of self experience; 2) feelings of continuity in spite of flux over time; 3) feelings of initiative in spite of setbacks; and 4) feelings of admiration for a flexible set of values and ideals in spite of disappointments. The initial sense of self emerges as the center of experience and initiative in response to repeated experiences in which selfobject needs are met by the caregiver. The internalization of selfobect functioning results in relative autonomy for the growing self. However, more-mature forms of **selfobject relationships** and **mutual selfobject exchange** are needed for self maintenance throughout life.

The concept of the **selfobject** is one of the central theoretical and clinical concepts in self psychology. It emphasizes that the self cannot be conceptualized outside of the **self-selfobject matrix**. It also emphasizes that narcissism is defined by the quality of the relationship, rather than whether the target of libido is the self or the object. In addition, the "discovery" of **selfobject transferences**, in which the analyst serves a vital function for the development and maintenance of the self, expanded the possibilities for psychoanalytic treatment to disorders of the self. When Kohut (1971) first coined the term *selfobject*, he initially spelled it "self-object." He later removed the hyphen to better convey the word's meaning: that the object is subjectively important, not in its "otherness," but in that it sustains the self. The term has shifted from its original intrapsychic meaning to an increasingly relational term that includes how another subject is experienced. The selfobject concept is distinct from merger fantasies or introjects, concepts that are embedded in ego psychology or object relations theory. It straddles the worlds of self and object, intrapsychic and interpersonal, with similarities to Winnicott's (1951) notion of transitional experience, in which questions about psychic attribution are never asked; or to M. Balint's (1952) primary love, offered with neither initiative nor awareness on the part of the child.

Kohut (1971) initially identified two major categories of selfobject function: mirroring and idealizing. Mirroring had three substages: merger, twinship, and mirroring proper. Later he viewed twinship as a selfobject need in its own right (1984). Mirroring is the experiencing of affective resonance, affirmation, and recognition from another. Twinship refers to the feeling of likeness to other human beings and of belonging through shared interests, affect, or activity. Idealizing is the need to admire and emulate significant others. The three selfobject functions contribute to affect regulation and to the organization of experience. These achievements, in turn, facilitate the development of skills directed to the pursuit of meaningful ambitions and goals. They also contribute to the capacities for sustained relationships and for living according to an internalized set of values and ideals. Every selfobject function is phase specific. For example, the child's successful navigation of the oedipal phase depends upon the optimal responsiveness of the **oedipal selfobject**. The child must be able to elicit optimal mirroring for his budding capacity to compete and for his sexual and affectionate strivings; he must also be able to idealize both the same-sex parent and the opposite-sex parent. Successful mirroring of the child's oedipal strivings results in a self with the capacity to pursue love interests with enthusiasm, experience pleasure in sexual desire, and contend with others. Successful idealization of his parents leads to the strengthening of values and ideals, as well as to the development of healthy self esteem related to gender-linked attributes.

When the selfobject needs of childhood are not adequately met, development is impaired; the individual seeks the fulfillment of early selfobject needs throughout life or defends against feelings of deficit and longing. In psychoanalytic treatment, hopes are mobilized that the missing selfobject functions will finally be provided. These hopes are expressed as selfobject transferences, in which the patient unconsciously turns to the analyst for provision of the missing mirroring, twinship, or idealizing functions.

The analyst's optimal response to the patient's selfobject transference includes allowing time for the mobilization of transference, as well as attending to the defenses against the unfolding of transference. When selfobject transferences emerge, the analyst conveys understanding and acceptance of the patient's **selfobject longings**, placing them in the context of both their developmental origins and the analyst's own failings. Any renewed loss of **selfobject experience** can evoke rage and despair. Even the most empathic interpretations and reconstructions constitute frustration for the patient because the interpretive process does not fulfill selfobject needs in their original form. However, the patient's frustration and disappointment, if manageable, can lead to a process of transmuting internalization, through which he becomes able to take over the selfobject functions previously provided by the analyst. An optimal frustration, rather than an injurious one, permits this transmuting internalization to take place. Optimal frustration occurs in the context of an empathic bond in which there is an experience of ongoing affective regulation (Kohut, 1971, 1977, 1984).

Following the death of Kohut, the selfobject concept has continued to develop. For example, Stolorow, Brandchaft, and Atwood (1987) have expanded the concept to include not just the three functions identified by Kohut but any relational experience that contributes to the establishment, maintenance, or enhancement of a sense of self. Other self psychologists have introduced additional types of selfobject needs, such as the need for an adversarial ally (Wolf, 1980), an efficacy need (Wolf, 1988), a selfdelineating need (Trop and Stolorow, 1992), and a validation need (Stolorow, Brandchaft, and Atwood, 1987). Other contemporary self psychologists have asked whether "archaic" and "mature" forms of selfobject functioning might call for different degrees of attunement.

Findings from infant research, attachment theory, and cognitive neuroscience (Sander, 2002; Schore, 2003; Decety and Jackson, 2006) have confirmed the centrality of selfobject relationships during development, lending support to the idea that the mind can carry out its self-organizing function only by becoming part of a larger system. This system consists of two individuals who, through their interactions with each other, co-create the experience of self, for one or for both. Indeed, many researchers studying infant-caregiver interactions (Lachmann and Beebe, 1996a, 1996b; Beebe, 2005; Trevarthen, 2009), and attachment theorists (D. N. Stern et al., 1998; Lyons-Ruth, 1999; Fonagy et al., 2002; Sander, 2002), as well as Stolorow et al.'s Dyadic Intersubjective Systems (Stolorow and Atwood, 1992a; Orange and Stolorow, 1998), and Lichtenberg et al.'s Nonlinear Dynamic Systems models (Lichtenberg 2002, Lichtenberg, Lachmann, and Fosshage, 2010) highlight the mutuality and bidirectionality of influence in infant-caretaker relationships. Reflecting these changes, self psychologists now describe clinical complexities in the mutual exchange of empathy and selfobject function (Sucharov, 1994; Bacal and Thomson, 1996; Lachmann and Beebe, 1996b; Mermelstein, 2000; Brothers and Lewinberg, 1999; Preston and Shumsky, 2002). Lachmann and Beebe (1992) have attempted to integrate the "transference organized by representational configurations," that is, the self with the other, with the selfobject dimension of the transference. They emphasize that patients may unconsciously seek specific selfobject responsiveness for particular attributes from a critical other.

In addition, toward the end of his life, Kohut (1984) began to explore dimensions of relating beyond selfobject experience. In line with this, many theorists and researchers have suggested that the qualities of attachment (Lyons-Ruth, 1991; Beebe, Lachmann, and Jaffe, 1997) and the presence or absence of intersubjective relatedness (D. N. Stern, 1985) should be additional dimensions of experience guiding the specificity of the analyst's response to the patient (Bacal, 1985, 1988, 1998; Lachmann and Beebe, 1996b; Lichtenberg, Lachmann, and Fosshage, 1996; Teicholz, 2001; Bacal and Herzog, 2003). Stolorow, Brandchaft, and Atwood (1987) have suggested that there might be different clinical approaches, based on whether the patient's selfobject needs are in the background or foreground, alternating with oedipal concerns.

Finally, many contemporary self psychologists see psychic structure accruing from ongoing experiences of mutual and self regulation, alternating with "heightened affective moments" and cycles of rupture and repair. These "principles of salience" (Lachmann and Beebe, 1996a) resonate with Kohut's (1984) description of optimal frustration. However, many other self psychologists reject the notion of frustration as a prerequisite for structure-building

internalizations. They argue that frustration is a carryover from Freudian drive theory, with its emphasis on the frustration of wishes rather than needs. Instead, they propose "optimal responsiveness" (Bacal, 1985, 1988, 1998; Terman, 1988; Wolf, 1988; Brandchaft, 1993; M. Shane and E. Shane, 1996; Teicholz, 1996), "fittedness" (A. Ornstein, 1988; M. Tolpin, 2002), and "specificity" of response (Bacal and Herzog, 2003; Sander, 2002).

Separation Anxiety is: 1) a normative developmental phenomenon of distress that appears in infants and young children when separated from their primary caregiver; also known as **stranger anxiety** or **eight-months anxiety**, its onset occurs at seven to nine months, peaking at thirteen to sixteen months, and disappearing usually by the end of the third year; observable manifestations of separation anxiety include crying and protest, clinging, and anxious facial expression; the fear of strangers appears independently at about the same time or somewhat earlier; 2) a disorder in older children characterized by unusual and excessive anxiety at separation from a primary caregiver or from home, beyond the age when it would be developmentally expectable; such a condition is manifested by the following symptoms: worry about losing attachment figures, school refusal, fear of being alone, fear of sleeping separately from attachment figures, separation nightmares, and complaints of physical symptoms when separated from attachment figures; 3) the intrapsychic experience of anxiety over loss, or fear of loss, of a love object, an experience that may occur at any age.

Separation anxiety plays a central role in psychoanalytic theorizing about anxiety, regarding its function in attachment behavior and in the development of object relations. Anxiety, in turn, plays a special role in the history of affect theory in psychoanalysis, serving as the paradigmatic affect starting with Freud. Situated at the interface of metapsychology and phenomenology, separation anxiety has been of interest to an eclectic array of theorists, clinicians, and infant researchers. Within psychoanalysis, efforts to elucidate the etiology of adult psychopathology inevitably led to theories of early mental experience. Coming from the other direction, infant researchers from a variety of disciplines have vetted such theories. The observation that infants become anxious when separated from their mothers became the cornerstone of such developmental theories as attachment theory (Bowlby, 1960b, 1969/1982, 1973, 1980) and separation-individuation theory (Mahler, Pine, and Bergman, 1975), among others. These theories importantly acknowledge the contribution of both internal (psychic) and external (in reality) experiences to early development.

Freud first mentioned separation anxiety early in his writings (1905b); however, it is in delineating his second theory of anxiety (1926a) that Freud accorded separation anxiety a central role. Freud described "fear of loss of the object" as the first danger situation in a developmental hierarchy of anxiety situations. In Klein's view, depressive anxieties are connected to loss and separation throughout development, beginning with birth and weaning (Segal, 1964, 1979a).

In subsequent years, the observation by infant researchers that infants become anxious when they are separated from their mothers figured prominently in their conceptualizations of the development of object relations. Such concepts as object permanence and object constancy were delineated, as well as the nature of early internal representations of the object. Psychoanalytic observers including Spitz, Winnicott, Mahler, Bowlby, Fraiberg, as well as Robertson (1952) were interested in how the actual relationship to the mother and separation from the mother affects the child's development. Spitz (1950) described the normal appearance of eight-months anxiety, or stranger anxiety, which he interpreted as fear of object loss. He theorized that this development marks the initiation of object constancy in the infant as well as the beginning awareness of the self. Spitz (1945; Spitz and Wolf, 1946a) also described anaclitic depression and hospitalism, two catastrophic disorders of infancy resulting from premature separation from the primary caregiver. Winnicott (1953, 1958a, 1958b) introduced the idea of the transitional object, the "me and not-me" object, which functions as a bridge between the infant and mother as the intrapsychic awareness of separation develops.

A. Freud (1965), in observing infants separated from parents during WWII, placed separation anxiety on a developmental continuum of anxieties, each representing a different developmental phase of object relations. She viewed the first phase as symbiotic and narcissistic, involving a biological unity of the mother-infant couple. Disruptions in this phase cause separation anxiety, and fixations result in intense separation anxiety later on. In the second phase, the infant relies on the mother to provide need satisfaction, and frustration may result in anaclitic depression or precocious ego development. By phase three, the infant has achieved object constancy, the development of a stable internal image, and is able to gradually tolerate separations. Bowlby proposed that separation anxiety is a primary anxiety, triggered

when the attachment figure is not available and the fear system is activated. The function of attachment behavior is to maintain the physical proximity of an infant to its caregiver and, therefore, to enhance survival. Mahler proposed her theory of object relations development based on longitudinal observations of mothers and babies and viewed separation anxiety as the characteristic fear of the separation-individuation process. Mahler used the term *separation* to refer to the intrapsychic awareness of separateness from the mother. Fraiberg (1969) viewed separation anxiety as an indicator of the development of an internal representation of the object that can be remembered when the object is not present. However, she noted that the onset of separation anxiety has implications for the processes of internalization and of memory, and suggested that separation anxiety can appear before object constancy, if recognition memory rather than evocative memory is involved. More recently Lyons-Ruth (1999) described the internal representations of early dyadic relationships as "implicit relational knowing." Quinodoz (1993) focused on the role of separation anxiety in the clinical situation, specifically within the transference, manifested throughout an analysis at ends of sessions, weekends, vacations, and termination. Neuroscience research suggests that the anxiety at eight months (including stranger fear and separation anxiety) is partly explained by the maturation of memory centers and fear centers in the amygdala and prefrontal cortex (Kalin, 2002).

Separation-Individuation is: 1) an intrapsychic process involving two interweaving tracks in the slowly unfolding psychological birth of the human infant; 2) a complex stage of development that occurs between six and twenty-four months of age, during which the process of separation-individuation occurs; 3) the developmental theory that features this process, which was introduced by Margaret Mahler. Separation consists of those intrapsychic processes that result in the formation of a mental representation of the self separate from the mental representation of the mother. Such processes include differentiation, distancing, boundary formation, and disengagement. Individuation consists of those intrapsychic processes by which the child attains intrapsychic autonomy, thereby distinguishing his or her own individual characteristics, so that the self not only becomes differentiated from the object but is also represented intrapsychically as a series of self representations. Such processes include the maturation and development of perception, memory, cognition and reality testing (Mahler, Pine, and Bergman, 1975). During the separation-individuation stage of development, four subphases are explicated: differentiation, practicing, rapprochement, and "on the way to libidinal object constancy." Before the separation-individuation stage occurs, there are two important forerunners: the autistic phase (birth to two months), in which the infant is relatively unresponsive to external stimuli; followed by the symbiotic phase (two to nine months), in which the infant establishes a specific affective attachment with the mother.

Separation-individuation, a concept introduced by Mahler (1952), is derived from an impressive body of detailed longitudinal mother-infant observation, which follows a psychoanalytic-anthropological approach rather than a structured experimental method. In her developmental theory, Mahler retained Freud's concepts of psychosexual development and drive theory, while expanding his ego psychological and object relational concepts. She built upon the infant observational research studies of Spitz (1946, 1959) and Bowlby (1969/1982, 1973, 1980), as well as the ideas of Piaget (1951, 1953, 1954), Erikson (1950), and Winnicott (1956a, 1965). Mahler's developmental theory may be contrasted with attachment theory, which also focuses on the early relationship between mother and infant but rejects Freud's concepts of psychosexual development and drive theory and replaces them with a motivational theory based upon attachment. Mahler's contributions catalyzed enormous interest in research, thought, and debate about child development and treatment, as evidenced by the almost two thousand articles in the psychoanalytic literature and a considerable number in the child-development literature referring to aspects of this theory. Mahler's contribution stretched more broadly to catalyze the study of adolescent and adult development and treatment, especially in the realm of the widening scope. Mahler's concepts have been challenged by subsequent experimental studies, from both inside and outside the psychoanalytic community, regarding the developmental capabilities of young infants and toddlers. In particular, her concepts of the autistic and symbiotic phases of development have been shaken by contemporary studies that have demonstrated the infant's very early capacities for making contact with the outside world and for differentiating others as separate entities (D. Silverman, 2005; Pine, 2005a; Striano, Henning, and Stahl, 2005).

Mahler's first two stages of child development—the autistic phase and the symbiotic phase—have been largely discredited. She modeled both stages upon her study of infantile psychosis, which no doubt contributed to her problematic formulations. Mahler described the autistic phase as a state of iso-lation in which the infant is relatively unresponsive to outside stimuli. Mahler described the major tasks of the symbiotic phase as the formation of the mother-infant bond, the development of basic trust, and the early delineation of the body image. This phase is characterized by the specific smiling response to the primary caregiver.

The separation-individuation stage of development begins with the differentiation subphase (six to nine months), in which the child differentiates himself bodily from the mother. This begins with "hatching," as the infant takes more of an interest in the surroundings and interacts with the environment in a more purposeful way (three to five months). The relationship to the mother is established, as indicated by the appearance of the social smile, followed by the use of transitional and checking back phenomena (Mahler, Pine, and Bergman, 1975). Additional characteristic features include "customs inspection," "single/double stimulation," "peekaboo," and "craning." The phase ends as stranger reactions and stranger anxiety appear (Pine, 2004).

In the practicing subphase (ten to fifteen months), the child tests and practices emerging autonomous ego functions, and experiments with differentiation by moving away, practicing motor activities, and exploring the ever-expanding environment at greater distances from mother. However, the infant still requires the availability of the mother for "emotional refueling," especially when tired. These activities result in constructive use of aggression, beginning empathy, sound secondary narcissism, a sense of omnipotence, and a "love affair with the world," demonstrated by a mood of elation.

All of this leads to the rapprochement subphase (fifteen to twenty-four months), with renewed wooing of the mother, underlining the intertwining of the two strands of this process. As individuation has proceeded rapidly and cognitive maturation has progressed, the child is capable of experiencing his own separateness. He experiences increased vulnerability in the form of separation anxiety and now demands mother's attention, often in a coercive controlling mode. This behavior leads to a fear of the loss of hard-earned separateness and independence. Mahler (1972) describes this tension as "ambitendency," which confuses the mother as well as the child and which ultimately leads to a rapprochement crisis, that is, an intrapsychic conflict between the wish to remain with the mother and the wish for autonomy that accompanies the awareness of the self as a separate individual. Others, such as Lyons-Ruth (1991), see this as the result of insecure attachment rather than as a normal developmental crisis. The awareness that mother's wishes are not always coincidental with one's own, an accomplishment of this stage, indicates a dawning capacity for understanding mind states (Bartsch and Wellman, 1995), known as mentalization.

Object constancy is attained when the child is able to maintain a constant relation with the object regardless of need or affective state. Mahler referred to this as "on the way to object constancy," as it is never permanently or fully achieved. Mahler understood object constancy to be a qualitatively new level of organization of object representations based on the concept of burgeoning relatedness, rather than purely on instinctual drive. She borrowed the term from Piaget's (1953) cognitive theory of object permanence, which is considered to be a necessary but not sufficient condition for the development of object constancy. Mahler, like Klein, believed this ability is reached when the child is able to integrate the defensively split-off all-bad representations of the mother with the all-good representations of the mother, and establishes a unified and constant internalized object that can retain its identity even when the mother does something displeasing to the child. For the child to do this, he must be able to carry not only internal representations of physical objects, but also must be able to carry representation of mental properties such as desires, beliefs, intentions, and emotions.

The challenge to Mahler's developmental theory has focused in large part on the validity of the autistic and symbiotic phases. Pine (2004) noted that the autistic phase is not a necessary part of Mahler's theory of separation and individuation, and therefore does not invalidate it. He further argued that "symbiosis" or "merger" is a powerful experience in infancy and might provide an important early template for deep intimate relationships. However, others argue that if Mahler's symbiotic stage is not valid, then her theoretical construct of the child's development of self and relationships as evolving from this symbiosis is seriously challenged. A paradox is created. On the one side is the ability of Mahler's concept to explain so much observational data and to have so much clinical utility. On the other side is empirical data that undercuts the concept of symbiosis upon which the separation-individuation process is built. Part of this dilemma may derive from difficulty reconciling experimental behavioral data used by developmental psychologists with naturalistic observations and interpretation of subjective states used by analysts in the clinical setting. Although Mahler began with assumptions that the neonate was not capable of apprehending the world,

her clinical descriptions and even her conceptual writing seems to anticipate some of these criticisms. Indeed, Mahler's own writings suggest that she was aware that the young infant was capable of discrimination between self and other, but she did not account for this observation. Coates (2004) and H. Blum (2004) noted that Mahler's concepts allow for the infant to have different capacities operating side by side.

Gergely (2000), a neurodevelopmental infant researcher, observed that the discredited concepts of autism and symbiosis do have some basis in early infant behavior. Gergely further noted that many aspects of Mahler's later stages of separation-individuation are consistent with recent empirical research regarding the child's development of awareness of mother's intentions as separate from his own, and in being able to represent those intentions in his mind, as in the work done on mentalization and theory of mind (Fonagy et al., 2002; Mayes and Cohen, 1996). D. N. Stern (1985) criticized the view of the infant as perceptually incapable of distinguishing self from other, and argued, based on his own research, that the infant is equipped at birth with preexisting emergent structures that lead to very early separate cognitive schemas of self and other. Lichtenberg (1982) added that the theory of symbiosis is contested by the active role of the infant as behavioral initiator of interaction. However, Mahler's concept of individuation is consistent with observations by Hofer (1995), who noted that the function of the direct emotion-regulative influence of parental interactions is eventually taken over by mental representations, which, as internalized aspects of the maternal environment, enable the child to regulate affect states independently.

It has been noted that contemporary experimental data do not offer any explanation for the steps and motivating forces necessary in the process of personality development. There are also aspects of symbiosis that give understanding to adult behaviors, particularly around the wish and fear to merge, as well as explaining the normative oceanic feelings originally described by Freud (1927a). Consequently, the concept of separation-individuation, with modifications, stands as a framework for thinking about the early development of the personality and its inner subjective states against which other conceptualizations have been compared and other observations tested.

Sexual Identity is the consolidation within an individual's self concept of his/her sexual orientation, sense of masculinity or femininity, and personal erotism expressed in sexual fantasies. It is a further refinement of gender identity, begins to form unconsciously during the oedipal phase of development, and coalesces during adolescence when erotic desires become conscious, experienced, and knowable. Sexual identity may be experienced as primarily positive and nonconflicted or with varying degrees of conflict. Prior to 1970, *sexual identity* was used in the psychoanalytic literature to refer to an individual's sense of maleness or femaleness. This early use of the term was gradually replaced by "gender identity," due to the influence of Stoller (1964, 1968c). During the 1970s, *sexual identity* gradually became used as an overarching term encompassing core gender identity, gender role identity, and sexual orientation (Frankel and Sherick, 1979; Roiphe and Galenson, 1981b).

The use of *sexual identity* to refer to the expression of an individual's sexual orientation as incorporated in his or her self concept became more prevalent as psychoanalysts devoted greater attention to homosexual development, recognizing that the experience of being different likely increases the developmental significance of sexual identity formation. While sexual identity remains constant for most people, some people experience variability across their lifespan. Flexibility and fluidity in sexual identity appears to be more prevalent in women than in men (Golden, 1987, 2003; Notman, 2002; L. Diamond, 2008). An individual might also engage in same- or opposite-sex erotic behavior or fantasy without such experiences being incorporated into his or her sexual identity.

Sexual Inhibition is a self-imposed inability to allow oneself to obtain sexual gratification, arising from inner conflict, usually unconscious. The inhibition may include difficulty in loving or a complete inability to love. A severe inhibition may be manifested in never gratifying the sexual impulse or never consciously feeling sexual desire. In less-severe sexual inhibition, sexual response and gratification are possible but with some restrictive conditions. Manifestations of sexual inhibition may be as common as not being able to have sex in certain positions or having sex and orgasm with little interest and pleasure, or as dramatic as the fetishist's need to look at a woman's high-heeled shoe in order to have sexual pleasure. The first formal definition was offered by H. Deutsch (1933a).

Sexual Orientation is the erotic attractions experienced by an individual based on the gender of the people the individual is attracted to, and categorized into heterosexual, bisexual, and homosexual.

Although often treated as distinct categories, these orientations occur along a continuum, ranging from exclusive heterosexuality, to varying degrees of bisexuality, to exclusive homosexuality. Comparable terms include *sexual-partner orientation, sexual preference, sexual-object choice,* and *love-object choice.* Some analysts have conceptualized sexual-partner orientation as an aspect of sexual-identity formation, the third component in a developmental line of gender-identity formation, following core gender identity and gender-role identity (P. Tyson, 1982a, 1982b; R. Fischer, 2002). In this model, love-object choice has its roots in preoedipal and oedipal object relations, is established during adolescence, and remains stable throughout life.

Classification of persons according to the gender of their sexual attractions is a relatively recent practice, beginning in the late-nineteenth century, although historical records, including manuscripts and art, document a variety of sexual behaviors. Such classification has emerged with the increased interest in homosexuality by the medical profession and society. Recent contributions to the understanding of sexual orientation have challenged the notion of distinct categories, or of a singular mode of expression and experience, preferring to conceptualize the multiplicity of sexual orientation in heterosexualities, homosexualities, and bisexualities (McDougall, 1986; Chodorow, 1992; Schuker, 1996). This approach recognizes that each person's path toward her or his adult sexual orientation is a unique one. In addition, contemporary psychoanalytic approaches to sexual orientation, in contrast to earlier models, recognize the potential for greater fluidity and flexibility in sexual orientation across the lifespan. This has been particularly evident in women (Golden, 1987, 2003; Notman, 2002; L. Diamond, 2008).

Sexualization/Desexualization: see EROTIZATION, PERVERSION, SUBLIMATION

Shadow: see JUNGIAN PSYCHOLOGY

Shame is a complex affect experienced when an individual's vulnerabilities, needs, and/or actions, felt as defects, are exposed to the real or fantasized critical regard of others. When an individual has the feeling of being held in diminished esteem by another, this feeling provokes a concordant drop in self-esteem. Shame is associated with anxiety as well as with depressive feelings. It is experienced on a spectrum from mild embarrassment to devastating humiliation and tormenting self consciousness. Shame is associated with suicide. Psychoanalysts, depending on their theoretical orientation, view shame as: 1) a reaction formation against exhibitionism and scopophilia; 2) a sense of failure due to an inability to meet the standards of the ego ideal; 3) the consequence of having one's exhibitionism unrecognized; or 4) a universal experience, with an innate component, central to the development of a sense of self. Shame can be distinguished from guilt, which involves anxiety over moral transgressions.

Mild shame reactions, experienced as moments of self consciousness can promote the development of self awareness. This self awareness leads to discretion, tact, and awareness of others. Some psychoanalysts distinguish shame from the **sense of shame** (Broucek, 1991) or **anticipatory shame** (Nathanson, 1987) (analogous to signal anxiety), which serves to regulate one's behavior. In this sense, shame preserves ideals and values that are specific not only for the individual but also for the culture. Groups may regard shame as a socially endorsed attribute of modesty. Shame may also become the source for violence against oneself or others.

Freud (Breuer and Freud, 1893/1895) initially observed that the experience of shame could be traumatic and become a motive for resistance or defense, noting that patients repress memories and sexual fantasies so as to avoid the painful shame, self reproach, and feeling of being harmed associated with them. He (1899a) also noted shame, along with fear and physical pain, as among the most frequent memories of childhood. Later, in "Three Essays on Sexuality," Freud (1905b) viewed shame as an innate source of resistance against the sexual instinct, more specifically as a defensive reaction formation against exhibitionistic wishes and other derivatives of the sexual drive. He (1908d, 1917d) also associated shame with the anal phase, describing how shame contributes to the reaction formations typical of the latency period. In "On Narcissism," Freud (1914e) introduced the concept of the ego ideal related to the experience of self regard, stating that repression proceeds from the self regard of the ego; again, he implied here that shame instigates defense. After Freud (1923a) introduced the structural theory, the capacity for guilt—a psychological achievement arising from the dissolution of the oedipus complex—became a dominant focus in psychoanalytic theory and practice and little was written about shame.

After Freud, ego psychologists such as Fenichel (1945) and Nunberg (1955) continued to see shame as a reaction formation against oral, anal, and phallic impulses. In his delineation of stages of development, Erikson (1950) emphasized autonomy versus shame and self doubt resulting from failure to man-

age anal-phase challenges successfully. Piers and Singer (1953) introduced a theoretical advance when they argued that shame arises out of tension between the ego and the ego ideal, while guilt arises out of conflict between the ego and the critical superego. Guilt occurs when the prohibitions of the superego are transgressed, leading to remorse and anxiety about punishment. Shame occurs when a goal set by the ego ideal is not met, leading to feelings of inadequacy and anxiety about abandonment. Failure to reach one's potential, established by the ego ideal, is consciously experienced as shame that betrays an unconscious anxiety that others will turn away in disgust and contempt. Following Piers and Singer, psychoanalysts continued to emphasize guilt over shame, arguing that guilt involved a more-complex developmental achievement with an internalized and depersonalized set of moral rules. Shame, in contrast, was thought of as a relatively superficial response to fear of other people's disapproval.

Following Kohut's (1971) *The Analysis of the Self* and Lewis's (1971) *Shame and Guilt in Neurosis,* and coinciding with greater interest among psychoanalysts in narcissism, an explosion of interest in shame occurred (Wurmser, 1981, 2004; Broucek, 1982, 1991; Nathanson, 1987; A. Morrison, 1989; Lansky, 1994, 1999). Psychoanalysts developed a more-complex understanding of the vicissitudes of the need for the object or other's acknowledgment and approval in establishing and sustaining a sense of self and self esteem, opening a door to a deeper understanding of shame.

Kohut's conceptualization of the self-affirming aspect of the object in the development of the self (the selfobject function) provided a psychoanalytic understanding of the disruption of self experience and the consequent shame. Kohut's (1977) clinical material is replete with descriptions of shame, describing shame as "guiltless despair." Kohut introduced a new psychoanalytic conceptualization of shame as arising from the unmet exhibitionism of the grandiose self. Kohut explicitly disagreed with Piers and Singer's proposal that shame results from the demands of a perfectionist ego ideal, and he also disputed the view that shame is a defense against exhibitionistic strivings. In Kohut's view, defense against the experience of shame through disavowal of wishes for recognition and affirmation of one's grandiosity creates a vertical split. He focused on the psychological legitimacy of being recognized, and avoided interpretations that implied that a patient's goals or ideals are too lofty or unrealistic or his superego too harsh. Shame is often a conscious or unconscious instigator of narcissistic rage, expressed as contempt or violence toward others in fantasy or behavior. Recognition of shame as a common experience in many people, not just those with severe narcissistic pathology, facilitates an appreciation of the role of shame resistance and stalemates in analysis.

Lewis's studies of verbatim transcripts of psychotherapy sessions contributed to the understanding of shame. She found a prevalence of shame over other affects in psychotherapy sessions. She also described (Lewis, 1987) unacknowledged shame or unconscious shame and its role in therapeutic stalemates. She provided clinical evidence for shame as part of a cycle that included aggression directed others or one's self. Lewis's ideas, like those of Broucek, Morrison, and others also highlighted the social and intersubjective context of shame experiences and how shame can lead either to isolation and alienation or to greater interest in maintaining relationships with others.

While Kohut focused on the role of narcissistic pathology in shame propensity, Broucek (1982) focused on the sense of shame in the development of the self. Broucek posited "objective self awareness" as a precursor to shame. Awareness of how one is seen by others can promote healthy self awareness or shame. He viewed shame as reflecting a disturbance in the interpersonal matrix out of which a sense of self develops. He used Kernberg's concept of the pathologic grandiose self to delineate how individuals defend against shame. Lansky and Wurmser have attempted to integrate Kohut's views of shame with ego psychology as **shame conflict** and **shame dynamics**. Lansky had highlighted the significant role of shame in fundamental concepts such as castration anxiety, which involve fear of sexual humiliation as well as fear of guilt and punishment. He argued that shame dynamics, while involving the self experience of defectiveness, cannot be separated from the inevitable sexual and aggressive conflicts arising from relationships. Wurmser has studied shame related to inner conflict, as well as shame causing inner conflict. Wurmser averred that linking shame exclusively with narcissism excludes the role of the superego, which he viewed as inevitability linked to shame dynamics.

Developmental psychoanalysts have also contributed to the study of shame. Shame is considered by many to develop in the child between eighteen and twenty-four months of age, coincident with the anal phase, rapprochement subphase, and early castration anxieties. It can be heightened by the narcissistic mortifications of the oedipal period (Arlow, 1980). The child may experience shame for exposing something in particular or for the act of exposing, and

may fear being rejected or being seen as small and insignificant, flawed, weak, or dirty. Often induced and maintained in the child by parents, siblings, peers, and teachers, early experiences of being exposed and shamed can contribute to the development of a shaming superego (Kennedy and Yorke, 1982; Yorke, 1990). Amsterdam and Levitt (1980) equated shame with painful self consciousness; they identified the negative parental reaction to the child's genital exploration or play as a major source of shame. Further, negative parental response to the child's exhibitionistic impulses, including displays of pride or pleasure in his or her body or bodily capacities can become a source of shame. While its early roots do not point to obvious gender differences, as awareness of gender and generational differences becomes consolidated, shame can become associated with a sense of organ deficiency seen more typically in girls. Developmental factors underlying a special proneness to shame include the nature and intensity of parental and social shaming influences; the recognition and awareness of physical or psychological disabilities or insufficiencies; and childhood illness or defects felt to be disgusting or devaluing. A child who is repeatedly humiliated may react with disruptive behavior that sometimes appears defensively shameless.

Elaborating on the connections drawn by Freud, Erikson, and others between shame and anal-phase development, Mahler, Pine, and Bergman (1975) emphasized the developments made in object relationships during the phase of sphincter control and the concurrent mental establishment of self boundaries. Correspondingly, it has been suggested that shame prominently involves a regressive breakdown of anal defensiveness, including the breakdown of a barrier between self and other, evident in the sense of nakedness typically accompanying shame.

Shame has also been conceptualized as operating in some form during the first year of life. From this perspective, the "stranger anxiety" identified by Spitz in the six-to-eight-month-old, featuring shyness, lowered eyes, and the action of hiding the face, is seen as a form of "anticipatory shame." Tomkins (1987) postulated that the trigger to the shame affect is any experience (such as failure to engage the mother) requiring a rapid suppression of interest, excitement, or joy, where the child desires to maintain the preexisting affect state. A form of "proto-shame," an affect that does not require an observer, has also been hypothesized as operating from infancy, serving to down-regulate excitement.

Increased shame, embarrassment, or shyness are prevalent during adolescence (Spero, 1984). Heightened narcissism and the recurrence of weak self boundaries characterize this stage and appear in the frequent adolescent experience of depersonalization in reaction to shame (Blos, 1962). During senescence or in terminal illness, increased shame is evoked by the perception that one's infirmities, loss of control, and body excrements are exposed. One defensive approach in old age is the withdrawal of libido from objects, resulting in self involvement (Levin, 1965).

Sibling Rivalry is the competition among siblings for the exclusive or preferred love of their parents. The term appears frequently in popular psychology and child-rearing books that discuss ways to manage and minimize sibling rivalry, but its dynamic underpinnings are usually not discussed. Sibling rivalry and sibling relationships in general are relatively neglected in the psychoanalytic literature, which relegates the sibling relationship to a byproduct of the oedipal parental relationship. In such a perspective, sibling rivalry is understood in terms of the parent as prize, and sibling love is seen as solely defensive, warding off feelings of aggression and anger. However, some contemporary psychoanalysts (J. Mitchell, 2003; Vivona, 2007) have attempted to correct this view by proposing a lateral (sibling/peer) dimension of mental life that is of equal importance to the vertical (parent-child) one. The lateral dimension concerns the developmental challenge of establishing one's uniqueness among similar others, a process in which the central role of differentiation (as opposed to identification) is emphasized in facilitating the formation of an identity different from one's siblings.

The term was used only once in Freud's (1914e) writings, in a letter to Abraham in which he referred to Reik's "sibling rivalry complex," suggesting the presence of a preexisting formulation. Although Freud did discuss sibling relationships subsequently, he tended to de-emphasize them relative to parental relationships. A. Freud and Dann (1951) observed that the aggression toward a sibling only generates conflict when the child realizes that in order to retain the love of his mother, he must renounce his most severe aggression and direct some libido toward the sibling. Neubauer (1983), differentiating rivalry from jealousy and envy, postulated that envy and jealousy are related to feelings of conflict and dissatisfaction that the child experiences with the primary psychological parent, whereas rivalry more closely reflects the sibling interaction.

Some clinicians have described a more-complex developmental role for sibling relationships, in which the sibling is not viewed solely as a rival or intruder. Abend (1984) described adult patients who exhibit a pattern of seeking out opposite-sex relationships that mimic the eroticized and dependent relationships they had with older siblings. During childhood these patients had emotionally unavailable parents, which fostered an intense sibling attachment. Sharpe and Rosenblatt (1994) postulated that oedipal-like triangles develop among siblings and between siblings and a parent, which are thought to exist parallel to and relatively independently from the oedipal "parental" triangle. These sibling relationships are thought to exert important influences on the individual's later identifications, choice of adult love object, and patterns of object relating.

Sharpe and Rosenblatt also described a developmental line for sibling relationships, distinguishing preoedipal sibling rivalry from oedipal sibling rivalry. They viewed preoedipal sibling rivalry as reflecting a dyadic level of object relating, in which the mother and rival sibling are not distinguished as whole objects and the sibling is regarded as an unwelcome intruder. In contrast, as oedipal sibling rivalry is developmentally on a higher level, the rival is ambivalently loved and hated, resulting in internal conflict and guilt. J. Mitchell (2003) proposed that every child—eldest, youngest, or middle—initially experiences himself as the center of the family and only arrives at the "crisis of non-uniqueness" through maturing awareness of the family organization. The result is that every child is confronted with the task of differentiating himself, and often relies on polarization of personality attributes to distinguish himself from his siblings.

Slip of the Tongue: see PARAPRAXIS, PRIMARY PROCESS

Social Constructivism/Social Paradigm: see RELATIONAL PSYCHOANALYSIS

Social Referencing: see INTERSUBJECTIVITY

Somatic Compliance: see PSYCHOSOMATIC DISORDERS

Somatization: see PSYCHOSOMATIC DISORDERS

Soul Murder: see TRAUMA

Splitting is a process by which a part of the experiencing mind is separated into two or more parts. The most common contemporary use of the term *splitting* is in the work of Kernberg (1966, 1975), who described splitting as a defense in borderline and other severe psychopathology. Kernberg defined splitting as "mutually dissociated ego states," wherein contradictory, conscious experiences (usually of self and/or object) coexist, side by side, without influencing each other. His view of splitting is based on Klein's concept of the defensive splitting of ego (self) and object into all-good and all-bad representations early in life, with the aim of protecting good experience from aggression. Kernberg contrasted splitting with repression, a healthier defense that depends on better integration of self and object representations, in which unacceptable feelings and/or thoughts are kept out of awareness.

The word *splitting* has a long history in psychoanalysis, used with many different meanings, including: 1) the **splitting of consciousness**," described by French psychopathologists as the cause of hysteria; 2) normal splitting of part of the mind, as in the normal use of self observation in introspection, or the willing suspension of disbelief in children at play; 3) a normal process of development leading to the differentiation of psychic structure, as in Freud's description of the split in the ego in the development of the "critical agency" (superego); 4) splitting of parts of the mind, usually into opposing pairs, as part of a defensive process (as in Freud's description of men who split the love object into a debased and an idealized image, or his description of the split in attitude toward the father, both feared and venerated, in the formation of taboo); 5) a defensive process (based on disavowal), which Freud called **splitting of the ego**, specifically directed against aspects of reality, so that two conflicting attitudes toward reality can exist side by side (as in his description of fetishism and psychosis); 6) an early defensive process described by Klein and her followers, including Kernberg, in which both ego (self) and object are split into all-good or all-bad parts; this process of splitting defends against anxieties associated with aggression and is part of the development of both self and object representations; and 7) the **vertical split** described by Kohut, manifested as coexisting contradictory self states of grandiosity and despair, which results when healthy narcissistic needs are frustrated by caretakers.

Many analysts have attempted to differentiate splitting from repression, disavowal, and dissociation, but none of these attempts has been completely successful. As Freud noted in one his last papers, splitting is likely involved in all defensive maneuvers (1938b). However, in his later description of splitting of the ego based on disavowal, Freud initiated an important and ongoing exploration of defensive processes at work in more serious psychopathology.

The concept of the "splitting of consciousness" was made famous by French psychopathologists, particularly Janet, in their descriptions of the "dual consciousness" characteristic of hysteria. Freud and Breuer used the term in this way in their early work (Breuer and Freud, 1893/1895). However, Freud quickly differentiated himself from the French by conceptualizing hysteria as the result of repression and/or conflict, and not as the result of a degenerate incapacity for synthesis. Nevertheless, Freud continued to use the word *splitting* in a variety of ways, including the splitting of the self in creative writers (1908a); some kinds of object choice, as for example, what came to be known as the "madonna-whore complex" (1910d); the development of fantasy as a type of thought that has been split off and kept apart from reality testing (1911b); the formation of totems and gods that are both feared and venerated (1913e); the splitting of thoughts into "words" and "things" (1915d); the splitting of the instinct into parts in perversion (1916/1917); the splitting of the ego in the formation of the superego (1917c); and the splitting of the ego into conscious and unconscious parts (1923a).

In 1927 and later, Freud (1927a, 1938a, 1938b) introduced a new idea, the splitting of the ego, contributing to both fetishism and psychosis. In exploring these phenomena, Freud described how it is possible for the ego to adopt contradictory attitudes toward aspects of reality through the use of splitting and disavowal. His most famous example was of the fetishist who believes simultaneously that the woman is "castrated" (without a penis) and that she possesses a penis, represented by the fetish object. While Freud never fully succeeded in differentiating between splitting and repression, his effort was to describe patients with more-severe types of psychopathology characterized by disturbances in the relationship to reality, which he understood as including "distortions" or "splits" in the ego itself, rather than conflict between ego and id.

The concept of splitting plays a major role in the theories of Klein and her followers. Klein used the concept of splitting of the object into all-good and all-bad parts as a defense against anxieties associated with aggression. She first observed this defensive use of splitting in her observations of children's play. Later, she described how splitting of the object contributes to the paranoid position during development; by contrast, the depressive position is characterized by better integration of good and bad experiences of the object into a coherent whole. In Klein's view, splitting plays a role in serious psychopathology, including borderline and paranoid states of mind, as well as in the "manic defense" against depression.

Fairbairn (1952), influenced by the work of Klein, applied the concept of splitting to the ego (self) as well as to the object. Fairbairn generalized from his work with very disturbed patients to describe the "schizoid core" of all people, based on the universal mechanism of splitting, mobilized in response to frustration in early relationships. In Fairbairn's view, an original "pristine ego" is split into three parts: 1) the "central ego," or "I," which is the seat of self observation and conscious experience; 2) the "libidinal ego," associated with libido; 3) the "antilibidinal ego," or "internal saboteur," associated with aggression, which attacks the libidinal ego. Each of these ego states is paired with a corresponding internal object. Fairbairn called this early phase of splitting the "schizoid position."

Klein soon adopted Fairbairn's ideas, renaming her paranoid position, the "paranoid-schizoid position"; in the process, she also adopted Fairbairn's view that the ego as well as the object is split in the normal course of development. Klein went on to elaborate on splitting in her description of fragmentation in schizophrenic patients, based on a defensive need to obliterate a feared object by splitting it into multiple pieces. Bion (1959) also elaborated on the concept of splitting in his views on defensive "attacks on linking."

As an aspect of self psychology, Kohut (1971) introduced the concept of the vertical split, a developmental split in the structure of the self, manifested as coexisting contradictory self states, such as grandiosity and diffidence, or unintegrated behaviors, such as perversions and infidelity. Interpersonal theorists such as P. Bromberg (1998a, 2006), D. B. Stern (1997), and others sometimes use the word *splitting* to describe the effects of their preferred concept, dissociation.

Strange Situation: see ATTACHMENT THEORY

Stranger Anxiety: see ANXIETY, SEPARATION ANXIETY

Structural Theory, also known as the **Tripartite Model**, is Freud's second and final model of the mind, in which the mind is organized into three systems, agencies, or structures—the id, ego and superego—defined by their relatively interdependent organizations and functions and their enduring motivational configurations. Structural theory does not reify or personify these structures, which have no material form or location, although the theory has been criticized, not infrequently, as doing so. This model, which has been further elaborated within ego psychology and conflict theory, has largely supplanted Freud's first theory, the topo-

graphic model, which divides the mind into agencies defined by their relation to consciousness. The ascendance of the structural theory represented an important shift in the aim of psychoanalytic treatment, from making the unconscious conscious to focusing on the analysis of conflict with the aim of strengthening the ego.

Many psychoanalysts regard structural theory as one of the most useful explanatory paradigms within psychoanalysis for understanding mind and behavior. The structural theory facilitated the exposition of ego psychology, including Hartmann's views on adaptation and Waelder's views on multiple function, as well as many other refinements of metapsychology, clinical technique, and developmental theory. For many years within the history of North American psychoanalysis, the hegemony of the structural theory and ego psychology remained unchallenged, even as it began to incorporate object relations theory (Jacobson, Kernberg), infant observation (Mahler), and relational influences (Loewald). Structural theory suffered some of its most significant criticism from within its own ranks. For example, C. Brenner, originally a major proponent, ultimately rejected structural theory, claiming that the utilization of the microstructure of compromise formation is sufficient for a full description of mental function. Others have disagreed, arguing the usefulness of structural theory particularly in elucidating psychopathology and development. Structural theory (and ego psychology) has also been rejected on the grounds that it is too mechanistic and too distant from the level of clinical discourse. Some contemporary theorists, such as relational and interpersonal theorists, do not utilize an elaborated metapsychology, as their focus is on the here-and-now intrapsychic and interpersonal experience of the analytic dyad. Structural theory does not contribute to their conceptualization of the clinical situation.

Freud articulated the structural model between 1920 and 1926, as a way of addressing the failure of his earlier topographic model to adequately account for numerous clinical observations, particularly regarding intrapsychic conflict. Freud's (1900, 1915d) topographic model had equated the unconscious with instinctual (essentially sexual) wishes, and had represented the anti-instinctual repressive forces that oppose those wishes as being part of the conscious (or preconscious) system of the mind. Yet, clinical observation revealed that the forces that oppose instinctual wishes are very often themselves unconscious. In addition, his observations of the role played by self-directed aggression and self-punitive trends in such clinical phenomena as melancholia, masochism, negative therapeutic reactions, and certain character types such as those "wrecked by success," would lead him both to recognize the centrality of aggression in mental life and to recognize that defenses, moral demands, and guilt, not just instinctual wishes, are themselves often unconscious. Thus, in 1920, in "Beyond the Pleasure Principle," Freud (1920a) not only introduced the idea of a destructive or death drive, but also first raised the idea that "much of the ego is itself unconscious." The elaboration of this latter idea and many of its consequences were more fully articulated in 1923 in "The Ego and the Id," in which Freud (1923a) presented his new structural hypothesis to better describe how the mind functions in situations of conflict.

In this new theory, Freud proposed that the mental apparatus is divided into three agencies or structures, characterized by their relatively stable and enduring sets of functions and relationships with each other and with the external world. Each of these structures—the id, ego, and superego—had a significant prehistory in Freud's earlier work (though the terms *id* and *superego* were new). The id, constituted by the mental representatives of the sexual and aggressive instinctual drives, has the characteristics of what Freud had previously called the system unconscious, operating with primary process modes of energy discharge according to the pleasure principle. Freud described the id as the earliest part of the mind, out of which the ego gradually differentiates under the impact of sensory stimuli from the outside world. The ego's role is always one of mediation between the id drives and the demands of external reality. The ego includes such functions as perception, control of motility, rational thought, language, reality testing, adaptation, affect modulation, and defenses against the drives. With individual development and maturation, the ego becomes progressively more coherent, synthetic, and organized in its functions. The ego is able both to carry out id wishes, as well as increasingly to oppose them when they come into conflict with the demands of the external world or with the moral prohibitions of the superego. The ego's role is always one of mediation between the id drives, the superego, and the demands of external reality. The ego's function as the central steering mechanism of the organism allows it to effect compromise solutions to the competing demands of id, superego, and reality so as to facilitate maximal satisfaction even in the face of competing aims. The ego develops a capacity to anticipate danger situations posed by instinctual wishes and to react to them with a signal of anxiety, thus initiating defense to avoid the development of more overwhelming traumatic anxiety (Freud, 1926a).

The third agency or structure in the mind, the superego, is a further division of the ego, comprised of functions involved with ideal aspirations, moral commands, and prohibitions. Although the superego has both earlier precursors and subsequent development, the essential structure is formed through identifications with parental prohibitions against incestuous and parenticidal wishes, which occur as part of the resolution of the oedipus complex. The superego makes use of aggressive energies of the id, redirecting the aggression against id wishes themselves, in the form of guilt and self punishment.

Freud's structural model had significant consequences for psychoanalytic theory and technique (Fenichel, 1941; Arlow and Brenner, 1964). In this model, anxiety is no longer conceptualized as the consequence of defense but rather the initiator of it. Repression is no longer synonymous with defense but is now one among many possible defense mechanisms. The concepts of overdetermination and compromise formation take on a larger and more-complex role within this new model. This led to Waelder's (1936) formulation of the principle of multiple function, which underlines the necessity of understanding the id, ego, and superego components involved in all mental products and behavior, as well as the ego's synthetic, problem-solving, and adaptational role. The structural model places an increased emphasis on developmental and genetic aspects of mental functioning, such as the history of the danger situations producing anxiety, and of ego and superego identifications. Most centrally, perhaps, it changes the very nature of the therapeutic task in analysis from making the unconscious conscious to enlarging and strengthening the functioning of the ego through a more-optimal integration of id and superego components. This change entails an expansion from the previous focus on unconscious drive wishes to one that includes defense, resistance, and superego analysis, as well as consideration of the ego's adaptive role.

Important contributions to the development of structural theory since Freud have included A. Freud's (1936) work on the defensive functions of the ego, and Hartmann's (1939a) focus on the role of the ego in adaptation. In contrast to Freud's hypothesis that the ego develops out of the id, Hartmann postulated that both structures develop from an earlier undifferentiated matrix. He viewed aspects of ego functioning, such as perception and motility, to have a drive-independent origin that is free from conflict and possesses primary autonomy. Hartmann proposed that other aspects of ego functioning attain secondary autonomy, or independence from conflict, during the course of development. Brenner (1982) also made central contributions to the development of structural theory, stressing the ubiquity of conflict and compromise formation in normality as well as pathology. He also pointed out that the structure of the superego is itself a compromise formation and argued that depressive affect as well as anxiety is involved in the initiation of defense.

Numerous criticisms of structural theory have been raised both by those who view it as a very useful model in need of modification and those who reject the model in more-fundamental ways. Many analysts have taken issue with, or entirely rejected, the energic concepts that are integral to Freud's version of the structural model. Most analysts have rejected Freud's hypothesis of a death drive as a useful explanation of aggressive drives (with the notable exception of the Kleinians). Similarly, few contemporary analysts invoke the id in thinking about drives, wishes, or other motivational forces. Many have felt that the structural model does not adequately address the concepts of affects, object relations, narcissism, or the self. Jacobson, Loewald, Mahler, Sandler, and Kernberg are all important analytic theorists whose work has attempted in various ways to better integrate these central concepts with structural theory. Schafer, G. Klein, Kohut, and most recently, Brenner offered fundamental critiques of the structural model. Schafer (1976) and G. Klein (1976) have both viewed structural theory as too abstract and clinically distant and also insufficiently focused on the individual's intentions and meanings. These authors proposed alternative approaches, such as the use of an action language or "schemata." The self psychology model proposes the self as a superordinate structure organizing the psyche, and focuses on deficits in self structure rather than conflict. In a shift from his earlier views, Brenner (2002) advocated retiring the structural model, arguing that the microstructures of conflict and compromise formation are concepts that adequately describe mental function and experience. Sullivan's (1953a) interpersonal theory rejected structural theory and any concept of individual psychic structure, instead focusing on the interpersonal field. Some contemporary interpersonal theorists and most relational theorists view structure as "created by the internalization of interpersonal regularities" (D. B. Stern, 1994) and utilize object relational structures without reference to the structural theory.

Structure or **Psychic Structure** is a relatively enduring, organized mental configuration or group of mental functions. Psychic structures are useful theoretical abstractions, inferred from the observation of persistent patterns in the flux of mental processes and behavior, and should not be regarded as reified or personified entities. Structures develop from the interaction of maturing constitutional givens and environmental influences, most importantly interactions with caregivers. In their development, psychic structures become progressively more complex and differentiated, through processes of internalization and externalization. Psychic structures are not meant to refer to or correlate with anatomical structures within the brain, although they may ultimately reflect underlying neurophysiologic processes. Psychic structure as a broad concept should be distinguished from the narrower concept of Freud's structural theory, which is established with the formation of the superego upon resolution of the oedipus complex. Developmental theorists recognize that the development of psychic structure begins with birth.

Different models of the mind conceptualize structure in different ways, elaborating different psychic structures as central in determining behavior. Examples of psychic structure include id, ego, and superego; unconscious fantasy; character; internalized object relations; self as a superordinate structure; among others. Psychic structures are central in the way psychoanalytic theories of mind account for the influence of the body on the mind, the past on the present, and interactions with the external world on the internal world.

Between 1920 and 1926, Freud articulated a revised model of the mind, eventually referred to as the **structural theory**, which divided the mind into three agencies or structures—the id, ego, and superego—defined by their relatively stable sets of interdependent functions. Freud himself never used the term *structural theory,* though he spoke of the "structural conditions of the mind" in describing the antithesis between the coherent ego and the id (Freud, 1923a), the "structural division of the mental apparatus" (Freud, 1926a), and later of the "structural relations" (Freud, 1933a) of the mind, in describing the interacting functions of id, ego, and superego.

Rapaport and Gill (1959) attempted to systematize Freud's metapsychological description by outlining the points of view considered necessary to adequately delineate mental phenomena. They defined the structural viewpoint as involving propositions concerning "abiding psychological configurations" that were described as "configurations of a slow rate of change" and "abiding patterns in the flux of processes." They suggested that not only id, ego, and superego were to be viewed as structures, but also configurations such as defenses and character traits, which reflected the enduring influence of the past on the present.

Over the ensuing decades, the term *structure* has been used at many different levels of complexity and conceptualization within psychoanalytic theory, creating a certain degree of confusion. Structure has been employed to refer to configurations that can be abstracted from behavior, as well as to underlying determinants of behavior. Structure has been variously defined as stable functions, as a group of functions that forms a coherent unit, as modes of organization in contrast to functions, as organizations of aims and motives, as the ordering of patterns of stimuli in the service of adaptation, as the interrelation of elements rather than the elements themselves, and as superordinate regulators of behavior (Levey, 1984). Boesky (1988) argued that it is misleading to consider all mental processes with stability and organization as structures. He proposed reserving the use of the term for id, ego, and superego, which are underlying "causative structures," rather than for entities such as character traits, transference, the self, and object representations, which are compromise formations resulting from the interactions of id, ego, and superego functions. Pulver (1988) proposed a dynamic definition for structure as an organized group of mental contents and/or processes that carries out a specific function, rather than the broader static definition of structure as any organized, patterned, enduring mental configuration or sequence of mental events.

To some extent, different psychoanalytic schools of thought can be distinguished by the psychic structures that they tend to privilege in their consideration of how the mind operates. However, within ego psychology there are controversies as to whether entities such as self and object representations within the ego, or compromise formations such as unconscious fantasy and character traits, should also properly be considered as structures. Object relations theories view internal object relations, made up of affectively linked self representations in interaction with object representations, as the central units of psychic structure. Self psychology considers the self to be the superordinate structure regulating behavior (rather than a substructure of the ego). Interpersonal theories are often viewed as rejecting structural concepts. However, D. N. Stern (1994) argued that interpersonal theory views structure as created by the internalization of interpersonal regularities, and that "people shape and discover the enduring aspects of themselves in interaction with others."

Sublimation is a defensive process that redirects unacceptable impulses toward socially acceptable aims. The concept of sublimation helps account for human activities that do not appear to be motivated by sexual or aggressive impulses (for example, artistic creation or intellectual activity) but which may, at least in part, be motivated by these impulses. Sublimation is considered one of the highest-level defenses, a mark of successful adaptation.

Freud (1905b) first used the term *sublimation* (along with *reaction formation*) in 1905, exploring its role in the development of the "civilized and normal individual" by diverting sexual impulses toward more acceptable aims. In this early period, sublimation was conceptualized simply as a vicissitude of the instinct (1915b); later it was viewed as a function of the ego, a special form of defense. In many of his works, Freud (1908b, 1927a, 1930) explored the contributions of sublimation not only to the formation of character but to the creation of art, science, philosophy, religion, and civilization itself. Earlier, in 1923, Freud (1923a) had broadened his definition of sublimation to include any desexualization of libidinal drive energy, going hand in hand with the transformation of object libido into narcissistic (or ego) libido (through the process of identification), after which libido can be redirected by the ego to any alternative aim. This change reflected his commitment to the idea that libidinal energy is the driving force for all psychic activity, including ego activity. Using the more general term *neutralization,* Hartmann, Kris, and Loewenstein (1949) extended Freud's theory of redirected instinctual energy to include aggressive drives. At the same time, by positing inborn ego functions with primary autonomy, Hartmann implicitly recognized that it is not necessary to assume that all behavior originally has sexual or aggressive aims. Thus, Hartmann restored the concept of sublimation to its original use, as describing only those culturally acceptable activities thought to involve redirected sexual or aggressive impulses. A. Freud (1936) included sublimation in her list of defense mechanisms, and it appears on almost every other well-known list of defenses. Klein (1940) argued that sublimation originates in the mechanism of reparation. While contemporary psychoanalysts have largely dispensed with the energic or drive implications of sublimation, the term is still widely used. Following Freud, Vaillant (1992b) considered sublimation, along with altruism, humor, and suppression to be among the more "mature" defenses. Others have criticized the concept of sublimation, arguing that it necessitates value judgments regarding the desirability of various activities (Kaywin, 1966).

Superego is one of three agencies of the structural or tripartite model of the mind, commonly known as the conscience. The functions of the superego include the ego ideal (a set of depersonified ideals and moral values), a limiting function that attempts to stop unacceptable behavior, and a punitive function. Superego formation occurs with the resolution of the oedipus complex, although precursors are established much earlier, and subsequent development and consolidation is thought by some analysts to continue throughout the life cycle. Closely tied to issues of self-esteem regulation, the superego measures the self according to values of the ego ideal and then either criticizes or rewards. Failure to live up to moral standards results in the painful affect of guilt; failure to live up to nonmoral standards associated with personal ideals of perfection results in the painful affect of shame. Derived in part from powerful id strivings, the superego is easily subject to regression and externalization onto authority figures, an issue of particular clinical significance in relationship to the transference. Derivatives of the superego are observable in phenomena metaphorically described as an inner voice, an inner authority, or inner judge.

The concept of the superego has important significance within the history of psychoanalytic theorizing. It is closely tied to Freud's view of the oedipus complex as a universal organizer of psychic experience, and the resolution of the oedipus complex as the formative influence in the development of morality. It is also linked to some of Freud's mistaken theories about female development, specifically his notion that the female superego is less stringent than that of the male. In contemporary discourse, the concept of the superego has contributed to views on affect development and the early development of intersubjectivity. Superego pathology contributes to a range of pathological conditions, including at its most severe end of the spectrum, sociopathy, masochism, and depression, but also to more subtle issues involving the regulation of self esteem. Clinical issues involving the superego often involve the management of aggression and associated guilt. Within the clinical situation, superego pathology has been linked to the negative therapeutic reaction, which is often conceptualized in terms of the need for punishment.

Freud (1923a) first employed the term *superego* in "The Ego and the Id." The superego designates the system of the mind that is defined, according to the principles of the structural theory, by its three interrelated component functions: conscience, self observation, and the ego ideal (or ideal function). However, both the term and the system had by 1923 undergone a long, and sometimes confusing, development from much earlier writings. Freud's (1913e) view of morality was first definitively described as the injunctions imposed by society, and transmitted from generation to generation by parental authority, in reaction to the biologically based oedipal impulsions toward incest and parenticide. Thus, at that time, according to Freud, morality and its core (the prohibitions against incest and parenticide) are not derived from internal developmental processes at all (except for the child's obedience to the parents out of love for them). Freud's (1914e) earliest mention of an internal moral agency was in "On Narcissism." A more truncated mention of such an agency occurred in "Mourning and Melancholia" (1917c). In those papers, especially the former, Freud put forward the notion of a mental agency that stands apart from the rest of the mind, critically observes it, and compares it with ideal standards of behavior set by the parents. Adhering to these ideal standards brings with it narcissistic enhancement, which corresponds to the primary narcissism experienced by the child before the establishment of object relations. This view was later expanded in "Group Psychology and the Analysis of the Ego" (1921), where Freud pointed to attitudes toward idealized objects, for example, leaders of authoritative/charismatically led groups, as being the externalized correlates of the internal agency.

Freud (1923a) formally defined and formulated the superego in 1923 with the publication of "The Ego and Id." What had been termed the *ego ideal* two years previously is now termed the *superego*. The superego is seen as the authoritative mental agency that forms with the resolution of the oedipus complex, and that embodies a prohibitive reaction formation against the oedipal wishes of incest and parenticide. Previous to the superego's formation, authoritative regulation is based upon the parents' injunctions. With the formation of the superego, authoritative regulation is now internalized through the child's identification with the parents. Correlated with this developmental vicissitude, Freud (1923b) interpolated a phallic psychosexual phase as occurring after the anal-sadistic phase and before the latency phase. The object relations characteristic of the phallic phase is triadic, in contrast to the dyadic object relations characteristic of the prephallic psychosexual phases. The major fantasied danger of that phase is castration, which is conceived by the child as the appropriate punishment for oedipal wishes. The conflict between oedipal wishes and the punitive threat of castration mobilizes the oedipus complex, which is resolved with the formation of the superego. This model works well in describing the boy's development, but in Freud's (1924b) view, the little girl, already perceiving herself to be castrated, has less to fear. For that reason, in Freud's view, her oedipus complex is not resolved as completely as that of the boy, and her superego is never "so inexorable and independent of its emotional origins as we require it to be in men."

Tension between the superego and the ego manifests itself as guilt (the successor of castration anxiety) and diminished self esteem. Conversely, adhering to the moral and perfectionist standards of the superego leads to enhanced self esteem. The function that guarantees that these moral and perfectionistic standards are met is termed the "ego ideal" or the "ideal function" or the "vehicle of the ego ideal" (Freud, 1933a). The critical and punitive orientation of the superego indicates that it operates mostly with aggressive drive energy. The harshness of the superego is not necessarily a reflection of the harshness of the parents but it is a reflection of the harshness of the rivalrous aggression of the child's oedipus complex. The general and persistent inhibition of aggression due to societal conformity continues the same process and induces in civilized humanity an ever-increasing burden of guilt, one of the major "discontents" of civilization (Freud, 1930).

While Freud's definitive formulation of the superego specified its three component functions (conscience, ego ideal, and self observation), this list had not always been so stable. In 1914 and 1921, Freud attributed reality testing to what was then called the "ego ideal," but in 1923, he finally attributed it to the ego. Most analysts following Freud have also considered self observation to be a function of the ego, although it is acknowledged as interdependent on the other superego functions. Thus, there has been a trend toward absorbing various superego functions into the concept of the ego.

Numerous controversies have been associated with the superego concept. The understanding of shame, as opposed to guilt, has remained problematic. Both affects result from the noncompliance with standards of perfection. Nevertheless, there are phenomenological differences between the two. Efforts have been made to formulate the differences on the basis of: drives (libido versus aggression), the drive direction (object orientation versus narcissism/masochism), and superego functions (conscience versus ego ideal). So far, there has not been any consensus in this regard (Piers and Singer, 1953). Another controversy concerns the issue of female superego development. Most contemporary analysts understand that the girl's superego is as stringent as that of the boy. The girl's anxieties with respect to her body are different, in keeping with her own anatomy, and her triangular situation differs in key respects from that of the boy. Consequently, her ways of relating to both mother and father and the demands she sets for herself may differ from the boy's (Gilligan, 1982; D. Bernstein, 1983; P. Tyson, 1994; P. Bernstein, 2004; Kulish and Holtzman, 2008). Freud neglected the fact that the superego often speaks in the mother's voice, in men as well as in women.

There is controversy over whether the superego as a structure forms or whether it develops slowly. Those analysts who endorse the formation concept emphasize the distinction between superego precursors and the superego proper (Hartmann and Loewenstein, 1962; Jacobson, 1964; D. Milrod, 2002). They describe the presence of two critical factors that permit the formation of a new psychic structure at the specific time that it occurs, which include the powerful stimulus of the oedipal crisis and the attainment of requisite ego capacities, such as the capacity for renunciation, conceptualization, and self observation. Klein (1927b) argued that superego functioning may be observed in extremely young children, a view that has precipitated very vigorous debate. J. Sandler (1960b) postulated a "preautonomous superego schema," which is a sort of cognitive blueprint of the externally imposed superego injunctions. However, this schema is devoid of internalized parental authority, which occurs only with the resolution of the oedipus complex.

Some contemporary analysts maintain that superego development is a lifelong process, identifying the internalization of parental expectations in young children long before the oedipal phase and tracing its further modification well into adulthood. Direct observation of the infant and young child's relationships with both parents has further illuminated the biological, psychodynamic, and social foundations of the superego. These findings call attention to the loving and beloved aspects of the superego (Schafer, 1960). Roots of moral development have been traced back to baby-caregiver affective communications that prevail from birth forward (Spitz, 1965; Emde, 1983; D. N. Stern, 1985). Everyday reciprocally negotiated interactions help with internal self regulation, guide behaviors, and promote shared imaginative creativity (Emde, 1991). Infants less than a year old reference the caregiver for guidance (via affective signals) in situations of uncertainty (Klinnert et al., 1982). The "do's" shape what is "right," enhancing the infant's self pride, while the "no's" block impulse expression—and may also elicit a willful counter-"no!" as one of the infant's first word-gestures (Spitz, 1959; Emde, Johnson, and Easterbrooks, 1988). Infants between eighteen and thirty-six months have already internalized some superego functions, as demonstrated by the preoedipal child's empathy for others, affective reactions to wrongdoing, prosocial behaviors and attitudes, and even the capacity to struggle with moral dilemmas (Emde and Buchsbaum, 1990)—though impulse control may be best maintained under the watchful eyes of the caregiver. Such observations, along with neuroscientific studies of modularly distributed procedural memory systems throughout the brain (Grigsby and Stevens, 2000; Westen and Gabbard, 2002) support Freud's insight that much of the superego operates outside conscious awareness.

During latency, harsh superego fantasies are gradually modified in accord with the child's ongoing socialization and cognitive development (Bornstein, 1951, 1953; Sarnoff, 1976). The adolescent passage involves the casting out of the parental superego and its reinternalization in accord with the young adult's self definitions, values, and autonomy (A. Freud, 1936; Blos, 1979b). Generally speaking, the various superego functions gradually become more impersonal (abstract) and attain greater autonomy from external objects. Still, moral sensibilities may be refined or corrupted through adulthood and old age as a function of experience. The Nazi movement illustrates the adult's vulnerability to authority and raises questions about the degree to which the superego is ever completely internalized and autonomous. Violence in every society, embraced in the name of "good," reminds us of the collusion between superego and id (B. Steele, 1970).

Clinically, superego development and the resolution of the triangular oedipus complex have been de-linked in the minds of some psychoanalysts, although superego functioning remains a key diagnostic dimension in assessing character and pathology (Coen, 1992; P. Tyson, 1996a). Dyadic relational issues, once thought an indicator of more-severe pathology, may prevail in some neurotic people, who nonetheless demonstrate the ability to take responsibility for their own behavior and for their failings. The oedipus complex is never fully resolved; it resurfaces in new iterations through the life cycle, to be reworked in the light of new experiences and life challenges (Loewald, 1979; Ogden, 2006).

Suppression is the deliberate, conscious attempt to drive specific thoughts, affects, and impulses out of awareness. Suppression is unique among defense mechanisms in that it operates consciously. It is considered a mature defense in that it takes into account the demands of reality while deferring attention to particular mental contents to a more opportune time (Vaillant, 1977). The volitional and conscious nature of suppression distinguishes it from repression and/or denial, both of which also expel unwelcome mental contents from awareness but which operate unconsciously.

While Freud (1900) did not clearly distinguish between suppression and repression in most of his early publications, in an early footnote, he noted that repression is more indebted to unconscious processes than is suppression. A. Freud (1936) did not include suppression in her inventory of defense mechanisms, presumably because it contradicted her view of defenses as, by definition, unconscious. C. Brenner (1955) argued against the sharp categorical distinction between repression and suppression, proposing instead a spectrum of intermediates between more- and less-conscious processes. The most extensive exploration of suppression was undertaken by Werman (1983), who emphasized that suppression operates in a wide variety of ways, both in the daily life of an individual and in psychoanalytic treatment. It may be used as resistance by the patient, or as a means for the analyst to maintain an optimal analytic stance. Werman also noted that suppression is not always indicative of "mature" adaption, as, for example, when it leads to ostrichlike behavior that serves to avoid taking necessary action. However, the empirical studies of Vaillant (1992a) support the classification of suppression as among the most mature defenses, associated with greater ego strength and higher global functioning. Anderson et al. (2004) proposed neuroanatomical correlates (hippocampus, dorsolateral prefrontal cortex) for a postulated continuum of suppression and repression.

Symbiotic Phase: see SEPARATION-INDIVIDUATION

Symbolism/Symbolization/Representation/ Symbolic Representation is a universal process or capacity of the human mind whereby one element is used to stand for another. The products of such processes are known as **symbols**, representations, or symbolic representations. Symbolic representation is a broad term that includes inanimate objects as well as self and object representations. Symbolic representations appear in dreams, art, literature, and cultural objects, as well as in psychological symptom formation.

The simplest form of a symbol is a signal, which stands for its referent in a one-to-one relationship. The form the signal takes may be related to the referent or it may be arbitrary. Complex signals may have many parts and denote many separate signals but still retain a one-to-one structure. Signals are usually consciously chosen according to secondary process rules of logic.

From a psychoanalytic perspective, a symbol is a complex representation that refers to a potentially infinite class of referents chosen and united by emotional meaning or theme. The resulting symbol is constructed using the primary processes of condensation and displacement. A representation in psychoanalysis usually refers to an intrapsychic symbolization of an experience of self and/or other, often in the interaction with each other. Symbolic representations of this sort are known as **self representations** and **object representations**. The domain of psychoanalytic theory that specifically focuses on representations of self and object and their relationship to each other is object relations theory. Representations of self and object experiences are generally stable and enduring but also develop over time in their contents, themes, relationships, and overall complexities. Representations are crucial aspects of any concept of psychic organization or structure. A psychoanalytic representation may be visual and is often a composite structure. A representation is comprised of both reality experience and emotional experience in variable proportion, and its content often includes a layering of past or present experience. It may be experienced consciously, preconsciously, or unconsciously, and is therefore varyingly organized by the primary, secondary, and tertiary processes. A representation may be comprised of reality details of self experience, or self in relationship to another individual, that may evoke, refer to, and/or symbolize complex emotional responses (H. Blum, 1978).

Representation is a basic concept in psychoanalysis and probably in all theories of mind. Because representation organizes human experience, all theories either explicitly or implicitly describe representations in their intrapsychic or behavioral manifestations. While the concept of representation is utilized in all mind sciences and in philosophy of mind, psychoanalysis is unique in its focus on the unconscious, affective, and developmental aspects of representation. Freud's earliest theories onward involved a description of inner experience that is now described as representation. Freud explored representational processes in relationship to dreams, to neurotic and psychotic symptomatology, and to literature, as well as to other areas of artistic expression.

Freud's (1895b) first use of the term *symbol* is in "The Project for a Scientific Psychology," where he described the use of symbolic displacements in hysterical symptom formation. However, it is in "The Interpretation of Dreams" that Freud (1900) described in greater detail the use of symbolization as a method of disguise used by the primary process to transform the original unconscious dream-thoughts and wishes into the manifest dream. Condensation and displacement are mental processes that organize the formation of symbols by the primary process mode.

In Strachey's translation, *symbol* is used to mean "signal" as it refers to a dream-image that always has the same unconscious referent, regardless of who is the dreamer. Strachey used the term **plastic representation** for Freud's use of what is now defined as a psychoanalytic symbol.

The term *representation* rarely appears in Freud's writing. Freud first discussed the concept of representation in "The Interpretation of Dreams" in the context of **representability**. Freud considered what aspects of an object or thing are "suitable" for use as a dream-symbol or as a representation. Those objects or things that are emotionally meaningful are preferentially chosen by the individual dreamer or symbolizer. However, the concept of representation is inherent in Freud's many discussions of the constituents of mental life, including references to memories, reality, and emotional experience—including, importantly, traumatic experience—which together comprise the experience of self in relationship to others.

Freud used the term **thing presentation** for visual and other concretely experienced symbolic representations of the unconscious. Freud (1895b) described the unconscious as organized in thing presentations. He explained that objects, animate or inanimate, in external reality or imaginary, are utilized for unconscious symbolic representation based on qualities of representability. Freud (1915d/Appendix C) used the term **word presentation** for the mental storage of language in the conscious mind. Freud also described the entry into consciousness of an unconscious idea, or thing presentation, via its registration as a word presentation.

Jones (1912) described how symbols may indirectly or metaphorically represent drive derivatives and conflicts of forbidden wishes. In his view, psychoanalytic symbols represent unconscious ideas that are linked to affective experience. For Klein, symbolic representation refers to unconscious object relations, primarily the representation of objects in their connection to drives, especially the aggressive drive. Klein regarded symbols as the representations of unconscious "phantasy," in the form of derivatives of the unconscious. Klein (1930) described the capacity to symbolize unconscious frightening, sadistic aggressive feelings for the object as an important step in ego development. Klein focused predominantly on the affect contents of drive derivatives rather than the forms or processes that are involved in symbol formation. However, Klein did describe two processes in the usage of symbols: splitting and projective identification. Segal (1957, 1979b) described how, in psychotic patients, symbols are equated with the thing symbolized, forming what she called **symbolic equations**. Later object relations theorists ascribe symbol formation to the ego, but their primary focus continues to be on contents, not forms or processes. Two exceptions are Sutherland and Kernberg, who stressed that self and object representations are linked by affects and organized by the primary process and splitting.

With the advent of Freud's (1923a) structural theory and the growth of ego psychology, conceptualizations of the ego shifted from the ego as self to the ego as the mediator of processes, particularly intersystemic conflict. A. Freud's (1936) focus on ego defenses, and Waelder's (1936) focus on multiple function, furthered this emphasis on ego processes that are involved in the mediation of conflict. Ego psychologists have generally been less focused than have the Kleinians on the representation of compromise entities such as unconscious object relations, and have been more focused on preconscious compromises of conflict and defensive processes based on repression.

Jacobson (1964) synthesized object relations and ego psychology by elaborating the object relational components of agency structures, the way in which object relations are organized by both the maturation and development of the drives and ego functions, the differentiation of ego functions and processes as they relate to severity of psychopathology, and the role of affect in all of these processes. In Jacobson's theorizing, the concept of self and object representations is fundamental to the contents of all structural considerations.

Other theorists who have made significant contributions to the conceptualization of mental representations include Schafer (1968b), who described self and object representations as compromise formations; Kernberg (1975), who, like Jacobson and Schafer, combined ego psychology and object relations theory by describing the development and structure of object relations and of agencies, especially in their relationship to affect; J. Sandler and Rosenblatt (1962), who carefully delineated, from the standpoint of the ego, the **representational world** of self and objects.

Modern ego psychology focuses on symbols, especially their dynamic contents and structures, the processes of symbol formation, and the ego capacities essential for the processes of symbolic representation. Symbols and symbolic representations are understood to be basic to human mental experience and information processing, especially as it is related to affect (Aragno, 1997). Symbol formation is regarded as a particularly crucial capacity for thinking in so-

phisticated ways and for appreciating the depth and range of subtle affective experience. This capacity is both the result of and a further stimulus to ego growth and development. Modern ego psychologists such as Sarnoff (1976) delineated an ego-based schema of the development of symbolic capacity. E. Marcus (1999, 2003) recognized that while Freud regarded thing presentations as present only in unconscious thought, they are, in fact, ubiquitously present in conscious thought. He further elaborated the concept of thing presentation by describing it as a type of symbolic representation in which affect is represented in a perceptual mode. Their presence is evident in the form of fantasy, dreams, art, and architecture, among others. Thing presentations are also central aspects of the mental representations characteristic of psychotic and near-psychotic psychopathology. Indeed, thing presentations are part of all human emotional experience that is symbolically represented.

In contrast, other psychoanalytic schools are considerably less focused on issues of mental representation and symbol formation. For example, C. Brenner's (2006) modern conflict theory eliminated all structural considerations other than the microstructure of compromise formation. Brenner rejected the notion that distinguishing compromise formations from one another (for example creative products from noncreative products) requires specific consideration, as the underlying emotional dynamics are the same. Similarly, self and object representations are not elaborated in modern conflict theory.

Self psychology, relational, interpersonal, and intersubjective theories tend to focus on the immediate, interactive, evoked experience, and there is, therefore, little need for concepts of representation or their structures. Such concepts are often regarded as mechanistic and are considered distractions from focus on the clinical moment. Instead, emphasis is placed on aspects of mental experience that are thought to be stored as implicit memories. In the view of theorists from these schools of thought, such experience cannot be symbolized but is experienced through processes described as "implicit relational knowing" and enactment.

In general psychology, particularly cognitive psychology, symbol is used most often to mean a signal. Representation is used to mean a mental modeling of reality to prepare for behavior adaptive to the physical environment. General psychology usage often omits the interpersonal, emotional, and social environment, which, however, is also of crucial importance for survival. Cognitive neuropsychology, specifically affective neuroscience, does address the study of affect, particularly the neural correlates of emotion. Because many emotional experiences are organized as representations, researchers in affective neuroscience have begun to study the representational process. An example of such work is Bucci's (1997) multiple code theory. Psychoanalytic understanding may be helpfully applied to this work.

The concept of symbol appears in other allied fields that study products of human symbolization, such as the philosophy of knowledge and the philosophy of mind (Langer, 1942; Cassirer, 1955; Werner and Kaplan, 1963), anthropology (Obeyeskere, 1990), and art (Kuhns, 1983; Waldheim, 1984). The application of psychoanalytic conceptualizations of symbolic representation to these intellectual fields may enrich them, particularly in their efforts to interpret symbolic representations. Interpretation in this context refers to the rules for understanding how to derive the latent emotional meaning from the manifest symbolic product.

Symptom/Symptom Formation/Symptomatic Act: see CHARACTER, DEFENSE, NEUROSIS, PARAPRAXIS, REPETITION COMPULSION

Syntaxic Mode: see INTERPERSONAL PSYCHOANALYSIS

T

Talking Cure is a colloquial synonym for psychoanalysis, first used by Breuer's famous patient Anna O. to describe the prepsychoanalytic, cathartic method of treatment. Breuer (Breuer and Freud, 1893/1895) noticed that when Anna O. was in hysterical states of "absence" (altered personality accompanied by confusion), she would often mutter a few words to herself. He would hypnotize her, repeat these words to her, and Anna O. would then report the trains of thought that had been occupying her mind during the "absences." This process seemed to restore her to near normal mental life. Anna O. aptly described this procedure as a "talking cure," and also referred to it jokingly as "chimney-sweeping." Although psychoanalysis itself is often popularly referred to as the "talking cure," neither the cathartic method nor hypnosis is a component of psychoanalysis.

Temperament: see MOOD, CONSTITUTIONAL FACTORS

Termination Phase is the final phase of an analytic treatment, during which time the work of the analysis invariably features the meaning of the anticipated loss of the analyst and the treatment; consequently, the work of termination has been compared to the work of mourning. While the experience of termination is influenced by the analysand's phase of life, fantasies about birth, death, pregnancy, and separation are common. The termination phase is often an intense and fruitful period of analysis, which may involve the reemergence of old symptoms; it represents the final reworking of conflicts and issues that have comprised the substance of the treatment. It is generally agreed that a complete analysis is a fantasy that may be held by both patient and analyst, and that feelings of disappointment and disillusionment that it has not been achieved may be present. In the "ideal" termination, the timing of the event is mutually agreed upon, with both the analysand and the analyst concluding that they have reached their goals. The following issues have been described as instrumental in decisions about readiness for termination: symptomatic improvement, structural change, assessment of the state of transference resolution, assessment of the countertransference, the analyst's

intuition, and a belief that termination can only be assessed on a trial-and-error basis (S. Firestein, 1974). A distinction has been made between termination that is mutually agreed upon by analyst and analysand, and the interruption of analysis. Interruptions are often unilaterally decided upon, by either analysand or analyst, but may be initiated by mutual agreement when the dyad agrees that nothing more can be gained by continuing the treatment.

Termination is a psychoanalytic concept that is primarily of contemporary significance, as analyses have become significantly longer and broader in their scope. It is also surrounded by some controversy. The criteria used to determine a patient's readiness to terminate are closely connected to the analyst's conceptualization of the treatment process and the analytic relationship. Furthermore, what goals are appropriately considered indications of readiness is also a matter of debate, reflected in the distinction that has been made between life goals and analytic goals.

Although Freud wrote of termination, it was not until the 1950s that a well-defined series of analytic phases (opening, mid, and termination phase) was described. Interestingly, the word *termination* is not listed in Strachey's general subject index of the *Standard Edition*. However, as early as April 16, 1900, Freud wrote to Fliess of the difficulties of ever terminating an analysis because of the unresolvable nature of transference (Masson, 1985b). Ironically, Freud's (1918a) most specific discussion of a termination phase involved the Wolf Man, a case that he considered stalemated. He imposed a forced termination as a "heroic measure" and described the major share of the analytic work as having taken place during the six-month termination phase of the four-year analysis. Freud (1937a), while never using the words *termination phase,* discussed the issue of termination in "Analysis Terminable and Interminable." As the title suggests, Freud viewed analysis as a lifelong process, as was his own self analysis. Freud described the limits of analysis imposed by constitutional factors and the influence of the death drive, and he also indicated that a successful treatment does not guarantee immunization from future need. He acknowledged that only active conflicts can be analyzed, and famously recommended that analysts should resume their own analyses at a frequency of every five years or so. Ferenczi's (1927) view was that analyses ended when they died from exhaustion, a graphic but not explicit view of what constitutes a proper time for termination or a defined structure for that period of analysis. Neither Ferenczi nor Freud described what ought to constitute a termination phase of an analysis.

With the publication of a symposium on termination in the *International Journal of Psychoanalysis* in 1950, discussions began on the criteria for termination, the characteristics of the termination phase, the standard technique of termination, and technical variations that might be employed (A. Reich, 1950). The concept of the termination phase was made explicit for the first time in E. Glover's (1955) *The Technique of Psychoanalysis*. He maintained that an individual was not successfully analyzed unless he had passed through a termination phase, and with that, the termination phase became the touchstone of a completed analysis.

Discussions then ensued that focused on the criteria for termination and on a theory of termination technique (H. Blum, 1989). Eventually the experience of termination also came to be correlated with analyzability and outcome (S. Weiss and Fleming, 1980). J. Novick (1982), in a review of termination, concluded that clinical assessment, the state of the transference, and the analyst's intuition play a role. Buxbaum (1950) focused on the state of the transference neurosis in relation to termination, and Dewald (1972) asserted that symptomatic change is reliable only when it is accompanied by shifts in the transference neurosis. This is a perspective that is viewed with considerable skepticism by many analysts, since many clinicians no longer believe that a transference neurosis is an inevitable occurrence within an analysis. Similarly, in the past, concepts such as the resolution of the infantile neurosis and the successful tracing and resolution of the childhood roots of conflict were criteria for considering termination (S. Firestein, 1974). Analysts whose ideas about therapeutic action stress other mechanisms challenge such views (Fonagy, 2003).

The work of the termination phase has been characterized by an increase in the tempo of the analytic work, regressive intensification of the transference, and an increased efficiency in the working alliance (J. Novick, 1982). The major tasks of the termination phase have been described by many authors as the working through and synthesizing of the insights gained (Ekstein, 1965), turning insight into effective and lasting action (Greenson, 1965b), and doing the work of mourning the loss of the analyst. Loewald (1962a) viewed the termination phase as a drawn-out leave-taking, with deprivation and autonomy juxtaposed.

For many decades, the recognition of the analytic relationship as an important feature of the therapeutic experience has been reflected in the view that the patient must endure the loss of the analyst, both as a transference object and as a real object (H. Blum, 1989). What weight is given to each component reflects the theoretical orientation of the analyst (Fonagy, 2003), but all would agree that the analytic relationship is a uniquely intimate and meaningful one for both the patient and the analyst. The analyst shares in the emotional experience of the termination process, and must also come to terms with loss; he must relinquish his attachment to his patient and to their work together and must also accept its limitations. For those patients with more significant psychopathology, whose need for the analyst as a supportive real object has been central throughout the analysis, termination presents additional challenges. In a follow-up study of patients interviewed many years after the termination of their analyses, Pfeffer (1993) described the transient but vivid recurrence of the transference neurosis accompanied by the reemergence of old symptoms. He concluded that there is a persisting mental representation of the analyst, created during the course of the analysis, as both an old and a new object.

Tertiary Process: see PRIMARY PROCESS, PSYCHOSIS, SYMBOLISM/SYMBOLIZATION/REPRESENTATION/ SYMBOLIC REPRESENTATION

Thanatos: see AGGRESSION, DEATH DRIVE

Theory of Mind: see MENTALIZATION, OBJECT CONSTANCY

Therapeutic Action is the means by which psychoanalytic treatment effects therapeutic gain. Each school of psychoanalysis explicates a theory of therapeutic action that is implicitly linked to a model of the mind and of pathogenesis. Theories of therapeutic action are explicitly linked to clinical theories of technique and to how therapeutic outcome is conceptualized. Contemporary theories of therapeutic action coalesce around the function of interpretation and the function of the analytic relationship, as well as whether and in what way the therapeutic relationship is to be interpreted. Any theory of therapeutic action must recognize the patient's contribution as an active participant who is consciously motivated for change. The relationship between theories of therapeutic action and the actual outcome of any psychoanalytic treatment remains speculative, as empirical studies are necessary to demonstrate the connection between any specific technique and its effect. Nonetheless, a wealth of salutary clinical experience among analysts of different theoretical persuasions strongly supports the argument that there are multiple modes of therapeutic action.

The history of psychoanalysis might well be described by the succession of theories of therapeutic action. While theoretical pluralism has been a feature of psychoanalysis from its inception, the extensive elaboration of multiple schools of psychoanalytic thinking has never been greater than in the present. The cross-fertilization of thinking that has resulted has, perhaps, been most apparent in the clinical situation. Analysts of different theoretical persuasions have utilized combined treatment strategies to effect therapeutic gain, independent of more-thorough reformulations of basic propositions. General trends in all psychoanalytic theories of therapeutic action have been toward greater emphasis on the significance of the analytic relationship, the value of the analyst's countertransference, and a focus on the here and now in facilitating change. Advances in cognitive neuroscience that describe how different kinds of experiences and memories are stored, as well as what leads to mind/brain plasticity, have also influenced theories of therapeutic action.

Although Freud did not explicitly discuss the issue of therapeutic action, the evolution of his theory entailed increasingly complex notions of how psychoanalysis works and under what conditions it fails. Breuer and Freud (1893/1895) formulated the earliest, preanalytic, model of therapeutic action—catharsis—in their treatment of hysterical patients. Using this method, hysterical symptoms are removed through the recovery of traumatic memories and the discharge of their linked affects. However, also notable is the doctor's active role through hypnosis or suggestion. Freud's first psychoanalytic model of mental organization, the topographic model, featured the lifting of repressions and making the unconscious conscious as agents of therapeutic action. Freud had replaced the memory of trauma, with the persistent effect of repressed, unacceptable childhood sexual wishes, as the instigator of neurosis. At that time he formulated that the analyst's role is to interpret the patient's resistance to anything that interferes with the flow of the treatment process, which Freud had come to recognize as motivated defense. A watershed in Freud's (1914b) theory occurred with his recognition of the complex relationship between transference and resistance and the role of transference as the strongest vehicle for cure. The significance of this

recognition forever changed the role of the analyst and the technique of psychoanalytic treatment, as the meaning of the patient's feelings about the analyst moved front and center. Freud had discovered the link between the patient's here-and-now experience in the analytic situation and his repressed early history of loving attachments. Therapeutic action resides in the patient's acquisition of insight associated with the lifting of repressions and the undoing of pathological fixations, facilitated by the analyst's interpretations, not suggestions. This latter point—that the analyst's role is to interpret and not to suggest—served for Freud and others as an important distinction between psychoanalysis and other forms of mental treatment. However, Freud (1912a) did also acknowledge use of the analytic relationship itself as a vehicle for change in his reference to the "unobjectionable" transference, by which he meant the nonsexual positive transference.

Freud's (1923a, 1926a) structural theory and second anxiety theory shifted the aim of treatment from making the unconscious conscious to a focus on the analysis of conflict. While therapeutic action was still thought to reside in the patient's acquisition of insight, this occurred through strengthening of ego capacities and modulation of the drives. Later in his theorizing, Freud (1937a) attributed the forces working against therapeutic gain to constitutional factors in the strength and rigidity of the ego's defenses and to the excessive mobility and adhesiveness of the drives.

With the further growth of ego psychology, represented by such psychoanalytic theorists as Fenichel, Hartmann, Kris, and Lowenstein, formulations about therapeutic action did not substantially change, however the goal of psychoanalysis was more explicitly formulated in terms of structural change. In a classical and much-quoted paper, J. Strachey (1934), influenced by Klein, located the site of maximal therapeutic action as the patient's superego, because it is that part of the patient's mind that is most subject to the influence of the analyst. Strachey described an interpretation as "mutative" when interpretation of the patient's hostile impulses toward the analyst enables the patient to achieve insight into the discrepancy between the archaic fantasy object that he has projected onto the analyst and the real object of the analyst. Strachey's formulation became used as an unintended rationale for the exclusive use of transference interpretation.

F. Alexander (F. Alexander and French, 1946; F. Alexander, 1950a) provoked considerable controversy among ego psychologists with his proposition that patients require a "corrective emotional experience" in which therapeutic benefit is attributed to the analyst's attitudinal and behavioral responses to the patient, rather than insight gained through interpretation. Some mainstream ego psychologists (Zetzel, 1956; Stone, 1961; Greenson and Wexler, 1969) introduced concepts of the "therapeutic alliance" and the "real relationship," which enlarged the view of therapeutic action to include the facilitation of nontransference aspects of the analytic relationship, without the analyst adopting artificial, specific attitudes and roles as suggested by Alexander. This broadened view of therapeutic action was given further impetus by increased focus on the preoedipal period, by both developmental theorists, such as Mahler (Mahler, Pine, and Bergman, 1975), and by psychoanalysts treating more severely disturbed patients, who located such pathology in the preoedipal period (Stone, 1961; Jacobson, 1964, 1971). Modifications in classical technique resulted from the understanding that strictly interpretive approaches are not therapeutic with more severely ill patients. In a more-profound reformulation of therapeutic action, Loewald (1960), coming from a Freudian background and tradition, emphasized the relationship between patient and analyst as a catalyst for change. He described the analyst as a "new object" for the patient, who becomes available for identification through the interpretation of transference distortions. Loewald likened the analytic relationship to the parent/child relationship, whereby the parent/analyst empathically facilitates the further integration and structuralization of the child's/patient's ego, self, and object relations. Furthermore, the analyst is able to hold something in mind about the patient's potential that the patient is not yet able to conceive.

Contemporary conflict theorists and modern ego psychologists espouse a spectrum of views about therapeutic action. Some adhere strictly to the view that emotionally compelling insight is gained through the interpretation of the transference which produces more adaptive compromise formations and structural change. However, this formulation is problematic because the relationship between insight and structural change has never been clearly delineated. Patients may gain one without the other, while both may be necessary for lasting therapeutic gain. Most contemporary conflict theorists and modern ego psychologists now recognize the role of the analytic relationship in facilitating therapeutic outcome, no longer viewing these issues from an either/or perspective; but the extent to which the relationship itself is viewed as serving a corrective function varies greatly. Similarly, some analysts have incorporated a contemporary emphasis on countertransference, issues of intersubjectivity, and co-construction, while others eschew such concepts (Abend, 2007).

Some object relations theorists (Winnicott, 1960b, 1969; Modell, 1976) attributed therapeutic action to the psychoanalytic situation itself, in which the analyst's constancy and reliability, his focus on the patient, his benign and nonretaliatory stance, and his capacity to understand the patient's affective states evoke the early maternal "holding environment." Modell noted that in the early stages of the analysis of narcissistic patients, who are responding to parental failures, insatiable, dependent demands are warded off with affective nonrelatedness and an illusion of self sufficiency. He maintained that the "holding environment" provided by the analyst, who neither interprets nor offers special support, provides safety, which facilitates the subsequent expression of those demands. This occurs through the patient's internalization of the analyst's function.

In the view of Kleinian theorists, first represented by Klein (1932), Heimann (1950), and Racker (1957), among others, the patient's insight derives from deep interpretation of currently active unconscious "phantasies," which represent the content of urges and feelings in relationship to objects and to parts of the self, and which are activated within the transference. From a Kleinian perspective, transference is both the background and foreground of experience in psychoanalytic work, creating a matrix of unconscious phantasy that the analyst must verbalize for the patient through interpretation, thereby reinstating the past in the patient's present experience. The goals of Kleinian treatment are that the patient will: reclaim split-off, projected parts of the self, leading to a greater sense of aliveness and integration; replace omnipotence with insight; and gain a more-integrated view of the object with whom he can then relate in greater depth. Kleinian analysts (Heimann, 1956; Money-Kyrle, 1956) introduced a fundamental revision of classical technique in the extensive use of countertransference as a primary source of data about the patient's unconscious phantasies, emphasizing the cycle of projective and introjective processes that constitute the parallel processes of transference and countertransference. Bion (1959) emphasized the analyst's "containing" function, a reparative process whereby the analyst takes in and modifies a part of the patient's mind that is experienced as intolerable. Hinshelwood (2007) argued that the Kleinian emphasis on the interpretation of primary destructive and self-destructive elements in the human psyche is required in a "to-and-fro" dynamic that slowly facilitates the integration of pathological ego splits organized around a "libidinal self" and a "destructive self."

Self psychologists view psychoanalysis from a developmental perspective, linking certain functions of the analyst to selfobject functions experienced as missing in caretakers and needed by the patient to facilitate the repair of pathological self states. The emphasis on the patient's need, rather than on unconscious unacceptable wishes, distinguishes self psychology from both conflict theory and object relations theory. This results in a view of treatment that legitimizes (selfobject) needs rather than interprets their unrealistic or distorted character. Kohut (1971) outlined a two-step interpretive process: understanding followed by explaining what has been understood through the analyst's efforts to listen from the patient's perspective. Central to therapeutic action is an examination of moments of disruption in the selfobject transference and an understanding by the patient and analyst of what is required for its repair. Later, Kohut (1984) considered the extent to which empathy, in addition to defining the field of psychoanalysis and serving as a mode of observation, has, in itself, a mutative and curative role in treatment. He concluded that empathy is neither a therapeutic technique nor an active agent of cure, but a method of gathering data. The communication and interpretation of this data to the patient, however, means that empathy is inevitably a requisite ingredient for psychological change and health. Furthermore, the analyst's empathic mode of observation diminishes the patient's need for defenses and expands the capacity for introspection, promoting the emergence of warded-off affects and memories. Self psychologists have integrated Kohut's formulations about optimal frustration with "optimal responsiveness" (Bacal, 1985) in their clinical practice. Others have argued for a reworking of the self psychological view of therapeutic action, conceptualizing faulty development not only in terms of the experience of the selfobject's interference with narcissistic strivings, but also in terms of the experience of the selfobject's mismanagement of affects and failure to contain them (D. Socarides and Stolorow, 1984; Newman, 2007). The analyst must recognize his additional function in managing intense negative affects that may otherwise retraumatize the patient in the clinical situation.

The emergence of interpersonal psychoanalysis in the 1950s and relational psychoanalysis in the 1980s represented a paradigm shift that moved the analytic dyad to the foreground of therapeutic action. Ferenczi (1933) focused on treatment as an interactive process, and the analyst's active role in it. He influenced Sullivan (1953a) in his formulation of an interpersonal theory of development and of treatment that

viewed the construction of the self through its relationship with others, and in the importance of social and cultural factors in human experience. For Sullivan, and for other interpersonal and relational analysts who followed, meaning is created within the interpersonal matrix in the here and now (Greenberg and Mitchell, 1983; Levenson, 1993; D. B. Stern, 1997; P. Bromberg, 2006). They posit that change does not occur as the result of the analyst's objective capacity to interpret what is unknown to the patient, but rather change occurs through co-created experience. The emphasis here is on interpsychic rather than on intrapsychic experience. Relational psychoanalysts describe these processes as intersubjectivity, the dynamic interaction between the patient's and the analyst's subjective experiences, and the capacity to understand, feel, participate in, and share the subjective experience of another person. Intersubjectivity describes the process by which meaning occurs and also describes its outcome, insofar as a deepened capacity for intersubjectivity is a desired outcome of treatment. Psychoanalytic exploration necessarily focuses on understanding the intersubjective field, including misunderstandings and processes of repair as well as "moments of meeting," as these unfold in the here and now of the psychoanalytic situation (Boston Change Process Study Group, 2002). This process has also been described as change in "implicit relational knowing," which can occur only through nonverbal modes of expression (Lyons-Ruth, 1999).

The technique of developmental help is based upon the assumption that therapeutic action takes place within the actual relationship between patient and analyst, rather than within the transference. The analyst's noninterpretive role as a "developmental object" (Tähkä, 1993; Hurry, 1998) or "new object" facilitates change through growth and consolidation of new organizations, rather than integrations obtained through insight. These concepts originated in A. Freud's notion of developmental disturbance in children, as well as the integration into analytic theory of developmental psychology, infant research, and attachment theory. The concept of the analyst as developmental or new object is similar to the analyst's function as auxiliary ego, but as a developmental object, the analyst works to promote the conditions for development to occur. The concept of new object or developmental object has been integrated into the clinical work of some ego psychologists, Kleinians, and relationalists with patients who have deficits or faulty developmental processes. The technical approach with adult patients suffering from developmental disturbances has been called psychodynamic developmental therapy (Fonagy and Target, 1996a) or developmentally based psychotherapy (Greenspan, 1997). The aim is for the patient, via the relationship with the analyst, to learn the ways his mind works. Methods have been formulated to promote interactions, to address primitive defenses and destructive behavior, and to develop capacities for self reflection and mentalization (Fonagy and Target, 1998), among others.

According to Gabbard and Westen (2003), the relationship versus interpretation argument has already waned, and we must now think about how to integrate multiple modes of therapeutic action that include the role of interpretation, the role of the analytic relationship, and various nonspecific strategies, all of which work synergistically. The emphasis on any specific mode of action is best thought of in terms of any patient's individual need at a specific time in his treatment. In their view, therapeutic action involves changing unconscious associative neural networks that represent problematic emotions, defenses, and interpersonal patterns, as well as conscious patterns of thought, affect, and motivation.

Westen and Gabbard (2002), Kernberg (2007), and others emphasized that empirical research is necessary to determine whether and when therapeutic strategies are effective. Psychoanalytic therapy research that is able to answer such questions combines the assessment of analytic outcomes with the close study of process within individual cases that may account for positive outcome. These are prospective studies that combine the use of instruments refined for assessing process in individual cases and group aggregated outcome studies (Wallerstein, 2005). Bucci (2005) reported that research that is able to identify vehicles for change is at an early stage. In a summary of the findings to date, she identified certain issues that have been suggested as critical for change, including the role of narratives of self in relation to others, especially when there are parallel patterns for the relationship with the therapist and with others; the accuracy of interpretations of those narratives; and the focus on painful affects associated with those narratives.

Therapeutic Alliance or **Working Alliance** is that aspect of the relationship between patient and analyst that depends upon the patient's capacity to sustain cooperative effort, independent of the emotional valence of the transference or the state of resistance. (The therapeutic alliance can be strong in the face of negative transference and weak in the face of positive transference.) The concept of the therapeutic alliance emerged with the growth of ego psychology, as it is based on recognition of the specific

ego capacities of the patient that are necessary for its maintenance. These include capacities that are considered relevant in the assessment of analyzability: basic trust; capacity for candor; capacity to establish, tolerate, and reflect on an intense transference experience; and ability to make beneficial use of the analyst's interpretive role. The ego functions that underlie such capacities include reality testing, affect and frustration tolerance, and self reflection. The therapeutic alliance has also been described as the core of the "real relationship." Others have argued that it is theoretically unsound to make a distinction between the transference and the therapeutic alliance. At the heart of this argument is the perspective that all thoughts, feelings, and attitudes have both conscious and unconscious motives. Some analysts, accepting that position, nonetheless view the concept of therapeutic alliance as a functionally useful one. It may be used to describe the patient's willingness to participate in the work of analysis at any particular point in the treatment, assuming his capacity to do so. Used in that way, therapeutic alliance is a dynamic concept, as it recognizes that therapeutic alliance is not a static structure during the course of the analysis.

The therapeutic and working alliance are important concepts in psychoanalysis because they attempt to parse questions about the contribution of transferential and extra-transferential issues to therapeutic process and gain. In fact, the issues associated with these terms are complex, as they refer to aspects of technique, as well as to considerations about patient capacities that are necessary for successful participation in an analytic treatment. The concept of therapeutic alliance is very rooted in ego psychology, however contemporary analysts of all schools are attentive in some way to the conditions of the analytic relationship that facilitate productive analytic work.

The term *therapeutic alliance* entered the psychoanalytic lexicon in 1956 in a paper by Zetzel (1956). Freud (1912a), however, established the basis for the concept in his paper "The Dynamics of Transference," where he discussed the role of the "unobjectionable" conscious component of the transference, which he described as the "vehicle of success" for the treatment. Freud contrasted this component with the part of the transference that is responsible for the resistance, that which includes both the negative transference and the repressed positive erotic transference. In "Analysis Terminable and Interminable," Freud (1937a) discussed the analyst's role in "allying" himself with the patient's ego in order "to subdue portions of his id." Sterba (1934) further developed this idea in describing the role of the patient's ego in the therapeutic process as a "therapeutic split." One portion of the patient's ego is involved in the regressive transference experience of analysis, and the other part is available for self observation. Sterba's focus on the split between instinctual motives and ego motives was similar to E. Bibring's (1937) concept of the analyst's alliance with that part of the patient's ego that has not been drawn into intrapsychic conflict.

The concept of the "widening scope" introduced in the 1950s (Stone, 1954, 1961) opened discussion to the treatment of patients with more-severe psychopathology and the technical modifications they require. As a result, attention became more focused on the analytic relationship and the necessary stance for the analyst to assume with such patients, particularly, what level of gratification is necessary and what level of frustration can be tolerated in order to promote a therapeutic outcome with patients who are described as having "preoedipal" or dyadic conflicts. Along these lines, Zetzel's (1956, 1958) concept of the therapeutic alliance refers to the patient's capacity to form a trusting object relationship with the analyst. She theorized that this capacity is the direct expression of the early maternal/child dyadic object relationship. Zetzel differentiated this early source of the therapeutic alliance from the patient's transference neurosis, which is based on later childhood experience and fantasy.

Greenson (1965a), who used the term *working alliance,* approached the issue from a different vantage point. In response to what he saw as excessively rigid and withholding analytic technique on the part of many analysts, Greenson argued that such technique serves to obstruct the patient's "non-neurotic, rational rapport" with the analyst, which promotes the patient's purposeful work in the analysis. Greenson also observed patients who appear to be doing analytic work by talking freely and manifesting transference feelings, but their analyses are stalemated. He attributed this to inauthentic participation in analysis, which is masked by pro forma compliance. When the transference resistance is recognized, it is successfully analyzed and a productive "working alliance" is established. Because Greenson was writing during a period in which analysts were focused primarily on patients' verbal associations, Greenson's observations were, in fact, a valuable contribution to the understanding of subtly enacted transference resistances.

Greenson and Wexler (1969) subsequently wrote about the "real relationship" between patient and analyst in psychoanalysis. Building on the concept of the "working alliance," Greenson and Wexler posited that an atmosphere in which both patient and analyst are authentically present facilitates an analytic technique that, nonetheless, focuses on the interpretation of transference. Anticipating aspects of relational psychoanalysis, Greenson and Wexler emphasized that patients regularly observe a great deal about their analyst's personality and that these observations can become part of the treatment in both transferential and nontransferential contexts. This "real" aspect of the patient's participation might lead to the analyst's self disclosure, an aspect of the analyst's noninterpretive, real relationship to the patient. For Greenson and Wexler, the analyst's spontaneity and personal engagement are not themselves curative but facilitate the interpretive analytic work.

Greenson's ideas were controversial, and mainstream ego psychology analysts (C. Brenner, 1979; M. Stein, 1981) were critical of his conceptualization of the nontransferential component of the patient's experience. They noted that there are transferential contributions to the patient's "rational rapport," which Greenson failed to address. They argued that no distinction can be made between transference and any other aspect of the analytic relationship. This view is similar to that of Kleinians, who interpret all aspects of the "total" analytic situation as transference. Although relational analysts do not use the term *therapeutic alliance,* they do address how the analyst's ability to negotiate ambiguities with the patient and establish an atmosphere of safety contributes to productive analytic work.

The concept of the therapeutic/working alliance has been one of the most intensely investigated concepts in psychotherapy process and outcome research. At least six scales have been developed that attempt to operationalize the concept, almost all based in part on its psychoanalytic conceptualization. The strength of the therapeutic alliance as a predictor for outcome across all kinds of psychotherapy (and also in pharmacotherapy) has been one of the most robust findings in psychotherapy research (Fenton et al., 2001).

Thing Presentation/Word Presentation: see SYMBOLISM/SYMBOLIZATION/REPRESENTATION/SYMBOLIC REPRESENTATION

Third: see LACAN (for Analytic Third: see INTERSUBJECTIVITY)

Topographic Theory is Freud's first theory of mental organization. It describes the mind as divided into three agencies or systems—the unconscious, preconscious, and conscious—defined by their relationships to consciousness. These systems are further characterized by: forms of mental functioning (primary versus secondary process), types of energy (free versus bound), and the regulatory principles according to which they operate (pleasure principle versus reality principle). For many analysts, the topographic model has been supplemented and largely superseded by a second topography, the tripartite model (id, ego, superego) of Freud's (1923a) structural theory.

The concept of the dynamic unconscious has remained the bedrock of most subsequent psychoanalytic thought. Freud's shift from the topographic to the structural model of mental organization reflected a critical shift in the aim of psychoanalysis; the goal of making the unconscious conscious was replaced by the goal of analyzing psychic conflict and bringing the id under the mastery of the ego. Nonetheless, the richness of Freud's topographic model is reflected in his revolutionary insights into the nature of dreams, primary process mentation, the motivating power of wish, and the dynamic properties of unconscious conflict.

Freud (1900) first introduced the topographic model in chapter 7 of "The Interpretation of Dreams." However, Freud (1915d) formally designated it as reflecting a **topographic point of view** fifteen years later in "The Unconscious." At that time Freud included the topographic point of view as one of three viewpoints (in addition to the dynamic and the economic points of view) constituting a metapsychological approach to understanding psychic phenomena. The topographic model, with its root *topo* derived from the Greek word for "place," reflected Freud's conception of the mind as consisting of "agencies" or "systems" that each occupy a particular "psychical locality" and function in a particular spatial relation to each other. One aspect of the model describes the mind as a kind of reflex arc with the capacity to transform perceptions into increasingly complex thoughts, and ultimately, motoric responses. In addition, Freud designated three systems that are defined by their relationship to consciousness, "located" along a metaphorical axis from the depth to the surface of the mind. Freud's topographic theory reflected his intellectual grounding in the fields of neurophysiology and anatomy; however, he repeatedly stressed that the elements of the model should not be correlated with particular areas of the physical brain.

The system unconscious (Ucs.) contains derivatives of the drives in the form of wishes and memories represented in a primary process mode, which operates according to the pleasure principle without regard for logic, degrees of certitude, negation or contradiction, or time. Primary process thoughts are not expressed in words (except in their most concrete form) but in imagery using symbolization, displacement, and condensation. It was largely through his study of dreams that Freud formulated a process mode of thinking. The system unconscious is separated from an adjacent area, the system preconscious (Pcs.) by dynamic forces variously referred to as the "critical agency," the "censorship," or the "forces of repression," which function to keep its unacceptable contents out of conscious awareness. The preconscious system contains thoughts and memories that are descriptively rather than dynamically unconscious, because they can become part of the system conscious (Cs.) without obstacle, as soon as attention is focused on them. The preconscious and conscious systems are closely related and operate according to the reality principle with the more organized, linear, and verbal form of thinking referred to as the secondary process.

Freud's topographic model would ultimately prove problematic because the division of the mind into conscious and unconscious regions did not adequately account for clinical observations regarding intrapsychic conflict. In particular, Freud found that not just instinctual wishes but defensive operations, moral demands, and guilt were themselves often unconscious. This observation led him to develop, between 1920 and 1926, his subsequent structural model of the mind, which ultimately replaced the topographic model as the dominant theory of mental life for most psychoanalysts in the ensuing decades (Gill, 1963; Arlow and C. Brenner, 1964). However, J. Sandler et al. (1997) and others have argued that many of the concepts put forth in the topographic model have retained a central place in psychoanalytic discourse, and that Freud's two theories offer complementary options for understanding various types of clinical situations and technical approaches.

Totemism: see MAGICAL THINKING, OMNIPOTENCE, PRIMAL HORDE, SPLITTING

Transference is the patient's conscious and unconscious experience of the analyst in the psychoanalytic situation as it is shaped by the patient's internalized early life experiences. Transference can be conceptualized both as the intrinsic, perceptual, and affective organizing function of internalized self and object representations, and the active wish to revivify or actualize intrapsychic, multidetermined object relations fantasies. While the experience of transference is a universal tendency, many analysts believe that the specific attributes of the analytic setting, including the asymmetries of the patient/analyst interaction, the patient's recumbent position, and the patient's need for help facilitate the activation of more **regressive transferences**, that is, transferences that express childhood feelings about early parental figures. A patient's transference usually includes the reactivation of more than one object relationship and more than one version of any object relationship. Transference is manifested not only in the patient's associations and subjective experience, but also in his unconscious attempts to enact conflictual, wished-for interactions with the analyst (J. Sandler, 1976a). The patient's conscious experience of the reactivation of internalized past relationships is that his feelings and thoughts are about the present-day relationship. Because transference includes intense and conflictual fantasies and memories associated with threatening and painful affects, patients unconsciously resist their elucidation. While some aspects of the patient's transference feelings may be accessible to consciousness and expressed in the patient/analyst interaction, these transference feelings are also understood to be defending against other transference feelings. Additionally, transference feelings may be defensively displaced onto people other than the analyst, or the awareness of transference feelings may be completely repressed and their presence inferred only by unconsciously determined, disguised allusions to them. Lastly, when patients experience conscious transference feelings about the analyst, they may resist the awareness that aspects of these feelings are determined by their own inner lives (Gill, 1982). Because of the interactive aspect of transference noted above, the analyst also plays some role in the expression or resistance to the awareness of a patient's transference. The patient may unconsciously recruit aspects of the analyst's personality so as to defensively emphasize one set of feelings, and thereby ward off more conflictual feelings. Also, the analyst's resistance to the awareness of his own countertransferences may heighten the patient's resistance to the awareness of feelings that might, in response to the analyst's stance, make certain feelings even less acceptable or even more threatening.

The goal of transference interpretation is the patient's increased understanding and acceptance of less defensively disguised versions of all the intrapsychic contributions to his transferences. The ability of transference interpretation to provide insight into the patient's persistent intrapsychic activation of early relationships is a core psychoanalytic discovery and a key feature of psychoanalytic treatment. The therapeutic benefit of the analysis of transference depends on the patient's ability to engage emotionally in the analytic experience and to understand that this engagement is largely shaped by his own psychic reality. Paradoxically, the therapeutic benefit also depends on the patient's ability to experience the analyst as a "new object," someone with whom old concerns may be addressed in a novel way.

Transference is a concept of central importance in psychoanalysis because it demonstrates vividly that the past lives within the present and exerts a powerful force upon it. While transference is a universal feature of mental life, its role within the analytic situation provides a unique experience for the patient, one that provides the greatest leverage for therapeutic gain. Historically, interpretation of the transference has distinguished psychoanalysis from all other treatments. While contemporary psychoanalytic schools differ in their approach to transference, all must account in some way for the intrapsychic importance that the analytic relationship holds for every patient.

Three fundamental controversies surround the concept of transference within contemporary psychoanalytic discourse. These include how transference is conceptualized, how the analyst's own subjectivity influences the patient's transferences, and how the transference is interpreted. The first controversy—how the transference is conceptualized—raises the following questions: 1) Is transference an inevitable aspect of all human relations, thrown into high relief by the analytic setting and analytic technique? 2) Is transference the manifestation of unconscious peremptory wishes and the defenses against them, or does it express the patient's need to repeat, and thereby master, traumatic aspects of his past? 3) Is transference the patient's attempt to heal and to continue his interrupted development? Is transference, therefore, a wish for a new experience in the context of the repetition of an old one (Loewald, 1960)? 4) Do transference fantasies exist fully formed in the patient's mind, or are they tendencies that find specific expression in interaction with a specific analyst (D. B. Stern, 1997) or perhaps even in plausible experiences of the analyst's behavior? 5) Are all aspects of the patient's experience the result of transference? Are aspects of the patient's experience better described as the expression of character defenses, which are not necessarily aspects of early relationship experience (J. Sandler, 1969)? 6) Does an underlying "primordial" (Stone, 1967) or "basic" (Greenacre, 1954) transference, the evocation of early mother/child interactions, appear in the analysis before the reactivation of developmentally later, discrete transferences? 7) Alternatively, does the patient form a "therapeutic alliance" (E. Bibring, 1937), that is, an identification with the analyzing function of the analyst? 8) Does the patient enter a "working relationship" (Greenson, 1965a) with the analyst, a mature wish to work with the analyst free of transference influences? These various characterizations of transference are not mutually contradictory, and analysts may include more than one conceptualization of transference in their clinical work.

The second controversy—how the analyst's own subjectivity influences the patient's transferences or the expression of those transferences—raises the following questions: 1) Is the analyst mainly the passive recipient of the patient's attitudes as distorted by the patient's inner life, or do the particularities of the analyst's personality, his countertransferences, and his theory facilitate the expression of one, rather than another, aspect of the patient's transference? 2) Do transference fantasies exist fully formed in the patient's mind, or are they tendencies that only find specific expression in a unique interaction with a specific analyst? 3) While the patient has specific transference fantasies, does the analyst's subjectivity result in a co-created transference experience that requires exploration of both of their contributions? 4) While the patient's transference fantasies have intrapsychic origins, are they best understood in their enactment within the dyad or in the analyst's subjective experience via projective identification?

The third controversy—how the transference is interpreted—raises the following questions: 1) Should the manifestations of transference be interpreted early in the treatment (Gill, 1982), or do such early interpretations inhibit the full expression of the transference? 2) Should transference be interpreted only when it becomes a resistance? 3) Should transference interpretations focus on the here-and-now expression of transference, or should they be genetic interpretations that link the patient's present experience with the past? 4) Should the interpretation of transference begin with the analyst's inquiries about what the patient might be responding to about himself? 5) Is the analyst in a position to know which aspects of the patient's transference feelings have intrapsychic origins and which are responses to the actual here-and-now analyst/patient interaction? 6) In addition to transference interpretations that address symbolized and repressed thoughts and affects, are there mutative interactions in analysis, "moments of meeting," that result in beneficial shifts in the patient's procedural "implicit relational knowing" (D. N. Stern et al., 1998)?

Freud wrote few papers on psychoanalytic technique and, despite the central role of transference in the theory of technique, he did not significantly revise his conceptualization of transference with other changes in theory. Freud (Breuer and Freud, 1893)

first used the word *transference* in 1893, describing it as a "false connection." Between 1893 and 1917, Freud conceptualized transference as the expression of the displacement of libido from one object (representation) to another. In 1900, in "The Interpretation of Dreams," that point was elaborated in Freud's (1900) description of transference as a principle of unconscious mental life. Repressed unconscious impulses seek points of attachment to nonforbidden preconscious thoughts, just as libido/forbidden fantasies seek gratification through displacement onto the person of the analyst. In 1905, Freud (1905a) described transferences as "new editions" of fantasies made conscious during analysis, ones that could become obstacles to treatment. In his "Papers on Technique," Freud (1914b) described both the resisting and facilitating functions of transference. **Positive transference**, or **erotic transference** (the expression of sexual wishes for the analyst), and **negative transference** (the expression of hostile or critical feelings) function as resistances because they are uncomfortable to talk about and appear tendentiously to stop the patient's free associations (Freud, 1912a). Freud contrasted erotic, positive transference with nonsexual positive feelings for the analyst, which the patient feels free to express; this positive **unobjectionable transference** does not function as a resistance. In fact, because this unobjectionable transference includes a positive regard for an authority figure, Freud viewed it as a component of "suggestion"—the therapeutic benefit of the analyst's influence. Because of this influence, the patient is more likely to accept the analyst's explanation that the patient's erotic and negative feelings about the analyst are displaced from important persons in the patient's early life. The nonthreatening positive regard of the unobjectionable transference also allies the patient with the analyst and supports the patient's motivation to remain in the analysis in the face of shame and frustration attached to his transference longings. Other analysts later elaborated these ideas as the concept of the therapeutic alliance. In 1914, Freud (1914c) linked transference to the compulsion to repeat rather than remember the past and clarified that transference is both a resistance to and a chief instrument of change in psychoanalysis. Transference serves resistance when a patient is intent on enacting (repeating) it with the analyst; it is the instrument of change when the patient gains insight into that repetition, thereby understanding (remembering) the historical origins of his conflicts. In 1914, Freud also explained that the repetition of transferences to past objects coalesce into a **transference neurosis**, whereby all of the libidinal attachments to past relationships are displaced into the analysis, and consequently the relationship to the analyst subsumes all the conflicts that had originally resulted in the patient's symptoms. The attachment to the analyst, Freud wrote, is ultimately "dissolved" through the interpretation of transference.

Freud's concept of transference was limited to the transference (or displacement) of wishes. A. Freud (1936) observed that not only wishes but also the original defenses against them are relived in the transference. These **transferences of defense** are more difficult to interpret because they have become integrated into the patient's character style, are consciously rationalized, and the patient does not experience them as motivated. A. Freud, following W. Reich (1933/1945) referred to the interpretation of the transference of defense as "character analysis." Ego psychological analysts after A. Freud have viewed transference as a compromise formation, the defensively distorted expression of past wishes, defenses, guilt, and self-esteem needs.

Several of Freud's views on transference have been modified or supplemented by later analysts. In general, contemporary analysts do not believe that a patient always needs to experience a transference neurosis as part of his treatment. Contemporary analysts also specifically oppose the therapeutic use of influence; they are alert to a patient's transference wish to be influenced and analyze its meaning.

Some additional varieties of transference have been named. **Erotized transference** refers to a patient's intense wish that the analyst respond to his erotic longings; the patient does not treat these wishes as complex expressions of his inner life but rather as urgent demands regarding current reality (H. Blum, 1973). **Transference psychosis** refers to a patient's experience of delusional ideas limited to the transference (Kernberg, 1967).

In the years following Freud, disparate views of transference have evolved. In the 1950s and 1960s, partially in response to the treatment of more-impaired patients, and in response to the unnecessarily depriving analytic technique practiced at that time, several analysts theorized that there were beneficial, nontransferential aspects of the relationship between analyst and patient. These were conceptualized as either the "real relationship" between analyst and patient (Greenson and Wexler, 1969) or expressions of a basic maternal transference to a healing figure (Greenacre, 1954); this aspect of the analytic relationship was not interpreted but rather viewed as necessary background for the analysis. Later analysts (Bird, 1972; C. Brenner, 1979; M. Stein, 1981) argued that transference pervades all aspects of the analytic relationship, including what appears to be the patient's basic sense of mutuality and cooperation in the analytic process. Loewald (1960) presented an important exception to this view. He posited that the patient's willingness to experience an intense and regressive transference is based on his trust in the analyst as a potential new object. Loewald also emphasized that the patient's growing ability to integrate conscious and repressed aspects of himself occurs in the context of a relationship with the analyst who can see "something more" in the patient than the patient is able to see himself.

Psychoanalysts conceptualize transference within their own theoretical tradition. Kleinian analysts view transference as the patient's constantly shifting feelings about the here-and-now relationship to the analyst; these feelings are expressed in everything the patient says and especially in nonverbal enactments that recruit the analyst through projective identification. The analyst learns about the patient's anxieties and his defenses against them by both being attuned to his own subjective experience and being attentive to how the patient listens to and uses the analyst's words. Genetic transference interpretations are offered only late in the analysis, after much is understood about the present (B. Joseph, 1985).

Self psychologists focus on transferences organized by the patient's needs for a selfobject, rather than by wishes and fears related to internalized object relationships. A selfobject is another person who is experienced as part of the self and who serves essential functions for the self. When the needs for selfobject functions are not met in childhood, an individual either seeks for their fulfillment with others or defends against the feelings of deficit and longing. **Selfobject transferences** include mirroring, twinship, and idealizing. Self psychologists interpret the defense against the emergence of these transferences, and when they have been mobilized, the analyst is empathic to the selfobject longings they express (Kohut, 1971, 1977).

Relational analysts describe the psychoanalytic situation as a two-person experience in which the patient's intrapsychic transferences and the analyst's subjectivity both contribute to the patient/analyst interaction. Relational analysts may interpret expressions of the patient's transferences but are sensitive to the potential for their own participation in the co-creation of that transference. Relational analysts also assume that aspects of their own intrapsychic lives are apparent to the patient and that the patient's transference is created partially in response to the patient's observation and knowledge of the analyst (S. Mitchell, 1997; I. Hoffman, 1994).

Contemporary analysts working from all theoretical perspectives are sensitive to the manner in which transference is expressed in the interaction between patient and analyst. Therefore, analysts do not only listen for the patient's verbal associations to the transference but are also alert to how transference fantasies are being enacted in the analytic setting. Consequently, analysts view their own subjective experience as an important source of information about enacted transferences.

Transmuting Internalization: see INTERNALIZATION, SELF PSYCHOLOGY, SELFOBJECT, THERAPEUTIC ACTION

Transsexualism is a gender identity of adulthood in which a person's subjective sense of gender differs from the gender assigned at birth and is characterized by the wish for sex reassignment. Such individuals are usually highly motivated to pursue biological interventions, such as hormonal treatment and plastic and sex-reassignment surgeries. While transsexuals do not deny their gender anatomy, they experience it as alien. Although transsexualism occurs in men and women, it is significantly more frequent in men. Transsexualism can be distinguished from transgenderism, which describes a wide range of gender variance and expression.

Transsexualism is an important concept in psychoanalysis, as it demonstrates the limits of contemporary knowledge about the variations of gender identity. While it is generally agreed that gender identity is the complex outcome of biological, psychodynamic, and social components, it is not known for any particular individual how to parse those various contributants. Psychoanalysts have limited ability to explore such conditions, as their access is restricted to a self-selected subset of a larger population. Whether transsexualism is a pathological condition remains controversial.

Hirschfeld (1923) first used the term *psychic transsexualism* in a German text, "*The Intersexual Constitution.*" Cauldwell (1949/2006) is credited with introducing the term in the United States with a single case study of a female who grew up thinking of herself as a boy and sought surgical intervention to become a male. Endocrinologist H. Benjamin (1966) published the first comprehensive text describing transsexualism, which became the dominant treatment approach to sex reassignment.

There are various theories that account for the occurrence of transsexualism, including the biological/imprint hypothesis, the nonconflictual identity hypothesis, and the conflict/defense hypothesis (Meyer, 1982). The biological/imprint hypothesis, based on animal models, advocated by Money, views transsexualism as a biologically based condition associated with a nonconflictual identity (Meyer, 1982). Stoller's studies of gender abnormalities were among the earliest psychoanalytic contributions to the study of transsexualism (Stoller 1966, 1968a, 1968b, 1973). Stoller considered transsexualism to be a disorder of gender identity, due to a very specific set of early infantile experiences with the parents. In his formulation, a nonconflictual female identity is formed in the male child such that there is no male identification and therefore no oedipal issues or attendant castration anxiety. He described the mother of the transsexual as bisexual, unconsciously wishing to prevent separation, and encouraging a feminine identification in her son. The father of the transsexual is either absent or does nothing to discourage the boy's femininity. Stoller distinguished transsexualism from effeminate homosexuality and sexual perversions in which conflict is present. Ovesey and Person (1973, 1976) considered transsexualism to be at the extreme end of a continuum of gender-identity disorders, followed by transvestism and effeminate homosexuality. They proposed that these disorders are the result of unresolved separation anxiety during the separation-individuation phase of infantile development. They differentiated primary transsexualism, in which an individual's transsexuality persists throughout his development, from secondary transsexualism, in which an effeminate homosexual or transvestite develops transsexual wishes only during periods of heightened stress. Meyer made a rare effort to offer a symmetrical explanation for the development of male and female transsexualism, based on his clinical experience with more than five hundred transsexual patients. Meyer emphasized early developmental trauma affecting body ego and sense of self, caused by the mother's fantasies of nonrecognition of the difference between the sexes, and her use of the child as a narcissistic extension. The healthier outcome of such mothering may be perversion, indicating that symbolic capacity remains intact. However, when symbolic capacities are impaired, the outcome is transsexualism, with its associated concreteness of representation and near-psychotic organization.

Contemporary contributions to the psychoanalytic understanding of transsexualism, though limited, attempt to broaden the appreciation of gender variance across cultures. Although most contributions continue to define transsexualism as a pathological condition best treated psychoanalytically (Ambrosio, 2009), there are exceptions where it is seen as a variance in gender expression and where sex-reassignment surgery and psychotherapy are seen as beneficial (Pfäfflin, 2009). Psychoanalytic feminist and gender theorists (Butler, 1990, 1993, 2004; Goldner, 1991; Harris, 1991, 2005a; Chodorow, 1994b, 1995), as well as queer theorists (G. Grossman, 2002), challenge a dichotomous model of gender categorization and caution against forming etiological explanations of transsexuality based on patient populations. More recent contributions argue for a psychoanalytic theory of gender that recognizes the actual degree and frequency of variance in human gender experience and expression (Corbett, 1996, 2009b; Ehrensaft, 2007).

Transvestism is the use of cross-dressing, or wearing the clothes of the opposite sex, as a requirement for sexual arousal and gratification. A transvestite's gender identity is concordant with his or her biological sex. Occurring more frequently in males than in females, male transvestism is also often associated with heterosexual object preference. Some authors emphasize conflicts at the oedipal level underlying transvestic behavior, particularly castration anxiety; others emphasize conflicts at the preoedipal level, particularly separation issues. In the analysis of male transvestites, the cross-dressing has been understood to serve multiple functions: expressing a feminine identification, as a punishment for incestuous oedipal wishes, and expressing the fantasy of the phallic woman, among others. The transvestite is distinguished from the transsexual or cross-dresser. A transsexual is an individual whose gender identity differs from his or her assigned biological sex. A cross-dresser is an individual who wears the clothing of the opposite sex for reasons other than sexual arousal or performance.

Transvestism is an illustration of the more-general concept of perversion. Freud's observations about the similarity between perversion, normal infantile sexuality, neurosis, and normal adult foreplay led to his radical reconceptualization of psychosexuality as a universal motivational force, present at birth as a polymorphously perverse disposition. Transvestism is also linked to the concept of fetishism, the study of which provided Freud (1927b) with important insights into the role of ego splitting in its defensive function.

Hirschfeld (1910/1991) coined the term *transvestite* to refer to individuals who voluntarily and habitually dressed in the clothing of the opposite sex. Through his case studies, Hirschfeld found that many, but not all, transvestites experienced sexual arousal from cross-dressing. Adopting Hirschfeld's term, Fenichel (1930), in the first comprehensive psychoanalytic exploration of transvestism published in English, classified it as a sexual perversion, comparable to fetishism in its underlying dynamics, with the distinction that the transvestite wears his fetishistic object, that is, the clothing of the opposite sex. In the presence of severe castration anxiety, the transvestite both imagines himself as a woman with a penis hidden under feminine garments and uses female clothing as a representation of the woman's penis. Together these constructions serve to maintain the unconscious fantasy that a woman has a penis, thus alleviating his castration anxiety.

Stoller (1964, 1965, 1966, 1968a, 1968b, 1973, 1979a, 1979b) devoted significant attention to transvestism and transsexuality in his studies of gender development. Like Fenichel, Stoller categorized transvestism in men as a fetishistic perversion. He described the transvestite's efforts to maintain a split identity in which he is both a potent heterosexual man and a woman with a phallus. Based on case examples and reconstructions of the early histories of adult transvestites, Stoller identified several etiological factors in childhood that contribute to the development of transvestism: the mother's unconscious need to feminize her son, her use of him as a transitional object, and her own gender-identity confusion; the father's collusion with mother in her feminization of their son and/or his absence. Stoller also described the life history of the transvestite in which the symptom becomes progressively more elaborated, from a circumscribed private fetishistic act into the need for public passing as a woman.

Ovesey and Person (Ovesey and Person, 1976; Person and Ovesey, 1978) viewed male transvestism in the context of a more-contemporary view of perversion in which the focus is on pathology of the ego, self, and object relations, rather than on castration anxiety alone. They regarded the etiology of transvestism as unknown, much like other sexual and gender pathology in which there are multiple determinants, including conflict, learning, cognitive development, and biology, as well as underlying psychodynamics. They also viewed transvestism on a developmental gradient between transsexualism at the most-severe end and effeminate homosexuality at the other. Despite their disavowal of etiology, they described a developmental history in which a failure in separation-individuation resulting in separation anxiety combines with intense aggressively infiltrated oedipal conflict with father and attendant castration anxiety. They described transvestites as men who are not effeminate in boyhood and in fact value their masculine assertiveness.

Trauma is the psychological disruption that occurs in response to a sudden overwhelming stimulus, either from without or from within, that exceeds capacities for active assimilation and has severe and pervasive negative impact on psychological function. The subjective mental state associated with trauma is one of helplessness, ranging from total apathy and withdrawal, to emotional storm accompanied by disorganized behavior bordering on panic. Many aspects of personality functioning may be affected, including the sense of self, the quality of object relations, the capacity for symbolization and fantasy, affect tolerance, reality testing, and secondary process thinking. The conditions under which trauma occurs are multiply determined by the nature of a real event, its psychological meaning to the individual, underlying vulnerability due to developmental factors and/or preexisting psychopathology, and the effect of prior trauma. The mental mechanism of trauma has been postulated as a breach in the stimulus barrier or protective shield of the ego, which is overwhelmed and loses its mediating capacity. In a broadening of its meaning, **shock trauma**, the experience of trauma after a single experience, has been distinguished from **stress trauma** or **strain trauma**, in which the experience of trauma emerges after a period of protracted lower-level traumatic experience resulting in psychological strain over time (Kris, 1956b), and from **cumulative trauma**, which results from the mother's failure to act as an external protective shield or stimulus barrier in relation to traumatizing experiences over the developmental life of the child (Khan, 1963).

The concept of trauma has had an important place in psychoanalytic theorizing from its beginning. Freud's early theories of neurosis emphasized the role of trauma in its etiology; in his seduction hypothesis, he attributed psychopathology to the impact of traumatic childhood sexual experience. Freud ultimately rejected this theory following his discovery that neurosis could result from the effects of unacceptable wishes in the form of unconscious sexual fantasies, without exposure to actual trauma. It was this recognition of the significance of psychic reality that initiated Freud's formulation of a truly psychoanalytic model of the mind, a model that asserts that psychopathology derives from a complex interplay between internal and external sources, or what Freud (1916/1917) referred to as the "complemental series." Freudian psychoanalysis has been misunderstood and at times criticized for diminishing or denying the impact of external reality, including trauma (Masson, 1985a), because it is a theory in which real experience is always considered along with its conscious and unconscious meaning to the individual. The extent to which real experience or intrapsychic experience is privileged as the primary

organizer and motivator of psychological structure and psychopathology differs greatly among psychoanalytic theories and has been the source of considerable controversy. For example, Kleinian theorists place major emphasis on the role of unconscious "phantasy" and the drives, while interpersonalists and self psychologists emphasize the traumatic impact of inadequate parenting. In fact, the evolution of psychoanalytic theorizing has followed a general trend toward greater emphasis on the impact of real experience, both during development and within the clinical situation.

Derived from a Greek word meaning "wound," *trauma* is a medical term referring to a bodily injury and its effects. Freud's earliest views on trauma were shaped by his exposure to the medical culture of late-nineteenth-century Europe, which was consumed by controversy over the origins of **traumatic hysteria**. Freud was influenced by the work of the French neurologist Charcot (and others), who had advanced a theory of hysteria, attributing it to the effects of trauma (which could include the traumatic effect of intense emotional states), in a mind made vulnerable by degenerative heredity, resulting in a state of dissociated ideas and somatic symptoms. Freud too explored the relationships among trauma, dissociation, and unconscious ideas. He defined **psychical trauma** as an intense "quota of affect" that exceeds the subject's capacities for discharge (Freud, 1888/1893). Freud (Breuer and Freud, 1893/1895) viewed "reminiscences" of traumas as the cause of psychical conflict that motivates defense, or the sequestering of ideas from ordinary consciousness. By 1896, Freud (1896c, 1898b) had arrived at his famous "seduction hypothesis," which explained hysterical symptoms as the sequelae of traumatic sexual seductions during childhood. Freud came to view traumatic seduction in two stages, the initial event occurring during childhood, in which the child experiences a sexual seduction by an adult, but without feeling sexually aroused. An experience in adolescence reevokes a memory of the original event, resulting in a state of overwhelming excitation of traumatic dimension. The childhood event becomes traumatic only through the process of deferred action (or *Nachträglichkeit*).

From about 1897 on, Freud (1905c) gradually abandoned the seduction hypothesis in favor of a revolutionary theory of internally generated overstimulation, in which unconscious fantasy, and eventually drive, became the primary motivator of conflict and defense. While the role of trauma became diminished in his views of neurosogenesis, it was never eliminated and appears as a topic of interest throughout his writings. Indeed, Freud's (1919a) interest in the traumatic etiology of neurosis gained renewed attention because of the high incidence of war neuroses and **traumatic neuroses** occasioned by the outbreak of World War I. However, he noted the similarity between the transference neuroses of peace and the traumatic war neuroses, citing the common factor of the ego's fear of being damaged. In the former case it is by the libido, and in the latter case by a danger that threatens from outside. Freud cited further similarities in the role of predisposition as well as the role of attempts at mastery of the trauma. In "Beyond the Pleasure Principle," Freud (1920a) further developed his notion of the stimulus barrier, a protective shield that serves to bind stimuli and to keep excitation at an optimal level. Freud described the strength of the stimulus barrier both in terms of constitutional factors and of its state of preparedness. Under conditions of trauma, the stimulus barrier is breached and the integrity of the individual is overwhelmed. The pleasure principle is no longer operative, and regression occurs as the individual attempts unsuccessfully to master the trauma. **Traumatic dreams** and other expressions of what Freud called the "repetition compulsion," represent this effort to master trauma.

In 1926, Freud (1926a) revised his theory of anxiety, proposing that the ego generates signal anxiety to protect it from being overwhelmed, thus avoiding the experience of trauma. In effect, signal anxiety serves as a protective mechanism against internally generated stimuli of traumatic potential, analogous to the stimulus barrier, which protects the ego from externally generated trauma. In this revision, Freud also added a developmental perspective to his view of trauma, regarding the original traumatic state as the **birth trauma** (along with Rank [1924]), or what he called "automatic anxiety," when the infant at birth is suddenly overwhelmed with stimulation. Subsequently, anxiety is experienced in either of two forms: a **traumatic anxiety** form that reproduces the trauma of birth, or an attenuated form (signal anxiety) that the ego initiates in the service of defense. Freud identified a sequence of developmentally predictable and potentially traumatic danger situations that elicit the ego's signal of anxiety: fear of being overwhelmed by stimuli, arising from the infant's utter helplessness; fear of the loss of the object upon whom the infant has become dependent; fear of the loss of the love of the object whose approval has become central to the child's sense of well-being; fear of castration in retaliation for oedipal desires; and finally, as the relationships are internalized, fear of the superego. However, no individual is immune to trauma; signal function may fail, because the capac-

ity to dispose of excessive quantities of excitation always reaches a limit. In a reprise of Freud's seduction hypothesis, Freud's contemporary, Ferenczi (1933), in a paper with the evocative title "Confusion of Tongues between Adults and the Child," proposed that psychopathology results from the trauma of abuse, particularly sexual abuse, on the part of parents, and their obfuscation of the child's experience of this abuse.

Freud laid the groundwork for much of the subsequent exploration of trauma, having focused upon the mechanisms operative at the time of its occurrence, contributions to vulnerability, and clinical sequelae. Contemporary literature has similarly focused on trauma proper, the preconditions for trauma, and the clinical effects of trauma. The concept of trauma has also become broader in its scope. This broadened perspective includes an emphasis on childhood trauma and, to a large extent, reflects the growth of developmental research, which emphasizes continuing processes rather than discrete events, the difficulty of distinguishing retrospectively between an acute and a chronic condition, and the lack of precise association between trauma and any particular type of psychological outcome (Furst, 1967).

Studies of childhood trauma focus on the developmental aspects of the predisposition to trauma, elaborating the conditions under which events are likely to have traumatic impact. Issues include phase specific temporal factors; predisposition to anxiety; frustration tolerance; preparedness of the ego; subliminatory capacity; rigidity of defenses; self esteem; degree of inner conflict; the resonance of actual experience with memories, wishes, and fantasies; superego severity; and the quality of object relations or attachment, to mention a few. All authors emphasize the state of vulnerability of the child's ego based on interacting constitutional, experiential, and dynamic factors. All emphasize the role of early caretakers in either perpetrating or protecting against trauma. For example, Shengold (1989) described the syndrome of "soul murder," or the deliberate attempt to interfere with the child's separate identity, joy in life, and capacity to love, caused by seduction, overstimulation, cruelty, indifference, and/or neglect.

The literature on the consequences of trauma is also complex. Some authors argue that trauma is inevitable and does not invariably result in pathology. For example, A. Freud (1967a), observing children exposed to wartime conditions, described the capacity for adaptation to increased stimuli in a shared social milieu. In a similar vein, she described the capacity of children to habituate to difficult parental handling, which might be experienced as traumatic if it were unexpected or unfamiliar. Many others have tried to explain the quality of resilience to trauma, for example, Rangell (1967b), who described the inevitability of trauma during early development and the possibility for mastery and increased capacities for adaptation. However, many also have argued that no traumatic event is ever fully integrated. While there is no pathological outcome specific to trauma, common sequelae include symptoms, inhibitions, massive repressions and/or dissociation, persistent regression, broad avoidance patterns, failures of mentalization, and other distortions of character. Many, including Freud (1920a) himself, have noted the association between trauma and repetition or enactment. Within the vast literature exploring the psychological effects of the Holocaust, Niederland (1968) has described a "survivor syndrome," which includes survivor guilt and other sequelae. Beginning in this context, others have explored the **intergenerational transmission of trauma** (H. Barocas and C. Barocas, 1979), or the unconscious process by which the effect of trauma in a parent is passed on to the child. Many have explored the specific psychopathology that accompanies severe childhood deprivation and associated syndromes of hospitalism and anaclitic depression (Spitz, 1945; Fraiberg, 1982). Others have explored the sequelae of object loss (Frankiel, 1994), sexual abuse (Davies and Frawley, 1992), and immigration (Akhtar, 1995). Many have noted a close association between a history of trauma and borderline personality disorder (Fonagy, 2000). Useful reviews of the subject include the work of Furst (1967), Krystal (1968, 1988), and Parens, Blum, and Salman (2008).

Dissociation theorists (Van der Kolk, 2000; Tutte, 2004; Bromberg, 2006) emphasize the relationship between childhood trauma and the phenomenon of dissociation in adult patients, even when massive trauma has not occurred. They theorize that trauma induces unsymbolized affect linked to self states that cannot reemerge as memories and can only be accessed through behavioral enactment. Such theories attribute therapeutic action to the exploration of interpersonally constructed enactments within the clinical situation. These formulations have also been linked to theories about procedural and implicit memory systems that may be activated preferentially during certain conditions, including trauma.

In the psychiatric literature (PDM Task Force, 2006), the term *traumatic neurosis* has been replaced by the diagnosis of **posttraumatic stress disorder (PTSD)**. PTSD is considered a syndrome with a set of characteristic features that occurs in a significant percentage of individuals under conditions of massive trauma. These include "intense fear or horror;

obligatory repetition and persistent re-experiencing of the traumatic event; avoidance of associated stimuli; internal numbing mechanisms, such as dissociation and alcoholism; symptoms of increased arousal; internal intrusions of associated memories and feelings; somatic states; and re-enactments." Interest in posttraumatic pathology gained considerable momentum in the aftermath of the Vietnam War and with the greater prevalence of acts of terrorism and torture, such that PTSD gained the status of a household term. While these conditions have been more prevalent among adults, similar posttraumatic stress disorder patterns have also been identified among children and adolescents. Some theorists have attempted to integrate the psychoanalytic point of view with evidence from developmental psychology and cognitive neuroscience (Schore, 2002).

Trial Identification: see COUNTERTRANSFERENCE, EMPATHY, IDENTIFICATION

Triangulation is the process by which a child experiences triadic interpersonal interactions with actual persons in his or her life and develops corresponding intrapsychic structures. Triangulation can be conceptualized as having earlier and later developmental formations concordant with the preoedipal and oedipal phases of development. Triangulation begins when the child goes beyond his dyadic attachment to a parent to include interactions with a "third," such as a father, and to perceive the attachment between mother and father in relation to himself. Triangulation is thus a developmental process whereby the individual's object relations advance to incorporate a complex, ambivalent relationship to two other important persons (typically the parents), which includes the awareness of their relationship to each other.

Triangulation is a central concept for any psychoanalytic theory that highlights the importance of the oedipus complex, but it does not require the latter to be recognized as a momentous developmental accomplishment. As a process, it marks the infant's earliest capacity to psychologically move beyond the mother/infant dyad, take in an "other," and sense feelings between two separate people outside of himself. As this process becomes consolidated as an interpersonal capacity, the child is capable of complex relationships and emotions, such as ambivalence, jealousy, and rivalry. Moreover, the child is forced to confront his own position in the family and to come to terms with the narcissistic injury he experiences by exclusion from the intimacy of the parental relationship he observes.

The term *triangulation* derives from trigonometry and did not appear regularly in the psychoanalytic literature until the 1970s, when Abelin (1971, 1975) gave it psychoanalytic meaning. He explicitly linked it to the developmental step in which the toddler grasps his relationship to mother, father, and their relationship to each other. Nonetheless, the notion of triangulation is present in Freud's earliest theorizing about the oedipus complex, although he himself did not use the term. Abelin's use of the term was embedded in Mahler's (1972) theory of separation-individuation. He described the earliest form of triangulation occurring when the child experiences the "other," usually the father, as serving two functions: to introduce the child to the wider world and to facilitate the child's separation from the dyadic relationship with the mother. Within Mahler's separation-individuation paradigm, the father facilitates the child's autonomy and the achievement of intrapsychic separation from the ambivalently experienced mother of the rapprochement subphase. The child requires an actual experience with a "third" in order to achieve intrapsychic representation of triadic relationships and triadic structures (Rupprecht-Schampera, 1995).

The sine qua non of the later phase of triangulation is Freud's oedipal phase of psychosexual development. The advanced triadic relations come into formation with the mobilization of sexual and aggressive drives in the developing child. Freud (1900, 1923a) described the boy's love for his mother and rivalry with his father and further elaborated on complex forms of triangulation in describing the negative or inverted oedipus complex. While Freud (1925b) initially considered boys' and girls' triangular development to be parallel, he (1931) later came to see girls' development as different from that of boys. Some theorists proposed that the Oedipus myth more aptly describes the triadic constellation in boys, and that the myth of Persephone and the myths of Athena and Medusa are more accurate paradigms for the triangulation process in girls' development during this period (Kulish and Holtzman, 1998; Seelig, 2002).

Theorists of different persuasions consider triangulation crucial for optimal development of a range of mental capacities. Abelin indicated that triangulation is the vehicle that propels the child's mental organization from the level of sensorimotor relationships toward representational and symbolic formations. With the change, the child develops a sense of the relationship between two others and therefore solidifies a sense of self image. While this might be considered akin to an oedipal level form of triangu-

lation, the emphasis here is on the sense of self rather than on imbuing triadic relationships with sexual and aggressive drive elements. Rupprecht-Schampera noted that the unique ego functions of emotional integration and contextualization supplied by a parent on behalf of a child help the child contend with frustrations and destabilizing affects. These auxiliary functions serve as a "triangular psychic function" while the child is otherwise engaged in a dyadic relationship with the same individual. When the parent fails to provide this triangular function, the child will seek an "other," such as a father, as a potential resource for these auxiliary ego functions. Britton (1989) identified the concept of triangulation as the basis for the capacity of self reflection, that is, seeing oneself in interaction with others and envisioning another perspective of oneself.

Lacan (1966/2006) and A. Green (1975) maintained that triadic structures exist from birth, inasmuch as the child recognizes that he or she is the product of the relationship between a mother and a father and that the mother desires someone other than the child. Lacan referred to the mother's object of desire as the "symbolic father," which represents anyone or any activity that separates the mother from the child. Thus he underscored the important role of triangulation in the development of symbolic functioning. In his view, the symbolic phallus and the father image facilitate the shift from the dyadic relationship of the "mirror stage" to the structural level of symbolic functioning of the "register." Green applied the triangulation concept to the development of the mind and its creative processes.

Research on infant development has focused on studying triadic interactions among infant, mother, and father. Using the Lausanne triadic-play experimental paradigm (Corboz-Warnery et al., 1993), microanalytic observations of the infant's gaze and affect expression in triadic interactions indicate that the infant demonstrates triangulation by nine months. The infant communicates his intention to achieve an expected goal in his interactions with each parent, using strategies of affect sharing, affect signaling and social referencing. Triangulation, in this model, is defined as a process whose function is to establish and maintain triadic interactions in high-affect situations (Fivaz-Depeursinge and Corboz-Warnery, 1999).

Tripartite Model: see STRUCTURAL THEORY

Turning against the Self is a defensive process whereby unacceptable aggressive feelings or impulses, originally aimed against others, are redirected toward the self. Without naming it as such, Freud (1905c) understood the self-deprecating ethnic humor of Jews as an example of turning against the self. Freud (1915b) identified "turning round upon the subject's own self" as one of the four vicissitudes of the instinct (in addition to repression, sublimation, and reversal into the opposite). Although Freud (1915b, 1917c, 1924a) did not use the term itself, he described the prominent role of turning against the self in the phenomena of depression and masochism. A. Freud (1936) coined the phrase "turning against the self," describing it as a form of the defense mechanism "turning active to passive." She also explored its close relationship to what she called "identification with the aggressor."

Twinship: see SELF, SELF IN SELF PSYCHOLOGY, SELF PSYCHOLOGY, SELFOBJECT

U

Uncanny is a strange feeling, especially a feeling of dread and horror, brought about by an experience in which something repressed threatens to return to awareness, and/or by a primitive belief or mode of thought that seems real. An uncanny experience is always both familiar and strange at the same time. It also always involves doubt as to whether what is experienced is real or fantastical. Examples of the uncanny include déjà vu; experiences of seeing one's "double," ghosts, dead bodies, machines that seem to come to life, or severed body parts; the "evil eye"; or repetitive coincidences. The uncanny is a common response to art.

Freud touched on the aspects of the uncanny in relation to déjà vu (1901), the child's experience of noises from the parents' bedroom (1905b), the experience of seeing one's double (1911c), and the boy's experience of seeing the girl's genitals (1910b). However, Freud's (1919d) most extensive exploration of the subject was in his paper "The 'Uncanny,'" in which he described two possible sources of uncanny experience, not always distinguishable from one another. One source derives from situations in which repressed infantile complexes are revived, especially the castration complex. The other results from situations in which the infantile belief in the "omnipotence of thoughts" seems plausible once again. Freud also related the uncanny to the compulsion to repeat, which creates an uncanny sense of coincidence.

Bergler (1934), who updated the concept of the uncanny in terms of structural theory, suggested that the feeling of the uncanny may be experienced masochistically as anxiety-pleasure. Sullivan (1953a) wrote about what he called "the uncanny emotions," or the dread, loathing, and horror experienced by the child in the face of the mother's own anxiety or disapproval. More recently, Kohut (1971) discussed the uncanny as a defensive effort to allay "apprehensions about the aliveness of self and body," with the assertion that the inanimate can also be alive. Bach (1975) suggested that uncanny experience results from a situation in which a person feels the lack of reciprocal dialogue with an internalized narcissistic selfobject, creating a sense of discontinuity of self. Terr (1985) explored the uncanny in relation to actual trauma, and Feigelson (1993) explored it in cases where personality changes create bizarre and distorting effects.

Unconscious is mental contents or processes of which the individual is unaware but which nonetheless exert an active effect on conscious experience. In psychoanalysis, **the unconscious** designates a hypothetical region of the mind where mental contents are denied access to awareness as a result of repression and which operates according to its own unique modes of functioning. Psychoanalysis is most interested in thoughts and feelings that are actively kept from awareness by motivational "force," specifically by wishes to not know about these thoughts and feelings; such thoughts and feelings make up what is called the **dynamic unconscious**. We know unconscious contents only through their disguised effects on conscious experience or behavior. The term **subconscious**, coined by the nineteenth-century French psychopathologist Janet, is used in common discourse but rarely in psychoanalysis.

Among the most important contributions of psychoanalysis to the study of psychology has been its radical denial of the "equation of the psychical with the conscious" (Freud, 1915d). While Freud was not the first to argue for the possibility of unconscious mental life, psychoanalysis was the first and, for many years, the only organized account of unconscious mental life describing both its unique contents and its specific modes of functioning (Ellenberger, 1970). While later psychoanalysts have modified many of Freud's ideas about unconscious mental life, the idea that all of mental life and behavior is, in large measure, determined by unconscious factors remains the most important shared feature of the psychoanalytic theory of mind, of psychopathology, and of treatment. Freud (1914d) himself is famous for having asserted that the theory of the dynamic unconscious, based on repression, was among the most original of his ideas, "the cornerstone on which the whole structure of psycho-analysis rests." In the early part of the twentieth century, the study of unconscious mental life became known as "depth psychology," a term credited to Bleuler and Jung (Freud, 1912e).

Freud's (Breuer and Freud, 1893) first recorded use of the word *unconscious* as an adjective appeared in an unpublished manuscript, "On the Psychical

Mechanism of Hysterical Phenomena," written in 1893. Freud's (Breuer and Freud, 1893/1895) first recorded use of the word as a noun appeared in "Studies in Hysteria." As early as 1896, in a letter to Fliess describing the idea of mental "registrations" characterized by "unconsciousness," Freud (1896b) noted that he was on his way to inventing a "new psychology." Freud's (1900) first organized account of the unconscious appears in chapter 7 of "The Interpretation of Dreams" and is developed most fully in "The Unconscious" (Freud, 1915d). These early discussions are elaborated within what is known as the topographic model of the mind, which conceives of the mind as consisting of three parts (or systems) differentiated according to their relationship to consciousness. These three systems are the system conscious (Cs.), the system preconscious (Pcs., sometimes called Cs-Pcs.), and the **system unconscious** (Ucs.). The conscious includes mental contents that are within awareness. The preconscious includes mental contents that are **descriptively unconscious**, in that they are not conscious at any given moment but can easily be brought to consciousness if attention is applied to them. By contrast, the unconscious is **dynamically unconscious**, meaning that its contents are actively denied access to consciousness because of repression.

In the topographic model, Freud described the Ucs. from a developmental perspective. Initially, "primal repression" works to deny some parts of mental life access to awareness, forming the Ucs. Later, through "repression proper," parts of mental life that have the potential to become conscious or have become conscious are subject to censorship because they are deemed unacceptable to consciousness. In Freud's view, in 1900, the contents of the Ucs. consist of both kinds of unacceptable wishes. After the invention of drive theory (Freud, 1905b), the contents of the Ucs. consist of derivatives of the drives. These repressed drive derivatives seek access to consciousness in a disguised form acceptable to the censor. They may become conscious in the form of neurotic symptoms, parapraxes, slips of the tongue, and, later, character and transference. Freud argued that dreams are the "**royal road to the unconscious**," because when the censor is asleep, it is possible to observe in dream life how unconscious wishes from childhood activate and organize the mind. Through his investigation of dreams, Freud was also able to observe a specific mode of functioning of the Ucs., which he called the "primary process." He considered primary process to be the most primitive form of mentation. It operates according to the pleasure principle (as opposed to the reality principle), without regard for

logic, degrees of certitude, negation, contradiction, or time. Thoughts are expressed not in words (except in their most concrete form), but in imagery using symbolization, displacement, and condensation. In contrast to the Ucs., the Cs.-Pcs. operates according to the secondary process, characterized by logical, language-based thought in line with the reality principle.

When mental contents have been subject to repression, they become sequestered from more logical parts of the mind, continuing to operate according to the primary process. They do not get "worn away" through exposure to reason and reality. Repressed unconscious thoughts and feelings exert an attractive force on other mental contents, which can be pulled down into the unconscious to form complexes of associated, repressed ideas. Even while repressed, these thoughts and feelings exert an ongoing, albeit disguised effect on conscious mental life. Mental contents that have been subject to excessive repression exert a pathogenic effect on the mind. These pathogenic effects include inhibitions, symptoms, and anxiety. Freud co-opted the term *neurosis* from the surrounding medical world, to describe the symptoms of hysteria, phobia, and syndromes characterized by obsessions and compulsions (the psychoneuroses), all based on the repression of unacceptable wishes and impulses that "return" to consciousness, disguised as symptoms. Repressed unconscious memories are often repeated rather than remembered, especially in the transference (Freud, 1914c). Later, Freud asserted that character also represents the effect of repressed unconscious drive derivatives.

Freud's (1896c) earliest model of treatment, based on this topographic model of the mind, focused on the aim of "making conscious what has so far been unconscious." Through the treatment process, repression is replaced by conscious assessment and judgment (Freud, 1909c). Repressed unconscious memories that are repeated (rather than consciously remembered) in life or in the transference are reconstructed with the aim of making them conscious (Freud, 1937b). However, as the psychoanalytic model of the mind changed and the theories of psychopathology and treatment became more complex, insight achieved through interpretation (defined as a statement about the patient's unconscious mental life) and reconstruction of repressed memories became seen as only part of the therapeutic action of psychoanalysis. However, the idea of helping the patient become more aware of aspects of mental life that are outside of awareness is part of every theory of treatment.

Freud (1923a) modified the topographic model of the mind in response to his observation that the unconscious includes not just the drives seeking gratification but also defensive processes (including repression itself) and moral imperatives (**unconscious guilt**). His new, structural model of the mind consists of three agencies—id, ego, and superego—each of which has an unconscious component. In this model, the id (now including both libido and aggression) assumes qualities previously attributed to the system Ucs.; the unconscious ego assumes functions previously attributed to the Cs.-Pcs. With the new structural model, it makes most sense to use the word *unconscious* as an adjective rather than as a noun (with the latter's implication of a coherent system). The term *the unconscious* continues to be used in psychoanalytic discourse, usually in the sense of **the dynamic unconscious**, referring to mental contents that are repressed but continue to influence mental life and behavior. When used this way, any implication of systemic properties of the unconscious are often left somewhat vague.

While all psychoanalytic theories include a view of unconscious mental life, schools of thought can be differentiated, in part, with regard to their various views about what is "in" the unconscious, or their views on the nature of unconscious mental life. For example, ego psychology, based on the structural model of the mind, understands all conscious mental life and behavior as the result of compromise formation reflecting **unconscious conflict** between id, ego and superego (Waelder, 1936; C. Brenner, 1982). Ego psychology also emphasizes the mediating role of **unconscious fantasy**, or narratives of the self, originating in childhood under the influence of id, ego, superego, and interactions with others (Arlow, 1969b). Kleinian analysts emphasize their own concept of **unconscious phantasy** as mental representatives of the drives connected with internalized object relations, beginning with the earliest nonverbal, somatic experience that they hold to be the basis for all psychic life (Isaacs, 1948). Most post-Freudian analysts, including most modern ego psychologists, retain the concepts of a dynamic unconscious, unconscious conflict, and unconscious fantasy but have moved away from the drives (at least as conceptualized by Freud), preferring to conceptualize psychic life as influenced by repressed thoughts, feelings, memories, and motives of all kinds organized with varying degrees of primary and secondary processes (concepts that have also undergone much revision). Object relations theories of all kinds consider the basic unit of experience, both conscious and unconscious, to be internalized object relations. Self psychologists focus on unconscious aspects of the self-selfobject matrix. J. Sandler and A. Sandler (1983, 1984) distinguished between the **past unconscious** and the **present unconscious**. Recently, psychoanalysts from interpersonal, relational, or intersubjectivist points of view conceive of nonconscious or nondynamically unconscious **implicit relational knowing**, which consists of interactions with caregivers that are encoded in procedural rather than declarative memory and therefore cannot be verbalized (D. N. Stern et al., 1998). Others talk about **unformulated experience**, which consists of experiences in childhood that are not acknowledged by caregivers and are therefore not allowed access to consciousness (D. B. Stern, 1997). Both implicit relational knowing and unformulated experience can be enacted in the treatment dyad. Relational self psychologists Stolorow and Atwood (1989) distinguished among a dynamic unconscious, defensively repressed because of its conflicted contents; the **prereflective unconscious**, consisting of organizing principles of subjective experience that originate in the early intersubjective dyad; and the **invalidated unconscious**, which cannot be articulated at all because of selfobject failure of validation. The analyst's participation within the intersubjectivity of the analytic situation enables the patient to investigate, articulate, validate, and reorganize his unconscious experience. Some contemporary analysts prefer to talk about a **two-person unconscious**, existing within the dyad itself (Lyons-Ruth, 1999). Jung (1921/1957) divided the unconscious into the **personal unconscious** and the **collective unconscious**, which consists of archetypes common to and inherited by all people.

The ascendance of cognitive science in contemporary psychology has brought with it a "rediscovery" of the unconscious. Concepts such as "tacit knowledge," "preattentive information processing," "automaticity," "subliminal perception," and "procedural" or "implicit memory" are all part of what is now called the **cognitive unconscious** (Kihlstrom, 1995; Hassin, Uleman, and Bargh, 2005). For the most part, cognitive scientists reject the notion of a dynamic or repressed unconscious. Recently, however, the cognitive unconscious has expanded to include "implicit emotions," "implicit motivations," and "motivated forgetting," bringing it closer to the psychoanalytic concept of a dynamic unconscious (Westen, 1999b). Sometimes the term **nonconscious** is used in psychology to refer either to the cognitive unconscious or to brain activities that influence mental life but are not in themselves psychological. Cognitive science has influenced psychoanalytic researchers such as J. Weinberger and L. Silverman (1990) and Shevrin et al. (1996), who have developed experimental paradigms that provide evidence for repression, primary process, and a dynamic unconscious.

Undoing is a defensive process whereby a forbidden or painful thought, wish, affect, impulse, or action is rendered "undone" by following it with a thought or action with the opposite meaning. For example, an insult might be followed with the disclaimer "I was only kidding." Undoing is closely related to reaction formation, with the difference that in reaction formation, the forbidden thought is repressed, whereas in undoing, the forbidden thought is conscious but its impact is "undone." In contrast to reparation, undoing occurs out of concern for oneself—for example, to avoid retaliation or self condemnation—whereas reparation is offered out of remorse, guilt, and concern for the harmed object (Klein, 1940; J. Sandler and A. Freud, 1981). In addition, in contrast to acts of reparation and normal atonement, undoing seeks to obliterate the reality of the misdeed or unacceptable thought. For this reason, it is conceptualized as involving an element of magical thinking. Like most defenses, undoing may be characterized as normal or pathological, depending on the context. For example, normal children frequently use undoing in the service of mastery and control of the environment, as first noted by Freud (1920a) in his description of the child's game of repeatedly throwing and retrieving a spool of thread in order to manage feelings of separation. Children may also make gestures aimed at repairing injury, for example, a child who has pulled out another child's hair may try to put it back in. In adult psychopathology, undoing is most common in obsessional disorders and psychosis.

Freud (1909d) first described undoing in his exploration of the Rat Man's compulsive act of repeatedly placing and removing a stone from the road where he anticipated his lady friend's carriage might pass, with the hope that the second act might neutralize the earlier act. Freud conceptualized this act of undoing as his patient's attempt to manage a conflict between equal amounts of love and hate. In 1926, Freud (1926a) officially named the process of undoing, describing it, along with isolation and reaction formation, as a defense characteristic of obsessional neurosis. A. Freud (1936) lists undoing in her inventory of defense mechanisms, asserting that it aims to prevent an outbreak of aggression while maintaining sexual impulses under strict moral oversight.

Unformulated Experience: see DEFENSE, DISSOCIATION, INTERPERSONAL PSYCHOANALYSIS, UNCONSCIOUS

V

Vertical Split, a developmental concept introduced by Kohut (1970/1978, 1971, 1977), is a structural alteration in the self representation or structure of the self that results when healthy narcissistic needs have been ignored or frustrated by caretakers. Kohut theorized that there are two types of splits—vertical and horizontal—in which the child's developmentally appropriate grandiosity and need for recognition become unavailable for the promotion of a healthy self. The vertical split is based on disavowal and isolation. In the vertical split, the child's grandiosity is co-opted and showcased by the parents for their own self aggrandizement, resulting in split-off grandiosity in the child and, later, in the adult. The vertical split explains the coexistence of fantasies of greatness or displays of grandiosity, with feelings of diffidence, hypochondriasis, or masochism. It allows for the coexistence of two incompatible self experiences, oblivious grandiosity and painful inadequacy. Using the vertical split, the individual defends himself from experiencing the inevitable shame and humiliation of unmet narcissistic demands while simultaneously enacting these demands and satisfying these wishes. A vertical split defends the individual from feelings of shame that result from unmet needs, while allowing him to enact these needs. The side of the split that contains the conscious experience of diffidence, depletion, and depression can also be horizontally split. The horizontal split is based on and created by the repression of needs to be recognized and mirrored that are not acceptable to caretakers. Both vertical and horizontal splits protect the individual from experiencing his own narcissistic demands for recognition, affirmation, and validation.

Kohut elaborated on Freud's (1927b, 1937b, 1938b) idea that disavowal causes a split in the ego when external reality arouses anxiety, so that one part of the ego acknowledges the reality and the other repudiates its meaning. Kohut argued that each side of a vertical split corresponds to a different self state that is linked to an unconscious constellation. The self experience of oblivious grandiosity is often accompanied by feelings of fraud; the self experience of painful inadequacy is linked with unconscious grandiose fantasies.

The concept of vertical and horizontal splits informs psychoanalytic technique in self psychology. Initially, the analyst addresses the vertical split by understanding and interpreting the patient's split-off behaviors as efforts to satisfy selfobject needs. With treatment of the vertical split, there is greater affective connection between the patient's feelings of expansiveness and his feelings of depletion. This facilitates the emergence of repressed affects and fantasies that allow for the interpretation of the horizontal split, resulting in healthy self esteem and self assertion.

In his later work, Kohut (1977) expanded the idea of the vertical split to explain not only the fate of unintegrated grandiosity in narcissistic personality disorders but also to explain disorders such as perversions and addictions. Goldberg (1995, 1999, 2000) continued the study of perversion, extending the concept of the vertical split to include behaviors that are often secretively split off, such as binge-eating, cross-dressing, and infidelity.

Voyeurism: see ACTIVE/PASSIVE, EXHIBITIONISM, INFANTILE GENITAL PHASE, PERVERSION, SHAME

W

"We" Psychology: see INTERSUBJECTIVITY, MOTIVATION

Widening Scope is a shorthand reference to the analysis of patients for whom psychoanalytic treatment might present both great difficulties and the potential for significant therapeutic benefit. This group includes, but is not limited to, patients with borderline and narcissistic personalities. The importance of the term *widening scope* is largely historical, as it appeared at a time when controversy surrounded the differentiation of psychoanalysis from psychotherapy, especially as applied to the treatment of more-disturbed patients.

Widening scope first appeared in the title of Stone's (1954) paper "The Widening Scope of Indications for Psychoanalysis." In that paper, Stone discussed the analytic treatment of patients with significantly compromised ego function, and the technical modifications that could make analysis useful for them. While Stone remained committed to the analysis of the transference for such patients, he also emphasized that successful analysis largely depended on the warmth and flexibility of an analyst who could provide the support necessary to facilitate the analysis. In positing this stance, he underscored the importance of the real relationship. In contrast, contemporaneously, K. Eissler (1953) presented his views on the use of "parameters," which he defined as a conscious and deliberate therapeutic intervention that departs from an analyst's usual stance or technique. However, Eissler's term carried negative implications, both for the technique and the patients who required such intervention, and has fallen out of use.

Many analysts from Kleinian, object relations, and self psychology points of view have described the psychoanalytic treatment of patients whose psychopathology overlaps with Stone's "widening scope" patients. However, these analysts are less likely to use this phrase, and they recommend technical interventions congruent with their own theoretical perspectives.

Wild Analysis (or Wild Psychoanalysis), first used by Freud (1910f), is psychoanalytic treatment conducted by an inadequately trained practitioner, and a psychoanalytic technique in which interpretations of unconscious mental content are ill timed, premature, or wrong. *Wild analysis* has been used imprecisely as a pejorative term for particular analysts and for the technical interventions of whole schools of thought (Beres, 1957). Because of the current plurality of psychoanalytic theory and the associated variation of technique, the term has an increasingly vague referent (Schafer, 1985). It is rarely, if ever, used in contemporary psychoanalytic discourse.

Donald W. Winnicott proposed a theory of object relations, particularly the development of object relations, which has had a profound influence on all of psychoanalysis. While Winnicott's theory is less systematized than some, his innovative style along with the evocative quality of his ideas have had lasting impact. Winnicott (1945, 1949, 1950, 1951, 1952, 1953, 1955, 1956b, 1956c, 1958a, 1958b, 1960b, 1965, 1969, 1971a, 1971b, 1975/1992, 1987) formulated his own lexicon of novel concepts—including "transitional object," "holding environment," and "good enough mother"—that have entered the psychoanalytic mainstream. Others, such as "impingement" and "false self" remain controversial but have been widely discussed. Beginning his career in the practice of pediatrics, Winnicott has been especially influential in child and developmental psychoanalysis. At the same time, his work with sicker patients brought him greater awareness of the impact of the caretaking environment on the developing child and the importance of his own behavior in the therapeutic action of analysis. Winnicott was a major influence on Kohut and the development of self psychology. He is famous for having stated, "There is no baby without the mother," a sentence often cited in relational psychoanalysis and the study of intersubjectivity. His work has also been influential in the areas of aesthetics and the study of creativity. Winnicott was heavily influenced by his study with Klein. However, working in the United Kingdom at the time of the Freud-Klein controversies, Winnicott helped to found the British Middle School, later known as the Independent Group (King and Steiner, 1991).

Throughout all of his writings, Winnicott emphasized the concept and the origin of the self, the development of the infant's subjective sense of self, and his sense of reality. He emphasized the dependence of the infant on the mother in psychic development. Like other independent thinkers who were his contemporaries, such as Balint and Fairbairn, Winnicott concentrated his attention on the early development of the infant, rejecting the notion of an infant who does not relate to his objects from the beginning. The reality of the infant's dependence on his environment determines his emotional development. Winnicott postulated three stages of dependency—absolute dependence, relative dependence, and toward independence. The successful negotiation of the first two stages relies on "good enough mothering," and they provide the basis for a mature sense of independence.

Winnicott suggested that the infant's primary experience oscillates between integrated and unintegrated pleasurable and unpleasurable affective states. The protective environment provided by the empathic presence of the "good enough mother" allows the infant to experience nontraumatic gratification of his needs, with gradual integration of his affect states into a stable sense of self and stable sense of reality. The mother approaches her infant in a normal state of "primary maternal preoccupation," which develops during pregnancy and lasts for the first few months of the infant's life. This attitude combined with her natural and spontaneous mothering behaviors allow her to be a "good enough mother," meaning, a mother who provides the infant with the optimal amount of comfort and frustration. The "good enough mother" provides appropriate physical handling of the infant's instinctual needs ("object mother"). She also provides appropriate emotional "holding" for his affective needs ("holding mother"). The "holding environment" is an essential feature of the infant's development, in that it provides sufficient security for the infant to tolerate the fury associated with inevitable failures in empathy, when "holding" is lost. It also allows for the infant's omnipotent fantasy that he alone creates the reality needed for satisfaction. The infant's omnipotent fantasy, or illusion, is essential for the development of his early self experience, as well as for the later development of "transitional space" and "transitional phenomena."

Indeed, among Winnicott's most important contributions to psychoanalysis are his related concepts of transitional space and "transitional object." These transitional phenomena are essential to the development of the child's sense of self, sense of reality, and creativity. *Transitional space* is Winnicott's term for a hypothetical area of mutual creativity that occurs between infant and mother. The space between infant and mother is only a "potential space," as its availability depends on good-enough maternal care. Transitional space is an area where distinctions between "me" and "not-me," "real" and "unreal," or "internal" and "external" are not made. It is a space where illusion thrives. The hungry baby and the feeding mother come together in a moment of illusion in which the baby is free to experience the satisfying breast either as a hallucination of his own creation, or as something belonging to the reality of the external world. Once established and used, this transitional space becomes a generative, intersubjective accomplishment internalized by the infant as a psychic attribute, so that he can create this potential area between himself and other objects. At first, transitional objects emerge; later, after further development, the capacity for symbolic play and creative aesthetic experience materializes.

The *transitional object* is the term Winnicott used to distinguish the intermediate area of experience for the infant between oral eroticism and the true relationship, that is, between thumb and teddy bear, "me" and "not-me." The transitional object is the infant's first "not-me" possession, inanimate but treasured, such as a blanket, a piece of cloth, or a teddy bear. The transitional object is not part of the infant's body, yet it is not yet fully recognized as belonging to external reality. It is especially important to the child at times of separation from the mother and at times of stress. The transitional object evokes the illusion of symbiosis with the mother at a period in development in which the self and object representations are only partially differentiated. It can serve as a psychic organizer for the process of separation-individuation; it delineates a boundary between the self and the world; and it aids in the creation of a body image. Through his relationship to the transitional object, the infant learns to tolerate ambivalent feelings toward the object and to develop a "capacity for concern." His initial "ruthlessness" toward the object subsides with development, especially as he is reassured that his aggression has not destroyed the object. In this way, the infant progresses from the paranoid-schizoid position to the depressive position, which Winnicott called the "stage of concern." The transitional object also contributes to the development of the child's "capacity to be alone," derived from what Winnicott called his capacity to be "alone in the presence of the mother," reassured by her ongoing availability and goodness. In Winnicott's view, failures in the development of transitional phenomena result in various kinds of psychopathology, ranging from mild to severe disturbances in the self, object relations, and relationship to reality.

Winnicott's key contributions to psychoanalysis also include his concepts of the "true self" and the "false self." These concepts have been foundational in the psychoanalytic psychology of feelings of authenticity and of authentic relationships with others, including those in the treatment situation. When the mother fails to react to the infant in an empathic way (fails to be "good enough"), allowing her own needs to dominate, the infant experiences a feeling of "impingement," which is traumatic. A basic defensive operation then occurs, in the formation of splitting between the infant's "true self," which withdraws into an internal world of fantasy, and his "false self," which adapts to the frustrating reality. Under excessively traumatic circumstances, an exaggerated false self may lead to a chronic sense of inauthenticity, supported by intellectualization and isolation of affect. In serious cases, it may lead to severe psychopathology, including antisocial personality.

Applications of Winnicott's theory have been important in several areas of psychoanalysis. For example, the concept of the "holding environment" has been generalized to include the nonspecific, supportive continuity provided by the analyst and the analytic situation, including the regularity of visits, rituals of coming and going, underlying empathy, steadiness of voice, continuity of the object, and spaces and textures of the analytic room (Modell, 1976). More generally, Winnicott's observations about the impact of the analyst's real behavior in the analysis, outside of his interpretive function, have been important in all modern conceptualizations of therapeutic action.

Developmental psychoanalysts have made many observations related to the child's experience of the transitional object, documenting that transitional objects first appear between four and twelve months of age. They are used in the service of defense against anxiety, especially when going to sleep. The importance of the object to the infant may continue into childhood especially at bedtime and times of loneliness or stress. At these times, the transitional object may be more important to the infant than the actual mother. The transitional object is subjected to affection, love, excitement, hate, and pure aggression. Eventually the child loses interest in the transitional object, which is given up without mourning; while it may not be forgotten, it is relegated to a limbo where it gradually loses its meaning.

Winnicott's ideas were important in the development of self psychology. His ideas about: the mirroring function of the mother's face, the holding environment, the ordinary devoted mother, the transitional object, the experience of omnipotence, potential space, illusion, and the false self all overlap with ideas developed by Kohut. Winnicott's ideas about the importance of illusion are central to theo-

ries about the development of the capacity for intersubjectivity.

Finally, the concepts of transitional space and transitional phenomena have been important to the study of creativity, echoed in such concepts as: virtual space, theatrical illusion, liminality, the suspension of disbelief, and negative capability.

Wish is an unconscious mental state of desire that operates in the mind to motivate human behavior. In Freud's topographic model of the mind, wishes are the basic unit of the mental contents of the system unconscious (Ucs.). In libido theory, wishes are conceptualized as derivatives of the instinctual drives. In the structural model of the mind, wishes (still conceptualized as derivatives of the drives) make up the content of the id. Wishes, along with defense, comprise one of the central components of dynamic conflict. Ego psychologists describe wishes as organized into fantasies through the process of compromise formation, in which the expression of wishes is modified by defensive operations. Need, in contrast to wish, is a state of internal tension that arises in response to the survival requirements of the individual. Need is not always accompanied by clear mental content and must be met through something provided by the external environment.

Wish has long been important in psychoanalysis, which from the beginning emphasized the role of unconscious motivation as a critical element in organizing mental life. Indeed, the concept of wish was central to Freud's (1900) views of thinking and motivation: "Nothing but a wish can set our mental apparatus at work." Every psychoanalytic theory includes a concept of wish. However, among the many critics of Freud's drive theory are those who prefer the concept of wish to drive, arguing that the former offers a better basis for a theory of motivation (Holt, 1976).

Freud (1895b) first talked about the functioning of wishes and of "wishful states" within the mind in his posthumously published "Project for a Scientific Psychology." His (1900) first published work outlining his theory of thinking, and the role of wishes and **wish-fulfillment** within it, was presented in chapter 7 of "The Interpretation of Dreams." Here, reviewing some of what he had already begun to formulate in the "Project," Freud described how a baby experiences "excitations produced by internal needs," which can only be relieved by an "experience of satisfaction." Later, when the infant experiences the need again, it will "seek to re-cathect the mnemic image of the perception and to re-evoke the perception itself . . . to re-establish the situation of the original satisfaction."

The impulse to do this is what Freud labels a "wish," and "the reappearance of the perception is the fulfillment of the wish." Freud postulated that the most primitive way in which the mind discharges the tension arising from internal needs is to hallucinate the perception of satisfaction, so that wishing ends in hallucinating, producing a "perceptual identity." He called this kind of satisfaction **hallucinatory wish-fulfillment**, based on the earliest and most primitive kind of thinking, called the primary process, which operates according to the pleasure principle. However, because hallucination does not produce an experience of lasting satisfaction, the mind begins to divert its excitations toward controlling voluntary movements, directed toward bringing about changes in the external world so that wishes may be satisfied in reality. Thus enters the "second system" of thinking, the secondary process, which operates in accord with reality. Dreams, which reflect a regression to the primary process mode of thinking, are an example of hallucinatory wish-fulfillment. Psychosis also reflects primary process wishful thinking, which occurs while the mind is awake. Neurotic symptoms represent more disguised forms of wish-fulfillment. Modern conflict theory views wishes as involved in the ubiquitous compromise formations of normal behavior.

Developmental psychoanalysts have continued to study wishes in connection with the concept of needs. Wishes, while aroused in relation to internal biological needs, are directed toward the representations of objects and are fulfilled through the establishment of internal identities of perception. Needs, however, must be met through something provided by the external environment. A need implies no level of mental development, whereas a wish is inextricably linked to memories of previous gratifications, thus requiring at least some level of psychic development. The infant has not only physiologic needs for food, hydration, and protection from the elements but also equally imperative psychological needs without which it cannot properly develop or even survive (Spitz, 1946). These needs include a good-enough caretaker who can provide conditions of psychic safety, reliability, and proper emotional responsiveness for the growing child (Winnicott, 1960b; A. Freud, 1965; Kohut, 1971; Mahler, Pine, and Bergman, 1975). Discussions of the distinction between needs and wishes are associated with long-standing controversies (Eagle, 1990; Akhtar, 1999). Among these controversies are various views as to whether the proper focus of psychoanalytic treatment is the interpretation of unconscious sexual and aggressive wishes and conflicts or the use of empathic understanding to understand unmet devel-

opmental needs that have resulted in defects in the structure and functioning of the self (C. Brenner, 1982; Kohut, 1984).

Womb Envy is a male's experience of envy of a woman's ability to become pregnant and deliver babies. Womb envy in little boys may commonly take the form of conscious pregnancy fantasies (Freud, 1909c; Kleeman, 1966), yet with development, such fantasies are usually subject to defensive processes. Reaction formations may transform envy into devaluation of women with an emphasis on what women cannot do (Horney, 1933; Chasseguet-Smirgel, 1993). Womb envy may also apply to women who, for various medical reasons, are infertile.

Womb envy is best understood in the context of the development of gender identity. Gender identity develops gradually as the child of each sex learns the limits and capacities that biology, sex, family, and society impose on his or her gender. In this context, the boy learns to accept that he cannot produce babies and must cope with the narcissistic blow and the envy that this realization brings (Fast, 1984). However, as with penis envy in girls and women, womb envy should not be taken at face value but must be understood to represent a compromise formation serving multiple functions.

The reverberations of womb envy are manifest in mythology, anthropology, practices such as couvade, and certain religious rituals (Lax, 1997). Horney (1926, 1933) was the first to articulate a psychoanalytic theory of womb envy in men, formulating that the male's depreciation of women stemmed from the boy's intense envy of motherhood. In elaborating a femininity complex in men, Boehm (1930) wondered if womb envy might be tied to narcissistic strivings or related to passive homosexual attachments to the father. Freud (1924a) viewed such passive attachments and wishes to be feminine or to take on feminine functions, as representing a homosexual attachment to the father, resulting from a passive regression from a more "active" phallic masculinity. More recently, psychoanalysts have attributed womb envy to the child's narcissistic ambition to be both sexes. Nelson (1956) described the boy's efforts to assume his mother's productive powers and his awe of her feminine functions. P. Tyson (1980) stated that womb envy is ubiquitous in little boys, but like penis envy in girls, it is not necessarily problematic or fixed.

Work Ego is the analyst's capacity to tolerate his regressive, preconscious fantasies, thoughts, and affects that arise in the process of his identifications with the patient (concordant identification) or the patient's objects (complementary identification), and the analyst's subsequent capacity to use this experience to better understand the patient. The work-ego concept includes the analyst's permissive superego stance regarding his conscious immersion in potentially conflictual mental experience and his temporary regression from higher-level ego function. The work ego also includes the function of the analyst's ego ideal, which embodies his dedication to his professional role. The ego ideal signals the requirement to end this experiential immersion and to work analytically, though this work may already have been accomplished preconsciously (Olinick et al., 1973). These functions are referred to as a work ego because it is assumed that the analyst does not ordinarily have access to these capacities in his extra-analytic functioning. The capacities of the work ego overlap with J. Sandler's (1976a) concept of "role-responsiveness." First used by Fliess (1942), work ego had a more restricted meaning: It referred only to the analyst's ability to empathically understand the patient via a purposeful and temporary trial identification, facilitated by the decreased censorship of the analyst's "working conscience." The contemporary meaning connotes an involuntary and more-prolonged experience.

Working Through is the necessary process within an analytic treatment that entails a cycle of interpretation followed by its repeated application to specific instances where those issues are demonstrated. Such repetition occurs within all domains of the analytic work, perhaps most importantly within the here and now of the transference, but also within the patient's psychological experience outside of the treatment situation and within his developmental history. The requirement for working through is manifest evidence of the gap between the attainment of intellectual insight and evidence of real change. In other words, a patient may be able to cogently identify his conflicts or problematic issues but may have little understanding of when and where those conflicts and issues are intrapsychically, behaviorally, and interpersonally expressed. What is ultimately required of the working-through process is the forging of affective conviction to intellectual insight. The necessity for the working-through process is linked to the concept of resistance, described broadly as all of the conscious and unconscious factors and forces that operate to maintain the status quo within a patient's psychological experience, despite his conscious motivation to change.

Working through is important within the history of psychoanalysis because the evolution of the concept traces the same arc as that of therapeutic action, the means by which psychoanalytic treatment accomplishes therapeutic gain. All psychoanalytic theoretical orientations recognize the necessity for a working-through process, whether or not they utilize the term, but they conceptualize the process differently depending upon their view of what impedes and what facilitates progress in treatment. Different theories emphasize variably the role of cognition, affect, internalizations, resumption of developmental processes, establishing meaningful life narratives, shifting implicit relational processes, intersubjectivity, and establishing feelings of safety, among many others.

Freud (1914c) coined the term "working-through" in his seminal paper "Remembering, Repeating and Working-Through," which set the stage for the continuing study of this concept. However, the concept of working through was implicitly present in Freud's work from the very beginning, as he struggled to understand the processes in the patient and the functions of the analyst that were required for recovery. Freud initially identified working through as: a united effort on the part of patient and analyst; a time-consuming and arduous process; the distinguishing feature of a psychoanalytic treatment, because other treatments utilized suggestion; and the necessary work for change to occur. Freud made few direct references to working through in his writings, however, in "Analysis Terminable and Interminable" (1937a), he acknowledged the limitations of analysis and examined under what conditions the working-through process is curtailed. These conditions involve the influence of resistances that cannot be understood solely within the realm of conflict and compromise but instead are derived from inherited dispositions. Freud included resistances of: the ego, in the characteristics of some defensive processes; the id, in the "adhesiveness" of libido and the lack of plasticity of the drives; and the superego, in destructive self-punishing forces that function beyond the pleasure principle.

Analysts within the ego psychology tradition have highlighted a succession of components of the working-through process, often with the suggestion that the most determinative aspect of the working-through process had been discovered. For example, Fenichel (1938a) argued that working through was essentially a matter of the arduous work of analyzing a patient's defenses. Greenacre (1956) considered that the reconstruction of traumatic events was critical to a successful culmination of the working-through process. For Greenson (1965a), the critical element was the establishment of a dependable working alliance. Dewald

(1976) cited the analyst's tolerant, analytic attitude as critical. Sedler (1983) stressed the patient's will to remember as a critical working-through process in the pursuit of the goal to triumph over neurotic barriers. C. Brenner (1987) countered the then-prevailing tendency to divide working through into phases and components. He noted that it is a construct that accounts for the analytic process in all of its components and aspects as they, of necessity, express themselves variously and with different emphases over the entire course of an analysis. Current writings recognize that working through is the analysis; working through is the total systematic analytic effort, in all its components in every analysis that is required to achieve the patient's fullest possible integrated personal growth and development.

From a self psychology perspective, working through occurs primarily during disruptions in a well-established selfobject transference, which the patient dreads because of his potential for retraumatization. When these disruptions occur at a point that the patient has tenuously acquired the capacity to change, they serve to demarcate for the patient and analyst the patient's anxieties and defenses. The working-through process is facilitated by reconstructive interpretations, focusing on the protective function of repetitive defenses, in addition to analysis and repair of the transference bond (A. Ornstein, 1990). Some interpersonal psychoanalysts reject the notion of resistance and emphasize that working through is the modification of interlocking facets of character that are expressed within the interpersonal field, and

is the reintegration of dissociated self states (A. Cooper, 1989; P. Bromberg, 1998a). Relational analysts emphasize the working-through process within the context of the experiential here-and-now relationship of the analytic dyad, which results in shifts in intrapsychic object relational configurations. Kleinian analysts emphasize that working through involves the interpretation of pathological projective and introjective cycles, in which the analyst functions as a container for the patient's projections, which are then returned to the patient in a more manageable form. Interpretive efforts are aimed at shifting unintegrated paranoid and depressive object relational configurations to the more-integrated internalized objects of the depressive position.

Based on his reading of approximately four hundred and fifty cases presented for certification to the American Psychoanalytic Association, Burland (1997) proposed that there are six elements that are invariably present in the working-through process, despite significant differences among the patients and analysts involved. He included self observation and insight, abreaction, mourning, disillusionment, desensitization, and the resumption of psychological development. The universality of these elements led Burland to conclude that they are fundamental aspects of the process of psychological repair, both within and outside of analysis, and throughout the life cycle.

Wrecked by Success: see CHARACTER, MASOCHISM, SUPEREGO

APPENDIX

Dictionaries/Encyclopedias of English-Language Psychoanalysis

Abram, J. (2007). *The language of Winnicott: A dictionary of Winnicott's use of words.* London: Karnac.

Akhtar, S. (2009). *Comprehensive dictionary of psychoanalysis.* London: Karnac.

Brenner, C. (1955). *An elementary textbook of psychoanalysis.* New York: International Universities Press.

Eidelberg, L., ed. (1968). *Encyclopedia of psychoanalysis.* New York: Free Press.

Elliot, A. (1994). *Psychoanalytic theory: An introduction.* Oxford: Blackwell.

English, H., and English, A. (1958). *A comprehensive dictionary of psychological and psychoanalytical terms.* New York: Longman's, Green.

Erwin, E., ed. (2002). *The Freud encyclopedia: Theory, therapy, and culture.* New York: Routledge.

Evans, D. (1996). *An introductory dictionary of Lacanian psychoanalysis.* New York: Routledge.

Fodor, N., and Gaynor, F. (1950). *Freud: Dictionary of psychoanalysis.* New York: Philosophical Library.

Frosh, S. (2003). *Key concepts in psychoanalysis.* New York: New York University Press.

Gabbard, G. (1994). *Psychodynamic psychiatry in clinical practice, DSM IV edition.* Washington, DC: American Psychiatric Press.

Gedo, J., and Goldberg, A. (1973). *Models of the mind: A psychoanalytic theory.* Chicago: University of Chicago Press.

Gilman, S., ed. (1982). *Introducing psychoanalytic theory.* New York: Brunner/Routledge.

Hall, C. (1954/1979). *A primer of Freudian psychology.* New York: HarperCollins / Mentor Books.

Hinshelwood, R. (1989). *A dictionary of Kleinian thought.* London: Free Association Books.

Kahn, S. (1942). *Psychological and neurological definitions and the unconscious.* Boston: Meador Publishing.

Klumpner, G. (1992). *A guide to the language of psychoanalysis: An empirical study of the relationships among psychoanalytic terms and concepts.* Madison, CT: International Universities Press.

Laplanche, J., and Pontalis, J. (1967/1973). *The language of psycho-analysis.* New York: W. W. Norton.

Lionells, M., Fiscalini, J., Mann, H., and Stern, D. B., eds. (1995). *Handbook of interpersonal psychoanalysis.* Hillsdale, NJ: Analytic Press.

Mijolla, A., ed. (2002/2005). *International dictionary of psychoanalysis.* Detroit, MI: Thomson Gale. Also available online at http://www.enotes.com/psychoanalysis-encyclopedia.

Moore, B., and Fine, B., eds. (1968). *A glossary of psychoanalytic terms and concepts* (2nd edition). New Haven, CT: Yale University Press.

Moore, B., and Fine, B., eds. (1990). *Psychoanalytic terms and concepts* (3rd edition). New Haven, CT: American Psychoanalytic Association.

Moore, B., and Fine, B., eds. (1995). *Psychoanalysis: The major concepts.* New Haven, CT: Yale University Press.

Nagera, H., ed. (1969/1971). *Basic psychoanalytic concepts.* New York: International Universities Press.

Nersessian, E., and Kopff, R., eds. (1996). *Textbook of psychoanalysis.* Washington, DC: American Psychiatric Press.

PDM Task Force. (2006). *Psychodynamic diagnostic manual.* Silver Spring, MD: Alliance of Psychoanalytic Organizations.

Person, E., Cooper, A. M., and Gabbard, G. (2005). *Textbook of psychoanalysis.* Washington, DC: American Psychiatric Publishing.

Rothstein, A., ed. (1987). *Models of the mind: Their relationship to clinical work.* Madison, CT: International Universities Press

Rycroft, C. (1968). *A critical dictionary of psychoanalysis.* New York: Basic Books.

Sandler, J., Dare, C., and Holder, A. (1992). *The patient and the analyst: The basis of psychoanalytic process* (2nd edition). Madison, CT: International Universities Press.

Skelton, R., ed. (2006). *The Edinburgh international encyclopedia of psychoanalysis.* Edinburgh, UK: Edinburgh University Press.

Spillius, E., Milton, J., Garvey, P., Couve, C., and Steiner, D., eds. (2011). *The new dictionary of Kleinian thought* (rev. edition of R. Hinshelwood's *A dictionary of Kleinian thought, 1991*). London: Routledge.

(We are especially grateful to the editors of this book for sharing it with us prior to publication.)

Sterba, R. (1936/1937). *Handwörterbuch der psychoanalyse.* Vienna: Internationaler Psychoanalytischer Verlag.

Strachey, A. (1943). A new German-English psycho-analytical vocabulary. *International Journal of Psychoanalysis,* 1 (S): 1–84.

Tuckett, D., and Levinson, N. A. (2010). PEP Consolidated Psychoanalytic Glossary. London: Psycho-analytic Electronic Publishing. Available online at http://www.pep-web.org/document.php?id=zbk .069.0000a.

Wolman, B., ed. (1977). *International encyclopedia of psychiatry, psychology, psychoanalysis, and neurology.* New York: Aesculapius Publishing.

Wolman, B., ed. (1996). *The encyclopedia of psychiatry, psychology, and psychoanalysis.* New York: Henry Holt.

REFERENCES

Works of Sigmund Freud cited from the *Standard Edition* are from Strachey, J., ed. (1953–1974) *The Standard Edition of the Complete Psychological Works of Sigmund Freud,* 24 vols. London: Hogarth Press and Institute of Psycho-Analysis.

Abelin, E. (1971). The role of the father in the separation-individuation process. In *Separation-individuation: Essays in honor of Margaret S. Mahler,* ed. J. McDevitt and C. Settlage (pp. 229–52). New York: International Universities Press.

Abelin, E. (1975). Some further observations and comments on the earliest role of the father. *International Journal of Psychoanalysis,* 56, 293–302.

Abend, S. (1979). Unconscious fantasy and theories of cures. *Journal of the American Psychoanalytic Association,* 27, 579–96.

Abend, S. (1984). Sibling love and object choice. *Psychoanalytic Quarterly,* 53, 425–30.

Abend, S. (2007). Therapeutic action in modern conflict theory. *Psychoanalytic Quarterly,* 76, 1417–42.

Abraham, K. (1911). Notes on the psychoanalytical investigation and treatment of manic-depressive insanity and allied conditions. In *Selected papers of Karl Abraham M.D.,* ed. E. Jones (pp. 137–56). London: Hogarth Press, 1948.

Abraham, K. (1916). The first pregenital stage of the libido. In *Selected papers of Karl Abraham M.D.,* ed. E. Jones (pp. 248–79). London: Hogarth Press, 1948.

Abraham, K. (1919). A particular form of neurotic resistance against the psycho-analytic method. In *Selected papers of Karl Abraham M.D.,* ed. E. Jones (pp. 303–11). London: Hogarth Press, 1948.

Abraham, K. (1921). Contributions to the theory of the anal character. In *Selected papers of Karl Abraham M.D.,* ed. E. Jones (pp. 370–92). London: Hogarth Press, 1948.

Abraham, K. (1924a). The influence of oral eroticism on character-formation. In *Selected papers of Karl Abraham M.D.,* ed. E. Jones (pp. 393–406). London: Hogarth Press, 1948.

Abraham, K. (1924b). A short study of the development of the libido, viewed in the light of mental disorders. In *Selected papers of Karl Abraham M.D.,* ed. E. Jones (pp. 418–501). London: Hogarth Press, 1948.

Abraham, K. (1924c). Letter from Karl Abraham to Sigmund Freud, November 12, 1924. In *The complete correspondence of Sigmund Freud to Karl Abraham, 1907–1925,* ed. S. Freud and K. Abraham (pp. 521–22). London: Karnac Books.

Abraham, K. (1925a). Character-formation on the genital level of the libido. In *Selected papers of Karl Abraham M.D.,* ed. E. Jones (pp. 407–17). London: Hogarth Press, 1948.

Abraham, K. (1925b). The history of an impostor in the light of psychoanalytical knowledge. In *Clinical papers and essays on psycho-analysis,* ed. H. Abraham (vol. 2, pp. 291–305). New York: Basic Books, 1956.

Abram, J. (2007). *The language of Winnicott: A dictionary of Winnicott's use of words.* London: Karnac Books.

Abrams, S. (1977). The genetic point of view: Antecedents and transformations. *Journal of the American Psychoanalytic Association,* 25, 417–25.

Abrams, S. (1983). Development. *Psychoanalytic Study of the Child,* 38, 113–39.

Abrams, S. (1987). The psychoanalytic process: A schematic model. *International Journal of Psychoanalysis,* 68, 441–52.

Adler, A. (1908). Der aggressionstrieb im leben und in der neurose. *Fortschritte der Medizin,* 226, 577–84.

Adler, A. (1924). *Individual psychology.* New York: Harcourt, Brace.

Adler, A. (1925). *The practice and theory of individual psychology.* London: Kegan Paul.

Adler, A. (1927). Feelings of inferiority and the striving for recognition. *Proceedings of the Royal Society of Medicine,* 20, 1181–1886.

Adler, G. (1979). The myth of the alliance with borderline patients. *American Journal of Psychiatry,* 136, 642–45.

Adler, G., and Buie, D., Jr. (1979). Aloneness and borderline psychopathology: The possible relevance of child development issues. *International Journal of Psychoanalysis,* 60, 83–96.

Adolphs, R. (2003). Cognitive neuroscience of human social behavior. *Nature Reviews Neuroscience,* 4, 165–78.

Aichhorn, A. (1925). *Wayward youth.* New York: Viking Press, 1965.

Ainsworth, M., Blehar, M., Waters, E., and Wall, S. (1978). *Patterns of attachment: Psychological study of the strange situation.* Mahwah, NJ: Lawrence Erlbaum Associates.

Akhtar, S. (1988). Some reflections on the theory of psychopathology and personality development in Kohut's self psychology. In *New concepts in psychoanalytic psychotherapy,* ed. J. Ross and W. Myers (pp. 227–52). Washington, DC: American Psychiatric Press.

Akhtar, S. (1994). Object constancy and adult psychopathology. *International Journal of Psychoanalysis,* 75, 441–55.

Akhtar, S. (1995). A third individuation: Immigration, identity, and the psychoanalytic process. *Journal of the American Psychoanalytic Association,* 43, 1051–84.

Akhtar, S. (1996). "Someday . . ." and "if only . . ." fantasies: Pathological optimism and inordinate nostalgia as related forms of idealization. *Journal of the American Psychoanalytic Association,* 44, 723–53.

Akhtar, S. (1999). The distinction between needs and wishes: Implications for psychoanalytic theory and technique. *Journal of the American Psychoanalytic Association,* 47, 113–57.

Akhtar, S. (2009). *Comprehensive dictionary of psychoanalysis.* London: Karnac Books.

Alexander, B., Feigelson, S., and Gorman, J. (2005). Integrating the psychoanalytic and neurobiological views of panic disorder. *Neuropsychoanalysis,* 7, 129–41.

Alexander, F. (1950a). Analysis of the therapeutic factors in psychoanalytic treatment. *Psychoanalytic Quarterly,* 19, 482–500.

Alexander, F. (1950b). *Psychosomatic medicine.* New York: W. W. Norton.

Alexander, F., and French, T. (1946). *Psychoanalytic therapy: Principles and application.* New York: Ronald Press.

Allegro, L. (1990). On the formulation of interpretations. *International Journal of Psychoanalysis,* 71, 421–33.

Altman, N., Briggs, R., Frankel, J., Gensler, D., and Pantone, P. (2002). *Relational child psychotherapy.* New York: Other Press.

Ambrosio, G. (2009). *Transvestism, transsexualism in the psychoanalytic dimension.* London: Karnac Books.

American Psychiatric Association. (1981). *Diagnostic and statistical manual of mental disorders* (3rd edition, text revision). Washington, DC: APA Press.

American Psychiatric Association. (1994). *Diagnostic and statistical manual of mental disorder* (4th edition). Washington, DC: APA Press.

Amsterdam, B., and Levitt, M. (1980). Consciousness of self and painful self-consciousness. *Psychoanalytic Study of the Child,* 35, 67–83.

Anderson, M., Ochsner, K., Kuhl, B., Cooper, J., Robertson, E., Gabrieli, S., Glover, G., and Gabrieli, J. (2004). Neural systems underlying the suppression of unwanted memories. *Science,* 303, 232–35.

Andreas-Salome, L. (1916). "Anal" und "sexual." *American Imago,* 4, 249.

Angel, A. (1934). Some remarks on optimism. *Internationale Zeitschrift für Psychoanalyse,* 20 (2), 191–99.

Applegarth, A., and Wolfson, A. (1987). Panel report: Toward the further understanding of homosexual women. *Journal of the American Psychoanalytic Association,* 35, 165–73.

Apprey, M. (1988). Concluding remarks: From an inchoate sense of entitlement to a mature attitude of entitlement. In *Attitudes of entitlement,* ed. V. Volkan and T. Rodgers. Charlottesville, VA: University Press of Virginia.

Aragno, A. (1997). *Symbolization: Proposing a developmental paradigm for a new psychoanalytic theory of mind.* Madison, CT: International Universities Press.

Arieti, S. (1967). *The intrapsychic self: Feeling, cognition, and creativity in health and mental illness.* New York: Basic Books.

Arieti, S. (1976). *Creativity: The magic synthesis.* New York: Basic Books.

Arlow, J. (1953). Masturbation and symptom formation. *Journal of the American Psychoanalytic Association,* 1, 45–58.

Arlow, J. (1958). Panel: The psychoanalytic theory of thinking. *Journal of the American Psychoanalytic Association,* 6, 145–53.

Arlow, J. (1969a). Fantasy, memory, and reality testing. *Psychoanalytic Quarterly,* 38, 28–51.

Arlow, J. (1969b). Unconscious fantasy and disturbances of conscious experience. *Psychoanalytic Quarterly,* 38, 1–27.

Arlow, J. (1971). Character perversion. In *Currents in psychoanalysis,* ed. I. Marcus (pp. 317–36). New York: International Universities Press.

Arlow, J. (1980). The revenge motive in the primal scene. *Journal of the American Psychoanalytic Association,* 28, 519–41.

Arlow, J. (1986). The poet as prophet: A psychoanalytic perspective. *Psychoanalytic Quarterly,* 55, 53–68.

Arlow, J. (1995). Unconscious fantasy. In *Psychoanalysis: The major concepts,* ed. B. Moore and B. Fine (pp. 155–62). New Haven, CT: Yale University Press.

Arlow, J. (1996). The concept of psychic reality—How useful? *International Journal of Psychoanalysis,* 77, 659–66.

Arlow, J., and Brenner, C. (1960). The concept "preconscious" and the structural theory: Meetings of the New York psychoanalytic society. *Psychoanalytic Quarterly, 29,* 447–48.

Arlow, J., and Brenner, C. (1964). *Psychoanalytic concepts and the structural theory.* New York: International Universities Press.

Arlow, J., and Brenner, C. (1990). The psychoanalytic process. *Psychoanalytic Quarterly, 59,* 678–92.

Arntz, A., and Veen, G. (2001). Evaluations of others by borderline patients. *Journal of Nervous and Mental Disease, 189* (8), 513–21.

Aron, L. (1990). Free association and changing models of mind. *Journal of the American Psychoanalytic Association, 18,* 439–59.

Aron, L. (1991). The patient's experience of the analyst's subjectivity. *Psychoanalytic Dialogues, 1,* 29–51.

Aron, L. (1992). From Ferenczi to Searles and contemporary relational approaches: Commentary on Mark Blechner's "Working in the countertransference." *Psychoanalytic Dialogues, 2,* 181–90.

Aron, L. (1996). *A meeting of minds: Mutuality in psychoanalysis.* Hillsdale, NJ: Analytic Press.

Atwood, G., and Stolorow, R. (1984). *Structures of subjectivity: Explorations in psychoanalytic phenomenology.* Hillsdale, NJ: Analytic Press.

Auchincloss, E., and Vaughan, S. (2001). Psychoanalysis and homosexuality: Do we need a new theory? *Journal of the American Psychoanalytic Association, 49,* 1157–86.

Auchincloss, E., and Weiss, R. (1992). Paranoid character and the intolerance of indifference. *Journal of the American Psychoanalytic Association, 40,* 1013–37.

Auerbach, J., and Blatt, S. (1996). Self-representation in severe psychopathology: The role of reflexive self-awareness. *Psychoanalytic Psychology, 13,* 297–341.

Auerhahn, N., and Laub, D. (1998). Intergenerational memory of the holocaust. In *International handbook of multigenerational legacies of trauma,* ed. Y. Danieli (pp. 21–41). New York: Plenum Press.

Bacal, H. (1985). Optimal responsiveness and the therapeutic process. *Progress in Self Psychology, 1,* 202–27.

Bacal, H. (1988). Reflections on "Optimum frustration." *Progress in Self Psychology, 4,* 127–31.

Bacal, H. (1998). Introduction: Relational self psychology. *Progress in Self Psychology, 14,* xiii–xviii.

Bacal, H., and Herzog, B. (2003). Specificity theory and optimal responsiveness: An outline. *Psychoanalytic Psychology, 20,* 635–48.

Bacal, H., and Thomson, P. (1996). The psychoanalyst's selfobject needs and the effect of their frustration on the treatment: A new view of countertransference. *Progress in Self Psychology, 12,* 17–35.

Bach, S. (1975). Narcissism, continuity and the uncanny. *International Journal of Psychoanalysis, 56,* 77–86.

Bachrach, H. (1983). On the concept of analyzability. *Psychoanalytic Quarterly, 52,* 180–203.

Bachrach, H., Galatzer-Levy, R., Skolnikoff, A., and Waldron, S. (1991). On the efficacy of psychoanalysis. *Journal of the American Psychoanalytic Association, 39,* 871–916.

Bachrach, H., and Leaff, L. (1978). "Analyzability": A systematic review of the clinical and quantitative literature. *Journal of the American Psychoanalytic Association, 26,* 881–920.

Bak, R. (1956). Aggression and perversion. In *Psychodynamics and therapy,* ed. S. Lorand and M. Balint (pp. 231–40). New York: Gramercy Publications.

Bak, R. (1968). The phallic woman: The ubiquitous fantasy in perversions. *Psychoanalytic Study of the Child, 23,* 15–16.

Bak, R. (1973). Being in love and object loss. *International Journal of Psychoanalysis, 54,* 1–7.

Balint, A. (1949). Love for the mother and mother-love. *International Journal of Psychoanalysis, 30,* 251–59.

Balint, M. (1935). Critical notes on the pregenital organization of the libido. In *Primary love and psychoanalytic technique,* ed. M. Balint (pp. 49–72). London: Hogarth Press and Institute of Psycho-Analysis, 1952.

Balint, M. (1948) On genital love. In *Primary love and psycho-analytic technique,* ed. M. Balint (pp.128–40). London: Hogarth Press and Institute of Psycho-Analysis, 1952.

Balint, M. (1950). Changing therapeutical aims and techniques in psycho-analysis. *International Journal of Psychoanalysis, 31,* 117–24.

Balint, M. (1952). *Primary love and psycho-analytic technique.* London: Hogarth Press and Institute of Psycho-Analysis.

Balint, M. (1968). *The basic fault: Therapeutic acts of regression.* London: Tavistock Publications.

Balsam, R. (2001). Integrating male and female elements in a woman's gender identity. *Journal of the American Psychoanalytic Association, 49,* 1335–60.

Baratis, S. (1988). The personal myth as a defense against internal primitive aggression. *International Journal of Psychoanalysis, 69,* 475–82.

Barnett, J. (1966). On cognitive disorders in the obsessional. *Contemporary Psychoanalysis, 2,* 122–33.

Barnett, J. (1980a). Cognitive repair in the treatment of the neuroses. *Journal of the American Psychoanalytic Association, 8,* 39–55.

Barnett, J. (1980b). Interpersonal processes, cognition, and the analysis of character. *Contemporary Psychoanalysis, 16,* 397–416.

Barocas, H., and Barocas, C. (1979). Wounds of the fathers: The next generation of Holocaust victims. *International Review of Psycho-Analysis,* 6, 331–40.

Bartlett, F. (1932). *Remembering: A study in experimental and social psychology.* Cambridge, UK: Cambridge University Press.

Bartlett, N., Vassey, P., and Bukowski, W. (2000). Is gender identity disorder in children a mental disorder? *Sex Roles,* 33, 753–85.

Bartsch, K., and Wellman, H. (1995). *Children talk about the mind.* Oxford: Oxford University Press.

Basch, M. (1976). The concept of affect: A reexamination. *Journal of the American Psychoanalytic Association,* 24, 759–77.

Basch, M. (1978). Psychic determinism and freedom of will. *International Review of Psycho-Analysis,* 5, 257–64.

Basch, M. (1983a). Empathic understanding: A review of the concept and some theoretical considerations. *Journal of the American Psychoanalytic Association,* 31, 101–26.

Basch, M. (1983b). The perception of reality and the disavowal of meaning. *The Annual of Psychoanalysis,* 11, 125–53.

Bass, A. (2001). It takes one to know one; or, whose unconscious is it anyway? *Psychoanalytic Dialogues,* 11, 683–702.

Bass, A. (2003). "E" enactments in psychoanalysis: Another medium, another message. *Psychoanalytic Dialogues,* 13, 657–75.

Bassin, D. (1996). Beyond the he and the she: Toward the reconciliation of masculinity and femininity in the postoedipal female mind. *Journal of the American Psychoanalytic Association,* 44 (S), 157–90.

Bateman, A., and Fonagy, P. (2004). *Psychotherapy for borderline personality disorder: Mentalization-based treatment.* Oxford: Oxford University Press.

Bateman, A., and Fonagy, P. (2006). *Mentalization-based treatment for borderline personality disorder: A practical guide.* Oxford: Oxford University Press.

Baudry, F. (1984). Character: A concept in search of an identity. *Journal of the American Psychoanalytic Association,* 32, 455–77.

Bayer, R. (1981). *Homosexuality and American psychiatry: The politics of diagnosis.* New York: Basic Books.

Beebe, B. (2005). Mother-infant research informs mother-infant treatment. *Psychoanalytic Study of the Child,* 60, 7–46.

Beebe, B., Jaffe, J., Buck, K., Chen, H., Cohen, P., Feldstein, S., and Andrews, H. (2008). Six-week postpartum depressive symptoms and 4-month mother-infant self- and interactive contingency. *Infant Mental Health Journal,* 29 (5), 442–71.

Beebe, B., Jaffe, J., and Lachmann, F. (1992). A dyadic systems view of communication. In *Relational perspectives in psychoanalysis,* ed. N. Skolnick and S. Warshaw (pp. 61–81). Hillsdale, NJ: Analytic Press.

Beebe, B., and Lachmann, F. (1988). The contribution of mother-infant mutual influence to the origins of self- and object representations. *Psychoanalytic Psychology,* 5, 305–37.

Beebe, B., and Lachmann, F. (1998). Co-constructing inner and relational processes: Self- and mutual regulation in infant research and adult treatment. *Psychoanalytic Psychology,* 15, 480–516.

Beebe, B., and Lachmann, F. (2003). The relational turn in psychoanalysis: A dyadic systems view from infant research. *Contemporary Psychoanalysis,* 39, 379–409.

Beebe, B., Lachmann, F., and Jaffe, J. (1997). Mother-infant interaction structures and presymbolic self- and object representations. *Psychoanalytic Dialogues,* 7, 133–82.

Beebe, B., and Stern, D. N. (1977). Engagement-disengagement and early object experience. In *Communicative structure and psychic structures,* ed. M. Freedman and S. Grenel (pp. 33–55). New York: Plenum Press.

Behrends, R., and Blatt, S. (1985). Internalization and psychological development throughout the life cycle. *Psychoanalytic Study of the Child,* 40, 11–39.

Bell, D. (1997). *Reason and passion: A celebration of the work of Hanna Segal.* London: Duckworth.

Bell, D. (1999). *Psychoanalysis and culture: A Kleinian perspective.* London: Duckworth.

Bell, D. (2001). Projective identification. In *Kleinian theory: A contemporary perspective,* ed. C. Bronstein (pp. 125–47). London: Whurr Books.

Bell, D. (2008). La pulsion di morte: Prospettive nella teoria Kleiniana contemporanea. *Revista di Psicoanalisi,* 54, 707–26.

Bellak, L., Hurvich, M., and Gediman, H. (1973). *Ego functions in schizophrenics, neurotics, and normals: A systematic study of conceptual, diagnostic, and therapeutic aspects.* New York: John Wiley and Sons.

Benedict, T. (1976). On the psychobiology of gender identity. *Annual of Psychoanalysis,* 4, 117–62.

Benjamin, H. (1966). *The transsexual phenomenon.* New York: Julian Press.

Benjamin, J. (1988). *The bonds of love: Psychoanalysis, feminism, and the problem of domination.* New York: Pantheon.

Benjamin, J. (1990). An outline of intersubjectivity: The development of recognition. *Psychoanalytic Psychology,* 7 (S), 33–46.

Benjamin, J. (1997). *The shadow of the other.* New York: Routledge.

Beratis, S. (1988). The personal myth as a defense against internal primitive aggression. *International Journal of Psychoanalysis*, 69, 475–82.

Beres, D. (1957). New directions in psychoanalysis: The significance of infant conflict in the pattern of adult behavior. *Psychoanalytic Quarterly*, 26, 406–11.

Beres, D. and Arlow, J. (1974). Fantasy and identification in empathy. *Psychoanalytic Quarterly*, 43, 26–50.

Berg, M. (1977). The externalizing transference. *International Journal of Psychoanalysis*, 58, 235–44.

Bergler, E. (1934). The psycho-analysis of the uncanny. *International Journal of Psychoanalysis*, 15, 215–44.

Bergler, E. (1938). Preliminary phases of the masculine beating fantasy. *Psychoanalytic Quarterly*, 7, 514–36.

Bergler, E. (1948a). *The battle of the conscience: A psychiatric study of the inner-working of the conscience.* Oxford: Monumental Printing.

Bergler, E. (1948b). Further studies on beating fantasies. *Psychoanalytic Quarterly*, 22, 480–86.

Bergler, E. (1949). *The basic neurosis: Oral regression and psychic masochism.* Oxford: Grune and Stratton.

Bergler, E. (1956). On "negative" exhibitionism. *Psychoanalytic Review*, 43, 454–57.

Bergler, E. (1961). *Curable and incurable neurotics: Problems of "neurotic" versus "malignant" psychic masochism.* New York: Liveright.

Bergman, A., and Harpaz-Rotem, I. (2004). Revisiting rapprochement in the light of contemporary developmental theories. *Journal of the American Psychoanalytic Association*, 52, 555–70.

Bergmann, M. (1971). Psychoanalytic observations on the capacity to love. In *Separation-individuation: Essays in honor of Margaret S. Mahler*, ed. J. McDevitt and C. Settlage. New York: International Universities Press.

Bergmann, M. (1980). On the intrapsychic function of falling in love. *Psychoanalytic Quarterly*, 49, 56–77.

Bergmann, M. (1982). Platonic love, transference love, and love in real life. *Journal of the American Psychoanalytic Association*, 30, 87–111.

Bergmann, M. (1987). *The anatomy of loving: The story of man's quest to know what love is.* New York: Columbia University Press.

Bergmann, M. (1988). Freud's three theories of love in the light of later development. *Journal of the American Psychoanalytic Association*, 36, 653–72.

Bergmann, M. (1995). On love and its enemies. *Psychoanalytic Review*, 82, 1–19.

Bergmann, M. (1997). Termination: The Achilles heel of psychoanalytic technique. *Psychoanalytic Psychology*, 14, 163–74.

Berliner, B. (1942). The concept of masochism. *Psychoanalytic Review*, 29, 386–400.

Bernfeld, S. (1944). Freud's earliest theories and the school of Helmholtz. *Psychoanalytic Quarterly*, 13, 341–62.

Bernstein, D. (1983). The female superego: A different perspective. *International Journal of Psychoanalysis*, 64, 187–201.

Bernstein, D. (1990). Female genital anxieties, conflicts and typical mastery modes. *International Journal of Psychoanalysis*, 71, 151–65.

Bernstein, D. (1993). *Female identity conflict in clinical practice.* Northvale, NJ: Jason Aronson.

Bernstein, I. (1975). Integrative aspects of masturbation. In *Masturbation: From infancy to senescence*, ed. I. Marcus and J. Francis (pp. 53–76). New York: International Universities Press.

Bernstein, P. (2004). Mothers and daughters from today's psychoanalytic perspective. *Psychoanalytic Inquiry*, 24, 601–28.

Bers, S., Blatt, S., Sayward, H., and Johnston, R. (1993). Normal and pathological aspects of self-descriptions and their change over long-term treatment. *Psychoanalytic Psychology*, 10, 17–37.

Bettelheim, B. (1983). *Freud and man's soul.* London: Chatto and Windus.

Bibring, E. (1937). Discussion of the concept of therapeutic alliance. In Symposium on the theory of the therapeutic results of psycho-analysis. *International Journal of Psychoanalysis*, 18, 125–89.

Bibring, E. (1954). Psychoanalysis and the dynamic psychotherapies. *Journal of the American Psychoanalytic Association*, 2, 745–70.

Bibring, G., Dwyer, T., Huntington, D., and Valenstein, A. (1961). A study of the psychological processes in pregnancy and of the earliest mother-child relationship—I. Some propositions and comments. *Psychoanalytic Study of the Child*, 16, 9–24.

Bick, E. (1986). Further considerations of the function of the skin in early object relations. *British Journal of Psychotherapy*, 2, 292–99.

Billow, R. (1999). An intersubjective approach to entitlement. *Psychoanalytic Quarterly*, 68, 441–61.

Bion, W. (1956/1967). Development of schizophrenic thought. *International Journal of Psychoanalysis*, 37, 344–46.

Bion, W. (1957). Differentiation of the psychotic from the non-psychotic personalities. *International Journal of Psychoanalysis*, 38, 266–75.

Bion, W. (1959). Attacks on linking. *International Journal of Psychoanalysis*, 40, 308–15.

Bion, W. (1961). *Experience in groups.* London: Tavistock.

Bion, W. (1962a). *Learning from experience.* London: Heinemann.

Bion, W. (1962b). The psycho-analytic study of thinking—II. A theory of thinking. *International Journal of Psychoanalysis*, 43, 306–10.

Bion, W. (1963). *Elements of psycho-analysis*. London: Heinemann.

Bion, W. (1965). *Transformations: Change from learning to growth*. London: Tavistock.

Bion, W. (1967). *Second thoughts: Selected papers on psycho-analysis*. London: Heinemann.

Bion, W. (1970). *Attention and interpretation: A scientific approach to insight in psycho-analysis and groups*. London: Tavistock.

Bion, W. (1991). *A memoir of the future*. London: Karnac Books.

Bird, B. (1972). Notes on transference: Universal phenomenon and hardest part of analysis. *Journal of the American Psychoanalytic Association*, 20, 267–301.

Birksted-Breen, D. (1996). Unconscious representation of femininity. *Journal of the American Psychoanalytic Association*, 44 (S), 119–32.

Blacker, K., and Tupin, J. (1977). Hysteria and hysterical structures: Developmental and social theories. In *Hysterical personality style and the histrionic personality disorder*, ed. M. Horowitz (pp. 17–66). Lanham, MD: Jason Aronson.

Blackman, J. (2004). *101 defenses: How the mind shields itself*. New York: Brunner/Routledge.

Blatt, S. (1974). Levels of object representation in anaclitic and introjective depression. *Psychoanalytic Study of the Child*, 24, 107–57.

Blatt, S., Auerbach, J., and Levy, K. (1997). Mental representations in personality development, psychopathology, and the therapeutic process. *Review of General Psychology*, 1, 351–74.

Blatt, S., Brenneis, L., Schimek, J., and Glick, M. (1976). Normal development and the psychopathological impairment of the concept of the object on the Rorschach. *Journal of Abnormal Psychology*, 85, 364–73.

Blatt, S., and Lerner, H. (1983). Investigations in the psychoanalytic theory of object relations and object representations. In *Empirical studies of psychoanalytic theories*, ed. F. Masling (pp. 189–249). Hillsdale, NJ: Lawrence Erlbaum Associates.

Blechner, M. (1987). Panel II. Entitlement and narcissism: Paradise sought. *Contemporary Psychoanalysis*, 23, 244–54.

Blechner, M. (2001). *The dream frontier*. Hillsdale, NJ: Analytic Press.

Blechner, M. (2005). The gay Harry Stack Sullivan: Interactions between his life, clinical work, and theory. *Contemporary Psychoanalysis*, 41, 1–20.

Bleiberg, E. (2003). Treating professionals in crisis: A framework based on promoting mentalization. *Bulletin of the Menninger Clinic*, 67, 212–26.

Bleuler, E. (1910). Vortrag über Ambivalenz. *Zentralblatt für Psychoanalyse*, 1, 266.

Blos, P. (1962). *On adolescence*. New York: Free Press.

Blos, P. (1968). Character formation in adolescence. *Psychoanalytic Study of the Child*, 23, 245–63.

Blos, P. (1972). The epigenesis of the adult neurosis. *Psychoanalytic Study of the Child*, 27, 106–35.

Blos, P. (1974). The genealogy of the ego ideal. *Psychoanalytic Study of the Child*, 29, 43–88.

Blos, P. (1979a). Prolonged male adolescence. In *The adolescent passage*. New York: International Universities Press.

Blos, P. (1979b). *The adolescent passage*. New York: International Universities Press.

Blum, E., and Blum, H. (1990). The development of autonomy and superego precursors. *International Journal of Psychoanalysis*, 71, 585–95.

Blum, H. (1973). The concept of erotized transference. *Journal of the American Psychoanalytic Association*, 21, 61–76.

Blum, H. (1976a). The changing use of dreams in psychoanalytic practice—Dreams and free association. *International Journal of Psychoanalysis*, 57, 315–24.

Blum, H. (1976b). Masochism, the ego ideal, and the psychology of women. *Journal of the American Psychoanalytic Association*, 24 (S), 157–91.

Blum, H. (1978). Symbolic processes and symbol formation. *International Journal of Psychoanalysis*, 59, 455–71.

Blum, H. (1979a). Foreword. *Journal of the American Psychoanalytic Association*, 27 (S), 5–17.

Blum, H. (1979b). On the concept and consequences of the primal scene. *Psychoanalytic Quarterly*, 48, 27–47.

Blum, H. (1980a). Paranoia and beating fantasy: An inquiry into the psychoanalytic theory of paranoia. *Journal of the American Psychoanalytic Association*, 28, 331–61.

Blum, H. (1980b). The value of reconstruction in adult psychoanalysis. *International Journal of Psychoanalysis*, 61, 39–52.

Blum, H. (1981). Object inconstancy and paranoid conspiracy. *Journal of the American Psychoanalytic Association*, 29, 789–813.

Blum, H. (1983). The position and value of extratransference interpretation. *Journal of the American Psychoanalytic Association*, 31, 587–617.

Blum, H. (1985). Superego formation, adolescent transformation, and the adult neurosis. *Journal of the American Psychoanalytic Association*, 33, 887–909.

Blum, H. (1989). The concept of the termination and the evolution of psychoanalytic thought. *Journal of the American Psychoanalytic Association*, 37, 275–95.

Blum, H. (1996). Female psychology in progress. *Journal of the American Psychoanalytic Association, 44* (S), 3–9.

Blum, H. (2000). The writing and interpretation of dreams. *Psychoanalytic Psychology, 17*, 651–66.

Blum, H. (2001). The "exceptions" reviewed: The formation and deformation of the privileged character. *Psychoanalytic Study of the Child, 56*, 123–36.

Blum, H. (2003). Response to Peter Fonagy. *International Journal of Psychoanalysis, 84*, 509–13.

Blum, H. (2004). Separation-individuation theory and attachment theory. *Journal of the American Psychoanalytic Association, 52*, 535–53.

Boehm, F. (1930). The femininity-complex in men. *International Journal of Psychoanalysis, 11*, 444–69.

Boesky, D. (1982). Acting out: A reconsideration of the concept. *International Journal of Psychoanalysis, 63*, 39–55.

Boesky, D. (1988). The concept of psychic structure. *Journal of the American Psychoanalytic Association, 36*, 113–35.

Boesky, D. (1990). The psychoanalytic process and its components. *Psychoanalytic Quarterly, 59*, 550–84.

Bonime, W. (1962). *The clinical use of dreams.* New York: Basic Books.

Bonovitz, C. (2009). Looking back, looking forward: A reexamination of Benjamin Wolstein's interlock and the emergence of intersubjectivity. *International Journal of Psychoanalysis, 90*, 463–85.

Book Notices. (1970a). *International Journal of Psychoanalysis, 51*, 558–59.

Book Notices. (1970b). *Journal of the American Psychoanalytic Association, 18*, 736–38.

Bornstein, B. (1945). Clinical notes on child analysis. *Psychoanalytic Study of the Child, 1*, 151–66.

Bornstein, B. (1949). The analysis of a phobic child—Some problems of theory and technique in child analysis. *Psychoanalytic Study of the Child, 3*, 181–226.

Bornstein, B. (1951). On latency. *Psychoanalytic Study of the Child, 6*, 279–85.

Bornstein, B. (1953). Masturbation in the latency period. *Psychoanalytic Study of the Child, 8*, 65–78.

Boston Change Process Study Group. (2002). Explicating the implicit: The local level and the microprocess of change in the analytic situation. *International Journal of Psychoanalysis, 83*, 1051–62.

Bouchard, M., Target, M., Lecours, S., Fonagy, P., Tremblay, L., Schachter, A., and Stein, H. (2008). Mentalization in adult attachment narratives: Reflective functioning, mental states, and affect elaboration compared. *Psychoanalytic Psychology, 25*, 47–66.

Bowlby, J. (1944). Forty-four juvenile thieves: Their characters and home-life. *International Journal of Psychoanalysis, 25*, 19–53, 107–28.

Bowlby, J. (1951). *Maternal care and maternal health.* Geneva: World Health Organization.

Bowlby, J. (1958). The nature of the child's tie to his mother. *International Journal of Psychoanalysis, 39*, 350–73.

Bowlby, J. (1960a). Grief and mourning in infancy and early childhood. *Psychoanalytic Study of the Child, 15*, 9–52.

Bowlby, J. (1960b). Separation anxiety. *International Journal of Psychoanalysis, 41*, 89–113.

Bowlby, J. (1961). Processes of mourning. *International Journal of Psychoanalysis, 42*, 317–40.

Bowlby, J. (1963). Pathological mourning and childhood mourning. *Journal of the American Psychoanalytic Association, 11*, 500–41.

Bowlby, J. (1969/1982). *Attachment and loss: Attachment* (vol. 1). New York: Basic Books.

Bowlby, J. (1973). *Attachment and loss: Separation* (vol. 2). New York: Basic Books.

Bowlby, J. (1980). *Attachment and loss: Loss* (vol. 3). New York: Basic Books

Brakel, L. (1997). Commentary on Solms's What is consciousness? *Journal of the American Psychoanalytic Association, 45*, 714–20.

Brakel, L. (2004). The psychoanalytic assumption of the primary process: Extrapsychoanalytic evidence and finding. *Journal of the American Psychoanalytic Association, 52*, 1131–1161.

Brakel, L., Kleinsorge, S., Snodgrass, M., and Shevrin, H. (2000). The primary process and the unconscious: Experimental evidence supporting two psychoanalytic presuppositions. *Journal of the American Psychoanalytic Association, 81*, 553–69.

Brakel, L., Shevrin, H., and Villa, K. (2002). The priority of primary process categorizing. *Journal of the American Psychoanalytic Association, 50*, 483–505.

Brandchaft, B. (1993). To free the spirit from its cell. *Progress in Self Psychology, 9*, 209–30.

Braun, A. (1999). The new neuropsychology of sleep commentary. *Neuropsychoanalysis, 1*, 196–201.

Brenman, E. (1985). Hysteria. *International Journal of Psychoanalysis, 66*, 423–32.

Brenner, C. (1955). *An elementary textbook of psychoanalysis.* New York: International Universities Press.

Brenner, C. (1959). The masochistic character: Genesis and treatment. *Journal of the American Psychoanalytic Association, 7*, 197–226.

Brenner, C. (1968). Psychoanalysis and science. *Journal of the American Psychoanalytic Association, 16*, 675–96.

Brenner, C. (1971). The psychoanalytic concept of aggression. *International Journal of Psychoanalysis, 52*, 137–44.

Brenner, C. (1974). Depression, anxiety and affect theory. *International Journal of Psychoanalysis,* 55, 25–32.

Brenner, C. (1975). Affects and psychic conflict. *Psychoanalytic Quarterly,* 44, 5–28.

Brenner, C. (1979). Working alliance, therapeutic alliance, and transference. *Journal of the American Psychoanalytic Association,* 27 (S), 137–57.

Brenner, C. (1980). Metapsychology and psychoanalytic theory. *Psychoanalytic Quarterly,* 49, 189–214.

Brenner, C. (1982). *The mind in conflict.* Madison, CT: International Universities Press.

Brenner, C. (1987). Working through, 1914–1984. *Psychoanalytic Quarterly,* 56, 88–108.

Brenner, C. (2002). Conflict, compromise formation, and structural theory. *Psychoanalytic Quarterly,* 71, 397–417.

Brenner, C. (2003). Is the structural model still useful? *International Journal of Psychoanalysis,* 84, 1093–96.

Brenner, C. (2006). *Psychoanalysis or mind and meaning.* New York: Psychoanalytic Quarterly.

Brenner, C. (2008). Aspects of psychoanalytic theory: Drives, defense, and the pleasure-unpleasure principle. *Psychoanalytic Quarterly,* 77, 707–17.

Brenner, I. (1994). The dissociative character: A reconsideration of "multiple personality." *Journal of the American Psychoanalytic Association,* 42, 819–46.

Bretherton, I. (1992). The origins of attachment theory: John Bowlby and Mary Ainsworth. *Developmental Psychology,* 28, 759–75.

Bretherton, I., McNew, S., and Beeghly-Smith, M. (1981). Early person knowledge as expressed in gestural and verbal communication: When do infants acquire a "theory of mind"? In *Infant social cognition: Empirical and theoretical considerations,* ed. M. E. Lamb and L. R. Sherrod (pp. 333–74). Hillsdale, NJ: Lawrence Erlbaum Associates.

Breuer, J., and Freud, S. (1893). On the psychical mechanism of hysterical phenomena. *Standard Edition,* 2, 1–17.

Breuer, J., and Freud, S. (1893/1895). Studies on hysteria. *Standard Edition,* 2, 1–335.

Brierley, M. (1945). Further notes on the implications of psycho-analysis: Metapsychology and personology. *International Journal of Psychoanalysis,* 26, 89–114.

Brierley, M. (1953). Developments in psycho-analysis. *International Journal of Psychoanalysis,* 34, 158–60.

Brill, A. (1914). *Psychoanalysis: Its theories and practical application* (2nd edition). London: W. B. Saunders.

Britton, R. (1989). The missing link: Parental sexuality in the oedipus complex. In *The oedipus complex today: Clinical implications,* ed. R. Britton, M.

Feldman, and E. O'Shaughnessy (pp. 83–101). London: Karnac Books.

Brody, M. (1956). Clinical manifestations of ambivalence. *Psychoanalytic Quarterly,* 25, 505–14.

Bromberg, P. (1984). On the occurrence of the Isakower phenomenon in a schizoid disorder. *Contemporary Psychoanalysis,* 20, 600–24.

Bromberg, P. (1991). On knowing one's patient inside out: The aesthetics of unconscious communication. *Psychoanalytic Dialogues,* 1, 399–422.

Bromberg, P. (1998a). *Standing in the spaces: Essays on clinical process, trauma, and dissociation.* Hillsdale, NJ: Analytic Press.

Bromberg, P. (1998b). Staying the same while changing: Reflections on clinical judgment. *Psychoanalytic Dialogues,* 8, 225–36.

Bromberg, P. (2006). *Awakening the dreamer: Clinical journeys.* Hillsdale, NJ: Analytic Press.

Bromberg, W. (1948). Dynamic aspects of psychopathic personality. *Psychoanalytic Quarterly,* 17, 58–70.

Brothers, D., and Lewinberg, E. (1999). The therapeutic partnership: A developmental view of self-psychological treatment as bilateral healing. *Progress in Self Psychology,* 15, 259–84.

Broucek, F. (1982). Shame and its relationship to early narcissistic developments. *International Journal of Psychoanalysis,* 63, 369–78.

Broucek, F. (1991). *Shame and the self.* New York: Guilford Press.

Brunswick, R. (1940). The preoedipal phase of the libido development. *Psychoanalytic Quarterly,* 9, 239–319.

Bucci, W. (1997). *Psychoanalysis and cognitive science: Multiple code theory.* New York: Guilford Press.

Bucci, W. (2001). Pathways of emotional communication. *Psychoanalytic Inquiry,* 21, 40–70.

Bucci, W. (2005). Process research. In *Textbook of psychoanalysis,* ed. E. Person, A. Cooper, and G. Gabbard (pp. 317–34). Washington, DC: American Psychiatric Publishing.

Bucci, W. (2007). Dissociation from the perspective of multiple code theory: Part 1, Psychological roots and implications for psychoanalytic treatment. *Contemporary Psychoanalysis,* 43, 165–84.

Buechler, S. (2004). *Clinical values: Emotions that guide psychoanalytic treatment.* New York: Routledge.

Buechler, S. (2008). *Making a difference in patients' lives: Emotional experience in the therapeutic setting.* New York: Routledge.

Bullitt, C., and Farber, B. (2002). Gender differences in defensive style. *Journal of the American Psychoanalytic Association,* 30, 35–51.

Burch, B. (1993a). Heterosexuality, bisexuality, and lesbianism: Rethinking psychoanalytic views of women's object choice. *Psychoanalytic Review, 80,* 83–99.

Burch, B. (1993b). Gender identities, lesbianism, and potential space. *Psychoanalytic Psychology,* 10, 359–75.

Burgner, M., and Edgcumbe, R. (1972). Some problems in the conceptualization of early object relationships—Part 2, The concept of object constancy. *Psychoanalytic Study of the Child,* 27, 315–33.

Burland, J. (1997). The role of working through in bringing about psychoanalytic change. *International Journal of Psychoanalysis,* 78, 469–84.

Burnham, D., Gladstone, A., and Gibson, R. (1969). *Schizophrenia and the need-fear dilemma.* New York: International Universities Press.

Busch, F. (1993). "In the neighborhood": Aspects of a good interpretation and a "developmental lag" in ego psychology. *Journal of the American Psychoanalytic Association,* 41, 151–77.

Busch, F. (1996). The ego and its significance in analytic interventions. *Journal of the American Psychoanalytic Association,* 44, 1073–99.

Busch, F. N., Rudden, M., and Shapiro, T. (2004). *Psychodynamic treatment of depression.* Arlington, VA: American Psychiatric Publishing.

Butler, J. (1990). *Gender trouble: Feminism and the subversion of identity.* New York: Routledge.

Butler, J. (1993). *Bodies that matter: On the discursive limits of "sex."* New York: Routledge.

Butler, J. (2004). *Undoing gender.* New York: Routledge.

Buxbaum, E. (1950). Technique of terminating analysis. *International Journal of Psychoanalysis,* 31, 184–90.

Bychowski, G. (1953). The problem of latent psychosis. *Journal of the American Psychoanalytic Association,* 1, 484–503.

Cahn, R. (1995). Subject and agency in psychoanalysis: Which is to be master? *International Journal of Psychoanalysis,* 76, 189–91.

Calabrese, M., Farber, B., and Westen, D. (2005). The relationship of adult attachment constructs to object relational patterns of representing self and others. *Journal of the American Psychoanalytic Association,* 33, 513–30.

Caligor, E., Diamond, D., Yeomans, F., and Kernberg, O. (2009). The interpretive process in the psychoanalytic psychotherapy of borderline personality pathology. *Journal of the American Psychoanalytic Association,* 57, 271–301.

Cassidy, J. (2008). The nature of the child's ties. In *The handbook of attachment theory and research* (2nd edition), ed. J. Cassidy and P. Shaver. New York: Guilford Press.

Cassirer, E. (1955). *The philosophy of symbolic forms.* New Haven, CT: Yale University Press.

Cauldwell, D. (1949/2006). Psychopathia transexualis. In *The transgender studies reader,* ed. S. Stryker and S. Whittle (pp. 40–44). New York: Routledge.

Cavell, M. (1997). Commentaries. *Journal of the American Psychoanalytic Association,* 45, 721–26.

Cavell, M. (2003). The social character of thinking. *Journal of the American Psychoanalytic Association,* 51, 803–24.

Chapin, H. (1915). Are institutions for infants necessary? *Journal of American Medical Association,* 64, 1–3.

Chasseguet-Smirgel, J. (1964). Feminine guilt and the oedipus complex. In *Female sexuality,* ed. J. Chasseguet-Smirgel (pp. 94–134). Ann Arbor, MI: University of Michigan Press.

Chasseguet-Smirgel, J. (1974). Perversion, idealization and sublimation. *International Journal of Psychoanalysis,* 55, 349–57.

Chasseguet-Smirgel, J. (1978). Reflexions on the connexions between perversion and sadism. *International Journal of Psychoanalysis,* 59, 27–38.

Chasseguet-Smirgel, J. (1984). *Creativity and perversion.* London: Free Association Books.

Chasseguet-Smirgel, J. (1991). Sadomasochism in the perversions: Some thoughts on the destruction of reality. *Journal of the American Psychoanalytic Association,* 39, 399–415.

Chasseguet-Smirgel, J. (1993). Woman's social status as a reflection of the internal relationship to mother and father in both sexes. *International Journal of Psychoanalysis,* 2, 24–29.

Chehrazi, S. (1986). Female psychology: A review. *Journal of the American Psychoanalytic Association,* 34, 141–62.

Chess, S., and Thomas, T. (1986). *Temperament in clinical practice.* New York: Guilford Press.

Chodorow, N. (1978). *The reproduction of mothering.* Berkeley, CA: University of California Press.

Chodorow, N. (1992). Heterosexuality as a compromise formation: Reflections on the psychoanalytic theory of sexual development. *Psychoanalysis and Contemporary Thought,* 15, 267–304.

Chodorow, N. (1994a). "Freud on women" and "Heterosexuality as a compromise formation." In *Femininities, masculinities, sexualities: Freud and beyond* (pp. 1–69). Lexington, KY: University Press of Kentucky.

Chodorow, N. (1994b). *Femininities, masculinities, sexualities: Freud and beyond.* Lexington, KY: University Press of Kentucky.

Chodorow, N. (1994c). Individuality and difference in how women and men love. In *Femininities, masculinities, sexualities: Freud and beyond* (pp. 70–92). Lexington, KY: University Press of Kentucky.

Chodorow, N. (1995). Multiplicities and uncertainties of gender: Commentary on Ruth Stein's "Analysis of a case of transsexualism." *Psychoanalytic Dialogues,* 5, 291–99.

Chodorow, N. (1996). Theoretical gender and clinical gender: Epistemological reflections on the psychology of women. *Journal of the American Psychoanalytic Association,* 44, 215–38.

Chodorow, N. (1999). *The power of feelings.* New Haven, CT: Yale University Press.

Chodorow, N. (2002). Gender as a personal and cultural construction. In *Gender in psychoanalytic space,* ed. M. Dimen and V. Goldner (pp. 237–61). New York: Other Press.

Chodorow, N. (2003). The psychoanalytic vision of Hans Loewald. *International Journal of Psychoanalysis,* 84, 897–913.

Chodorow, N., and Hacker, A. (2003). Homosexualities as compromise formations: Theoretical and clinical complexity in portraying and understanding homosexualities. *Revue Française de Psychanalyse,* 67, 41–64.

Chused, J. (1987). Idealization of the analyst by the young adult. *Journal of the American Psychoanalytic Association,* 35, 839–59.

Chused, J. (1988). The transference neurosis in child analysis. *Psychoanalytic Study of the Child,* 43, 51–81.

Chused, J. (1991). The evocative power of enactments. *Journal of the American Psychoanalytic Association,* 39, 615–39.

Clarkin, J., Levy, K., Lenzenweger, M., and Kernberg, O. (2007). Evaluating three treatments for borderline personality disorder: A multiwave study. *American Journal of Psychiatry,* 164, 922–28.

Clarkin, J., Yeomans, F., and Kernberg, O. (1999). *Psychotherapy for borderline personality.* New York: John Wiley and Sons.

Clarkin, J., Yeomans, F., and Kernberg, O. (2006). *Psychotherapy for borderline personality: Focusing on object relations.* Washington, DC: American Psychiatric Press.

Cleckley, H. (1941). *The mask of sanity: An attempt to reinterpret the so-called psychopathic personality.* St. Louis, MO: Mosby.

Clower, V. (1970). Panel report: The development of the child's sense of his sexual identity. *Journal of the American Psychoanalytic Association,* 18, 165–76.

Coates, S. (1990). Ontogenesis of boyhood gender identity disorder. *Journal of the American Academy of Psychoanalysis,* 18, 414–38.

Coates, S. (1997). Is it time to jettison the concept of developmental lines? *Gender and Psychoanalysis,* 2, 35–53.

Coates, S. (1998). Having a mind of one's own and holding the other in mind: Commentary on paper by Peter Fonagy and Mary Target. *Psychoanalytic Dialogues,* 8, 115–48.

Coates, S. (2004). John Bowlby and Margaret S. Mahler: Their lives and theories. *Journal of the American Psychoanalytic Association,* 52, 571–601.

Coates, S., Friedman, R., and Wolfe, S. (1991). The etiology of boyhood gender identity disorder: A model for integrating temperament, development, and psychodynamics. *Psychoanalytic Dialogues,* 1, 481–523.

Coates, S., and Wolfe, S. (1995). The etiology of boyhood gender identity disorder in boys: The interface of constitution and early experience. *Psychoanalytic Inquiry,* 15, 6–38.

Coen, S. (1981). Sexualization as a predominant mode of defense. *Journal of the American Psychoanalytic Association,* 29, 893–920.

Coen, S. (1986). The sense of defect. *Journal of the American Psychoanalytic Association,* 34, 47–67.

Coen, S. (1988). Superego aspects of entitlement (in rigid characters). *Journal of the American Psychoanalytic Association,* 36, 409–27.

Coen, S. (1989). Intolerance of responsibility for internal conflict. *Journal of the American Psychoanalytic Association,* 37, 943–64.

Coen, S. (1992). *The misuse of persons: Analyzing pathological dependency.* Hillsdale, NJ: Analytic Press.

Coen, S. (1998). Perverse defenses in neurotic patients. *Journal of the American Psychoanalytic Association,* 46, 1169–94.

Cohler, B., and Galatzer-Levy, R. (2000). *The course of gay and lesbian lives: Social and psychoanalytic perspectives.* Chicago: University of Chicago Press.

Cohn, F. (1940). Practical approach to the problem of narcissistic neuroses. *Psychoanalytic Quarterly,* 9, 64–79.

Colarusso, C., and Nemiroff, R. (1981). *Adult development: A new dimension in psychodynamic theory and practice.* New York: Plenum Press.

Cooper, A. (1989). Working through. *Contemporary Psychoanalysis,* 25, 34–62.

Cooper, A. M. (1985). A historical review of psychoanalytic paradigms. In *Models of the mind: Their relationship to clinical work,* ed. A. Rothstein (pp. 5–20). Madison, CT: International Universities Press.

Cooper, A. M. (1987a). The transference neurosis: A concept ready for retirement. *Psychoanalytic Inquiry,* 7, 569–85.

Cooper, A. M. (1987b). Changes in psychoanalytic ideas: Transference interpretation. *Journal of the American Psychoanalytic Association,* 35, 77–98.

Cooper, A. M. (1988). The narcissistic-masochistic character. In *Masochism: Current psychoanalytic perspectives,* ed. R. Glick and D. Meyers (pp. 117–38). Hillsdale, NJ: Analytic Press.

Cooper, A. M. (1993a). Psychotherapeutic approaches to masochism. *Journal of Psychotherapy Practice and Research,* 2 (1), 51–63.

Cooper, A. M. (1993b). Paranoia: A part of most analyses. *Journal of the American Psychoanalytic Association,* 41, 423–42.

Cooper, S. (1998). Analyst subjectivity, analyst disclosure, and the aims of psychoanalysis. *Psychoanalytic Quarterly,* 67, 379–406.

Cooper, S., and Levit, D. (1998). Old and new objects in Fairbairnian and American relational theory. *Psychoanalytic Dialogues,* 8, 603–24.

Corbett, K. (1993). The mystery of homosexuality. *Psychoanalytic Psychology,* 10, 345–57.

Corbett, K. (1996). Homosexual boyhoods: Notes on girlyboys. *Gender and Psychoanalysis,* 1, 429–61.

Corbett, K. (2008). Gender now. *Psychoanalytic Dialogues,* 18, 838–56.

Corbett, K. (2009a). Boyhood femininity, gender identity disorder, masculine presuppositions, and the anxiety of regulation. *Psychoanalytic Dialogues,* 19, 353–70.

Corbett, K. (2009b). *Boyhoods: Rethinking masculinities.* New Haven, CT: Yale University Press.

Corboz-Warnery, A., Fivaz-Depeursinge, E., Gertsch-Betterns, C., and Favez, N. (1993). Systemic analysis of father-mother-baby interactions: The Lausanne triadic play. *Infant Mental Health Journal,* 14, 298–316.

Cramer, P. (2006). *Protecting the self: Defense mechanisms in action.* New York: Guilford Press.

Damasio, A. (1994). *Descartes' error: Emotion, reason, and the human brain.* New York: Putnam.

Damasio, A. (1999). *The feeling of what happens.* New York: Harcourt, Brace.

Dann, O. (1992). The Isakower phenomenon revisited: A case study. *International Journal of Psychoanalysis,* 73, 481–91.

Davies, J. (1994). Love in the afternoon: A relational reconsideration of desire and dread in the countertransference. *Psychoanalytic Dialogues,* 4, 153–70.

Davies, J. (2004). Whose bad objects are we anyway?: Repetition and our elusive love affair with evil. *Psychoanalytic Dialogues,* 14, 711–32.

Davies, J., and Frawley, M. (1992). Dissociative processes and transference-countertransference paradigms in the psychoanalytically oriented treatment of adult survivors of childhood sexual abuse. *Psychoanalytic Dialogues,* 2, 5–36.

Davison, W., Bristol, C., and Pray, M. (1986). Turning aggression on the self: Study of psychoanalytic process. *Psychoanalytic Quarterly,* 55, 273–95.

De Folch, T. (1984). The hysteric's use and misuse of observation. *International Journal of Psychoanalysis,* 65 (4), 399–410.

Decety, J., and Jackson, P. (2006). A social-neuroscience perspective on empathy. *Current Directions in Psychological Science,* 15, 54–58.

Defries, Z. (1978). Political lesbianism and sexual politics. *Journal of the American Psychoanalytic Association,* 6, 71–78.

Defries, Z. (1979). A comparison of political and apolitical lesbians. *Journal of the American Psychoanalytic Association,* 7, 57–66.

Deklyen, M., and Greenberg, M. (2008). Attachment and psychopathology in childhood. In *Handbook of attachment: Theory, research, and clinical applications* (2nd edition), ed. J. Cassidy and P. Shaver (pp. 637–65). New York: Guilford Press.

DeMarneffe, D. (1997). Bodies and words: A study of young children's genital and gender knowledge. *Gender and Psychoanalysis,* 2, 3–33.

Demos, E. (1996). Expanding the interpersonal perspective. *Contemporary Psychoanalysis,* 32, 649–63.

Depue, R., and Lenzenweger, M. (2001/2005). A neurobehavioral dimensional model of personality disturbance. In *Handbook of personality disorders,* ed. W. Livesley (pp. 136–76). New York: Guilford Press.

Deutsch, F. (1939). The choice of organ in organ neuroses. *International Journal of Psychoanalysis,* 20, 252–62.

Deutsch, H. (1926). Occult processes occurring during psychoanalysis. In *Psychoanalysis and the occult,* ed. G. Devereux (pp. 133–46). New York: International Universities Press, 1970.

Deutsch, H. (1929). The genesis of agoraphobia. *International Journal of Psychoanalysis,* 10, 51–69.

Deutsch, H. (1933a). Motherhood and sexuality. *Psychoanalytic Quarterly,* 2, 476–88.

Deutsch, H. (1933b). The psychology of manic depressive states with particular reference to hypomania. In *Neuroses and character types: Clinical psychoanalytic studies* (pp. 203–17). New York: International Universities Press, 1965.

Deutsch, H. (1934). Some forms of emotional disturbances and their relationship to schizophrenia. In *Neuroses and character types: Clinical psychoanalytic studies* (pp. 262–81). New York: International Universities Press, 1965.

Deutsch, H. (1942). Some forms of emotional disturbance and their relationships to schizophrenia. *Psychoanalytic Quarterly,* 11, 301–21.

Deutsch, H. (1944). *The psychology of women.* New York: Grune and Stratton.

Deutsch, H. (1955). The impostor: Contribution to ego psychology of a type of psychopath. In *Neuroses and character types: Clinical psychoanalytic studies* (pp. 319–38). New York: International Universities Press, 1965.

Deutsch, H. (1965). *Neurosis and character types: Clinical psychoanalytic studies.* New York: International Universities Press.

Deutsch, H. (1982). George Sand: A woman's destiny. *International Review of Psycho-Analysis, 9,* 445–46.

Devereux, G. (1951). Some criteria for the timing of confrontations and interpretations. *International Journal of Psychoanalysis, 32,* 19–24.

Dewald, P. (1964). *Psychotherapy: A dynamic approach.* New York: Basic Books.

Dewald, P. (1972). The clinical assessment of structural change. *Journal of the American Psychoanalytic Association, 20,* 302–24.

Dewald, P. (1976). Transference regression and real experience in the psychoanalytic process. *Psychoanalytic Quarterly, 45,* 213–30.

Dewald, P. (1978). The psychoanalytic process in adult patients. *Psychoanalytic Study of the Child, 33,* 323–32.

Diamond, D., Stovall-McClough, C., Clarkin J., and Levy, K. (2003). Patient-therapist attachment in the treatment of borderline personality disorder. *Bulletin of the Menninger Clinic, 67* (3), 224–57.

Diamond, L. (2008). *Sexual fluidity: Understanding women's love and desire.* Cambridge, MA: Harvard University Press.

Diamond, M. (2006). Masculinity unraveled: The roots of male gender identity and shifting of male ego ideals throughout life. *Journal of the American Psychoanalytic Association, 54,* 1099–1130.

Dimen, M. (1991). Deconstructing difference: Gender, splitting, and transitional space. *Psychoanalytic Dialogues, 1,* 335–52.

Doi, T. (1973). *The anatomy of dependence.* New York: Kodansha International.

Donegan, N., Sanislow, C., Blumberg, H., Fulbright, R., Lacadie, C., Skudlarski, P., Gore, J., Olston, I., McGlashan, T., and Wexler, B. (2003). Amygdala hyperreactivity in borderline personality disorder: Implications for emotional dysregulation. *Biological Psychiatry, 54* (11), 1284–93.

Dorpat, T. (2001). Primary process communication. *Psychoanalytic Inquiry, 21,* 448–63.

Dorsey, D. (1996). Castration anxiety or genital anxiety? The psychology of women: Psychoanalytic perspectives. *Journal of the American Psychoanalytic Association, 44* (S), 283–302.

Dowling, A. (2004). A reconsideration of the concept of regression. *Psychoanalytic Study of the Child, 59,* 191–210.

Downey, J., and Friedman, R. (1998). Female homosexuality reconsidered. *Journal of the American Psychoanalytic Association, 46,* 471–506.

Drescher, J. (2009). Queer diagnoses: Parallels and contrasts in the history of homosexuality, gender variance, and the *Diagnostic and Statistical Manual. Archives of Sexual Behavior, 39,* 427–60.

Dunbar, H. (1938). *Emotions and bodily changes.* New York: Columbia University Press.

Dunn, J. (1995). Intersubjectivity in psychoanalysis: A critical review. *International Journal of Psychoanalysis, 76,* 723–38.

Dupont, J., ed. (1988). *The Clinical Diary of Sándor Ferenczi.* Cambridge, MA: Belknap Press.

Eagle, M. (1984). *Recent developments in psychoanalysis: A critical evaluation.* New York: McGraw-Hill.

Eagle, M. (1990). Concepts of need and wish in self psychology. *Psychoanalytic Psychology, 7,* 71–88.

Eagle, M. (2000). Repression, part 2 of 2. *Psychoanalytic Review, 87,* 161–87.

Eagle, M., Migone, P., and Gallese, V. (2007). Intentional attunement: Mirror neurons and the neural underpinnings of interpersonal relations. *Journal of the American Psychoanalytic Association, 55,* 131–76.

Eagle, M., Wolitzky D., and Wakefield, J. (2001). The analyst's knowledge and authority: A critique of the "new view" in psychoanalysis. *Journal of the American Psychoanalytic Association, 49,* 457–89.

Easser, B., and Lesser, S. R. (1965). Hysterical personality: A re-evaluation. *Psychoanalytic Quarterly 34,* 390–405.

Edelman, G., and Tononi, G. (2000). *A universe of consciousness.* New York: Basic Books.

Edelson, M. (1985). The hermeneutic turn and the single case study in psychoanalysis. *Psychoanalysis and Contemporary Thought, 8,* 567–614.

Edelstein, D. (1990). The dream screen transference. *Annual of Psychoanalysis, 18,* 89–98.

Edgcumbe, R. (1995). The history of Anna Freud's thinking on developmental disturbances. *Bulletin of the Anna Freud Centre, 18,* 21–34.

Edgcumbe, R. (2000). *Anna Freud: A view of development.* London: Routledge.

Edgcumbe, R., and Burgner, M. (1975). The phallicnarcissistic phase—A differentiation between preoedipal and oedipal aspects of phallic development. *Psychoanalytic Study of the Child, 30,* 161–80.

Ehrenberg, D. (1992). *The intimate edge: Extending the reach of psychoanalytic interaction.* New York: W. W. Norton.

Ehrensaft, D. (2007). Raising girlyboys: A parent's perspective. *Studies in Gender and Sexuality, 8,* 269–302.

Eidelberg, L. (1959). Humiliation in masochism. *Journal of the American Psychoanalytic Association, 7,* 274–83.

Eidelberg, L., ed. (1968). *Encyclopedia of psychoanalysis.* New York: Free Press.

Eigen, M. (1974). On pre-oedipal castration anxiety. *International Review of Psycho-Analysis,* 1, 489–98.

Eissler, K. (1953). The effect of the structure of the ego on psychoanalytic technique. *Journal of the American Psychoanalytic Association,* 1, 104–43.

Eissler, R. (1949). Scapegoats of society. In *Searchlights on delinquency,* ed. K. Eissler (pp. 288–305). Madison, CT: International Universities Press.

Ekman, P. (1983). Autonomic nervous system activity distinguishes among emotions. *Science,* 221, 1208–10.

Ekstein, R. (1965). Working through and termination of analysis. *Journal of the American Psychoanalytic Association,* 13, 57–78.

Elise, D. (1997). Primary femininity, bisexuality, and the female ego ideal: A re-examination of female developmental theory. *Psychoanalytic Quarterly,* 66, 489–517.

Elise, D. (1998). Gender repertoire: Body, mind, and bisexuality. *Psychoanalytic Dialogues,* 8, 353–71.

Elise, D. (2000). Generating gender: Response to Harris. *Studies in Gender and Sexuality,* 1, 157–65.

Elise, D. (2002). The primary maternal oedipal situation and female homoerotic desire. *Psychoanalytic Inquiry,* 22, 209–28.

Ellenberger, H. (1970). *The discovery of the unconscious: The history and evolution of dynamic psychiatry.* New York: Basic Books.

Elliot, A. (1994). *Psychoanalytic theory: An introduction.* Oxford: Blackwell.

Ellis, H., and Symonds, J. (1897). *Sexual Inversion.* London: Wilson and Macmillan.

Emde, R. (1983). The prerepresentational self and its affective core. *Psychoanalytic Study of the Child,* 38, 165–92.

Emde, R. (1985). From adolescence to midlife: Remodeling the structure of adult development. *Journal of the American Psychoanalytic Association,* 33 (S), 59–112.

Emde, R. (1988). Development terminable and interminable—I. Innate and motivational factors from infancy. *International Journal of Psychoanalysis,* 69, 23–42.

Emde, R. (1990). Mobilizing fundamental modes of development: Empathic availability and therapeutic action. *Journal of the American Psychoanalytic Association,* 28, 881–913.

Emde, R. (1991). Positive emotions for psychoanalytic theory: Surprises from infancy research and new directions. *Journal of the American Psychoanalytic Association,* 39 (S), 5–44.

Emde, R. (1992). Social referencing research: Uncertainty, self, and the search for meaning. In *Social referencing and the social construction of reality in infancy,* ed. S. Feinman (pp. 79–94). New York: Plenum Press.

Emde, R. (1999). Moving ahead: Integrating influences of affective processes for development and for psychoanalysis. *International Journal of Psychoanalysis,* 80, 317–39.

Emde, R., Biringen, Z., Clyman, R., and Oppenheim, D. (1991). The moral self of infancy: Affective core and procedural knowledge. *Developmental Review,* 11, 251–70.

Emde, R., and Buchsbaum, H. (1990). "Didn't you hear my mommy?" Autonomy with connectedness in moral self-emergence. In *The self in transition: Infancy to childhood,* ed. D. Ciccheti and M. Beeghly (pp. 35–60). Chicago: University of Chicago Press, 1990.

Emde, R., Johnson, W., and Easterbrooks, M. (1988). The do's and don'ts of early moral development: Psychoanalytic tradition and current research. In *The emergence of morality,* ed. E. Kagan and S. Lamb (pp. 245–76). Chicago: University of Chicago Press.

Engel, R. (1961). Is grief a disease? *Psychosomatic Medicine,* 23, 18–22.

English, H., and English, A. (1958). *A comprehensive dictionary of psychological and psychoanalytical terms.* New York: Longman's, Green.

Erdelyi, M. (1985). *Psychoanalysis: Freud's cognitive psychology.* New York: W. H. Freeman.

Erikson, E. (1945). Childhood and tradition in two American Indian tribes—A comparative abstract, with conclusions. *Psychoanalytic Study of the Child,* 1, 319–50.

Erikson, E. (1946). Ego development and historical change—Clinical notes. *Psychoanalytic Study of the Child,* 2, 359–96.

Erikson, E. (1950). *Childhood and society.* New York: W. W. Norton.

Erikson, E. (1956). The problem of ego identity. *Journal of the American Psychoanalytic Association,* 4, 56–121.

Erikson, E. (1959). *Identity and the life cycle: Selected papers.* New York: International Universities Press.

Erreich, A. (2003). A modest proposal: (Re)defining unconscious fantasy. *Psychoanalytic Quarterly,* 72, 541–74.

Erwin, E., ed. (2002). *The Freud encyclopedia: Theory, therapy, and culture.* New York: Routledge.

Escalona, S. (1963). Patterns of infantile experience and the developmental process. *Psychoanalytic Study of the Child,* 18, 197–243.

Esman, A. (1973). The primal scene—A review and reconsideration. *Psychoanalytic Study of the Child,* 28, 49–81.

Evans, D. (1996). *An introductory dictionary of Lacanian psychoanalysis.* New York: Routledge.

Fajardo, B. (1993). Conditions for the relevance of infant research to clinical psychoanalysis. *International Journal of Psychoanalysis,* 74, 975–91.

Fajardo, B. (1998). A new view of developmental research for psychoanalysts. *Journal of the American Psychoanalytic Association, 46,* 185–207.

Fairbairn, W. (1941). A revised psychopathology of the psychoses and the psychoneuroses. In *An object relations theory of the personality* (pp. 28–58). New York: Basic Books, 1954.

Fairbairn, W. (1952). *Psychoanalytic studies of the personality.* London: Tavistock Publications.

Fairbairn, W. (1954). *An object-relations theory of the personality.* New York: Basic Books.

Fast, I. (1978). Developments in gender identity: The original matrix. *International Review of Psycho-Analysis, 5,* 265–73.

Fast, I. (1984). *Gender identity: A differentiation model.* Hillsdale, NJ: Analytic Press.

Fast, I. (1990). Aspects of early gender development: Toward a reformulation. *Psychoanalytic Psychology, 7,* 105–17.

Fast, I. (1999). Aspects of core gender identity. *Psychoanalytic Dialogues, 9,* 633–62.

Federn, P. (1926). Some variations in ego-feeling. *International Journal of Psychoanalysis, 7,* 434–44.

Federn, P. (1952). *Ego psychology and the psychoses,* ed. E. Weiss. New York: Basic Books.

Feigelson, C. (1993). Personality death, object loss, and the uncanny. *International Journal of Psychoanalysis, 74,* 331–45.

Feiner, A. (2000). *Interpersonal psychoanalytic perspectives on relevance, dismissal and self-definition.* New York: Jessica Kingsley Publishers.

Feldman, M. (1997). Projective identification: The analyst's involvement. *International Journal of Psychoanalysis, 78,* 227–41.

Felman, S. (1987). *Jacques Lacan and the adventure of insight: Psychoanalysis in contemporary culture.* Cambridge, MA: Harvard University Press.

Fenichel, O. (1930). The psychology of transvestism. *International Journal of Psychoanalysis, 11,* 211–26.

Fenichel, O. (1932). Outline of clinical psychoanalysis. *Psychoanalytic Quarterly, 1,* 121–65, 292–342, 545–652.

Fenichel, O. (1938a). Ego disturbances and their treatment. *International Journal of Psychoanalysis, 19,* 416–38.

Fenichel, O. (1938b). Problems of psychoanalytic technique. *Psychoanalytic Quarterly, 7,* 421–42.

Fenichel, O. (1939a). The counter-phobic attitude. *International Journal of Psychoanalysis, 20,* 263–74.

Fenichel, O. (1939b). Problems of psychoanalytic technique. *Psychoanalytic Quarterly, 8,* 438–70.

Fenichel, O. (1941). The ego and the affects. *Psychoanalytic Review, 28,* 47–60.

Fenichel, O. (1945). *The psychoanalytic theory of neurosis.* New York: W. W. Norton.

Fenichel, O. (1954). Psychoanalysis of character. In *The collected papers of Otto Fenichel,* 2nd series, ed. H. Fenichel and D. Rapaport (pp. 198–214). New York: W. W. Norton.

Fenton, L., Cecero, J., Nich, C., Frankforter, T., and Carroll, K. (2001). Perspective is everything: The predictive validity of six working alliance instruments. *Journal of Psychotherapy Practice and Research, 10,* 4.

Ferenczi, S. (1909). Introjection and transference. In *First contributions to psycho-analysis* (pp. 35–93). New York: Brunner/Mazel, 1952.

Ferenczi, S. (1913/1952). Stages in the development of a sense of reality. In *First contributions to psycho-analysis* (pp. 213–39). New York: Brunner/Mazel.

Ferenczi, S. (1919). Technical difficulties in the analysis of a case of hysteria. In *Further contributions to the theory and technique of psychoanalysis,* ed. J. Rickman (pp. 189–97). New York: Brunner/Mazel, 1980 (reprint of 1926 edition).

Ferenczi, S. (1920). The further development of an active therapy in psycho-analysis. In *Further contributions to the theory and technique of psychoanalysis,* ed. J. Rickman (pp. 198–216). New York, Brunner/Mazel, 1980 (original published in 1926).

Ferenczi, S. (1925). Psycho-analysis of sexual habits. *International Journal of Psychoanalysis, 6,* 372–404.

Ferenczi, S. (1927). The problems of termination of the analysis. In *Final contributions to the problems and methods of psychoanalysis,* ed. M. Balint (pp. 77–86). New York: Brunner/Mazel, 1955.

Ferenczi, S. (1928). The elasticity of psychoanalytic technique. In *Final contributions to the problems and methods of psychoanalysis,* ed. M. Balint (pp. 87–101). New York: Brunner/Mazel, 1955.

Ferenczi, S. (1929). The unwelcome child and his death instinct. In *Final contributions to the problems and methods of psychoanalysis,* ed. M. Balint (pp. 102–7). New York: Brunner/Mazel, 1955.

Ferenczi, S. (1930). The principle of relaxation and neocatharsis. *International Journal of Psychoanalysis, 11,* 428–43.

Ferenczi, S. (1931). Child-analysis in the analysis of adults. *International Journal of Psychoanalysis, 12,* 468–82.

Ferenczi, S. (1932). *The clinical diary of Sándor Ferenczi,* ed. E. Dupont. Cambridge, MA: Harvard University Press, 1988.

Ferenczi, S. (1933). Confusion of tongues between adults and the child. In *Final contributions to the problems and methods of psychoanalysis,* ed. M. Balint (pp. 156–67). New York: Brunner/Mazel, 1955.

Ferenczi, S. (1938). *Thalassa: A theory of genitality.* London: Karnac Books, 1989.

Ferenczi, S., and Rank, O. (1925). *The development of psychoanalysis. Nervous and mental disease.* New York: Nervous and Mental Disease Publishing.

Fertuck, E., Jekal, A., Song, I., Wyman, B., Morris, M., Wilson, S., Brodsky, B., and Stanley, B. (2009). Enhanced "reading the mind in the eyes" in borderline personality disorder compared to healthy controls. *Psychological Medicine,* 39 (12), 1979–88.

Fertuck, E., Lenzenweger, M., Clarkin, J., Hoermann, S., and Stanley, B. (2006). Executive neurocognition, memory systems, and borderline personality disorder. *Clinical Psychology Review,* 26 (3), 346–75.

Fertuck, E., Target, M., Mergenthaler, E., and Clarkin, J. (2004). The development of a computerized linguistic analysis instrument of the reflective functioning measure. *Journal of the American Psychoanalytic Association,* 52, 473–75.

Firestein, B. (1996). *Bisexuality: The psychology and politics of an invisible minority.* Thousand Oaks, CA: Sage Publications.

Firestein, S. (1974). Termination of psychoanalysis of adults: A review of the literature. *Journal of the American Psychoanalytic Association,* 22, 873–94.

Fiscalini, J. (2004). *Coparticipant psychoanalysis: Toward a new theory of clinical inquiry.* New York: Columbia University Press.

Fischer, R. (2002). Lesbianism: Some developmental and psychodynamic considerations. *Psychoanalytic Inquiry,* 22, 278–95.

Fisher, C. (1954). Dreams and perception—The role of preconscious and primary modes of perception in dream formation. *Journal of the American Psychoanalytic Association,* 2, 389–445.

Fisher, C. (1965). Psychoanalytic implications of recent research on sleep and dreaming—Part 1, Empirical findings; and Part 2, Implications for psychoanalytic theory. *Journal of the American Psychoanalytic Association,* 13, 197–303.

Fisher, C., and Paul, I. (1959). The effect of subliminal visual stimulation on images and dreams: A validation study. *Journal of the American Psychoanalytic Association,* 7, 35–83.

Fivaz-Depeursinge, E., and Corboz-Warnery, A. (1999). *The primary triangle: A developmental systems view of mothers, fathers, and infants.* New York: Basic Books.

Flax, J. (1990). *Thinking fragments: Psychoanalysis, feminism, and postmodernism in the contemporary west.* Berkeley, CA: University of California Press.

Fleming, J. (1975). Some observations on object constancy in the psychoanalysis of adults. *Journal of the American Psychoanalytic Association,* 23, 743–59.

Fliess, R. (1942). The metapsychology of the analyst. *Psychoanalytic Quarterly,* 11, 211–27.

Fodor, N., and Gaynor, F. (1950). *Freud: Dictionary of psychoanalysis.* New York: Philosophical Library.

Fogel, G. (1998). Interiority and inner genital space in men: What else can be lost in castration. *Psychoanalytic Quarterly,* 67, 662–97.

Fonagy, P. (1995). Playing with reality: The development of psychic reality and its malfunction in borderline personalities. *International Journal of Psychoanalysis,* 76, 39–44.

Fonagy, P. (1996). The future of an empirical psychoanalysis. *British Journal of Psychotherapy,* 13, 106–18.

Fonagy, P. (1999). Memory and therapeutic action. *International Journal of Psychoanalysis,* 80, 215–23.

Fonagy, P. (2000). Attachment and borderline personality disorder. *Journal of the American Psychoanalytic Association,* 48, 1129–46.

Fonagy, P. (2001). *Attachment theory and psychoanalysis.* New York: Other Press.

Fonagy, P. (2003). Rejoinder to Harold Blum. *International Journal of Psychoanalysis,* 84, 503–9.

Fonagy, P. (2008). A genuinely developmental theory of sexual enjoyment and its implications for psychoanalytic technique. *Journal of the American Psychoanalytic Association,* 56, 11–36.

Fonagy, P., Gergely, G., Jurist, E., and Target, M. (2002). *Affect regulation, mentalization, and the development of the self.* New York: Other Press.

Fonagy, P., Leigh, T., Steele, M., Steele, H., Kennedy, R., Mattoon, G., Target, M., and Gerber, A. (1996). The relation of attachment status, psychiatric classification, and response to psychotherapy. *Journal of Consulting and Clinical Psychology,* 64, 22–31.

Fonagy, P., and Moran, G. (1991). Understanding psychic change in child psychoanalysis. *International Journal of Psychoanalysis,* 72, 15–22.

Fonagy, P., Moran, G., Edgcumbe, R., Kennedy, H., and Target, M. (1993). The roles of mental representations and mental processes in therapeutic action. *Psychoanalytic Study of the Child,* 48, 9–48.

Fonagy, P., Steele, M., Moran, G., Steele, H., and Higgitt, A. (1993). Measuring the ghost in the nursery: An empirical study of the relation between parents' mental representations of childhood experiences and their infants' security of attachment. *Journal of the American Psychoanalytic Association,* 41, 929–89.

Fonagy, P., and Target, M. (1996a). A contemporary psychoanalytical perspective: Psychodynamic developmental therapy. In *Psychosocial treatment for child and adolescent disorders,* ed. E. Hibbs and P. Jensen (pp. 619–38). Washington, DC: American Psychological Association.

Fonagy, P., and Target, M. (1996b). Playing with reality: I. Theory of mind and the normal development of psychic reality. *International Journal of Psychoanalysis*, 77, 217–33.

Fonagy, P., and Target, M. (1998). Mentalization and the changing aims of child psychoanalysis. *Psychoanalytic Dialogues*, 8, 87–114.

Fonagy, P., Target, M., Gergely, G., Allen, J., and Bateman, A. (2003). The developmental roots of borderline personality disorder in early attachment relationships: A theory and some evidence. *Psychoanalytic Inquiry*, 23, 412–59.

Fox, R. (1984). The principle of abstinence reconsidered. *International Review of Psycho-Analysis*, 11, 227–36.

Fraiberg, S. (1966). Further considerations of the role of transference in latency. *Psychoanalytic Study of the Child*, 21, 213–36.

Fraiberg, S. (1969). Libidinal object constancy and mental representation. *Psychoanalytic Study of the Child*, 24, 9–47.

Fraiberg, S. (1972). Some characteristics of genital arousal and discharge in latency girls. *Psychoanalytic Study of the Child*, 27, 439–75.

Fraiberg, S. (1982). Pathological defenses in infancy. *Psychoanalytic Quarterly*, 51, 612–35.

Fraiberg, S., Adelson, E., and Shapiro, V. (1975). Ghosts in the nursery: A psychoanalytic approach to the problems of impaired infant-mother relationships. *Journal of the American Academy of Child and Adolescent Psychiatry*, 15, 387–421.

Frankel, J. (1998). Are interpersonal and relational psychoanalysis the same? *Contemporary Psychoanalysis*, 34, 485–500.

Frankel, S., and Sherick, I. (1979). Observations of the emerging sexual identity of three- and four-year-old children: With emphasis on female sexual identity. *International Review of Psycho-Analysis*, 6, 297–309.

Frankiel, R., ed. (1994). *Essential papers on object loss*. New York: New York University Press.

Frenkel, R. (1996). A reconsideration of object choice in women: Phallus or fallacy. *Journal of the American Psychoanalytic Association*, 44 (S), 133–56.

Freud, A. (1927). Four lectures on child analysis. In *The writings of Anna Freud* (vol. 1, pp. 3–69). New York: International Universities Press, 1974.

Freud, A. (1936). *The ego and the mechanisms of defence*. In *The writings of Anna Freud* (vol. 2, pp. 3–176). New York: International Universities Press, 1974.

Freud, A. (1945). Indications for child analysis. *Psychoanalytic Study of the Child*, 1, 127–49.

Freud, A. (1948). *Psycho-analytical treatment of children*. London: Imago Publishing.

Freud, A. (1952). The mutual influences in the development of ego and id. In *The writings of Anna Freud* (vol. 4, pp. 230–44). New York: International Universities Press, 1968.

Freud, A. (1954). Psychoanalysis and education. *Psychoanalytic Study of the Child*, 9, 9–15.

Freud, A. (1958). Adolescence. *Psychoanalytic Study of the Child*, 13, 255–78.

Freud, A. (1963). The concept of developmental lines. *Psychoanalytic Study of the Child*, 18, 245–65.

Freud, A. (1965). *Normality and pathology in childhood*. In *The writings of Anna Freud*. (vol. 6, pp. 3–235). New York: International Universities Press.

Freud, A. (1966). Obsessional neurosis: A summary of psycho-analytic views as presented at the congress. *International Journal of Psychoanalysis*, 47, 116–22.

Freud, A. (1967a). Comments on trauma. In *Psychic trauma*, ed. S. Furst (pp. 235–47). New York: Basic Books.

Freud, A. (1967b). About losing and being lost. *Psychoanalytic Study of the Child*, 22, 9–19.

Freud, A. (1970). The symptomatology of childhood—A preliminary attempt at classification. *Psychoanalytic Study of the Child*, 25, 19–41.

Freud, A. (1971). The infantile neurosis—Genetic and dynamic considerations. *Psychoanalytic Study of the Child*, 26, 79–90.

Freud, A. (1974). A psychoanalytic view of developmental psychopathology. In *The writings of Anna Freud* (vol. 8, pp. 57–74). New York: International Universities Press, 1981.

Freud, A. (1977). Fears, anxieties, and phobic phenomena. *Psychoanalytic Study of the Child*, 32, 85–90.

Freud, A. (1978). The principle task of child analysis. In *The writings of Anna Freud* (vol. 8, pp. 201–5). New York: International Universities Press, 1981.

Freud, A. (1979). Child analysis as the study of mental growth, normal and abnormal. In *The writings of Anna Freud* (vol. 8, pp. 119–36). New York: International Universities Press, 1981.

Freud, A. (1981). The concept of developmental lines—Their diagnostic significance. *Psychoanalytic Study of the Child*, 36, 129–36.

Freud, A., and Dann, S. (1951). An experiment in group upbringing. *Psychoanalytic Study of the Child*, 6, 127–66.

Freud, S. (1882). Sketches for the "preliminary communication" of 1893. [A] letter to Josef Breuer. *Standard Edition*, 1, 147–48.

Freud, S. (1886). Observation of a severe case of hemianaesthesia in a hysterical male. *Standard Edition*, 1, 23–31.

Freud, S. (1888a). Hysteria. *Standard Edition*, 1, 37–59.

Freud, S. (1888b). Preface to the translation of Bernheim's suggestion. *Standard Edition*, 1, 73–87.

Freud, S. (1888/1893). Some points for a comparative study of organic and hysterical motor paralyses. *Standard Edition*, 1, 157–72.

Freud, S. (1892/1899). Extracts from the Fliess papers. *Standard Edition*, 1, 175–280.

Freud, S. (1893/1895). The psychotherapy of hysteria. In Studies on Hysteria, ed. J. Breuer and S. Freud. *Standard Edition*, 2, 253–305.

Freud, S. (1894a). Letter 18 (Extracts from the Fliess papers). *Standard Edition*, 1, 188–89.

Freud, S. (1894b). Draft E: How anxiety originates (Extracts from the Fliess papers). *Standard Edition*, 1, 189–95.

Freud, S. (1894c). The neuro-psychoses of defence. *Standard Edition*, 3, 41–61.

Freud, S. (1894d). On the grounds for detaching a particular syndrome from neurasthenia under the description "anxiety neurosis." *Standard Edition*, 3, 85–115.

Freud, S. (1894e). Obsessions and phobias. *Standard Edition*, 3, 69–82.

Freud, S. (1895a). Draft H: Paranoia (Extracts from the Fliess papers). *Standard Edition*, 1, 206–12.

Freud, S. (1895b). Project for a scientific psychology. *Standard Edition*, 1, 295–343.

Freud, S. (1895c). A reply to criticisms of my paper on anxiety neurosis. *Standard Edition*, 3, 119–39.

Freud, S. (1896a). Draft K: The neuroses of defence (Extracts from the Fliess papers). *Standard Edition*, 1, 220–29.

Freud, S. (1896b). Letter 52 (Extracts from the Fliess papers). *Standard Edition*, 1, 233.

Freud, S. (1896c). Further remarks on the neuropsychoses of defence. *Standard Edition*, 3, 157–85.

Freud, S. (1896d). Heredity and the aetiology of the neuroses. *Standard Edition*, 3, 141–56.

Freud, S. (1897a). Draft M [Notes II] (Extracts from the Fliess papers). *Standard Edition*, 1, 250–53.

Freud, S. (1897b). Letter 55 (Extracts from the Fliess papers). *Standard Edition*, 1, 240–41.

Freud, S. (1897c). Letters 56 and 57 (Extracts from the Fliess papers). *Standard Edition*, 1, 242–43.

Freud, S. (1897d). Letter 66 (Extracts from the Fliess papers). *Standard Edition*, 1, 257–58.

Freud, S. (1897e). Letter 69 (Extracts from the Fliess papers). *Standard Edition*, 1, 259–60.

Freud, S. (1897f). Letters 70 and 71 (Extracts from the Fliess papers). *Standard Edition*, 1, 261–65.

Freud, S. (1897g). Letter 79 (Extracts from the Fliess papers). *Standard Edition*, 1, 272–73.

Freud, S. (1898a). Letter 84 (Extracts from the Fliess papers). *Standard Edition*, 1, 274.

Freud, S. (1898b). Sexuality in the aetiology of the neuroses. *Standard Edition*, 3, 259–85.

Freud, S. (1899a). Screen memories. *Standard Edition*, 3, 301–22.

Freud, S. (1899b). Letter 125 (Extracts from the Fliess papers). *Standard Edition*, 1, 279–80.

Freud, S. (1900). The interpretation of dreams. *Standard Edition*, 4–5, 1–626.

Freud, S. (1901). The psychopathology of everyday life. *Standard Edition*, 6, 1–310.

Freud, S. (1904) On psychotherapy. *Standard Edition*, 7, 257–68.

Freud, S. (1905a). Fragment of an analysis of a case of hysteria. *Standard Edition*, 7, 1–122.

Freud, S. (1905b). Three essays on the theory of sexuality. *Standard Edition*, 7, 123–246.

Freud, S. (1905c). My views on the part played by sexuality in the aetiology of the neuroses. *Standard Edition*, 7, 271–82.

Freud, S. (1905d). Jokes and their relation to the unconscious. *Standard Edition*, 8, 1–247.

Freud, S. (1906). Psycho-analysis and the establishment of the facts in legal proceedings. *Standard Edition*, 9, 97–114.

Freud, S. (1907a). Letter from Sigmund Freud to Karl Abraham, November 26, 1907. In *The complete correspondence of Sigmund Freud and Karl Abraham, 1907–1925*, ed. E. Falzeder (p. 13). London: Karnac Books, 2002.

Freud, S. (1907b). Obsessive actions and religious practices. *Standard Edition*, 9, 115–28.

Freud, S. (1907c). The sexual enlightenment of children. *Standard Edition*, 9, 129–40.

Freud, S. (1907d). Delusions and dreams in Jensen's *Gradiva*. *Standard Edition*, 9, 1–93.

Freud, S. (1908a). Creative writers and day-dreaming. *Standard Edition*, 9, 141–54.

Freud, S. (1908b). Character and anal erotism. *Standard Edition*, 9, 167–76.

Freud, S. (1908c). On the sexual theories of children. *Standard Edition*, 9, 207–26.

Freud, S. (1908d). Preface to Wilhelm Stekel's nervous anxiety-states and their treatment. *Standard Edition*, 9, 250–51.

Freud, S. (1908e). Hysterical phantasies and their relation to bisexuality. *Standard Edition*, 9, 155–66.

Freud, S. (1908f). "Civilized" sexual morality and modern nervous illness. *Standard Edition*, 9, 177–204.

Freud, S. (1909a). Family romances. *Standard Edition*, 9, 235–42.

Freud, S. (1909b). Some general remarks on hysterical attacks. *Standard Edition*, 9, 227–34.

Freud, S. (1909c). Analysis of a phobia in a five-year-old boy. *Standard Edition*, 10, 1–150.

Freud, S. (1909d). Notes upon a case of obsessional neurosis. *Standard Edition*, 10, 151–318.

Freud, S. (1910a). Five lectures on psycho-analysis. *Standard Edition*, 11, 1–56.

Freud, S. (1910b). Leonardo da Vinci and a memory of his childhood. *Standard Edition*, 11, 59–138.

Freud, S. (1910c). The future prospects of psycho-analytic therapy. *Standard Edition*, 11, 139–52.

Freud, S. (1910d). A special type of choice of object made by men. *Standard Edition*, 11, 163–76.

Freud, S. (1910e). The psycho-analytic view of psychogenic disturbance of vision. *Standard Edition*, 11, 209–18.

Freud, S. (1910f). "Wild" psycho-analysis. *Standard Edition*, 11, 219–30.

Freud, S. (1911a). Psycho-analytic notes on an autobiographical account of a case of paranoia (dementia paranoides). *Standard Edition*, 12, 1–82.

Freud, S. (1911b). Formulations on the two principles of mental functioning. *Standard Edition*, 12, 213–26.

Freud, S. (1911c). Dreams in folklore. *Standard Edition*, 12, 175–204.

Freud, S. (1912a). The dynamics of transference. *Standard Edition*, 12, 97–108.

Freud, S. (1912b). Recommendations to physicians practicing psychoanalysis. *Standard Edition*, 12, 109–20.

Freud, S. (1912c). Contributions to a discussion on masturbation. *Standard Edition*, 12, 239–54.

Freud, S. (1912d). On the universal tendency to debasement in the sphere of love. *Standard Edition*, 11, 178–90.

Freud, S. (1912e). Letter from Sigmund Freud to C. G. Jung, February 29, 1912. In *The Freud/Jung Letters: The correspondence between Sigmund Freud and C. G. Jung* (W. McGuire, Ed.) (pp. 488–89). Princeton, NJ: Princeton University Press, 1974, 1979.

Freud, S. (1912f). Letter from Sigmund Freud to Ernest Jones, August 1, 1912. In *The complete correspondence of Sigmund Freud and Ernest Jones, 1908–1939* (R. Paskauskas, Ed.) (pp. 147–48). Cambridge, MA: Harvard University Press, 1993.

Freud, S. (1913a). On beginning the treatment. *Standard Edition*, 12, 121–44.

Freud, S. (1913b). On psycho-analysis. *Standard Edition*, 12, 205–12.

Freud, S. (1913c). The claims of psycho-analysis to scientific interest. *Standard Edition*, 12, 163–90.

Freud, S. (1913d). The disposition to obsessional neurosis. *Standard Edition*, 12, 311–26.

Freud, S. (1913e). Totem and taboo. *Standard Edition*, 12, 1–161.

Freud, S. (1913f). Observations and examples from analytic practice. *Standard Edition*, 13, 192–98.

Freud, S. (1914a). Letter from Sigmund Freud to Karl Abraham, July 15, 1914. In *The complete correspondence of Sigmund Freud and Karl Abraham, 1907–1925* (E. Falzeder, Ed.) (pp. 256–57). London: Karnac Books, 2002.

Freud, S. (1914b). Papers on technique. *Standard Edition*, 12, 85–174.

Freud, S. (1914c). Remembering, repeating and working-through (further recommendations on the technique of psycho-analysis II). *Standard Edition*, 12, 145–56.

Freud, S. (1914d). On the history of the psycho-analytic movement. *Standard Edition*, 14, 1–66.

Freud, S. (1914e). On narcissism. *Standard Edition*, 14, 67–102.

Freud, S. (1915a). Observations on transference-love (further recommendations on the technique of psycho-analysis III). *Standard Edition*, 12, 157–71.

Freud, S. (1915b). Instincts and their vicissitudes. *Standard Edition*, 14, 109–40.

Freud, S. (1915c). Repression. *Standard Edition*, 14, 141–58.

Freud, S. (1915d). The unconscious. *Standard Edition*, 14, 159–215.

Freud, S. (1915e). A case of paranoia running counter to the psycho-analytic theory of the disease. *Standard Edition*, 14, 263–72.

Freud, S. (1915f). On transience. *Standard Edition*, 14, 303–8.

Freud, S. (1915g). Papers on metapsychology. *Standard Edition*, 14, 103–236.

Freud, S. (1915/1916). Introductory lectures on psycho-analysis (parts I and II). *Standard Edition*, 15, 1–240.

Freud, S. (1916). Some character-types met with in psycho-analytic work. *Standard Edition*, 14, 309–33.

Freud, S. (1916/1917). Introductory lectures (part 3). *Standard Edition*, 16, 241–463.

Freud, S. (1917a). A difficulty in the path of psycho-analysis. *Standard Edition*, 17, 135–44.

Freud, S. (1917b). A metapsychological supplement to the theory of dreams. *Standard Edition*, 14, 217–35.

Freud, S. (1917c). Mourning and melancholia. *Standard Edition*, 14, 237–58.

Freud, S. (1917d). On transformations of instincts as exemplified in anal erotism. *Standard Edition*, 17, 125–33.

Freud, S. (1918a). From the history of an infantile neurosis. *Standard Edition*, 17, 1–124.

Freud, S. (1918b). The taboo of virginity. *Standard Edition*, 11, 191–208.

Freud, S. (1919a). Lines of advance in psychoanalytic therapy. *Standard Edition*, 17, 157–68.

Freud, S. (1919b). A child is being beaten. *Standard Edition*, 17, 175–204.

Freud, S. (1919c). Introduction to psycho-analysis and the war neuroses. *Standard Edition*, 17, 205–16.

Freud, S. (1919d). The "uncanny." *Standard Edition*, 17, 217–56.

Freud, S. (1919e). Preface to Reik's ritual: Psychoanalytic studies. *Standard Edition*, 17, 257–64.

Freud, S. (1920a). Beyond the pleasure principle. *Standard Edition*, 18, 1–64.

Freud, S. (1920b). The psychogenesis of a case of homosexuality in a woman. *Standard Edition*, 18, 145–72.

Freud, S. (1921). Group psychology and the analysis of the ego. *Standard Edition*, 18, 65–144.

Freud, S. (1922). Some neurotic mechanisms in jealousy, paranoia and homosexuality. *Standard Edition*, 18, 221–32.

Freud, S. (1923a). The ego and the id. *Standard Edition*, 19, 1–66.

Freud, S. (1923b). The infantile genital organization (an interpolation into the theory of sexuality). *Standard Edition*, 19, 139–46.

Freud, S. (1923c). Two encyclopaedia articles. *Standard Edition*, 19, 233–60.

Freud, S. (1924a). The economic problem of masochism. *Standard Edition*, 19, 155–70.

Freud, S. (1924b). The dissolution of the oedipus complex. *Standard Edition*, 19, 171–80.

Freud, S. (1924c). The loss of reality in neurosis and psychosis. *Standard Edition*, 19, 181–88.

Freud, S. (1925a). Negation. *Standard Edition*, 19, 233–40.

Freud, S. (1925b). Some psychical consequences of the anatomical distinction between the sexes. *Standard Edition*, 19, 241–58.

Freud, S. (1925c). Preface to Aichhorn's *Wayward Youth. Standard Edition*, 19, 271–76.

Freud, S. (1925d). Some additional notes on dream-interpretation as a whole. *Standard Edition*, 19, 123–38.

Freud, S. (1925e). An autobiographical study. *Standard Edition*, 20, 1–74.

Freud, S. (1926a). Inhibitions, symptoms and anxiety. *Standard Edition*, 20, 77–175.

Freud, S. (1926b). The question of lay analysis. *Standard Edition*, 20, 177–258.

Freud, S. (1927a). The future of an illusion. *Standard Edition*, 21, 1–56.

Freud, S. (1927b). Fetishism. *Standard Edition*, 21, 147–58.

Freud, S (1928). Dostoevsky and parricide. *Standard Edition*, 21, 173–94.

Freud, S. (1930). Civilization and its discontents. *Standard Edition*, 21, 57–146.

Freud, S. (1931a). Female sexuality. *Standard Edition*, 21, 221–44.

Freud, S. (1931b). Libidinal types. *Standard Edition*, 21, 215–20.

Freud, S. (1933a). New introductory lectures on psychoanalysis. *Standard Edition*, 22, 1–182.

Freud, S. (1933b). Why war? *Standard Edition*, 22, 195–218.

Freud, S. (1933c). Revision of the theory of dreams. *Standard Edition*, 22, 7–30.

Freud, S. (1936a). A disturbance of memory on the acropolis. *Standard Edition*, 22, 237–48.

Freud, S. (1936b). Preface to Richard Sterba's dictionary of psycho-analysis. *Standard Edition*, 22, 253.

Freud, S. (1937a). Analysis terminable and interminable. *Standard Edition*, 23, 209–53.

Freud, S. (1937b). Constructions in analysis. *Standard Edition*, 23, 255–69.

Freud, S. (1938a). An outline of psycho-analysis. *Standard Edition*, 23, 139–208.

Freud, S. (1938b). Splitting of the ego in the process of defence. *Standard Edition*, 23, 271–78.

Freud, S. (1939). Moses and monotheism. *Standard Edition*, 23, 1–138.

Freudental, G. (1996). Pluralism or relativism? *Science in Contest*, 9, 151–63.

Friedman, L. (1982). The humanistic trend in recent psychoanalytic theory. *Psychoanalytic Quarterly*, 51, 353–71.

Friedman, L. (2000). Modern hermeneutics and psychoanalysis. *Psychoanalytic Quarterly*, 69, 225–64.

Friedman, L. (2005). Is there a special psychoanalytic love? *Journal of the American Psychoanalytic Association*, 53, 349–75.

Friedman, R. (1988). *Male homosexuality: A contemporary psychoanalytic perspective.* New Haven, CT: Yale University Press.

Friedman, R. (2001). Psychoanalysis and human sexuality. *Journal of the American Psychoanalytic Association*, 49, 1115–32.

Friedman, R., and Downey, J. (1993). Neurobiology and sexual orientation: Current relationships. *Journal of Neuropsychiatry and Clinical Neurosciences*, 5, 131–53.

Friedman, R., and Downey, J. (2002a). *Sexual orientation and psychoanalysis: Sexual science and clinical practice.* New York: Columbia University Press.

Friedman. R., and Downey, J. (2002b). *Late childhood: The significance of postoedipal development. Sexual orientation and psychoanalysis.* New York: Columbia University Press.

Friedman, R., and Downey, J. (2004). On: Homosexuality: Coming out of the confusion. *International Journal of Psychoanalysis*, 85, 521–22.

Friedrich, W., Fisher, C., Broughton, D., Houston, M., and Shafran, C. (1998). Normative sexual behavior in children: A contemporary sample. *Pediatrics*, 101 (4), 9–18.

Friend, M., Schiddel, L., Klein, B., and Dunaeff, D. (1954). Observations on the development of transvestism in boys. *American Journal of Orthopsychiatry*, 24, 563–74.

Fromm, E. (1941). *Escape from freedom.* New York: Rinehart.

Fromm, E. (1947). *Man for himself: An inquiry into the psychology of ethics.* New York: Rinehart.

Fromm, E. (1951). *The forgotten language: An introduction to the understanding of dreams, fairy tales, and myths.* New York: Rinehart.

Fromm, E. (1955a). *The sane society.* New York: Holt, Rinehart and Winston.

Fromm, E. (1955b). Remarks on the problem of free association. In *Pioneers of interpersonal psychoanalysis,* ed. D. B. Stern, C. Mann, S. Kantor, and G. Schlesinger. Hillsdale, NJ: Analytic Press, 1995.

Fromm, E. (1957). *The art of loving: An inquiry into the nature of love.* New York: Harper and Row.

Fromm-Reichmann, F. (1943). Psychoanalytic psychotherapy with psychotics. *Psychiatry,* 6, 277–79.

Fromm-Reichmann, F. (1950). *Principles of intensive psychotherapy.* Chicago: University of Chicago Press.

Frosch, J. (1959a). The psychotic character: Psychoanalytic considerations presented at the American Psychoanalytic Association. *Journal of the American Psychoanalytic Association,* 8, 544–48.

Frosch, J. (1959b). Transference derivatives of the family romance. *Journal of the American Psychoanalytic Association,* 7, 503–22.

Frosch, J. (1964). The psychotic character: Clinical psychiatric considerations. *Psychiatric Quarterly,* 38, 91–96.

Frosch, J. (1981). The role of unconscious homosexuality in the paranoid constellation. *Psychoanalytic Quarterly,* 50, 587–613.

Frosh, S. (2003). *Key concepts in psychoanalysis.* New York: New York University Press.

Furst, S. (1967). Psychic trauma: A survey. In *Psychic trauma,* ed. S. Furst (pp. 3–50). New York: Basic Books.

Furst, S. (1998). A psychoanalytic study of aggression. *Psychoanalytic Study of the Child,* 53, 159–78.

Gabbard, G. (1994a). *Psychodynamic psychiatry in clinical practice, DSM IV edition.* Washington, DC: American Psychiatric Press.

Gabbard, G. (1994b). Psychotherapists who transgress sexual boundaries with patients. *Bulletin of the Menninger Clinic,* 58, 124–35.

Gabbard, G. (1996). Nominal gender and gender fluidity in the psychoanalytic situation. *Gender and Psychoanalysis,* 1, 463–81.

Gabbard, G. (2006a). *Psychodynamic psychiatry in clinical practice* (4th edition). Washington, DC: American Psychiatric Press.

Gabbard, G. (2006b). When is transference work useful in dynamic psychotherapy? *American Journal of Psychiatry,* 163 (10), 1667–69.

Gabbard, G., and Westen, D. (2003). Rethinking therapeutic action. *International Journal of Psychoanalysis,* 84, 823–41.

Galatzer-Levy, R. (1995). Psychoanalysis and dynamical systems theory: Prediction and self similarity. *Journal of the American Psychoanalytic Association,* 43, 1085–1113.

Galatzer-Levy, R. (1997a). Book review of *Understanding nonlinear dynamics,* by D. Kaplan and L. Glass. *Psychoanalytic Quarterly,* 66, 737.

Galatzer-Levy, R. (1997b). The witch and her children: Metapsychology's fate. *Annual of Psychoanalysis,* 25, 27–48.

Galatzer-Levy, R. (2002). Emergence. *Psychoanalytic Inquiry,* 22, 708–27.

Galatzer-Levy, R. (2004). Chaotic possibilities: Toward a new model of development. *International Journal of Psychoanalysis,* 85, 419–41.

Galatzer-Levy, R., and Cohler, B. (2002). Making a gay identity: Coming out, social context, and psychodynamics. *Annual of Psychoanalysis,* 30, 255–87.

Galenson, E. (1986). Some thoughts about infant psychopathology and aggressive development. *International Review of Psycho-Analysis,* 13, 349–54.

Galenson, E., and Roiphe, H. (1976). Some suggested revisions concerning early female development. *Journal of the American Psychoanalytic Association,* 24 (S), 29–57.

Gallese, V. (2006). Mirror neurons and intentional attunement: Commentary on Olds. *Journal of the American Psychoanalytic Association,* 54, 47–57.

Gallese, V., and Umiltà, M. (2002). From self-modeling to the self model: Agency and the representation of the self. *Neuropsychoanalysis,* 4 (2), 35–40.

Gassner, S., Sampson, H., Weiss, J., and Brumer, S. (1982). The emergence of warded-off contents. *Psychoanalysis and Contemporary Thought,* 5, 55–75.

Gediman, H. (1985). Imposture, inauthenticity, and feeling fraudulent. *Journal of the American Psychoanalytic Association,* 33 (4), 911–35.

Gedo, J. (2005). *Psychoanalysis as biological science: A comprehensive theory.* Baltimore, MD: Johns Hopkins University Press.

Gedo, J., and Goldberg, A. (1973). *Models of the mind: A psychoanalytic theory.* Chicago: University of Chicago Press.

Gedo, P., and Schaffer, N. (1989). An empirical approach to studying psychoanalytic process. *Psychoanalytical Psychology,* 6, 277–91.

Geissmann, C., and Geissmann, P. (1998). *A history of child psychoanalysis.* London: Routledge.

Gelman, S. (2003). *The essential child: Origins of essentialism in everyday thought. New York*: Oxford University Press.

George, C., Kaplan, N., and Main, M. (1985). The Berkeley adult attachment interview. Unpublished manuscript, Department of Psychology, University of California, Berkeley.

Gergely, G. (1992). Developmental reconstructions: Infancy from the point of view of psychoanalysis and developmental psychology. *Psychoanalysis and Contemporary Thought*, 15, 3–55.

Gergely, G. (2000). Reapproaching Mahler: New perspectives on normal autism, symbiosis, splitting and libidinal object constancy from cognitive developmental theory. *Journal of the American Psychoanalytic Association*, 48, 1197–1226.

Gergely, G., and Watson, J. (1996). The social biofeedback theory of parental affect-mirroring: The development of emotional self-awareness and self-control in infancy. *International Journal of Psychoanalysis*, 77, 1181–1212.

Gill, M. (1954). Psychoanalysis and exploratory psychotherapy. *Journal of the American Psychoanalytic Association*, 2, 771–97.

Gill, M. (1963). *Topography and systems in psychoanalytic theory*. Psychological Issues (Monograph 10). New York: International Universities Press.

Gill, M. (1976). Metapsychology is not psychology. In *Psychology versus metapsychology*, ed. M. Gill and P. Holzman. Psychological Issues (Monograph 36, pp. 71–105). New York: International Universities Press.

Gill, M. (1977). Psychic energy reconsidered—Discussion. *Journal of the American Psychoanalytic Association*, 25, 581–97.

Gill, M. (1982). *Analysis of transference: Theory and technique*. Psychological Issues (Monograph 53). New York: International Universities Press.

Gill, M. (1988). Metapsychology revisited. *Annual of Psychoanalysis*, 16, 35–48.

Gill, M., and Hoffmann, I. (1982). A method for studying the analysis of aspects of the patient's experience of the relationship in psychoanalysis and psychotherapy. *Journal of the American Psychoanalytic Association*, 30, 137–67.

Gilligan, C. (1982). *In a different voice: Psychological theory and women's development*. Cambridge, MA: Harvard University Press.

Gilligan, C. (2002). *The birth of pleasure*. New York: Alfred A. Knopf.

Gilman, S., ed. (1982). *Introducing psychoanalytic theory*. New York: Brunner/Routledge.

Gilmore, K. (1995). Gender identity disorder in a girl: Insights from adoption. *Journal of the American Psychoanalytic Association*, 43, 39–59.

Gilmore, K. (2000). A psychoanalytic perspective on attention-deficit/hyperactivity disorder. *Journal of the American Psychoanalytic Association*, 48, 1259–93.

Gilmore, K. (2002). Diagnosis, dynamics, and development: Considerations in the psychoanalytic assessment of children with AD/HD. *Psychoanalytic Inquiry*, 22, 372–90.

Gilmore, K. (2005). Play in the psychoanalytic setting: Ego capacity, ego state, and vehicle for intersubjective exchange. *Psychoanalytic Study of the Child*, 60, 213–38.

Gilmore, K. (2008). Psychoanalytic developmental theory: A contemporary reconsideration. *Journal of the American Psychoanalytic Association*, 56, 885–907.

Gitelson, M. (1952). The emotional position of the psychoanalyst in the psychoanalytic situation. *International Journal of Psychoanalysis*, 33, 1–10.

Gitelson, M. (1962). The curative factors in psychoanalysis. *International Journal of Psychoanalysis*, 43, 194–205.

Gitelson, M. (1964). On the identity crisis in American psychoanalysis. *Journal of the American Psychoanalytic Association*, 12, 451–76.

Glover, E. (1943). The concept of dissociation. *International Journal of Psychoanalysis*, 24, 7–13.

Glover, E. (1955). *The technique of psychoanalysis*. New York: International Universities Press.

Glover, E. (1958). Ego-distortion. *International Journal of Psychoanalysis*, 39, 260–64.

Glover, E. (1964). Freudian or neofreudian. *Psychoanalytic Quarterly*, 33, 97–109.

Glover, J. (1926). Divergent tendencies in psychotherapy. *British Journal of Medical Psychology*, 6 (2), 93–109.

Glover, L., and Mendell, D. (1982). A suggested developmental sequence for a preoedipal genital phase. In *Early female development*, ed. D. Mendell (pp. 127–74). New York: S P Medical and Scientific Books.

Goldberg, A. (1983). Sexualization and desexualization. *Psychoanalytic Quarterly*, 62, 383–99.

Goldberg, A. (1995). *The problem of perversion: The view from self psychology*. New Haven, CT: Yale University Press.

Goldberg, A. (1999). *Being of two minds: The vertical split in psychoanalysis and psychotherapy*. Hillsdale, NJ: Analytic Press.

Goldberg, A. (2000). *Errant selves*. Hillsdale, NJ: Analytic Press.

Goldberg, A. (2001). Depathologizing homosexuality. *Journal of the American Psychoanalytic Association*, 49 (4), 1109–14.

Goldberger, M. (1996). *Danger and defense: The technique of close process attention*. Northvale, NJ: Jason Aronson.

Golden, C. (1987). Diversity and variability in women's sexual identities. In *Lesbian psychologies*, ed. Boston

Lesbian Psychologies Collective (pp. 18–34). Urbana, IL: University of Illinois Press.

Golden, C. (2003). Improbable possibilities. *Psychoanalytic Inquiry*, 23, 624–41.

Goldings, H. (1974). Jump-rope rhymes and the rhythm of latency development in girls. *Psychoanalytic Study of the Child*, 29, 431–50.

Goldner, V. (1991). Toward a critical relational theory of gender. *Psychoanalytic Dialogues*, 1, 249–72.

Goldner, V. (2004). Review essay: Attachment and Eros: Opposed or synergistic? *Psychoanalytic Dialogues*, 14, 381–96.

Goldner, V. (2005). Ironic gender, authentic sex. In *Psychoanalytic reflections on a gender-free case: Into the void*, ed. E. Toronto (pp. 243–255). London: Routledge.

Goldstein, E., and Horowitz, L. (2003). *Lesbian identity and contemporary psychotherapy: A framework for clinical practice*. Hillsdale, NJ: Analytic Press.

Govrin, A. (2006). The dilemma of contemporary psychoanalysis: Toward a "knowing" postpostmodernism. *Journal of the American Psychoanalytic Association*, 54, 507–35.

Graham, S., and Clark, M. (2006). Self-esteem and organization of valenced information about others: The "Jekyll and Hyde"-ing of relationship partners. *Journal of Personality and Social Psychology*, 90 (4), 652–65.

Gray, P. (1973). Psychoanalytic technique and the ego's capacity for viewing intrapsychic activity. *Journal of the American Psychoanalytic Association*, 21, 474–94.

Gray, P. (1982). "Developmental lag" in the evolution of technique for psychoanalysis of neurotic conflict. *Journal of the American Psychoanalytic Association*, 30, 621–55.

Gray, P. (1994). *The ego and the analysis of defense*. Northvale, NJ: Jason Aronson.

Gray, P. (1996). Undoing the lag in the technique of conflict and defense analysis. *Psychoanalytic Study of the Child*, 51, 87–101.

Green, A. (1974). Surface analysis, deep analysis (the role of the preconscious in psychoanalytic technique). *International Review of Psycho-Analysis*, 1, 415–23.

Green, A. (1975). The analyst, symbolization and absence in the analytic setting (On changes in analytic practice and analytic experience)—In memory of D. W. Winnicott. *International Journal of Psychoanalysis*, 56, 1–22.

Green, J. (1996). *Chasing the sun: Dictionary-makers and the dictionaries they made* (1st American edition). New York: Henry Holt.

Green, R. (1975). The significance of feminine behavior in boys. *Journal of Child Psychology and Psychiatry*, 16, 341–44.

Greenacre, P. (1950a). Special problems of early female sexual development. *Psychoanalytic Study of the Child*, 5, 122–38.

Greenacre, P. (1950b). General problems of acting out. *Psychoanalytic Quarterly*, 19, 455–67.

Greenacre, P. (1954). The role of transference—Practical considerations in relation to psychoanalytic therapy. *Journal of the American Psychoanalytic Association*, 2, 671–84.

Greenacre, P. (1955). Further considerations regarding fetishism. *Psychoanalytic Study of the Child*, 10, 187–94.

Greenacre, P. (1956). Re-evaluation of the process of working through. *International Journal of Psychoanalysis*, 37, 439–44.

Greenacre, P. (1957). The childhood of the artist—Libidinal phase development and giftedness. *Psychoanalytic Study of the Child*, 12, 47–72.

Greenacre, P. (1958a). Early physical determinants in the development of the sense of identity. *Journal of the American Psychoanalytic Association*, 6, 612–27.

Greenacre, P. (1958b). The impostor. In *Emotional growth: Psychoanalytic studies of the gifted and a great variety of other individuals* (vol. 1, pp. 93–112). New York: International Universities Press, 1971.

Greenacre, P. (1968). Perversions: General consideration regarding their genetic and dynamic background. In *Emotional growth: Psychoanalytic studies of the gifted and a great variety of other individuals* (vol. 1, pp. 300–14). New York: International Universities Press, 1971.

Greenacre, P. (1975). On reconstruction. *Journal of the American Psychoanalytic Association*, 23, 693–712.

Greenberg, J. (1986). Theoretical models and the analyst's neutrality. *Contemporary Psychoanalysis*, 22 (1), 87–106.

Greenberg, J. (1991). *Oedipus and beyond: A clinical theory*. Cambridge, MA: Harvard University Press.

Greenberg, J., and Mitchell, S. (1983). *Object relations in psychoanalytic theory*. Boston: Harvard University Press.

Greenson, R. (1954). The struggle against identification. *Journal of the American Psychoanalytic Association*, 2, 200–17.

Greenson, R. (1960). Empathy and its vicissitudes. *International Journal of Psychoanalysis*, 41, 418–24.

Greenson, R. (1965a). The working alliance and the transference neurosis. *Psychoanalytic Quarterly*, 34, 155–81.

Greenson, R. (1965b). The problems of working through. In *Drives, affects, behavior,* ed. M. Schur (vol. 2, pp. 277–314). New York: International Universities Press.

Greenson, R. (1966). A transvestite boy and a hypothesis. *International Journal of Psychoanalysis,* 47, 396–403.

Greenson, R. (1967). *The technique and practice of psychoanalysis* (vol. 1). New York: International Universities Press.

Greenson, R. (1968). Disidentifying from mother: Its special importance for the boy. *International Journal of Psychoanalysis,* 49, 370–76.

Greenson, R., and Wexler, M. (1969). The non-transference relationship in the psychoanalytic situation. *International Journal of Psychoanalysis,* 50, 27–39.

Greenspan, S. (1997). *Developmentally based psychotherapy.* Madison, CT: International Universities Press.

Grigsby, J., and Stevens, D. (2000). *The neurodynamics of personality.* New York: Guilford Press.

Grinker, R., Werble, B., and Drye, R. (1968). *The borderline syndrome.* New York: Basic Books.

Grossman, G. (2001). Contemporary views of bisexuality in clinical work. *Journal of the American Psychoanalytic Association,* 49, 1361–1377.

Grossman, G. (2002). Queering psychoanalysis. *Annual of Psychoanalysis,* 30, 287–99.

Grossman, L. (1996). "Psychic reality" and reality testing in the analysis of perverse defences. *International Journal of Psychoanalysis,* 77, 509–17.

Grossman, W. (1982). The self as fantasy: Fantasy as theory. *Journal of the American Psychoanalytic Association,* 30, 919–37.

Grossman, W. (1998). Freud's presentation of "the psychoanalytic mode of thought" in *Totem and Taboo* and his technical papers. *International Journal of Psychoanalysis,* 79, 469–86.

Grossman, W., and Simon, B. (1969). Anthropomorphism—Motive, meaning, and causality in psychoanalytic theory. *Psychoanalytic Study of the Child,* 24, 78–111.

Grossman, W., and Stewart, W. (1976). Penis envy: From childhood wish to developmental metaphor. *Journal of the American Psychoanalytic Association,* 24 (S), 193–212.

Grubrich-Simitis, I. (1986). Six letters of Sigmund Freud and Sándor Ferenczi on the interrelationship of psychoanalytic theory and technique. *International Journal of Psychoanalysis,* 13, 259–77.

Grünbaum, A. (1979). Epistemological liabilities of the clinical appraisal of psychoanalytic theory. *Psychoanalysis and Contemporary Thought,* 2, 451–526.

Grünbaum, A. (1982). Can psychoanalytic theory be cogently tested "on the couch"? *Psychoanalysis and Contemporary Thought,* 5, 311–436.

Grünbaum, A. (2006). Is Sigmund Freud's psychoanalytic edifice relevant to the 21st century? *Psychoanalytic Psychology,* 23, 257–84.

Gunderson, J. (2009). Borderline personality disorder: Ontogeny of a diagnosis. *American Journal of Psychiatry,* 166, 530–39.

Gunderson, J., and Kolb, J. (1978). Discriminating features of borderline patients. *American Journal of Psychiatry,* 135, 792–96.

Gunderson, J., and Singer, M. (1975). Defining borderline patients: An overview. *American Journal of Psychiatry,* 132, 1–10.

Guntrip, H. (1961). *Personality structure and human interaction.* London: Hogarth Press.

Guntrip, H. (1969). *Schizoid phenomena, object-relations and the self.* New York: International Universities Press.

Halberstadt-Freud, H. (1998). Electra versus Oedipus: Femininity reconsidered. *International Journal of Psychoanalysis,* 79, 41–56.

Hall, C. (1954/1979). *A primer of Freudian psychology.* New York: HarperCollins / Mentor Books.

Hanly, C. (1990). The concept of truth in psychoanalysis. *International Journal of Psychoanalysis,* 71, 375–83.

Hanly, C., and Hanly, M. (2001). Critical realism: Distinguishing the psychological subjectivity of the analyst from epistemological subjectivism. *Journal of the American Psychoanalytic Association,* 49, 515–32.

Hare, R. (1980). A research scale for the assessment of psychopathy in criminal populations. *Personality and Individual Differences,* 1, 111–20.

Hargreaves, E., and Varchevker, A. (2004). *In pursuit of psychic change.* London: Routledge.

Harley, M. (1967). Fragments from the analysis of a dog phobia in a latency child. *Bulletin of the Philadelphia Association for Child Psychoanalysis,* 17, 127–29.

Harris, A. (1991). Gender as contradiction. *Psychoanalytic Dialogues,* 1, 197–294.

Harris, A. (2005a). *Gender as soft assembly.* Hillsdale, NJ: Analytic Press.

Harris, A. (2005b). Gender as a strange attractor: Gender's multidimensionality. *Relational Perspectives Book Series,* 25, 155–73.

Harris, A. (2005c). Laws, desires, and contaminations—Mutuality with a price: Commentary on paper by Taras Babiak. *Studies in Gender and Sexuality,* 6, 145–53.

Harris, A., and Aron, L. (1997). Ferenczi's semiotic theory: Previews of postmodernism. *Psychoanalytic Inquiry,* 17, 522–34.

Harrison, A., and Tronick, E. (2007). Contributions to understanding therapeutic change: Now we have a playground. *Journal of the American Psychoanalytic Association,* 55, 853–74.

Hartmann, H. (1927). Understanding and explanation. In *Essays on ego psychology* (pp. 369–403). New York: International Universities Press, 1964.

Hartmann, H. (1939a). *Ego psychology and the problem of adaptation.* New York: International Universities Press, 1958.

Hartmann, H. (1939b). Psycho-analysis and the concept of health. *International Journal of Psychoanalysis,* 20, 308–21.

Hartmann, H. (1950). Comments on the psychoanalytic theory of the ego. *Psychoanalytic Study of the Child,* 5, 74–96.

Hartmann, H. (1952). The mutual influences in the development of ego and id. *Psychoanalytic Study of the Child,* 7, 9–30.

Hartmann, H. (1953). Contribution to the metapsychology of schizophrenia. *Psychoanalytic Study of the Child,* 8, 177–98.

Hartmann, H. (1964). *Essays on ego psychology.* New York: International Universities Press.

Hartmann, H., Kris, E., and Loewenstein, R. (1949). Notes on the theory of aggression. *Psychoanalytic Study of the Child,* 3, 9–36.

Hartmann, H., and Loewenstein, R. (1962). Notes on the superego. *Psychoanalytic Study of the Child,* 17, 42–81.

Hartocollis, P., and Graham, I. (1991). *The personal myth in psychoanalytic theory.* Madison, CT: International Universities Press.

Hassin, R., Uleman, J., and Bargh, J., eds. (2005). *The new unconscious.* New York: Oxford University Press.

Hayman, A. (1994). Some remarks about the "controversial discussions." *International Journal of Psychoanalysis,* 75, 343–58.

Heilbrunn, G. (1953). Fusion of the Isakower phenomena with the dream screen. *Psychoanalytic Quarterly,* 22, 200–204.

Heimann, P. (1942). A contribution to the problem of sublimation and its relation to processes of internalization. *International Journal of Psychoanalysis,* 23, 8–17.

Heimann, P. (1950). On counter-transference. *International Journal of Psychoanalysis,* 31, 81–84.

Heimann, P. (1956). Dynamics of transference interpretations. *International Journal of Psychoanalysis,* 37, 303–10.

Hendrick, I. (1943a). The discussion of the "instinct to master"—A letter to the editors. *Psychoanalytic Quarterly,* 12, 561–65.

Hendrick, I. (1943b). Work and the pleasure principle. *International Journal of Psychoanalysis,* 26, 181.

Herman, J. (1992). Trauma and recovery. *Psychiatric Quarterly,* 23, 248–76.

Herzog, J. (1980). Sleep disturbance and father hunger in 18-to-28-month-old boys—The Erlkonig syndrome. *Psychoanalytic Study of the Child,* 35, 219–33.

Herzog, J. (1984). Fathers and young children: Fathering daughters and fathering sons. In *Frontiers of infant psychiatry,* ed. J. Call, E. Galenson, and R. Tyson (vol. 11, pp. 335–43). New York: Basic Books.

Herzog, J. (2001). *Father hunger: Explorations with adults and children.* Hillsdale, NJ: Analytic Press.

Hesse, E., and Main, M. (2000). Disorganized infant, child, and adult attachment: Collapse in behavioral and attentional strategies. *American Psychoanalytic Association,* 48, 1097–1127.

Hinshelwood, R. (1989). *A dictionary of Kleinian thought.* London: Free Association Books.

Hinshelwood, R. (2007). The Kleinian theory of therapeutic action. *Psychoanalytic Study of the Child,* 76, 1479–98.

Hirsch, I. (1985). The rediscovery of the advantages of the participant-observation model. *Psychoanalysis and Contemporary Thought,* 8, 441–59.

Hirsch, I. (1996). Observing-participation, mutual enactment, and the new classical models ART. *Contemporary Psychoanalysis,* 32, 359–83.

Hirsch, I. (2000). Interview with Benjamin Wolstein. *Contemporary Psychoanalysis,* 36, 187–232.

Hirsch, I. (2002). Beyond interpretation: Analytic interaction in the interpersonal tradition. *Contemporary Psychoanalysis,* 38, 573–588.

Hirsch, I. (2008). *Coasting in the countertransference: Conflicts of self interest between analyst and patient.* New York: Routledge.

Hirschfeld, M. (1910/1991). *Transvestites: The erotic drive to cross-dress.* New York: Prometheus Books.

Hirschfeld, M. (1923). The intersexual constitution. *Yearbook of Sexual Intermediates,* 23, 3–27.

Hirst, W. (1995). Cognitive aspects of consciousness. In *The cognitive neurosciences,* ed. M. Gazzaniga (pp. 1307–19). Cambridge, MA: MIT Press.

Hobson, J. (1988). *The dreaming brain.* New York: Basic Books.

Hobson, J. (1994). *The chemistry of conscious states.* Boston: Little Brown.

Hoch, P., and Polatin, P. (1949). Pseudoneurotic forms of schizophrenia. *Psychiatric Quarterly,* 23, 248–76.

Hofer, M. (1995). Hidden regulators: Implications for a new understanding of attachment, separation, and loss. In *Attachment theory: Social, developmental, and clinical perspectives,* ed. S. Goldberg, R. Muir, and J. Kerr (pp. 203–30). Hillsdale, NJ: Analytic Press.

Hoffer, A. (1985). Toward a definition of psychoanalytic neutrality. *Journal of the American Psychoanalytic Association, 33,* 771–95.

Hoffman, I. (1983). The patient as interpreter of the analyst's experience. *Contemporary Psychoanalysis, 19,* 389–422.

Hoffman, I. (1994). Dialectical thinking and therapeutic action in the psychoanalytic process. *Psychoanalytic Quarterly, 63,* 187–218.

Hoffman, I. (1996). The intimate and ironic authority of the psychoanalyst's presence. *Psychoanalytic Quarterly, 65,* 102–36.

Hoffman, I. (1998). *Ritual and spontaneity in the psychoanalytic process.* Hillsdale, NJ: Analytic Press.

Hoffman, L. (2007). Do children get better when we interpret their defenses against painful feelings? *Psychoanalytic Study of the Child, 62,* 291–313.

Holder, A. (1975). Theoretical and clinical aspects of ambivalence. *Psychoanalytic Study of the Child, 30,* 197–220.

Holder, A. (1982). Preoedipal contributions to the formation of the superego. *Psychoanalytic Study of the Child, 37,* 245–72.

Holmes, J. (1993) Attachment theory: A biological basis for psychotherapy. *British Journal of Psychiatry, 163,* 430–38.

Holt, R. (1962). A critical examination of Freud's concept of bound vs. free cathexis. *Journal of the American Psychoanalytic Association, 10,* 475–525.

Holt, R. (1967). The development of the primary process; A structural view. In *Motives and thought: Essays in honor of David Rapaport,* ed. R. Holt. Psychological Issues (Monographs 18/19, pp. 344–84). New York: International Universities Press.

Holt, R. (1976). Drive or wish? A reconsideration of the psychoanalytic theory of motivation. In *Psychology vs. metapsychology: Psychoanalytic essays in memory of George S. Klein, ed.* M. Gill and P. Holzman (pp. 158–97). New York: International Universities Press.

Holt, R. (2002). Quantitative research on the primary process: Method and findings. *Journal of the American Psychoanalytic Association, 50,* 457–82.

Holtzman, D., and Kulish, N. (2000). The feminization of the female oedipal complex: Part 1, A reconsideration of the significance of separation issues. *Journal of the American Psychoanalytic Association, 48,* 1413–37.

Horney, K. (1924). On the genesis on the castration complex in women. *International Journal of Psychoanalysis, 5,* 50–65.

Horney, K. (1926). The flight from womanhood: The masculinity-complex in women, as viewed by men and by women. *International Journal of Psychoanalysis, 7,* 324–39.

Horney, K. (1933). The denial of the vagina—A contribution to the genital anxieties specific to women. *International Journal of Psychoanalysis, 14,* 57–70.

Horney, K. (1936). The problem of the negative therapeutic reaction. *Psychoanalytic Quarterly, 5,* 29–44.

Horney, K. (1945). *Our inner conflicts.* New York: W. W. Norton.

Horowitz, M. (1977). Hysterical personality: Cognitive structure and the processes of change. *International Review of Psycho-Analysis, 4,* 23–49.

Horowitz, M. (1987). *States of mind: Configurational analysis of individual psychology.* Critical Issues in Psychiatry. New York: Springer.

Horowitz, M. (1991). *Role-relationship modes: Person schemas and maladaptive interpersonal patterns.* Chicago: University of Chicago Press.

Horowitz, M. (1998). *Cognitive psychodynamics: From conflict to character.* New York: John Wiley and Sons.

Hurry, A. (1998). Psychoanalysis and developmental therapy. In *Psychoanalysis and developmental therapy,* ed. A. Hurry (pp. 32–73). London: Karnac Books.

Hyman, M. (1975). In defense of libido theory. *Annual of Psychoanalysis, 3,* 21–36.

Inderbitzin, L., and Levy, S. (1994). On grist for the mill: External reality as defense. *Journal of the American Psychoanalytic Association, 42,* 763–88.

Inderbitzin, L., and Levy, S. (2000). Regression and psychoanalytic technique: The concretization of a concept. *Psychoanalytic Quarterly, 69,* 195–223.

Irigaray, L. (1991). *Marine lover of Friedrich Nietzsche.* New York: Columbia University Press.

Isaacs, S. (1933). *The social development of young children: A study of beginnings.* London: Routledge.

Isaacs, S. (1948). The nature and function of phantasy. *International Journal of Psychoanalysis, 29,* 73–97.

Isakower, O. (1938). A contribution to the pathopsychology of phenomena associated with falling asleep. *International Journal of Psychoanalysis, 19,* 331–45.

Isay, R. (1986). The development of sexual identity in homosexual men. *Psychoanalytic Study of the Child, 41,* 467–89.

Isay, R. (1987). Fathers and their homosexually inclined sons in childhood. *Psychoanalytic Study of the Child, 42,* 275–94.

Isay, R. (1989). *Being homosexual: Gay men and their development.* New York: Farrar, Strauss and Giroux.

Isay, R. (1996). *Becoming gay: The journey to self-acceptance.* New York: Pantheon Books.

Isay, R., and Friedman, R. (1986). Toward a further understanding of homosexual men. *Journal of the American Psychoanalytic Association, 34,* 193–208.

Jacobs, T. (1986). On countertransference enactments. *Journal of the American Psychoanalytic Association, 34,* 289–307.

Jacobs, T. (1999). Countertransference past and present: A review of the concept. *International Journal of Psychoanalysis, 80,* 575–94.

Jacobson, E. (1953). Contribution to the metapsychology of cyclothymic depression. In *Affective disorders: Psychoanalytic contributions to their study,* ed. P. Greenacre. Oxford, England: International Universities Press.

Jacobson, E. (1957). Normal and pathological moods: Their nature and functions. *Psychoanalytic Study of the Child, 12,* 73–113.

Jacobson, E. (1959). The "exceptions"—An elaboration of Freud's character study. *Psychoanalytic Study of the Child, 14,* 135–53.

Jacobson, E. (1961). Adolescent moods and the remodeling of psychic structures in adolescence. *Psychoanalytic Study of the Child, 16,* 164–83.

Jacobson, E. (1964). *The self and the object world.* New York: International Universities Press.

Jacobson, E. (1971). *Depression: Comparative studies of normal, neurotic, and psychotic conditions.* New York: International Universities Press.

Jacques, E. (1965). Death and the mid-life crises. *International Journal of Psychoanalysis, 46,* 502–14.

Janet, P. (1889). *Psychological healing: A historical and clinical study.* London: G. Allen and Unwin.

Jeffrey, W. (1992). The psychoanalytic review. LXXVII, 1990: The preconscious and potential space. *Psychoanalytic Quarterly, 61,* 685.

Johnson, A. (1949). Sanctions for superego lacunae of adolescents. In *The mark of Cain: Psychoanalytic insight and the psychopath,* ed. J. Meloy (pp. 91–113). Hillsdale, NJ: Analytic Press/Taylor and Francis Group, 2001.

Johnson, S. (1755/2002). *Samuel Johnson's dictionary: Selections from the 1755 work that defined the English language,* ed. J. Lynch. New York: Levenger Press / Walker and Company, 2002.

Jones, E. (1908). Rationalization in everyday life. *Journal of Abnormal Psychology, 3,* 161–69.

Jones, E. (1912). The theory of symbolism. In *Papers on Psychoanalysis,* ed. H. Loewald (pp. 87–144). Baltimore, MD: William and Wilkins, 1948.

Jones, E. (1913a). *Papers on psycho-analysis.* London: Bailliere, Tindall and Cox.

Jones, E. (1913b) The God complex: The belief that one is God and the resulting character traits. In *Essays in applied psychoanalysis,* ed. G. Butler (vol. 2, pp. 244–65). London: Hogarth Press, 1951.

Jones, E. (1918a). Hate and anal erotism in the obsessional neurosis. In *Essential papers on obsessive-compulsive disorder,* ed. D. J. Stern and M. Stern (pp. 65–72). New York: NYU Press, 1997.

Jones, E. (1918b). Anal erotic character traits. *Journal of Abnormal Psychology, 13* (5), 261–84.

Jones, E. (1918c). *Papers on psychoanalysis* (2nd edition). London: Bailliere, Tindall and Cox.

Jones, E., ed. (1924). *Glossary for the use of translators of psychoanalytical works.* London: International Psychoanalytic Press.

Jones, E. (1927). The early development of female sexuality. *International Journal of Psychoanalysis, 8,* 459–72.

Jones, E. (1933). The phallic phase. *International Journal of Psychoanalysis, 14,* 1–13.

Jones, E. (1946). A valedictory address. *International Journal of Psychoanalysis, 27,* 7–12.

Jones, E. (1981). *The life and work of Sigmund Freud* (vols. 1–3). New York: Basic Books.

Jones, E., and Maeder, A. (1913). Besetzungsvorschläge der gebräuchlichsten psychoanalytischen. *Internationale Zeitschrift für Ärztliche Psychoanalyse,* 1–415.

Joseph, B. (1975). The patient who is difficult to reach. In *Tactics and techniques in psychoanalytic therapy,* ed. P. Giovacchini (vol. 2, pp. 205–16). New York: Jason Aronson.

Joseph, B. (1985). Transference: The total situation. *International Journal of Psychoanalysis, 66,* 447–54.

Joseph, B. (1989). *Psychic equilibrium and psychic change.* London: Routledge.

Joseph, B. (2000). Agreeableness as obstacle. *International Journal of Psychoanalysis, 81,* 641–49.

Joseph, E. (1965). *Beating fantasies: Regressive ego phenomena in psychoanalysis.* New York: International Universities Press.

Josselson, R. (1996). *Revising herself: The story of women's identity from college to midlife.* New York: Oxford University Press.

Jung, C. (1906). *Studies in word-association.* New York: Moffat, Yard, 1919.

Jung, C. (1921/1957). *Collected works of C. G. Jung.* Princeton, NJ . Princeton University Press.

Jung, C. (1934). *A review of the complex theory: Collected works of C. G. Jung* (vol. 8). New York: Pantheon Books, 1960.

Jung, C. (1963). *Memories, dreams, reflections.* New York: Pantheon.

Kahn, S. (1942). *Psychological and neurological definitions and the unconscious.* Boston: Meador Publishing.

Kalin, N. (2002). The neurobiology of fear. *Scientific American, 268,* 94–103.

Kantrowitz, J. (1986). The role of the patient-analyst "match" in the outcome of psychoanalysis. *Annual of Psychoanalysis*, 14, 273–97.

Kantrowitz, J. (1999). The role of the preconscious in psychoanalysis. *Journal of the American Psychoanalytic Association*, 47, 65–89.

Kanzer, M. (1957). Panel reports—Acting out and its relation to impulse disorders. *Journal of the American Psychoanalytic Association*, 5, 136–45.

Kaplan, L. (1991). *Female perversions: The temptations of Emma Bovary*. New York: Doubleday.

Kardiner, A., Karush, A., and Ovesey, L. (1959). A methodological study of Freudian theory. *Journal of Nervous and Mental Disorders*, 129, 341–56.

Karon, B., and Widener, A. (2001). Repressed memories. *Psychoanalytic Psychology*, 18, 161–64.

Karpman, B. (1950). A case of paedophilea (legally rape) cured by psychoanalysis. *Psychoanalytic Review*, 37, 235–76.

Katz, J. (1995). *The invention of heterosexuality*. New York: Dutton.

Katz, W. (2009). Payment as perverse defense. *Psychoanalytic Quarterly*, 78, 843–69.

Kay, P. (1971). A survey of recent contributions on transference and transference neurosis in child analysis. In *The unconscious today*, ed. M. Kanzer (pp. 386–99). New York: International Universities Press.

Kaywin, L. (1966). Problems of sublimation. *Journal of the American Psychoanalytic Association*, 14, 313–34.

Kennedy, H., and Yorke, C. (1982). Steps from outer to inner conflict viewed as superego precursors. *Psychoanalytic Study of the Child*, 37, 221–22.

Kernberg, O. (1966). Structural derivatives of object relationships. *International Journal of Psychoanalysis*, 47 (2–3), 236–53.

Kernberg, O. (1967). Borderline personality organization. *Journal of the American Psychoanalytic Association*, 15, 641–85.

Kernberg, O. (1970a). A psychoanalytic classification of character pathology. *Journal of the American Psychoanalytic Association*, 18, 800–22.

Kernberg, O. (1970b). Factors in the psychoanalytic treatment of narcissistic personalities. *Journal of the American Psychoanalytic Association*, 18, 51–85.

Kernberg, O. (1971). Prognostic considerations regarding borderline personality organization. *Journal of the American Psychoanalytic Association*, 19, 595–635.

Kernberg, O. (1974a). Mature love: Prerequisites and characteristics. *Journal of the American Psychoanalytic Association*, 22, 743–68.

Kernberg, O. (1974b). Barriers to falling and remaining in love. *Journal of the American Psychoanalytic Association*, 22, 486–511.

Kernberg, O. (1975). *Borderline conditions and pathological narcissism*. New York: Jason Aronson.

Kernberg, O. (1976a). *Object relations theory and clinical psychoanalysis*. New York: Jason Aronson.

Kernberg, O. (1976b). Technical considerations in the treatment of borderline personality organization. *Journal of the American Psychoanalytic Association*, 24, 795–829.

Kernberg, O. (1977). Boundaries and structure in love relations. *Journal of the American Psychoanalytic Association*, 25, 81–114.

Kernberg, O. (1980). *Internal world and external reality: Object relations theory applied*. New York: Jason Aronson.

Kernberg, O. (1982). Self, ego, affects, and drives. *Journal of the American Psychoanalytic Association*, 30, 893–917.

Kernberg, O. (1984). *Severe personality disorders: Psychotherapeutic strategies*. New Haven, CT: Yale University Press.

Kernberg, O. (1985). *Internal world and external reality: Object relations theory applied*. Northvale, NJ: Jason Aronson.

Kernberg, O. (1988). Between conventionality and aggression: The boundaries of passion. In *Passionate attachments: Thinking about love*, ed. W. Gaylin and E. Person (pp. 63–84), New York: Free Press.

Kernberg, O. (1995). Omnipotence in the transference and in the countertransference. *The Scandinavian Psychoanalytic Review*, 18, 2–21.

Kernberg, O. (1998). Aggression, hatred, and social violence. *Canadian Journal of Psychoanalysis*, 6, 191–206.

Kernberg, O. (1999). Psychoanalysis, psychoanalytic psychotherapy and supportive psychotherapy. *International Journal of Psychoanalysis*, 80, 1075–91.

Kernberg, O. (2000). The influence of the gender of patient and analyst in the psychoanalytic relationship. *Journal of the American Psychoanalytic Association*, 48, 859–83.

Kernberg, O. (2007). The therapeutic action of psychoanalysis: Controversies and challenges. *Psychoanalytic Quarterly*, 76, 1689–1723.

Kernberg, O. (2010). Some observations on the process of mourning. *International Journal of Psychoanalysis*, 91, 601–19.

Kernberg, O. (2011). Limitations to the capacity of love. *International Journal of Psychoanalysis*, 92, 1501–15. doi: 10.1111/j.1745–8315. 2001.00456.x.

Kessler, R. (1996). Panic disorder and the retreat from meaning. *Journal of Clinical Psychoanalysis*, 5, 505–28.

Kestenberg, J. (1968). Outside and inside, male and female. *Journal of the American Psychoanalytic Association,* 16, 457–520.

Kestenberg, J. (1982). The inner genital phase: Prephallic and preoedipal. In *Early female development,* ed. D. Mendell (pp. 71–126). New York: S P Medical and Scientific Books.

Khan, M. (1963). The concept of cumulative trauma. *Psychoanalytic Study of the Child,* 18, 286–306.

Khan, M. (1969). Role of the "collated internal object" in perversion-formations. *International Journal of Psychoanalysis,* 50, 555–65.

Kihlstrom, J. (1995). The rediscovery of the unconscious. In *The mind, the brain, and complex adaptive systems,* ed. H. Morowitz and J. Singer (vol. 22, pp. 123–43). Reading, MA: Addison-Wesley.

King, P., and Steiner, R., eds. (1991). *The Freud-Klein controversies 1941–45.* London: Tavistock/Routledge.

King-Casas, B., Sharp, C., Lomax-Bream, L., Lohrenz, T., Fonagy, P., and Montague, P. (2008). The rupture and repair of cooperation in borderline personality disorder. *Science,* 321 (5890), 806–10.

Kinsey, A. (1941). Homosexuality: Criteria for a hormonal explanation of the homosexual. *Journal of Clinical Endocrinology,* 1 (5), 424–28.

Kinsey, A., Pomeroy, W., and Martin, C. (1948). *Sexual behavior in the human male.* Bloomington, IN: Indiana University Press.

Kirkpatrick, M. (2002). Clinical notes on the diversity in lesbian lives. *Psychoanalytic Inquiry,* 22 (2), 196–208.

Kirkpatrick, M. (2003). The nature and nurture of gender. *Psychoanalytic Inquiry,* 23, 558–71.

Kitson, H. (1925). Review of "Dynamic psychology: An introduction to modern theory and Practice," by T. Moore (1924). *Journal of Applied Psychology,* 9 (1), 101–4.

Klaus, M., and Kennell, J. (1976/1982). *Parent-infant bonding.* St. Louis, MO: C. V. Mosby.

Kleeman, J. (1966). Genital self-discovery during a boy's second year—A follow-up. *Psychoanalytic Study of the Child,* 21, 358–92.

Kleeman, J. (1976). Freud's views on early female sexuality in the light of direct child observation. *Journal of the American Psychoanalytic Association,* 24 (S), 3–26.

Klein, G. (1959). Consciousness in psychoanalytic theory: Some implications for current research in perception. *Journal of the American Psychoanalytic Association,* 7, 5–34.

Klein, G. (1970). *Perception, motives, and personality.* New York: Knopf.

Klein, G. (1976). *Psychoanalytic theory: An exploration of essentials.* New York: International Universities Press.

Klein, M. (1927a). Criminal tendencies in normal children. In *Love, guilt and reparation: And other works 1921–1945* (pp. 170–85). London: Hogarth Press, 1975.

Klein, M. (1927b). Symposium on child analysis. In *Contributions to psycho-analysis, 1921–1945* (pp. 152–84). London: Hogarth Press, 1948.

Klein, M. (1927c). The psychological principles of infant analysis. *International Journal of Psychoanalysis,* 8, 25–37.

Klein, M. (1928). Early stages of the oedipus conflict. *International Journal of Psychoanalysis,* 9, 167–80.

Klein, M. (1929). Personification in the play of children. *International Journal of Psychoanalysis,* 10, 193–204.

Klein, M. (1930). The importance of symbol-formation in the development of the ego. *International Journal of Psychoanalysis,* 11, 24–39.

Klein, M. (1932). *The psycho-analysis of children.* London: Hogarth Press.

Klein, M. (1935). A contribution to the psychogenesis of manic-depressive states. *International Journal of Psychoanalysis,* 16, 145–74.

Klein, M. (1937). Love guilt and reparation. In *Love, guilt and reparation: And other works 1921–1945* (pp. 306–42). London: Hogarth Press, 1975.

Klein, M. (1940). Mourning and its relation to manic-depressive states. *International Journal of Psychoanalysis,* 21, 125–53.

Klein, M. (1945). The oedipus complex in the light of early anxieties. *International Journal of Psychoanalysis,* 26, 11–33.

Klein, M. (1946). Notes on some schizoid mechanisms. *International Journal of Psychoanalysis,* 27, 99–110.

Klein, M. (1948a). *Contributions to psycho-analysis, 1921–1945.* London: Hogarth Press.

Klein, M. (1948b). A contribution to the theory of anxiety and guilt. *International Journal of Psychoanalysis,* 29, 114–23.

Klein, M. (1952). Some theoretical conclusions regarding the emotional life of the infant. In *Envy and gratitude: And other works 1946–1963* (pp. 61–93). London: Hogarth Press, 1975.

Klein, M. (1955). On identification. In *The writings of Melanie Klein,* ed. R. Money-Kyrle, B. Joseph, E. O'Shaughnessy, and H. Segal (vol. 3, pp. 141–75). London: Hogarth Press, 1975.

Klein, M. (1957). Envy and gratitude. In *Envy and gratitude: And other works 1946–1963* (pp. 176–235). London: Hogarth Press, 1975.

Klein, M. (1958). On the development of mental functioning. *International Journal of Psychoanalysis,* 39, 84–90.

Klein, M. (1975). *Envy and gratitude: And other works 1946–1963.* London: Hogarth Press.

Klinnert, M., Campos, J., Sorce, J., Emde, R., and Svedja, M. (1982). Social referencing: Emotional expressions as behavior regulators. In *Emotion: Theory, research, and experience,* vol. 2: *Emotions in early development,* ed. R. Plutchik and H. Kellerman (pp. 57–86). Orlando, FL: Academic Press.

Klumpner, G. (1992). *A guide to the language of psychoanalysis: An empirical study of the relationships among psychoanalytic terms and concepts.* Madison, CT: International Universities Press.

Knapp, P. (1995). Somatization. In *Psychoanalysis: The major concepts,* ed. B. Moore and B. Fine (pp. 221–493). New Haven, CT: Yale University Press.

Knight, R. (1940). The relationship of latent homosexuality to the mechanisms of paranoid delusions. *Bulletin of the Menninger Clinic,* 4, 149–59.

Knight, R. (1946). Determinism, "freedom," and psychotherapy. *Psychiatry,* 9, 251–62.

Knight, R. (1953). Borderline states. *Bulletin of the Menninger Clinic,* 17, 1–12.

Koch, E. (1991). Nature-nurture issues in Freud's writings: "The complemental series." *International Review of Psycho-Analysis,* 18, 473–87.

Kogan, I. (1992). From acting out to words and meaning. *International Journal of Psychoanalysis,* 73, 455–65.

Kohlberg, L. (1963). Moral development and identification. In *Child Psychology,* ed. H. Stevenson et al. Sixty-second Yearbook of the National Society for the Study of Education (part 1, pp. 277–332). Chicago: University of Chicago Press.

Kohut, H. (1959). Introspection, empathy, and psychoanalysis. *Journal of the American Psychoanalytic Association,* 7, 459–83.

Kohut, H. (1966). Forms and transformations of narcissism. *Journal of the American Psychoanalytic Association,* 14, 243–72.

Kohut, H. (1970/1978). Narcissism as a resistance and as a driving force in psychoanalysis. In *The search for the self: Selected writings of Heinz Kohut, 1950–1978,* ed. P. Ornstein (pp. 547–62). New York: International Universities Press.

Kohut, H. (1971). *The analysis of the self: A systematic approach to the psychoanalytic treatment of narcissistic personality disorders.* London: Hogarth Press.

Kohut, H. (1972). Thoughts on narcissism and narcissistic rage. *Psychoanalytic Study of the Child,* 27, 360–400.

Kohut, H. (1973). Psychoanalysis in a troubled world. *Annual of Psychoanalysis,* 1, 3–25.

Kohut, H. (1977). *The restoration of the self.* New York: International Universities Press.

Kohut, H. (1982). Introspection, empathy, and the semi-circle of mental health. *International Journal of Psychoanalysis,* 63, 395–407.

Kohut, H. (1984). *How does analysis cure?* Chicago: University of Chicago Press.

Kohut, H., and Wolf, E. (1978). The disorders of the self and their treatment: An outline. *International Journal of Psychoanalysis,* 59, 413–25.

Krausz, R. (1994). The invisible woman. *International Journal of Psychoanalysis,* 75, 59–72.

Kreisler, L. (1984). Fundamentals for a psychosomatic pathology of infants. In *Frontiers of infant psychiatry, ed.* J. Call, E. Galenson, and R. Tyson (vol. 2, pp. 447–54). New York: Basic Books.

Kris, A. (1976). On wanting too much: The "exceptions" revisited. *International Journal of Psychoanalysis,* 57, 85–95.

Kris, A. (1984). The conflicts of ambivalence. *Psychoanalytic Study of the Child,* 39, 213–34.

Kris, A. (1990). The analyst's stance and the method of free association. *Psychoanalytic Study of the Child,* 45, 25–41.

Kris, E. (1936). The psychology of caricature. *International Journal of Psychoanalysis,* 17, 285–303.

Kris, E. (1947). The nature of psychoanalytic propositions and their validation. In *Selected papers of Ernst Kris.* New Haven, CT: Yale University Press, 1975.

Kris, E. (1950a). Notes on the development and on some current problems of psychoanalytic child psychology. *Psychoanalytic Study of the Child,* 5, 24–46.

Kris, E. (1950b). On preconscious mental processes. *Psychoanalytic Quarterly,* 19, 540–60.

Kris, E. (1951). Some comments and observations on early autoerotic activities. *Psychoanalytic Study of the Child,* 6, 95–116.

Kris, E. (1956a). The personal myth—A problem in psychoanalytic technique. *Journal of the American Psychoanalytic Association,* 4, 653–81.

Kris, E. (1956b). The recovery of childhood memories in psychoanalysis. *Psychoanalytic Study of the Child,* 11, 54–88.

Krystal, H. (1968). *Massive psychic trauma.* New York: International Universities Press.

Krystal, H. (1975). Affect tolerance. *Annual of Psychoanalysis,* 3, 179–219.

Krystal, H. (1988). *Integration and self-healing: Affect, trauma, alexithymia.* Hillsdale, NJ: Analytic Press.

Krystal, H. (1997). Desomatization and the consequences of infantile psychic trauma. *Psychoanalytic Inquiry,* 17, 126–50.

Kubie, L. (1947). The fallacious use of quantitative concepts in dynamic psychology. *Psychoanalytic Quarterly,* 16, 507–18.

Kubie, L. (1968). Unsolved problems in the resolution of the transference. *Psychoanalytic Quarterly,* 37, 331–52.

Kubie, L. (1974). The drive to become both sexes. *Psychoanalytic Quarterly, 43*, 349–426.

Kubie, L. (1975). The language tools of psychoanalysis. *International Review of Psycho-Analysis, 2*, 11–24.

Kuhns, R. (1983). *Psychoanalytic theory of art: A philosophy of art on developmental principles.* New York: Columbia University Press.

Kulish, N. (1998). Book review: *Femininities, masculinities, sexualities: Freud and beyond,* by N. Chodorow. *Psychoanalytic Quarterly, 67*, 174–77.

Kulish, N. (2000). Primary femininity: Clinical advances and theoretical ambiguities. *Journal of the American Psychoanalytic Association, 48*, 1355–79.

Kulish, N. (2003). Countertransference and the female triangular situation. *International Journal of Psychoanalysis, 84*, 563–77.

Kulish, N., and Holtzman, D. (1998). Persephone, the loss of virginity and the female oedipal complex. *International Journal of Psychoanalysis, 79*, 57–71.

Kulish, N., and Holtzman, D. (2008). *A story of her own: The female oedipus complex reexamined and renamed.* New York: Jason Aronson.

Lacan, J. (1956a). The function of language in psychoanalysis. In *The language of the self,* ed. A. Wilden (pp. 28–54). Baltimore, MD: Johns Hopkins Press, 1968.

Lacan, J. (1956b). Seminar on "The Purloined Letter." In *The purloined Poe: Lacan, Derrida, and psychoanalytic reading,* ed. J. Muller and W. Richardson (pp. 28–54). Baltimore, MD: Johns Hopkins Press, 1988.

Lacan, J. (1959). On a question preliminary to any possible treatment of psychosis. In *Écrits: A selection* (pp. 179–225). New York: W. W. Norton, 1966, 2006.

Lacan, J. (1966/2006). *Écrits: The first complete edition in English.* New York: W. W. Norton.

Lachmann, F. (2000). *Transforming aggression.* New York: Jason Aronson.

Lachmann, F., and Beebe, B. (1992). Representational and selfobject transferences: A developmental perspective. *Progress in Self Psychology, 8*, 3–15.

Lachmann, F., and Beebe, B. (1996a). Three principles of salience in the organization of the patient-analyst interaction. *Psychoanalytic Psychology, 13*, 1–22.

Lachmann, F., and Beebe, B. (1996b). The contribution of self- and mutual regulation to therapeutic action: A case illustration. *Progress in Self Psychology, 12*, 123–40.

Laing, R. (1965). Mystification, confusion and conflict. In *Intensive family therapy,* ed. I. Boszormenyi-Nagy, and J. Framo (pp. 343–64). New York: Harper and Row.

Lamb, M. (2004). How do fathers influence children's development? Let me count the ways. In *The role of the father in child development* (4th edition), ed. M. Lamb (pp. 1–26). Hoboken, NJ: Wiley.

Lampl-De Groot, J. (1927). The evolution of the oedipus complex in women. In *The development of the mind: Psychoanalytic papers on clinical and theoretical problems* (pp. 3–18). New York: International Universities Press, 1965.

Lampl-De Groot, J. (1950). On masturbation and its influence on general development. *Psychoanalytic Study of the Child, 5*, 153–74.

Langer, S. (1942). *Philosophy in a new key.* Cambridge, MA: Harvard University Press.

Langer, S. J., and Martin, J. (2004). How dresses can make you mentally ill: Examining gender identity disorder in children. *Child and Adolescent Social Work Journal, 22*, 5–23.

Lansky, M. (1994). Shame: Contemporary psychoanalytic perspectives. *Journal of the American Academy of Psychoanalysis, 22*, 433–41.

Lansky, M. (1999) Shame and the idea of a central affect. *Psychoanalytic Inquiry, 19*, 347–61.

Laplanche, J. (1976). *Life and death in psychoanalysis.* Baltimore, MD: Johns Hopkins University Press.

Laplanche, J. (1991). Notes on afterwardsness. In *Jean Laplanche: Seduction, translation, and the drives,* ed. J. Laplanche, J. Fletcher, and M. Stanton. London: Institute of Contemporary Arts, 1992.

Laplanche, J. (1997). The theory of seduction and the problem of the other. *International Journal of Psychoanalysis, 78*, 653–66.

Laplanche, J., and Pontalis, J. (1967/1973). *The language of psycho-analysis.* New York: W. W. Norton.

Laufer, M. (1976). The central masturbation fantasy, the final sexual organization and adolescence. *Psychoanalytic Study of the Child, 31*, 297–316.

Laufer, M., and Laufer, M. E. (1984). *Adolescence and developmental breakdown: A psychoanalytic view.* New Haven, CT: Yale University Press.

Laughlin, H. (1956). *The neuroses in clinical practice.* Oxford: W. B. Saunders.

Lax, R. (1994). Aspects of primary and secondary genital feelings and anxieties in girls during the preoedipal and early oedipal phases. *Psychoanalytic Quarterly, 63*, 271–96.

Lax, R. (1997). Boys' envy of mother and the consequences of the narcissistic mortification. *Psychoanalytic Study of the Child, 52*, 118–39.

Layton, L. (2000). The psychopolitics of bisexuality. *Studies in Gender and Sexuality, 1*, 41–60.

Layton, L. (2002). Cultural hierarchies, splitting, and the heterosexist unconscious. In *Bringing the plague: Toward a postmodern psychoanalysis,* ed. S. Fairfield, L. Layton, and C. Stack (pp. 195–223). New York: Other Press.

Lear, J. (1990). *Love and its place in nature: A philosophical interpretation of Freudian psychoanalysis.* New Haven, CT: Yale University Press.

Leavy, S. (1977). The significance of Jacques Lacan. *Psychoanalytic Quarterly,* 46, 201–19.

Lecours, S., and Bouchard, M. (1997). Dimensions of mentalisation: Outlining levels of psychic transformation. *International Journal of Psychoanalysis,* 78, 855–75.

LeDoux, J. (1996). *The emotional brain.* New York: Simon and Schuster.

Lenzenweger, M., Clarkin, J., Fertuck, E., and Kernberg, O. (2004). Executive neurocognitive functioning and neurobehavioral systems indicators in borderline personality disorder: A preliminary study. *Journal of Personality Disorders,* 18 (5), 421–38.

Lenzenweger, M., Clarkin, J., Kernberg, O., and Foelsch, P. (2001). The inventory of personality organization: Psychometric properties, factorial composition, and criterion relations with affect, aggressive dyscontrol, psychosis proneness, and self-domains in a nonclinical sample. *Psychological Assessment,* 13 (4), 577–91.

Lepore, J. (2006). Noah's mark: Webster and the original dictionary wars. *New Yorker,* November 6, 78–87.

Leslie, A. (1987). Pretense and representation. *Psychological Review,* 94, 412–26.

Lester, E. (1986). Narcissism and the personal myth. *Psychoanalytic Quarterly,* 55, 452–73.

Lester, E. (2002). Sappho of lesbos: The complexity of female sexuality. *Psychoanalytic Inquiry,* 22, 10–181.

Levenson, E. (1972). *The fallacy of understanding.* New York: Basic Books.

Levenson, E. (1983). *The ambiguity of change.* New York: Basic Books.

Levenson, E. (1987). The purloined self. *Journal of the American Academy of Psychoanalysis,* 15, 481–90

Levenson, E. (1993). Shoot the messenger—Interpersonal aspects of the analyst's interpretations. *Contemporary Psychoanalysis,* 29, 383–96.

Levenson, E., Hirsch, I., and Iannuzzi, V. (2005). Interview with Edgar A. Levenson, January 24, 2004. *Contemporary Psychoanalysis,* 41, 593–644.

Levey, M. (1984). The concept of structure in psychoanalysis. *Annual of Psychoanalysis,* 12, 137–53.

Levin, F. (1997). Commentary on Solms's "What is consciousness?" *Journal of the American Psychoanalytic Association,* 45, 732–39.

Levin, S. (1965). Some comments on the distribution of narcissistic and object libido in the aged. *International Journal of Psychoanalysis,* 46, 200–208.

Levinson, D., Darrow, C., Klein, E., Levinson, M., and McKee, B. (1978). *The seasons in a man's life.* New York: Knopf.

Levy, D. (1943). *Maternal overprotection.* New York: W. W. Norton.

Levy, D. (1956). Developmental and psychodynamic aspects of oppositional behavior. In *Changing concepts of psychoanalytic medicine,* ed. S. Rado and G. Daniels (pp. 114–34). New York: Grune and Stratton.

Levy, K., Meehan, K., Kelly, K., Reynoso, J., Weber, M., Clarkin, J., and Kernberg, O. (2006). Change in attachment patterns and reflective function in a randomized control trial of transference focused psychotherapy for borderline personality disorder. *Journal of Consulting and Clinical Psychology,* 74 (6), 1027–40.

Levy, K., Wasserman, R., Scott, L., Zach, S., White, C., Cain, N., Fischer, C., Carter, C., Clarkin, J., and Kernberg, O. (2006). The development of a measure to assess putative mechanisms of change in the treatment of borderline personality disorder. *Journal of the American Psychoanalytic Association,* 54, 1325–30.

Levy, S., and Inderbitzin, L. (1992). Neutrality, interpretation, and therapeutic intent. *Journal of the American Psychoanalytic Association,* 40, 989–1011.

Levy-Warren, M. (2000). *The adolescent journey.* New York: Jason Aronson.

Lewes, K. (1988). *The psychoanalytic theory of male homosexuality.* New York: Simon and Schuster.

Lewin, B. (1932). Analysis and structure of a transient hypomania. *Psychoanalytic Quarterly,* 1, 43–58.

Lewin, B. (1933). The body as phallus. *Psychoanalytic Quarterly,* 2, 24–47.

Lewin, B. (1946). Sleep, the mouth, and the dream screen. *Psychoanalytic Quarterly,* 15, 419–34.

Lewin, B. (1950). *The psychoanalysis of elation.* New York: W. W. Norton.

Lewin, B. (1952). Phobic symptoms and dream interpretation. In *Selected writings of Bertram D. Lewin,* ed. J. Arlow (pp. 187–213). New York: The Psychoanalytic Quarterly, 1973.

Lewin, B. (1953). Reconsideration of the dream screen. *Psychoanalytic Quarterly,* 22, 174–99.

Lewin, B., and Ross, H. (1960). *Psychoanalytic education in the United States.* New York: W. W. Norton.

Lewin, R., and Schultz, C. (1992). *Losing and fusing: Borderline transitional object and self relations.* Northvale, NJ: Jason Aronson.

Lewis, H. (1971). *Shame and guilt in neurosis.* New York: International Universities Press.

Lewis, H. (1987). *The role of shame in symptom formation.* Hillsdale, NJ: Lawrence Erlbaum Associates.

Libet, B., Gleason, C., Wright, E., and Pearl, D. (1983). Time of conscious intention to act in relation to onset of cerebral activity (readiness potential): The unconscious initiation of a freely voluntary act. *Brain,* 106, 623–42.

Lichtenberg, J. (1981). Implications of psychoanalytic theory of research on the neonate. *International Review of Psycho-Analysis,* 8, 35–52.

Lichtenberg, J. (1982). Reflections on the first year of life. *Psychoanalytic Inquiry,* 1, 695–729.

Lichtenberg, J. (1983). *Psychoanalysis and infant research.* Hillsdale, NJ: Analytic Press.

Lichtenberg, J. (1989). *Psychoanalysis and motivation.* Hillsdale, NJ: Analytic Press.

Lichtenberg, J. (2002). Values, consciousness, and language. *Psychoanalytic Inquiry,* 22, 841–56.

Lichtenberg, J., Bornstein, M., and Silver, D. (1984). *Empathy I and II.* Hillsdale, NJ: Analytic Press.

Lichtenberg, J., Lachmann, F., and Fosshage, J. (1996). *The clinical exchange: Techniques derived from self and motivational systems.* Hillsdale, NJ: Analytic Press.

Lichtenberg, J., Lachmann, F., and Fosshage, J.(2010) *Psychoanalysis and motivational systems: A new look.* Psychoanalytic Inquiry Book Series. New York and London: Routledge.

Lichtenstein, H. (1961). Identity and sexuality—A study of their interrelationship in man. *Journal of the American Psychoanalytic Association,* 9, 179–260.

Likierman, M. (1990). "Translation in transition": Some issues surrounding the Strachey translation of Freud's works. *International Review of Psycho-Analysis,* 17, 115–20.

Lillard, A. (1993). Pretend play skills and the child's theory of mind. *Child Development,* 64, 348–71.

Lindemann, E. (1944). Symptomatology and management of acute grief. *American Journal of Psychiatry,* 101, 141–48.

Lionells, M., Fiscalini, J., Mann, H., and Stern, D. B., eds. (1995). *Handbook of interpersonal psychoanalysis.* Hillsdale, NJ: Analytic Press.

Lippmann, P. (2002). *Nocturnes: On listening to dreams.* New York: Routledge.

Lipton, S. (1955). A note on the compatibility of psychic determinism and freedom of will. *International Journal of Psychoanalysis,* 36, 355–56.

Lipton, S. (1977). The advantages of Freud's technique as shown in his analysis of the Rat Man. *International Journal of Psychoanalysis,* 58, 255–73.

Litowitz, B. (1998). An expanded developmental line for negation: Rejection, refusal, denial. *Journal of the American Psychoanalytic Association,* 46 (1), 121–48.

Litowitz, B. (2007). Unconscious fantasy: A once and future concept. *Journal of the American Psychoanalytic Association,* 55, 199–228.

Loewald, H. (1951). Ego and reality. *International Journal of Psychoanalysis,* 32, 10–18.

Loewald, H. (1960). On the therapeutic action of psychoanalysis. *International Journal of Psychoanalysis,* 41, 16–33.

Loewald, H. (1962a). Internalization, separation, mourning, and the superego. *Psychoanalytic Quarterly,* 31, 483–504.

Loewald, H. (1962b). The superego and the ego-ideal. *International Journal of Psychoanalysis,* 43, 264–68.

Loewald, H. (1970). Psychoanalytic theory and the psychoanalytic process. *Psychoanalytic Study of the Child,* 25, 45–68.

Loewald, H. (1971). On motivation and instinct theory. *Psychoanalytic Study of the Child,* 26, 91–128.

Loewald, H. (1972). Freud's conception of the negative therapeutic reaction, with comments on instinct theory. *Journal of the American Psychoanalytic Association,* 20, 235–45.

Loewald, H. (1973a). *Papers on psychoanalysis.* New Haven, CT: Yale University Press, 1980.

Loewald, H. (1973b). On internalization. In *Papers on psychoanalysis* (pp. 69–86). New Haven, CT: Yale University Press, 1980.

Loewald, H. (1974). Current status of the concept of infantile neurosis—Discussion. *Psychoanalytic Study of the Child,* 29, 183–88.

Loewald, H. (1978). Primary process, secondary process, and language. In *Papers on psychoanalysis* (pp. 178–206). New Haven, CT: Yale University Press, 1980.

Loewald, H. (1979). The waning of the oedipus complex. In *Papers on psychoanalysis* (pp. 384–404). New Haven, CT: Yale University Press, 1980.

Loewenstein, R. (1957). A contribution to the psychoanalytic theory of masochism. *Journal of the American Psychoanalytic Association,* 5, 197–234.

Long, K. (2005). The changing language of female development. *Journal of the American Psychoanalytic Association,* 53, 1161–74.

Low, B. (1920). *Psycho-analysis: A brief account of the Freudian theory.* London: Allen and Unwin.

Luborsky, L. (1984). *Principles of psychoanalytic psychotherapy: A manual for supportive-expressive treatment.* New York: Basic Books.

Lynch, P. (2002). Yearning for love and cruising for sex: Returning to Freud to understand some gay men. *Annual of Psychoanalysis,* 30, 175–90.

Lyons-Ruth, K. (1991). Rapprochement or approchement: Mahler's theory reconsidered from the vantage point of recent research on early attachment relationships. *Psychoanalytic Psychology,* 8, 1–23.

Lyons-Ruth, K. (1999). The two-person unconscious: Intersubjective dialogue, enactive relational representation, and the emergence of new forms of relational organization. *Psychoanalytic Inquiry*, 19, 576–617.

Lyons-Ruth, K., and Jacobvitz, D. (2008). Attachment disorganization: Genetic factors, parenting contexts, and developmental transformation from infancy to adulthood. In *The handbook of attachment theory and research* (2nd edition), ed. J. Cassidy and P. Shaver (pp. 666–97). New York: Guilford Press.

MacKinnon, R., and Michels, R. (1971). *The psychiatric interview in clinical practice*. Philadelphia: W. B. Saunders.

Maddox, B. (2006). *Freud's wizard: Ernest Jones and the transformation of psychoanalysis*. London: John Murray.

Magee, M., and Miller, D. (1997). *Lesbian lives: Psychoanalytic narratives old and new*. Hillsdale, NJ: Analytic Press.

Mahler, M. (1952). On child psychosis and schizophrenia—Autistic and symbiotic infantile psychoses. *Psychoanalytic Study of the Child*, 7, 286–305.

Mahler, M. (1966). Notes on the development of basic mood: The depressive mood. In *Psychoanalysis—A general psychology: Essays in honor of Heinz Hartmann*, ed. R. Loewenstein, L. Newman, M. Schur, and A. Solnit (pp. 152–68). New York: International Universities Press.

Mahler, M. (1967). On human symbiosis and the vicissitudes of individuation. *Journal of the American Psychoanalytic Association*, 15, 740–63.

Mahler, M. (1968). *On human symbiosis and the vicissitudes of individuation: Infantile psychosis* (vol. 1). New York: International Universities Press.

Mahler, M. (1972). On the first three subphases of the separation-individuation process. *International Journal of Psychoanalysis*, 53, 333–38.

Mahler, M. (1975). On the current status of the infantile neurosis. *Journal of the American Psychoanalytic Association*, 23, 327–33.

Mahler, M., and McDevitt, J. (1982). Thoughts on the emergence of the sense of self, with particular emphasis on the body self. *Journal of the American Psychoanalytic Association*, 30, 827–48.

Mahler, M., Pine, F., and Bergman, A. (1975). *The psychological birth of the human infant*. New York: Basic Books.

Mahony, P. (1979). The boundaries of free association. *Psychoanalysis and Contemporary Thought*, 2, 151–98.

Mahony, P. (1993). Some transatlantic reflections on language in psychoanalysis. *Journal of the American Psychoanalytic Association*, 21, 433–40.

Main, M. (1993). Discourse, prediction, and recent studies in attachment: Implications for psychoanalysis. *Journal of the American Psychoanalytic Association*, 41 (S), 209–44.

Main, M. (1999). Epilogue: Attachment theory: Eighteen points with suggestions for future studies. In *Handbook of attachment: Theory, research, and clinical applications*, ed. J. Cassidy and P. Shaver (pp. 845–87). New York: Guilford Press.

Main, M., Kaplan, N., and Cassidy, J. (1985). Security in infancy, childhood and adulthood: A move to the level of representation. In *Growing points of attachment theory and research*, ed. I. Bretherton and E. Waters. Monographs of the Society for Research in Child Development (pp. 61–104). Chicago: University of Chicago Press.

Main, T. (1946). The hospital as a therapeutic institution. *Bulletin of the Menninger Clinic*, 10, 66–70.

Main, T. (1989). *The ailment and other psychoanalytic essays*. London: Free Association Books.

Makari, G. (1997). Current conceptions of neutrality and abstinence. *Journal of the American Psychoanalytic Association*, 45, 1231–39.

Malyon, A. (1982). Psychotherapeutic implications of internalized homophobia in gay men. *Journal of Homosexuality*, 7, 59–69.

Marcovitz, E. (1963). The concept of the id (panel report). *Journal of the American Psychoanalytic Association*, 11, 151–60.

Marcus, E. (1992). *Psychosis and near psychosis: Ego function, symbol structure, treatment*. New York: Springer-Verlag.

Marcus, E. (1999). Modern ego psychology. *Journal of the American Psychoanalytic Association*, 48, 843–71.

Marcus, E. (2003). Medical student dreams about medical school: The unconscious developmental process of becoming a physician. *International Journal of Psychoanalysis*, 84, 367–86.

Margolis, G. (1966). Secrecy and identity. *International Journal of Psychoanalysis*, 47, 517–22.

Marmor, J. (1953). Orality in the hysterical personality. *Journal of the American Psychoanalytic Association*, 1, 656–70.

Marmor, J. (1972). Homosexuality: Mental illness or moral dilemma? *International Journal of Psychoanalysis*, 10, 114–17.

Marshall, B. (2000). *Configuring gender: Explorations in theory and practice*. Peterborough, ON: Broadview Press.

Marty, P., and de M'Uzan, M. (1963). La pensée opératoire. *Psychoanalytic Review*, 27, 1345–56.

Masson, J. (1985a). *The assault on truth: Freud's suppression of the seduction theory*. New York: Penguin Press.

Masson, J. (1985b). *The complete letters of Sigmund Freud to Wilhelm Fliess, 1887–1904.* Cambridge, MA: Belknap Press / Harvard University Press.

Masterson, J. (1981). *The narcissistic and borderline disorders.* New York: Brunner/Mazel.

Maudsley, H. (1874). *Responsibility in mental disease.* London: Henry S. King.

Mayer, E. (1985). Everybody must be just like me: Observations on female castration anxiety. *International Journal of Psychoanalysis,* 66, 331–48.

Mayer, E. (1991). Towers and enclosed spaces. *Psychoanalytic Inquiry,* 11, 480–510.

Mayer, E. (1995). The phallic castration complex and primary femininity: Paired developmental lines toward female gender identity. *Journal of the American Psychoanalytic Association,* 43, 17–38.

Mayes, L. (1994). Understanding adaptive processes in a developmental context: A reappraisal of Hartmann's problem of adaptation. *Psychoanalytic Study of the Child,* 49, 12–35.

Mayes, L. (1999). Clocks, engines, and quarks—Love, dreams, and genes: What makes development happen? *Psychoanalytic Study of the Child,* 54, 169–92.

Mayes, L. (2001). The twin poles of order and chaos: Development as a dynamic, self-ordering system. *Psychoanalytic Study of the Child,* 56, 137–70.

Mayes, L., and Cohen, D. (1992). The development of a capacity for imagination in early childhood. *Psychoanalytic Study of the Child,* 47, 23–47.

Mayes, L., and Cohen, D. (1996). Children's developing theory of mind. *Journal of the American Psychoanalytic Association,* 44, 117–42.

McDevitt, J. (1975). Separation-individuation and object constancy. *Journal of the American Psychoanalytic Association,* 23, 713–42.

McDougall, J. (1972). Primal scene and sexual perversion. *International Journal of Psychoanalysis,* 53, 371–84.

McDougall, J. (1980). *Plea for a measure of abnormality.* New York: International Universities Press.

McDougall, J. (1985). *Theaters of the mind: Illusion and truth on the psychoanalytic stage.* Philadelphia: Brunner/Mazel.

McDougall, J. (1986). Identifications, neoneeds, and neosexualities. *International Journal of Psychoanalysis,* 67, 19–30.

McDougall, J. (1995). *The many faces of Eros: A psychoanalytic exploration of human sexuality.* New York: W. W. Norton.

McLaughlin, J. (1981). Transference, psychic reality, and countertransference. *Psychoanalytic Quarterly,* 50, 639–64.

McLaughlin, J. (1987). The play of transference: Some reflections on enactment in the psychoanalytic situation. *Journal of the American Psychoanalytic Association,* 35, 557–82.

McLaughlin, J. (1991). Clinical and theoretical aspects of enactment. *Journal of the American Psychoanalytic Association,* 39, 595–614.

Meissner, M. (2001). Becoming 100 percent straight. In *Men's lives,* ed. M. Kimmel (pp. 401–6). Boston: Allyn and Bacon Press.

Meissner, W. (1983). Book review: *Preconscious processing,* by N. Dixon. *Psychoanalytic Quarterly,* 52, 107–11.

Meissner, W. (1993). Self-as-agent in psychoanalysis. *Psychoanalysis and Contemporary Thought,* 16, 459–95.

Meissner, W. (2000). Reflection on psychic reality. *International Journal of Psychoanalysis,* 81, 1117–38.

Melnick, B. (1997). Metaphor and the theory of libidinal development. *International Journal of Psychoanalysis,* 78, 997–1015.

Meltzer, D. (1975). Adhesive identification. *Contemporary Psychoanalysis,* 11, 289–310.

Mermelstein, J. (2000). Easy listening, prolonged empathic immersion, and the selfobject needs of the analyst. *Progress in Self Psychology,* 16, 175–98.

Meyer, J. (1982). The theory of gender identity disorders. *Journal of the American Psychoanalytic Association,* 30, 381–418.

Meyer-Bahlburg, H. (2010). From mental disorder to iatrogenic hypogonadism: Dilemmas in conceptualizing gender identity variants as psychiatric conditions. *Archives of Sexual Behavior,* 39, 461–76.

Michaels, J., and Stiver, I. (1965). The impulsive psychopathic character according to the diagnostic profile. *Psychoanalytic Study of the Child,* 20, 124–41.

Michels, R. (1985). Introduction to panel: Perspectives on the nature of psychic reality. *Journal of the American Psychoanalytic Association,* 33, 515–19.

Michels, R. (1999). Psychoanalysts' theories. In *Psychoanalysis on the move: The work of Joseph Sandler,* ed. P. Fonagy, A. Cooper, and R. Wallerstein (pp. 187–200). London: Hogarth Press.

Mijolla, A., ed. (2002/2005). *International dictionary of psychoanalysis.* Detroit, MI: Thomson Gale. Also available online at http://www.enotes.com/psychoanalysis-encyclopedia.

Milrod, B. (2007). Emptiness in agoraphobia patients. *Journal of the American Psychoanalytic Association,* 55, 1007–26.

Milrod, B., Busch, F., Cooper, A., and Shapiro, T. (1997). *Manual of panic—focused psychodynamic psychotherapy.* Washington, DC: American Psychological Association Press.

Milrod, D. (1988). A current view of the psychoanalytic theory of depression—with notes on the roles of identification, orality, and anxiety. *Psychoanalytic Study of the Child*, 43, 83–99.

Milrod, D. (1990). The ego ideal. *Psychoanalytic Study of the Child*, 45, 43–60.

Milrod, D. (2002). The superego: Its formation, structure, and functioning. *Psychoanalytic Study of the Child*, 57, 131–47.

Minter, S. (1999). Diagnosis and treatment of gender identity disorder in children. In *Sissies and tomboys: Gender nonconformity and homosexual childhood*, ed. M. Rottnek (pp. 9–33). New York: New York University Press.

Minzenberg, M., Poole, J., and Vinogradov, S. (2006). Adult social attachment disturbance is related to childhood maltreatment and current symptoms in borderline personality disorder. *Journal of Nervous and Mental Disease*, 194 (5), 341–48.

Mitchell, J. (2003). *Siblings: Sex and violence*. Oxford: Polity Press.

Mitchell, S. (1978). Psychodynamics, homosexuality, and the question of pathology. *Psychiatry*, 41, 254–63.

Mitchell, S. (1984). Object relations theories and the developmental tilt. *Contemporary Psychoanalysis*, 20, 473–99.

Mitchell, S. (1988). *Relational concepts in psychoanalysis: An integration*. Cambridge, MA: Harvard University Press.

Mitchell, S. (1991). Wishes, needs, and interpersonal negotiations. *Psychoanalytic Inquiry*, 11, 147–70.

Mitchell, S. (1993). *Hope and dread in psychoanalysis*. New York: Basic Books.

Mitchell, S. (1997). *Influence and autonomy in psychoanalysis*. Hillsdale, NJ: Analytic Press.

Mitchell, S. (2000). *Relationality: From attachment to intersubjectivity*. Hillsdale, NJ: Analytic Press.

Mitchell, S. (2002). *Can love last?: The fate of romance over time*. New York: W. W. Norton.

Modell, A. (1976). "The holding environment" and the therapeutic action of psychoanalysis. *Journal of the American Psychoanalytic Association*, 24, 285–307.

Modell, A. (1984). *Psychoanalysis in a new context*. New York: International Universities Press.

Money, J. (1965). *Sex research: New developments*. New York: Holt, Reinhart and Winston.

Money, J. (1973). Gender role, gender identity, core gender identity: Usage and definition of terms. *Journal of the American Psychoanalytic Association*, 1, 397–402.

Money, J., and Ehrhardt, A. (1972). *Man and woman, boy and girl: Differentiation and dimorphism of gender identity from conception to maturity*. Baltimore, MD: Johns Hopkins University Press.

Money, J., and Hampson, J. (1955). An examination of some basic sex concepts: The evidence of human hermaphroditism. *Bulletin of Johns Hopkins Hospital*, 97, 301–19.

Money-Kyrle, R. (1956). Normal counter-transference and some of its deviations. *International Universities Press*, 37, 360–66.

Moore, B. (1990). The problem of definition in psychoanalysis. In *Psychoanalytic terms and concepts*, ed. B. Moore and B. Fine (pp. xix–xxv). New Haven, CT: Yale University Press.

Moore, B., and Fine, B., eds. (1968). *A glossary of psychoanalytic terms and concepts* (2nd edition). New Haven, CT: Yale University Press.

Moore, B., and Fine, B., eds. (1990). *Psychoanalytic terms and concepts* (3rd edition). New Haven, CT: American Psychoanalytic Association.

Moore, B., and Fine, B., eds. (1995). *Psychoanalysis: The major concepts*. New Haven, CT: Yale University Press.

Morrison, A. (1989). *Shame: The underside of narcissism*. Hillsdale, NJ: Analytic Press.

Morrison, A. (1997). Ten years of doing psychotherapy while living with a life-threatening illness: Self-disclosure and other ramifications. *Psychoanalytic Dialogues*, 7, 225–41.

Moss, D. (2003). *Hating in the first person plural: Psychoanalytic essays on racism, homophobia, misogyny, and terror*. New York: Other Press.

Motley, M. (2002). Slips, theory of. In *The Freud encyclopedia*, ed. E. Erwin (pp. 530–33). New York: Routledge.

Muller, J. (2007). A view from Riggs: Treatment resistance and patient authority—IV: Why the pair needs the third. *Journal of the American Academy of Psychoanalysis and Dynamic Psychiatry*, 35 (2), 221–24.

Nagera, H. (1966). *Early childhood disturbances, the infantile neurosis, and the adulthood disturbances*. New York: International Universities Press.

Nagera, H., ed. (1969/1971). *Basic psychoanalytic concepts*. New York: International Universities Press.

Nathanson, D. (1987). "A timetable for shame" in *The many faces of shame*. New York: Guilford Press.

Nelson, J. (1956). Anlage of productiveness in boys: Womb envy. In *Childhood psychopathology*, ed. S. Harrison and J. McDermott (p. 360). New York: International Universities Press, 1972.

Nersessian, E., and Kopff, R., eds. (1996). *Textbook of psychoanalysis*. Washington, DC: American Psychiatric Press.

Neubauer, P. (1982). Rivalry, envy, and jealousy. *Psychoanalytic Study of the Child*, 37, 121–42.

Neubauer, P. (1983). The importance of the sibling experience. *Psychoanalytic Study of the Child*, 38, 325–36.

Neubauer, P. (1984). Anna Freud's concept of developmental lines. *Psychoanalytic Study of the Child,* 39, 15–27.

Neubauer, P. (1994). The role of displacement in psychoanalysis. *Psychoanalytic Study of the Child,* 49, 107–19.

Neubauer, P. (2003). Some notes on the role of development in psychoanalytic assistance, differentiation, and regression. *Psychoanalytic Study of the Child,* 58, 165–71.

Newmann, K. (2007). Therapeutic action in self psychology. *Psychoanalytic Quarterly,* 76, 1513–46.

New York Psychoanalytic Institute. (1956). Problems of infantile neurosis: A discussion. *The Psychoanalytic Study of the Child,* 9, 16–71.

Niederland, W. (1951). Three notes on the Schreber case. *Psychoanalytic Quarterly,* 20, 579–59.

Niederland, W. (1968). Clinical observations on the "survivor syndrome." *International Journal of Psychoanalysis,* 49, 313–15.

Nigg, J., Lohr, N., Westen, D., Gold, L., and Silk, K. (1992). Malevolent object representation in borderline personality disorder and major depression. *Journal of Abnormal Psychology,* 101, 61–67.

Northoff, G., and Boeker, H. (2006). Principles of neuronal integration and defense mechanisms: Neuropsychoanalytic hypothesis. *Neuropsychoanalysis,* 8, 69–84.

Notman, M. (2002). Changes in sexual orientation and object choice in midlife women. *Psychoanalytic Inquiry,* 22 (2), 182–95.

Novick, J. (1982). Termination: Themes and issues. *Psychoanalytic Inquiry,* 2, 329–65.

Novick, J., and Kelly, K. (1970). Projection and externalization. *Psychoanalytic Study of the Child,* 25, 69–95.

Novick, J., and Novick, K. (1972). Beating fantasies in children. *International Journal of Psychoanalysis,* 53, 237–52.

Novick, J., and Novick, K. (2001). Two systems of self-regulation. *Journal of Psychoanalytic Social Work,* 8, 95–122.

Novick, K. (2001). Book review: *The sadomasochism of everyday life: Why we hurt ourselves—and others—and how to stop,* by J. Ross. *Journal of the American Psychoanalytic Association,* 49, 1459–62.

Novick, K., and Novick, J. (1987). The essence of masochism. *Psychoanalytic Study of the Child,* 42, 353–84.

Novick, K., and Novick, J. (1991). Some comments on masochism and the illusion of omnipotence from a developmental perspective. *Journal of the American Psychoanalytic Association,* 39, 307–31.

Novick, K., and Novick, J. (1998). An application of the concept of the therapeutic alliance to sado-masochistic pathology. *Journal of the American Psychoanalytic Association,* 46, 813–46.

Novick, K., and Novick, J. (2005). *Working with parents makes therapy work.* New York: Jason Aronson.

Nunberg, H. (1926). The sense of guilt and the need for punishment. *International Journal of Psychoanalysis,* 7, 420–32.

Nunberg, H. (1931). The synthetic function of the ego. *International Journal of Psychoanalysis,* 12, 123–40.

Nunberg, H. (1934). The feeling of guilt. *Psychoanalytic Quarterly,* 3, 589–604.

Nunberg, H. (1942). Ego strength and ego weakness. *American Imago,* 3, 25–40.

Nunberg, H. (1955). *Principles of psychoanalysis.* New York: International Universities Press.

Oates, J., and Grayson, A. (2004). *Cognitive and language development in children.* Hoboken, NJ: Wiley-Blackwell.

Oberndorf, C. (1946). Constant elements in psychotherapy. *Psychoanalytic Quarterly,* 15, 435–49.

Obeyeskere, G. (1990). *The work of culture: Symbolic transformations in psychoanalysis and culture.* Chicago: University of Chicago Press.

O'Connor, N., and Ryan, J. (1993). *Wild desires and mistaken identities: Lesbianism and psychoanalysis.* New York: Columbia University Press.

Offer, D., Offer, J., Ostrov, E. (1975). *From teenage to young manhood.* New York: Basic Books.

Ogden, T. (1979). On projective identification. *International Journal of Psychoanalysis,* 60, 357–73.

Ogden, T. (1994). The analytic third: Working with intersubjective clinical facts. *International Journal of Psychoanalysis,* 75, 3–19.

Ogden, T. (1996a). The perverse subject of analysis. *Journal of the American Psychoanalytic Association,* 44, 1121–46.

Ogden, T. (1996b). *Subjects of analysis.* Northvale, NJ, and London: Jason Aronson.

Ogden, T. (2006). Reading Loewald: Oedipus reconceived. *International Journal of Psychoanalysis,* 87, 651–66.

Olden, C. (1958). Notes on the development of empathy. *Psychoanalytic Quarterly,* 13, 505–18.

Olds, D. (1992). Consciousness: A brain-centered informational approach. *Psychoanalytic Inquiry,* 12, 419–44.

Olds, D. (1994). Connectionism and psychoanalysis. *Journal of the American Psychoanalytic Association,* 42, 581–611.

Olds, D. (2003). Affect as a sign system. *Neuropsychoanalysis,* 5, 81–95.

Olds, D. (2006). Identification: Psychoanalytic and biological perspectives. *Journal of the American Psychoanalytic Association,* 54, 17–46.

Olesker, W. (1998a). Conflict and compromise in gender identity formation: A longitudinal study. *Psychoanalytic Study of the Child,* 53, 212–30.

Olesker, W. (1998b). Female genital anxieties: Views from the nursery and the couch. *Psychoanalytic Quarterly,* 67, 276–94.

Oliner, M. (1998). Jacques Lacan: The language of alienation. In *Psychoanalytic versions of the human condition,* ed. P. Marvus and A. Rosenberg (pp. 362–91). New York: NYU Press.

Olinick, S. (1964). The negative therapeutic reaction. *International Journal of Psychoanalysis,* 45, 540–48.

Olinick, S., Poland, W., Grigg, K., Granatir, W. (1973). The psychoanalytic work ego: Process and interpretation. *International Journal of Psychoanalysis,* 54, 143–51.

Orange, D. (2003). Why language matters to psychoanalysis. *Psychoanalytic Dialogues,* 13, 77–103.

Orange, D., Atwood, G., and Stolorow, R. (1997). *Working intersubjectively: Contextualism in psychoanalytic practice.* Hillsdale, NJ: Analytic Press.

Orange, D., and Stolorow, R. (1998). Self-disclosure from the perspective of intersubjectivity theory. *Psychoanalytic Inquiry,* 18, 530–37.

Ornstein, A. (1983). Idealizing transference from the oedipal phase. In *Reflections on self psychology,* ed. J. Lichtenberg and S. Kaplan (pp. 135–48). Hillsdale, NJ: Analytic Press.

Ornstein, A. (1985). Survival and recovery. *Psychoanalytic Inquiry,* 5, 99–130.

Ornstein, A. (1988). Optimal responsiveness and the theory of cure. *Progress in Self Psychology,* 4, 155–60.

Ornstein, A. (1990). Selfobject transferences and the process of working through. *Progress in Self Psychology,* 6, 41–58.

Ornstein, A. (1991). The dread to repeat: Comments on the working-through process in psychoanalysis. *Journal of the American Psychoanalytical Association,* 39, 377–98.

Ornstein, A. (1998). The fate of narcissistic rage in the treatment process. *Psychoanalytic Inquiry,* 18, 55–70.

Ornstein, P. (1990). How to "enter" a psychoanalytic process conducted by another analyst: A self psychology view. *Psychoanalytic Inquiry,* 10, 478–97.

Ornstein, P. (1993). Chapter 12: Chronic rage from underground: Reflections on its structure and treatment. *Progression in Self Psychology,* 9, 143–57.

Ornstein, P., and Ornstein, A. (1980). Formulating interpretations in clinical psychoanalysis. *International Journal of Psychoanalysis,* 61, 203–11.

Ornstein, P., and Ornstein, A. (1985). Clinical understanding and explaining. *Progress in Self Psychology,* 1, 43–61.

Ornstein, P., and Ornstein, A. (1993). Assertiveness, anger, rage, and destructive aggression: A perspective from the treatment process. In *Rage, power, and aggression,* ed. R. Glick and S. Roose (pp. 102–17). New Haven, CT: Yale University Press.

Ornston, D. (1982). Strachey's influence. *International Journal of Psychoanalysis,* 63, 409–26.

Ornston, D. (1985). Freud's conception is different from Strachey's. *Journal of the American Psychoanalytic Association,* 33, 379–412.

Ornston, D. (1988). How standard is the "standard edition"? In *Freud in exile: Psychoanalysis and its vicissitudes,* ed. E. Timms and N. Segal (pp. 196–209). New Haven, CT, and London: Yale University Press.

Osofsky, J. (1993). Applied psychoanalysis: How research with infants and adolescents at high psychosocial risk informs psychoanalysis. *Journal of the American Psychoanalytic Association,* 41 (S), 193–207.

Ostow, M., and Turnbull, O. (2004). Founders of neuropsychoanalysis. *Neuropsychoanalysis,* 6, 209–16.

Ovesey, L., and Person, E. (1973). Gender identity and sexual psychopathology in men: A psychodynamic analysis of homosexuality, transsexualism, and transvestitism. *Journal of the American Psychoanalytic Association,* 1, 3–72.

Ovesey, L., and Person, E. (1976). Transvestism: A disorder of the sense of self. *International Journal of Psychoanalytic Psychotherapy,* 5, 219–35.

Pally, R., and Olds, D. (1998). Consciousness: A neuroscience perspective. *International Journal of Psychoanalysis,* 79, 971–989.

Panksepp, J. (1999). Emotions as viewed by psychoanalysis and neuroscience: An exercise in consilience. *Neuropsychoanalysis,* 1, 15–38.

Pantone, P. (1995). Preadolescence and adolescence. In *Handbook of interpersonal psychoanalysis,* ed. M. Lionells, J. Fiscalini, C. Mann, and D. B. Stern (pp. 277–92). Hillsdale, NJ: Analytic Press.

Parens, H. (1973). Aggression. *Journal of the American Psychoanalytic Association,* 21, 34–60.

Parens, H. (1979). *The development of aggression in early childhood.* New York: Jason Aronson.

Parens, H. (1980). An exploration of the relations of instinctual drives and the symbiosis / separation-individuation process. *Journal of the American Psychoanalytic Association,* 28, 89–113.

Parens, H. (1990). On the girl's psychosexual development: Reconsiderations suggested from direct observation. *Journal of the American Psychoanalytic Association,* 38, 743–72.

Parens, H., Blum, H., and Salman, A. (2008). *The unbroken soul: Tragedy, trauma, and resilience.* Lanham, MD: Jason Aronson.

Parens, H., Pollock, L., Stern, J., and Kramer, S. (1976). On the girl's entry into the oedipus complex. *Journal of the American Psychoanalytic Association,* 24 (S), 79–107.

Paris, J. (2008). *Treatment of borderline personality disorder.* New York: Guilford Press.

Parsons, M. (2000). Sexuality and perversion a hundred years on. *International Journal of Psychoanalysis,* 81, 37–49.

PDM Task Force. (2006). *Psychodynamic diagnostic manual.* Silver Spring, MD: Alliance of Psychoanalytic Organizations.

Perry, J., and Lanni, F. (2008). Observer-rated measures of defense mechanisms. *Journal of Personality,* 66, 993–1024.

Person, E. (1988). *Dreams of love and fateful encounters: The power of romantic passion.* New York: Penguin.

Person, E. (1991). Romantic love: At the intersection of the psyche and the cultural unconscious. *Journal of the American Psychoanalytic Association,* 39 (S), 383–411.

Person, E. (1995). *By force of fantasy: How we make our lives.* New York: Basic Books.

Person, E. (1999). *The sexual century.* New Haven, CT: Yale University Press.

Person, E. (2006). Masculinities, plural. *Journal of the American Psychoanalytic Association,* 54, 1165–86.

Person, E., Cooper, A. M., and Gabbard, G. (2005). *Textbook of psychoanalysis.* Washington, DC: American Psychiatric Publishing.

Person, E., and Ovesey, L. (1974). The transsexual syndrome in males. Part 1: Primary transsexualism. *American Journal of Psychotherapy,* 8, 4–20.

Person, E., and Ovesey, L. (1978). Transvestism: New perspectives. *Journal of the American Academy of Psychoanalysis and Dynamic Psychiatry,* 6, 301–23.

Person, E., and Ovesey, L. (1983). Psychoanalytic theories of gender identity. *Journal of the American Academy of Psychoanalysis and Dynamic Psychiatry,* 11, 203–26.

Peskin, M. (1997). Drive theory revisited. *Psychoanalytic Quarterly,* 66, 377–402.

Pfäfflin, F. (2009). Research, research politics, and clinical experience with transsexual patients. In *Identity, gender, and sexuality: 150 years after Freud,* ed. P. Fonagy, R. Krause, and M. Leuzinger-Bohleber (pp. 139–56). London: Karnac Books.

Pfeffer, A. (1993). After the analysis: Analyst as both old and new object. *Journal of the American Academy of Psychoanalysis and Dynamic Psychiatry,* 41, 323–37.

Phillips, M. (1981). Freud, psychic determinism and freedom. *International Review of Psycho-Analysis,* 8, 449–55.

Phillips, S. (2001). The overstimulation of everyday life. 1: New aspects of male homosexuality. *Journal of the American Psychoanalytic Association,* 49, 1235–68.

Phillips, S. (2006). Paul Gray's narrowing scope: A "developmental lag" in his theory and technique. *Journal of the American Psychoanalytic Association,* 54, 137–70.

Piaget, J. (1932). *The moral judgment of the child.* New York: Free Press.

Piaget, J. (1937). *The construction of reality in the child.* New York: Basic Books.

Piaget, J. (1951). *Play, dreams and imitation in childhood.* London: Heinemann.

Piaget, J. (1953). *Origins of intelligence in the child.* London: Routledge and Kegan Paul.

Piaget, J. (1954). *Construction of reality in the child.* London: Routledge and Kegan Paul.

Piaget, J. (1969). *The psychology of the child.* New York: Basic Books.

Pick, I. (1985). Working through in the countertransference. *International Journal of Psychoanalysis,* 66, 157–66.

Piers, G., and Singer, M. (1953). *Shame and guilt: A psychoanalytic and a cultural study.* Springfield, IL: Charles C. Thomas.

Pigman, G. (1995). Freud and the history of empathy. *International Journal of Psychoanalysis,* 76, 237–56.

Pine, F. (1974). On the concept "borderline" in children—a clinical essay. *Psychoanalytic Study of the Child,* 29, 341–68.

Pine, F. (1994). Some impressions regarding conflict, defect, and deficit. *Psychoanalytic Study of the Child,* 49, 222–40.

Pine, F. (2004). Mahler's concepts of "symbiosis" and separation-individuation: revisited, reevaluated, refined. *Journal of the American Psychoanalytic Association,* 52, 511–33.

Pine, F. (2005a). Theories of motivation in psychoanalysis. In *Textbook of psychoanalysis,* ed. E. Person, A. M. Cooper, and G. Gabbard (pp. 3–20). Washington, DC: APA Publishing.

Pine, F. (2005b). Response to Doris Silverman. *Journal of the American Psychoanalytic Association,* 53, 253–55.

Pine, F. (2006). The psychoanalytic dictionary: A position paper on diversity and its unifiers. *Journal of the American Psychoanalytic Association,* 54, 463–91.

Pines, M. (1988). The question of revising the *Standard Edition.* In *Freud in exile: Psychoanalysis and its vicissitudes,* ed. E. Timms and N. Segal (pp. 177–80). New Haven, CT: Yale University Press.

Poland, W. (1984). On the analyst's neutrality. *Journal of the American Psychoanalytic Association,* 32, 283–99.

Poland, W. (2006). The analyst's fears. *American Imago,* 63, 201–17.

Pollock, G. (1961). Mourning and adaptation. *International Journal of Psychoanalysis, 42*, 341–61.

Pontalis, J. (1980). The negative therapeutic reaction: An attempt at definition. *European Psycho-Analytical Federation, 15*, 19–30.

Porcerelli, J., Shahar, G., Blatt, S., Ford, R., Mezza, J., and Greenlee, L. (2005). Abstracts of the 2005 poster session of the American Psychoanalytic Association winter meeting. *Journal of the American Psychoanalytic Association, 53*, 1323–25.

Posner, M., Rothbart, M., Vizueta, N., Levy, K., Evans, D., Thomas, K., and Clarkin, J. (2002). Attentional mechanisms of borderline personality disorder. *Procedures of the National Academy of Science, 99*, 16366–370.

Potamianou, A. (1985). The personal myth—Points and counterpoints. *Psychoanalytic Study of the Child, 40*, 285–96.

Powell, S. (1993). Electra: The dark side of the moon. *Journal of the American Psychoanalytic Association, 38*, 155–74.

Premack, D., and Woodruff, G. (1978). Does the chimpanzee have a theory of mind? *Behavioral and Brain Sciences, 1*, 515–26.

Preston, L., and Shumsky, E. (2002). From an empathic stance to an empathic dance: Empathy as a bidirectional negotiation. *Progress in Self Psychology, 18*, 47–61.

Provence, S., and Lipton, R. (1962). *Infants in institutions. A comparison of their development with family-reared infants during the first year.* New York: International Universities Press.

Pruett, K., and Dahl, E. (1982) Psychotherapy of gender identity conflict in young boys. *Journal of the American Academy of Child Psychiatry, 21*, 65–70.

Pulver, S. (1988). Psychic structure, function, process, and content: Toward a definition. *Journal of the American Psychoanalytic Association, 36*, 165–88.

Purcell, S. (2006). The analyst's excitement in the analysis of perversion. *International Journal of Psychoanalysis, 87*, 105–23.

Quinodoz, J. (1993). *The taming of solitude: Separation anxiety in psychoanalysis.* New York: Routledge.

Racker, H. (1957). The meanings and uses of countertransference. *Psychoanalytic Quarterly, 26*, 303–57.

Rado, S. (1928). The problem of melancholia. *International Journal of Psychoanalysis, 9*, 420–438.

Rado, S. (1956a). Adaptational psychodynamics: A basic science. In *Changing concepts of psychoanalytic medicine,* ed. S. Rado and G. Daniels (pp. 332–46). New York: Grune and Stratton, 1956.

Rado, S. (1956b). *Psychoanalysis of behavior: Collected papers.* New York: Grune and Stratton.

Rangell, L. (1954). Similarities and differences between psychoanalysis and the dynamic psychotherapy. *Journal of the American Psychoanalytic Association, 2*, 734–44.

Rangell, L. (1963). Structural problems in intrapsychic conflict. *Psychoanalytic Study of the Child, 18*, 103–38.

Rangell, L. (1967a). Psychoanalysis, affects, and the "human core"—On the relationship of psychoanalysis to the behavioral sciences. *Psychoanalytic Quarterly, 36*, 172–202.

Rangell, L. (1967b). The metapsychology of psychic trauma. In *Psychic trauma,* ed. S. Furst (pp. 51–84). New York: Basic Books.

Rangell, L. (1992). The psychoanalytic theory of change. *International Journal of Psychoanalysis, 73*, 415–28.

Rangell, L. (2007). *The road to unity in psychoanalytic theory.* Northvale, NJ: Jason Aronson.

Rank, O. (1909). *The myth of the birth of the hero: A psychological exploration of myth.* Baltimore, MD: Johns Hopkins Press, 2004.

Rank, O. (1924). The trauma of birth in its importance for psychoanalytic therapy. *Psychoanalytic Review, 11*, 241–45.

Rapaport, D. (1944). The scientific methodology of psychoanalysis In *The collected papers of David Rapaport,* ed. M. Gill (pp. 165–220). New York: Basic Books, 1967.

Rapaport, D. (1951). *Organization and pathology of thought.* New York: Columbia University Press.

Rapaport, D. (1953). On the psychoanalytic theory of affects. *International Journal of Psychoanalysis, 34*, 177–98.

Rapaport, D., and Gill, M. (1959). The points of view and assumptions of metapsychology. *International Journal of Psychoanalysis, 40*, 153–62.

Reed, G. (1997). The analyst's interpretation as fetish. *Journal of the American Psychoanalytic Association, 45*, 1153–81.

Reed, K. (2002). Listening to themes in a review of psychoanalytic literature about lesbianism. *Psychoanalytic Inquiry, 22* (2), 229–58.

Reich, A. (1950). On the termination of analysis. *International Journal of Psychoanalysis, 31*, 179–83.

Reich, A. (1951). On counter-transference. *International Journal of Psychoanalysis, 32*, 25–31.

Reich, A. (1953). Narcissistic object choice in women. *Journal of the American Psychoanalytic Association, 1*, 22–44.

Reich, A. (1954). Early identifications as archaic elements in the superego. *Journal of the American Psychoanalytic Association, 2*, 218–38.

Reich, A. (1960). Pathological forms of self-esteem regulation. *Psychoanalytic Study of the Child, 15*, 215–32.

Reich, W. (1931). The characterological mastery of the oedipus complex. *International Journal of Psychoanalysis,* 12, 452–67.

Reich, W. (1933/1945). *Character analysis.* New York: Simon and Schuster.

Reichbart, R. (2006). On men crying. *Journal of the American Psychoanalytic Association,* 54, 1067–98.

Reik, T. (1924). Some remarks on the study of resistances. *International Journal of Psychoanalysis,* 5, 141–54.

Reik, T. (1939). The characteristics of masochism. *American Imago,* 1A, 26–59.

Renik, O. (1993). Analytic interaction: Conceptualizing technique in light of the analyst's irreducible subjectivity. *Psychoanalytic Quarterly,* 62, 553–51.

Renik, O. (1995). The ideal of the anonymous analyst and the problem of self-disclosure. *Psychoanalytic Quarterly,* 64, 466–95.

Reports of discussions of acting out. (1968). *International Journal of Psychoanalysis,* 49, 224–30.

Ribble, M. (1943). *The rights of infants: Early psychological needs and their satisfactions.* New York: Columbia University Press.

Rice, A. (1963). *The enterprise and its environment.* London: Tavistock.

Richards, A. (1992). The influence of sphincter control and genital sensation on body image and gender identity in women. *Psychoanalytic Quarterly,* 61, 331–51.

Richards, A. (1996). Primary femininity and female genital anxiety. The psychology of women: Psychoanalytic perspectives. *Journal of the American Psychoanalytic Association,* 44 (S), 261–81.

Ricoeur, P. (1970). *Freud and philosophy.* New Haven, CT: Yale University Press.

Ritvo, S. (1971). Late adolescence—Developmental and clinical considerations. *Psychoanalytic Study of the Child,* 26, 241–63.

Ritvo, S. (1974). Current status of the concept of infantile neurosis—Implications for diagnosis and technique. *Psychoanalytic Study of the Child,* 29, 159–80.

Ritvo, S. (2003). Conflicts of aggression in coming of age: Developmental and analytic considerations; observations on reanalysis. *Journal of Clinical Psychoanalysis,* 12, 31–54.

Riviere, J. (1936). A contribution to the analysis of the negative therapeutic reaction. *International Journal of Psychoanalysis,* 17, 304–20.

Robbins, M. (1996). Nature, nurture, and core gender identity. *Journal of the American Psychoanalytic Association,* 44, 93–117.

Robertson, J. (1952). *A two-year-old goes to hospital.* Tavistock Child Development Research Unit. London: NYU Film Library. Robertson Films.

Rockland, L. (1992). *Supportive therapy for borderline patients.* New York: Guilford Press.

Roiphe, H. (1968). On an early genital phase—With an addendum on genesis. *Psychoanalytic Study of the Child,* 23, 348–65.

Roiphe, H., and Galenson, E. (1981a). Genital-drive development in the second year. In *Infantile origins of sexual identity* (pp. 243–66). New York: International Universities Press.

Roiphe, H., and Galenson, E. (1981b). *Infantile origins of sexual identity.* New York: International Universities Press.

Rosenblatt, A., and Thickstun, J. (1970). A study of the concept of psychic energy. *International Journal of Psychoanalysis,* 51, 265–78.

Rosenblatt, A., and Thickstun, J. (1977). *Modern psychoanalytic concepts in a general psychology: Psychological Issues* (Monograph 11). New York: International Universities Press.

Rosenfeld, H. (1947). Analysis of a schizophrenic state with depersonalization. *International Journal of Psychoanalysis,* 28, 130–39.

Rosenfeld, H. (1950). Notes on the psychopathology of confusional states in chronic schizophrenias. *International Journal of Psychoanalysis,* 31, 132–37.

Rosenfeld, H. (1952). Notes on the psycho-analysis of the super-ego conflict of an acute schizophrenic patient. *International Journal of Psychoanalysis,* 33, 111–31.

Rosenfeld, H. (1954). Considerations regarding the psycho-analytic approach to acute and chronic schizophrenia. *International Journal of Psychoanalysis,* 35, 135–40.

Rosenfeld, H. (1964). On the psychopathology of narcissism: A clinical approach. *International Journal of Psychoanalysis,* 45, 332–37.

Rosenfeld, H. (1971a). A clinical approach to the psychoanalytic theory of the life and death instincts: An investigation into the aggressive aspects of narcissism. *International Journal of Psychoanalysis,* 52, 169–78.

Rosenfeld, H. (1971b). Contribution to the psychopathology of psychotic states: The importance of projective identification in the ego structure and the object relations of the psychotic patient. In *Problems of psychosis,* ed. P. Doucet and C. Laurin (pp. 103–18). The Hague: Excerpt Medica, 1988.

Rosenfeld, H. (1983). Primitive object relations and mechanisms. *International Journal of Psychoanalysis,* 64, 261–67.

Rosenfeld, H. (1987). *Impasse and interpretation.* London: Tavistock Press.

Ross, J. (2003). Preconscious defence analysis, memory and structural change. *International Journal of Psychoanalysis,* 84, 59–76.

Ross, N. (1970). The primacy of genitality in the light of ego psychology—Introductory remarks. *Journal of the American Psychoanalytic Association,* 18, 267–84.

Rothstein, A., ed. (1987). *Models of the mind: Their relationship to clinical work.* Madison, CT: International Universities Press.

Rothstein, A. (1998). Neuropsychological dysfunction and psychological conflict. *Psychoanalytic Quarterly,* 67, 218–39.

Rothstein, A. (2006). Reflections on the concept "analyzability." *Psychoanalytic Review,* 93, 827–33.

Roy, C., Perry, J., Luborsky, L., Banon, E. (2009). Changes in defensive functioning in completed psychoanalyses: The Penn psychoanalytic treatment collection. *Journal of the American Psychoanalytic Association,* 57, 399–415.

Rubin, L. (1973/1971). Shame and guilt: A psychoanalytic and a cultural study by G. Piers and M. Singer. *Psychoanalytic Quarterly,* 42, 301–3.

Rubinfine, D. (1958). Problems of identity. *Journal of the American Psychoanalytic Association,* 6, 131–42.

Rubovits-Seitz, P. (1992). Interpretive methodology: Some problems, limitations, and remedial strategies. *Journal of the American Psychoanalytic Association,* 40, 139–68.

Rupprecht-Schampera, U. (1995). The concept of "early triangulation" as a key to a unified model of hysteria. *International Journal of Psychoanalysis,* 76, 457–73.

Rycroft, C. (1951). A contribution to the study of the dream screen. *International Journal of Psychoanalysis,* 32, 178–84.

Rycroft, C. (1968). *A critical dictionary of psychoanalysis.* New York: Basic Books.

Ryle, G. (1971). *Collected papers.* London: Hutchinson.

Sachs, L. (1962). A case of castration anxiety beginning at eighteen months. *Journal of the American Psychoanalytic Association,* 10, 329–37.

Saft, D. (2007). Raising girlyboys: A parent's perspective. *Studies in Gender and Sexuality,* 8, 269–302.

Samberg, E. (2004). Resistance: How do we think of it in the twenty-first century? *Journal of the American Psychoanalytic Association,* 52, 243–53.

Samberg, E., and Marcus, E. (2005). Process, resistance, and interpretation. In *Textbook of psychoanalysis,* ed. E. Person, A. Cooper, and G. Gabbard (pp. 229–240). Washington, DC: American Psychiatric Publishing.

Sameroff, A., and Fiese, B. (2000). Models of development and developmental risk. In *Handbook of mental health,* ed. C. Zeanah (pp. 3–19). New York: Guilford Press.

Sander, L. (1997). Paradox and resolution. In *Handbook of child and adolescent psychiatry,* ed. J. Osofsky (pp. 153–60). New York: John Wiley and Sons.

Sander, L. (2002). Thinking differently: Principles of process in living and the specificity of being known. *Psychoanalytic Dialogues,* 12, 11–42.

Sandler, A. (1977). Beyond eight-month anxiety. *International Journal of Psychoanalysis,* 58, 195–207.

Sandler, J. (1960a). The background of safety. *International Journal of Psychoanalysis,* 41, 352–56.

Sandler, J. (1960b). On the concept of the superego. *Psychoanalytic Study of the Child,* 15, 128–62.

Sandler, J. (1969). Notes on some theoretical and clinical aspects of transference. *International Journal of Psychoanalysis,* 50, 633–45.

Sandler, J. (1976a), Countertransference and role-responsiveness. *International Review of Psycho-Analysis,* 3, 43–47.

Sandler, J. (1976b). Actualization and object relationships. *Philadelphia Association for Psychoanalysis,* 3, 59–70.

Sandler, J. (1980). The negative therapeutic reaction: An introduction. *European Psycho-Analytical Federation,* 15, 13–18.

Sandler, J. (1987a). *From safety to superego.* New York and London: Guilford Press.

Sandler, J. (1987b). The concept of projective identification. *Bulletin for Anna Freud Centre,* 10, 33–49.

Sandler, J., Dare, C., and Holder, A. (1973). *The patient and the analyst.* New York: International Universities Press.

Sandler, J., Dare, C., and Holder, A. (1992). *The patient and the analyst: The basis of psychoanalytic process* (2nd edition). Madison, CT: International Universities Press.

Sandler, J., and Freud, A. (1981). Discussions in Hampstead index on "The ego and the mechanisms of defence": The mechanisms of defence, part 1. *Bulletin for the Hampstead Clinic,* 4, 151.

Sandler, J., Holder, A., Dare, C., and Dreher, A. (1997). *Freud's models of the mind.* Madison, CT: International Universities Press.

Sandler, J., Holder, A., and Meers, D. (1963). The ego ideal and the ideal self. *Psychoanalytic Study of the Child,* 18, 139–58.

Sandler, J., and Joffe, W. (1965). Notes on childhood depression. *International Journal of Psychoanalysis,* 46, 88–96.

Sandler, J., Kennedy, H., and Tyson, R. (1980). Interpretations and other interventions. In *The technique of child psychoanalysis: Discussions with Anna Freud,* ed. J. Sandler, H. Kennedy, and R. Tyson (pp. 78–104). Cambridge, MA: Harvard University Press.

Sandler, J., and Rosenblatt, B. (1962). The concept of the representational world. *Psychoanalytic Study of the Child,* 17, 128–45.

Sandler, J., and Sandler, A. (1983). The "second censorship," the "three box model" and some technical implications. *International Journal of Psychoanalysis,* 64, 413–25.

Sandler, J., and Sandler, A. (1984). The past unconscious, the present unconscious, and interpretation of the transference. *Psychoanalytic Inquiry,* 4, 367–99.

Sandler, J., Sandler, A., and Davies, R. (2000). *Clinical and observational psychoanalytic research: Roots of a controversy.* London: Karnac Books.

Sarnoff, C. (1976). *On latency.* New York: Jason Aronson.

Scarlett, W. (1994). Play, cure, and development: A developmental perspective on the psychoanalytic treatment of young children. In *Children at play: Clinical and developmental approaches to meaning and representation,* ed. A. Slade and D. Wolf (pp. 48–61). New York: Oxford University Press.

Schachtel, E. (1959/2001). *Metamorphosis: On the conflict of human development and the development of creativity.* New York: Basic Books.

Schachtel, E. (1966/2001). *Experiential foundations of Rorschach's test.* New York: Basic Books.

Schafer, R. (1959). Generative empathy in the treatment situation. *Psychoanalytic Quarterly,* 28, 342–73.

Schafer, R. (1960). The loving and beloved superego in Freud's structural theory. *Psychoanalytic Study of the Child,* 15, 163–88.

Schafer, R. (1968a). The mechanisms of defense. *International Journal of Psychoanalysis,* 49, 49–62.

Schafer, R. (1968b). *Aspects of internalization.* New York: International Universities Press.

Schafer, R. (1970). The psychoanalytic vision of reality. *International Journal of Psychoanalysis,* 51, 279–97.

Schafer, R. (1974). Problems in Freud's psychology of women. *Journal of the American Psychoanalytic Association,* 22, 459–85.

Schafer, R. (1976). *A new language for psychoanalysis.* New Haven, CT: Yale University Press.

Schafer, R. (1982). The relevance of the "here and now" transference interpretation to the reconstruction of early development. *International Journal of Psychoanalysis,* 63, 77–82.

Schafer, R. (1983). *The analytic attitude.* New York: Basic Books.

Schafer, R. (1985). Wild analysis. *Journal of the American Psychoanalytic Association,* 33, 275–99.

Schafer, R. (1997). *The contemporary Kleinians of London.* Madison, CT: International Universities Press.

Schechter, D., Zygmunt, A., Coates, S., Davies, M., Trabka, K., McCaw, J., Kolodji, A., and Robinson, J. (2007). Caregiver traumatization adversely impacts young children's mental representations of self and others. *Attachment and Human Development,* 9 (3), 187–205.

Schecter, M., and Combrinck-Graham, L. (1980). The normal development of the seven- to ten-year-old child. In *The course of life,* ed. S. Greenspan and G. Pollock, vol. 2: *Latency, adolescence and youth,* (pp. 93–108). Madison, CT: International Universities Press.

Scheeringa, M., and Zeanah, C. (2001). A relational perspective on PTSD in early childhood. *Journal of Traumatic Stress,* 14, 799–815.

Schmideberg, M. (1948). On fantasies of being beaten. *Psychoanalytic Review,* 35, 303–8.

Schore, A. (1994). *Affect regulation and the origin of the self: The neurobiology of emotional development.* Hillsdale, NJ: Lawrence Erlbaum Associates.

Schore, A. (2002). Advances in neuropsychoanalysis, attachment theory, and trauma research. *Psychoanalytic Inquiry,* 22, 433–84.

Schore, A. (2003). *Affect dysregulation and disorders of the self;* and *Affect regulation and the repair of the self* (2-vol. set). New York: W. W. Norton.

Schuker, E. (1996). Toward a further understanding of lesbian patients. *Journal of the American Psychoanalytic Association,* 44, 484–508.

Schur, M. (1955). Comments on the metapsychology of somatization. *Psychoanalytic Study of the Child,* 10, 119–64.

Schur, M. (1966). *The id and the regulatory principles of mental functioning.* New York: International Universities Press.

Schwaber, E. (1981). Empathy: A mode of analytic listening. *Psychoanalytic Inquiry,* 1, 357–92.

Schwaber, E. (2010). Reflections on Heinz Kohut's last presentation. *International Journal of Psychoanalytic Self Psychology,* 5, 160–76.

Searles, H. (1965). *Collected papers on schizophrenia and related subjects.* Madison, CT: International Universities Press.

Sedler, M. (1983). Freud's concept of the working through. *Psychoanalytic Quarterly,* 52, 73–98.

Seelig, B. (2002). The rape of Medusa in the temple of Athena: Aspects of triangulation in the girl. *International Journal of Psychoanalysis,* 83, 895–911.

Seelig, B., and Rosof, L. (2001). Normal and pathological altruism. *Journal of the American Psychoanalytic Association,* 49, 933–59.

Segal, H. (1952). A psycho-analytic approach to aesthetics. *International Journal of Psychoanalysis,* 33, 196–207.

Segal, H. (1957). Notes on symbol formation. *International Journal of Psychoanalysis,* 38, 391–97.

Segal, H. (1964). *An introduction to the work of Melanie Klein.* London: Karnac Books.

Segal, H. (1974). Delusion and artistic creativity: Some reflexions on reading *The Spire* by William Gold-ing. *International Review of Psycho-Analysis,* 1, 135–41.

Segal, H. (1978). On symbolism. *International Journal of Psychoanalysis,* 59, 315–19.

Segal, H. (1979a). *Melanie Klein.* London: Karnac Books.

Segal, H. (1979b). Postscript to "Notes on symbol formation." In *The work of Hanna Segal* (pp. 60–65). London: Jason Aronson, 1981.

Segal, H. (1981). *The work of Hanna Segal.* New York: Jason Aronson.

Segal, H. (1987). Silence is the real crime. *International Review of Psycho-Analysis,* 14, 3–12.

Segal, H. (1991). On symbolism. In *Psychoanalysis, literature and war: Papers 1972–1995,* ed. J. Steiner (pp. 33–38). London: Routledge, 1997.

Segal, H. (1993). The clinical usefulness of the concept of the death instinct. In *Psychoanalysis, literature and war: Papers 1972–1995,* ed. J. Steiner (pp. 14–21). London: Routledge, 1997.

Segal, H. (1997). From Hiroshima to the Gulf War and after: Socio-political expressions of ambivalence. In *Psychoanalysis, literature and war: Papers 1972–1995, ed.* J. Steiner (pp. 129–138). London: Routledge, 1997.

Segal, H. (2001) *An interview with Hanna Segal.* Retrieved from http://www.melanie-klein-trust.org.uk/segalinterview2001.htm.

Segal, H. (2007). *Yesterday, today and tomorrow.* London: Routledge.

Settlage, C. (1993). Therapeutic process and developmental process in the restructuring of object and self constancy. *Journal of the American Psychoanalytic Association,* 41, 473–92.

Settlage, C., Curtis, J., Lozoff, M., Silberschatz, G., and Simburg, E. (1988). Conceptualizing adult development. *Journal of the American Psychoanalytic Association,* 36, 347–69.

Shane, M., and Shane, E. (1994). Discussion of "The myth of the isolated mind." *Progress in Self Psychology,* 10, 257–62.

Shane, M., and Shane, E. (1996). Self psychology in search of the optimal: A consideration of optimal responsiveness, optimal provision, optimal gratification, and optimal restraint in the clinical situation. *Progress in Self Psychology,* 12, 37–54.

Shank, R., and Abelson, R. (1977). *Scripts, plans, goals, and understanding.* Hillsdale, NJ: Lawrence Erlbaum Associates.

Shapiro, D. (1965). *Neurotic styles.* Oxford: Basic Books.

Shapiro, T. (1974). The development and distortions of empathy. *Psychoanalytic Quarterly,* 43, 4–25.

Shapiro, T. (1976). Latency revisited—The age 7 plus or minus 1. *Psychoanalytic Study of the Child,* 31, 79–105.

Shapiro, T. (1977). Oedipal distortions in severe character pathologies: Developmental and theoretical considerations. *Psychoanalytic Quarterly,* 46, 559–79.

Sharp, C., Williams, L., Ha, C., Baumgardner, J., Michonski, J., Seals, R., Patel, A., Bleiberg, E., and Fonagy, P. (2009). The development of a mentalization-based outcomes and research protocol for an adolescent inpatient unit. *Bulletin of the Menninger Clinic,* 73 (4), 311–38.

Sharpe, S., and Rosenblatt, A. (1994). Oedipal sibling triangles. *Journal of the American Psychoanalytic Association,* 42, 491–523.

Shear, K. (2005). Commentary on "Integrating the psychoanalytic and neurobiological views of panic disorder." *Neuropsychoanalysis,* 7, 162–63.

Shedler, J. (2002). A new language for psychoanalytic diagnosis. *Journal of the American Psychoanalytic Association,* 50, 429–56.

Shedler, J., and Westen, D. (1998). Refining the measurement of axis II: A Q-sort procedure for assessing personality pathology. *Assessment,* 5, 335–353.

Shedler, J., and Westen, D. (2004). Refining personality disorder diagnosis: Integrating science and practice. *American Journal of Psychiatry,* 161, 1350–65.

Shengold, L. (1979). Child abuse and deprivation soul murder. *Journal of the American Psychoanalytic Association,* 27, 533–59.

Shengold, L. (1985). Anality and anal narcissism. *International Journal of Psychoanalysis,* 66, 47–73.

Shengold, L. (1989). *Soul murder: The effects of childhood abuse and deprivation.* New Haven, CT: Yale University Press.

Shevrin, H. (1978). Semblance of feeling: The imagery of affect in empathy, dreams, and unconscious processes—a revision of Freud's several affect theories. In *The human mind revisited,* ed. S. Smith (pp. 263–94). New York: International Universities Press.

Shevrin, H. (1997). Commentaries. *Journal of the American Psychoanalytic Association* 45, 746–53.

Shevrin, H. (2003). The consequences of abandoning a comprehensive psychoanalytic theory: Revisiting Rapaport's systematizing attempt. *Journal of the American Psychoanalytic Association,* 51, 1005–20.

Shevrin, H., Bond, J., Brakel, L., Hertel, R., and Williams, W. (1996). *Conscious and unconscious processes: Psychodynamic, cognitive, and neurophysiological convergences.* New York: Guilford Press.

Shulman, M. (1987). On the problem of the id in psychoanalytic theory. *International Journal of Psychoanalysis,* 68, 161–73.

Siegler, R. (1996). *Emerging minds: The process of change in children's thinking.* New York: Oxford University Press.

Sifneos, P. (1973). The prevalence of "alexithymia" characteristics in psychosomatic patients. *Psychotherapy and Psychosomatics,* 22, 255–62.

Silbersweig, D., Clarkin, J., Goldstein, M., Kernberg, O., Tuescher, O., Levy, K., Brendel, G., Pan, H., Beutel, M., Pavony, M., Epstein, J., Lenzenweger, M., Thomas, K., Posner, M., and Stern, E. (2007). Failure of frontolimbic inhibitory function in the context of negative emotion in borderline personality disorder. *The American Journal of Psychiatry,* 164 (12), 1832–41.

Silverman, D. (2005). Early developmental issues reconsidered. Commentary on Pine's ideas on symbiosis. *Journal of the American Psychoanalytic Association,* 53, 239–51.

Silverman, M. (1981). Cognitive development and female psychology. *Journal of the American Psychoanalytic Association,* 29, 581–605.

Silverman, M., and Bernstein, P. (1993). Gender identity disorder in boys. *Journal of the American Psychoanalytic Association,* 41, 729–42.

Simmel, E. (1929). Psycho-analytic treatment in a sanatorium. *International Journal of Psychoanalysis,* 10, 70–89.

Simon, B. (1991). Is the oedipus complex still the cornerstone of psychoanalysis? Three obstacles to answering the question. *Journal of the American Psychoanalytic Association,* 39, 641–68.

Singer, K. (1995). *Repression and dissociation: Implications for personality theory, psychopathology, and health.* Chicago: University of Chicago Press.

Skelton, R., ed. (2006). *The Edinburgh international encyclopedia of psychoanalysis.* Edinburgh, UK: Edinburgh University Press.

Slade, A. (1994). Making meaning and making believe. In *Children at play: Clinical and developmental approaches to meaning and representation,* ed. A. Slade and D. Wolf (pp. 81–107). New York: Oxford University Press.

Slade, A. (2000). The development and organization of attachment: Implications for Psychoanalysis. *Journal of the American Psychoanalytic Association,* 48, 1147–74.

Slade, A. (2008). The implications of attachment theory and research for adult psychotherapy: Research and clinical perspectives. In *The handbook of attachment: Theory, research, and clinical applications,* ed. J. Cassidy and P. Shaver (2nd edition, pp. 575–94). New York: Guilford Press.

Smith, H. (2002a). Creating the psychoanalytic process incorporating three panel reports: Opening the process, being in the process and closing the process. *International Journal of Psychoanalysis,* 83, 211–27.

Smith, H. (2002b). On psychic bisexuality. *Psychoanalytic Quarterly,* 71, 549–58.

Smith, H. (2006). Analyzing disavowed action: The fundamental resistance of analysis. *Journal of the American Psychoanalytic Association,* 54, 713–37.

Socarides, C. (1960). Theoretical and clinical aspects of overt male homosexuality. *Journal of the American Psychoanalytic Association,* 8, 552–66.

Socarides, D., and Stolorow, R. (1984). Affects and selfobjects. *Annual of Psychoanalysis,* 12, 105–19.

Sohn, L. (1985). Narcissistic organization, projective identification, and the formation of the identificate. *International Journal of Psychoanalysis,* 66, 201–13.

Solms, M. (1997a). *The neuropsychology of dreams: A clinico-anatomical study.* Mahwah, NJ: Lawrence Erlbaum Associates.

Solms, M. (1997b). What is consciousness? *Journal of the American Psychoanalytic Association,* 45, 681–703.

Solms, M. (1999). Controversies in Freud translation. *Psychoanalysis and History,* 1, 28–43.

Solms, M. (2000a). Dreaming and REM sleep are controlled by different brain mechanism. *Behavioral Brain Science,* 23, 843–50.

Solms, M. (2000b). Preliminaries for an integration of psychoanalysis and neuroscience. *Annual of Psychoanalysis,* 28, 179–200.

Solms, M., and Saling, M. (1990). *A moment of transition.* London: Karnac Books and the Institute of Psycho-Analysis.

Solnit, A. (1982). Developmental perspectives on self and object constancy. *Psychoanalytic Study of the Child,* 37, 201–18.

Solnit, A., Cohen, D., and Neubauer, P. (1993). *The many meanings of play.* New Haven, CT: Yale University Press.

Spence, D. (1982). *Narrative truth and historical truth: Meaning and interpretation in psychoanalysis.* New York: W. W. Norton.

Spero, M. (1984). Shame—An object-relational formulation. *Psychoanalytic Study of the Child,* 39, 259–82.

Spezzano, C. (1995). "Classical" versus "contemporary" theory—The differences that matter clinically. *Contemporary Psychoanalysis,* 31, 20.

Spillius, E. (1988). *Melanie Klein today: Mainly theory* (vol. 1). London: Routledge.

Spillius, E. (1993). Varieties of envious experience. *International Journal of Psychoanalysis,* 74, 199–212.

Spillius, E. (2001). Freud and Klein on the concept of phantasy. *International Journal of Psychoanalysis,* 82, 361–73.

Spillius, E., Milton, J., Garvey, P., Couve, C., and Steiner, D., eds. (2011). *The new dictionary of Kleinian thought* (rev. edition of R. Hinshelwood's *A dictionary of Kleinian thought,* 1989). London: Routledge.

Spitz, R. (1945). Hospitalism—An inquiry into the genesis of psychiatric conditions in early childhood. *Psychoanalytic Study of the Child,* 1, 53–74.

Spitz, R. (1946). Hospitalism—A follow-up report on investigation described in volume I, 1945. *Psychoanalytic Study of the Child*, 2, 113–17.

Spitz, R. (1950). Anxiety in infancy: A study of its manifestations in the first year of life. *International Journal of Psychoanalysis*, 31, 138–43.

Spitz, R. (1959). *A genetic theory of ego formation*. New York: International Universities Press.

Spitz, R. (1961). Some early prototypes of ego defenses. *Journal of the American Psychoanalytic Association*, 9, 626–51.

Spitz, R. (1965). *The first year of life*. New York: International Universities Press.

Spitz, R. (1969). *A genetic field theory of ego formation*. New York: International Universities Press.

Spitz, R., and Wolf, K. (1946a). Anaclitic depression—An inquiry into the genesis of psychiatric conditions in early childhood. *Psychoanalytic Study of the Child*, 2, 313–42.

Spitz, R., and Wolf, K. (1946b). The smiling response: A contribution to the ontogenesis of social relations. *Genetic Psychology Monographs*, 34, 57–125.

Spruiell, V. (1995). Self. In *Psychoanalysis: The major concepts*, ed. B. Moore and B. Fine (pp. 421–32). New Haven, CT: Yale University Press.

Stechler, G. (1982). The dawn of awareness. *Psychoanalytic Inquiry*, 1, 503–32.

Stechler, G. (1987). Clinical applications of a psychoanalytic system model of assertion and aggression. *Psychoanalytic Inquiry*, 1, 348–363.

Stechler, G., and Kaplan, S. (1980). The development of the self. *Psychoanalytic Study of the Child*, 35, 85–106. New Haven, CT: Yale University Press.

Steele, B. (1970). Violence in our society. *The Pharos of Alpha Omega Alpha*, 33, 41–48.

Steele, M. (2003). Attachment, actual experience and mental representation. In *Emotional development in psychoanalysis, attachment theory and neuroscience: Creating connections*, ed. V. Green (pp. 86–106). New York: Brunner/Routledge.

Stein, D., and Hollander, E. (2001). *Textbook of anxiety disorders*. Washington, DC: American Psychiatric Press.

Stein, E. (1999). *The mismeasure of desire: The science, theory, and ethics of sexual orientation*. New York: Oxford University Press.

Stein, M. (1981). The unobjectionable part of the transference. *Journal of the American Psychiatric Association*, 29, 869–92.

Stein, R. (2006). Unforgetting and excess, the re-creation and re-finding of suppressed sexuality. *Psychoanalytic Dialogues*, 16, 763–78.

Steiner, J. (1993). *Psychic retreats. Pathological organizations in psychotic, neurotic, and borderline patients*. London and New York: Routledge and the Institute of Psycho-Analysis.

Steiner, R. (1987). A world wide international trade mark of genuineness? *International Journal of Psychoanalysis*, 14, 33–102.

Steiner, R. (1991). To explain our point of view to English readers in English words. *International Review of Psycho-Analysis*, 18, 351–92.

Steiner, R. (1994). "The Tower of Babel" or "After Babel in contemporary psychoanalysis"?—Some historical and theoretical notes on the linguistic and cultural strategies implied by the foundation of the *International Journal of Psycho-Analysis*, and on its relevance today. *International Journal of Psychoanalysis*, 75, 883–901.

Sterba, R. (1934). The fate of the ego in analytic therapy. *International Journal of Psychoanalysis*, 15, 117–26.

Sterba, R. (1936/1937). *Handwörterbuch der psychoanalyse*. Vienna: Internationaler Psychoanalytischer Verlag.

Sterba, R. (1953). Clinical and therapeutic aspects of character resistance. *Psychoanalytic Quarterly*, 22, 1–20.

Stern, A. (1938). Psychoanalytic investigation of and therapy in the borderline group of neuroses. *Psychoanalytic Quarterly*, 7, 467–68.

Stern, B., Caligor, E., Clarkin, J., Critchfield, K., Horz, S., MacCornack, V., Lenzenweger, M., and Kernberg, O. (2010). Structured interview of personality organization (STIPO): Preliminary psychometrics in a clinical sample. *Journal of Personality Assessment*, 92 (1), 35–44.

Stern, D. B. (1994). Conceptions of structure in interpersonal psychoanalysis—A reading of the literature. *Contemporary Psychoanalysis*, 30, 255–300.

Stern, D. B. (1995). Cognition and language. In *The handbook of interpersonal psychoanalysis*, ed. M. Lionells, J. Fiscalini, C. Mann, and D. B. Stern (pp. 79–138). Hillsdale, NJ: Analytic Press.

Stern, D. B. (1997). *Unformulated experience: From dissociation to imagination in psychoanalysis*. Hillsdale, NJ: Analytic Press.

Stern, D. B. (2010). *Partners in thought: Working with unformulated experience, dissociation, and enactment*. New York: Routledge.

Stern, D. N. (1977). *The first relationship: Mother and infant*. Cambridge, MA: Harvard University Press.

Stern, D. N. (1985). *The interpersonal world of the infant*. New York: Basic Books.

Stern, D. N. (1992). The "pre-narrative envelope": An alternative view of "unconscious phantasy" in infancy. *Bulletin of the Anna Freud Centre*, 15, 291–318.

Stern, D. N. (1994). One way to build a clinically relevant baby. *Infant Mental Health Journal*, 15, 36–54.

Stern, D. N. (2003). *The present moment in psychotherapy and everyday life*. New York: W. W. Norton.

Stern, D. N. (2005). Intersubjectivity. In *The American Psychiatric Publishing Textbook of Psychoanalysis*, ed. E. Person, A. M. Cooper, and G. Gabbard (pp. 77–92). Washington, DC: American Psychiatric Publishers.

Stern, D. N., Sander, L., Nahum, J., Harrison, A., Lyons-Ruth, K., Morgan, A., Bruschweilerstern, N., and Tronick, E. (1998). Non-interpretive mechanisms in psychoanalytic therapy: The "something more" than interpretation. *International Journal of Psychoanalysis, 79,* 903–21.

Stoller, R. (1964). A contribution to the study of gender identity. *International Journal of Psychoanalysis, 45,* 220–26.

Stoller, R. (1965). The sense of maleness. *Psychoanalytic Quarterly, 35,* 207–18.

Stoller, R. (1966). The mother's contribution to infantile transvestic behaviour. *International Journal of Psychoanalysis, 47,* 384–95.

Stoller, R. (1967). It's only a phase: Femininity in boys. *Journal of the American Psychoanalytic Association, 201* (5), 314–15.

Stoller, R. (1968a). A further contribution to the study of gender identity. *International Journal of Psychotherapy, 49,* 364–68.

Stoller, R. (1968b). *Sex and gender: On the development of masculinity and femininity.* New York: Science House.

Stoller, R. (1968c). The sense of femaleness. *Psychoanalytic Quarterly, 37,* 42–55.

Stoller, R. (1973). The male transsexual as "experiment." *International Journal of Psychoanalysis, 54,* 215–25.

Stoller, R. (1975a). *Perversion: The erotic form of hatred.* New York: Pantheon Books.

Stoller, R. (1975b). *Sex and gender: The transsexual experiment* (vol. 2). New York: Aronson.

Stoller, R. (1975c). The language of psycho-analysis. *International Journal of Psychoanalysis, 56,* 103–4.

Stoller, R. (1976). Primary femininity. *Journal of the American Psychoanalytic Association, 24* (S), 59–78.

Stoller, R. (1979a). A contribution to the study of gender identity: Follow-up. *International Journal of Psychoanalysis, 60,* 433–41.

Stoller, R. (1979b). Fathers of transsexual children. *Journal of the American Psychoanalytic Association, 27,* 837–66.

Stoller, R. (1985). *One homosexual woman: Observing the erotic imagination.* New Haven, CT: Yale University Press.

Stoller, R. (1991). *Pain and passion: A psychoanalyst explores the world of S and M.* New York: Plenum.

Stolorow, R. (1984). Varieties of selfobject experience. In *Kohut's legacy: Contributions to self psychology,* ed. P. Stepansky and A. Goldberg (pp. 43–50). Hillsdale, NJ: Analytic Press.

Stolorow, R. (1986). On experiencing an object: A multidimensional perspective. *Progress in Self Psychology, 2,* 273–79.

Stolorow, R., and Atwood, G. (1979). *Faces in a cloud: Subjectivity in personality theory.* New York: Jason Aronson.

Stolorow, R., and Atwood, G. (1989). The unconscious and unconscious fantasy: An intersubjective-developmental perspective. *Psychoanalytic Inquiry, 9,* 364–74.

Stolorow, R., and Atwood, G. (1992a). *Contexts of being: The intersubjective foundations of psychological life.* Hillsdale, NJ: Analytic Press.

Stolorow, R., and Atwood, G. (1992b). Three realms of the unconscious. In *Contexts of being: The intersubjective foundations of psychological life* (pp. 29–40). Hillsdale, NJ: Analytic Press.

Stolorow, R., and Atwood, G. (1996). The intersubjective perspective. *Psychoanalytic Review, 83,* 181–94.

Stolorow, R., Atwood, G., and Orange, D. (1999). Kohut and contextualism: Toward a post-Cartesian psychoanalytic theory. *Psychoanalytic Psychology, 16,* 380–88.

Stolorow, R., Brandchaft, G., and Atwood, G. (1987). *Psychoanalytic treatment: An intersubjective approach.* Hillsdale, NJ: Analytic Press.

Stone, L. (1954). The widening scope of indications for psychoanalysis. *Journal of the American Psychoanalytic Association, 2,* 567–94.

Stone, L. (1961). *The psychoanalytic situation.* New York: International Universities Press.

Stone, L. (1967). The psychoanalytic situation and transference—Postscript to an earlier communication. *Journal of the American Psychoanalytic Association, 15,* 3–58.

Stone, L. (1981). Notes on the non-interpretative elements in the psychoanalytic situation and process. *Journal of the American Psychoanalytic Association, 29,* 10–118.

Strachey, A. (1941). A note on the use of the word "internal." *International Journal of Psychoanalysis, 22,* 37–43.

Strachey, A. (1943). A new German-English psychoanalytical vocabulary. *International Journal of Psychoanalysis, 1* (S), 1–84.

Strachey, J. (1934). The nature of the therapeutic action of psycho-analysis. *International Journal of Psychoanalysis, 15,* 127–59.

Strachey, J. (1966). *General preface: The standard edition of the complete psychological works of Sigmund Freud, 1886–1899: Pre-psycho-analytic publications and unpublished drafts* (vol. 1, pp. xiii–xxvi). London: Hogarth Press.

Striano, T., Henning, A., and Stahl, D. (2005). Sensitivity to social contingencies between 1 and 3 months of age. *Developmental Science, 8,* 509–18.

Sucharov, M. (1994). Psychoanalysis, self psychology, and intersubjectivity. In *The intersubjective perspective*, ed. R. Stolorow, G. Atwood, and B. Brandchaft (pp. 187–202). Northvale, NJ: Jason Aronson.

Sugarman, A. (1997). Dynamic underpinnings of father hunger as illuminated in the analysis of an adolescent boy. *Psychoanalytic Study of the Child*, 52, 227–43.

Sugarman, A. (2003). A new model for conceptualizing insightfulness in the psychoanalysis of young children. *Psychoanalytic Quarterly*, 72, 325–55.

Sugarman, A. (2006). Mentalization, insightfulness, and therapeutic action: The importance of mental organization. *International Journal of Psychoanalysis*, 87, 965–87.

Sullivan, H. (1940). *Conceptions of modern psychiatry*. New York: W. W. Norton.

Sullivan, H. (1947). *Conceptions of modern psychiatry* (2nd edition). Washington, DC: The William Alanson White Psychiatric Foundation.

Sullivan, H. (1953a). *The interpersonal theory of psychiatry*. New York: W. W. Norton.

Sullivan, H. (1953b). *The psychiatric interview*. New York: W. W. Norton.

Sullivan, H. (1956a). *Clinical studies in psychiatry*. New York: W. W. Norton.

Sullivan, H. (1956b). Selective inattention. In *Clinical studies in psychiatry*, ed. H. Perry, M. Gawel, and M. Gibbon (pp. 38–76). New York: W. W. Norton.

Sutherland, J. (1963). Object-relations theory and the conceptual model of psychoanalysis. *British Journal of Medical Psychology*, 36, 109–25.

Tähkä, V. (1988). On the early formation of the mind—II. From differentiation to self and object constancy. *Psychoanalytic Study of the Child*, 43, 101–134.

Tähkä, V. (1993). *Mind and its treatment*. Madison, CT: International Universities Press.

Tarachow, S. (1962). Interpretation and reality in psychotherapy. *International Journal of Psychoanalysis*, 43, 377–87.

Target, M., and Fonagy, P. (1996). Playing with reality: II. The development of psychic reality from a theoretical perspective. *International Journal of Psychoanalysis*, 77, 459–79.

Tauber, E., and Green, M. (1959/2008). *Prelogical experience*. New York: Basic Books.

Teicholz, J. (1996). Optimal responsiveness: Its role in psychic growth and change. In *Understanding therapeutic action*, ed. L. Lifson (pp. 139–64). Hillsdale, NJ: Analytic Press.

Teicholz, J. (2001). The many meanings of intersubjectivity and their implications for analyst self-expression and self-disclosure. *Progress in Self Psychology*, 17, 9–42.

Teller, V., and Dahl, H. (1981). The framework for a model of psychoanalytic inference. *Proceedings of the 7th International Joint Conference on Artificial Intelligence*, 1, 394–400.

Terman, D. (1988). Optimum frustration: Structuralization and the therapeutic process. *Progress in Self Psychology*, 4, 113–25.

Terr, L. C. (1985). Remembered images and trauma—A psychology of the supernatural. *Psychoanalytic Study of the Child*, 40, 493–533.

Thomas, A., and Chess, S. (1977). *Temperament and development*. New York: Brunner/Mazel.

Ticho, E. (1982). The alternate schools and the self. *Journal of the American Psychoanalytic Association*, 30, 840–62.

Timms, E., and Segal, N. (1988). *Freud in exile: Psychoanalysis and its vicissitudes*. New Haven, CT, and London: Yale University Press.

Tolpin, M. (1970). The infantile neurosis—A metapsychological concept and a paradigmatic case history. *Psychoanalytic Study of the Child*, 25, 273–305.

Tolpin, M. (1997). Compensatory structures: Paths to the restoration of the self. *Progress in Self Psychology*, 13, 3–19.

Tolpin, M. (2002). Doing psychoanalysis of normal development: Forward edge transferences. *Progress in Self Psychology*, 18, 167–90.

Tolpin, P. (1988). Optimal affective engagement: The analyst's role in therapy. *Progress in Self Psychology*, 4, 160–68.

Tomkins, S. (1979). Script theory: Differential magnification of affects. In *Nebraska symposium on motivation*, ed. H. Howe Jr., and R. Dienstbier (vol. 26, pp. 201–36). Lincoln, NE: University of Nebraska Press.

Tomkins, S. (1987). Shame. In *The many faces of shame*, ed. D. Nathanson (pp. 131–61). New York: Guilford Press.

Tori, C., and Bilmes, M. (2002). Multiculturalism and psychoanalytic psychology: The validation of a defense mechanisms measure in an Asian population. *Psychoanalytic Psychology*, 19, 701–721.

Toronto, E. (2005). Introduction to *Psychoanalytic reflections on a gender-free case: Into the void*, ed. E. Toronto, G. Ainslie, M. Donovan, M. Kelly, C. Kieffer, and N. McWilliams (pp. 1–7). London and New York: Routledge.

Torsti, M. (1998). Femininity and Masculinity in postmodernism. *International Journal of Psychoanalysis*, 79, 140–43.

Trevarthen, C. (1980). The foundations of intersubjectivity: Development of interpersonal and cooperative understanding in infants. In *The social foundations of language and thought*, ed. D. Olson (pp. 216–242). New York: W. W. Norton.

Trevarthen, C. (1993). Brain, science and the human spirit. In *Brain, culture, and the human spirit, ed. J. Ashbrook* (pp. 129–181). Lanham, MD: University Press of America.

Trevarthen, C. (2009). The intersubjective psychobiology of human meaning: Learning of culture depends on interest for co-operative practical work—and affection for the joyful art of good company. *Psychoanalytic Dialogues,* 19, 507–18.

Tronick, E. (1989). Emotions and emotional communication in infants. *American Psychology,* 44, 112–19.

Tronick, E. (2001). Emotional connection and dyadic consciousness in infant-mother and patient-therapist interactions: Commentary of paper by Frank M. Lachman. *Psychoanalytic Dialogues,* 11, 187–95.

Tronick, E. (2003). "Of course all relationships are unique": How co-creative processes generate unique mother-infant and patient-therapist relationships and change other relationships. *Psychoanalytic Inquiries,* 23, 473–91.

Tronick, E. (2007). *The neurobehavioral and social-emotional development of infants and children.* New York: W. W. Norton.

Trop, J., and Stolorow, R. (1992). Defense analysis in self psychology: A developmental view. *Psychoanalytic Dialogues,* 2, 427–42.

Tuckett, D., and Levinson, N. A. (2010). PEP Consolidated Psychoanalytic Glossary. London: Psychoanalytic Electronic Publishing. Available online at http://www.pep-web.org/document.php?id=zbk.069.0000a.

Tulving, E. (1972). Episodic and semantic memory. In *Organization of memory,* ed. E. Tulving and W. Donaldson (pp. 381–403). New York: Academic Press.

Tutte, J. (2004). The concept of psychical trauma: A bridge in interdisciplinary space. *International Journal of Psychoanalysis,* 85, 897–921.

Tyson, P. (1980). The gender of the analyst—In relation to transference and countertransference manifestations in prelatency children. *Psychoanalytic Study of the Child,* 35, 321–38.

Tyson, P. (1982a). A developmental line of gender identity, gender role, and choice of love object. *Journal of the American Psychoanalytic Association,* 30, 61–86.

Tyson, P. (1982b). On sexuality: Psychoanalytic observations. *Psychoanalytic Quarterly,* 51, 303–8.

Tyson, P. (1994). Bedrock and beyond: An examination of the clinical utility of contemporary theories of female psychology. *Journal of the American Psychoanalytic Association,* 42, 447–68.

Tyson, P. (1996a). Neurosis in childhood and in psychoanalysis: A developmental reformulation. *Journal of the American Psychoanalytic Association,* 44, 143–65.

Tyson, P. (1996b). Object relations, affect management, and psychic structure formation: The concept of object constancy. *Psychoanalytic Study of the Child,* 51, 172–89.

Tyson, P. (2002). The challenges of psychoanalytic developmental theory. *Journal of the American Psychoanalytic Association,* 50, 19–52.

Tyson, P., and Tyson, R. (1990). *Psychoanalytic theories of development: An integration.* New Haven, CT: Yale University Press.

Tyson, P., and Tyson, R. (1995). Development. In *Psychoanalysis: The major concepts,* ed. B. Moore and B. Fine (pp. 411–12). New Haven, CT: Yale University Press.

Ullman, M. (1996). *Appreciating dreams: A group approach.* Thousand Oaks, CA: Sage Publications.

Vaillant, G. (1977). *Adaptation to life.* Boston: Little, Brown.

Vaillant, G. (1992a). *Ego mechanisms of defense: A guide for clinicians and researchers.* Washington, DC: American Psychology Press.

Vaillant, G. (1992b). The historical origins and future potential of Sigmund Freud's concept of the mechanisms of defence. *International Review of Psycho-Analysis,* 19, 35–50.

Vaillant, G. (1993). *The wisdom of the ego.* Cambridge, MA: Harvard University Press.

Van der Kolk, B. (2000). Trauma, neuroscience, and the etiology of hysteria. *Journal of the American Academy of Psychoanalysis,* 28, 237–62.

Van Der Waals, H. (1965). Problems of narcissism. *Bulletin of the Menninger Clinic,* 29, 293–311.

Veen, G., and Arntz, A. (2000). Multidimensional dichotomous thinking characterizes borderline personality disorder. *Cognitive Therapy and Research,* 24, 23–45.

Vivona, J. (2007). Sibling differentiation, identity development, and the lateral dimension of psychic life. *Journal of the American Psychoanalytic Association,* 55, 1191–1215.

Von Krafft-Ebing, R. (1886/1999). *Psychopathia sexualis.* Burbank, CA: Bloat Publishing.

Waelder, R. (1936). The principle of multiple function: Observations on over-determination. *Psychoanalytic Quarterly,* 5, 45–62.

Waelder, R. (1962). Psychoanalysis, scientific method, and philosophy. *Journal of the American Psychoanalytic Association,* 10, 610–37.

Wagonfeld, S., and Emde, R. (1982). Anaclitic depression—A follow-up from infancy to puberty. *Psychoanalytic Study of the Child,* 37, 67–94.

Waldheim, R. (1984). *The thread of life.* Cambridge, MA: Harvard University Press.

Waldinger, R. (1987). Intensive psychodynamic psychotherapy with borderline patients: An overview. *American Journal of Psychiatry*, 144, 267–74.

Wallerstein, R. (1983a). Defenses, defense mechanisms, and the structure of the mind. *Journal of the American Psychoanalytic Association*, 31 (S), 201–25.

Wallerstein, R. (1983b). Reality and its attributes as psychoanalytic concepts: An historical overview. *International Review of Psycho-Analysis*, 10, 125–44.

Wallerstein, R. (1992). *The common ground of psychoanalysis*. Northvale, NJ: Jason Aronson.

Wallerstein, R. (1993). The effectiveness of psychotherapy and psychoanalysis: Conceptual issues and empirical work. *Journal of the American Psychoanalytic Association*, 41 (S), 299–312.

Wallerstein, R. (1998). Erikson's concept of ego identity reconsidered. *Journal of the American Psychoanalytic Association*, 46, 229–47.

Wallerstein, R. (2002). The growth and transformation of American ego psychology. *Journal of the American Psychoanalytic Association*, 50, 135–69.

Wallerstein, R. (2005). Outcome research. In *Textbook of psychoanalysis*, ed. E. Person, A. Cooper, and G. Gabbard (pp. 301–33). Washington, DC: American Psychiatric Publishing.

Wallerstein, R. (2009). What kind of research in psychoanalytic science? *International Journal of Psycho-Analysis*, 90, 109–13.

Warme, G. (1982). The methodology of psychoanalytic theorizing: A natural science or personal agency model? *International Review of Psycho-Analysis*, 9, 343–54.

Weil, A. (1970). The basic core. *Psychoanalytic Study of the Child*, 25, 442–460.

Weil, A. (1978). Maturational variations and genetic-dynamic issues. *Journal of the American Psychoanalytic Association*, 26, 461–91.

Weinberger, D., Schwartz, G., and Davidson, R. (1979). Low-anxious, high-anxious, and repressive coping styles: Psychometric patterns and behavioral and physiological responses to stress. *Journal of the American Psychoanalytic Association*, 88, 369–80.

Weinberger, J., and Silverman, L. (1990). Testability and empirical verification of psychoanalytic dynamic propositions through subliminal psychodynamic activation. *Psychoanalytic Psychology*, 7, 299–339.

Weinshel, E. (1984). Some observations on the psychoanalytic process. *Psychoanalytic Quarterly*, 53, 63–92.

Weiss, E. (1932). Regression and projection in the super-ego. *International Journal of Psychoanalysis*, 13, 449–78.

Weiss, E. (1935). Todestrieb und masochismus. *American Imago*, 21, 393.

Weiss, J. (1990). Unconscious mental functioning. *Scientific American*, 262 (3), 103–9.

Weiss, J. (1998). Bondage fantasies and beating fantasies. *Psychoanalytic Quarterly*, 67, 626–44.

Weiss, J., and Sampson, H. (1986). *The psychoanalytic process: Theory, clinical observation and empirical research*. New York: Guilford Press.

Weiss, J., Sampson, H., and Caston, J. (1976). *Research on the psychoanalytic process: An overview*. Psychotherapy Research Group, Department of Psychiatry, Mt. Zion Hospital and Medical Center, San Francisco, CA.

Weiss, S., and Fleming, J. (1980). On the teaching and learning of termination in psychoanalysis. *Annual of Psychoanalysis*, 8, 37–55.

Werman, D. (1983). Suppression as a defense. *Journal of the American Psychoanalytic Association*, 31 (S), 405–15.

Werner, H., and Kaplan, B. (1963). *Symbol formation*. New York: John Wiley and Sons.

Westen, D. (1985). *Self and society: Narcissism, collectivism, and the development of morals*. New York: Cambridge University Press.

Westen, D. (1990a). The relations among narcissism, egocentrism, self-concept, and self-esteem. *Psychoanalysis and Contemporary Thought*, 13, 183–239.

Westen, D. (1990b). Towards a revised theory of borderline object relations: Contributions of empirical research. *International Journal of Psychoanalysis*, 71, 661–93.

Westen, D. (1991a). Clinical assessment of object relations using the TAT. *Journal of Personality Assessment*, 56, 56–74.

Westen, D. (1991b). Social cognition and object relations. *Psychological Bulletin*, 109, 429–55.

Westen, D. (1995). *Social cognition and object relations scale: Q-sort for projective stories (SCORS-Q)*. Unpublished Manuscript, Department of Psychiatry, Cambridge Hospital and Harvard Medical School, Cambridge, MA.

Westen, D. (1997). Towards a clinically and empirically sound theory of motivation. *International Journal of Psychoanalysis*, 78, 521–48.

Westen, D. (1999a). Psychodynamic theory and technique in relation to research on cognition and emotion: Mutual implications. In *Handbook of cognition and emotion*, ed. T. Dalgleish and M. Power (pp. 727–46). Chichester, UK: John Wiley and Sons.

Westen, D. (1999b). The scientific status of unconscious processes: Is Freud really dead? *Journal of the American Psychoanalytic Association*, 47, 1061–1106.

Westen, D. (2002). The language of psychoanalytic discourse. *Psychoanalytic Dialogues*, 12, 857–98.

Westen, D., and Gabbard, G. (2002). Developments in cognitive neuroscience: 1. Conflict, compromise, and connectionism. *Journal of the American Psychoanalytic Association, 50,* 53–98.

Westerman, M., and Steen, E. (2009). Revisiting conflict and defense from an interpersonal perspective: Using structured role plays to investigate the effects of conflict on defensive interpersonal behavior. *Psychoanalytic Psychology, 26,* 379–401.

White, R. (1963). *Ego and reality in psychoanalytic theory: Psychological Issues (*Monograph 11). New York: International Universities Press.

Widzer, M. (1977). The comic-book superhero—A study of the family romance fantasy. *Psychoanalytic Study of the Child, 32,* 565–603.

Wieder, H. (1977). The family romance fantasies of adopted children. *Psychoanalytic Quarterly, 46,* 185–200.

Wilkinson-Ryan, T., and Westen, D. (2000). Identity disturbance in borderline personality disorder: An empirical investigation. *American Journal of Psychiatry, 157,* 528–41.

Will, O.(1965). The schizophrenic patient, the psychotherapist and the consultant. *Contemporary Psychoanalysis, 1,* 110–35.

Willick, M. (1983). On the concept of primitive defenses. *Journal of the American Psychoanalytic Association, 31* (S), 175–200.

Willick, M. (2001). Psychoanalysis and schizophrenia: A cautionary tale. *Journal of the American Psychoanalytic Association, 49,* 27–56.

Wilson, E. (1987). Did Strachey invent Freud? *International Journal of Psychoanalysis, 14,* 299–315.

Winnicott, D. (1945). Primitive emotional development. *International Journal of Psychoanalysis, 26,* 137–45.

Winnicott, D. (1949). Hate in the counter-transference. *International Journal of Psychoanalysis, 30,* 69–74.

Winnicott, D. (1950). Aggression in relation to emotional development. In *Through paediatrics to psycho-analysis: Collected papers* (pp. 204–218). New York: Brunner/Mazel, 1975, 1992.

Winnicott, D. (1951). Transitional objects and transitional phenomena. In *Through paediatrics to psycho-analysis: Collected papers* (pp. 229–242). New York: Brunner/Mazel, 1975, 1992.

Winnicott, D. (1952). Anxiety associated with insecurity. In *Through paediatrics to psycho-analysis: Collected papers* (pp. 97–100). New York: Brunner/Mazel, 1975, 1992.

Winnicott, D. (1953). Transitional Objects and Transitional Phenomena. *International Journal of Psychoanalysis, 34,* 89–97.

Winnicott, D. (1955). Metapsychological and clinical aspects of regression within the psycho-analytical set-up. *International Journal of Psychoanalysis, 36,* 16–26.

Winnicott, D. (1956a). Primary maternal preoccupation. In *Through paediatrics to psycho-analysis: Collected papers* (pp. 300–305). New York: Brunner/Mazel, 1975, 1992.

Winnicott, D. (1956b). On transference. *International Journal of Psychoanalysis, 37,* 386–88.

Winnicott, D. (1956c). The anti-social tendency. In *Through paediatrics to psycho-analysis: Collected papers.* (pp. 305–315). New York: Brunner/Mazel, 1975, 1992.

Winnicott, D. (1958a). Pyscho-analysis and the sense of guilt. In *Psycho-analysis and contemporary thought,* ed. J. Sutherland (pp. 15–28). London: Hogarth Press.

Winnicott, D. (1958b). The capacity to be alone. *International Journal of Psychoanalysis, 39,* 416–20.

Winnicott, D. (1960a). Ego distortion in terms of true and false self. In *The maturational processes and the facilitating environment* (pp. 140–152). New York: International Universities Press, 1965.

Winnicott, D. (1960b). The theory of the parent-infant relationship. *International Journal of Psychoanalysis, 41,* 585–95.

Winnicott, D. (1962). Ego integration in child development. In *The maturational processes and the facilitating environment* (pp. 56–63). New York: International Universities Press, 1965.

Winnicott, D. (1963a). Dependence in infant care, in child care, and in the psycho-analytic setting. *International Journal of Psychoanalysis, 44,* 339–44.

Winnicott, D. (1963b). From dependence towards independence in the development of the individual. In *The maturational processes and the facilitating environment* (pp. 83–92). New York: International Universities Press, 1965.

Winnicott, D. (1965). *The maturational processes and the facilitating environment.* New York: International Universities Press.

Winnicott, D. (1967). The mirror role of the mother and family in child development. In *Playing and reality* (pp. 111–18) New York: Basic Books, 1971.

Winnicott, D. (1969). The use of an object and relating through identification. In *Playing and reality* (pp. 86–94). New York: Basic Books, 1971.

Winnicott, D. (1971a). *Therapeutic consultations in child psychiatry.* New York: Basic Books.

Winnicott, D. (1971b). *Playing and reality.* New York: Basic Books.

Winnicott, D. (1974). Fear of breakdown. *International Review of Psycho-Analysis, 1,* 103–7.

Winnicott, D. (1975/1992). *Through paediatrics to psychoanalysis: Collected papers.* New York: Brunner/Mazel

Winnicott, D. (1987). *The spontaneous gesture: Selected letters of D. W. Winnicott,* ed. F. Rodman. Cambridge, MA: Harvard University Press.

Wittels, F. (1930). The hysterical character. *Medical Review of Reviews,* 36, 186.

Wittels, F. (1934a). Mona Lisa and feminine beauty: A study in bisexuality. *International Journal of Psychoanalysis,* 15, 25–40.

Wittels, F. (1934b). Motherhood and bisexuality. *Psychoanalytic Review,* 21, 180–93.

Wittels, F. (1935). A type of woman with a three-fold love life. *International Journal of Psychoanalysis,* 16, 462–73.

Wittgenstein, L. (1953/2001). *Philosophical investigations.* Oxford: Blackwell Publishing.

Wolf, E. (1980). On the developmental line of selfobject relations. In *Advances in self psychology,* ed. A. Goldberg (pp. 117–32). New York: International Universities Press.

Wolf, E. (1988). Problems of therapeutic orientation. *Progress in Self Psychology,* 4, 168–74.

Wolff, P. (1996). The irrelevance of infant observations for psychoanalysis. *Journal of the American Psychoanalytic Association,* 44, 369–92.

Wollheim, R. (1984). *The thread of life* (William James lectures). Cambridge, MA: Harvard University Press.

Wolman, B., ed. (1977). *International encyclopedia of psychiatry, psychology, psychoanalysis, and neurology.* New York: Aesculapius Publishing.

Wolman, B., ed. (1996). *The encyclopedia of psychiatry, psychology, and psychoanalysis.* New York: Henry Holt.

Wolstein, B. (1959). *Countertransference.* New York: Grune and Stratton.

Wolstein, B. (1981). The psychic realism of psychoanalytic inquiry. *Contemporary Psychoanalysis,* 17, 399–412, 595–606.

Wolstein, B. (1983). The first person in interpersonal relations. *Contemporary Psychoanalysis,* 19, 522–35.

Wolstein, B. (1987). Experience, interpretation, self-knowledge: The lost uniqueness of Kohut's self psychology. *Contemporary Psychoanalysis,* 23, 329–49.

Woods, M. (2003). Developmental considerations in an adult analysis. In *Emotional development in psychoanalysis, attachment theory and neuroscience: Creating connections,* ed. V. Green (pp. 206–25). New York: Brunner/Routledge.

Wurmser, L. (1981). *The mask of shame.* Baltimore, MD: Johns Hopkins University Press.

Wurmser, L. (2000). *The power of the inner judge.* New York: Jason Aronson.

Wurmser, L. (2004). Superego revisited. *Psychoanalytic Inquiry,* 24, 183–205.

Wurmser, L. (2007). *Torment me, but don't abandon me: Psychoanalysis of the severe neurosis in a new key.* New York: Jason Aronson / Rowman and Littlefield.

Yanof, J. (1996). Language, communication, and transference in child analysis. I: Selective mutism: The medium is the message; II: Is child analysis really analysis? *Journal of the American Psychoanalytic Association,* 44, 79–116.

Yanof, J. (2005). Technique in child analysis. In *Textbook of psychoanalysis,* ed. E. Person, A. M. Cooper, and G. Gabbard (pp. 267–80). Washington DC: American Psychiatric Publishing.

Yorke, C. (1990). The development and functioning of the sense of shame. *Psychoanalytic Study of the Child,* 45, 377–409.

Young-Bruehl, E. (2003). *Where do we fall when we fall in love?* New York: Other Press.

Young-Bruehl, E., and Bethelard, F. (2000). *Cherishment: A psychology of the heart.* New York: Free Press.

Zajonc, R. (1984). On the primacy of affect. *American Psychology,* 39, 117–23.

Zeligs, M. (1957). Acting in—A contribution to the meaning of some postural attitudes during analysis. *Journal of the American Psychoanalytic Association,* 5, 685–706.

Zerbe, K. (2007). Psychotherapy and psychoanalysis: Fifty years later. *Journal of the American Psychoanalytic Association,* 55, 229–38.

Zetzel, E. (1949). Anxiety and the capacity to bear it. *International Journal of Psychoanalysis,* 30, 1–12.

Zetzel, E. (1956). Current concepts of transference. *International Journal of Psychoanalysis,* 37, 369–75.

Zetzel, E. (1958). Technical aspects of transference. *Journal of the American Psychoanalytic Association,* 6, 560–66.

Zetzel, E. (1968). The so-called good hysteric. *International Journal of Psychoanalysis,* 49 (2–3), 256–60.

Zetzel, E. (1970). *The capacity for emotional growth.* New York: International Universities Press.

Zimmer, R. (2003). Perverse modes of thought. *Psychoanalytic Quarterly,* 72, 905–38.

Zucker, K. (2010). The DSM diagnostic criteria for gender identity disorder in children. *Archives of Sexual Behavior,* 39, 477–98.